Lecture Notes in Computer Science 6074

Commenced Publication in 1973
Founding and Former Series Editors:
Gerhard Goos, Juris Hartmanis, and Jan van Leeuwen

Evgeny Osipov   Andreas Kassler
Thomas Michael Bohnert   Xavier Masip-Bruin
(Eds.)

Wired/Wireless Internet Communications

8th International Conference, WWIC 2010
Luleå, Sweden, June 1-3, 2010
Proceedings

 Springer

Volume Editors

Evgeny Osipov
Luleå University of Technology
Luleå, Sweden
E-mail: evgeny.osipov@ltu.se

Andreas Kassler
Karlstad University
Karlstad, Sweden
E-mail: kassler@ieee.org

Thomas Michael Bohnert
CEC Zurich
Zurich, Switzerland
E-mail: thomas.michael.bohnert@sap.com

Xavier Masip-Bruin
Universitat Politècnica de Catalunya
Barcelona, Spain
E-mail: xmasip@ac.upc.edu

Library of Congress Control Number: Applied for

CR Subject Classification (1998): C.2, H.4, D.4.4, H.3.5, I.2, D.2, H.5, K.6.4

LNCS Sublibrary: SL 5 – Computer Communication Networks
and Telecommunications

ISSN   0302-9743
ISBN-10   3-642-13314-2 Springer Berlin Heidelberg New York
ISBN-13   978-3-642-13314-5 Springer Berlin Heidelberg New York

springer.com

© Springer-Verlag Berlin Heidelberg 2010
Printed in Germany

Typesetting: Camera-ready by author, data conversion by Scientific Publishing Services, Chennai, India
Printed on acid-free paper   06/3180

Preface

Beginning with the first event in 2002, the International Conference on Wired/Wireless Internet Communications (WWIC) has continuously been established as a highly selective conference focusing on integration and co-existence of rapidly developing wireless network technologies and their applications related to the Internet. To do so WWIC provides an international forum for presenting and discussing cutting-edge research in this domain, and the 8th edition of WWIC, held at Luleå University in June 2010, continued this tradition.

The WWIC 2010 call for papers attracted 45 submissions from more than 25 countries and each contribution was subject to thorough peer review by recognized international experts that acted as members of the Technical Program Committee. The selection process resulted in 16 accepted papers, which were thematically grouped into 5 technical sessions. The major themes of WWIC 2010 were cooperation, management of multimedia traffic, advancing IEEE 802.11, cognitive optimization, mesh and multi-hop networks, security, signaling, control, and wireless sensor networks.

We are grateful to our two outstanding keynote speakers, Mario Gerla (UCLA, USA) and Henning Schulzrinne (Columbia University, USA). This year's conference also featured three invited sessions on cognitive multihop networks (organized by Andreas Kassler from Karlstad University and Merouane Debbah from Supelec), on QoS trends in networking and network monitoring and measurement systems (organized by Edmundo Monteiro from the University of Coimbra and Xavi Masip from the Universitat Politecnica de Catalunya) and on network monitoring and management systems (organized by Christian Callegari from the University of Pisa and Rene Serral-Gracia from the Universitat Politecnica de Catalunya). In line with the tradition of previous editions of WWIC, this year's conference gladly hosted the 4th ERCIM workshop on eMobility, which took place on May 31, 2010 and was organized by Torsten Braun from the University of Bern.

We thank all authors for contributing to the technical excellence of WWIC 2010 and all the members of the Technical Program Committee for their effort in providing timely and constructive reviews, which ensured the scientific excellence of the event. Further, Springer LNCS is gratefully acknowledged for their continued commitment to publishing the WWIC proceedings. Special gratitude goes to the financial sponsors of WWIC 2010, Ericsson and CDT (Centre for Distance-spanning Technologies) for providing their support. Luleå University of Technology, the Local Organizing Committee and its chair Laurynas Riliskis are gratefully acknowledged for their dedication in making WWIC 2010 a success.

We hope that all conference delegates enjoyed the scientific program and the unforgettable experience of the midnight sun. Next year we look forward to welcoming you to WWIC 2011 in Vilanova i la Geltrú, Barcelona, Spain

April 2010

Evgeny Osipov
Andreas Kassler
Xavi Masip-Bruin
Thomas Michael Bohnert

Organization

WWIC was organized by Luleå University of Technology in June 2010. Luleå University of Technology is the northernmost university of technology in Scandinavia and has a world-class standard of research and education. Luleå University of Technology conducts research in the Faculty of Engineering and the Faculty of Arts and Social Sciences. Both major international and national companies and small enterprises in the region are involved in the university's research and development projects.

General Co-chairs

Evgeny Osipov	Luleå University of Technology, Sweden
Andreas Kassler	Karlstad University, Sweden

Steering Committee

Torsten Braun	University of Bern, Switzerland
Georg Carle	TU München, Germany
Geert Heijenk	University of Twente, The Netherlands
Yevgeni Koucheryavy	Tampere University of Technology, Finland
Peter Langendörfer	IHP Microelectronics, Germany
Ibrahim Matta	Boston University, USA
Vassilis Tsaoussidis	Demokritos University, Greece

Technical Program Co-chairs

Thomas Michael Bohnert	SAP, Switzerland
Xavier Masip-Bruin	Universitat Politècnica de Catalunya, Spain

Technical Program Committee

Ozgur B. Akan	Middle East Technical University, Turkey
Khalid Al-Begain	University of Glamorgan, UK
Onur Altintas	Toyota InfoTechnology Center, Japan
Leonardo Badia	IMT Lucca Institute for Advanced Studies, Italy
Mortaza Bargh	Novay, The Netherlands
Carlos Bernardos	Universidad Carlos III de Madrid, Spain
Bharat Bhargava	Purdue University, USA
Fernando Boavida	University of Coimbra, Portugal
Thomas Michael Bohnert	SAP Research, Switzerland
Richard Boucherie	Universiteit Twente, The Netherlands
Torsten Braun	University of Bern, Switzerland

Rafaelle Bruno	IIT-CNR, Italy
Wojciech Burakowski	Warsaw University of Technology, Poland
Maria Calderon	Universidad Carlos III de Madrid, Spain
Bong Dae Choi	Korea University, Korea
Nicola Ciulli	Nextworks, Italy
Mieso Denko	University of Guelph, Canada
Michel Diaz	LAAS-CNRS, France
Magda El Zarki	University of California, Irvine, USA
Erik Fledderus	TNO ICT, The Netherlands
Jarmo Harju	Tampere University of Technology, Finland
Sonia Heemstra de Groot	Twente Institute for Wireless and Mobile Communications/TU Delft, The Netherlands
Geert Heijenk	University of Twente, The Netherlands
Markus Hofmann	Bell Labs / Alcatel-Lucent, USA
Michael Howarth	University of Surrey, Guildford, Surrey
Yuming Jiang	Norwegian University of Science and Technology, Norway
Andreas Kassler	Karlstad University, Sweden
Byung Kim	University of Massachusetts at Lowell, USA
Yevgeni Koucheryavy	Tampere University of Technology, Finland
Rolf Kraemer	IHP Microelectronics, Germany
Peter Kropf	University of Neuchâtel, Switzerland
Fernando Kuipers	Delft University, The Netherlands
Giada Landi	Nextworks, Italy
Peter Langendoerfer	IHP Microelectronics, Germany
Remco Litjens	TNO ICT, The Netherlands
Hai Liu	Hong Kong Baptist University, Hong Kong
Pascal Lorenz	University of Haute Alsace, France
Christian Maihöfer	Daimler AG, Germany
Lefteris Mamatas	University College London, UK
Saverio Mascolo	Politecnico di Bari, Italy
Xavi Masip-Bruin	Universitat Politecnica de Catalunya, Spain
Abdelhamid Mellouk	University Paris XII, France
Enzo Mingozzi	University of Pisa, Italy
Dmitri Moltchanov	Tampere University of Technology, Finland
Edmundo Monteiro	University of Coimbra, Portugal
Liam Murphy	University College Dublin, Ireland
Marc Necker	Universität Stuttgart, Germany
Ioanis Nikolaidis	University of Alberta, Canada
Guevara Noubir	Northeastern University, USA
Evgeny Osipov	Luleå University of Technology, Sweden
Philippe Owezarski	LAAS-CNRS, France
George Pavlou	University College London, UK
Guenter Schaefer	TU Ilmenau, Germany
Jochen Schiller	Free University Berlin, Germany
Patrick Sénac	ISAE, France
Dimitrios Serpanos	University of Patras, Greece

Vasilios Siris	Athens University of Economics and Business / FORTH-ICS, Greece
Dirk Staehle	University of Würzburg, Germany
Burkhard Stiller	University of Zurich and ETH Zurich, Switzerland
Vassilis Tsaoussidis	Demokritos University, Greece
Hans van den Berg	TNO ICT / University of Twente, The Netherlands
Rob van der Mei	Centre for Mathematics and Computer Science, The Netherlands
Miki Yamamoto	Kansai University, Japan
Marcelo Yannuzzi	Universitat Politecnica de Catalunya, Spain
Chi Zhang	Juniper Networks, USA

Publicity Chairs

Mieso Denko	University of Guelph, Canada
Zhisheng Niu	Tsinghua University, China
Yan Zhang	Simula Research, Norway

Publication Chair

Eva Marin-Tordera	Universitat Politècnica de Catalunya, Spain

Local Organization Chair

Laurynas Riliskis	Luleå University of Technology, Sweden

Workshop Chair

Torsten Braun (4th ERCIM eMobility Workshop)

Reviewers

Akan, Ozgur	Burakowski, Wojciech
Altintas, Onur	Calderon, Maria
Andreev, Sergey	Chai, Wei Koong
Badia, Leonardo	Choi, Bong Dae
Bargh, Mortaza	Ciulli, Nicola
Baryun, Abdussalam	Cunche, Mathieu
Bernardos, Carlos	Denko, Mieso
Berthou, Pascal	El Zarki, Magda
Bezirgiannidis, Nikolaos	Ergul, Ozgur
Bhargava, Bharat	Fledderus, Erik
Boavida, Fernando	Fragkiadakis, Alexandros
Boucherie, Richard	Francès, Fabrice
Braun, Torsten	Harju, Jarmo
Bruno, Raffaele	Heemstra de Groot, Sonia

Heijenk, Geert
Hofmann, Markus
Howarth, Michael
Jiang, Yuming
Kim, Byung-Guk
Kinalis, Athanasios
Kraemer, Rolf
Kropf, Peter
Kuipers, Fernando
Kuwadekar, Alhad
Landi, Giada
Langendoerfer, Peter
Lenas, Sotirios-Aggelos
Litjens, Remco
Liu, Hai
Lo, Anthony
Lorenz, Pascal
Maihöfer, Christian
Mascolo, Saverio
Mellouk, Abdelhamid
Mingozzi, Enzo
Moltchanov, Dmitri
Monteiro, Edmundo

Mueller, Christian
Murphy, Liam
Necker, Marc
Nikolaidis, Ioanis
Noubir, Guevara
Owezarski, Philippe
Pavlou, George
Portman, Marius
Prabhu, Balakrishna
Schiller, Jochen
Schmidt, Robert
Senac, Patrick
Serpanos, Dimitrios
Staehle, Dirk
Stiller, Burkhard
Tragos, Elias
van den Berg, Hans
van der Mei, Rob
Vassileva, Natalia
Yamamoto, Miki
Yannuzzi, Marcelo
Zhang, Chi

Sponsoring Institutions

Table of Contents

Cognitive Multihop Networks-I

Cognitive Multihop Networks-II

Security, Control and Signaling

QoE Trends in Networking

Monitoring and Measurements Systems

Wireless Sensor Networks

Unicast versus Multicast for Live TV Delivery in Networks with Tree Topology

Alireza Abdollahpouri[1,2], Bernd E. Wolfinger[1], and Junyu Lai[1]

[1] Department of Computer Science - TKRN
University of Hamburg - Germany
[2] University of Kurdistan - Sanandaj - Iran
{Abdollahpouri,Wolfinger,Lai}@informatik.uni-hamburg.de

Abstract. Multicasting is an essential technology in applications like IPTV or online multiplayer gaming and has been studied extensively in different networks. In this article, we introduce a new performance criterion, called multicast gain, which can be used for computing multicast efficiency. We analyze multicast transmission for delivery of live TV channels in tree-based networks representing, e.g., multicast trees, and determine the gain of subtrees and links in order to quantify the benefits of multicasting. We also define a threshold in order to identify cases in which unicasting might be preferable. We show that although multicasting can usually outperform multiple unicasting in terms of bandwidth usage, due to the inherent overhead in establishing and maintaining multicast connections, in special cases, using multiple unicast flows can be a better choice.

1 Introduction

Traditional IP networks involve communication between two end-systems. However, emerging applications like IPTV [1], multiplayer online gaming, remote education or video conferencing, require communication among groups of users. Meanwhile, demand for such applications has been explosive in the last decade.

Multicasting is a key technology that may provide beneficial services for these types of applications. Multicast allows the sender to transmit a message (destined for multiple receivers) only once, instead of sending it to each end-point separately. In the case of live TV, each channel would be associated to a unique IP multicast group.

Multicasting methods have been studied widely in the literature [2][3][4]. Traditionally, multicasting is handled by routers, and therefore it may be considered as a network layer mechanism. However, some efforts to support multicast have been done in other layers. K. S. Lee et al. proposed a MAC layer approach for multicasting in WiMAX networks [3]. Application layer multicasting or peer to peer (P2P) multicasting is also widely studied by many researchers [4][5]. In P2P multicasting, each individual client is potentially a server and it multicasts received content to other clients. An evaluation of multicast gain over unicast in cellular networks is done by J. Aaltonen et al., who used Monte-Carlo simulation for multicast sessions and the traditional Engset model for the unicast traffic [6].

E. Osipov et al. (Eds.): WWIC 2010, LNCS 6074, pp. 1–14, 2010.

T. Qiu et al. in [7] studied a large-scale IPTV service provider in the United States, with more than one million subscribers and over 500 different live TV channels. They showed that channel popularity is highly skewed and can be captured quite well by a Zipf-like distribution, such that, if all channels are sorted in descending order of popularity, the resulting distribution is typically close to Zipf-like [8]. M. Cha et al. showed that the top 10% of channels account for nearly 80% of viewers, which reflects the Pareto principal or 80-20 rule [9]. This property is also useful in designing CDNs (Content Delivery Networks) and cache systems where popular channels will be available close to the customer while a rarely watched channel may only be available further up in the hierarchically structured network.

In terms of bandwidth efficiency, using a multicast session usually outperforms multiple unicast sessions. However, there are several challenges in multicasting as mentioned below:

• UDP is widely used as the transport layer protocol for multicast communications. Therefore, if no additional mechanism is built on top of UDP in order to ensure responsiveness, multicast flows are unresponsive to packet loss and congestion.

• The sending rate for multicasting is usually lower than unicasting. For example, in IEEE 802.11b, the maximum multicast rate is 2Mbps which is the lowest rate of this standard [10].

• In IP-based wireless networks, due to time-varying channel conditions, burst errors and mobility of the nodes, IGMP may encounter service interruptions [11].

• Building multicast trees and pruning/grafting strategies [12] impose extra load to the network and therefore, consume valuable resources such as network bandwidth, especially in the case of sparse multicast trees.

• Saving power consumption in energy-constrained mobile nodes, especially in sensor networks, is critical. Therefore, a mobile node is allowed to enter its sleep mode when there is no data for it. However, IGMP membership query messages can disrupt the sleep mode and unnecessarily force the mobile node to wake up [11].

• In some networks, there exists a limitation in assigning multicast addresses, for example, in WiMAX, only a rather small range of Connection IDentifiers (CID) is allocated for multicast purpose [3]. Therefore, assigning a multicast address to a rarely watched channel is not reasonable.

So, it is quite reasonable to use unicasting for rarely watched and unpopular channels and the interesting question arises at which bound (in terms of channel popularity), usage of multicast seems to be advisable.

The rest of this paper is organized as follows. Section 2, gives a definition of the problem and required assumptions. In Section 3, we introduce and define our new measure of multicast gain for a single link as well as for subnetworks. Section 4, describes our calculation method of multicast gain for general tree-based networks. In Section 5, we show that calculation of gain can be simplified significantly for K-ary trees. Section 6, presents some numerical results and case studies of our analysis; and finally we conclude the paper in Section 7.

2 Definition of the Problem and Basic Assumptions

Traditional one-way broadcasting of TV programs no longer satisfies viewers. There will be a gradual paradigm shift from push-based media broadcasting to pull-based media streaming. We briefly explain Internet Protocol TV (IPTV) as an example. IPTV makes use of multicasting to deliver TV programs to subscribers. The video stream is broken up into IP packets and dumped into the core network. Every time a subscriber changes the channel, two steps need to be carried out, namely a leave process followed by a join process. The set-top box will first terminate access to the previously watched channel and sends a *leave previous multicasting group message* to the node in the upstream path (e.g., DSLAM, Edge router) using the IGMP protocol. After receiving this message, the node will take care of the termination of channel streaming if there is no user left in its downstream access network watching this channel. Then the set-top box will send a *join new channel message* to the upstream node. After receiving the request, the upstream node checks whether the requested channel is already available. If not, the request will be forwarded to the higher level node where the requested channel is available. On the other hand, if the subscriber just turns on the set-top box and no channel was watched by her/him previously, only the join process described above will be conducted [13].

Let us now introduce the scenarios and basic assumptions for which we are evaluating the benefits and the gain of multicasting. Assume that N users exist, each of which watches TV (i.e., accesses a given channel C) with probability p and that each user behaves independently of the other users. A user may be either active (watching channel C), or inactive. These users can access the TV service via one of the **access nodes** (e.g., WiFi AP or DSLAM) and send their request for the channels. If the program is already available at the access node (at least one user in this access network is watching this channel), then the user can watch the channel immediately; otherwise, the request is forwarded to the gateway (GW). Users may be fixed (using set-top boxes and TV sets) or mobile (using PDAs or mobile phones).

Without loss of generality and for the sake of simplicity, we assume that only one live TV server that provides TV programs, exists in the network. We also assume a tree structure in our investigation because multicast packets are forwarded via a tree topology, although the physical topology may be different. In addition, we assume that the live TV server is directly attached to the Gateway or it can be accessed via the Internet without bandwidth or latency constraints (Fig. 1). The links depicted in the Fig. 1 can be wired (e.g., fiber optic) or wireless. In the case of wireless communication, the gateway can use directional antennas to communicate with lower level nodes. The benefit of such a system is more spatial reuse and also less interference. Furthermore, access nodes can be WiFi APs in a hotspot and **relay nodes** can be WiMAX Base Stations or Relay Stations that provide a tree-structured backhaul for WiFi hotspots [14].

We also make the following assumptions about live TV channels:

- Each channel is considered to be a stream with constant bit rate.
- Access probability of each channel is defined by its popularity (which could, e.g., have a Zipf-like distribution).
- Streams are unidirectional and are transmitted from the server to the TV clients, so that, only the downlink traffic is considered.

Note that, although in general there exist a lot of different TV channels in the server, analysis is the same for all channels, because they are only different in their access probability. So, without loss of generality, we restrict ourselves to a single (arbitrary) channel C with access probability p in the rest of the paper. Furthermore, since we are modeling the network at an arbitrarily chosen (but then fixed) instant of time, we don't have to care about arrival and departure rates of clients.

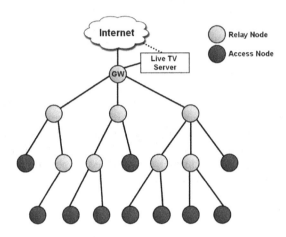

Fig. 1. Tree-structured network to deliver TV programs

3   A New Measure to Quantify the Gain of Multicast

Although benefit and efficiency of multicasting has been extensively studied in the literature, not much effort has been spent to quantitatively compare the performance of multicast and unicast transmission schemes. Gain measurement is conducted in order to find out whether it is worthwhile to use multicasting or not. In the cases where no significant gain is obtained, there is no need for multicast.

In [6], J. Aaltonen et al. evaluated the multicasting gain over unicast in cellular networks, for cells with a specific target call blocking probability. They modeled a mobile cell as a single transmission link and calculated the number of users that can be served with a given link capacity in unicast and multicast cases. They used the ratio N_{mc}/N_{uc} as multicast gain where N_{mc} and N_{uc} are the number of served clients in multicast and unicast schemes, respectively.

A. Phonphoem and L. Suchaisri in [15] used a 2-dimensional Markov model for both unicast and multicast to derive analytical expressions for the steady state behavior of a live streaming media system. They showed that multicast outperforms unicast with lower bandwidth per session and also a lower blocking probability.

In networks, bandwidth represents one of the most important resources. Therefore, in this paper, we let our measure of multicast gain focus on the bandwidth requirement for multicast versus unicast transmissions. In particular, we define multicast gain as amount of saved bandwidth by using multicast instead of multiple unicast. In order to refine our definition of multicast gain, let us concentrate on an arbitrary link L^* between an access node and a relay node as shown in Fig. 2. Assume multiple unicasting is used instead of multicasting, so i concurrent video streams (i instances of TV channel C) belonging to i different users in access network Net_j are transmitted via this link with probability P_i. Thus, multicast gain for this link (also called Link Gain and abbreviated as LG) would be the *difference between the required bandwidth for i streams and the required bandwidth for one stream* and is equal to:

$$LG = \sum_{i=2}^{N} P_i (i-1) b_c \tag{1}$$

Since we assumed that each client behaves independently of the others, and watching behavior of a client does not affect other clients, we can use a binomial random variable to calculate P_i. Therefore: $P_i = \binom{N}{i} p^i (1-p)^{N-i}$,

where N is the maximum number of active clients in access network Net_j, p is the watching probability of TV channel C and b_c is the constant bandwidth requirement for transmitting the video stream representing channel C. b_c depends on the format of TV programs. For a TV program in CIF format, b_c is at constant bit rate of about 500 Kbps and for standard definition (SD) with MPEG-2 encoding, it is about 3.75 Mbps.

It is quite obvious that when the number of users that watch TV channel C, is less than two, no gain is obtained; and that is why the lower bound of i in Equation (1) starts from two.

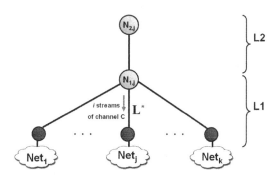

Fig. 2. Access networks and lowest levels (L1, L2) of the tree

The multicast gain of a network is the sum of the gains of its links. We use a simple example in Fig. 3 to illustrate the formula. The numbers shown as the label of the links indicate the number of concurrent streams or permanently active users watching channel C. In Fig. 3(a), multicast gain for the left and right links below node $N_{1,1}$ is equal to $3b_c$ and 0, respectively. Note that, if the number of streams is less than two, no gain is obtained. Thus, the total multicast gain of the tree is equal to $17b_c$.

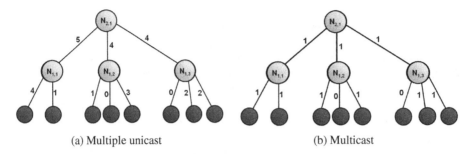

(a) Multiple unicast   (b) Multicast

Fig. 3. Number of unicast and multicast flows

4   Calculating Multicast Gain in General Tree Topologies

Recall from Section 2, we consider tree topologies for the following reasons:

- Regardless of the physical topology of a network, multicasting is done based on a tree structure called multicast tree.
- Tree topology is general enough and is widely used to construct hierarchical networks. Meanwhile, in some cases like WiMAX in Mobile Multi-hop Relay (MMR) mode, relay stations are organized in a tree-based structure [14].

We use the following notations to do our analysis:

Net_1 , …, Net_k: Access networks (e.g., IEEE 802.3, IEEE 802.11).
$U(Net_j)$: Number of users in the network Net_j which, in principle, might watch channel C at an arbitrarily chosen instant of time.
p: Probability for the TV channel C to be actually watched by one of its potential users (channel popularity); p is the same for all users in the access networks.
$N_{k,j}$: Node j of level k of the tree hierarchy.
P_i: Probability that exactly i users are watching TV channel C in an access network.
$ST_{i,j}$: Subtree below node $N_{i,j}$.
$U(ST_{i,j})$: Number of users in subtree $ST_{i,j}$.
$STG(ST_{i,j})$: Gain of subtree $ST_{i,j}$.
$LG(N_{i,j} , N_{l,k})$: Gain of link between $N_{i,j}$ and $N_{l,k}$ (or: link $N_{i,j}$-$N_{l,k}$ for short)
$P_i (N_{k,j})$: Probability of having to satisfy exactly i users watching channel C by means of node $N_{k,j}$.

4.1   Multicast Gain in Access Networks

Access networks can be categorized as either *point to point* or *broadcast*.

o   Point to point access networks. Clients have a point to point connection with access nodes. Therefore, the same amount of bandwidth and the same number of transmissions between access nodes and clients is required for both multicast and multiple unicast cases, as depicted in Fig. 4(a). In this case, no multicast gain is obtained within the access network.

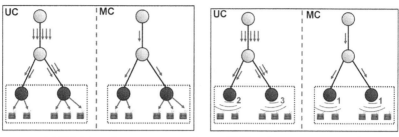

(a) Point-to-point access network   (b) Broadcast access network

Fig. 4. Multicast gain in access networks (UC: Unicast, MC: Multicast)

o Broadcast access networks. In this case, active clients content for the shared bandwidth. Fig. 4(b) shows a case in which two and three active clients exist in the left and right access networks, respectively. As depicted by the figure, in this type of access networks, required bandwidth is different for multicast and multiple unicast cases. The multicast gain for a broadcast access network is equal to the multicast gain of its upper link in the tree (link between access node and relay node) and can be calculated from Equation (1), which depends on the number of active clients, channel popularity (watching probability) and required bandwidth for a TV stream.

4.2 Multicast Gain on Level-1 of the Distribution Network

Now, let us concentrate on the lowest level of the distribution network (links between access nodes and relay nodes). First we need to calculate the gain of links at this level.

Assume that a set of k access networks, Net_1, ..., Net_k exist at the lowest level providing access for clients via their access nodes. Consider an arbitrary link between Net_j and $N_{1,j}$ (see link L^* in Fig. 2). Multicast gain for this link can be calculated by means of the following formula which is similar to Equation (1):

$$\sum_{i=2}^{U(Net_j)} \binom{U(Net_j)}{i} p^i (1-p)^{U(Net_j)-i} (i-1)b_c, \qquad (2)$$

where, again p denotes the watching probability (per user) of TV channel C.

Therefore, the multicast gain of level one is equal to the sum of the multicast gain of all links in this level:

$$L1Gain = \sum_{j=1}^{k} \sum_{i=2}^{U(Net_j)} \binom{U(Net_j)}{i} p^i (1-p)^{U(Net_j)-i} (i-1)b_c. \qquad (3)$$

Therefore, to calculate the gain at the level one, the following information is required:

- k: The number of access networks Net_j at the lowest level; j=1,...,k
- $U(Net_j)$: The number of concurrent live TV service clients in Net_j; j=1,...,k
- p: Watching probability of TV channel C

4.3 Multicast Gain on Level-2

To calculate the multicast gain on Level-2 (L2) links, we can consider the case that i users are active in subtree $ST_{1,1}$, c.f., Fig. 5. Then, the probability of having to deliver i different instances of channel C to these users via the link between $N_{1,1}$ and $N_{2,1}$ equals $P_i(N_{1,1})$.

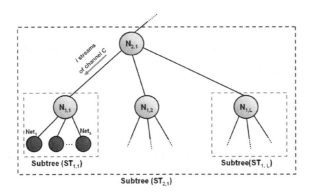

Fig. 5. Level one and level two subtrees

- **Calculation of multicast gain for link $N_{1,1}$-$N_{2,1}$**

The total number of users below node $N_{1,1}$ which is equal to $U(ST_{1,1})$ is calculated as follows:

$$U(ST_{1,1}) = \sum_{i=1}^{k} U(Net_i) \cdot \tag{4}$$

Therefore, $LG(N_{1,1}, N_{2,1})$, the multicast gain for a Level-2 link between nodes $N_{1,1}$ and $N_{2,1}$ can be calculated by using the formula below:

$$LG(N_{1,1}, N_{2,1}) = \sum_{i=2}^{U(ST_{1,1})} P_i(N_{1,1})(i-1)b_c = \sum_{i=2}^{U(ST_{1,1})} \binom{U(ST_{1,1})}{i} p^i (1-p)^{U(ST_{1,1})-i} (i-1)b_c \cdot \tag{5}$$

Note that, although the number of users in subtree $ST_{1,1}$ is equal to the number of users that use link $N_{1,1}$-$N_{1,2}$ (users below node $N_{1,1}$), the multicast gain in subtree $ST_{1,1}$ is not equal to the multicast gain for link $N_{1,1}$-$N_{1,2}$.

Now that we have calculated the multicast gain of L2-links, we can continue with calculating the gain of the complete subtrees.

- **Calculating gain in subtree ($ST_{2,1}$)**

Denote $STG(ST_{2,1})$ as the gain in subtree $ST_{2,1}$. To calculate this value, we need the gain in Level-1 subtrees. The gain in a Level-1 subtree (e.g., $ST_{1,1}$), is the sum of the gains of its links.

We can calculate the gain in subtree $ST_{2,1}$ by summing the gains of all Level-1 subtrees and the gains of all Level-2 links:

$$STG(ST_{2,1}) = \sum_{j=1}^{L} \left[STG(ST_{1,j}) + \sum_{i=2}^{U(ST_{1,j})} \binom{U(ST_{1,j})}{i} p^i (1-p)^{U(ST_{1,j})-i} (i-1)b_c \right]. \quad (6)$$

Therefore, the information required to calculate the multicast gain in subtree ($ST_{2,1}$) are as follows:

- L: number of Level-1 subtrees ($ST_{1,j}$); j=1,...,L
- $U(ST_{1,j})$: constant number of users in subtree $ST_{1,j}$
- p: watching probability of TV channel C

These iterated calculations can be repeated to calculate the gain of the complete tree. For example, for an arbitrary level k which has L subtrees, we have:

$$STG(ST_{k,1}) = \sum_{j=1}^{L} \left[STG(ST_{k-1,j}) + \sum_{i=2}^{U(ST_{k-1,j})} \binom{U(ST_{k-1,j})}{i} p^i (1-p)^{U(ST_{k-1,j})-i} (i-1)b_c \right]. \quad (7)$$

In Fig. 3(a), the total bandwidth requirement is equal to $26b_c$ when unicasting is used. In case multicasting is used, the bandwidth requirement is equal to $9b_c$ according to Fig. 3(b). So:

$STG(ST_{1,1}) = 3b_c$, $STG(ST_{1,2}) = 2b_c$, $STG(ST_{1,3}) = 2b_c$
$LG(N_{1,1}, N_{2,1}) = 4b_c$, $LG(N_{1,2}, N_{2,1}) = 3b_c$, $LG(N_{1,3}, N_{2,1}) = 3b_c$

$STG(ST_{2,1})$ is equal to the sum of multicast gains at links of Level-2 and multicast gains of subtrees, so: $STG(ST_{2,1}) = (4 + 3 + 3 + 3 + 2 + 2)b_c = 17b_c$.

To summarize our calculation method, the multicast gain of a complete network consisting of L levels can be calculated as follows:

Starting from the lowest level, one has to calculate the gain of links and subtrees in this level from the aforementioned formulae; then using Equation (7), one continues with calculating the gain of upper levels using the information from lower levels.

5 Multicast Gain in K-ary Trees with L Levels

In special cases when the structure of the tree is regular or the number of the users in all access networks is equal, we can simplify the formulae. In the following, we investigate these cases.

a) Tree structures
Tree structure can be regular K-ary tree with K outgoing arcs and L levels. In general, there exist K^L nodes in the lowest level. For example, for the case of K=2, if we suppose that the maximum number of hops between access nodes and gateway is not more than 5 (L ≤ 5), the maximum number of leaves would be equal to 32. In such trees, all access nodes are at lowest level.

b) Distribution of clients
Users can be randomly or equally distributed among leaf nodes. Here, we assume that the number of users at each leaf node is the same.

If we combine the above cases, where users are equally distributed on leaves of a K-ary tree with L levels, then, $m = \dfrac{N}{K^L}$, where, N denotes the total number of active users, and m is the number of users in each access network. (N is chosen such that m will be an integer value).

The gain of each level can be calculated from the following formulae:

$$\text{Level-1 gain} = K^L \sum_{i=2}^{m} \binom{m}{i} p^i (1-p)^{m-i} (i-1) b_c$$

$$\text{Level-2 gain} = K^{L-1} \sum_{i=2}^{Km} \binom{Km}{i} p^i (1-p)^{Km-i} (i-1) b_c$$

$$\vdots$$

$$\text{Level-L gain} = K \sum_{i=2}^{K^{L-1}m} \binom{K^{L-1}m}{i} p^i (1-p)^{K^{L-1}m-i} (i-1) b_c \tag{8}$$

$$\text{Total gain} = \sum_{i=1}^{L} \text{Level-}i \text{ gain} \tag{9}$$

For example, assume a 3-ary tree with 3 levels and total number of 540 users that are equally distributed among the leaves (20 users in each leaf). Furthermore, assume these users want to watch a TV channel with a watching probability of 0.01.

Then: N = 540, K= 3, L=3, m=20, p=0.01

$$\text{Level-1 gain} = 3^3 \sum_{i=2}^{20} \binom{20}{i} 0.01^i (0.99)^{20-i} (i-1) b_c \approx 81.311 \, b_c$$

And similarly:

Level-2 gain = $99 b_c$, Level -3 gain=$105 b_c$. So, the total multicast gain $\approx 285.311 b_c$.

6   Case Studies and Numerical Results

In this section, we want to discuss some numerical results based on the analytical formulae obtained in Section 4.

We designed an algorithm that constructs different tree structures and calculates multicast gain for all the links as well as the total multicast gain of the tree. We implemented it by using the C++ programming language. One of the trees generated by our algorithm, is shown in Fig. 6 and will be studied as an example.

6.1   Effect of Client Distribution and Watching Probability on Multicast Gain

To evaluate the effect of client distribution, we test the algorithm for different number of clients in the access networks. A total number of 200 clients are distributed among the access networks. Four different cases are studied:

Case 1: Equal distribution of users among access nodes (20 clients per each access network).
Case 2: Moderately unbalanced distribution of users (according to Fig. 6).

Case 3: Unequal and completely unbalanced distribution of clients in access networks (155 clients in access network X and 5 clients in each of the other access networks). *Case 4:* All 200 clients are in access network X.

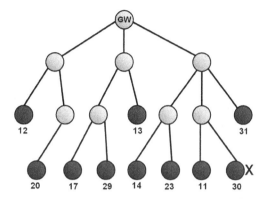

Fig. 6. Effect of different client distributions in access networks on multicast gain

We vary the watching probability (channel popularity) from a rarely watched channel (p=0.001) to a popular channel (p=0.1). The results are shown in Fig. 7(a). As can be concluded from the figure, the least gain is obtained for case 1, when all users are equally distributed among access nodes. Furthermore, for case 4, the maximum gain is obtained. In fact, all other curves will be between these two extreme cases. We call the area between the curves of case 1 and case 4, *Multicast Gain Area* which is depicted in Fig. 7(a). Also, it can be seen from the figure that for channels with watching probability less than 0.01, no considerable gain is obtained in any case. We repeated the test for numerous other types of trees and obtained similar results. Therefore, it is quite clear that for channels with low watching probability, multicasting is not reasonable.

6.2 Effect of Number of Clients and Watching Probability on Multicast Gain

To analyze and evaluate the effect of number of clients on multicast gain, we vary the watching probability from a very popular channel to a rarely watched channel and calculate the multicast gain for different number of clients that are equally distributed in the access nodes and the result is shown in Fig. 7(b). It clearly makes sense that the more clients in the network, the higher the multicast gain would be; because then it is more probable that two or more clients watch the same channel simultaneously. Similarly, in all cases, for the channels with watching probability less than 0.01, multicast gain is insignificant.

In order to take into account the effect of the number of links in the tree structure on multicast gain, we introduce the mean link multicast gain $\overline{LG}$, and define:

$$\overline{LG} = \frac{1}{n_L} Total\ Gain,$$ where, n_L = Total number of links. For the tree in Fig. 6, n_L =17.

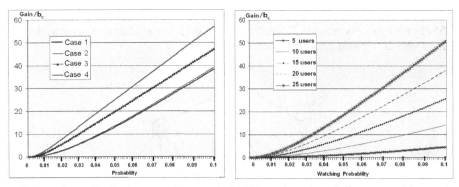

(a) Effect of user distribution on multicast gain (b) Effect of number of clients on multicast gain

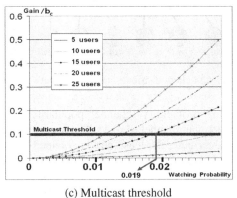

(c) Multicast threshold

Fig. 7. Numerical results for multicast gain and multicast threshold

A possible strategy for channel distribution could be based on the value of $\overline{LG}$. The decision of whether a channel is assigned to a dedicated multicast group or is unicasted based on the demand of the clients, is up to the service provider. For example, if the service provider aims for at least $10\%b_c$ of average gain per link, the threshold value should be set to 0.1 to identify which channels should be unicasted as shown in Fig. 7(c). This figure depicts the average multicast gain per link for the curves in Fig. 7(b) with a closer look at rarely watched channels with probability less than 0.03. The multicast threshold defines the border between multicasting and unicasting. For instance, when the number of active users in each access node is about 15, for the channels with watching probability less than 0.019, unicasting would be a better strategy than multicasting (see Fig. 7(c)).

Finally, we conclude that the potential advantage of multicast vs. unicast depends on:

- Tree structure (number of levels and branches).
- Watching probabilities of channels.
- Number and distribution of users at leaf nodes.
- Bandwidth requirement (b_c) to transmit the desired channel in a unicast mode.

7 Conclusion

Multicast can reduce the steady state bandwidth requirement on network links in TV streaming systems from one stream per viewer to one stream per TV channel. We introduced a new performance criterion, the multicast gain, to compare multicast and unicast efficiency. Based on this new measure, we analyzed the benefits of multicasting in tree-based topologies and proposed a method to calculate multicast gain for tree-structured networks. We also defined a strategy to decide when to use unicast or multicast sessions. Since TV channel watching probability often matches a Zipf-like distribution, most of the channels are among the unpopular channels with a very low watching probability. Due to overheads and problems of multicasting mechanisms, assigning a multicast group address to these types of channels may often be not reasonable. Although in this paper we discussed live TV channels, our results can be applied in a straight-forward manner to other applications that use multicasting. Since in a real network, not all the links have the same capacity, and the importance of the gain will depend on the capacity of the link, considering the gain relatively to the link capacity will be investigated in future work. We also plan to validate our numerical results by comparing them to simulation results or to measurements of existing IPTV networks.

References

1. Al-Khatib, M., Alam, M.S.: IPTV Multimedia Networks: Concepts, Developments, and Design. IEC Publ. (2007)
2. Pragyansmita, P., Raghavan, S.V.: Survey of multicast routing algorithms and protocols. In: Proceedings of the 15th Int. Conf. on Computer Communication, pp. 902–926 (2002)
3. Lee, K.S., Rhee, S.W., Youn, H.Y.: A MAC Layer Multicasting Approach for WiMAX Access Networks. In: PerCom (2008)
4. Hosseini, M., Ahmed, D.T., Shirmohammadi, S., Georganas, N.D.: A Survey of Application-Layer Multicast Protocols. IEEE Communications Surveys & Tutorials 9(3), 58–74 (2007)
5. Liu, Y., Guo, Y., Liang, C.: A survey on peer-to-peer video streaming systems. Peer-to-Peer Networking and Applications 1(1), 18–28 (2008)
6. Aaltonen, J., Karvo, J., Aalto, S.: Multicasting vs. Unicasting in Mobile Communication Systems. In: Proc. WoWMoM'02 (2002)
7. Qiu, T., Ge, Z., Lee, S., Wang, J., Zhao, Q., Xu, J.: Modeling Channel Popularity Dynamics in a Large IPTV System. In: SIGMETRICS/Performance'09, Seattle, WA, USA (2009)
8. Saichev, A., Malevergne, Y., Sornette, D.: Theory of Zipf's Law and Beyond. Springer, Heidelberg (2009)
9. Cha, M., et al.: Watching Television Over an IP Network. In: ACM IMC (2008)
10. IEEE 802.11b WG, Part 11: Wireless LAN Medium Access Control (MAC) and Physical Layer (PHY) specifications, IEEE Std. 802.11b- 1999/Cor 1-2001 (November 2001)
11. Liao, N., Shi, Y., Cheng, J., Li, J.: Optimized multicast service management in a mobile WiMAX TV system. In: Proc. CCNC 2009 (2009)
12. Kurose, J.F., Ross, K.: Computer Networking: A Top-Down Approach, 5th edn. Addison-Wesley, Reading (2010)

13. Xiao, Y., Du, X., Zhang, J., Hu, F., Guizani, F.: Internet Protocol Television (IPTV): The Killer Application for the Next-Generation Internet. IEEE in Communications Magazine, IEEE 45(11), 126–134 (2007)
14. IEEE 802.16 Relay Task Group (2008), `http://www.ieee802.org/16/relay/` (last access March 2010)
15. Phonphoem, A., Suchaisri, L.: Performance Analysis and Comparison between Multicast and Unicast over Infrastructure Wireless LAN. In: Second Asian Internet Engineering Conference, AINTEC (2006)

Dual Mobile-IP Tunnels for Video Stream Splitting and Merging in Wireless Handoffs

Tsang-Ling Sheu and Yang-Shun Hsu

Department of Electrical Engineering
National Sun Yat-Sen University
Kaohsiung, Taiwan
sheu@ee.nsysu.edu.tw

Abstract. In this paper, we design and develop a dual-tunnel scheme by setting up a secondary tunnel such that HA can perform load sharing by splitting and redirecting video packets from the primary tunnel to the secondary tunnel when the former encounters extremely high traffic load. The splitting of MPEG-4 video streams is performed progressively based on their frame types, I, B, and P; i.e., splitting B and P-frames first, and followed by even-numbered I-frames. Video receiver at MN will have to merge these divided video packets and then playback the video stream utterly. For the purpose of demonstration, we implement the dual-tunnel schemes on Linux platform. Experiments are conducted with different scenarios of stream splitting by varying the ratio of on-off background traffic. From the experimental results, we prove that the proposed dual-tunnel schemes can significantly improve the quality of video streams even under severe traffic load.

Keywords: Mobile IP, Wireless handoff, Dual tunnels, Load sharing, MPEG-4, Stream splitting and merging.

1 Introduction

Due to the fast development in wireless technologies, it has increasing possibility for a small and light mobile device (such as cellular phone, PDA, and notebook PC) to move away from its connection through another AP/BS. Thus, a mobile device may encounter sudden interruption during handoffs when receiving real-time video streams. Mobile IP [1-2] was developed by IETF to support seamless handoffs if an MH (mobile host) lost the connection with the original AP (belonging to one IP subnet) and reconnects to another AP (belonging to another IP subnet). In mobile IP, a reconnected MH is assigned a CoA (care of address) in a foreign network. Through CoA, the MH can re-establish the communication with CN (correspondent node) after home agent (HA) sets up an IP tunnel to foreign agent (FA). Even though mobile IP can support seamless handoffs for mobile devices, unfortunately, since only one tunnel at a time can be established between HA and FA, a large percentage of video packets over a single IP tunnel could be lost if wireless network becomes heavily congested. Consequently, the quality of video streams may be seriously degraded. This paper therefore presents a dual-tunnel approach for Mobile IP to offer load sharing by establishing a secondary tunnel in addition to the primary tunnel if another FA can be nearby located by MH.

E. Osipov et al. (Eds.): WWIC 2010, LNCS 6074, pp. 15–26, 2010.

Previous works on improving the quality of video streaming over wireless networks during handoffs include different aspects. Kashibuchi et al. [3] proposed a method to improve video quality during handoff. By predicting when to handoff using a modified RTCP report, his method can estimate the amount of bandwidth available to the MN after handoff. To overcome the problem of fast moving speed, Chao et al. [4] proposed a handoff strategy to minimize ping-pong effect between two base stations. Similarly, Mohanty et al. [5] proposed a method that combines layer-2 signal strength and layer-3 parameters to improve handoff efficiency.

Other than the improvement of handoff efficiency, many papers have focused on load sharing by dividing a video stream into many sub-streams. Tu et al. [6] proposed a method of adaptive split transmission for video streams in wireless mesh networks. Based on the estimation of available bandwidth, his method can determine whether splitting a video stream into several sub-streams is substantially helpful. By fully utilizing the multi-layer characteristics of MPEG-4, Chilamkurti et al. [7-9] improved video quality through FEC (Forward Error Correction) techniques. Pan et al. [10] proposed an end-to-end multipath smooth handoff scheme for video streaming. The basic idea behind his approach is to duplicate the critical data, such as I-frames, and then place these critical data on different multiple paths. To deal with load sharing over multiple paths, Leung et al. [11-12] proposed two algorithms. The first algorithm is to divide the traffic based on the relative importance of data packets. The second algorithm, on the contrary, is to weight the multiple paths for different traffic loads. Finally, Son et al. [13] proposed a soft load-balancing scheme, with which IP packets can be split evenly and placed over multiple paths.

The main goal of this paper, different from the previous works, is to build a secondary tunnel for Mobile IP to offer load sharing when the primary tunnel gets congested. Thus, one of the novelties presented by this paper is to split video streams over two Mobile-IP tunnels by classifying MPEG-4 VOP (Video Object Planes) frame types, I-, B-, and P-VOP. The splitting of video streams is performed progressively along with the increasing background traffic; i.e., splitting B- and P-VOP frames first, and then followed by even-numbered I-VOP frames. Video receiver at MN will have to merge these divided video packets and playback the video stream successively. For the purpose of demonstration, we design and implement the dual-tunnel Mobile IP schemes on Linux platform by C/C++ coding. Experiments and measurements are conducted with different scenarios of stream splitting and merging by varying the ratio of on-off background traffic on FA through the primary tunnel.

The remainder of this paper is organized as follows. In Section 2, we introduce the encapsulation of MPEG-4 VOP frame within an IP packet. In Section 3, we present the proposed stream splitting and merging (SSM) scheme with dual Mobile IP tunnels. In Section 4, the implementations of the SSM scheme on Linux platform is described, and the experimental results are discussed. Finally, we conclude this paper in Section 5.

2   VOP in MPEG-4

Different from the traditional encoding scheme, a video picture in MPEG-4 [14] is divided into many different video objects (VO). Each VO is then compressed into three types of Video Object Plane (VOP), I-VOP, B-VOP, and P-VOP. Similar to I, B, and P frame in MPEG-2, I-VOP can be decoded independently, while P-VOP will have to rely on I-VOP or other P-VOP, and B-VOP will have to rely on I-VOP and P-VOP. Thus, among the three types of VOP, I-VOP is considered as the most important one for decoder to playback the original MPEG stream. Delivering a video stream with these three types of VOP frames from a server to a client over IP network requires the encapsulation process. Figure 1 shows how I-VOP frames be segmented into IP packets to adapt to an MTU (Maximum Transfer Unit) of a physical network.

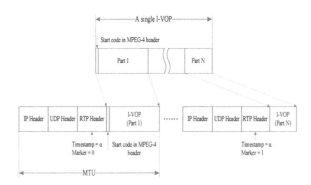

Fig. 1. I-VOP of MPEG-4 encapsulated within IP packets

As illustrated in Figure 1, the start code (0x000001B6) within the MPEG-4 header is used to determine the beginning of an I-VOP frame. Unfortunately, the start code exists only in the first IP packet after segmentation. Thus, to reassemble all the segmented IP packets into the original I-VOP frame, a receiver will have to examine the 32-bit RTP (Real-time Transport Protocol) timestamp of every IP packet, for the packets belonging to the same VOP frame all possess the same RTP timestamp. Additional, to determine whether the packet is the last one of a VOP frame, the one-bit marker, denoting the end of a video frame, is examined.

3 Stream Splitting and Merging

In Today's Mobile IP, there exists a single tunnel between FA and HA, which may become performance bottleneck if high-quality video streams are delivered over the single tunnel. Thus, this Section aims at designing an effective stream splitting and merging (SSM) scheme over multiple tunnels during handoff.

3.1 Network Topology

Figure 2 shows the topology of stream splitting and merging by setting up a secondary tunnel in addition to the primary tunnel. As illustrated, when MN moves away from its HA and approaches to an area where many FAs signals can be sensed. FA with the strongest signal will be selected by MN to acquire its CoA, through which

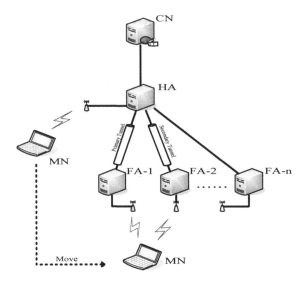

Fig. 2. Mobile IP architectures with dual tunnels

the primary tunnel is built. When the traffic on the primary tunnel increases very quickly and exceeds the tunnel capacity, an FA with the second strongest signal will set up the secondary tunnel with HA to share the load.

3.2   The Proposed SSM Algorithms

To split video stream on HA and merge the stream on MN, we propose the stream splitting and merging (SSM) algorithms as shown in Figure 3. Three states exist in the proposed SSM algorithm state-1 (S1) represents the normal traffic condition, i.e., stream splitting is not required. State-2 (S2) is the state when queue length of FA has exceeded the first threshold (qlen_threshold_A) beyond which video quality is degraded. Thus, the proposed SSM algorithm will begin to split P and B-VOP from the original stream and place them on the established secondary tunnel. When traffic load on the primary tunnel continues to increase and the queue length of FA has exceeded the second threshold (qlen_threshold_B), the system changes from moderate traffic load to severe traffic load. Thus, State-3 (S3) represents the condition where I-VOP may be dropped due to severe traffic load on the primary tunnel. At this moment, SSM begins to place even-numbered I-VOP on the secondary tunnel. Finally, when the queue length of FA drops below qlen_threshold_A, the system automatically goes back to the normal state (S1). Thus, the proposed SSM consists of two sub-algorithms to be performed on HA.

  1. Modified handoff scheme,
  2. Classification of VOP frames.

3.2.1   Modified Mobile-IP Handoff Scheme

Since the proposed SSM supports dual tunnels between HA and FA, the original Mobile IP software at MN and HA requires some modifications.

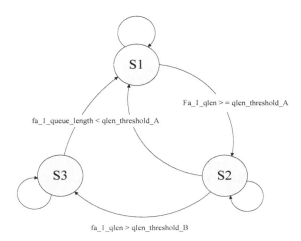

Fig. 3. Three-state transitions of the SSM

```
WHILE (1) {
IF (receive_advertisement())
{// If a received Advertisement Broadcast message
IF(advertisement_from_ha())
// Identify whether it is from HA or not
update_mn_location();  // Update MN Location
IF(advertisement_from_fa())
{// Identify whether it is from FA or not
IF (get_mn_location() == leave_ha)
{// If MN is leaving HA
IF (registed_coa < 2)
// If the number of registered CoA is less than 2
register_coa();    // Register CoA}}}
ELSE
update_mn_location();
// Update MN location
}
```

Fig. 4. Operations of a mobile node

As shown in Figure 4, an MN will first determine whether the advertisement message is from HA or FA. If MN has moved away from HA, it will register two CoAs from two different FA, respectively. As shown in Figure 5, HA first periodically broadcast advertisement message, and at the same time it receives CoA binding message from FA. HA then builds the primary tunnel for the first CoA binding, and in turn builds the secondary tunnel for the second CoA. At last, HA reroutes packets to MN through the primary and the secondary tunnels by classifying VOP frame.

```
WHILE(1) {
broadcast_advertisement(); // Broadcast advertisement
IF (receive_register())
{// If  a received registration message
IF(registed_coa() < 2)
{// If the number of registered CoA is less than 2
IF (!pri_tun_exist()) {// If the primary tunnel not setup
setup_pri_tun();  // Set up the primary tunnel
re-route_pkt_to_pri_coa();
// Reroute packets to the primary tunnel
} ELSE // If the primary tunnel has been setup
setup_sec_tun(); // Set up the secondary tunnel
re-route_pkt_to_sec_coa();
// Reroute packet to the secondary tunnel
}}
IF (pri_tun_exist() && sec_tun_exist())
// If these two tunnels have been setup
activate_stream_split_mechanism();}
```

Fig. 5. Operations of HA

3.2.2 VOP Classification Algorithm

The start code of MPEG-4 header can be used to classify the three types of VOP. As shown in Table 1, I-VOP has two start codes, 0x000001B3 and 0x000001B6 with next 2 bits 00, while P-VOP and B-VOP has the same start code 0x000001B6 but different in the next two bits (01 for P-VOP and 10 for B-VOP). It is noticed that a VOP may consists of more than one IP packets.

Table 1. MPEG start code

RTP Payload Data		Frame
Start code	Next 2 bits	Types
0x000001B3	Don't care	I
0x000001B6	00	
	01	P
	10	B

In this case, the start code exists only in the first IP packet. Thus, no start codes can be used to distinguish the VOP types for the rest of IP packets of the same VOP. Fortunately, we observe that all the IP packets of the same VOP possess the same timestamp within RTP header. Hence, split a video stream into two sub-streams based on VOP types becomes possible when network becomes congested. Figure 6 shows the VOP classification performed by HA. As it can be observed, start codes and RTP timestamps are used to classify different VOPs. Additionally when network becomes severely congested, as shown in Figure 7, SSM will switch from S2 to S3. At S3, I-VOP is further classified into two types; even-numbered and odd-numbered I-VOP.

```
IF (receive_packet()) {// Receive a packet
IF (packet_transmission_header() == udp_header) {// Is it a UDP packet?
IF((packet _data() == rtp_header) && (rtp_payload_type == mpeg4))
{// It is RTP packet, and payload type is MPEG-4
IF (rtp_payload() == 0x000001B6) {// Is it a start code?
IF (mpeg4_vop_type(packet) == 0) {// Is it an I-frame?
RETURN i_frame_odd_even_process();
// Call i_frame_odd_even_process()
} ELSE IF (mpeg4_vop_type() == 1) {// Is it a P-frame?
p_frame_timestamp = rtp_timestamp;
// Record the timestamp of P-frame
RETURN p_frame_match();
} ELSE IF (mpeg4_vop_type() == 2) {// Is it a B-frame?
b_frame_timestamp = rtp_timestamp;
// Record the timestamp of B-frame
RETURN b_frame_match();
}} ELSE IF (rtp_payload() == 0x000001B3)
{// It is an I-frame in a Group of VOP
RETURN i_frame_odd_even_process();
// Call i_frame_odd_even_process()
} ELSE IF {// Identify whether the same timestamp
IF (rtp_timestamp() == odd_i_frame_timestamp)
RETURN odd_i_frame_match();
ELSE IF (rtp_timestamp() == even_i_frame_timestamp)
RETURN even_i_frame_match();
ELSE IF (rtp_timestamp() == p_frame_timestamp)
RETURN p_frame_match();
ELSE IF (rtp_timestamp() == b_frame_timestamp)
RETURN b_frame_match();}}}}
```

Fig. 6. VOP frame classifications

Even-numbered I-VOP will be redirected to the secondary tunnel, while odd-numbered I-VOP will stay in the primary tunnel.

4 Implementations and Analyses

Figure 8 shows the topology of experiments. Initially, MN is connected to HA over wireless link (IEEE 802.11g). MN then moves into the overlapping area of FA-1 and FA-2. To purposely vary the traffic load on FA-1, background traffic is generated by a notebook PC by passing through a Hub to FA-1. Note that in the topology, six different IP networks are used (i.e., 192.168.0.0/24 to 192.168.5.0/24) to demonstrate the handoff of an MN while receiving video streams. Figure 9 shows the flow chart of the proposed SSM modules inserted through Pre-routing, one of the Net-filter hook [15] provided by Linux kernel for external interface. Developed new SSM modules are described as below.

```
i_frame_odd_even_process() {
IF (is_odd_i_frame) {// If it is an odd-numbered
odd_i_frame_timestamp = rtp_timestamp;
// Record the timestamp of an odd-numbered I-frame
RETURN odd_i_frame_match();
} ELSE
{// If it is an even-numbered
even_i_frame_timestamp = rtp_timestamp;
// Record the timestamp of an even-numbered  I-frame
RETURN even_i_frame_match();
}}
```

Fig. 7. I-VOP re-marked with odd and even

1. ip_dest_match( ): Packet received from ip_rev( ) are examined whether its destination address matches with MN's.

2. ip_dest_swarp_PT( ): If the destination address of an IP packet matches with IP address of MN, it is swapped with the CoA of the primary tunnel.

3. mepg4_match( ): With this module, IP packets can be differentiated by I/P/B-VOP. Thus, B-VOP and P-VOP packets are redirected to the secondary tunnel, if traffic load on FA-1 has exceeded the minimum threshold.

4. ip_dest_swarp_ST( ): If the destination address of an IP packet matches with the IP address of MN, it is swapped with the CoA of the secondary tunnel.

Two experiments are performed. The first experiment observes the improvement of video quality when the proposed SSM with dual tunnels is employed. The second experiment estimates how many percentages of I, B, and P-VOP frames being split to the secondary tunnel when different ratios of on-off background traffic are generated. HA will periodically detect the queue length of FA-1, where background traffic is generated by iperf [16] through a hub in an on-off fashion. Initially, HA remains in state-1 (S1), and it will enter state-2 (S2) when the queue length of FA-1 exceeds 30,000 bytes. At this time, the SSM algorithm is invoked to split B and P-VOP to the secondary tunnel. When the queue length of FA-1 continues to increase and exceeds 50,000 bytes, the system enters state-3 (S3). At S3, only odd-numbered I-VOP frame remains in the primary tunnel, while B, P, and even-numbered I-VOP frames are split to the secondary tunnel.

Table 2 shows the number and size of I, P, B-VOP frames of a video film used in the experiment. As an example, if I-VOP frames of the film are examined, there are total 806 frames with total frame size 9,184,548 bytes. The 806 I-VOP frames are segmented into 6,534 IP packets with average packet size 1,405.65 bytes. To compare the difference in video quality, Figure 10 (a) shows four consecutive frames by using the proposed SSM with dual tunnels, while Figure 10 (b) shows the same consecutive four frames without employing the SSM. As it can be observed from the figures, mosaic and lag phenomenon in Figure 10 (b) was removed and video quality is improved.

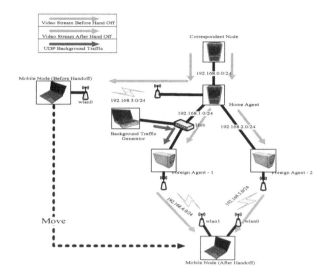

Fig. 8. Topology for the SSM experiment

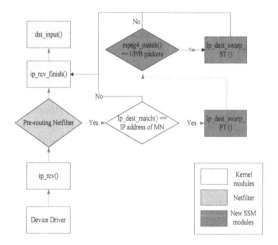

Fig. 9. Developed SSM modules on Linux

Table 2. The number and size of I, P, and B-VOP

VOP Frame Types	Number of Frames	Total Frame Size (Bytes)	Average Frame Size (Bytes)	Total Number of IP Packets	Average IP Packet Size (Bytes)
I	806	9,184,548	11,395.22	6,534	1,405.65
P	4,022	28,959,285	7,200.22	21,466	1,349.07
B	9,652	36,006,345	3,730.45	29,062	1,238.95

(a) With the SSM

(b) Without the SSM

Fig. 10. Four consecutive video frames

Figure 11 validates the effect of stream splitting and merging. By increasing the ratio of on-off background traffic on FA-1 from 10% to 100%, bit rates over the primary tunnel has been decreased from 1270 Kbps down to 1160 Kbps; it is about 113 Kbps traffic load relief in the primary tunnel.

Figure 12 shows the bit rate variations on the secondary tunnel between state-2 and state-3. During the 480-sec experiment, the total amount of data received at FA-2 is 511.84 Mbits for state-2, and it is 547.93 Mbits for stste-3. If we deduct the second number from the first number, the difference is the size of even-numbered I-VOP frames, which are split from the primary to the secondary tunnel.

Finally, by increasing the ratio of background traffic from 10% to 100%, Figure 13 shows the percentage of I, B, P-VOP frames received from the secondary tunnel. When the ratio of on-off traffic is smaller than 30%, it is observed that no I-VOP frames are redirected to the secondary tunnel. However, the percentage of I-VOP frames received from the secondary tunnel increases gradually when the ratio of on-off traffic increases. In fact, it is about 49% of I-VOP frames and about 96% of B/P-VOP frames, which are redirected to the secondary tunnel when the ratio increases to 100%. From the percentage of I, B, and P-VOP frames received from the secondary tunnel, we also found out that it is about 1% of I-VOP frames and 4% of B/P-VOP frames lost during the wireless handoff.

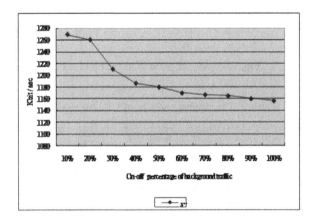

Fig. 11. Bit rates versus background traffic

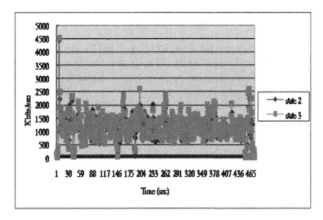

Fig. 12. Bit rate variations on the secondary tunnel

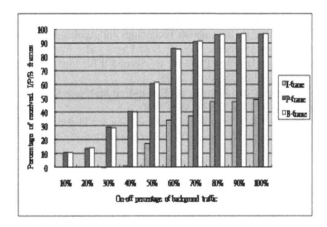

Fig. 13. Percentages of received I, P, and B frames

5 Conclusions

In this paper, we have presented a stream splitting and merging (SSM) scheme for Mobile-IP with dual tunnels to share the load when network traffic becomes severely congested. To build the secondary tunnel in addition to the primary tunnel, we have modified Today's mobile IP so that two different CoAs can be bind concurrently on HA. For the purpose of evaluation, we implemented the proposed SSM scheme with dual tunnels on Linux platform. The implementations include the modified mobile IP handoff module and I/B/P-VOP frame classification module. By purposely injecting different percentages of on-off background traffic on the primary tunnel, we observed that, with the proposed SSM scheme, the traffic load on the primary tunnel has been evenly split to the secondary tunnel. Because of the load sharing between the two tunnels, video quality can be substantially improved even in a heavily congested traffic condition.

References

1. Perkins, C.: IP Mobility Support for IPv4. RFC 3344, IETF (August 2002)
2. Perkins, C., Microsystems, S.: Mobile IP. IEEE Comm. Magazine (May 1997)
3. Kashibuchi, K., Taleb, T., Jamalipour, A., Nemoto, Y., Kato, N.: A New Smooth Handoff Scheme for Mobile Multimedia Streaming Using RTP Dummy Packets and RTCP Explicit Handoff Notification. IEEE Wireless Communications and Networking Conference (2006)
4. Chao, H.-C., Huang, C.-Y.: Micro-Mobility Mechanism for Sooth Handoffs in an Integrated Ad-Hoc and Cellular IPv6 Network Under High-Speed Movement. IEEE Transactions on Vehicular Technology 52(6) (November 2003)
5. Mohanty, S., Akyildiz, I.F.: A Cross-Layer (Layer 2 + 3) Handoff Management Protocol for Next-Generation Wireless Systems. IEEE Transactions on Mobile Computing 5(10) (October 2006)
6. Tu, W., Sreenan, C.J.: Adaptive Split Transmission for Video Streams in Wireless Mesh Networks. In: IEEE Wireless Communications and Networking Conference (2008)
7. Chilamkurti, N.K., Soh, B., Auley, A.M.: Video Multicasting Using Layered FEC on Split Protocol. In: IEEE Region 10 Conference (2004)
8. Chilamkurti, N.K., Soh, B.: Multimedia Multicast Using SPLIT and Layered FEC. In: Third International Conf. on Information Technology and Applications (2005)
9. Brennan, S.C., Chilamkurti, N.K., Soh, B.: Split-Layer Video Multicast Protocol: A New Receiver-Based Rate-Adaptation Protocol. In: Second IEEE International Symposium on Network Computing and Applications (2003)
10. Pan, Y., Lee, M., Kim, J.-B., Suda, T.: An End-to-End Multipath Smooth Handoff Scheme for Stream Media. IEEE JSAC 22(4) (May 2004)
11. Leung, K.-C., Li, V.O.K.: Generalized Load Sharing for Packet-Switching Networks I: Theory and Packet-Based Algorithm. IEEE Transactions on Parallel and Distributed Systems 17(7) (July 2006)
12. Leung, K.-C., Li, V.O.K.: Generalized Load Sharing for Packet-Switching Networks II: Flow-Based Algorithms. IEEE Trans. on Parallel and Distributed Systems 17(7) (July 2006)
13. Son, H., Lee, S., Kim, S.-C., Shin, Y.-S.: Soft Load Balancing Over Heterogeneous Wireless Networks. IEEE Trans. on Vehicular Technology 57(4) (July 2008)
14. Koenen, R.: MPEG-4 Overview- (V.21-Jeju Version). ISO/IEC JTC1/SC29/WG11 N4668 (March 2002)
15. iptables, http://www.netfilter.org/
16. iperf, http://iperf.sourceforge.net/

Distributed Cooperation and Diversity for Hybrid Wireless Networks

H. Javaheri, G. Noubir, and Y. Wang

College of Computer and Information Science
Northeastern University, Boston, MA 02115 USA
{hooman,noubir,yin}@ccs.neu.edu

Abstract. In this paper, we propose a new Distributed Cooperation and Diversity Combining framework. Our focus is heterogeneous networks with devices equipped with two types of radio frequency (RF) links: short-range high-rate interface (e.g., IEEE802.11), and a long-range low-rate interface (e.g., cellular) communicating in fading channels. Within this framework, we propose and evaluate a set of distributed cooperation techniques operating at different hierarchical levels with resource constraints such as short-range RF bandwidth. We propose a Priority Maximum-Ratio Combining (PMRC) for pre-demodulation combining, a post soft-demodulation combining, and a decode-and-forward technique. We show that the proposed techniques achieve significant improvements on Signal to Noise Ratio (SNR), Bit Error Rate (BER) and throughput through analysis, simulation, and experimentation on our platform prototype. Our results also indicate that, under several communication scenarios we are considering, PMRC can improve the throughput performance by over an order of magnitude.

Keywords: Diversity, Cooperation, Hybrid Wireless Networks.

1 Introduction

Wireless communication networks are enabling an ever increasing set of applications. The service quality and scalability of these applications is limited by fundamental constraints. These include a scarce radio-frequency spectrum, signal propagation effects such as fading and shadowing resulting in areas with limited coverage, and the small form factor of mobile devices with limited energy capacity and antenna diversity. Recently due to the increasing demand of mobile services such as mobile cloud computing and video streaming, improving the robustness and throughput of cellular systems has become more critical. Many technologies including dynamic power control, adaptive coding and modulation, smart antenna, etc., have been proposed or adopted, nevertheless the cooperation gain has yet been exploited completely. To improve the spectrum efficiency, one of the solutions used by operators is to deploy additional base stations [1], but this strategy is ineffective and costly. In this paper, we propose to explore a new communication model, where multiple mobile nodes *cooperate*

E. Osipov et al. (Eds.): WWIC 2010, LNCS 6074, pp. 27–39, 2010.

with each other and with the base stations. We will investigate communication strategies that exploit the channel diversity across a set of cooperating mobile nodes equipped with multiple radio interfaces.

Diversity and cooperation, as general mechanisms to improve the robustness and efficiency of wireless communication systems, have been studied for many years [2,3,4], but very little research has been done for distributed wireless systems with multiple types of air-interfaces and considering the unique characteristics of each interfaces. With the increased hardware integration, faster computation, and high users density, the cooperation between nearby devices is becoming possible and even necessary given the increased demand for bandwidth.

Unlike traditional diversity paradigms, our approach combines the physical layer information from multiple distributed receivers using the short-range high data-rate wireless network. It exploits both the antenna gain and the fading independence. This cooperation can significantly improve the Signal to Noise Ratio (SNR), Bit Error Rate (BER) and throughput. It leads to improved coverage, capacity boost and reduction of interference.

Contributions: We propose a distributed cooperation framework - Hierarchical Priority Combining, which allows multiple levels of cooperation depending on the channel conditions and resource constraints. It consists of three combining techniques: pre-demodulation combining, post soft-demodulation combining, and decode-and-forward. We also propose Priority Maximum Ratio Combining (PMRC) as an implementation of pre-demodulation combining, and show orders of magnitude improvement of the SNR, outage probability, BER and throughput even with limited short-range bandwidth. We also show that most of the benefit of the traditional single device Maximum-Ratio Combining (MRC) can be achieved by PMRC with the contribution from a small group of neighbouring nodes. In addition, we simulate its performance using a pilot-based channel estimator and show that a significant gain can be achieved. We also implemented the post soft-demodulation combining prototype on the USRP/GNU radio and revealed substantial gain for channels with moderate fading.

Related work: While, cellular have been benefiting from continuous improvements of the physical link-layer between a mobile station and one or multiple base stations (through various coding, modulation, and antenna technologies), it is only recently that distributed cooperation started to attract more interest from the wireless communications and networking research community [5]. Some studies have addressed specific cases such as diversity with *homogeneous* interfaces where the combining occurs over the air [6, 7, 8]. Several interesting approaches demonstrate the benefits of distributed cooperation in *ad hoc networks* with *homogeneous* wireless interfaces and challenged the community to investigate the full benefits of distributed cooperation [9, 10, 5]. Distributed MIMO in ad hoc network has also been theoretically studied in [11]. The use of cooperating *heterogeneous* air-interfaces was advocated in [12, 13]. Cooperation of multi-radio access networks has also been researched in [14] to enhance the transmission robustness. More recently, several post soft-demodulation techniques were proposed [15, 16]. In our previous work [17], we have introduced Threshold Maximum-Ratio Combining and studied its performance. In this paper, we significantly extend our previously proposed distributed cross-layer diversity framework to hierarchical combining (HPC) and introduce PMRC a substantially superior combining technique.

2   System Model

We consider a hybrid network where the mobile nodes are equipped with two radio interfaces: a long-range, low data-rate cellular interface, and a short-range, high data-rate interface. The performance of long-range cellular links is limited by the shadowing and channel fading caused by multipath propagation and mobility. These are critical problems in cellular communication as they result in dead-signal areas and localized poor system performance. *RF-channel diversity* is a typical approach to overcome them through independent transmission paths. Many existing technologies, such as MIMO, require multiple antennas to be co-located at the same device. Due to the minimum spatial separation (0.4λ [4]) and high cost of RF front ends, however, it is impractical to implement these schemes on a single small form factor device such as a cell phone [6]. Our cooperation strategy intends to make use of the RF front ends of a group of geographically separated devices. This cooperation operates at the physical-link layer, and it is transparent to applications. Therefore the existing applications would have an improved performance without requiring any awareness or modifications.

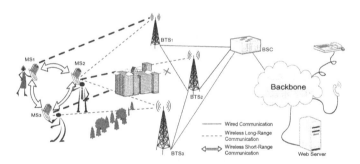

Fig. 1. Example of setup for distributed cross-layer diversity

Currently, most smart-phones are equipped with a WiFi interface besides their cellular interface. The high speed local network makes the distributed cooperation with a small group of nearby users possible. For example, consider the scenario depicted in Figure 1. Three mobile users, each with a cellular phone, suffer from the typical channel fading and shadowing, that impairs urban cellular communication, and also from path loss (attenuation) due to the distance to the base station. In this scenario, the long-range cellular signals are (1) independently received at each node, (2) relayed through the high speed local wireless network, and (3) combined at the destination node.

The existing techniques introduced in the past (e.g., Maximum Ratio Combining, and Generalized Selective Combining [18, 2, 4]) were designed for antennas that are wired to a central combiner and not restricted by the local communication limitations. The proposed cooperation strategy allows the nodes to forward information to other nodes through a local wireless network. This raises interesting questions on how to maximize the system performance with the constraints on the local network bandwidth, computation and energy consumption. We propose a novel cooperation framework that improve the long-range communication performance while accounting for the local bandwidth constraint.

For the proposed cooperation to be used in practice, other mechanisms need to be developed to address the issues regarding security, privacy and fairness. They will be in our future work. In this paper, we mainly focus on the performance analysis, protocol design and evaluation.

3   Hierarchical Priority Combining

In this section, we introduce a distributed cooperation framework - Hierarchical Priority Combining (HPC). It incorporates three levels of combining: *decode-and-forward*, *post soft-demodulation*, and *pre-demodulation*. We first outline the three combining techniques used in HPC; then describe the proposed HPC protocol; followed by performance analysis, and simulation and experiment results.

Decode-and-forward: if at least one of the assisting nodes can demodulate the packet and verify its integrity, then the decoded packet can be relayed to the master node through the local network. This level of combining uses the minimum local bandwidth, but can only be used when the overall signal strength is high while the mobile nodes are experiencing strong uneven fading or shadowing. This could be the case of a group of moving people in a car, bus, or train.

Post soft-demodulation combining: at this level, the signal received by the assisting nodes is already strong enough for demodulation but still has a significant number of errors. In this case, *some* of the assisting nodes, with the strongest received signals, send the soft-decision output of the demodulator to the master node. Combining at this level can be very efficient at correcting errors when the signal strength is relatively high and has the advantage of requiring only a moderate local communication bandwidth.

Pre-demodulation combining: at this level, *some* of the assisting nodes with the strongest SNR transmit the sampled down-converted RF-signal to the master node to combine with the master's signal. Combining at this level delivers the best error correction result, but transmitting the sampled waveform requires a large local bandwidth. Therefore, it is more appropriate in the scenarios where the long-range radio signal is weak and experiences strong fading. We introduce *Priority Maximum Ratio Combining* as an implementation candidate for pre-demodulation combining.

HPC protocol decides which level of combining to use based on the received signal quality at each node. It runs in two phases. In Phase I, the nodes exchange information with each other about the quality of the received signals. In phase II, each node decides if and what level of combining to operate. The high-level description of the protocol is provided below. M is the total number of nodes involved in the cooperation. N is the number of signal sources involved in combining. Note that since the cooperation always includes the master node, $N - 1$ is the actual number of remote assisting nodes.

Phase I: The master node broadcasts a cooperation request beacon if it is unable to decode the packet. Upon recipience of the cooperation-request beacon, the assisting node measures the SNR of the received signal (denoted by γ) from the long-range air interface and compares it with a predefined value γ_D, the threshold above which demodulating the packet is feasible.) If $\gamma < \gamma_D$ the assisting node just broadcasts the SNR to others. If $\gamma > \gamma_D$, it will try to demodulate the packet and verify its integrity using a CRC-like checksum. Finally, the assisting node will broadcast both the SNR and the CRC verification result. Each node is assigned to a time slot during this phase to avoid collisions.

Phase II: In this phase each node makes a decision after hearing other assisting nodes' report of signal quality. If at least one assisting node can demodulate the long-range RF signal and also pass the CRC check, one of them with the highest ID will relay the decoded packet to the master. If no one passes the CRC check and the total number of assisting nodes with $\gamma > \gamma_D$ is more than a predefined value, the top $N_{soft} - 1$ nodes with the strongest SNR transmit their soft decision values to the master, in the order of their IDs, for post soft-demodulation combining, and the value $N_{soft} - 1$ is limited by the local bandwidth. Last, if none of the above cases happen, the top $N_{pre} - 1$ nodes with strongest SNR send the sampled waveform to the master for pre-demodulation combining. N_{pre} is also limited by the local bandwidth. N_{soft} and N_{pre} are usually different, depending on system parameters. For simplicity of notation, in the following discussion we may use N to represent either.

3.1 Priority Maximum-Ratio Combining

We introduce Priority Maximum-Ratio Combining (PMRC) as an implementation of pre-demodulation combining scheme. In PMRC, a subset of the assisting nodes with strongest SNR relay their signals to the master to combine with the signal received at the master node. The complete protocol is described in Algorithm 1 and 2. As the master's signal does not need to be transmitted, there is no bandwidth consumption for it. Therefore, we first introduce SPMRC, which is a special case of PMRC, where the signals are combined without the master's contribution. Then we will use SPMRC to derive PMRC.

Consider a system of M mobile nodes in cooperation. For each packet (or time slot) PMRC first identifies the $N - 1$ strongest signals out of the $M - 1$ cooperating neighbours and then combines their sampled signals with the signal received by the master node (destination) before demodulation. The selected signals are combined by *Maximum Ratio Combining* (MRC) [2]. In the following we denote by (M, N)-PMRC a scheme where the master's signal is combined with the signal from $N - 1$ remote cooperating nodes. $(M, 1)$-PMRC is the non-cooperative case. (M, M)-PMRC is the traditional MRC with M branches. We will show that $(M, N < M)$-PMRC (e.g. $M = 5, N = 3$) are the most interesting schemes that benefit from distributed diversity at low bandwidth/energy cost. We first study the distribution of the combined SNR. This allows us to compute the outage probability, BER, frame error rate (FER) as well as throughput. Our analysis of PMRC is in two steps. First, we derive the SNR distribution of the combined signal from only the $N - 1$ strongest remote assisting nodes $((M, N)$-SPMRC), and then compute the actual SNR distribution at the master node where it is also combined with the master's own signal.

Algorithm 1: Protocol 1. PMRC - master node protocol

Initialize the cooperative network with M nodes
Broadcast the cooperation control packet -*CCINFO*
/* CCINFO contains the info. such as frequency, modulation, GSM time slot allocation, and parameters (M, N) for the PMRC
    cooperation scheme.   */
begin
    while *until the session ends* **do**
        $buf[0]$ ←receive signal at the next expected time slot from the long-range interface;
        $\Gamma[0]$ ← the SNR γ of the received signal;
        $\Delta[0]$ ← 1 if $\gamma > \gamma_D$. and CRC correct;
        if $\Delta[0] = 1$ **then**
            Broadcast to cancel cooperation;
            out ← $decode(buf[0])$; **return**;
        Broadcast the *Phase I* beacon to all nodes through the short-range interface;
        $\Gamma[1...M]$ ← collect γs from all branches;
        $\Delta[1...M]$ ← collect δs from all branches;
        if $sum(\Delta[1...M]) > 1$ **then**
            out←Received data at *Phase II*; **return**.
        if $num(\gamma' > \gamma_D) \geq S, \gamma' \in \Gamma[1...M]$ **then**
            out← soft decision decode on the aggregated data from N strongest neighboring nodes;
            return;
        $buf[1...N - 1]$ ← collect the sampled signals with the top $(N - 1)$ SNRs from assisting nodes;
        out←$decode(MRC(buf, \gamma))$;
        /* out is the output data   */
end

Algorithm 2: Protocol 2. PMRC - assisting nodes protocol

Receive the cooperation control packet - *CCINFO*.
begin
    while *until the session ends* **do**
        buf←receive signal at the next master's time slot from the long-range interface;
        γ ← the SNR of the received signal;
        δ ← the result from CRC check if $\gamma > \gamma_D$;
        Wait for the *Phase I* beacon from the master;
            Receive the $\Gamma[1...M]$ and $\Delta[1...M]$ from all other assisting nodes;
            Broadcast γ and δ at its dedicated time slot;
        Wait for the *Phase II* beacon from the master;
        if *it's the highest ID with $\delta = 1$* **then**
            Send the decoded packet to master; **return**;
        if *other nodes pass the CRC check* **then return**;
        if $\gamma > \gamma_D$ *and $num(\gamma' > \gamma_D) \geq S, \gamma' \in \Gamma[]$ and γ is among the N strongest signal branches* **then**
            send **soft decision decoding values to the master**
            return;
        if γ *is within N^{th} strongest SNR of all assisting nodes* **then**
            transmit buf to the master in the ith time slot through the short-range interface.
end

3.2   Channel Model

We consider a typical channel propagation model for cellular communications-Rayleigh channel [4]. We assume that frame can be delayed and aligned at the destination node for constructive combining. In this model, the distribution function of the signal to noise ratio (SNR denoted by γ) is as a function of the long run average SNR (denoted by $\bar{\gamma}$).

$$p(\gamma \leq t) = \int_0^t \frac{1}{\bar{\gamma}} e^{-\frac{\gamma}{\bar{\gamma}}} \, d\gamma = 1 - e^{-\frac{t}{\bar{\gamma}}}$$

In practice the average SNR might not be the same for each node, e.g. shadowing, but to demonstrate the potential gain our analysis assumes equal average SNR for each node with the noise power spectral density $\mathcal{N}_0/2$. Due to the spatial separation, the fading channel for each node is independent. The probability that the signals received by all nodes have an SNR less than t is:

$$p(\gamma_1 \leq t, \cdots, \gamma_M \leq t) = p(\gamma_1 \leq t) \cdots p(\gamma_M \leq t) = (1 - e^{-\frac{t}{\bar{\gamma}}})^M$$

3.3   SPMRC: SNR Distribution for N=1, 2, 3

Let (M, N)-SPMRC, be the combined signal of the N strongest assisting nodes excluding the master node. Let X, Y, Z denote the random variable for the highest, second highest and third highest SNR among all M neighbors. In the case of $(M, 1)$-SPMRC, this is traditionally known as *Selective Combining* [4].

$$p_X(x) = \frac{M}{\bar{\gamma}} e^{-\frac{x}{\bar{\gamma}}} (1 - e^{-\frac{x}{\bar{\gamma}}})^{M-1}$$

In the case of $(M, 2)$-SPMRC, the master collects the two strongest signals from the M neighboring nodes. The joint probability density function (PDF) is:

$$p_{X,Y}(x, y) = \begin{cases} \frac{M}{\bar{\gamma}} e^{-\frac{x}{\bar{\gamma}}} \frac{(M-1)}{\bar{\gamma}} e^{-\frac{y}{\bar{\gamma}}} \times (1 - e^{-\frac{y}{\bar{\gamma}}})^{M-2}, & x \geq y \\ 0, & \text{else} \end{cases}$$

Applying MRC to the two strongest signals X and Y gives, $\gamma_\Sigma = X + Y$ [18]:

$$p_{\gamma_\Sigma}(\gamma) = \int_0^\gamma p_{X,Y}(\gamma - y, y) \, dy$$

$$= \frac{M(M-1)e^{-\frac{\gamma}{\bar{\gamma}}}}{\bar{\gamma}} \times \left(\frac{\gamma}{2\bar{\gamma}} + \sum_{i=1}^{M-2} \frac{(-1)^i}{i} \binom{M-2}{i} (1 - e^{-\frac{i\gamma}{2\bar{\gamma}}}) \right)$$

Similarly for $(M, 3)$-SPMRC:

$$p_{X,Y,Z}(x, y, z) = \begin{cases} \frac{M}{\bar{\gamma}} e^{-\frac{x}{\bar{\gamma}}} \frac{(M-1)}{\bar{\gamma}} e^{-\frac{y}{\bar{\gamma}}} \frac{(M-2)}{\bar{\gamma}} e^{-\frac{z}{\bar{\gamma}}} \times (1 - e^{-\frac{z}{\bar{\gamma}}})^{M-3}, & x \geq y \geq z \\ 0, & \text{else} \end{cases}$$

$$p_{\gamma_\Sigma}(\gamma) = \iint_{D_{y,z}} p_{X,Y,Z}(\gamma - y - z, y, z) \, dy \, dz$$

$$= \frac{1}{2} M(M-1)(M-2)(\frac{1}{\bar{\gamma}})^3 e^{-\frac{\gamma}{\bar{\gamma}}} \times$$

$$\left(\frac{\gamma^2}{6} + \sum_{i=1}^{M-3} \frac{(-1)^i}{i} \binom{M-3}{i} \left((1 - e^{-\frac{i\gamma}{3\bar{\gamma}}})(\bar{\gamma}\gamma - \frac{3\bar{\gamma}^2}{i}) + \bar{\gamma}\gamma e^{-\frac{i\gamma}{3\bar{\gamma}}} \right) \right)$$

3.4   PMRC: SNR Distribution for N=2, 3, 4

In PMRC, the master's signal does not need to transmit, so the master always combines its own received signal with the $N-1$ strongest signals from the remote nodes. Let $\gamma_{\Sigma'}$ denote the SNR of PMRC at the master node: $\gamma_{\Sigma'} = \gamma_{\Sigma} + \gamma$.

The distribution of the sum of two independent random variables is the convolution of these two random variables' distributions. Therefore, for $N = 2, 3, 4$ of PMRC we have $p_{\gamma_{\Sigma'}}(\gamma) = \int_0^\gamma p_{\gamma_\Sigma}(\tau) \cdot p(\gamma - \tau)\, d\tau$, where p_{γ_Σ} was derived in the previous section. Computing the SNR distribution for higher values of N is hard to obtain analytically in a closed form formula. However, we will show that small values of N are sufficient to obtain most of the diversity gain.

3.5   Outage Probability

Outage probability can effectively measure the performance of communication systems. Assume that γ_0 is the minimum SNR that can be tolerated by the decoding scheme. Outage probability is defined as $P_{out}(\bar{\gamma}) = p_{\gamma_{\Sigma'}}(\gamma \leq \gamma_0)$, where $\bar{\gamma}$ is the average SNR. Figure 2, shows the performance of $(5, N)$ PMRC for $N = 2, 3, 4$ and compares it with the non-cooperative scheme and the traditional MRC. For example, for a target $P_{out} = 10^{-2}$, in $(5, 2)$-PMRC the average transmission energy can be reduced by more than $17dB$ comparing to non-cooperative scheme, which is 50 times low energy. From this graph we conclude that most of the benefit of the diversity gain can be acquired by requesting the contribution from only a few neighbors with strong signals.

We also studied the impact of the number of cooperating nodes on the outage probability. Figure 3, shows that increasing M significantly reduces the outage probability. For example, although 5-MRC outperforms $(5, 3)$-PMRC, increasing M by 1 gives $(6, 3)$-PMRC which not only outperforms 5-PMRC (by 2dB at $P_{out} = 10^{-7}$) but also requires only 2 cooperating nodes to send their contributions instead of totally 4 nodes in the case of 5-MRC. Therefore 5-MRC requires 100% more bandwidth for lesser performance than $(6, 3)$-PMRC. We observe

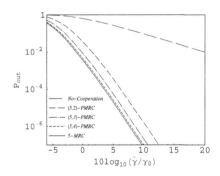
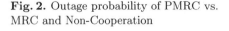
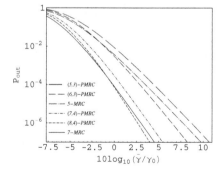

Fig. 2. Outage probability of PMRC vs. MRC and Non-Cooperation

Fig. 3. Impact of M on the performance of PMRC

that when the average SNR increases, $(M', 1)$ will eventually outperform M-MRC (or any $(M, N) - PMRC$)) as long as $M' > M$. Note that M-MRC (i.e., MRC with M branches) is identical to (M, M)-PMRC.

3.6   Bit Error Rate and Throughput

Bit Error Rate (BER) is another important measure of the performance of communication systems. We consider the coherent Minimum-Shift Keying (MSK) modulation, which is similar to GMSK used in GSM system, with uncoded communication. To compute BER, We assume a pulse shaping transmission with bit duration equal to $1/W$ such as raised cosine pulses (similar to $sinc()$, but it is widely used in practice [2].) with $\beta = 1$ (where W is the used frequency bandwidth). Therefore $E_b/\mathcal{N}_0 = \gamma$ and the $BER = Q(\sqrt{\frac{2E_b}{\mathcal{N}_0}}) = Q(\sqrt{2\gamma})$.

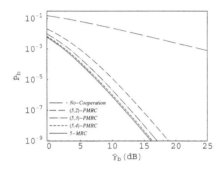 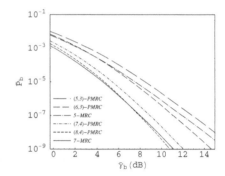

Fig. 4. BER of MSK demodulator under PMRC vs. MRC and Non-Cooperation

Fig. 5. Impact of M on the performance of PMRC in terms of BER

We compare the performance of PMRC to the non-cooperative mode and the traditional MRC. The BER performance of PMRC is consistent with the outage probability. Figure 4 shows that for a target BER of 10^{-3}, $(5,2)$-PMRC requires 20dB (100 times) less power and with the contribution from only one cooperating neighbor. Higher gains are achievable when the target BER is lower. Most of the gain of MRC is obtained using the 2 to 3 strongest signals from neighboring nodes. Figure 5, shows the impact of increasing M. Similarly, to the outage probability, increasing the number of cooperating nodes outperforms the benefit by increasing N, the number of nodes who are effectively sending their contributions.

To measure the throughput of PMRC, we only consider the overhead of 32 bits CRC necessary for error detection. To compare the various PMRC schemes with fairness, the packet size is normalized to maximizes throughput. Figure 6 shows that the throughput of the master node can be significantly increased (over an order of magnitude) by signal combining with a limited number of cooperation nodes. We also find that PMRC gives comparable performance of

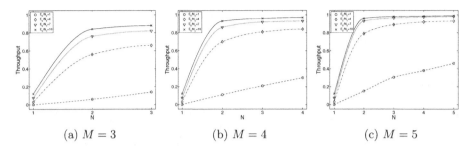

(a) $M = 3$ (b) $M = 4$ (c) $M = 5$

Fig. 6. Throughput in different cooperation scenarios and $E_b/\mathcal{N}_0(\text{dB})$

MRC by using fewer active branches. For example of $N = 3$ and $M = 5$, besides the master's branch it uses only two active branches out of the four external diversity branches, but it achieves more than 90% the performance given by MRC with a fairly low $E_b/\mathcal{N}_0$ (4 or above) while it uses only half of the bandwidth required by MRC. For a very low $E_b/\mathcal{N}_0$ at value 1,it still maintains at least 65% throughput.

$$Throughput = \frac{(L - OH)(1 - BER)^L}{L}, OH \text{ is the CRC length, } L \text{ is the frame length}$$

3.7   Local Bandwidth Consumption

To compute the local bandwidth consumption, we consider a 2-level HPC strategy which consists of only decode-and-forward and pre-demodulation combining. The local bandwidth can be computed by considering three cases. 1)The master can correctly decode the frame/packet (with probability $1 - FER$). 2)The master fails to decode the packet but at least one of the $M - 1$ assisting nodes is capable of decoding it (with probability $FER \times (1 - FER^{M-1})$). 3)None of the nodes can correctly decode the packet, so nodes execute $PMRC$ combining. The N assisting nodes with the strongest signals send their sampled signals to the master (with probability FER^M). The average local traffic is:

$$Avg - Throughput_{local} = L \times FER \times (1 - FER^{M-1}) + N \times L \times R \times FER^M$$

where L denotes the frame size and R denotes the average number of bits used to represent each sampled signal. R can be 8 bits in the case of a non-coherent decoding, and as high as 96 bits for coherent decoding (4 over-sampling factor, 12 bits quantization for I and Q).

4   Simulation and Experiment Results

4.1   PMRC with Imperfect Channel Knowledge

In Section 3.6, we show that PMRC can significantly reduce the BER. Like many other combining techniques, it assumes perfect phase synchronization among the signal branches. However, in practical it is well known to be a challenging task. To solve this problem, we use a pilot-based technique for estimating the channel condition and adjusting the phase of each signals. We consider a long range communication link using the Gaussian Minimum Shift Keying modulation (such as used in the GSM cellular communication standard) with a 200 KHz frequency band, and a symbol rate of 250 Kbps. For channel estimation, we supplement the data signals with a pilot tone (i.e., non modulated sin wave) separated by 200KHz from the center of the communication band. Similar technique is commonly used in many communication systems such as IEEE802.11a (4 pilots for 48 carriers), and WiMax (8 pilots for 256 carriers). Note that a single pilot tone can be shared by multiple frequency bands. On the receiver side, the pilot tone is filtered and used to estimate the channel to resynchronize the master and assisting nodes signals before combining. We use an over-sampling rate of 4 samples per bit. Figure 7, summarizes the performance of PMRC when simulated with the Matlab Simulink environment for $M = 5$. The simulation results confirm that significant gains can be achieved by combining the master data with the two strongest assisting nodes. A gain of 10 dB (order of magnitude reduction in energy cost) is reachable. We also note that due to the imperfection of the phase synchronization technique a full MRC has poorer results than (5, 4)-PMRC, so it is preferable to only combine the strongest signals.

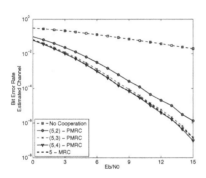

Fig. 7. BER performance of PMRC with pilot-based channel estimation

Table 1. Experimental results for post soft-demodulation combining. Note that the signal synchronization imperfections, can in some cases, lead to a (5, 4)-PMRC performance lower then the (5, 2)-PMRC.

TX Amp	Bit errors non-coop	Bit errors PMRC2	Bit errors PMRC3	Bit errors PMRC4
2000	1145	109	89	46
3000	289	3	8	18
4000	92	0	0	8
5000	70	0	0	0

4.2 Post Soft Decoding on Prototype

We have implemented a testbed prototype based on USRP/GNU Radio [19], and measured the performance of the post soft-demodulation combining on this platform. We use a GMSK modulation at 500 Kbps on the 915MHz ISM band. The GMSK demodulator is modified to extract the soft decision values and combine the master bits with the N strongest signals from the assisting nodes. We conducted experiments with various transmission power levels where the cooperating nodes are fairly distant from the transmitter and located in a different office (around 50 feet away) allowing for significant multi-path fading effects.

Table 1 summarizes the results for four transmission power levels (values are normalized to 2, 3, 4, 5). Each shows the number of bits in error of 1 megabit data. The experiment results demonstrate the number of bits in error can be significantly reduced by combining the soft decision values obtained from two assisting nodes with strongest signals.

5   Conclusions

In this paper, we introduced a framework for distributed cooperation and diversity. We proposed and studied several combining techniques that can be used in multiple levels of decoding process. We proposed and analysed PMRC in terms of SNR gain, outage probability, bit error rate, and throughput. Our results from the simulation for PMRC with a pilot-based channel estimation, as well as experiments for a post soft-demodulation combining, reveal that the cooperation between devices with a combination of cellular and short-range air-interfaces is a promising approach to increase network capacity and mitigate the effects of channel fading and shadowing. Still, our results are only a first step towards understanding the potential of distributed cooperation and diversity. Future work will consider complete trade-offs in terms of local communications and overall performance improvement, and more realistic channels and node distributions.

References

1. Rumney, M.: Identifying technology to deliver the next 100x capacity growth in wireless. The 3rd LTE World Summit (2008)
2. Proakis, J.: Digital Communications, 4th edn. McGraw-Hill, New York (2000)
3. Rappaport, T.S.: Wireless Communications: Principles and Practice, 2nd edn.
4. Goldsmith, A.: Wireless Communications. Cambridge University Press, Cambridge (2005)
5. Fitzek, F.H.P., Katz, M.D.: Cooperation in Wireless Networks: Principles and Applications: Real Egoistic Behavior is to Cooperate! Springer, Heidelberg (2006)
6. Sendonaris, A., Erkip, E., Aazhang, B.: User cooperation diversity– part i and part ii. IEEE Transactions on Communications 51(11), 1927–1948 (2003)
7. Laneman, J.N., Wornell, G.W.: Energy-efficient antenna sharing and relaying for wireless networks. In: Proc. IEEE WCNC (September 2000)
8. Hunter, T.E., Nosratinia, A.: Diversity through coded cooperation. IEEE Trans. on Wireless Commun. 5(2) (2006)
9. Khandani, A., Modiano, E., Abounadi, J., Zheng, L.: Reliability and route diversity in wireless networks. In: Conference on Information Science and System (2005)
10. Ramanathan, R.: Challenges: A radically new architecture for next generation mobile ad hoc networks. In: Proceedings of ACM Mobicom (2005)
11. Ozgür, A., Lévêque, O., Tse, D.: Hierarchical Cooperation Achieves Optimal Capacity Scaling in Ad Hoc Networks. IEEE Trans. on Information Theory (2007)
12. Bahl, P., Adya, A., Padhye, J., Walman, A.: Reconsidering wireless systems with multiple radios. SIGCOMM Comput. Commun. Rev. 34(5), 39–46 (2004)
13. Luo, H., Ramjee, R., Sinha, P., Li, L.E., Lu, S.: Ucan: a unified cellular and ad-hoc network architecture. In: MobiCom '03 (2003)

14. Dimou, K., et al.: Generic link layer: A solution for multi-radio transmission diversity in communication networks beyond 3g. In: Vehicular Technology Conference, vol. 3 (2005)
15. Woo, G., Kheradpour, P., Shen, D., Katabi, D.: Beyond the bits: Cooperative packet recovery using physical layer information. In: MOBICOM (2007)
16. Kyle, J., Balakrishnan, H.: Partial packet recovery for wireless networks. In: SIG-COMM (2007)
17. Hooman, J., Noubir, G., Wang, Y.: Cross-layer distributed diversity for heterogeneous wireless. In: Boavida, F., Monteiro, E., Mascolo, S., Koucheryavy, Y. (eds.) WWIC 2007. LNCS, vol. 4517, pp. 259–270. Springer, Heidelberg (2007)
18. Brennan, D.G.: Linear diversity combining techniques. Proc. IEEE 91(2) (2003)
19. The GNU Software Defined Radio, http://www.gnu.org/software/gnuradio

A Multi-hop Aware Weighted Scheduling Mechanism for HSDPA and IEEE 802.11 Integrated Network

Jinglong Zhou, Anthony Lo, Jiazhen Hao, and Ignas Niemegeers

Faculty of Electrical Engineering, Mathematics, Computer Science,
Delft University of Technology, Mekelweg 4, 2600 GA Delft, The Netherlands
{J.L.Zhou,A.Lo,J.Hao,I.Niemegeers}@tudelft.nl

Abstract. Next-generation communication networks will comprise third-generation (3G) cellular and multi-hop ad hoc networks. This integrated network can be seen as an extension to the cellular network and uses two different technologies, HSDPA and IEEE 802.11. Compared to the traditional cellular network, there is a new problem that nodes in IEEE 802.11 ad hoc network may not always be fairly served due to the different channel quality. This is because the traditional scheduling mechanisms for HSDPA are not multi-hop aware. The paper proposes to use a multi-hop aware weighted scheduling mechanism which considers the parameters in both the IEEE 802.11 ad hoc network and HSDPA network, namely the number of hops away from the gateway, and the packet delivery error in ad hoc network. Based on simulation results, our proposed mechanism achieved better throughput fairness in the simulated scenarios.

1 Introduction

Recent developments in wireless technology enable electronic devices to connect with each other and the Internet using different radio technologies. Widespread deployment of the third-generation (3G) cellular networks such as Universal Mobile Telecommunications System (UMTS) and High Speed Downlink Packet Access (HSDPA) [1] enables high speed access to Internet. Meanwhile, the IEEE 802.11 technology enables short range high speed connection between the devices. The idea of integrating these two technologies was proposed in previous work [2], and this network scenario is depicted in Fig. 1. Both technologies have its own advantages and disadvantages, the 3G cellular network can provide wide range coverage and high mobility but its data rate is limited (peak data rate 14.4 Mbps for HSDPA enhancement). Nevertheless, not every device has a 3G radio interface. IEEE 802.11 can offer high data rates (54 Mbps for IEEE 802.11g) and it is a popular technology. Therefore, integrating those two technologies can provide Internet access to those devices that do not have 3G cellular network interface. Further, the integration allows load balancing in the 3G cellular networks, relaying traffic for devices that experiencing bad UMTS/HSDPA channel conditions.

E. Osipov et al. (Eds.): WWIC 2010, LNCS 6074, pp. 40–51, 2010.
© Springer-Verlag Berlin Heidelberg 2010

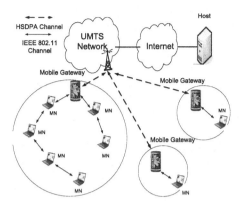

Fig. 1. Integrated network system architecture overview

For this new integrated network, a new problem emerged. That is, the end-to-end performance between nodes in the ad hoc network and the host in Internet may be poor due to several reasons, namely bad HSDPA channel quality, large number of hops away from hybrid gateway, and bad channel quality on IEEE 802.11 links. Moreover, TCP will aggravate this unfairness due to its characteristics, i.e., the slow start mechanism. This unfairness will make sharing the radio resources by different users highly dependent on link quality in both types of channels and IEEE 802.11 network topologies. Users that are far away from the gateway can hardly access the Internet. However, this unfairness problem is not well addressed previously.

In this paper, we propose to use a weighted scheduling mechanism with a novel weights calculation method for this HSDPA and IEEE 802.11 integrated network. The mechanism takes into account the HSDPA channel quality, the number of hops away from the gateway, and the IEEE 802.11 link quality. The weighted scheduler decides the transmission probability of the incoming packets from different traffic flows whose end points are the nodes in the ad hoc network. The weight for each TCP flow is decided by the two types channel quality. Our contribution is that we revealed this unfairness problem in the new integrated network and shows how much unfairness it can introduce to the system via simulation. We also show how much this unfairness can be mitigated by considering more factors other than the HSDPA channel information along. The rest of paper is organized as follows: Section 2 will introduce the architecture of HSDPA, IEEE 802.11 integrated network and introduce some simulation result to show the unfairness in this new network. Our new multi-hop aware weighted scheduling mechanism will be introduced in Section 3. In Section 4, we present our simulation results for parameter selection and fairness improvement in different scenarios. The related work is introduced in Section 5, The paper is concluded in Section 6.

2   HSDPA and IEEE 802.11 Integrated Network

2.1   Integrated Network Architecture

The new integrated network is shown in Fig. 1. A host in the Internet is connected to the UMTS network. The UMTS/HSDPA network and the IEEE 802.11 ad hoc networks are interconnected via a hybrid device called HSDPA-802.11 Ad-hoc gateway, which has two different network interfaces, we call it mobile gateway for short. The traditional UMTS User Equipment (UE) and the new mobile gateways will share the HSDPA channel. To enable the nodes in ad hoc network to find and select the mobile gateway, a gateway discovery protocol is implemented over the IP layer in the mobile gateway. The mobile gateway implements the ad hoc routing protocol to relay packets for ad hoc networks. The mobile nodes belonging to different gateways may interfere with each other if the distance between two ad hoc networks are very small.

2.2   Unfairness in the Integrated Network

In Fig. 1, we can see that the nodes in ad hoc network may connect to the Internet via the same or different mobile gateways. The IEEE 802.11 link quality in different ad hoc networks or between different nodes may be different. Meanwhile, the nodes in the ad hoc networks may be several hops away from the mobile gateways or just have an one hop connection with the gateways. Those factors will all effect the end-to-end TCP performance between the nodes in ad hoc network and nodes in the Internet. Current UMTS/HSDPA system uses scheduling mechanisms to allocate transmission resources among different UEs. However, those mechanisms do not consider the differences among each flow, which may use different topology. We use the simulations to investigate the end-to-end TCP performance between nodes in ad hoc networks and nodes in Internet. The fairness index [3] is used to evaluate the fairness for each flow, which is defined as

$$f = \frac{\left(\sum_{i=1}^{n} x_i\right)^2}{n \sum_{i=1}^{n} x_i^2}, \tag{1}$$

where n is the number of concurrent FTP flows and x_i denotes the throughput achieved by the ith flow. The result ranges from $1/n$ (worst case) to 1 (best case). We use this metric for our system fairness performance evaluation.

In the simulation, we used four flows and three of them used the same topology configuration, and the destinations of those flows in IEEE 802.11 ad hoc networks were one hop away from the mobile gateways. We call it Flow 2, Flow 3 and Flow 4. Another flow which is called Flow 1 was configured differently. The destination of this flow in IEEE 802.11 ad hoc network can be 1, 2, 3 or 4 hops away from the mobile gateway. The gateway's HSDPA channel quality of this flow can be also different from other flows' channels. We assumed the error rates for all IEEE 802.11 links are the same. The default round robin scheduling mechanism was used. The detailed description of simulation configuration can be found in Section 3.2. We divide the simulations to four groups:

Group1: The mobile gateways had the same HSDPA channel condition (average SNR 50dB), no error in IEEE 802.11 links.

Group2: The mobile gateways had the same HSDPA channel condition, (average SNR 50dB), 5% error in IEEE 802.11 links.

Group3: The mobile gateways had different HSDPA channel condition, (flow 1 with average SNR 0.18 dB and other flows still with 50dB). No error in IEEE 802.11 links.

Group4: The mobile gateways had different HSDPA channel condition, (flow 1 with average SNR 0.18 dB and other flows still with 50dB). 5% error in IEEE 802.11 links.

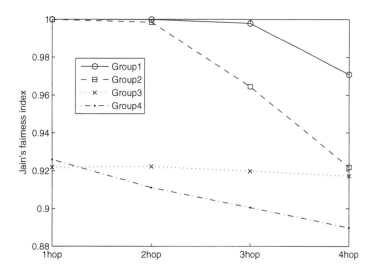

Fig. 2. Fairness index with round robin scheduling

The simulation results are shown in Fig. 2, we can see that with number of hops increases for the Flow 1, the fairness index decreased in all groups. It is very obvious to see that when both conditions are worse for the Flow 1 in Group4, the fairness index decreased the most compared to other groups. We show the throughput values in Table. 1, we can see that in the most serious situation, the Flow 1 only got 31% of throughput compared to other flows.

3   Multi-hop Aware Weighted Scheduling Mechanism

3.1   Proposed Multi-hop Aware Weight Calculation Method

To overcome the unfairness of the resource allocation in UMTS/HSDPA system caused by different configurations, we decided to use the weighted scheduling mechanism to schedule the packets in UMTS/HSDPA base station. Flows that

Table 1. Throughput for all the flows in Group4 simulation

	1hop	2hop	3hop	4hop
Flow1 (Mbps)	0.302254	0.267396	0.258655	0.236356
Flow2 (Mbps)	0.691216	0.689961	0.713423	0.732889
Flow3 (Mbps)	0.689207	0.687961	0.733722	0.724923
Flow4 (Mbps)	0.687228	0.686334	0.730843	0.725637

are treated unfairly by the base station will be assigned larger weight, which means they will get more chances to transmit packets in each TTI. The weight for each flow is decided by the three factors, the HSDPA channel quality, which is indicated by the Channel Quality Indicator (CQI), the number of hops away from the mobile gateway (H_N) and the IEEE 802.11 error rate (E_{80211}). For a certain flow i, we use the following formula to decide the weight,

$$w_i = CQI_i * (H_{N_i})^\alpha * (E_{80211})^{H_{N_i}\beta}, \tag{2}$$

in which α and β are the parameters which control H_N and E_{80211}. If the E_{80211} is 0 which means the IEEE 802.11 channel has perfect quality and the β value is not calculated. In this mechanism, the topology and link quality in IEEE 802.11 is also taken into the consideration. After each flow achieves its own weight w_i, the probability that a certain flow can transmit its packet in a TTI is determined as $R_i = \frac{w_i}{\sum_{i=1}^{n} w_i}$. In this way, the flows whose TCP receivers are further away from the mobile gateways and suffer more packet loss will get more chances to transmit their packets in the scheduler. Therefore, the Round-Trip Time (RTT) for those TCP flows can be reduced. The mechanism use the α and β parameters to determine how the resources are allocated between each flow and try to reduce the difference between each flow's RTT. The next question is how can we determine the proper α and β values, and how much performance improvement can be achieved. Different simulation scenarios are used to investigate previous questions and the simulation methodology is presented in the following section.

3.2   Simulation Methodology

The HSDPA and IEEE 802.11 simulation model is described in detail in [4] and [5]. Here, we only introduce our simulation configurations. The integrated network architecture in NS-2 is introduced in [6]. The difference of the simulations between this paper and previous work [7] is that we used multiple mobile gateways in the simulations. The simulations topology is shown in Fig. 3. We used the Serving GPRS Support Node (SGSN) as our TCP traffic source. The setting is to simplify the simulation topology, since the packet delay between SGSN node to the Host in the Internet is much smaller compared to the packet delay in HSDPA channel if the HSDPA channel quality is very bad. The maximum HSDPA downlink data rate is 3.36 Mbps and the real data rates depend on the average SNR values. In the ad hoc network, a chain topology is used

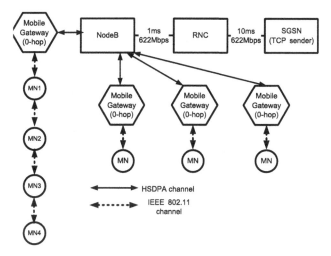

Fig. 3. Simulation Topology

to connect the IEEE 802.11 nodes. The TCP Flow1's receiver can be the mobile gateway, or from MN1 to MN4. We name them correspondingly as 0hop to 4hop. The configuration of the wireless links can be found in Table 2. In the simulations, the IEEE 802.11b's highest data rate was used, this is because we assumed our application scenarios are outdoor and the distance between IEEE 802.11 nodes are long (130m in simulation). Previous literature indicated that the 802.11g radio channel quality are very bad in those conditions [8]. In the simulation, we assumed the packet error rate is constant in IEEE 802.11b links.

4   Performance Evaluation

The α and β in Eq. 2 can increase the transmission probability for certain flows that suffer the large RTT. However, larger α or β values will allocate too much resources for the "weak" flows and reduce the transmission chances for other flows, which introduce unfairness for other flows. To determine what are the best parameters to be used in Eq. 2, we carried out extensive simulations. In this section, we will first present the optimal α and β selections in different groups. Then, we present how much improvement these parameters can be achieved compared to the round robin scheduling scheme.

4.1   The Optimal Parameter Selection

For the simulations Group1 and Group3, since there were no error in the IEEE 802.11 links, the β values in Eq. 2 will not take effect. Therefore, we only used different α values to tune the system. We used some preliminary simulations to decide the suitable range of α and then select ten values for the simulations. The results for Group1 and Group3 are shown in Fig. 4 and Fig. 5. For Group1, we

Table 2. Simulation parameters

HSDPA	Values
Distance from NodeB	0-700m
Path loss component (n)	3.52
Mobile gateway speed	3km/h
Mobile gateway move pattern	circle
Standard deviation in shadow fading (N)	8dB
Maximum buffer size at NodeB	1000kbytes
Downlink TTI	2ms
Uplink bandwidth	384Kbps
UPlink TTI	10ms
IEEE 802.11	Values
IEEE 802.11 bandwidth	11Mbps
RTS\CTS Threshold	3000Bytes
TCP Reno	Values
TCP window size	128 segments
TCP packet size	512Bytes

can see that if we used the α values smaller than 0.2, the 1, 2 and 3hop scenarios will show obviously fairness among different flows. This is because there was not much unfairness for these scenarios originally, since the HSDPA channel quality for all the flows were the same and there was no error for IEEE 802.11 links. However, for the 4hop scenario, the fairness index was still around 0.98, which was similar to the scenario when round robin scheduling performance. This indicates that α values lower than 0.2 still result too small weight for the 4hop flow. We can see that the best α for this scenario was 0.3, at which all the flows can achieve fairness index higher than 0.99.

In Group3 scenario, since the HSDPA channel quality was quite different between Flow 1 and other flows, round robin scheduling will cause obvious unfairness for Flow 1 (see Fig. 2). After we used our special weighted scheduling mechanism, all scenarios except 1hop scenario got performance enhancement. The 1hop scenario did not improve due to the fact that all the flows were one hop connection with gateways and α can do nothing help. For other hops scenario, the fairness indexes all reached 1 when the α was 1.0. Also, too large α will further decrease the fairness index to the lowest point 0.25 when the α was 5.0 for the 4hop scenario.

For the Group2 and Group4 scenarios, since the IEEE 802.11 links are also erroneous, we had to select the best α and β combinations. We used 100 different α and β combinations in Eq. 2 and plot the fairness indexes for Group2 and Group4 in Fig. 6 and Fig. 7. Only the 4hop scenario's result is plotted in both figures. For Group2' 4hop scenario, the best α and β combination was 0.2 and 0.25. We can also clearly see that larger or smaller α and β will result in very small fairness index for the system. For the Group4's 4hop scenario, we got similar conclusion and the best α and β combination was 0.07 and 0.3.

Based on result from Fig. 4 to Fig. 7, we can see that the rule for selecting the best α and β are different for different Groups, which suggests scheduling mechanism have to be adaptive for different scenarios. However, the difference in results between optimal and suboptimal α or β values is not very big, which suggests that for a certain topology, we only need one group of α and β value.

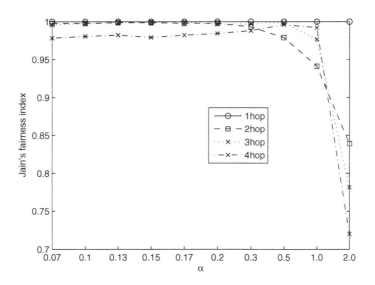

Fig. 4. The α selection in Group1

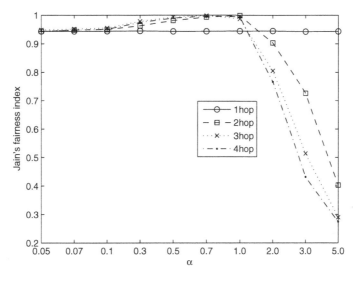

Fig. 5. The α selection in Group3

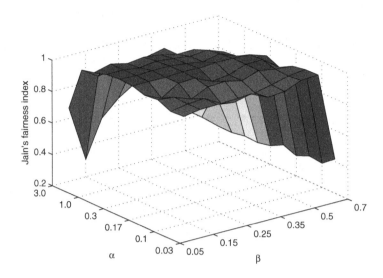

Fig. 6. The α and β selection in Group2

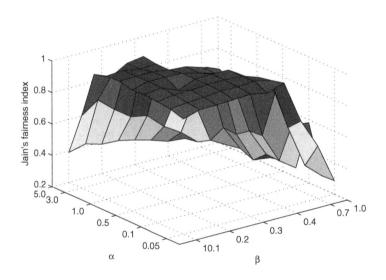

Fig. 7. The α and β selection in Group4

4.2   Fairness Index Improvement

In the previous section, we selected the best α and β for all the simulation groups. We used the groups' scenarios as in Fig. 2 and applied our Eq. 2. For the Group2 and Group4, we used the best α and β calculated for the 4hop scenario in other scenarios. We got the following result shown in Fig. 8. We can see that almost

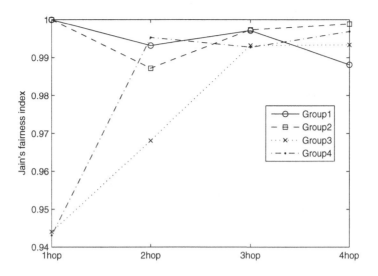

Fig. 8. Fairness index with the new multi-hop aware scheduling

for all the scenarios, the fairness index increased, especially for the Group4, 4hop scenario, the fairness index increased from 0.88 to 0.987.

We also list the throughput results for the Group4 scenario in Table 3. We can see that for all the scenarios, the Flow 1's throughput increased and shared the resources more fairly among other flows.

Table 3. Throughput for all the flows in Group4 simulation with multi-hop aware weighted scheduling scheme

	1hop	2hop	3hop	4hop
Flow1 (Mbps)	0.412079	0.589823	0.481410	0.455753
Flow2 (Mbps)	0.795520	0.655644	0.546789	0.431752
Flow3 (Mbps)	0.794990	0.659287	0.550830	0.428043
Flow4 (Mbps)	0.849219	0.717423	0.614155	0.491479
Improvement (Flow1)	36%	123%	92%	95%

4.3 Algorithm Discussion

Based on previous simulation, it is obvious to see that with better parameter settings, the optimal α or β will result in higher fairness index. There are two methods for the system to determine these two parameters. Either via simulation method or using a mathematical model. The scheduler does not have to be always absolutely fair for all the users in all the scenarios. Our mechanism is designed for those users need long time TCP downloading services. With the computation ability increases, the base station may have the computation power to use the simulation method to get suitable parameters setting for certain scenarios. Meanwhile, the link quality of the HSDPA, IEEE 802.11 channel may be dynamic, also the number of hops may changed. The system should set a threshold that under what circumstance the parameters have to be recalculated again.

5   Related Work

A great deal of effort was expended to analyze the performance of transport protocols (TCP and UDP) over these two networks by means of mathematical model, simulation and measurement. The end-to-end performance of this integrated network has been extensively investigated in [2] and [7]. However, the simulation scenarios in [2] and [7] just have single TCP flows. Multiple flows scenarios have not yet been investigated. There are also lots of literature on the scheduling algorithms in HSDPA. The Maximum SINR serves the users with best channel condition, Proportional Fair (PF) [9] serve the user with best relative channel quality. Modified Largest Weighted Delay First (M-LWDF) [10] keep the probability of delayed packets exceeding the discard bound. The performance of different scheduling algorithms are compared in [11], [12]. Those algorithms mainly consider the channel quality of HSDPA. However, none of them consider the configuration of the node in IEEE 802.11 ad hoc networks. The number of hops in IEEE 802.11 network and link quality for 802.11 links are not considered in previous work.

6   Conclusion

The integrated HSDPA and IEEE 802.11 network can provide seamless Internet access for end users and can also help the operators to balance the load between cellular network cells. Due to complex topology and link quality differences between different traffic flows, a fair sharing of radio resources among all the users became a new problem. Simulation results reveal that the Jain's fairness index can be as low as 0.88 in certain scenarios. Traditional scheduling algorithms in HSDPA only consider the HSDPA channel quality when it allocates resources for different flows, which can not fairly allocate the resources and some users in the ad hoc network can hardly access the Internet. We propose to use a multi-hop aware weighted scheduling mechanism which can consider the HSDPA channel quality, number of hops and channel quality of IEEE 802.11 links. Using the proposed scheduler, the fairness indexes among the flows could be improved by 14% and the throughput for the unfair flow can be increased by as high as 123%.

For future work, we will further consider using the mathematical method instead of simulations to determine the weights in our mechanism. The mathematical model will let the mechanism to be more scalable and adaptive to be used in large set of scenarios. The comparison with other algorithm for the relaying network will be done. Lastly, we will design a new signaling protocol which can inform the scheduler the number of hops and the channel quality on each hop.

References

1. HSDPA overall description (Rel.5), 3GPP TS 25.308, vol. 5.2.0 (March 2002)
2. Lo, A., Zhou, J., Niemegeers, I.: Simulation-Based Analysis of TCP Over Beyond 3G Cellular Multi-Hop Networks. In: Proc. IEEE PIMRC'06, Helsinki, Finland (September 2006)
3. Jain, R.: The Art of Computer Systems Performance Analysis. John Wiley and Sons, Chichester (1991)
4. Eurane, http://www.ti-wmc.nl/eurane/
5. The network simulator ns-2, http://www.isi.edu/nsnam/ns/
6. Lo, A., Zhou, J., Jacobsson, M., Niemegeers, I.: ns-2 models for simulating a novel beyond 3G cellular multi-hop network. In: Proc. ACM WNS2'06, Pisa, Italy (October 2006)
7. Zhou, J., Lo, A., Liu, Z., Niemegeers, I.: TCP Performance Evaluation Over Multihop Cellular Network: HSDPA and IEEE 802.11. In: Proc. IEEE ISWCS 2008, Reykjavik, Iceland, October 21-24 (2008)
8. Bianchi, G., Formisano, F., Giustiniano, D.: 802.11 b/g Link Level Measurements for an Outdoor Wireless Campus Network. In: Proc. IEEE WoWMoM'06, Washington, DC, USA, pp. 525–530 (2006)
9. Holtzman, J., Inc, Q., San Diego, C.: CDMA forward link waterfilling power control. In: Proc. IEEE VTC 2000-Spring, Tokyo, Japan, September 2000, vol. 3, pp. 1663–1667 (2000)
10. Andrews, M., Kumaran, K., Ramanan, K., Stolyar, A., Whiting, P., Vijayakumar, R.: Providing quality of service over a shared wireless link. IEEE Communications magazine 39(2), 150–154 (2001)
11. Necker, M.: A comparison of scheduling mechanisms for service class differentiation in HSDPA networks. AEUE-International Journal of Electronics and Communications 60(2), 136–141 (2006)
12. Malkowski, M., Kemper, A., Wang, X.: Performance of Scheduling Algorithms for HSDPA. In: Proc. CHINACOM'07, pp. 1052–1056 (2007)

Enhanced Mobility Support for Roaming Users: Extending the IEEE 802.21 Information Service

Karl Andersson[1], Andrea G. Forte[2], and Henning Schulzrinne[2]

[1] Luleå University of Technology
Division of Mobile Networking and Computing
SE-931 87 Skellefteå, Sweden
karl.andersson@ltu.se
[2] Columbia University
Department of Computer Science
New York, NY 10027, USA
{andreaf,hgs}@cs.columbia.edu

Abstract. Many cell-phones and Personal Digital Assistants (PDAs) are equipped with multiple radio interfaces. Because of this, devices need to have ways of efficiently selecting the most suitable access network across multiple technologies based on the physical location of the device as well as user-defined parameters such as cost, bandwidth, and battery consumption. The IEEE has standardized the 802.21 framework for media-independent handovers where dynamic selection of network interfaces is an important feature. This paper describes and evaluates a novel architecture which extends the IEEE 802.21 information service. The architecture is based on a three-layer structure with Location-to-Service Translation (LoST) servers, service provider servers and independent evaluator servers. Evaluator servers are populated with information on coverage and quality of service as provided by trusted users. The proposed architecture allows for competition at all levels and scales well due to its distributed nature. A prototype has been developed and is presented in the paper.

Keywords: Heterogeneous wireless environments, Media-independent handover services, IEEE 802.21 information service.

1 Introduction

In the near future, mobile users will likely have access to many different wireless access technologies, from 4G LTE to WiMAX, offering broad coverage, and hot spots offering IEEE 802.11 connectivity for smaller areas. Each of these networks offers a trade-off of cost, convenience and performance. For example, a user may decide to walk to a nearby hot spot rather than pay high per-MB cellular data rates to perform some data-intensive task. Also, the performance of the same kind of network differs by geographic location; data rates in dense metropolitan areas may be lower than outside those areas. However, currently, mobile users or their devices have no good way to make such choices without elaborate web searches and manual tariff comparisons. We propose a new model for automating the decision process that not only take

E. Osipov et al. (Eds.): WWIC 2010, LNCS 6074, pp. 52–63, 2010.

into account static information, such as cost, but also allows to incorporate the experience real users have had with the network in that particular geographic area.

The rest of the paper is organized as follows. Section 2 presents an overview of mobility management schemes and the IEEE 802.21 standard while Section 3 presents the Location-to-Service Translation (LoST) protocol. Section 4 presents the proposed architecture while Section 5 evaluates the work by describing the prototype built, experiments being conducted, and results achieved. Finally, Section 6 contains related work, while Section 7 concludes the work and indicates future work.

2   Mobility Management and the IEEE 802.21 Standard

Seamless mobility is achieved by applying a suitable mobility management scheme handled at the link layer, the network layer [1, 2], the transport layer [3, 4], or the application layer [5]. Also, proposals on new layers for handling mobility exist [6] as well as proposals on handling mobility in the network [7], instead of using host-based solutions.

To improve handover performance in heterogeneous environments, the IEEE decided to standardize a media-independent handover (MIH) framework under the name of 802.21 [8]. It defines mechanisms for exchanging handover-related events, commands, and information. Handover initiation and handover preparation are covered but not the actual handover execution. It should also be noted that the mobility management mechanism can be of any type, working at either the network, transport or application layers. Finally, the IEEE 802.21 standard allows for both network-controlled handovers and host-controlled handovers and it defines three main services: Media-independent Event Services (MIES), Media-independent Command Services (MICS) and Media-independent Information Services (MIIS).

2.1   Media-Independent Event Services (MIES)

MIES define events representing changes in the link characteristics either originated from the link layer or from the MIH function. Such characteristics could be information on link status or link quality, for example. Events can be subscribed to and be either local or remote. They may indicate changes in the state and transmission behavior of the physical, data-link and logical-link layers. Events can also predict state changes of these layers. Remote events are transported over the network in MIH protocol messages and typically contain information on link events originated from the point of attachment that the user subscribed to earlier.

2.2   Media-Independent Command Service (MICS)

The MICS defines commands for controlling the link state and can be invoked either locally or remotely. By using the MICS, the user may control the configuration and selection of a specific link. Remote commands are, like remote events, transported over the network by MIH protocol messages and may result in a link command or an MIH indication in the peer Media-Independent Handover Function (MIHF) entity.

2.3 Media-Independent Information Service (MIIS)

The MIIS defines a set of information elements (IEs), their structure and their representation. Furthermore, it defines a query-response-based mechanism for information
retrieval. Such information can be used to take more accurate handover decisions that
is, using information on available access networks in the proximity of the user may
help to radically improve the decision-making process for handovers.

Information is exchanged through binary type-length-value (TLV) coded messages. Also, complex queries are supported through the Resource Description Framework (RDF) query language SPARQL [9].

IEs can be of general type indicating either the network type, operator identifier, or
a service-provider identifier. They can also be access-network specific by providing
specific information on Quality of Service (QoS), security characteristics, revisions of
current technology standards in use, cost, and roaming partners. Also, some IE types
deliver Point-of-Attachment (PoA)-specific information such as the MAC address of
the PoA, its geographical location, data rates offered, and channel information. IEs
may also be vendor-specific.

Figure 1 shows the MIH framework and communication between local and remote
MIHF entities.

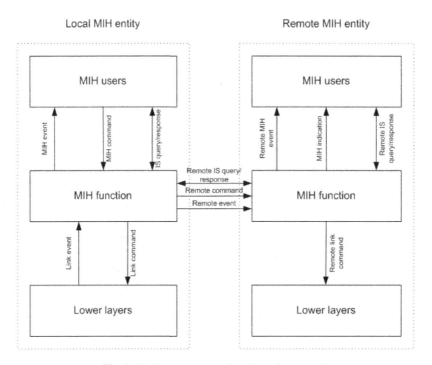

Fig. 1. Media-independent handover framework

The interfaces in the architecture are defined by a number of Service Access Points
(SAPs) in the IEEE 802.21 standard. The interface between MIH users and the MIH
function is referred to as the MIH_SAP while the interface to the lower layers is

referred to as the MIH_LINK_SAP which is generic to all access technologies. The primitives in the MIH_LINK_SAP are mapped to technology-specific primitives included in the IEEE 802.21 standard. MIH_NET_SAP defines the exchange of messages between MIH entities.

MIH protocol messages are either sent at layer 2 or by using higher layer communication mechanisms [10, 11, 12, 13].

Currently, security extensions are being standardized (IEEE 802.21a), as well as handling of handovers for downlink only technologies (IEEE 802.21b).

3   Overview of the Location-to-Service Translation (LoST) Protocol

The Location-to-Service Translation (LoST) protocol [14] was originally developed to map location information into Uniform Resource Locators (URLs) representing Public Safety Answering Points (PSAPs) for emergency calling. Although targeted for a specific application, LoST offers great flexibility and is not at all limited to its initially targeted application. Therefore, a generalized Location-to-URL Mapping Architecture and Framework was also developed [15]. Furthermore, methods for finding LoST servers were described [16]. Ongoing work includes definition of LoST extensions [17], labels for common location-based services [18], and a policy for defining new service-identifying labels [19].

LoST uses a distributed architecture relaying heavily on caching. Protocol messages are carried in HTTP messages. The LoST architecture consists of seekers, resolvers, forest guides, and authoritative mapping servers (AMSs). Queries originate from seekers that want a location to be mapped into a URL. Resolvers are special servers with information on various jurisdictions and cached data typically operated by the Internet Service Provider (ISP) or an enterprise. Forest guides acts as a lightweight directory service for trees of AMSs, who in turn performs the mapping functionality, see Figure 2.

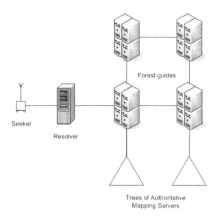

Fig. 2. Location-to-Service Translation (LoST) Architecture

LoST is an XML-based protocol. The LoST client performing a query is called a seeker. Typically, a seeker sends a query to its resolver in order to find a mapping for the specified type of service, given the device physical location. If the resolver does not have such information it forwards the request one step up in the hierarchy to a forest guide. The forest guide knows the coverage area of all trees and can therefore propagate the query down to the correct tree. Eventually, in the tree the query will reach an authoritative server which will be able to send a reply. Such reply propagates back to the seeker by traversing the same servers traversed by the query but in reverse order. The path of the query is stored in <via> elements allowing the response to follow the path in the opposite direction. There is also an iterative version of the query protocol allowing for servers to respond with addresses of other servers instead of actually delivering the answer to the query. This feature allows the seeker to iterate over a set of servers. The query <findService> is the core query type in LoST.

4   Proposed Architecture

The core contribution of this paper is the architecture proposal presented in this section. The architecture is built on a three-layer structure. At the top layer there are LoST top-level servers serving a specific geographic region. These servers perform location-to-service mapping to servers of the second and third layer. At the second layer service-provider-owned servers deliver information on each service provider's access network. Finally, at the third layer servers run by independent evaluators deliver aggregated information on available access networks that is, networks provided by national providers but also by local service providers (i.e., the local bookstore's WiFi network). Aggregated information is collected with users submitting reports which contain information on coverage and quality of service as they are experienced by users, see Figure 3.

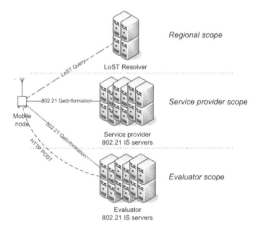

Fig. 3. Architecture proposal

In a typical scenario the end node sends a LoST <findService> query to the
LoST resolver; such query containing current location of the end-user, a certain area
within which the user wants to find points of service, and the 802.21 service URN.
Figure 4 shows an example of a LoST <findService> geodetic query. In particular, with this query we are asking the LoST server to find IEEE 802.21 IS servers
handling information about points of attachment within 200 meters from our current
position.

```
<?xml version="1.0" encoding="UTF-8"?>
<findService
  xmlns="urn:ietf:params:xml:ns:lost1"
  xmlns:p2="http://www.opengis.net/gml"
  serviceBoundary="value"
  recursive="true">
  <location id="6020688f1ce1896d" profile="geodetic-2d">
    <p2:Circle srsName="urn:ogc:def:crs:EPSG::4326">
      <p2:pos>37.775 -122.422</p2:pos>
      <p2:radius uom="urn:ogc:def:uom:EPSG::9001">
        200
      </p2:radius>
    </p2:Circle>
  </location>
  <service>urn:service:communication.internet.80221</service>
</findService>
```

Fig. 4. LoST query example

The LoST server responds with a list of 802.21 IS servers corresponding to the
service-provider 802.21 IS servers and evaluator-built 802.21 servers within the geographical area specified by the end-user in the query. After getting such list, the end
node directly queries the chosen 802.21 IS server(s) in order to obtain a list of available networks and points of attachment. Also, end nodes may filter the list of points of
attachment based on some criteria such as preferred network. At this point they would
select the local interface to use and the network to connect to based on cost, battery
consumption and performance. Required performance may change depending on the
application to be used at a specific time.

For contributing information to evaluator-built 802.21 IS servers, selected identified users may submit reports at three levels. On one level such users can passively
scan the medium and submit reports on points of attachment, including information
such as MAC address/cell id, channels used, type of encryption used. On a second
level, these selected users can submit extended reports for those access points or base
stations they are actually connected to. This second type of reports would contain
information such as achieved data rates, delay, jitter, or packet loss rate. Both types
of reports include the location of the user and allow the server to estimate the location
of the access points or base stations. The third and last type of report is the error report. Error reports are sent by clients to inform the 802.21 IS server that the received
information was wrong. After receiving a certain number of error reports from different clients regarding the same access point or base station, the 802.21 IS server may
decide to remove information regarding that access point or base station from its
database.

Reports are sent over HTTP-based POST messages to the 802.21 IS server which has been extended to handle this. The structure of these types of messages is following the IEEE 802.21 basic schema [20]. Figure 5 exemplifies an extended report.

```
<?xml version="1.0" ?>
<rdf:RDF xmlns:rdf="http://www.w3.org/1999/02/22-rdf-syntax-ns#"
xmlns:rdfs="http://www.w3.org/2000/01/rdf-schema#"
xmlns:m="http://script.tt.ltu.se/~karand/2010/01/draft-ohba802dot21-
basic-schema-07.rdf#" xmlns:owl="http://www.w3.org/2002/07/owl#"
xmlns:xsd="http://www.w3.org/2001/XMLSchema#">
  <m:NETWORK>
    <m:NETWORK_TYPE m:link_type="1" m:subtype="4" m:type_ext="7"
m:country_code="US" />
    <m:OPERATOR_ID m:op_name="Verizon Wireless" m:op_name_space="1" />
    <m:COST m:cost_unit="8" m:cost_value="25" m:cost_currency="USD" />
    <m:QOS_LIST>
      <m:COS m:cos_id="1" m:cos_value="4" m:min_pk_tx_delay="100"
m:avg_pk_tx_delay="150"
        m:max_pk_tx_delay="200" m:pk_delay_jitter="15"
m:pk_loss_rate="200" />
    </m:QOS_LIST>
    <m:IP_CONFIG m:ip_cfg_mthds="1" />
  </m:NETWORK>
  <m:POA m:LINK_ADDR="c8:ed:0f:fe:43:78" m:LOCATION_CELL_ID="5432" />
</rdf:RDF>
```

Fig. 5. Example report to an evaluator-built 802.21 IS server

By collecting such reports, an 802.21 IS server builds up its own independent database containing as rich data as any service-provider-owned 802.21 IS server could, while not being operator-network specific. Also, such independent 802.21 IS servers because of the way they are built and maintained, might be able to update their content faster than a manually-administered system.

Figure 6 shows messages exchanged between an end user and an evaluator-built 802.21 IS server.

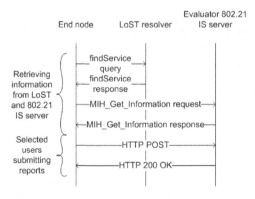

Fig. 6. Message exchange between end-users and Evaluator 802.21 IS servers

Both LoST and IEEE 802.21 can handle provisioning of location-based services. Because of this, two architectural options are possible. One option is to have LoST provide coarse-grained information as well as fine-grained information. The first would be information regarding the available 802.21 IS servers to query, given the end-user's physical location while the latter would be about points of attachment the end-user could connect to. IEEE 802.21 IS servers would then take care only of QoS-related information. In other words, reports about points of attachment would be sent to the LoST server and later queried via the LoST protocol, while reports about QoS information would be sent to IEEE 802.21 IS servers and later queried via the IEEE 802.21 MIH protocol.

In our proposed architecture, however, we follow a second option, which is to use LoST for the discovery of available 802.21 IS servers, given the end-user's current physical location, and then use 802.21 IS servers to deliver information to end-users about available points of attachment as well as QoS-related information. The reason for choosing this second approach is simply that we wanted to be consistent with the IEEE 802.21 framework without creating a special case based on LoST for the evaluator scope only, while having the other two scopes as IEEE 802.21 centric.

Furthermore, one issue with our proposal may be operators allowing access to their IEEE 802.21 IS servers only to closed user groups. Since subscribers most likely will be members of such user groups this is not a problem.

Finally, security and trust issues may occur when allowing users to contribute QoS-related information to Evaluator 802.21 IS servers. This aspect is, however, out of the scope of this paper.

5 Experiments

In order to evaluate our proposal, a prototype was built and tested in an experimental test-bed.

5.1 Experimental Set-Up

Our prototype was designed to demonstrate the key features of the proposed architecture in an experimental environment. The mobile node was implemented on a laptop running Linux Fedora core 12. Code for queries to the LoST system and the IEEE 802.21 IS servers was integrated with a commercial GPS system from Globalsat (BU-353). For the LoST client/server we used the Columbia University LoST reference implementation [21]. An experimental 802.21 IS server was implemented using Python version 3.0 where Python classes for each 802.21 IE type were implemented and installed on a Linux server running Linux Fedora version 12. MIH protocol messages were transported over TCP using binary data transmission and TLV representation of IEs. The experimental 802.21 IS server was extended with web server capabilities for the handling of user-contributed reports on access networks over HTTP. Access network selection in the mobile node was performed by reusing principles from an earlier prototype [22] calculating policy values for each access technology taking the weighted sum of normalized values for cost, performance, and battery consumption into account. The access technology with lowest policy value was selected at each decision time.

First, a trusted user follows a certain path and contributes with reports to the evaluator-operated IEEE 802.21 IS server. It provides information regarding the available points of attachment on that path. Sometime later, a regular user follows the same path and connects to those points of attachment discovered using the information provided by the evaluator-operated IEEE 802.21 IS server. Figures 7 a-f indicate the path followed by such an end-user and the points of attachment provided by the IEEE 802.21 IS server on the path. Each time the user performs a query to the IEEE 802.21 IS server it specifies a circular area within which to search for points of attachment. Once the end-user reaches the limit of such circular area, new queries are issued.

Fig. 7. a-f. Path followed by the end-user. The position of the end-user and points of attachment provided by the 802.21 IS server are indicated by different markers.

5.2 Experimental Results

Applying a make-before-break IP mobility management scheme with a multihomed mobile node as described in [22] avoided handoff delays and packet losses. Access to the evaluator-owned IEEE 802.21 IS server typically took an average of 22 ms for multiple-location queries. Such queries provide information on all the points of attachment present along the entire path. This is possible if the user already knows the entire path he or she will follow. Single location queries took an average of 19 ms and were performed so that new queries for points of attachment within 150 meters from the user's current location were made each 100 meters along the path.

6 Related Work

To the best of our knowledge, the idea of helping roaming users by the delivery of IEEE 802.21 information services from independent evaluators is new. Also, the idea of looking up IEEE 802.21 IS servers through the LoST protocol is new. In the following we present some related work on IEEE 802.21 assisted handovers.

Eastwood et al. [23] showed how the requirements in the IMT-Advanced network (a.k.a. 4G) can be met by integrating 802.11VHT and 802.16m radio access technologies with the IEEE 802.21 handover support technology. Five use cases were identified and MIIS was used explicitly in the case where the user was decelerating while running an application whose performance was increasing at higher data rates.

Kim et al. [24] proposed a framework for seamless mobility across WIBRO and HSDPA networks using the IEEE 802.21 standard. The proposal was evaluated running Skype and a Video on Demand application in a multi-radio environment with a make-before-break handover policy. Results from a stationary test reported neither packet losses, nor any disruption of either voice or video streams. When driving at 60 km/h service disruption occurred during handover in specific places, but overall performance was reported to be acceptable with no service quality degradation in the general case. The MIIS database was updated with data from users detecting a base station not yet included. This particular detail shows some similarity to the principles of our proposal. On the other hand, the approach of Kim et al. is to use a network-centric access network selection mechanism which is not the case in our proposal.

Finally, there are quite a few papers where the IEEE 802.21 event and command services are used to improve handover performance. Cacace et al. [25] introduced the concept of a Mobility Manager (MM) interfacing with the MIH function in the mobile node. The MM included functionality for user policies, link quality, handoff decisions, and power management. By implementing a prototype on a Linux platform the proposal was tested in a UMTS/802.11 network environment. Adaptive streaming was also adopted, so that the bit-rates of the streams were adapted to the characteristics of the access technology being used for the moment. Also, adaptive VoIP applications were tested in the same manner. Results showed that connection and application quality improved.

Dutta et al. [26] described an experimental testbed including IEEE 802.21 features for network discovery and network selection. Experiments were performed with a VoIP application using a SIP-based mobility mechanism. Total handover delay was reported to 14 ms and only one single audio packet was lost at each handover.

On the commercial side, a number of web based Wi-Fi finder applications exist, but non-web-page versions being automated are not common. However, special applications for high end handsets like the Apple iPhone and its competitors exist [27]. The degree of automation in such applications varies a lot and standards-based solutions, like ours building on IEEE 802.21 and LoST, are not available.

Our approach combining the strengths of the LoST protocol and the IEEE 802.21 standard, and also allowing for independent evaluators to deliver information of interest when taking handover decisions makes it a very practical and useful solution to large groups of end-users.

7   Conclusions and Future Work

The architecture proposed in this paper was described and evaluated through a proto-type implementation and experiments in a live environment. It is a generic solution, allows for competition at all levels, and scales well due to the distributed nature of the proposed architecture. End-users will ultimately experience improved quality and lower costs. Also, as a consequence of basing the proposal on the IEEE 802.21 standard, the need for scanning has been minimized thus allowing for lower battery consumption.

Future work will include investigations on integrating the ideas presented in this paper with software defined radio (SDR) that is, solutions aiming to deliver "cellular on demand" services to end-users.

Acknowledgement

This work was supported in part by the National Science Foundation under award 07-51094 and in part by Skellefteå Kraft within the Hybrinet project. The collaboration between Luleå University of Technology and Columbia University was financially supported by Nordea Norrland Foundation.

References

1. Perkins, C. (ed.): IP Mobility Support for IPv4, IETF, RFC 3344 (August 2002)
2. Johnson, D., Perkins, C., Arkko, J.: IP Mobility Support in IPv6, IETF, RFC 3775 (June 2004)
3. Stewart, R., Xie, Q., Morneault, K., Sharp, C., Schwarzbauer, H., Taylor, T., Rytina, I., Kalla, M., Zhang, L., Paxson, V.: Stream Control Transmission Protocol, IETF, RFC 2960 (October 2000)
4. Koh, S.J., Chang, M.J., Lee, M.: mSCTP for Soft Handover in Transport Layer. IEEE Communications Letters 8(3), 189–191 (2004)
5. Schulzrinne, H., Wedlund, E.: Application-layer mobility using SIP. Mobile Computing and Communications Review archive 4(3), 47–57 (2000)
6. Moskowitz, R., Nikander, P.: Host Identity Protocol (HIP) Architecture, IETF, RFC 4423 (May 2006)
7. Gundavelli, S. (ed.): Proxy Mobile IPv6, IETF, RFC 5213 (August 2008)
8. IEEE Standard for Local and metropolitan area networks—Part 21: Media Independent Handover Services (January 2009)
9. SPARQL Query Language for RDF, W3C Recommendation (January 2008), http://www.w3.org/TR/2008/REC-rdf-sparql-query-20080115/
10. Melia, T. (ed.): Mobility Services Transport: Problem Statement, IETF, RFC 5164 (March 2008)
11. Melia, T.(ed.), Bajko, G., Das, S., Golmie, N., Zuniga, J.: IEEE 802.21 Mobility Services Framework Design (MSFD), IETF, RFC 5677 (December 2009)
12. Bajko, G., Das, S.: Dynamic Host Configuration Protocol (DHCPv4 and DHCPv6) Options for IEEE 802.21 Mobility Services (MoS) Discovery, IETF, RFC 5678 (December 2009)
13. Bajko, G.: Locating IEEE 802.21 Mobility Services Using DNS, IETF, RFC 5679

14. Hardie, T., Newton, A., Schulzrinne, H., Tschofenig, H.: LoST: A Location-to-Service Translation Protocol, IETF, RFC 5222 (August 2008)

15. Schulzrinne, H.: Location-to-URL Mapping Architecture and Framework, IETF, RFC 5582 (September 2009)

16. Schulzrinne, H., Polk, J., Tschofenig, H.: Discovering Location-to-Service Translation (LoST) Servers Using the Dynamic Host Configuration Protocol (DHCP), IETF, RFC 5223 (August 2008)

17. Forte, A., Schulzrinne, H.: Location-to-Service Translation Protocol (LoST) Extensions, Internet Draft, draft-forte-ecrit-lost-extensions-02.txt (March 2009)

18. Forte, A., Schulzrinne, H.: Labels for Common Location-based Services, Internet Draft, draft-forte-ecrit-service-classification-02.txt (March 2009)

19. Forte, A., Schulzrinne, H.: Policy for defining new service-identifying labels, Internet Draft, draft-forte-ecrit-service-urn-policy-00.txt (March 2009)

20. Taniuchi, K., Ohba, Y., Das, S.: IEEE 802.21 Basic Schema, Internet Draft, draft-ohba-802dot21-basic-schema-07.txt (December 2009)

21. Columbia University LoST Reference Implementation, http://lost.cs.columbia.edu

22. Andersson, K., Granlund, D., Åhlund, C.: M^4: MultiMedia Mobility Manager - a seamless mobility management architecture supporting multimedia applications. In: Proceedings of the 6th International Conference on Mobile and Ubiquitous Multimedia, MUM2007, Oulu, Finland, December 2007. ACM International Conference Proceeding Series (2007)

23. Eastwood, L., Migaldi, S., Xie, Q., Gupta, V.: Mobility Using IEEE 802.21 In A Heterogeneous IEEE 802.16/802.11-based, IMT-Advanced (4G) Network. IEEE Wireless Communications 15(2), 26–34 (2008)

24. Kim, K., Hong, J.Y., Choi, Y., Kim, Y.H., Lee, S.: Design and Implementation of IEEE 802.21 Framework for WIBRO-HSDPA Seamless Mobility. In: Proceedings of 2009 International Conference on New Trends in Information and Service Science, Beijing, China (July 2009)

25. Cacace, F., Vollero, L.: Managing mobility and adaptation in upcoming 802.21 enabled devices. In: Proceedings of the 4th international Workshop on Wireless Mobile Applications and Services on WLAN Hotspots, Los Angeles, CA, USA (September 2006)

26. Dutta, A., Das, S., Famolari, D., Ohba, Y., Taniuchi, K., Kodama, T., Schulzrinne, H.: Seamless handover across heterogeneous networks - an IEEE 802.21 centric approach. In: Proceedings of the 8th International Symposium on Wireless Personal Multimedia Communications, Aalborg, Denmark (September 2005)

27. Wi-Fi Finder, http://www.jiwire.com

Error-Sensitive Adaptive Frame Aggregation in 802.11n WLAN

Melody Moh*, Teng-Sheng Moh, and Ken Chan

Department of Computer Science
San Jose State University, San Jose, CA 95192-0249 USA
moh@cs.sjsu.edu

Abstract. IEEE 802.11n is an emerging standard for high data-rate wireless local area networks (WLAN). Frame aggregation is vital for enhancing its MAC layer efficiency. A large frame size can usually boost network throughput, yet it also causes a high frame-error rate (FER), which is undesirable for many real-time applications. This paper proposes a novel scheme, the Error-Sensitive Adaptive Frame Aggregation (ESAFA). The ESAFA utilizes the two-layer frame aggregation method specified in 802.11n. It dynamically adjusts the frame aggregation size according to the current channel conditions to satisfy the FER level required by the application. Performance evaluation shows that, when compared with an existing scheme, OFA (Optimal Frame Aggregation), ESAFA greatly improves network throughput and decreases delay, especially in error-prone channels. It also satisfies the FER required by applications in most conditions. We believe that the proposed method is significant for supporting ubiquitous, seamless multimedia services over high-speed WLAN.

Keywords: Frame error rate, frame aggregation, IEEE 802.11n, wireless local area networks.

1 Introduction

An IEEE 802.11 Wireless Local Area Network (WLAN) provides wireless communication over short distances. WLAN have become ubiquitous as they are easily deployed and simple to use. Many existing enterprises and home users have switched from using wired networks to using 802.11 WLAN as their primary Internet connection media. The traditional 802.11 a/b/g WLANs use the Distributed Co-ordination Function (DCF) for accessing the shared wireless medium, which employs the CSMA/CA (Carrier Sense Multiple Accesses with Collision Avoidance) algorithm. However, research has shown that the MAC layer overhead is the main reason for their inefficiency [6] [16] [7].

With the increasing demand of data-intensive applications over wireless networks, the IEEE 802.11n WLAN is being standardized with new medium access control (MAC) and physical (PHY) specifications [5]. Its primary design goal is to increase the WLAN net throughput above 100Mbps, comparable to 100Mbps Fast Ethernet

---

* Corresponding author.

E. Osipov et al. (Eds.): WWIC 2010, LNCS 6074, pp. 64–76, 2010.
© Springer-Verlag Berlin Heidelberg 2010

[15]. Backward compatibility with legacy 802.11 a/b/g devices is also a critical design requirement. These goals are aided by improvements in radio technology, such as the Orthogonal Frequency-Division Multiplexing (OFDM) modulation method and the Multiple-Input-Multiple-Output (MIMO) smart antenna. The effective management of the enhanced PHY mode (40MHz channel bonding) also helps. 802.11n can provide a network with a longer range and a higher PHY speed and is expected to have a maximum raw PHY data rate of 600Mbps, compared to the 54Mbps data rate in the previous 802.11 a/b/g standards.

Even though a significant improvement for the PHY transmission rate can be reached, one cannot achieve a real throughput boost without using frame aggregation techniques. This is because with a higher speed in the PHY layer, the DCF overhead in the MAC layer is even greater. Frame aggregation techniques can help reduce the known MAC overhead and utilize the increased PHY speed.

To further increase throughput, Lin and Wong proposed the Optimal Frame Aggregation (OFA) scheme for 802.11n [12]. The OFA calculates the optimal frame size with respect to different bit error rates (BER) to reach maximum throughput. While a large frame size may raise throughput, it leads to a much larger frame error rate (FER), as illustrated formally in Section 4.1. Note that a high FER either severely degrades the receiving quality or requires frequent retransmissions, and is thus undesirable for many applications.

Most applications have specific quality-of-services (QoS) requirements. Real-time applications, including voice and video, are particularly QoS-sensitive; the quality of audio or video is directly influenced by the QoS offered by the carrying networks. For example, Voice over IP (VoIP) traffic is delay-sensitive and they tolerate less than 2% of packets with a delay greater than 30ms [17][2]; they can tolerate about 2% -5% of loss depending on compression status and the type of compression [1]. Streaming video traffic, on the other hand, is sensitive to loss and the loss rate should be within 5%. The latency should be no more than 5 seconds [17].

We proposed the Error-Sensitive Adaptive Frame Aggregation (ESAFA) scheme based on the above observations . It is designed to satisfy the FER required by the application. By utilizing the two-layer frame aggregation of 802.11n [5], it dynamically adjusts the frame aggregation size based on the current channel condition to achieve the design goal.

The rest of the paper is organized as follows. Section 2 covers background information and related studies. Section 3 presents the rationale and description of the ESAFA. Section 4 illustrates performance evaluation. Finally, we conclude the paper in Section 5.

2 Background and Related Studies

This section includes two parts. First, background information including various 802.11n frame aggregation methods is briefly described. Next, related studies, in terms of analyzing 802.11 aggregation and enhancements for voice and video supports, are presented.

2.1 Background

In this section, we will briefly describe the latest 802.11n Draft 4.0 specifications on the A-MSDU (Aggregated MAC Service Data Unit), the AMPDU (Aggregated MAC Protocol Data Unit), the two-level frame aggregation, and the Block Acknowledgement (BA) technique [5].

2.1.1 A-MSDU Frame Aggregation

The A-MSDU is designed to allow multiple MSDU frames to be sent to the same receiver concatenated in a single MPDU. The top MAC layer receives packets from the Link Layer; these buffered packets are then aggregated to form a single A-MSDU. The AMSDU aggregation is only allowed for packets with same source and destination.

Figure 1 shows the frame format for an A-MSDU frame. Each MSDU subframe in an A-MSDU frame consists of the Subframe Header, the MSDU data payload and the Padding field. The Subframe Header is formed by the Destination Address field, the Source Address field, and Length field, where indicates the length of the MSDU data payload. A single A-MSDU frame is then transferred after adding the Physical Header (Physical Layer Convergence Protocol (PLCP) Preamble, PLCP Header), the MAC header and the FCS field into the packet.

Note that each MSDU subframe does not have its individual FCS field. Only the AMSDU frame has an FCS field at the end. This implies that corrupting any bit in an MSDU subframe will corrupt the entire AMSDU frame. There is no retransmission mechanism for a MSDU subframe.

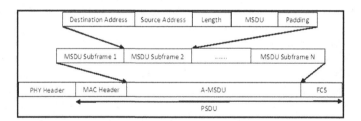

Fig. 1. A-MSDU Frame Format

2.1.2 A-MPSU Frame Aggregation

The purpose of an A-MPDU is to join multiple MPDU subframes with a single leading PHY header to reduce the PHY header overhead. All the MPDU subframes within an A-MPDU must be addressed to the same receiver, but these MPDU subframes can have different source addresses. Figure 2 shows the A-MPDU frame format. Each MPDU subframe includes the MPDU delimiter and padding bytes. The MPDU delimiter is used to calibrate the MPDU's position. It also contains the CRC value for error control. The maximum AMPDU size is 64KB. The maximum number of MPDU subframes in an AMPDU is 64; this is constrained by the 128 bitmap in the BA Frame.

When the receiver de-aggregates an A-MPDU frame, it checks the frame error of *each* MPDU subframe based on the CRC value in the MPDU delimiter. Those that contain errors will be handled by BA for retransmission, as described after the two-level frame aggregation illustrated below

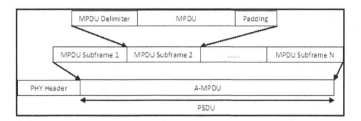

Fig. 2. A-MPDU Frame Format

2.1.3 Two-Level Frame Aggregation

The idea is to combine both the benefits of the A-MSDU and the A-MPDU aggregation to further reduce the overhead of the 802.11n protocol. Figure 3 shows the two-level frame aggregation process. An A-MSDU frame with its MAC header and FCS are treated as a single MPDU payload, which together with the MPDU delimiter and padding bytes form a single MPDU subframe. Finally, multiple MPDU subframes are concatenated to form one A-MPDU frame.

By combining the two aggregations, both PHY and MAC overhead are significantly reduced in a high speed network. Note that the shaded part of Figure 3 is the focused of our proposed algorithm, which we adaptively adjust according to the channel condition to satisfy the desired FER level, as will be explained in Section 3.

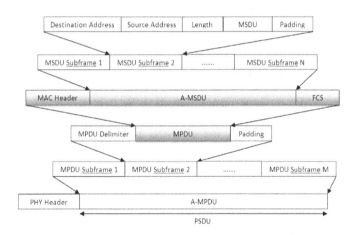

Fig. 3. Two-Level Frame Aggregation

2.1.4 Block Acknowledgment (BA)

IEEE 802.11n introduces a mechanism to acknowledge a block of packets effectively, and is applied to the A-MPDU. A sender can send an Add Block Acknowledgment (ADDBA) frame to the receiver. This frame includes the starting frame sequence number (SN) and the size of the frame SN's that the receiver should expect during the transmission. The receiver accepts frames that have SN's within the current window. During the A-MPDU de-aggregation process, the receiver updates the status of each MPDU subframe in the bitmap of the BA frame and sends back the BA to indicate the

SN's that have been successfully received. Upon receiving the BA, the sender checks the BA bitmap. All the corrupted subframes will be retransmitted.

2.2 Related Studies

Paul and Ogunfunmi described the evolutions of the 802.11n amendments and the evaluation of different new PHY and MAC frame aggregation techniques [15]. Kim, Hwang and Sung investigated the throughput performance of the AMSDU and the AMPDU frame aggregations [8].

Lee proposed a multiple-receiver frame aggregation for boosting video capacity on the 802.11n network [9]. Different video frames were encapsulated in a single A-MPDU. MPDU subframes in the same A-MPDU could have different destination addresses. The client receiving this A-MPDU would acknowledge only the MPDU subframes that were destined for it. Unfortunately, this was incompatible with the 802.11n draft 2.0, and required unnecessary processing at receivers.

Hegde proposed an algorithm to improve the VoIP performance in the 802.11n network [4]. The scheme altered the behavior of the Access Point (AP) at the time of receiving the ACK frames. Following the reception of a voice packet from a station, the AP sent an ACK frame as a usual DCF operation. However, after another SIFS period, it transmitted an extra voice packet from its own buffer. This scheme needed some modification on the AP and it created a traffic fairness problem when there was a mix of VoIP and data traffic in the network.

Note that the above two schemes both required some behavioral changes to the current 802.11n frame aggregation, whereas the proposed ESAFA algorithm requires minimal changes.

Optimal Frame Aggregation (OFA)

Below, we give a more detailed description of the OFA algorithm, since it was compared with the ESAFA for performance evaluation (Section 4).

Wong and Lin suggested an Optimal Frame Size for the A-MSDU Aggregation in 802.11n [12]. The rationale is that the A-MSDU aggregation may reach a maximum throughput under different BER conditions, and there is an optimal aggregated frame size $L*$ for maximizing the AMSDU throughput with respect to BER.

The OFA algorithm may be described as follows: First, it constructs the $L*$-BER curve from the analytical model using N, the average number of stations in the network. Next, the signal-to-noise ratio (SNR) value is obtained from the closed loop receiver-assisted link adaptation of 802.11n. Before transmitting an aggregated A-MSDU frame, the sending station will obtain an estimation of the channel BER from the SNR. After that, it will consult the $L*$-BER curve for an optimal frame size $L*$ corresponding to the estimated BER. An AMSDU frame with size $L*$ is then constructed. According to the OFA, the optimal AMSDU frame size in BER channels of 10^{-6}, 10^{-5}, 2×10^{-5}, 5×10^{-5}, and 10^{-4} are 8000bytes, 4500bytes, 2500bytes, 1500bytes and 1000bytes respectively (see Table 1 of Section 3).

Nevertheless, that there are some limitations associated with the algorithm: First, the $L*$-BER curve from the analytical model is obtained by using N, the average number of stations in the network. The curve is static and pre-determined. The $L*$ value may not be appropriate if N is not close to the current number of stations.

Secondly, the algorithm uses the BER-SNR relationship, which assumes the closed-loop receiver-assisted link adaptation feature in 802.11n. In the proposed ESAFA algorithm, we simply utilize the feedback from the BA. Third, the work did not utilize or evaluate the two-level aggregation in 802.11n.

3 Error-Sensitive Adaptive Frame Aggregation (ESAFA)

In this section, we first describe the design rationale. A detailed description of the algorithm is then presented.

3.1 Design Rationale

The ESAFA is designed based on three important principles:

1. To support application-specified QoS (in terms of loss rate FER)
2. To observe the relationship among channel BER, application-required FER, and frame length
3. To utilize 802.11n two-level frame aggregation

These three principles are discussed in the following subsections.

3.1.1 Rationale 1: Supporting Application-Specified QoS (in Terms of FER)

Applications have specific QoS requirements. Real-time applications, including voice and video, are particularly sensitive. Their quality is directly influenced by the QoS offered by the carrying networks, including loss rate and delay. The proposed ESAFA takes the FER requirement of an application as a parameter for its frame size adjustment. By limiting the frame size to satisfy the FER, it also greatly reduces delay since most retransmissions were eliminated. As a result, the quality is much improved.

3.1.2 Rationale 2: The Relationship among Channel BER, Application-Specified FER, and Frame Length

We noted that the OFA algorithm computed an L^*-BER $curve$; i.e., it calculated the optimal frame size based on the channel BER value to achieve the maximum throughput [12]. Nonetheless, it is important to observe the relationship among FER, BER, and Frame Size (FS). In OFA, a low BER implies a large FS. Yet, a large FS leads to a very high FER (see Table 1 below), which is undesirable. This is explained more formally below.

A frame is considered to be an error frame if at least one bit of error is detected. Under the assumption that bit errors are independent, identically distributed events, then the relationship among BER, FER and FS is expressed in the following equations:

Equation 1: Given BER and BPF, FER can be calculated as,

$$FER = 1 - (1 - BER)^{FS} \qquad (1)$$

Equation 2: From Equation (1), given FER and FS, we derive BER:
$$(1 - BER)^{FS} = 1 - FER$$
$$FS \, log_{10} \, (1\text{-}BER) = log_{10} \, (1 - FER)$$
$$log_{10} \, (1\text{-}BER) = (log_{10} \, (1 - FER)) / \, FS$$
$$BER = 1 - 10 \, \char94 \, (\, (log_{10} \, (1 - FER)) \, / \, FS) \tag{2}$$

Equation 3: From Equation (1), given FER and BER, then FS:
$$FS = log_{10} \, (1 - FER) \, / \, log_{10} \, (1 - BER) \tag{3}$$

By using the suggested Optimal Frame Size (OFS) in the Optimal OFA scheme [12], we calculate the corresponding FER in table 1. The results show that FER would increase rapidly when using the suggested OFS. These FER results are not acceptable when applied to voice/video multimedia traffic where the FER requirement would normally be within 5% [17][1].

Table 1. FER with respect to the optimal frame size in different BER channels

BER	10^{-6}	$1*10^{-5}$	$2*10^{-5}$	$5*10^{-5}$	10^{-4}
OFS	8000*8	4500*8	2500*8	1500*8	1000*8
FER	6.19%	30.23%	32.96%	45.12%	55.07%

To further investigate this relationship, Tables 2 (a), 2(b), and 2(c) show more sample data between FER and FS (i.e., MPDU subframe size) under various BER channels.

Table 2. FER with respect to different MPDU subframe sizes (FS)

(a) BER = 10^{-6}

FS	120*8	480*8	959*8	1918*8	3839*8
FER	0.09%	0.38%	0.76%	1.5%	3%

(b) BER = 10^{-5}

FS	120*8	480*8	959*8	1918*8	3839*8
FER	0.95%	3.8%	7.3%	14%	26%

(c) BER = 10^{-4}

FS	120*8	480*8	959*8	1918*8	3839*8
FER	9%	31%	53%	78%	95%

Clearly, the value of FER depend on the current BER and FS. In order to achieve a FER the application traffic can tolerate, it is necessary to consider the current BER and to adjust the FS accordingly. This forms the basis of the proposed ESAFA, in which the size of the MPDU subframe is adjusted based on the maximum FER tolerance specified by the application.

3.1.3 Rationale 3: Utilizing 802.11n Two-Level Frame Aggregation

In order to reduce both MAC and PHY overhead and to achieve the best efficiency, ESAFA adapts the two-level frame aggregation (described in Section 2.2.4). Recall that, in the first level, AMSDU, no corrupted MSDU subframes is retransmitted; i.e., a single bit error triggers the drop of the entire AMSDU frame. In the second level, AMPDU, however, the receiver retransmits any corrupted MPDU subframes through the BA mechanism.

Based on the above observation, it is clear that there is no benefit for adjusting the subframe size of the first level (MSDU). Instead, it is more profitable to adjust the size of the second level subframe; i.e., MPDU subframe, according to the current channel BER and the FER specified by the application. A smaller MPDU subframe size will used in the high BER, error-prone channel condition. This will reduce the probability of frame corruption and the frequency of retransmissions. When the channel condition is good, then a larger MPDU subframe size will be used to increase throughput.

3.2 ESAFA Description

Based on the above three design principles, ESAFA adjusts the second-level MPDU subframe size based on the channel BER and the desired FER specified by the application. The ESAFA algorithm is first presented, followed by its description.

> Let **X** be the maximum FER specified by the application (maximum tolerable loss),
> **Y** (Y < X) be the minimum FER below which the frame size can be increased to boost throughput,
> **R** be the current FER, using the average ratio of corrupted sub-frames in an AMPDU
>> R = (Total number of corrupted sub-frames in an AMPDU)/ (Total number of sub-frames in an AMPDU)
> **mBER** be the measured current BER calculated from R by the sender using equation (2), and
> **currentFS** be the current MPDU subframe size

Note that R may be calculated by the sender based on the BA frame received from the receiver, and is taken as the current FER, which determines whether to increase, decrease, or maintain the current aggregation size MPDU (refer to Fig 3).

ESAFA Algorithm

1. **Obtain *mBER* in the network by substituting *R* and the *currentFS* into equation (2)**
   $mBER = 1 - 10 ^\wedge ((log_{10} (1 - R)) / currentFS)$
2. **Adjust MPDU subframe size to satisfy the FER requirement *X*, based on current FER, *R***
   a. *If R > X*
      //Bad channel condition; decrease the MPDU size by using X in equation (3)
         $currentFS := log_{10}(1 - X) / log_{10}(1 - mBER)$

    b. *else if R < Y*
        //Good channel condition; increase the MPDU size by using Y in equation
        (3) to boost throughput
            currentFS = log_{10} (1 - Y) / log_{10} (1 - mBER)
    c. *Use currentFS for the next MPDU size*
        //Note that no frame adjustment is needed for the condition $Y \le R \le X$

The above ESAFA algorithm is explained below. First, in Step 1, the current BER (mBER) of the channel may be calculated by using R (obtained from the bitmap of BA) and the current MPDU subframe size, substituting into equation (2). In Step 2, the MPDU subframe size is adjusted to satisfy X, the FER requirement specified by the application, based on the channel BER. If the current channel FER, R, is greater than X (Step 2a), then it is a noisy channel, and the MPDU size is reduced based on the channel BER, using equation (3). If, on the other hand, the channel condition is good and R is smaller than Y, which is a parameter below which the aggregation frame size can be increased to boost throughput; this is handled in Step 2b, and the MPDU size is increased, also using equation (3). Note that if R is between X and Y, nothing needs to be done. Finally, the adjusted MPDU size is used in the next transmission.

In Step 2b, instead of increasing the frame size by directly following equation (3), one can simply increase the frame size by, for example, 100 bytes, to smoothly increase the frame size. This may also prevent unfairness in the network. Thus,

Alternate Step 2b: Smooth Increase of Frame Size
    b. *else if R < Y*
        //Smoothly increase the MPDU size to gradually raise throughput
            currentFS = current FS + 100 bytes

Finally, recall that one AMPDU frame can contain a maximum of 64 MPDU subframes. Changing MPDU subframe size also changes the total AMPDU size, and helps an overall reduction of loss or an overall increase of throughput. According to the specification [5], the number of MPDU subframes in one AMPDU frame should not be fixed and the number is adjusted based on the channel conditions. Adjusting this number is left for future extensions.

4 Performance Evaluation

4.1 Simulation Settings

To simulate the 802.11n frame aggregation, we implemented both the proposed ESAFA and the existing OFA on NS-2 [13], using version 2.30 [14], while referring to a detailed description of the MAC code in NS-2 [19]. The network topology is a typical WLAN with a single AP and multiple mobile, wireless clients moving in the Random Way Point Model. The AP and the clients are within the transmission range of each other. The data rate is 144Mbps. We set X to be 5%, as most multimedia traffic including voice have loss tolerance within is 5% [17][3]. Y is set to be 0.8X; i.e.,

Y = 4%. Note that Y is a tunable parameter, depending on the application-specific preference and on channel conditions. All the wireless nodes are saturated with Constant Bit Rate (CBR) traffic, for which there is no application-level acknowledgment or retransmission; it is therefore suitable for evaluating MAC-layer performance. We conduct the simulation under different BER conditions and each simulation run lasts for 10 seconds.

In the simulation, we measure throughput, average delay, percentage delay, and *FER*, as described below:

- The *throughput* refers to the maximum rate at which the MAC layer can *successfully* transfer packets from the senders to the receivers.
- The *average delay* refers to the average duration from the time a packet is ready to be sent at the sender's interface queue until it is correctly received by the receiver. The average delay also includes the retransmission time.
- The *Percentage delay* refers to the percentage of packets where the delay is greater than a delay upper limit [10]. This is a useful metric for real-time applications such as VoIP where delay is a critical performance [17]. We selected 30ms as the delay upper limit in the percentage delay.
- Finally, the *measured FER* represents the average percentage of corrupted MPDU sub-frames in an AMPDU. It also reflects the average loss rate in the wireless LAN. It is evaluated to see if the ESAFA satisfies the application FER requirement.

4.2 Simulation Results

In the following, we show the simulation results and compare two frame aggregation schemes. On the figures, "Optimal frame Aggregation" refers to the OFA [12], and "Adaptive Frame Aggregation" refers to the ESAFA. The BER varied, raging from 10^{-6} (denoted by 1E-06) to 10^{-4} (denoted by 1E-04).

Figure 3 shows the throughput comparison. At low BER, both schemes stay at high throughput. As the BER increases, their performance both degraded. Yet, the throughput of the OFA decreases much more rapidly than that of the ESAFA. This is mainly because in high-BER channels, the ESAFA adaptively reduces MPDU frame size and successfully minimizes the chance of frame corruptions.

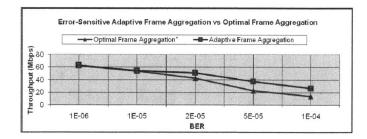

Fig. 3. Throughput of ESAFA and OFA in different BER channels

Figure 4 shows the average delay. We observed that the OFA has a higher average delay under high-BER channels, while the ESAFA maintains a much lower average delay. This is because the ESAFA adaptively reduces the MPDU subframe size in high BER channels. This greatly reduced the probability of frame corruption and, consequently, the number of packet retransmissions. In fact, when compared to the OFA, the ESAFA reduces the average delay by about 50% in each case except for the very low BER case.

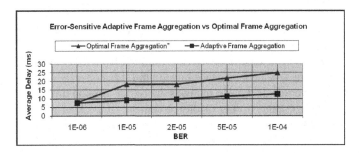

Fig. 4. Average Delay of ESAFA and OFA in different BER channels

Figure 5 shows the percentage delay, which is the percentage of packets that experienced a delay of more than 30 msec. Both schemes experienced a higher percentage delay when BER increases since more MPDU subframes are corrupted and need to be retransmitted. Note, however, that the ESAFA is able to maintain a 5% -10% percentage of delay, whereas the OFA suffers a much higher percentage of delay, up to 30%. This again shows that the ESAFA has successfully adjusted frame aggregation size under different channel conditions and is well suited for real-time applications.

Finally, Figure 6 shows the resulting FER measured in the MAC layer. This is an important metric since it evaluates how well the ESAFA can support the application FER requirement. FER = 5% is achieved under low to medium BER, while approximately 10% is achieved under very high BER. This shows that ESAFA has successfully controlled the FER under high channel errors, which is significant for real-time multimedia applications. On the other hand, the results of OFA are much higher, up to 50%. These OFA simulation results are close to the analytical FER data shown in Table 1.

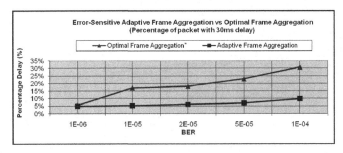

Fig. 5. Percentage of packets with more than 30ms delay for ESAFA and OFA in different BER channels

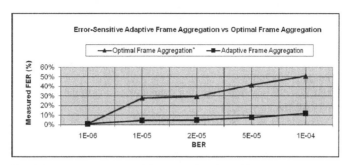

Fig. 6. Measured FER for ESAFA and OFA in different BER channels

5 Conclusion

We have proposed the ESAFA, an adaptive scheme that adds the factor of maximum FER tolerable by a particular application into frame aggregation. The ESAFA is based on and compatible with the 802.11n two-layer frame aggregation. It dynamically adjusts frame aggregation size in responding to channel conditions to meet a set FER level. Simulation results show that ESAFA has outperformed the existing OFA by significantly improving both delay and net throughput in the 802.11n WLAN. It has maintained FER performance at about the same level required by the application. These performance improvements are clear especially in severely error-prone networks. Future works may include careful studies of the complexity and backward compatibility of the proposed scheme, the effect of frame-aggregation adjusting frequency, assessment of the scheme based on dynamically changing BER, and based on actual test networks. We may also extend ESAFA for 802.11n-based Mesh and MANET environments [11], and integrating ESAFA with 802.11e QoS requirements.

References

[1] Audin, G.: VoIP – A question of perspective (2009),
    http://www.securitytechnet.com/resource/hot-opic/voip/Quest-of-Persp.pdf (retrieved May 1, 2009)
[2] Cisco: QoS requirements of Voice (2009a),
    http://www.ciscopress.com/articles/article.asp?p=357102
    (retrieved May 1, 2009)
[3] Cisco: QoS requirements of Video (2009b),
    http://www.ciscopress.com/articles/article.asp?p=357102&seqNum=2 (retrieved May 1, 2009)
[4] Hegde, N.: Evolution of WLANs towards VoIP traffic and higher throughputs. In: ACM In Proceedings of the 1st international Conference on Access Networks AcessNets '06, vol. 267 (2006)
[5] IEEE (2008) IEEE Draft STANDARD for Information Technology-Telecommunications and information exchange between systems-Local and metropolitan area networks-Specific requirements-Part 11: Wireless LAN Medium Access Control (MAC) and Physical Layer (PHY) specifications: Amendment 4: Enhancements for Higher Throughput, IEEE 802.1n TGn Sync. Working Group, P802.11n/D4.00 (March 2008)

[6] IEEE (2007) IEEE Standard for Information technology-Telecommunications and information exchange between systems-Local and metropolitan area networks-Specific requirements - Part 11: Wireless LAN Medium Access Control (MAC) and Physical Layer (PHY) Specifications, IEEE Std 802.11-2007 (Revision of IEEE Std 802.11-1999), pp.C1-1184, June 12 (2007)

[7] IEEE (2005) WWiSE proposal: High throughput extension to the 802.11 standard, IEEE 802.11n WWiSE (January 2005)

[8] Kim, B.S., Hwang, H.H.Y., Sung, D.K.: MAC 15-3 - Effect of Frame Ag-gregation on the Throughput Performance of IEEE 802.11n. In: IEEE Wireless Communications and Networking Conference, WCNC 2008, pp. 1740–1744 (March 31-April 3, 2008)

[9] Lee, K., Sangki, Y., Kim, H.: Boosting Video Capacity of IEEE 802.11n through Multiple Receiver Frame Aggregation. In: IEEE Vehicular Technology Conference, Spring 2008, pp. 2587–2591 (May 11-14, 2008)

[10] Li, Q., Ni, Q., Malone, D., Leith, D., Xiao, Y., Turletti, T.: A new MAC scheme for very high-speed WLANs. In: International Symposium on a World of Wireless Mobile and Multimedia Networks, WoWMoM 2006, June 26-29, p. 10 (2006)

[11] Li, Y., Safwat, A.M.: On high-throughput and fair multi-hop wireless ad hoc networks with MIMO. In: ACM In Proceedings of the 3rd international Conference on Mobile Technology, Applications &Amp. Systems Mobility '06, vol. 270 (2006)

[12] Lin, Y., Wong, V.W.S.: Frame Aggregation and Optimal Frame Size Adaptation for IEEE 802.11n WLANs. In: IEEE GLOBECOM '06, pp. 1–6 (November 27-December, 12006)

[13] Network Simulator NS-2 Wiki, http://www.isi.edu/nsnam/ns/ (retrieved May 1, 2009); Network Simulator NS-2 version 2.30 download link, http://sourceforge.net/project/showfiles.php?group_id=149743 &package_id=169689&release_id=450423 (retrieved May 1, 2009)

[14] Paul, T.K., Ogunfunmi, T.: Wireless LAN Comes of Age: Understanding the IEEE 802.11n Amendment. IEEE Circuits and Systems Magazine 8(1), 28–54 (First Quarter 2008)

[15] Skordoulis, D., Ni, Q., Chen, H.-S., Stephens, A.P., Liu, C., Jamalipour, A.: IEEE 802.11n MAC frame aggregation mechanisms for next-generation high-throughput WLANs [medium access control protocols for wireless LANs]. IEEE Wireless Communications 15(1), 40–47 (2008)

[16] Stephens, A.P., et al.: IEEE P802.11 Wireless LANs: Usage Models. IEEE 802.11-03/802r23 (May 2004)

[17] Villavicencio, O., Lu, K., Zhu, H., Sastri, K.: Performance of IEEE 802.11n in Multi-Channel Multi-Radio Wireless Ad Hoc Network. In: IEEE Military Communications Conference, MILCOM 2007, pp. 1–6 (October 29-31, 2007)

SHORT: A Static-Hybrid Approach for Routing Real Time Applications over Multichannel, Multihop Wireless Networks⋆

Vijay Raman and Nitin H. Vaidya

ECE & Coordinated Science Lab
University of Illinois at Urbana-Champaign
Urbana, IL 61801, USA
{vraman3,nhv}@illinois.edu

Abstract. Many of the existing multichannel wireless network implementations rely on channel switching capability of the wireless radios to ensure network connectivity. However, due to both software and hardware restrictions switching channels incur a significant delay, which can be prohibitive for many delay sensitive, real time applications, such as VoIP and interactive gaming. The situation can be worse in the case of a multihop network, as every node along the traffic path may require a channel switch that adds up to the overall end-to-end delay. This motivates the need for efficient routing strategies that can make use of the flexibilities of a multichannel network while favoring delay sensitive applications by routing them on low delay paths. In this paper, we propose SHORT, a *S*tatic-*H*ybrid approach for r*O*uting *R*eal *T*ime applications over multichannel, multihop wireless networks, which ensures low delay paths for delay sensitive applications. Using measurements on a real multichannel testbed, we show that our protocol can provide significantly low delay multihop paths for delay sensitive applications (eg., VoIP) without degrading the throughput performance of non-delay sensitive, best effort traffic, such as TCP that may co-exist in a network.

Keywords: Multichannel routing, VoIP over multichannel, channel switch delay, static channel allocation.

1 Introduction

Multichannel wireless networks are gaining popularity due to the variety of flexibilities that they can offer [1, 2]. For instance, when nodes in a network are tuned to different channels, the amount of contention on any single channel is reduced. Moreover, when we use orthogonal channels, the overall interference in the network can also be reduced. Additionally, most of the multichannel deployments propose to use multiple radios on each nodes [3, 4, 5, 6, 7]. By ensuring that the radios within a node are always operated on different, orthogonal channels, a node can effectively transmit and receive simultaneously.

⋆ This work was supported in part by NSF grant 06-27074.

E. Osipov et al. (Eds.): WWIC 2010, LNCS 6074, pp. 77–94, 2010.

Three popular channel and interface allocation strategies exist in the literature, namely common control channel approach [8] (where nodes decide on communication channel prior to a transmission using control messages on a common channel), static channel approach [9, 10] (in which the channels for all the radios of a node are fixed), and hybrid channel approach [11] (in which the channels for only a subset of radios are fixed apriori and that for the remaining radios are varied dynamically during communication). Among these three approaches, the hybrid multichannel protocol has been shown to be efficient in providing higher system throughput [11]. However, the hybrid channel allocation approach are not optimized for providing low delays for real time applications, such as VoIP. This is because, while a static channel allocation achieves network connectivity by a careful topology preserving channel selection [9], a hybrid channel allocation relies on the radios of a node to switch across channels to maintain network connectivity. Even with a fast hardware, the latencies associated with channel switching (as explained later) is prohibitive for delay sensitive application such as VoIP or interactive gaming, especially in the case of a multihop operation. Because no such channel switch delays exist in a static channel approach, such a scheme may be beneficial for delay sensitive applications. However, a purely static channel-based approach is not suitable for providing higher throughput values for non-delay sensitive applications. Moreover, a pure-static channel approach is not suitable in a network where the link characteristics keep varying that can make the network topology change with time (as in a mobile network). Therefore, we need a newer scheme that can exploit the advantages of both the static and the hybrid channel allocation schemes.

Routing real time applications over multichannel wireless networks has been handled in several different ways in literature. Most of the existing approaches concentrate on provisioning QoS in multichannel wireless networks [12, 13]. The authors in [13], for instance, propose a topology control and QoS routing approach with a goal for providing bandwidth aware routing for real time flows. However, the approach requires significant topology information for its execution, and hence not wholly suitable for an unmanaged network. In [12], the authors provide a QoS-aware multichannel scheduling algorithm for providing higher priorities for VoIP packets, by which they are scheduled more often than non-real time packets. A similar approach for scheduling delay sensitive flows more often than non-delay sensitive flows is proposed in [14]. In [15], the authors propose a gateway controlled channel allocation scheme, where the channel allocation to the nodes are determined by the gateway based on the flows in the network. However, the scheme does not differentiate between real time and non-real time flows. In this paper, we propose a mechanism that can provide low delay routes for real time applications and high throughput routes for non-real time applications, which can complement any of the existing QoS mechanisms. The goal is to consider practical difficulties (such as hardware delays) that may exist in a network, which many of the existing QoS mechanisms overlook.

We propose a mechanism called SHORT that exploits the benefits of a static channel approach for providing lower delay paths for real time applications, while at the same time utilizes the flexibilities of a hybrid channel approach for providing higher throughputs for non-delay sensitive applications. According to this approach, we design a protocol that can, depending on the type of traffic being routed, control the channel allocation strategy of the nodes. More specifically, when routing a delay sensitive flow, the routing protocol, after determining the route to be taken for the flow, forces the nodes on the path to behave as in a static channel approach. In other words, the radios in the nodes are controlled in such a way to prevent them from switching across channels for the duration of the real time flow. A hybrid channel allocation scheme is used for routing non delay-sensitive flows. We modify the multichannel AODV routing protocol proposed in [11] for this purpose. Note that, while our protocol enables the nodes on a real time flow's path to behave as in the static channel mechanism, the actual path is not determined by our approach and is taken care by the multichannel routing protocol [11], discussed briefly in the Section 2 that is complemented by the hybrid channel allocation protocol (hence the name static-hybrid approach).

Using actual implementations on a multichannel mesh testbed, called Net-X [5] we show that the end-to-end delays of real time applications is significantly lower in SHORT when compared to a purely hybrid approach. Furthermore, we show that the throughput of non-delay sensitive applications is also not degraded.

2   Background

In this section, we provide a brief overview of the hybrid channel allocation protocol, called HMCP and the multichannel routing protocol [11] that are used in the testbed on which we carry out our experiments. In the discussion that follows, we assume that every node is equipped with two radios or interfaces (the terms interfaces and radios are used interchangeably in this paper and both mean a wireless radio).

2.1   Hybrid Multichannel Protocol Operation

The main challenge in a multichannel network implementation lies in ensuring that nodes operating on different channels can coordinate and communicate with other without much overhead. The hybrid multichannel protocol (HMCP) [11] ensures connectivity between nodes by allowing one of the two wireless interfaces to switch across channels as required. The other interface remains fixed on a channel as long as the channel is perceived to be good. We call the interface that may switch often across channels as the *switchable* interface and the interface that operates on a fixed channel as the *fixed* interface. Only the fixed interface is used for data reception. However, a data transmission can be from any of the two interfaces, fixed or switchable; this depends on the channel of the fixed interface on the neighboring node to which a multi-hop flow is directed. In general, if a neighboring node is operating on the same fixed channel as the current node, then the transmission can be through the fixed interface, otherwise the switchable interface is used for transmission after switching its channel to the fixed channel of the neighboring node. Thus, a node can potentially transmit and receive simultaneously, if the channels on which they transmit and receive are different. The necessary control messages that are exchanged to communicate the channel information between the nodes is discussed later in this section. Once a node switches to a channel, it stays on that channel for a pre-determined amount of time before switching to the next channel. The amount of time spent by the switchable interface may vary depending on the availability of packets to be sent on that channel. Because the channel on which a

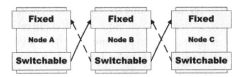

Fig. 1. Example multichannel protocol operation

switchable interface operates depends on the channel allocated to the fixed interface of a neighboring node, it is clear that we need to allocate channels only to the fixed interface of a node. Figure 1 shows an example of our protocol operation for a bidirectional data transmission from node A to node C, with node B as an intermediate node. (Solid lines indicate transmission form A to C and dotted lines indicate the transmission from C to A. The switchable radio in B switches between the two directions.)

The HMCP protocol operation requires that every node be aware of the (fixed) channels on which their neighboring nodes are listening. In other words, two neighboring nodes cannot communicate with each other even if one of them is not aware of the channel of the other. The nodes are made aware of the neighbor channels by the exchange of a broadcast `hello` message that contains the channel information. Any broadcast message sent by a node is transmitted on all the channels so that all of a node's neighbor that may be listening on any of the channels may receive the broadcast message. To help in load-balancing among the channels that are used within a neighborhood, the `hello` messages are propagated over two-hops. This allows every node to be aware of the channel information of all the neighbors that are up to two hops away.

The HMCP protocol also defines a channel allocation mechanism for allocating channels to the fixed interface. Briefly, the channel allocation algorithm works by using the two hop channel information exchanged using the broadcast `hello` messages for choosing a channel that is used by the least number of nodes in its (two hop) neighborhood. This helps in fairly balancing the number of nodes that are on each of the channels. Due to space restrictions we skip the details of the channel allocation mechanism. However, interested readers can refer to [5] for more information on the channel allocation algorithm.

2.2 Multichannel Routing Protocol

The routing mechanism used currently in our testbed is an AODV protocol, modified for multichannel operation. The modifications to the original AODV protocol include incorporating a mechanism for finding a channel diverse route, avoiding bottlenecks, and reducing the overall expected transmission time in addition to reducing the number of hops. More specifically, to utilize the benefit of using multiple channels, it is necessary to make sure that a flow experiences minimum intra-flow interference (interference due to transmissions of the same flow on adjacent hops). This requires that the route taken by the flows is such that the adjacent hops are on different channels as much as possible. Furthermore, it is preferable to avoid routing multiple flows through a single node, as this may result in the node requiring to switch its transmission channel frequently for routing the flows, which may possibly be targeted at neighbors on different channels.

These requirements are incorporated in the form of a routing metric, called the MCR metric [5], as the traditional routing metric based on hop count is not suitable. The MCR metric, in brief, uses the statistics of channel usage from the interface drivers and uses it to calculate the cost for switching the channels for routing a flow. Additionally, the cost of a link per channel is estimated using the popular ETT metric [16] on every channel, which when coupled with the switching costs and summed up over the entire path results in the MCR routing metric. If $SC(c_i)$ is the channel switching cost of channel c_i used in the ith hop of transmission, and ETT_i is the estimated transmission time in the ith hop, then the MCR metric is given by,

$$\text{MCR} = (1 - \beta) * \sum_{i=1}^{h} (ETT_i + SC(c_i)) + \beta * \max_{1 \leq j \leq c} X_j$$

where, β is a weight between 0 and 1, h is the number of hops on the path, and c is the total number of channels. X_j is the total ETT cost on channel j and is given by,

$$X_j = \sum_{\forall i \text{ such that } c_i = j} ETT_i.$$

The ETT of a link is given by, $ETT = ETX * \frac{S}{B}$, where ETX is the expected number of transmission attempts (including re-transmissions) required to transmit a packet, S is the average packet size and B is the data rate of the link. The expected number of transmissions is estimated based on the loss in the link.

The multichannel protocol also incorporates few other modifications. For instance, when a routing entry is created for a node, it is also necessary now to indicate the channel and the actual interface to use for reaching the next hop. The multichannel routing protocol incorporates the appropriate mechanism for creating the route entries. Furthermore, optimizations such as route caching, available in the original AODV protocol, is not performed as the channel allocations and the corresponding costs may change frequently, which can be estimated accurately only at the destination. Finally, the multichannel routing protocol incorporates a procedure called "Route Refresh", by which a source node initiates a route discovery periodically (currently every 30 seconds in our testbed) for learning routes with better costs or for updating the costs of the current route.

3   Problem Statement

A pure-hybrid channel allocation approach (such as HMCP [11]) is optimized for providing higher system throughputs for non-delay sensitive applications. However, a main drawback with the hybrid channel allocation approach is the channel switching delays associated with the wireless radio hardware and software. For instance, the channel switching delay currently in our hardware, T_s is 5 ms. This includes several components such as, delays due to stopping interrupt service routines of the driver, tuning to the new frequency, re-starting the interrupt service routines and sensing the medium. To compensate for the higher switching delays, it is advisable to spend at least a minimum amount of time in a channel, before switching to another channel for amortizing the switching costs. Additionally, consider a scenario where there are multiple packets to be sent by a node, each on a different channel. In this case, while sufficient time has to be spent transmitting packets on the current channel before switching to the next channel, there has to be a limit on the time spent on any single channel. In the network used for our experiments, the minimum time spent on a channel, T_{min} is 20 ms, and the maximum time spent, T_{max} on a channel before switching to another channel that has packets waiting to be spent is 60 ms. The relevance of these parameters and the procedure used for choosing these values are discussed in more detail in [17]. Thus, the channel switching delay, T_s along with T_{min} and T_{max} together may add to the overall transmission time of a packet.

To illustrate more on the switching delays, we discuss the following simple experiment.

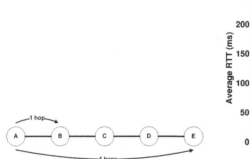

Fig. 2. Topology used for ping experiments   **Fig. 3.** Results for pinging the nodes in flooding mode

3.1   Ping Experiment

In this experiment, we use up to five wireless nodes that are placed across different offices in our lab and arranged linearly as shown in the Figure 2, each of which are one hop apart from their neighbors, and we initiate one hop, two hop, three hop, and four hop pings in flooding mode with 1500 byte packets. (A node is said to be one hop away from another node if they can have a direct communication between them. If two nodes require k one hop communications between them, through other intermediate nodes, then they are said to be k hops away from each other.) We plot in Figure 3, the resulting average round trip time (RTT) returned by ping when all the nodes use the same fixed channel (labeled as 'Fixed' in the plot), when the nodes are assigned channels using a static channel allocation (labeled as 'Static'), and when the hybrid multichannel protocol with five channels (labeled as 'HMCP5') and two channels (labeled as 'HMCP2') is used for allocation. Note that in the case of HMCP2, the switchable radio do not switch channels as they always operate on only channel (the other channel is allocated to the fixed radio). In the case of 'Fixed', the switchable radios are free to switch across the remaining channels. We can readily observe from the plot that the average RTT in the case of HMCP5 is significantly higher than the other channel allocations. Furthermore, we observe that the RTTs become worse as the number of hops increase. Finally, we also observe that the RTTs in the case of HMCP2 is much lower than HMCP5 and the same fixed channel allocations, though the actual values are higher than a static allocation. The reason for the increased RTTs in the case of HMCP5 is because of the following factors:

1. A transmission from one node to another that are on different fixed channels requires a channel switching. This can take place at every single hop of the path taken by the flow.

2. Because a periodic broadcast message, such as `hello` or a route refresh has to be sent on every channel, the associated switching delay adds up, at every hop, to the end-to-end delay.

Thus, by assuming a channel switching delay of 5 ms, and by assuming that only a T_{min} amount of time is spent on each of the channel and observing the fact that a message broadcast on the fixed interface do not incur any channel switching delay, a message broadcast on five channels incur a delay of $((5-1) \times 5 + (5-1) \times 20 = 100ms)$ and that broadcast on 2 channels incur $((2-1) \times 5 + (2-1) \times 20 = 25ms)$. Thus, the broadcast messages alone can cause round trip delays of up to $200ms$ and $50ms$, respectively. This is the reason for HMCP2 to have a lower delay when compared to HMCP5. The reason for higher RTTs in the case of 'Fixed' channel allocation is due to two reasons. The first reason is that the adjacent hops of a flow has to contend for channel access as they are both transmitted on the same channel. The second reason is due to hardware restrictions. Specifically, the wireless driver can schedule a transmission from only one of the two radios at a time. Consequently, a packet queued up on a fixed radio has to share its transmission opportunities with that in the switchable radio, resulting in a higher RTT.

The resulting delays, mainly in the case of HMCP5, are prohibitive for real time, delay sensitive applications such as VoIP or interactive gaming, and therefore alternate mechanisms has to be formulated for routing such applications. However, we should also ensure sufficient throughput for non-delay sensitive applications that may co-exist in the network. This motivates a routing approach that can improve both the delay and throughput performance depending on the type of application. From Figure 3, we see that a static channel allocation may be advantageous for real time applications, as it results in the least RTTs among the four mechanisms compared. Our proposed protocol exploits the advantages of this allocation. In this paper, we assume a dense network scenario that has a predominantly non-delay sensitive traffic with fewer delay sensitive applications. In fact, this mimics a real network scenario, as most of the flows in the present day internet are HTTP or FTP-type best effort traffic.

4   Proposed Approach

Motivated by our initial ping experiments, we develop a new routing strategy, called SHORT for controlling the wireless radios and the underlying channel allocation mechanism. The idea is to make the wireless radios behave as in a static channel allocation mechanism for real time applications and to follow the hybrid channel allocation mechanism for non-real time applications. Accordingly, the nodes in the network operate on one of two modes, namely normal mode and static mode. The normal mode of operation is exactly as explained in Section 2.1 and shown in Figure 1, wherein only the 'fixed' radio is used for receiving data and the 'switchable' radio is used only for transmitting data, after switching to the corresponding channel. This mode of operation is used for non-delay sensitive traffic. For delay sensitive flows, the static mode of operation is used. In this mode, the 'switchable' interface is not allowed to switch channels for the duration of the delay sensitive flow. Rather, after the route for the flow is determined, it remains fixed on the channel of the previous hop's[1] fixed interface. Furthermore, both the fixed and the switchable radios are allowed to receive and transmit. In other words, the switchable interface also behaves like a 'fixed' interface for the duration of the delay sensitive flow. Note that only those nodes that lie in the path of a delay sensitive flow operate in static mode. The remaining nodes in the network continue to behave as in the normal mode. Furthermore, the nodes that are in static mode revert back to normal mode of operation once the delay sensitive flow ends. The associated protocol steps for getting back to normal mode is trivial and not discussed in this paper. While the channel allocations in our protocol are based on HMCP to simplify implementation, any existing dynamic channel allocation can be used, in general.

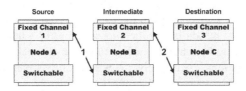

Fig. 4. SHORT protocol operation

We wish to explain this concept more clearly using the illustration in Figure 4. The figure shows a traffic flow from node A to C via node B. Let the channels allocated to the fixed radios of the nodes A, B. and C be labeled 1, 2, and 3, respectively. Accordingly, during the static mode of operation, the switchable radio of node C is fixed to channel 2, which is the fixed channel of node B. Similarly, the switchable radio of node B is fixed to the channel 1, which is the fixed channel of node A. Thus, traffic from A to B flows on channel 1, and that from B to C flows on channel 2. Moreover, the switchable radios on nodes B and C receive the traffic on these channels transmitted by the fixed radios of nodes A and B, respectively. Observe that any traffic from C to A can be routed using the same configuration, except that the switchable radios will be sending traffic that will now be received by the fixed interface of the nodes B and A. Thus, this setting enables a bi-directional flow without requiring any channel switching. We would like to point out that the switchable interface of node A is not required to be fixed on any channel in this example, and is free to switch across channels as in the normal mode. Because in

---

[1] The terms 'previous hop' and 'next hop' imply the appropriate nodes in the path as seen by a node in the 'source to destination' direction of the flow.

this example, the nodes B and C behave as in a static channel allocation (both the radios are non-switchable and every node on the path shares a channel with the adjacent hop nodes), we call this as static mode.

In the static mode of operation, a node does not send a broadcast message on all the channels (unlike the normal mode of operation, see Section 2.1). Instead, it simply forwards them on the channels to which the two radios are fixed. Note that this may result in few nodes not being aware of the channel used by their neighboring nodes. Because we require in our protocol that two nodes involved in a direct communication be aware of each other channels (as otherwise the nodes cannot decide on which channel to transmit), this may result in a node losing connectivity with the nodes that are on a channel different from those on which the broadcast messages are sent. When several such nodes lose connectivity with each other, this can eventually result in a network partition. To avoid such a scenario, we propose a channel re-selection mechanism that works in tandem with the routing protocol. More details of the channel re-selection mechanism is explained later in this section.

4.1 SHORT Protocol Operation

We now discuss the details of the SHORT protocol. We assume that the information whether the flow being routed is delay-sensitive or not is available at the routing layer of the source node. Such an information can be passed on from the upper layers by, for instance by setting the ToS (type of service) field in the IP header. The actual mechanism on how this information is passed on from the application to the routing layer is beyond the scope of this paper. We just present the protocol sequence executed for a delay sensitive flow. The sequence of procedures carried out for a non-delay sensitive flow is as done in the multichannel routing protocol, explained in [18] and is not reproduced here. The protocol mechanisms described for delay sensitive flows, however, is a modification of the multichannel routing protocol and to avoid duplication of work, we present only the relevant modifications to the multichannel routing protocol.

Once the source node determines that it is a delay sensitive flow, the following is performed:

1. The source node checks if a route is already available for the destination. If not, it initiates a route request message (RREQ) along with a special flag, isRealTime to indicate that the request is for a real time flow and broadcasts it on all channels.

2. Any intermediate node, that is not the destination, simply re-broadcasts the RREQ message on all channels.

3. The destination, upon receiving the RREQ, creates a route response (RREP) message and unicasts the RREP along with the isRealTime flag (copied from RREQ) to the node from which the corresponding RREQ was received. Additionally, it takes the following actions only if the channel on which the RREP is unicast (which is the fixed channel of the previous hop node in this path) is different from its own fixed channel:

a. The node sends a broadcast hello message as described in Section 2.1 on all the channels. However, in this case, the node includes the flag isRealTime along with two channel information. One is the fixed channel that it has been operating on, and the other is the channel over which the RREP is unicast. (Note that the original hello message described in Section 2.1 contains only the fixed channel information.) The cost associated with this broadcast is one time and shall be considered as part of the route setup cost, which does not affect the delay experienced by the delay sensitive packets.

b. The node fixes its switchable interface on the channel over which the RREP message is unicast (which is the fixed channel of the previous hop node in this path). The routing entry created for the previous hop node is informed to use the switchable interface in this (reverse) direction.

c. The switchable interface is also informed to start receiving packets on this channel.
4. Any intermediate, upon receiving the RREP along with the isRealTime flag, also forwards the RREP message to the node from which it received the corresponding RREQ message. Furthermore, the intermediate node, in addition to performing the set of operations described in Step (3) when the RREP is unicast on a channel different from its own fixed channel, also performs the following:

d. The node creates a routing entry for the next hop node and is informed to use the fixed interface in this direction of flow (forward direction).
5. The source node, upon receiving the RREP starts sending the packets, after creating the routing entry for the next hop node through its fixed interface.

Once the radios of the corresponding nodes in the real time flows path are fixed based on the above steps, any transmission by these nodes (including broadcasts) are restricted to the two fixed channels. Observe that any non-real time flow that has been existing in the chosen real time path prior to the arrival of the real time flow may be affected because of this protocol. In particular, an existing non-real time flow may be dropped during the above process as the radios on the corresponding path will no longer be allowed to switch across channels. We handle this situation by initiating a RERR message, which gets forwarded to the source. The source can then re-initiate a new RREQ message to find a new route. Because of the channel re-selection mechanism (described in the next sub-section), finding a new route will not be difficult and we did not see a significant throughput loss, as a result, during our experimentation.

4.2   Channel Re-selection Mechanism

The channel re-selection mechanism is introduced to maintain network connectivity in spite of nodes in static mode restricting their broadcast to only the two channels that their interfaces are fixed on. The channel re-selection mechanism is only executed by those nodes that lie adjacent to the path chosen for the real time applications and are in the normal mode. For this purpose, the nodes make use of the broadcast hello message with a isRealTime flag broadcast by a node in the path of a real time flow before switching to the static mode (see Section 4.1 step 3a.). Upon receiving the broadcast message with a isRealTime flag, the nodes performing channel re-selection perform the following steps:

1. The node first checks if both of the channels contained in the hello message is different from its fixed channel. If its fixed channel is same as one of the channels in the hello message, the node discards the message and takes no further steps.

2. If both the channels in the `hello` message are different from the node's fixed channel, then the node selects one of the two channels, chosen uniformly at random, as its new fixed channel.

3. If more than one `hello` message with a `isRealTime` flag is received (which may happen when a node is adjoining two nodes that lie in the path of a real time flow), then the node first tries to choose the channel that is common to a majority of the `hello` messages. Thus, the channel re-selection mechanism is designed to maintain connectivity with a majority of the nodes in the network. If none of the channel is common to the `hello` messages, then the node just selects one of the channels contained in the `hello` messages, uniformly at random, as its fixed channel.

When the majority of flows in the network are real time, the channel re-selection mechanism will tend to make the overall network behave as in a pure-static approach, while when the majority of flows in the network are non-real time, the network behaves as in a pure-hybrid approach, as required.

4.3   Implementation Specific Details

The architecture of our multichannel protocol along with the SHORT implementation is shown in Figure 5. The SHORT protocol consists of two main components, namely the SHORT controller or *C-SHORT* and the SHORT executor or *E-SHORT*. The *C-SHORT* is implemented in the user level and interacts with the multichannel routing protocol for creating routing entries compatible with the static mode of operation whenever a real time flow is to be routed. Furthermore, it is also responsible for setting the *isRealTime* flag when a new route discovery for a real time flow is initiated. Finally, *C-SHORT* indicates to the *E-SHORT* component, through a special IOCTL control message, whether to transition to static mode or revert back to normal mode. (IOCTL messages are used standardly in linux for any interaction between the user space and kernel space code.) If the message is for transitioning to static mode, then the channel to which the switchable radio has to be fixed from now on is also specified.

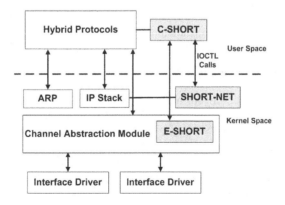

Fig. 5. System architecture with SHORT-specific components in gray

The *E-SHORT* component, on the other hand, is implemented as a kernel module and resides as part of the linux 'bonding' module[2]. The *E-SHORT* component is responsible for fixing the switchable radio to the channel supplied by the *C-SHORT* component and for restoring the switchable radio back to normal mode, depending on the message from the *C-SHORT* component.

In addition to the two main components, SHORT protocol also consists of a smaller third component, called SHORT-NET, which interacts with the linux netfilter hooks for making the switchable interface behave like a fixed interface for real time flows. In normal mode, the netfilter hook is designed to drop any incoming packets on the switchable radio. The SHORT-NET overrides this and lets the switchable radio to accept the packets while in static mode. The relevant control messages are passed on from the *C-SHORT* as an IOCTL message.

5   Experimental Results

In this section, we present the experimental results to illustrate the performance benefits of the SHORT protocol. Before proceeding further, we first present an overview of our testbed and the associated hardware.

5.1   Testbed Overview

We use a multi-channel, multi-interface, and multi-hop wireless testbed called Net-X, developed by the Wireless Networking Group at the University of Illinois at Urbana-Champaign (UIUC). The testbed consists of 20+ Soekris net4521 boxes distributed across various offices on the fourth floor of the Coordinated Science Lab (CSL) in UIUC. Each of the testbed node has a 133 MHz microprocessor, a compact flash (CF) card slot, two PCMCIA slots, and one mini-PCI slot. We run Linux kernel 2.4.26-based operating system on each of these boards. For our experiments, we equip the test nodes with one mini-PCI and one PCMCIA wireless card. These wireless cards are based on Atheros chipsets and are driven by madwifi drivers. The cards operate in the IEEE 802.11a mode. The mini-PCI cards make use of a pair of external antennas, and the PCMCIA card has its own internal antenna for communication.

5.2   Experimental Methodology

Traffic Details: For evaluating our protocol, we used different traffic sources for generating real time and non-real time traffic. For real time traffic, we used a tool called D-ITG [19] for generating G.711 codec type VoIP packets for 50 seconds. The tool generates about 100 byte VoIP packets every 20 ms. The same D-ITG tools is used generating non-delay sensitive TCP and UDP type packets. The UDP flows are always generated at a rate of 6 Mbps and the packet sizes are fixed at 512 bytes. The size of the TCP packets on the other hand are uniformly distributed between 500 and 1000

---

[2] The bonding module has been modified in our system to enable multi-radio operation and the details can be found in [5].

bytes, and are generated at the rate of 1000 packets per second. Both UDP and TCP packets are generated for a duration of 50 seconds. Every wireless radio transmits at the maximum power and the physical rate of transmission are fixed at 6 Mbps. For all the experiments we use five orthogonal 802.11a channels, namely 36, 48, 64, 149, and 161 for allocation.

Protocols Compared: We compare the performance of our SHORT protocol with HMCP and two other protocols as described below:

Static channel allocation: For this case, we allocate channels to the radios using a centralized static channel allocation methodology. In other words, knowing the connectivity graph among the nodes, we allocated channels to the two radios in a node such that every node having an edge in the connectivity graph has at least one channel in common. The channel allocation technique is based on the scheme proposed in [9].

Fixed channel for real time traffic: This is a protocol similar, but simpler than SHORT. In this protocol, while generating a route discovery for a real time flow, the source node also includes its current fixed channel in the RREQ message. Every intermediate node re-broadcasts the RREQ message, as usual. However, while forwarding the RREP message the corresponding node changes its fixed channel to that of the source node (which is embedded in the RREP message). Thus, all the nodes in the path of a real time flow use their fixed interface for routing. The advantage of this scheme is that the switchable radios in the nodes need not be fixed and can remain switchable as in normal mode. As a result, unlike SHORT there will be no loss of connectivity. We call this as 'fixed' mode of operation. Figure 6 illustrates this protocol.

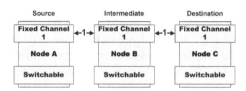

Fig. 6. Fixed mode operation

Performance Metrics: The D-ITG tool is capable of generating per flow statistics on the minimum, maximum, and average delays, average jitter, and throughput achieved. Because throughput is not of concern for real time flows, and delays are not important for non-real time flows, we measure the average and maximum delays, and jitters (which is the variance in time of arrivals of adjacent packets at the destination) for real time traffic and the throughput values for the non-real time traffic. However, due to space restrictions, we only present the average delay values for real time applications. The maximum delay and jitter values can be referred from [20].

Time Synchronization: For measuring delays it is important to have a common notion of clock between the traffic sources and destinations. However, the wireless nodes used have imperfect clocks and proper time synchronization is necessary for measuring time delay values between the sender and receiver. We therefore use `ntpdate` periodically on these nodes for synchronizing their time values. Because the nodes are not connected to the internet, we use a desktop computer as the ntp server and synchronize all the nodes relative to this server. We use the local wired LAN connectivity for time synchronization between the nodes and the desktop ntp server.

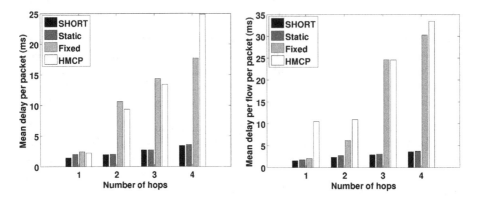

Fig. 7. Average delay for unidirectional flows   **Fig. 8.** Average delay for bidirectional flows

5.3   Performance Results

We now discuss in detail the experimental setup and the performance results.

Multihop Experiments: For each of the experiments in this section, we generate flows between a pair of nodes that are separated by one, two, three, and four hops away. Owing to the size of our network, we cannot realize a route that is farther than 4 hops. For each of the scenarios, we chose 10 different source and destination pairs, each of which are picked from different locations in the network, and are separated by different distances.

Unidirectional flows
For this experiment we generate a VoIP flow between a source and a destination that is located one hop away from the source. We then repeat this for destinations that are two hops, three hops, and four hops away from the source node. In each case, we measure the average delay experienced by the packets, and the results averaged over the 10 different source-destinations pairs are plotted in Figure 7. In all the figures presented in this section, the plots corresponding to the static channel allocation are labeled as 'Static' and those obtained for the case where we use the fixed channel for real time flows are labeled as 'Fixed'.

From Figure 7, we first observe that the average delays experienced by the VoIP packets in the case of SHORT and Static are always lower than 5 ms, irrespective of the number of hops. We also observe that the delays in the case of Fixed and HMCP allocations are much higher than SHORT or Static allocation, and the difference increases significantly as the number of hops increase. As mentioned in Section 3, the main reason for higher delays in the case of HMCP is the need to switch the channels at every hop along the multihop path. In the case of Fixed channel allocation, the delays are comparatively lower than HMCP owing to the fact that the fixed radios are used for transmitting the VoIP packets. However, the delays are still high when compared to SHORT or Static. One reason for this is that the fixed radio has to share its transmission opportunity with that of the packets in the switchable radio, as explained in Section 3. Though the average delay of about 38 ms in the case of HMCP for the 4 hop case is acceptable for VoIP packets, the rate at which the delay grows with the number of hops is significant and the delays may become unacceptable in the case of real multichannel deployments, where more than 4 hops may be common. Even in the case of 4 hops, we observed that there were packets that experience more than 200 ms delays (not shown here), which is, certainly unacceptable for VoIP.

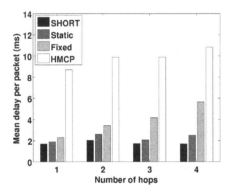
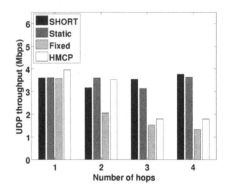

Fig. 9. Average delay of VoIP packets sent with a UDP flow   **Fig. 10.** Throughput of UDP flow went with a VoIP flow

Bidirectional flows

In this case, we generate two VoIP flows, one from a source to the destination and the other from the destination to the source. The delay values averaged over all the flows and over 10 different pairs of nodes, chosen from different location in the network for each scenario, are plotted in Figure 8. We first observe that the delays in the case of SHORT and Static mechanisms are similar to that in the unidirectional case. This is because, in the case of SHORT protocol, once a route is established between two nodes, the same route is used both for the forward and reverse traffic. The same is true in the case of Static mechanism. The delays in the case of HMCP is higher than that in the unidirectional case. This is because a significant time is spent by the switchable radio in switching between the forward and reverse traffic.

VoIP with UDP and TCP (non-delay sensitive)

For this experiment, we first generate a VoIP flow along with a UDP flow, both from the same source and targeted at the same destination. Figure 9 shows the average delay experienced by the VoIP packets, and Figure 10 when the throughput achieved by the

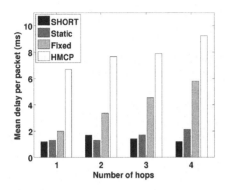 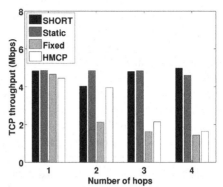

Fig. 11. Average delay of VoIP packets sent with a TCP flow   **Fig. 12.** Throughput of TCP flow went with a VoIP flow

UDP packets, all averaged over 10 different source-destination pairs. Next we generate a VoIP flow along with a TCP flow as before, and the delay and throughput values of the VoIP and TCP packets, respectively are plotted in Figures 11 and 12. We observe from the plots that the throughputs for both UDP and TCP flows remain almost the same, irrespective of the number of hops, in the case of SHORT and Static protocols. However, we observe that the throughputs reduce with the number of hops in the case of Fixed and HMCP. In the case of TCP flows, this is because of the increased RTTs between the source and destination, which in turn affects the packet generation rate at the source. In the case of UDP, this is due to loss of packets during channel switching. Furthermore, in the case of fixed mode, adjacent hops of the same flow contend for transmission as they are on the same channel. This, in turn affects the throughput achieved.

Single hop experiments: We now evaluate the capability of the protocols in supporting multiple flows from the same source node, as such a scenario may usually involve several channel switches when each flow is sent on a different channel. For this purpose, we choose a source node and four other nodes that are within one hop from each other and generate multiple VoIP flows (varied from one to four) between them. Once gain, we choose 10 different sets of nodes situated at different locations in our network and present the average values. The average delay values per flow are plotted in Figures 13. For this case, we also present the average jitter values in Figure 14. We observe from the delay plots that the average and maximum delay values do not vary much with number of flows in the case of SHORT, Static, and Fixed mechanisms, while it increases significantly for HMCP. (The improper variations in throughputs with the number of hops in the case of SHORT and Static are due to averaging.) This shows that HMCP is not capable of multiple real time flows all from the same source, as it requires significant channel switching. From the jitter values, we observe that HMCP performs poorly while handling multiple flows. Higher jitter values mean that the amount of jitter buffer at the receiving side should also be higher, so as to prevent packet losses. The jitter performance for SHORT and Static are fairly stable irrespective of the number of flows and allows for better codec design.

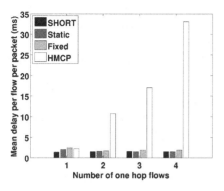 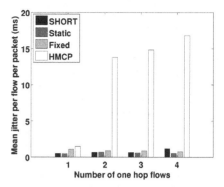

Fig. 13. Average delays for multiple one hop flows from a node

Fig. 14. Average jitters for multiple one hop flows from a node

We also performed some measurements to evaluate if the number of hops taken by a non-delay sensitive application is higher than that taken by HMCP. However, we found that there were no significant throughput losses because of SHORT protocol. We do not provide those results in this paper due to space restrictions. Moreover, our main goal in this paper is to demonstrate the delay performance of SHORT.

6 Conclusion

In this paper, we proposed SHORT, a routing approach that exploits the benefits of both static and hybrid channel allocation strategies. We have implemented the protocol on a real multichannel testbed and using extensive experimental data we have demonstrated the performance benefits of the SHORT protocol over a hybrid channel allocation protocol, called HMCP. All our experimental results illustrate the abilities of SHORT protocol in providing low delay multihop paths for real time traffic, while not affecting the throughputs of non-real time traffic. Our results show that the performance of SHORT protocol is comparable to that of a static channel allocation method. As a future work, we wish to demonstrate the benefits of SHORT using real voice traffic, which has not been possible right now due to hardware restrictions.

References

[1] Raniwala, A., Chiueh, T.c.: Architecture and algorithms for an IEEE 802.11-based multi-channel wireless mesh network. In: IEEE Infocom (2005)
[2] Maheshwari, R., Gupta, H., Das, S.: Multichannel mac protocols for wireless networks. In: IEEE SECON (2006)
[3] Bahl, P., Adya, A., Padhye, J., Wolman, A.: Reconsidering wireless systems with multiple radios. In: ACM SIGCOMM (2004)
[4] Ramachandran, K., Sheriff, I., Belding, E., Almeroth, K.: A multi-radio 802.11 mesh network architecture. MONET journal (2008)

[5] Kyasanur, P., Chereddi, C., Vaidya, N.: Net-x: System extensions for supporting multiple channels, multiple interfaces, and other interface capabilities (2006), http://www.crhc.uiuc.edu/wireless/groupPubs.html

[6] Ramachandran, K., Almeroth, K., -Royer, E.M.B.: A novel framework for the management of large-scale wireless network testbeds. In: WinMee Workshop (2005)

[7] Navda, V., Kashyap, A., Das, S.: Design and evaluation of imesh: an infrastructure-mode wireless mesh network. In: IEEE WoWMoM Symposium (2005)

[8] So, J., Vaidya, N.: Multi-channel mac for ad hoc networks: Handling multi-channel hidden terminals using a single transceiver. In: ACM MobiHoc (2004)

[9] Das, A., Vijayakumar, R., Roy, S.: Static channel assignment in multi-radio multi-channel 802.11 wireless mesh networks: Issues, metrics and algorithms. In: IEEE Globecom (2006)

[10] Marina, M., Das, S.: A topology control approach to using directional antennas in wireless mesh networks. In: Broadnets (2005)

[11] Kyasanur, P., Vaidya, N.: Routing and link-layer protocols for multi-channel multi-interface ad hoc wireless networks. In: ACM MC2R (2006)

[12] Castro, M., Dely, P., Kassler, A., Vaidya, N.: Qos-aware channel scheduling for multi-radio/multi-channel wireless mesh networks. In: WinTech (2009)

[13] Tang, J., Xue, G., Zhang, W.: Interference-aware topology control and qos routing in multi-channel wireless mesh networks. In: ACM MobiHoc (2005)

[14] Shen, T.-Y.: Experiments on a multichannel multi-interface wireless network. M.S. Thesis, UIUC (2008)

[15] Dhananjay, A., Zhang, H., Li, J., Subramanian, L.: Practical, distributed channel assignment and routing in dual-radio mesh networks. In: ACM Sigcomm (2009)

[16] Draves, R., Padhye, J., Zill, B.: Routing in multi-radio, multi-hop wireless networks. In: ACM MobiCom (2004)

[17] Chereddi, C.: System architecture for multichannel multi-interface wireless networks. M.S. Thesis, UIUC (2006)

[18] Kyasanur, P.: Multichannel wireless networks: Capacity and protocols. Ph.D. Dissertation, UIUC (2006)

[19] Botta, A., Dainotti, A., Pescape, A.: Multi-protocol and multi-platform traffic generation and measurement. In: IEEE Infocom (2007)

[20] Raman, V., Vaidya, N.: A static-hybrid approach for providing low delay routing for real time applications (2009), http://www.crhc.uiuc.edu/wireless/groupPubs.html

Multiuser Scheduling via Dynamic Optimization

T. Heikkinen

University of Helsinki, Department of Computer Science
P.O. Box 68 FIN-00014, Finland
tiina.heikkinen@cs.helsinki.fi

Abstract. This paper studies optimal scheduling in a multiuser wireless network, allowing for simultaneous transmission of sets of users. The approach is based on dynamic optimization. The multiuser scheduling problem is solved numerically as a dynamic programming problem with user-specific power constraints, assuming deterministic channel information during a given scheduling window. The dynamic programming approach enables to solve for both an optimal discrete power allocation and scheduling. Numerical examples suggest that previous results on optimal scheduling based on decomposing a T-period scheduling problem to T separate problems do not hold in general when decomposing the problem to a smaller number of larger problems. An auction-based algorithm for distributed scheduling is proposed, achieving an optimal schedule, assuming one-at-a-time transmission.

Keywords: Wireless scheduling, power control, dynamic programming, game theory.

1 Introduction

Scheduling is a classical resource allocation mechanism in a wireless network, enabling to improve the network throughput and also providing a tool for service differentiation. Much work has been done on opportunistic scheduling exploiting channel variability [14], assuming one-at-a-time transmission. Emerging wireless networks such as ad hoc networks have brought new challenges to the wireless scheduling problem. Motivated by such networks, this paper focuses on the optimal multiuser scheduling problem, allowing for simultaneous transmission of sets of users.

As part of the scheduling problem, the determination of efficient transmitting sets of users has been addressed in [12] in a CDMA packet data system and recently in [10] in the context of an ad hoc MIMO network. In order to find efficient transmitting sets both [12] and [10] make simplifying assumptions that will be relaxed in this study. First, results on [12] are based on assuming the dynamic scheduling problem can be decomposed to a series of similar single period scheduling problems. Second, instead of optimizing over all possible transmitting sets of users [10] only considers sets of at most two transmitters. The novelty of

E. Osipov et al. (Eds.): WWIC 2010, LNCS 6074, pp. 95–106, 2010.

this paper is to study the optimal scheduling of users over time and over all user sets using dynamic optimization[1].

This paper applies numerical dynamic programming (DP) to solve for optimal multiuser scheduling in a time window small enough to validate the assumption of a constant channel. Assuming a constant or a highly time-correlated channel, an optimal transmission schedule can be obtained using DP, assuming the set of discrete power levels and/or the set of users is not large. The dimensionality problem of DP suggests that simplifications (such as assuming only a few possible power levels) of the scheduling problem are necessary. To simplify the scheduling problem, [12] considers a scheduling time window consisting of just a single point (time slot). A larger time window is considered in this paper, to see whether the results based on decomposing a T-period scheduling problem to T separate problems in [12] continue to hold when decomposing the problem to a smaller number of larger problems (in terms of the number of time slots to be scheduled). Numerical examples suggest that the optimal scheduling policies implied by the two models are only partly similar. More work is still needed to establish general conclusions regarding optimal scheduling. Optimal solutions are not easily obtainable in practice, motivating the development of efficient heuristics as in [12].

Decentralized "self-organizing" networks such as wireless ad hoc networks require distributed solutions to resource allocation. Motivated by the DP-model distributed scheduling is studied as an auction model, assuming one-at-a-time transmission. The auction model is efficient, maximizing the delay-discounted sum of utilities over users over the scheduling horizon. Furthermore, the auction algorithm is known to highly efficient for solving the underlying assignment problem [3]. The extension of the DP model to the distributed scheduling of coalitions of users is left for future work.

The organization is as follows. Section 2 summarizes the wireless scheduling problem and introduces a dynamic programming approach to optimal dynamic resource allocation. Section 3 presents numerical examples. Section 4 studies distributed scheduling via an auction game. Conclusions are presented in section 5.

2   Scheduling in a Packet-Data Network

In a survey on wireless scheduling, [1] identifies two characteristic traffic models: first, in an infinitely backlogged model each user always has data to transmit, and the scheduler needs to determine at each time slot the user(s) allowed to transmit, based on channel information regarding channel state of each user; second, in a model based on an arrival process the scheduler receives a vector describing the amount of data for each user in addition to a channel-state vector. This paper focuses on scheduling in an infinitely backlogged model with perfect

---

[1] Previous work on wireless scheduling has observed the applicability of the dynamic programming (DP) approach; however, due to the dimensionality problem of DP, the focus has been on developing various heuristics mainly to deal with a time-varying channel, see e.g [11].

channel information during the scheduling interval. Performance is studied in terms of a weighted sum of sum of rates where the weights capture a delay cost.

Section 2.1 introduces the scheduling problem in an infinitely backlogged packet data network. In a distributed self-organizing network there is no centralized scheduler to determine the transmission schedule; section 4 discusses distributed scheduling scheme based on game theory. A DP model of optimal scheduling is presented in 2.2.

2.1   Multiuser Scheduling Problem

Consider the scheduling problem in a time-slotted multipoint-to-point interference channel (e.g. CDMA) with m users. Denote the link gain between node i and the destination node at time slot t by $g_i(t)$ and denote by $x_i(t)$ the transmit power of node i at time t. The link gain parameters $g_i(t)$ are (until section 4) assumed to be known during the scheduling window. Denote an orthogonality factor between transmitting users by f, capturing nonorthogonal signalling e.g. spreading codes. The signal-to-noise ratio (SNR) of node i at time i is

$$\gamma_i(t) = \frac{g_i(t)x_i(t)}{f\sum_{j\neq i} g_j(t)x_j(t) + e(t)} \tag{1}$$

where $e(t)$ is external noise power at time t. In a multi-receiver model (1) can be more generally written as

$$\gamma_i(t) = \frac{g_{ii}(t)x_i(t)}{f\sum_{j\neq i} g_{ij}(t)x_j(t) + e(t)}, \tag{2}$$

where g_{ij} denotes the received power of user j's transmission at user i's receiver. The interference power at user is receiver is defined as

$$I_i(t) = \sum_{j\neq i} g_j(t)x_j(t). \tag{3}$$

For simplicity, the orthogonality factor f, modifying $I_i(t)$ in (1) and (2) will be assumed to be a fixed constant, same across users.

Let

$$\alpha_i(t) = \log_2(1 + \gamma_i(t)) \tag{4}$$

denote the transmission rate of node i at t. Define sequence x_i as

$$x_i = \{x_i(t)\}_{t=1,\dots,T}, \tag{5}$$

where $T < \infty$ denotes the scheduling horizon. Letting $\{w_i(t)\}$ denote a given set of user weights at t, the centralized scheduling problem can be stated e.g. as:

$$\max_{\{x_i\}_{i=1,\dots,m}} \sum_t \sum_i w_i(t)\alpha_i(t) \text{ s.t. } x_i(t) \in S_i, \sum_t x_i(t) \leq R_i, \tag{6}$$

where S_i denotes the set of discrete power levels available to user i and R_i is the aggregate resource constraint of i. For example, in [9],

$$w_i(t) = b_i(t) \tag{7}$$

where $b_i(t) = b_i^t$ and $b_i \in [0,1]$ denotes the delay-discount factor of node i. Formulation (6) captures joint scheduling and (discrete) power allocation; as a special case, scheduling with constant power can be considered at each t, with an upper power constraint $\bar{x}_i = 1$, $i = 1, ..., m$ [2]. The focus will be on optimal scheduling assuming a deterministic (constant) channel during the scheduling window and assuming $R_i \leq T$, $i = 1, ..., m$.

Related work in [12] formulates a general optimal scheduling problem as

$$\max \sum_i w_i \alpha_i, \tag{8}$$

subject to maximum power constraints

$$x_i \leq \bar{x}_i, \ i = 1, ..., m,$$

and subject to QoS-constraints

$$\alpha_i \geq \bar{\alpha}_i, \ i = 1, .., m, \tag{9}$$

where $\bar{\alpha}_i$ is the rate target of i. [12] observed that a low complexity approximation QRP can be applied to obtain close to optimal solutions; the QRP $algorithm$ can be summarized as follows:

- users are sorted in decreasing order of the measure

$$v_i = \frac{w_i \alpha_i^0}{\bar{x}_i}, \tag{10}$$

  ignoring interference when computing α_i^0, and
- users are added to the set of transmitting users starting from the top of the list until the weighted sum of rates (now taking interference into account) no longer can be improved. The set of transmitting users use their peak powers.

In [12], the weight of i in (10) is defined as the queue length of i. This paper considers rate sum maximization over time, modelling the delay by a discount cost parameter $b_i(t)$ (7). The performance of the proposed dynamic optimization approach will be discussed relative to QRP in numerical examples in section 4.

Note that formulation (8) (with $\bar{\alpha}_i = 0$ in (9)) can be seen as a special case (with $T = 1$) of the dynamic optimization problem in (6) studied in this paper. Results in sections 3 and 4 suggest that fairness in dynamic formulation (6) can be achieved via resource restrictions formalized by S_i and R_i.

---

[2] Previous work in [9] considered discrete choice with $x_i(t) \in \{0, 1\}$ $\forall i$ $\forall t$. For simplicity [9] was based on assuming the interference of i (3) includes the received power of i, $I_i = \sum_i g_i x_i$, where each g_i either denotes a constant or a memoryless link gain process.

2.2 A Dynamic Programming Formulation

The optimal scheduling problem in (6) can be solved using dynamic programming as follows. Define the state space Y in terms of the possible amounts of available resources (remaining transmit power) of each user. In the absence of period-specific maximum power constraints, $\max S_i = R_i$. In this case the control space X coincides with state space $Y = S_1 \times S_2 \times ... \times S_m$. For example, with m users each with n discrete power levels to choose from, the size of both Y and X is n^m. To alleviate the dimensionality problem of the dynamic programming approach, either the number of users can be restricted and/or the strategy sets S_i can be simplified. For example, constant transmission power can be modelled assuming binary strategy sets

$$S_i = \{0, 1\}, \ i = 1, ..., m, \tag{11}$$

reducing the size of the control space S to 2^m. The corresponding state space is $Y = \{0, 1, 2, ..., R\}^m$, assuming $R_i = R, \ i = 1, ..., m$.

The Bellman equation for the scheduling problem can be stated as:

$$v(y(t)) = \max_{\{x_i(t)\}_i} \{\sum_i \alpha_i(t) + bv(y(t+1))\},$$

where v denotes the value function and $y(t) \in Y$ is the state of the system at time t.

An advantage of the DP approach is that it enables to deal both with variable and with discrete power allocation ([12]) assumed continuous power).

3 Numerical Examples

In what follows, the scheduling problem will be studied using the dynamic programming approach both with constant power and with variable discrete power control ([12]) assumed continuous power). All examples of the dynamic programming model are based on applying numerical dynamic programming [5].

3.1 Optimal Scheduling with Constant Power

Consider a set of $m = 5$ transmitters, each with a binary strategy set S_i in (11). The optimal scheduling of the users over a period of $T = 5$ slots will be studied, assuming a single-receiver model (1). In [12] two scheduling regions according to the value of the orthogonality factor f were observed: letting $f \in [0, 0.5)$ favors simultaneous transmission and at power levels less than maximum whereas with $f \in [0, 5, 1]$ transmitting users transmit with full power. In order to exemplify both cases, in the numerical simulations consider two values of the orthogonality factor: $f = 0.3$ or $f = 0.6$ (according to [12] in practice coding implies $f \approx 0.6$.)

Without loss of generality, arrange users according to the channel gain, assuming user 1 is weakest in terms of the power of its channel gain $g_1(t)$ and users 4 and 5 are strongest. Problem (6) subject to (11) was solved numerically with $R_i = 4$, $1 = 1, .., 5$, assuming $w_i(t) = 0.96^t$. The optimal transmission schedule is exemplified in Table 1, assuming constant channel ($g_i(t) = i, i = 1, 2, 3, 4, g_5(t) = 4$). One-at-a-time-transmission results assuming weak orthogonality with $f = 0.6$; however, when $f = 0.3$:

- users 1-4 simultaneously transmit during slots 1-4;
- user 5 transmits during slots 1-3 simultaneously with other users and alone at slot 5.

The QRP-algorithm (summarized in section 2.1) implies at-at-a-time transmission by users 4 or 5. The sum of rates obtained in this example via dynamic programming is approximately 5 % higher than that obtained using the QRP algorithm [12] (assuming equal queue sizes over the short horizon).

Recall the main result in [12], derived assuming instantaneous rate-sum maximization at each time slot: users with weak channels should transmit simultaneously whereas users with strong channels should transmit one-at-a-time. However, above model permits simultaneous transmission of all (weak and strong) at some slots (t=1,2,3 with f=0.3) while also allowing for one-at-a-time transmission (t=5) during the same scheduling window. Not surprisingly, the length of the scheduling window and the available aggregate amounts of resources (power budgets) during the window both affect the optimal transmitting sets. General rules regarding optimal transmitting sets are harder to define in the extended model studied here.

Table 1. Scheduled users when $f \in [0.3, 0.6]$

time slot	scheduled users when f=0.3	scheduled users when f=0.6
t=1	1,2,3,4,5	4
t=2	1,2,3,4,5	4
t=3	1,2,3,4,5	4
t=4	1,2,3,4	4
t=5	5	5

3.2   Optimal Scheduling with Variable Power

Consider the preceding example, modifying it by allowing for a variable discrete power. Consider two cases, first letting $x_i(t) \in [0, 0.5, 1]$, $i = 1, ..., m$ when $R_1 = 1$, and second letting $x_i(t) \in [0, 2, 4]$, $i = 1, ..., m$ when $R_i = 4$, $i = 1, ..., 5$.

In both examples the state space Y coincides with the control space X. The corresponding optimal schedules for $f = 0.3$ are listed in Table 2.

Comparing the outcomes in Tables 1 and 2 for the same total transmit energy constraint $R_i = 4$, $i = 1, ..., m$, simultaneous transmission appears rationalized when the maximum power restrictions are stringent (Table 1) whereas allowing all resources to be used at once, one-at-a-time transmission becomes optimal (Table 2). Likewise, in the absence of power limitations, [12] argue that one-at-a-time transmission is optimal; the DP model has an analogous outcome:

Remark 1. Numerical examples, assuming the absence of power restrictions $R_i = \infty$, $i = 1, ..., m$ in (6), suggest the optimality of single-user transmission when optimizing the transmitting set of users over a set of time slots.

Table 2. $\{x_i(t)^*\}$ with f=0.3

time slot	$R_i = 1$, $S_i = [0, 0.5, 1]$ $\forall i$	$R_i = 4$, $S_i = [0, 2, 4]$ $\forall i$
t=1	$x_4(1) = 1$, $x_{j \neq 4}(1) = 0$	$x_4(1) = 4$, $x_{j \neq 4}(1) = 0$
t=2	$x_3(2) = 1$, $x_{j \neq 3}(2) = 0$	$x_5(2) = 4$, $x_{j \neq 5}(2) = 0$
t=3	$x_2(3) = 1, x_1(3) = 0.5$, $x_{j \neq 2,1}(3) = 0$	$x_3(3) = 4, x_{j \neq 3}(3) = 0$
t=4	$x_1(4) = 0.5, x_5(4) = 0.5$, $x_{j \neq 2,1}(4) = 0$	$x_2(4) = 4, x_{j \neq 2}(4) = 0$
t=5	$x_5(5) = 0.5, x_{j \neq 5}(5) = 0$	$x_1(5) = 4, x_{j \neq 1}(5) = 0$

Consider the outcome with a smaller aggregate resource constraint $R_i = 1$, $i = 1, .., m$, also summarized in Table 2. This example suggests that it need not be optimal to transmit at full power at all times (cf. users 1 and 5). However, letting $f \geq 0.35$ changes the optimal solution (not depicted) to a corner point of transmitting at full power like in the case in right column. This is reminiscent of the results in [12], arguing that $f \in [0, 0.5)$ favors transmission at power levels less than peak whereas with $f \geq 0.5$ transmitting users use maximum power; however, the range of orthogonality values where full power transmission is optimal seems larger in the DP model.

Note that the optimal schedule in the right column of Table 2 coincides with that implied by the QRP-algorithm (section 2.1), taking resource constraints into account. There is no straightforward way of comparing the sum of rates resulting from the left-column solution to the optimal solution in [12] since continuous power is assumed in the latter. The gain of the DP-solution relative to QRP is less than 1 % in this example.

In summary, the numerical examples demonstrate the applicability of DP to solving optimal scheduling and power allocation. The dimensionality problem necessitates simplifications, making it difficult to obtain general efficient scheduling rules. Much more work, both numerical and analytical, is still needed to establish general conclusions on optimal scheduling.

3.3 Heuristics for Optimal Transmitting Sets of Users

Numerical DP can be applied to obtain an optimal solution to joint power allocation and scheduling, provided the number of users m and/or the number of available power strategies n are not too large. However, both the DP model and the optimal scheduling model in [12] are too complex to apply in practice; efficient heuristics are needed. In emerging distributed networks, distributed scheduling heuristics are applicable to decompose the scheduling problem to a game problem with m objectives. This approach will be studied in what follows.

4 Distributed Scheduling

In a distributed system there is no centralized scheduler to make the scheduling decisions; furthermore, in a fully distributed network (e.g. ad hoc network) there is only local information available for decision-making. In a distributed wireless network the scheduling decisions are made by the nodes themselves, based on local information on interference and link parameters.

To model distributed resource allocation, noncooperative game theory [13] is applicable. A noncooperative game is defined in terms of a set of players M (users $i = 1, ..., m$), strategy sets S_i of players $i = 1, .., m$ and utility functions of players. The utility optimization of user $i = 1, .., m$ in a dynamic scheduling problem can be stated as

$$\max_{x_i \in \{0,1\}^T} \sum_{t=1}^{T} b^t \alpha_i(x_i(t)), \ x_i(t) \in \{0,1\}, \tag{12}$$

where for simplicity only binary strategies are considered. Define the sequence x_i as in equation (5), and let

$$x_{-i}(t) = \{x_1(t), .., x_{i-1}(t), x_{i+1}(t), .., x_m(t)\},$$

$$x_{-i} = \{x_{-i}(t)\}_t \text{ and}$$

$$V_i(x_i, x_{-i}) = \sum_{t=1}^{T} b^t \alpha_i(x_i(t), x_{-i}(t)).$$

Definition 1. *Nash equilibrium (NE) for the scheduling game defined by m objective functions (12) is defined as a vector $\{x_i^*\}$ satisfying for each $i = 1, ..., m$,*

$$V_i(x_i^*, x_{-i}^*) \geq V_i(x_i, x_{-i}^*), \ \forall x_i \in S_i^T. \tag{13}$$

An Auction Algorithm for One-at-a-Time Transmission

Numerical examples such as those discussed above suggested the optimality of one-at-a-time transmission when the resource budgets of the transmitters are large (Remark 1 and Table 2). Thus, assuming large power budgets the multiuser scheduling problem in (6) can be approximated by:

$$\max \sum_i \sum_t b_i^t \log_2(1 + \frac{g_i(t)x_i(t)}{e}), \tag{14}$$

subject to

$$\sum_i x_i(t) = 1, \ t = 1, .., T, \tag{15}$$

imposing one-at-a-time transmission, and subject to

$$\sum_t x_i(t) \le R_i, \ i = 1, ..., m, \tag{16}$$

In the special case when $R_i = 1$, $i = 1, .., m$ in (16), problem (14)-(16) is the classical *assignment problem* in operations research [3]. When allowing for user-specific power budgets R_i, problem (14)-(16) is a so called transportation problem that can be transformed to an assignment problem [3].

Considering the scheduling problem as an assignment problem, it can be solved in a distributed way as a noncooperative game using an auction [4]. In an auction game, the transmitters are the players, making bids for the available transmission slots given local channel information $\{g_i(t)\}_t$ and delay preferences as captured by the parameters b_i^t, $i = 1, .., m$.

Previous work in [15] has observed the applicability of the auction algorithm in [4] to distributed resource allocation in OFDMA systems. [15] did not consider the game-theoretic aspect of the auction model whereas the focus in this paper is on a resource allocation game between noncooperative users, each associated with a delay-parameter b_i that is private information to user i. The auction algorithm starts with any assignment of time slots to users and any set of prices $\{p_t\}_t$. User i prefers the slot offering the maximal value:

$$\max_t \{b_i^t \log(1 + \frac{g_i(t)}{e}) - p_t\}.$$

If all users obtain their preferred slots, then the prices and allocations are at equilibrium and the process stops. Otherwise, a user k that is not happy with his assignment is chosen to find the slot with maximal utility

$$t_k = arg \max_t \{b_k^t \log(1 + \frac{g_k(t)}{e}) - p_t\}.$$

User k then exchanges his slot with the user assigned to slot t_k. The price p_{t_k} is updated to a level where user k is indifferent between t_k and its second best slot. This sequence is repeated until all user obtain their preferred allocations at the given prices.

The auction algorithm solves the assignment problem, thus offering the maximal utility to the users [4]. Computationally, the auction algorithm has been observed to outperform its main competitors (such as the primal-dual algorithm with complexity $O(n^4)$) [4]. The scheduling problem can thus be solved efficiently over any horizon over which the channel can be considered deterministic. An alternative approach, capable of dealing with a time-varying channel environment, is summarized in what follows.

Threshold-Based Scheduling

An alternative approach to auction-based scheduling, applicable in a time-varying channel environment, is summarized in what follows. Assuming a stationary link gain process $\{g_i(t)\}$, $i = 1, .., m$ [9] considers a dynamic programming model for the distributed scheduling problem defined by utility functions as in (12): in a stage game a time t each user $i = 1, .., m$ solves

$$v_{i,t}(\alpha_i(t)) = \max_{x_i(t) \in \{0,1\}} \{\alpha_i(t), bEv_{i,t+1}(\alpha_i(t+1))\}, \tag{17}$$

where $v_{i,t}$ denotes the value function of i at t and where for simplicity a constant discount factor is assumed: $b_i(t) = b$, $i = 1, ..., m$. Threshold-based scheduling according to (17) implies setting

$$x_i(t) = \begin{cases} 1 & \text{if } \alpha_i(t) \geq \bar{\alpha}_i \\ 0 & \text{otherwise,} \end{cases} \tag{18}$$

where the transmission threshold $\bar{\alpha}(t)$ is defined as the solution to the fixed point equation (cf. [9,16]):

$$\bar{\alpha}_i(t) = bE(v_i(\bar{\alpha}_i(t))) = b[\int_0^{\bar{\alpha}_i(t)} \bar{\alpha}_i(t)f(\alpha(t))d\alpha(t) + \int_{\bar{\alpha}_i(t)}^\infty \alpha_i(t)f(\alpha(t))d\alpha(t)]. \tag{19}$$

According to (18), it is optimal for user i to use its scarce resource at t only if its rate at t meets its scheduling threshold at t. Otherwise, it is better to postpone transmission.

A key difference to the optimal stopping scheduling rules in [9,16] in equations (18)-(19) is a time-dependent threshold $\bar{\alpha}_i(t)$, due to assuming a time-varying load (and/or a time-correlated Rayleigh channel environment)[3]. Also, the DP model studied in this paper implies time-dependent optimal scheduling rules, due to discrete power strategy sets and asymmetric users. General scheduling rules like in [12], applicable at ant scheduling time, would be appealing in practice. The quantitative significance of time-dependent scheduling rules is a topic for future work.

5   Conclusion

This paper has studied scheduling via dynamic optimization. The dimensionality problem necessitates simplifications, making it difficult to obtain general efficient

---

[3] Preliminary work on efficient thresholds $\bar{\alpha}_i(t)$ is presented in [8].

scheduling rules. Even though some of the results derived assuming slot-wise optimization of the scheduling rule continue to hold when extending the resource optimization to multiple slots, there are some differences. For example, in an optimal transmission schedule, both simultaneous transmission and one-at-a-time transmission can appear in an optimal solution when the size of the scheduling window is larger than a single time slot. More work is still needed to establish general rules regarding optimal scheduling.

Two approaches based on distributed scheduling were discussed: auction-based scheduling and threshold-based scheduling. Auction-based scheduling enables to obtain an optimal schedule efficiently, assuming one-at-a-time transmission. The DP model suggests that the optimality of one-at-a-time transmission only holds in the absence of power constraints. For future work, the significance of energy considerations motivates the study of distributed scheduling under stringent resource restrictions. Another topic for future work, motivated by the complexity of the multiuser scheduling problem, is the study of efficient scheduling heuristics for emerging networks.

Acknowledgements. T. Heikkinen acknowledges financial support from Finnish Cultural Foundation.

References

1. Andrews, M.: A Survey of Scheduling Theory in Wireless Networks. In: IMA (Institute for Mathematics and its Applications) summer workshop on wireless communications (2005)
2. Basar, T., Olsder, G.: Dynamic noncooperative game theory. Academic Press, London (1995)
3. Bazaraa, M., Jarvis, J., Sherali, H.: Linear Programming and Network Flows. Wiley, Chichester (1990)
4. Bertsekas, D.: Auction Algorithms. In: Floudas, C.A., Pardalos, P.M. (eds.) Encyclopedia of Optimization, pp. 128–132 (2009)
5. Fackler, P.: Compecon Toolbox for Matlab,
   http://www4.ncsu.edu/~pfackler/compecon/toolbox.html
6. Han, S., Kim, H., Han, Y.: Distributed Utility Maximization using a Resource Pricing Power Control in Uplink DS-CDMA. IEEE Communication Letters 12(4), 286–288 (2008)
7. Heikkinen, T., Hottinen, A.: Distributed Scheduling via Pricing with Partial Orthogonality. In: Proc. 6th International Conference on Advances in Mobile Computing and Multimedia (MoMM 2008), Linz, Austria, November 2008, pp. 248–253 (2008)
8. Heikkinen, T., Hottinen, A.: Distributed scheduling in a Time-Varying Ad hoc Network. Journal of Mobile Multimedia 5(3), 238–254 (2009)
9. Heikkinen, T.: Distributed Scheduling and Dynamic Pricing in a Communication Network. Wireless Networks 10(3), 233–244 (2004)
10. Hottinen, A., Viterbo, E., Heikkinen, T.: Device Collaboration in ad-hoc MIMO Networks. In: Proc. International ITG Workshop on Smart Antennas (WSA), Berlin, Germany, February 16-18 (2009)

11. Kulkarni, S., Rosenberg, C.: Opportunistic scheduling policies for wireless systems with short term fairness constraints. In: Proc. GLOBECOM 2003 - IEEE Global Telecommunications Conference, December 2003, vol. (1), pp. 533–537 (2003)
12. Kumaran, K., Qian, L.: Uplink Scheduling in CDMA Packet-Data Systems. Wireless Networks 12, 33–34 (2006)
13. Osborne, M., Rubinstein, A.: A Course in Game Theory. The MIT Press, Cambridge (1994)
14. Viswanath, P., Tse, D., Laroia, R.: Opportunistic Beamforming using Dumb Antennas. IEEE Transactions on Information Theory 48(6) (2002)
15. Yang, K., Prasad, N., Wang, X.: An Auction Approach to Resource Allocation in Uplink Multi-Cell OFDMA Systems. In: Proceedings of the Global Communications Conference, GLOBECOM 2008, New Orleans, LA, USA, November 30-December 4 (2008)
16. Zheng, D., Ge, W., Zhang, J.: Distributed Opportunistic Scheduling for Ad Hoc Networks with Random Access: An Optimal Stopping Approach. IEEE Tr. on Information Theory 55, 205–222 (2009)
17. Zhu, H., Tang, Y., Chlamtac, I.: Unified Collision-Free Coordinated Distributed Scheduling (CF-CDS) in IEEE 802.16 Mesh Networks. IEEE Tr. on Wireless Communications 7(10), 3889–3903 (2008)

Scalable Packet Loss Recovery for Mobile P2P Streaming

Jani Peltotalo[1], Jarmo Harju[1], Lassi Väätämöinen[1],
Imed Bouazizi[2], Igor D.D. Curcio[2], and Joep van Gassel[2]

[1] Tampere University of Technology, Department of Communications Engineering
P.O.Box 553, FI-33101 Tampere, Finland
{jani.peltotalo,jarmo.harju,lassi.vaatamoinen}@tut.fi
[2] Nokia Research Center
P.O.Box 1000, FI-33721 Tampere, Finland
{imed.bouazizi,igor.curcio,joep.van.gassel}@nokia.com

Abstract. In a real-time peer-to-peer streaming system peers in the overlay network may arrive and depart in a very dynamic fashion especially in mobile environment. This manifests itself by a sudden uncontrolled disappearance of a sender and, as a consequence, packets being lost at the receiving side. To ensure seamless media playback the data should not have interruptions. Therefore, if some data packets are missing those should be requested and retrieved from other peers before the playback point reaches the gap in the reception buffer. This paper presents a scalable two-stage packet loss recovery mechanism for a real-time peer-to-peer streaming system using RTCP and RTSP.

Keywords: Real-Time, Peer-to-Peer, Streaming, Packet Loss Recovery, RTP, RTCP, RTSP.

1 Introduction

In traditional streaming applications based on the Real-time Transport Protocol (RTP) / RTP Control Protocol (RTCP) [7], one or more receivers are connected to a single sender. Although there can be multiple senders in a multi-party communication, a receiver of a particular RTP session is only retrieving data from a single sender. In such applications, failures in the network path between sender and receiver can cause packet losses. Special mechanisms are available for the retransmission of those lost packets. This procedure consists of signalling the losses by the receiver and retransmitting the lost packets by the sender. One method to signal packet losses to the sender is using the Generic NACK RTCP message, as specified in [3]. In addition [6] specifies how the lost packets can be retransmitted by delivering them in a separate stream.

In [4] results from experimental test with some of the currently existing P2P streaming application, such as Octoshape [2] and SopCast [10], shows that improvements are needed to enhance the mobile usage. Our real-time Peer-to-Peer (P2P) streaming system [5] contains several important improvements, like small

E. Osipov et al. (Eds.): WWIC 2010, LNCS 6074, pp. 107–120, 2010.

ten seconds initial buffering time, ten seconds buffer size due to the RTP usage, and the partial RTP stream concept where the original RTP sessions related to a media delivery are split into a number of so-called partial RTP streams which allow a single media stream, like an audio or video component, to be received simultaneously from multiple senders.

Because these peers may join and leave the service at their own will, streams being sent to a receiver may be temporarily interrupted, introducing another reason for packet losses in a P2P streaming system. Hence, in a multi-sender P2P streaming environment two different causes, due to which packet loss may be experienced, can be distinguished: (a) network failure, and (b) peer churn. Upon detection of packet loss by a receiving peer, the peer does not necessarily know which one of the two options described above is causing the experienced packet loss. Therefore, the traditional RTCP-based packet loss signalling is insufficient in the P2P streaming case. This is due to the fact that when a sender completely leaves the network, it does not make sense to keep sending Generic NACK RTCP messages to signal lost packets since they will never be received by the departed sender.

An additional requirement is that the packet loss recovery mechanism should be scalable. Once a single connection becomes unavailable, all the peers in an isolated region may start signalling packet losses or explicitly start to request retransmissions. This occurs when one peer along the path back to the original data source departs from the overlay network. In that case, not only peers directly receiving from the departed peer, but also all other peers down the supply chain would start signalling packet losses or requesting retransmission of the same data. Such message propagation throughout the system is undesirable and should be avoided, or kept to the minimum, in order to allow the packet loss recovery mechanism to scale to large network sizes.

The structure of the remainder of this paper is as follows. Packet loss recovery mechanisms based on RTCP and Real Time Streaming Protocol (RTSP) [8] are presented in Sections 2 and 3, respectively. Then, a scalable two-stage packet loss recovery mechanism combining RTCP and RTSP is presented in Sections 4 and 5. After that, results from the performance experiments are presented in Section 6. Finally, Section 7 gives a concluding summary and a look into future developments.

2   RTCP-Based Packet Loss Recovery Mechanism

Generic NACK RTCP messages are used to signal packet losses from the receiver to the sender in a traditional streaming application. A number of variations on how to use RTCP in the P2P streaming system for this purpose is illustrated in Fig. 1, where Peer Y is receiving *audio*, *video partial 0* and *video partial 1* from the Audio, Video 0, and Video 1 peers, respectively. In this particular example, Peer Y has detected packet losses from the Video 0 sender. Using RTCP the peer may signal packet losses to other peers using RTCP in the following three ways:

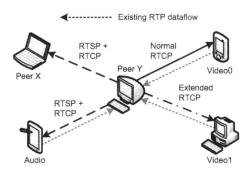

Fig. 1. Packet loss recovery mechanism based on RTCP

1. *Normal RTCP*, as specified in [3] by sending Generic NACK RTCP Receiver Reports (RRs). The receiver, i.e., `Peer Y` in Fig. 1, uses RTCP RRs to signal the losses to the sending peer from which it was expecting to retrieve the lost packets, i.e., `Video` 0 sender in Fig. 1. This can be considered as normal operation according to [3].
2. *Extended RTCP*, in which case the receiver uses RTCP RRs to signal the losses to a peer that was not serving the missing packets in the first place. However, the peer receiving the RTCP messages was serving a different partial from the same RTP session, i.e., `Video` 1 sender in Fig. 1. Note, that this extends the scope of the original RTCP specification beyond its normal use.
3. *RTSP + RTCP*. Since RTCP can only be used in the presence of an RTP connection, RTSP must be used to set up an RTP session between peers if no media stream was set up beforehand, i.e., `Audio` sender and `Peer X` in Fig. 1. In this case the sole purpose of providing an RTP stream is the retransmission of lost packets.

To summarize, RTCP is only suitable for requesting retransmission of data in the case where the sending peer is still available. Otherwise, a new stream would have to be set up using RTSP. Furthermore, it should be noted that RTCP is already in place in most implementations so this is a fairly low-impact way of signalling packet losses which is completely in line with current specifications. The amount of overhead is small, since the Generic NACK messages are sent along with the normal RTCP RRs in compound RTCP messages. However, a peer does not explicitly request retransmission; it only signals which packets have been lost to the sender, and it is up to the sender to decide how to deal with this information.

3   RTSP-Based Packet Loss Recovery Mechanism

Alternatively to the RTCP-based packet loss signalling, the `RTSP PLAY` message can be used for requesting retransmission of lost packets. However, the current

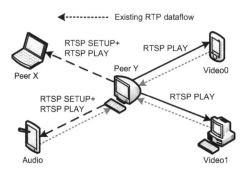

Fig. 2. Packet loss recovery mechanism based on RTSP

syntax of the `Range` header field does not allow requesting retransmission of individual packets or a limited set of packet ranges; it allows time-based ranges but these do not suffice to uniquely identify single packets. This paper proposes the necessary header field extension to make the RTSP-based packet loss signalling possible. The format of a `Packet-Range` header field in ABNF is given below. This format overrides the format specified in [5], where the `Packet-Range` header field was used to signal the play-after value to the replacement peer, without the possibility to specify any missing packet preceding the last received packet from the departed peer.

```
Packet-Range = "Packet-Range:" SP 1*range-specifier CRLF
range-specifier = 1*DIGIT ["-" [1*DIGIT]] ";"
```

In Fig. 2 `Peer Y` has experienced packet losses from the `Video 0` sender and may request retransmission of the lost packets from alternative source peers in the following two ways by means of RTSP:

1. *RTSP PLAY.* This is the case where a suitable media stream was already set up using RTSP beforehand, i.e., `Video 0` and `Video 1` senders in Fig. 2. The peer sends an `RTSP PLAY` message with a `Packet-Range` header field containing sequence numbers of the missing packets directly to the candidate source peer.
2. *RTSP SETUP + RTSP PLAY.* This is the case where a new peer, which was not serving a suitable media stream that could be used for retransmission, i.e., `Audio` sender or `Peer X` in Fig. 2, is selected among the candidate source peers. In this case an `RTSP SETUP` message is first used to create a connection between peers, and an `RTSP PLAY` message with a `Packet-Range` header field is subsequently used to request the lost packets.

The candidate source peer will respond with a 200 `OK` message if all of the requested data is available and the requested packets will be streamed to the requesting peer. A 206 `Partial Content` message will be sent if the requested data is partially available, and the available packets will be sent to the requesting peer. The 206 `Partial Content` message contains also information on what parts are actually streamed using the `Packet-Range` header field. Otherwise, a `204 No Content` message will be returned if the candidate source peer does not have the requested packets, or a `453 Not Enough Bandwidth` message if the candidate source peer does not have enough bandwidth available to successfully handle the given request.

Note that in order to speed up the reconnecting process, the `RTSP SETUP` and `RTSP PLAY` messages could be combined using pipelining as specified in [9] and [1]. In relation to the earlier described RTCP-based method, the RTSP-based method generates more message overhead and latencies. However, because of the request and response nature of RTSP signalling, a peer will always receive information about the sender's capability to actually retransmit the requested packets.

4   Scalable Two-Stage Packet Loss Recovery Mechanism

To ensure seamless media playback the data should not have interruptions. Therefore, if some data packets are missing, those should be requested from other peers before the playback point reaches the gap in the reception buffer. In order to allow for scalable and efficient retransmission of lost packets in the presence of network failure and unexpected peer churn, a simple two-stage packet loss recovery mechanism is proposed in this section. Scalability is necessary to prevent a ripple through effect of retransmission requests and redundant retransmissions in case many peers start simultaneously requesting lost packets due to a single cause, like a failing or departed peer. The proposed packet loss recovery mechanism consists of two stages:

1. Use RTCP in the normal and extended way to signal packet losses to the sending peers.
2. In case lost packets are not received during a certain time-out value T_W, use RTSP to set up new connections and to request the retransmission of the missing packets.

In combination with the above mentioned two stages, a special signalling of pending retransmission requests and resolved packet losses can be applied to enhance the scalability of the proposed packet loss recovery mechanism.

4.1   Stage One

Every RTP session, such as audio, video or subtitle streams of the entire multimedia session is split into smaller pieces, each consisting of a group of RTP packets, along the time axis. Every piece has a fixed duration T_P which is expressed in time. The N partial streams are constructed by assigning pieces sequentially one by one into the partial streams *0...N-1* and then continuing again with partial stream *0*, etc.

The time-out value T_L, defined by (1), is signalling the amount of time that is waited until the packet is considered lost. This value consists of the normal network delay T_N, that can be calculated for example from RTSP request response pairs, and an extra time T_E given to peers to patch their missing packets to avoid overloading the network with retransmission requests for packets that might still be forwarded in the network. If the missing packet is the last packet of the piece, then the time $T_B = T_P * (N - 1)$ between two pieces belonging to the same partial RTP stream will be also added to the time-out value.

$$T_L = \begin{cases} T_N + T_E, & \text{not last packet in the piece,} \\ T_N + T_E + T_B, & \text{last packet in the piece.} \end{cases} \tag{1}$$

After the time-out value T_L has expired, the signalling of packet losses using RTCP is started. Firstly, the packet losses are signalled back to the peer it was expected to receive the missing packets from. Alternatively or simultaneously, a similar RTCP RR may be sent to other peers serving different partial RTP streams from the same RTP session.

4.2 Stage Two

If the packets that have been signalled as lost using RTCP do not arrive within a certain waiting time T_W, the receiving peer selects a new candidate source peer and starts to request retransmission of the lost packets by means of RTSP. This occurs for instance when a sending peer departs without signing off from the network, for example due to malfunctioning, or when the used network path is broken. Note that in case a source peer departs in a controlled way, the peer will also reconnect to an alternative source peer and resume playback from the point of interruption as specified in [5]. However, this is considered to be normal operation of the peer-to-peer streaming system. If the waiting time T_W is set to zero, then the peer will directly go to the stage two, of course after the time-out value T_L is expired, and start to request missing packets from the candidate source peers using RTSP.

The candidate source peers can be peers that are already serving the receiving peer with other media streams of the same service, for example the `Audio` peer in Fig. 2, or completely different peers, like `Peer X` in Fig. 2. Note however, that these cannot be peers that are already serving other partials from the same RTP session, since in that case RTCP RRs should be used as described in stage one. Retransmissions from the new peers are explicitly requested by setting up a new RTP connection using `RTSP SETUP` and `RTSP PLAY` messages.

The new RTP connection can either be set up permanently, or used only to retrieve missing packets. In the former case the old existing RTP connection is discarded and playback resumes with the new peer possibly after individual missed packets have been received. In the latter case, the new connection will be torn down using the `RTSP TEARDOWN` message after the lost packets have been retransmitted. In order to improve the speed of retransmissions, backup RTSP connections can be kept open, without actual streaming taking place, just for the purpose of requesting retransmission of lost packets in case other peers fail. This allows faster error recovery, since the set up time is eliminated from the retransmission procedure. Alternatively, similar performance improvements can also be realized by pipelining the `RTSP SETUP` and `RTSP PLAY` messages.

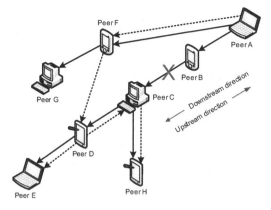

Fig. 3. Recovery of broken streaming path of a partial RTP stream

4.3 Avoiding Retransmission Request Overload

In order to avoid multiple peers, downstream from the point of failure in a broken path, from signalling lost packets due to the same root cause, such as a malfunctioning peer, or a peer departed in an uncontrolled way or cut off from the network connection, a special signalling mechanism is devised. The proposed mechanism includes two aspects. The first aspect is the signalling of pending retransmission requests downstream, i.e., in the direction of the data flow from the original data source to the leaf nodes. Hence, in the absence of packets, the information is signalled to indicate to the receiving peers that the sender is aware of the losses. Secondly, it includes the signalling of the recovered packets both downstream and upstream. This information can be utilized by the recipients to efficiently reconnect to other peers which have signalled that they have resolved the problem.

Fig. 3 illustrates a delivery flow of a particular partial RTP stream using solid edges. In the figure, `Peer B` is malfunctioning and causing `Peer C`, `Peer D`, `Peer E` and `Peer H` further downstream to experience packet losses. Note that the packet losses could also be caused by a failing network link between `Peer B` and `Peer C`. This situation may cause all of these peers to start signalling packet losses or requesting retransmissions and, as a consequence, this will flood the network with redundant retransmissions of the same lost packets. If packet retransmission is handled in such uncoordinated way, the efficiency and scalability of the system is seriously jeopardized. Therefore, the peers will signal pending retransmission requests downstream and recovery of lost packets both up- and downstream. This is achieved by enhancing the RTCP feedback messages specified in [3].

The common packet format for feedback messages is depicted in Fig. 4. Both pending retransmission request and recovered packet loss messages are using RTPFB value (205, transport layer feedback message, specified in [3]) in the Packet Type (PT) field. The first synchronization source (SSRC) identifier

```
0                   1                   2                   3
0 1 2 3 4 5 6 7 8 9 0 1 2 3 4 5 6 7 8 9 0 1 2 3 4 5 6 7 8 9 0 1
+-+-+-+-+-+-+-+-+-+-+-+-+-+-+-+-+-+-+-+-+-+-+-+-+-+-+-+-+-+-+-+-+
|V=2|P|  FMT   |       PT      |            length             |
+-+-+-+-+-+-+-+-+-+-+-+-+-+-+-+-+-+-+-+-+-+-+-+-+-+-+-+-+-+-+-+-+
|               SSRC (peer ID) of FB packet sender              |
+-+-+-+-+-+-+-+-+-+-+-+-+-+-+-+-+-+-+-+-+-+-+-+-+-+-+-+-+-+-+-+-+
|               SSRC (peer ID) of media source                  |
+-+-+-+-+-+-+-+-+-+-+-+-+-+-+-+-+-+-+-+-+-+-+-+-+-+-+-+-+-+-+-+-+
:               Feedback Control Information                    :
+-+-+-+-+-+-+-+-+-+-+-+-+-+-+-+-+-+-+-+-+-+-+-+-+-+-+-+-+-+-+-+-+
```

Fig. 4. Common packet format for feedback messages

identifies the sender of the feedback message and the second SSRC identifies the original sender of the media data.

A single feedback control information block can be repeated multiple times and has the format shown in Fig. 5. The Packet IDentifier (PID) specifies the sequence number of the first lost or recovered packet. The feedback message type (FMT) will be used to distinguish between pending retransmission request and recovered packet loss messages. The semantics of the feedback control information can be given either in the NPLR field (Number of Packets Lost or Recovered) or in the BLP field (Bitmask of following Lost Packets). The NPLR field represents the number of packets lost or recovered from PID onwards excluding the packet with PID itself. The BLP field represents a bit mask identical to the syntax and semantics of the BLP field used in the Generic NACK message specified in [3].

```
0                   1                   2                   3
0 1 2 3 4 5 6 7 8 9 0 1 2 3 4 5 6 7 8 9 0 1 2 3 4 5 6 7 8 9 0 1
+-+-+-+-+-+-+-+-+-+-+-+-+-+-+-+-+-+-+-+-+-+-+-+-+-+-+-+-+-+-+-+-+
|              PID              |            NPLR/BLP           |
+-+-+-+-+-+-+-+-+-+-+-+-+-+-+-+-+-+-+-+-+-+-+-+-+-+-+-+-+-+-+-+-+
```

Fig. 5. Feedback control information block

It is the responsibility of a receiving peer to aggregate this information from the incoming streams and send it out to the outgoing streams. This is especially important if the configuration of the partial streams is not constant within the service. In practice, this is the case when a particular media stream is portioned into a different number of partials on the incoming and outgoing connections of a peer. The explicit signalling of packet loss to downstream peers also reduces the time it takes for a particular peer to detect a packet loss. This is due to the fact that in the absence of packets, signalling is available to indicate these losses. Hence, the peer does not need to wait too long before it can conclude that packets have been lost somewhere upstream.

In case a peer discovers pending retransmission requests, it may either wait until these lost packets arrive from the sending peer, or it may choose to start its own packet loss recovery mechanism. The former occurs when the upstream peer has found an alternative source or the original sending peer has recovered from the problematic situation. Once any peer has successfully recovered lost packets by reconnecting to a new peer, it will signal this both up- and downstream. This improves the self-healing capability of the peer-to-peer streaming system. In this way, the overlay may be reorganized jointly by the distributed peers in a coordinated effort. This is illustrated in Fig. 3, where **Peer D** discovers an alternative source (**Peer F**) before the sending peer (**Peer C**) solves the problem. After **Peer D** has signalled packet loss recovery upstream to the **Peer C**, **Peer C** may for instance decide to switch roles and use **Peer D** as a new source for this particular partial RTP stream. This means in practice that a new data flow, indicated by the dashed edges in the figure, is constructed jointly by the involved peers.

5   Peer Operation

The operation of a peer using the two-stage packet loss recovery mechanism including signalling of pending retransmissions and recovered packets is depicted in detail in Fig. 6. A peer receives RTP packets in a normal manner (block 1). When it determines that packets have been lost (block 2), i.e., the time-out value T_L for some missing packets has expired, it enters to the first stage of the two-stage packet loss recovery mechanism.

In the first stage, an additional scalability mechanism utilising active and passive modes can be used to avoid overload of packet loss signalling. In the passive mode a peer may wait for the stream path issues to be resolved, while in the active mode (block 3) it tries to actively resolve the stream path issues. If the peer is in the passive mode, it waits for a period of time T_D (block 4), defined by (2), to allow the stream path issues to be resolved. $Peer_{position}$ is the position of the peer in the path from the original data source. This position can be indicated for example by the Contributing Source (CSRC) header field in the RTP packet. Max_{depth} is the maximum allowed depth for the stream path set by the P2P streaming system operator, and in the current implementation it is set to 15. In (2), $\alpha \in (0, 1)$ is a random coefficient to diversify the delay time among peers in the same level of the stream path. D_{max} is the maximum delay which still allows to recover from the packet loss before the playback point reaches the gap in the reception buffer and is dependent on the used initial buffering time.

$$T_D = \frac{Peer_{position}}{Max_{depth}} * (1 - \alpha) * D_{max} \qquad (2)$$

After T_D has elapsed, the peer in the passive mode checks whether an indication of a pending retransmission request has been made (block 5). If such an indication has been received for the missing packets in question, the peer waits for another small period of time (block 6) to allow an upstream peer to retrieve and forward the lost packets. If the lost packets are received (block 7), the peer can stop the packet loss recovery mechanism for packets in question. If the lost packets are not received, the peer returns to the block 6 and waits again for the small period of time. This is continued until the playback point reaches the

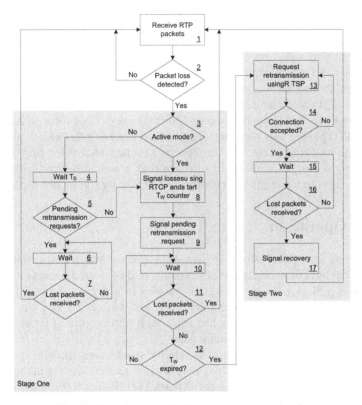

Fig. 6. Two-stage packet loss recovery mechanism

missing packets. On the other hand, if pending retransmission requests have not been signalled (block 5), the peer proceeds to signal an indication of lost packets using RTCP (block 8) to the upstream peer. Similarly, if the peer is in an active mode (block 3), the peer proceeds to the block 8 and starts the T_W counter.

Next, the peer signals to the downstream peers an indication of a pending retransmission request (block 9). The peer then waits for a small period of time (block 10) and checks whether the lost packets have been received (block 11). If the packets have been received, the peer can again stop the packet loss recovery for the packets in question. On the other hand, if the lost packets have not been received, the peer checks whether a threshold period of time T_W has expired (block 11). If the threshold period of time has not expired, the peer repeats blocks 10, 11 and 12. If the threshold period of time has expired, the peer enters to the second stage of the two-stage process.

In the second stage, the peer sends a request for RTP packet retransmission using RTSP (block 13). Next, the peer will discover whether an RTSP connection has been accepted (block 14). If the connection is not accepted, the peer returns to block 13 until the connection is accepted. Once the connection is accepted, the peer waits (block 15) and determines whether the lost packets have been received (block 16). Once the lost packets are received, the peer signals an indication of

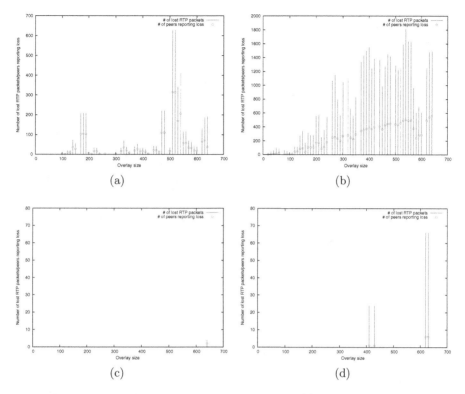

Fig. 7. The number of lost packets with churning peers, (a) audio stream without loss recovery, (b) video stream without loss recovery, (c) audio stream with loss recovery, and (d) video stream with loss recovery

the packet loss recovery both to up- and downstream peers (block 16), and the peer can stop the packet loss recovery for the packets in question.

6   Performance Evaluation

Currently our P2P streaming system contains only an RTSP-based packet loss recovery mechanism, specified in Section 3, in addition to the peer replacement presented in [5]. So the results presented in this section illustrate the benefits of that kind of packet loss recovery, but the overall system performance could be enhanced with a complete two-stage packet loss recovery mechanism.

As in [5], a laboratory network environment with 17 desktop PCs has been utilized to evaluate the operation of the system with and without the RTSP-based packet loss recovery mechanism. 16 hosts were used to run 40 peers in each host together with one host acting as an original data source. The length for one live streaming service was roughly one hour, and T_P was set to 100 milliseconds and N was set one for audio stream and, correspondingly, 400 milliseconds and

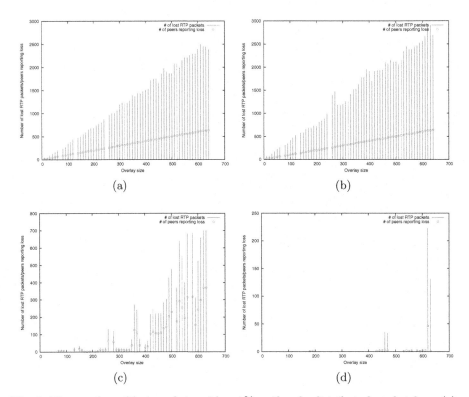

Fig. 8. The number of lost packets with a 1% uniformly distributed packet loss, (a) audio stream without loss recovery, (b) video stream without loss recovery, (c) audio stream with loss recovery, and (d) video stream with loss recovery

four for video stream. The maximum cluster size was set to 70 peers, and peers were started in 40 cycles with five seconds starting interval: first one peer was started at each host, then a second one and so on. To simulate churning caused by the real mobile nodes, a timer functionality which randomly shuts down and restarts nodes was used. After a peer had joined to the service, it stayed randomly up to 30 seconds in the service and then left the service and joined back randomly after one to ten seconds.

The number of lost packets per peer as a function of the overlay size with and without RTSP-based packet loss recovery are shown in Fig. 7 (with churning peers) and Fig. 8 (with a 1% uniformly distributed packet loss). From the figures we can see that the improvement with a packet loss recovery is remarkable. With churning peers, only few packets remain lost with the packet loss recovery. This loss is due to the fact that also some of the selected new source peers departs before sending all of the requested missing packets and the small ten seconds initial buffering time does not allow requesting some of the missing packets again. With a 1% uniformly distributed packet loss, retransmitted packets are also affected by the packet loss and causes some amount of packets to remain

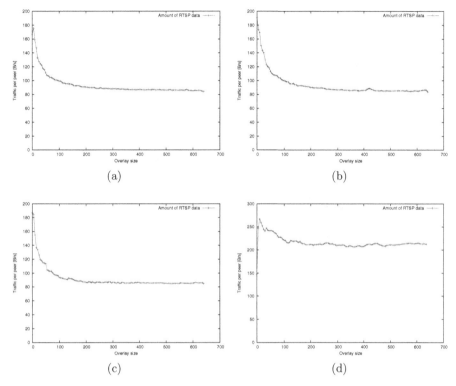

Fig. 9. The amount of sent RTSP data, (a) churning peers without packet loss recovery, (b) churning peers with packet loss recovery, (c) 1% uniformly distributed packet loss without loss recovery, and (d) 1% uniformly distributed packet loss with loss recovery

lost also with the packet loss recovery. It should be noted that the packet interval for both audio and video streams is circa 55 milliseconds, but the payload size and the total amount of lost bytes is larger for the video stream.

The amount of sent RTSP data in bytes per peer with and without RTSP-based packet loss recovery as a function of overlay size is shown in Fig. 9. From the figure we can see that with churning peers the values follow the same trend, but the packet loss recovery causes small overall increase to the signalling data. With a 1% uniformly distributed packet loss, the amount of RTSP data is more than doubled, but is still quite minimal compared to the combined bit rate 112kbps of the original RTP sessions.

7   Conclusions and Further Work

In a traditional streaming application based on RTP / RTCP, special mechanisms are available for signalling of packet losses and retransmission of lost packets. The traditional RTCP-based packet loss signalling is however insufficient in the peer-to-peer streaming case, since when a sender completely leaves the network, it does not make sense to signal lost packets since they will never be received by the departed sender. This paper presents a scalable two-stage packet loss recovery mechanism for a real-time peer-to-peer streaming system using RTCP and RTSP.

Laboratory tests with the current RTSP-based packet loss recovery mechanism have shown that it is beneficial to try to ensure seamless media playback using packet retransmissions. Full implementation level support for the two-stage packet loss recovery mechanism is still needed to be able to verify the operation of the packet loss recovery mechanism and to be able to fine tune all parameters in the system, such as initial buffering time, partial RTP stream duration T_P and all waiting times in the two-stage packet recovery mechanism, to maximize the quality and minimize the data delivered in the network.

Mechanisms for handling packet losses using Forward Error Correction (FEC) in an RTSP-based P2P streaming system needs to be studied to find out the benefits and drawbacks of using FEC in addition to the current mechanisms based on packet retransmissions and peer replacement before the reception buffer underflows.

More advanced laboratory tests with different latencies, packet losses and throughputs between peers will highlight possible bottlenecks and usability issues in the system.

References

1. 3GPP: Transparent end-to-end Packet-switched Streaming Service (PSS); Protocols and codecs. TS 26.234, 3rd Generation Partnership Project (3GPP) (March 2009)
2. Octoshape Homepage (March 2010), http://www.octoshape.com/
3. Ott, J., Wenger, S., Sato, N., Burmeister, C., Rey, J.: Extended RTP Profile for Real-time Transport Control Protocol (RTCP)-Based Feedback (RTP/AVPF). RFC 4585, Internet Engineering Task Force (July 2006)
4. Peltotalo, J., Bouazizi, I., Curcio, I., Hannuksela, M., Harju, J., Jantunen, A., Saukko, M., Väätämöinen, L.: Peer-to-Peer Streaming Technology Survey. In: Proceeding of the Seventh International Conference on Networking (ICN 2008), pp. 342–350 (April 2008) doi: 10.1109/ICN.2008.86
5. Peltotalo, J., Harju, J., Väätämöinen, L., Curcio, I., Bouazizi, I.: RTSP-based Mobile Peer-to-Peer Streaming System. International Journal of Digital Multimedia Broadcasting 2010, 15 pages (2010); Article ID 470813, doi:10.1155/2010/470813
6. Rey, J., Leon, D., Miyazaki, A., Varsa, V., Hakenberg, R.: RTP Retransmission Payload Format. RFC 4588, Internet Engineering Task Force (July 2006)
7. Schulzrinne, H., Casner, S., Frederick, R., Jacobson, V.: RTP: A Transport Protocol for Real-Time Applications. RFC 3550, Internet Engineering Task Force (July 2003)
8. Schulzrinne, H., Rao, A., Lanphier, R.: Real Time Streaming Protocol (RTSP). RFC 2326, Internet Engineering Task Force (April 1998)
9. Schulzrinne, H., Rao, A., Lanphier, R., Westerlund, M., Stiemerling, M.: Real Time Streaming Protocol 2.0 (RTSP). Internet-Draft draft-ietf-mmusic-rfc2326bis-23, Internet Engineering Task Force (March 2010) (Work in progress)
10. SopCast Homepage (March 2010), http://www.sopcast.org/

Aggressive Joint Access and Backhaul Design for Distributed-Cognition 1Gbps/km2 System Architecture

Pol Blasco, Lorenza Giupponi, Ana Galindo-Serrano, and Mischa Dohler

Centre Tecnològic de Telecomunicacions de Catalunya (CTTC)
Castelldefels, Barcelona, Spain
name.surname@cttc.es

Abstract. Capacity calculations reveal that required data rates in urban environments are in the order of 1 Gbps/km2, which is beyond any forward looking state-of-the-art. Following the BuNGee [1] design approach, we propose in this paper to follow an aggressive joint access and backhaul design which allows one powerful hub base station to feed several distributed access base stations at the same time as these communicate with associated user − all using the same band. The hence resulting interference environment is extremely dynamic and has eluded a viable communication strategy thus far. We propose however a novel distributed cognitive mechanism, which facilitates the capacity needs to be satisfied at these dynamics whilst being of low complexity and high reliability. Simulation results corroborate our findings.

1 Introduction

The prime driver for innovative communication systems are some promising applications and market requirements, i.e., dense high-data rate indoor usage, support of mobility, high expected traffic levels and emerging bandwidth-intensive applications. These, in turn, dictate ubiquitous coverage and high throughput, which are central to the expectations of potential beyond next generation networking users across markets worldwide. Focusing e.g., on the market demand in dense urban areas during business hours, it has been calculated in [1] that 800 Mbps/km2 are required. This is an order of magnitude higher than the forward looking current state of the art. It is essentially the need and inspiration to deliver 1 Gbps/km2 anywhere in the cell.

The aim is thus to design an architecture which is cost efficient whilst providing a capacity density of 1 Gbps/km2. To facilitate this goal to be achieved, it is proposed to utilize the same spectral bands for the access as well as backhaul links. Here, the backhaul links are formed between a hub base station (HBS) and several below-rooftop access base stations (ABSs) which in turn serve associated mobile stations (MSs). WiMAX naturally lends itself to such an architectural design for the following reasons:

E. Osipov et al. (Eds.): WWIC 2010, LNCS 6074, pp. 121–132, 2010.

1. In its original standards formulation, i.e., IEEE 802.16-2004 or IEEE 802.16d, WiMAX has been designed for high-capacity wireless links.
2. In a subsequent standards edition, i.e., IEEE 802.16e-2005 or simply IEEE 802.16e, mobility has been introduced thus allowing for true mobile cellular access provision.
3. In a recent amendment of the standard, i.e., IEEE 802.16j-2009, multihop relaying functionalities are facilitated which are fundamentally required when relaying data traffic from the HBS to the MS via the ABS or a set of ABSs.

However, whilst the architectural building blocks are available, some serious challenges remain to be addressed and thus constitute the prime focus of our design:

1. The multihop option of IEEE 802.16j-2009 allows only time-division relaying, i.e., the HBS first needs to communicate to the ABSs and only then can the ABSs communicate to the MSs. The spectral efficiency is thus roughly halved. A more aggressive approach would be to allow both backhaul as well as access links to communicate simultaneously. This, however, constitutes a serious challenge in interference management, i.e., interference avoidance, mitigation and suppression.
2. The complexity of the complete system at hand is very large. Notably, the system to be optimized will be composed of at least one HBS, several decentralized ABSs and a fairly large amount of MSs. In addition, the optimization scope will include the operation over license and license-exempt bands, presenting different interference conditions. If the optimization problem can be formalized, it is likely to be NP-hard and/or non-convex and thus a solution eludes the majority of tools available to date dealing with system optimization.
3. The system as a whole is highly dynamic, likely to yield non-stationary effects in both observation as well as actions to be taken by the involved parties. This means that the system should be sufficiently adaptive and self-organizing in the sense that changes in the operational conditions should be handled well by the system. Another implication is that most theoretical toolboxes break down and more computerized solving methods, such as machine learning, have to be invoked to yield viable results. The prime problem here is that most machine learning approaches assume perfect knowledge of the entire system and coordination between the involved parties.
4. The memory and coherence of the system is not negligible in that a specific action taken by the system (such as instructing a specific ABS to transmit at a given power level) is correlated with the action taken at a subsequent time instant as well as with the action taken under similarly occurring circumstances. This implies that using fixed or simple (memory-less) opportunistic strategies are inherently sub-optimal. We thus concentrate on truly cognitive approaches which capitalize on the peculiarities of the system under consideration. The prime problem with cognitive approaches, however, is the poor convergence in time and to the set target.

In summary, we assume that a) the architecture uses the same frequency band for the wireless backhaul and access links; b) decisions are taken in a distributed fashion; and c) the system obeys as much as possible the WiMAX specs. We will aim to formulate the problem in such a way that a) a solution in form of decisions can be found, even if only iteratively and numerically; b) these decision yield clear instructions on radio resource management functionalities to all involved parties; and c) these decisions are based on truly cognitive algorithms with elements of memory, learning and intelligent decision taking.

To this end, the paper is organized as follows. In Section 2, we briefly detail the system model in quantifying the signal-to-noise-and-interference-ratios (SINRs) and resulting capacities. In Section 3, we describe the distributed Q-learning algorithm in sufficient details. In Section 4, we discuss a large set of simulation results. Finally, Section 5 concludes the paper.

2   System Model

We consider an urban area with one HBS, providing service and coexisting with N ABSs. Each ABS provides service to its Q associated MSs. We consider orthogonal frequency division multiplexing (OFDM) symbols grouped into R subchannels. Both HBS and ABS systems operate in the same frequency band and have the same amount R of available sub-channels, which allows to increase the spectral efficiency per area through spatial frequency re-use. We focus only on the downlink operation.

We denote by $\mathbf{p}^{i,A} = (p_1^{i,A}, \ldots, p_R^{i,A})$ and $\mathbf{p}^H = (p_1^H, \ldots, p_R^H)$ the transmission power vector of ABS i and the HBS with $p_r^{i,A}$ and p_r^H denoting the downlink transmission power of ABS and HBS respectively in sub-channel r.

2.1   Signal-to-Noise-and-Interference Ratios

We analyze the system performance in terms of signal interference noise ratio (SINR) and capacity given in (bits/s). The SINR at MS $q \in Q$ allocated in sub-channel r of ABS i is:

$$\gamma_r^{i,u} = \frac{p_r^{i,A} h_{ii,r}^{Au}}{p_r^H h_{i,r}^{Hu} + \sum_{j=1, j \neq i}^{N} p_r^{j,A} h_{ji,r}^{Au} + \sigma^2} \tag{1}$$

with $i = 1, \ldots, N$. Here $h_{ii,r}^{Au}$ indicates the link gain between the transmitting ABS i and its MS u; $h_{i,r}^{H,u}$ indicates the link gain between the interfering HBS and MS u in ABS i; $h_{ji,r}^{Au}$ indicates the link gain between the interfering ABS j and MS u of ABS i, finally σ^2 is the noise power. The SINR of ABS i in sub-channel r is:

$$\gamma_r^{i,A} = \frac{p_r^H h_{i,r}^{HA}}{\sum_{j=1, j \neq i}^{N} p_r^{j,A} h_{ji,r}^{AA} + \sigma^2} \tag{2}$$

with $i = 1, \ldots, N$. Here, $h_{i,r}^{HA}$ indicates the link gain between the transmitting HBS and the receiving ABS i, in sub-channel r and $h_{ji,r}^{AA}$ indicates the link gain between interfering ABS j and ABS i.

2.2   Link Capacities

As for the resulting capacities, the capacity of ABS i used for its Q MSs is:

$$\widehat{C^{i,A}} = \sum_{r=0}^{R} \frac{BW}{R} \log_2(1 + \gamma_r^{i,u}) \tag{3}$$

with $i = 1, \ldots, N$. The capacity of the self-backhaul to ABS i is

$$C^{i,A} = \sum_{r=0}^{R} \frac{BW}{R} \log_2(1 + \gamma_r^{i,A}). \tag{4}$$

The capacity of the HBS and the entire self-backhaul is:

$$C^H = \sum_{i=0}^{N} C^{i,A} \tag{5}$$

The capacity of the self-backhaul and the sum of the capacities of the ABSs have to satisfy the following constraints:

$$C^{i,A} \geq \widehat{C^{i,A}} \tag{6}$$

$$C^H \geq \sum_{i=0}^{N} \widehat{C^{i,A}} \tag{7}$$

which is to guarantee that there is no buffer overflow in the ABSs.

3   General Learning Process

In this section we describe the system learning process for the self-adaptation of the transmission power associated with the ABSs. We propose a decentralized reinforcement learning (RL) scheme, where the ABSs are multiple agents aiming at learning an optimal control policy by repeatedly interacting with the controlled environment in such a way that their performances, evaluated by scalar costs, are minimized [2]. There exist several RL algorithms. For our particular problem, we consider the decentralized Q-learning as an accurate algorithm to implement interference control in the proposed scenario. We consider that each agent is characterized by as many learning processes as available sub-channels. In the following, we first introduce the Q-learning algorithm and then we describe in details the power allocation scheme proposed in this paper for each sub-channel.

3.1   Q-Learning

It is assumed that the environment is a finite-state, discrete-time stochastic dynamical system. Let $\mathcal{S}$ be the set of l possible states $\mathcal{S} = \{s_1^r, s_2^r, \ldots, s_l^r\}$, and $\mathcal{A}$ be a set of m possible actions $\mathcal{A} = \{a_1^r, a_2^r, \ldots, a_m^r\}$ that each agent i may choose with respect to a given sub-channel r. The interactions between the multi-agent system and the environment at each time instant t corresponding to sub-channel r consist of the following sequence:

- The agent i senses the state $s_t^{i,r} = s \in \mathcal{S}$.
- Based on s, agent i selects an action $a_t^{i,r} = a \in \mathcal{A}$.
- The environment thus makes a transition to the new state $s_{t+1}^{i,r} = v \in \mathcal{S}$.
- The transition to the state v generates a cost $c_t^{i,r} = c \in \mathbb{R}$, for agent i.
- The cost c is fed back to the agent and the process is repeated.

The objective of each agent is to find an optimal policy $\pi^*(s) \in \mathcal{A}$ for each s, to minimize some cumulative measure of the cost $c_t^{i,r} = c(s, a)$ received over time. For each agent i and learning process r, we define an evaluation function, denoted by $Q^{i,r}(s, a)$, as the expected total discount cost over an infinite time. To simplify the notation, in the following we refer to $Q^{i,r}(s, a)$ as $Q(s, a)$:

$$Q(s, a) = \mathbb{E}\left\{\sum_{t=0}^{\infty} \gamma^t c(s_t, \pi(s)) | s_0 = s\right\} \qquad (8)$$

where $0 \leq \gamma < 1$ is a discount factor. If the selected action a at time t following the policy $\pi(s)$ corresponds to the optimal policy $\pi^*(s)$, the Q-function is minimized with respect to the current state.

Let $P_{s,v}(a)$ be the transition probability from state s to state v, when action a is executed. Then, (8) can be expressed as:

$$Q(s, a) = \mathbb{E}\{c(s, a)\} + \gamma \sum_{v \in \mathcal{S}} P_{s,v}(a) Q(v, b) \qquad (9)$$

where $\mathbb{E}\{c(s, a)\}$ denotes the expected value of $c(s, a)$. Equation (9) indicates that the Q-function of the current state-action pair, for each agent i and learning process r, can be represented in terms of the expected immediate cost of the current state-action pair and the Q-function of the next state-action pairs. The task of Q-learning is to determine an optimal stationary policy π^* without knowing $\mathbb{E}\{c(s, a)\}$ and $P_{s,v}(a)$, which makes it well suited for learning a power allocation policy in the considered scenario. the objective is obtained in a recursive manner. The Q-learning rule to update the Q-values relative to agent i and learning process r is:

$$Q(s, a) \leftarrow Q(s, a) + \alpha[c + \gamma \min_a Q(v, a) - Q(s, a)] \qquad (10)$$

where α is the learning rate. For more details about RL and Q-learning the reader is referred to [2,3].

3.2   Learning for Power Allocation

In our system, the multiple agents with learning capabilities are the ABSs, so that for each sub-channel they are in charge of identifying the current environment state, select the action based on the Q-learning methodology and execute it. In the following, for each agent $i = 1, 2, \ldots, N$ and sub-channel $r = 1, 2, \ldots, R$ we define system state, action, associated cost and next state. To simplify the notation we will refer in the following to a system with only one sub-channel.

1. **State.** The system state for agent i consists of two parts: the individual state of agent i and the global state of the self-backhaul capacity, to achieve both the capacity constraints (6). In particular, at time t the state for ABS i is defined in the Table 1.

   To parameterize the global state of the self-backhaul, C^H is normalized with respect to the ideal maximum upper bound capacity C_{ub}^H. C_{ub}^H is computed equivalently to C^H but assuming the interference terms to be negligible. As a result, we define the normalized capacity of the system's self-backhaul as:

$$\widehat{C}^H = \frac{C^H}{C_{ub}^H} \tag{11}$$

   We will consider that this normalized parameter can take four possible values: "High" i.e., above 0.7; "Mid-High" i.e., between 0.7 and 0.5; "Mid-low" i.e., between 0.5 and 0.25 and "Low" i.e., for values below 0.25. In addition, we consider two different situations: the self-backhaul capacity to ABS i is above or below the capacity of the ABS i to the MSs. However, even if the local constraint is fulfilled and the capacity of ABS i to its users $\widehat{C^{i,A}}$ is below the self-backhaul capacity to ABS i, $C^{i,A}$, there may be a waste of self-backhaul capacity, and ideally $\widehat{C^{i,A}}$ should be equal to $C^{i,A}$. For this reason, a third situation is considered, i.e., $C^{i,A}$ is 10% above $\widehat{C^{i,A}}$, which we will consider as the most efficient state.

Table 1. Definition of states

	High $\hat{C}^H$	Mid-high $\hat{C}^H$	Mid-low $\hat{C}^H$	Low $\hat{C}^H$
$\widehat{C^{i,A}} > C^{i,A}$	State 1	State 2	State 3	State 4
$\widehat{C^{i,A}} \simeq< C^{i,A}$	State 5	State 6	State 7	State 8
$\widehat{C^{i,A}} < C^{i,A}$	State 9	State 10	State 11	State 12

2. **Actions.** The set of possible actions consists of: *maintain, increase* or *decrease* $p_r^{i,A}$ by one dBm.
3. **Cost.** The cost assesses the immediate return incurred due to the assignment of action a at state s. The aim of the learning algorithm is to find the optimal $p_r^{i,A}$ that maximizes the capacity C^H at the same time that (6) is satisfied. The cost function may be of the form:

$$c(s, a) = \frac{|C^{i,A} - \widehat{C^{i,A}}|^2}{C^H}. \tag{12}$$

The cost decreases while capacity C^H increases and $C^{i,A}$ gets closer to $\widehat{C^{i,A}}$. Nevertheless it may happen that $\widehat{C^{i,A}}$ remains infinitely close and above $C^{i,A}$, so that the constraint is not fulfilled, but the cost C is infinitely small. For this reason, we introduce some modifications in the expression of the cost. There are notably some states that are more desirable than others. In particular, states 1 to 4 are not convenient since here the system does not satisfy the capacity constraint. On the other hand, states 5 to 8 are more convenient since here the constraint is satisfied and $C^{i,A}$ is efficiently utilized by the MSs. As a result, we modify the cost function as follows:

$$C = \begin{cases} |100(C^{i,A} - \widehat{C^{i,A}})|^2 \gamma_{ec} + \alpha_{ec} & \text{states 1 to 4} \\[2ex] \dfrac{|100(C^{i,A} - \widehat{C^{i,A}})|^2 - \alpha_d}{\gamma_d (1 + \hat{C}^H)} & \text{states 5 to 8} \\[2ex] \dfrac{|100(C^{i,A} - \widehat{C^{i,A}})|^2}{1 + \hat{C}^H} & \text{states 9 to 12} \end{cases} \tag{13}$$

Here, γ_{ec} and α_{ec} increase the cost of states 1 to 4, and γ_d and α_d decrease the cost of states 5 to 8.

4. **Next State.** The state transition from s to v is determined by the power allocation policy.

With this Q-learning allocation strategy at hand, we proceed to the discussion of the simulation results.

4 Simulation Results

4.1 High-Capacity Scenario

The scenario considered for evaluation consists of one HBS and 16 ABSs, placed in a 4×4 matrix form. The separation between ABSs is 350 m and the HBS is located at 1350 m in the y direction from the center of the ABSs distribution. We consider one MS q for each ABS, which is randomly located within a 200 m radius coverage area of each ABS. The downlink transmission power p_r^H of the HBS is fixed at 46 dBm; additionally the downlink transmission powers $p_r^{i,A}$ of the ABSs can be adaptively fixed between 1 dBm and 31 dBm at a 1 dBm step.

A suitable model for a Beyond-3G short range urban scenario is the COST-WI model [4]. This model has also been accepted by the ITU-R and was selected as Urban/Alternative Flat Suburban path-loss model in the IEEE 802.16 standard for fixed wireless access [5]. The model distinguishes between LOS (Line of Sight) and NLOS (Non Line of Sight) situations. Here, we assume that the channel gains $h_{i,r}^{HA}$ between the transmitting HBS and the receiving ABS i, in sub-channel r and $h_{ii,r}^{Aq}$ between the transmitting ABS i and its user q are LOS with short-range path-loss (PL) model $PL(dB) = 30.18 + 26.0 \log_{10}(d)$. Alternatively, it is assumed that the channel gains $h_{i,r}^{H,q}$ between the interfering HBS and MS

q in ABS i, $h_{ji,r}^{Aq}$ between the interfering ABS j and user q of ABS i and $h_{ji,r}^{AA}$ between interfering ABS j and ABS i are NLOS with short-range path-loss model $PL(dB) = 11.14 + 38.0 \log_{10}(d)$. Here, d is the distance (in meters) between the transmitter and the receiver.

4.2   Learning Algorithm Configuration

The Q-learning learning process is usually organized in two phases, the *exploration*, i.e., the phase in which the algorithm makes random decisions and hence explores (visits) new states, avoiding being trapped in a small group of states and so in local maxima/minima of the problem solution, and the *exploitation*, which is the phase when the algorithm does not make random decisions but tries to minimize the cost. The considered Q-learning passes through 3 different stages: high exploration stage (20% random decisions) during the first third of iterations; a low exploration stage (10% random decisions) during the second third; and finally an exploitation stage with no random decisions. The important parameters configuring the learning algorithm are the number of iterations, i.e., 200000, $\alpha = 0.5$, $\gamma = 0.9$ and the initial values of the Q-table i.e, 10000. The extra cost parameters are: $\gamma_{ec} = 1.4(1 + \frac{r_{1,4}}{r_T})$ and $\alpha_{ec} = 1 + \frac{r_{1,4}}{r_T}$, where $\frac{r_{1,4}}{r_T}$ is the ratio of number of visits to states 1 to 4 to the total number of visits to all the states. The discount parameters are: $\gamma_d = 1.43$ and $\alpha_d = -0.57$.

4.3   Discussion on Performance

Figure 1 shows the number of ABSs satisfying the constraint (6). After a sufficient number of iterations, 15 and later 16 ABSs have learned the optimal decision policy.

Figure 2 compares the total access capacity of the MSs allocated by the N ABSs, normalized with respect to the maximum upper bound capacity of the

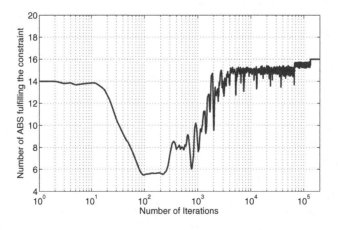

Fig. 1. Number of ABSs satisfying the constraints (6)

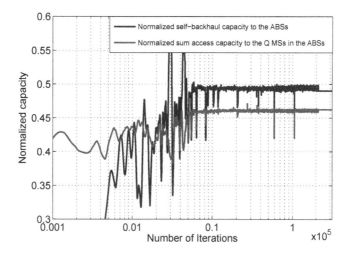

Fig. 2. Normalized total self-backhaul capacity $\hat{C}^H$ compared to the sum of the normalized capacity used for the Q MS allocated in all the ABSs

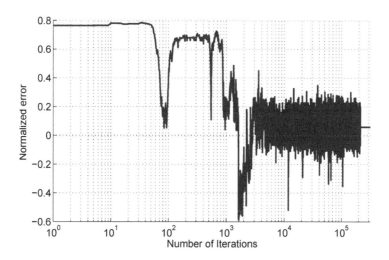

Fig. 3. Normalized error for ABS 4

self-backhaul C_{ub}^H, i.e., $\frac{1}{C_{ub}^H} \sum_{i=1}^{N} \widehat{C^{i,A}}$, to the total normalized capacity of the self-backhaul link $\widehat{C^H}$. It can be observed that the self-backhaul link is about 6 % larger than the access link capacity, which indicates that the designed decentralized system operates effectively.

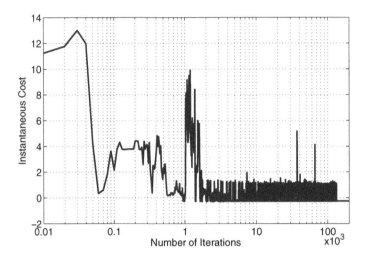

Fig. 4. Instantaneous Cost for ABS 4

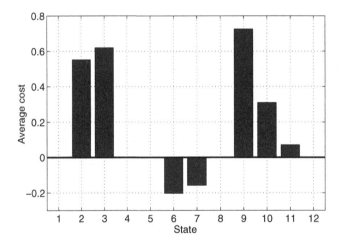

Fig. 5. Average cost value for each state, for ABS 4

In Figure 3, we show the normalized error between $\widehat{C^{i,A}}$ and $C^{i,A}$, defined as:

$$\epsilon = \frac{C^{i,A} - \widehat{C^{i,A}}}{C^{i,A}}. \tag{14}$$

It can be observed that the normalized error is reduced by the learning algorithm, and the oscillations around zero are reduced whilst increasing the number of iterations. Finally, some iterations after the beginning of the exploitation stage, the error remains constant.

Figure 4 shows the instantaneous cost value of one ABS, e.g., ABS 4. The cost is reduced whilst the iterations increase to finally remain level off. There is a clear correspondence between the cost plot and the normalized error plot in Figure 3. For instance, at iteration 1000 a negative peak can be observed in Figure 3, which translates into a stage with a large cost in Figure 4.

In Figure 5, the average values of the cost $c(s, a)$ are shown by states. Here, we can easily distinguish among three groups of states: states 6 and 7 with a small (negative) average cost, states 10 and 11 with an intermediate average cost, and states 2, 3 and 9 with large average costs. This is consistent with the cost function definition in 13.

Finally, Figure 6 shows the final Q-values $Q(s, a)$. Notice that the states with smallest Q-values are states 6, 7, 10 and 11. These correspond to the states where the capacity constraints are accomplished and the $\widehat{C}^H$ achieved is between 0.7 and 0.25 (see Table 1). What is noteworthy is that the two state-action pairs with very small Q-values correspond to states 6 and 7 with the *maintain* power action. This is consistent with the fact that once the ABS has reached a stationary behavior and found the optimal policy, the action most likely to maintain the system in the same conditions is to *maintain* the power at the selected level.

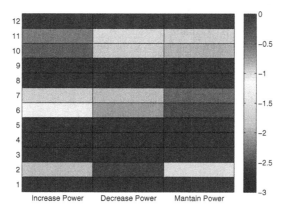

Fig. 6. Final Q-values for ABS 4

5   Conclusions

The prime of this paper was to prove that a stable and decentralized resource allocation is possible in a system where access and backhaul utilize the same time-frequency resources. This is seen as a facilitator for Gbps/km2 systems as the number of ABSs can be scaled with the capacity needs without jeopardizing operational conditions. This fairly aggressive joint access-backhaul cross-segment design contrasts prior resource allocation schemes; a worst case scenario is e.g., the allocation of maximum power which yields an extremely high interference and thus poor performance (not shown in this paper). Future work pertains to the reduction of the number of iterations needed to reach the target performance. A suitable approach could be via the emerging concept of docitive networks [6], where expert nodes teach less expert nodes to improve the learning process.

Acknowledgements

This work was partially supported by BuNGee ICT-248267, the funding of which is gratefully acknowledged.

References

1. The BuNGee website (2010), http://www.ict-bungee.eu/
2. Harmon, M.E., Harmon, S.S.: Reinforcement learning: A tutorial (2000)
3. Watkins, C.J., Dayan, P.: Technical note: Q-learning. Machine Learning 8, 279–292 (1992)
4. Baum, H., Galdo, D., Miljoevic, S., Kyösti: An interim channel model for beyond-3G systems. IEEE (2005)
5. Erceg, V., Hari, K.V.S., Smith, M.S., Baum, D.S.: Channel models for fixed wireless applications. IEEE Broad Band Wireless Working Group, Tech. Rep. 21, 139–150 (2001)
6. Dohler, M., Giupponi, L., Galindo-Serrano, A., Blasco, P.: Docitive networks: A novel framework beyond cognition. IEEE Communications Society, Multimdia Communications TC, E-Letter (January 2010)

Learning-Based Spectrum Selection in Cognitive Radio Ad Hoc Networks

Marco Di Felice[1], Kaushik Roy Chowdhury[2], Cheng Wu[2], Luciano Bononi[1], and Waleed Meleis[2]

[1] Department of Computer Science, University of Bologna, Italy
[2] Department of Electrical and Computer Engineering, Northeastern University, Boston, USA

Abstract. Cognitive Radio Ad Hoc Networks (CRAHNs) must identify the best operational characteristics based on the local spectrum availability, reachability with other nodes, choice of spectrum, while maintaining an acceptable end-to-end performance. The distributed nature of the operation forces each node to act autonomously, and yet has a goal of optimizing the overall network performance. These unique characteristics of CRAHNs make reinforcement learning (RL) techniques an attractive choice as a tool for protocol design. In this paper, we survey the state-of-the-art in the existing RL schemes that can be applied to CRAHNs, and propose modifications from the viewpoint of routing, and link layer spectrum-aware operations. We provide a framework of applying RL techniques for joint power and spectrum allocation as an example of Q-learning. Finally, through simulation study, we demonstrate the benefits of using RL schemes in dynamic spectrum conditions.

Keywords: Reinforcement Learning, Cognitive Radio Ad Hoc Networks, Routing, Spectrum Decision, Spectrum Sensing.

1 Introduction

Recent advances in Software Define Radio (SDR) technology have given an impetus towards developing a new generation of highly reconfigurable wireless devices, leading to the novel paradigm of "intelligent" radio systems. Here, the word "intelligence" refers to the ability of radio devices to learn from and adapt to their environment. Cognitive Radio (CR) constitutes the most promising and investigated approach in this research area. A CR device can be formally defined as a radio which changes its transmitter parameters based on interaction with the environment in which it operates [1]. CR technology is envisaged to solve the current problems of inefficiency in spectrum allocation and usage, by implementing dynamic spectrum access (DSA) techniques and often relying on opportunistic transmission in the licensed frequencies. Moreover, it provides reconfigurability at each layer of the protocol stack, in order to support different transmission access technologies and to dynamically meet the Quality of Service (QoS) requirements of end-users. The CR concept is extended in Cognitive Radio Ad Hoc Networks (CRAHNs), in which the network is deployed in an ad-hoc

E. Osipov et al. (Eds.): WWIC 2010, LNCS 6074, pp. 133–145, 2010.
© Springer-Verlag Berlin Heidelberg 2010

manner with no centralized controllers [1]. However, the benefits in terms of spectrum usage come at the price of higher complexity in the effective deployment of CRAHNs. The problems of how such a network self-organizes and adapts to the dynamic topologies changes and varying spectrum availability are some of the key distinguishing factors. Current research on CRAHNs demonstrates the need for a novel generation of adaptive protocols and algorithms, which should cope with the high fluctuation in the spectrum availability, as well as with diverse QoS requirements [16].

Reinforcement Learning (RL) is a biologically inspired machine learning technique (ML), in which an agent acquires its knowledge through trial-and-error interactions with its environment [2,12]. At each step, the agent performs an action and gets a feedback from the environment, which can be used to optimize its behaviour in the future. The dynamic interaction with the environment and the adaptivity of the learning process are two of the main features which make RL techniques appealing for CRAHNs applications, mainly for routing and spectrum decision tasks [7,9]. In some cases, the RL-based solutions are proved to work better than traditional solutions [3,17,22]. However, a comprehensive analysis of benefits and risks of RL techniques over CRAHNs is still missing.

This paper investigates the application of RL techniques over CRAHNs, as a general framework for the deployment of intelligent and reconfigurable radio networks. We provide three main contributions in this research field. First, we analyze benefits and drawbacks of RL approach over CRAHNs (Section 2), by identifying the RL techniques which are best suitable for protocol design (Section 3). Second, we review existing RL-based proposals, for these CRAHNs issues: routing (Section 4.1), spectrum sensing (Section 4.2) and spectrum decision (Section 4.3). Most of the solutions are single-layer, and try to learn the optimal configuration of a single parameter (e.g. spectrum in the spectrum decision problem, next-hop node in routing). Third, we show in Section 5 how RL techniques can be applied for solving complex problems like interference-control in CRAHNs, where each CR user should learn the optimal combination of multiple parameters (e.g. power and spectrum), in a distributed way. We conclude our work in Section 6.

2   RLs over CRAHNs: Benefits and Challenges

Cognitive Radio Ad Hoc Networks (CRAHNs) are multi-hop wireless networks, composed of two kind of users: cognitive radio (CR) users and primary users (PUs) [1]. PUs have license to access the licensed spectrum. CR users may opportunistically transmit in the spectrum holes. The effective deployment of multi-hop CRAHNs depends on the design of efficient spectrum sensing and selection techniques, and of novel routing and transport layer protocols [16]. RL techniques are suitable for protocol design in CRAHNs, as demonstrated by numerous prior works in the literature (Section 4). The main benefits provided by the RL approach are:

- *Adaptivity.* RL techniques help a node to adapt its behavior to the dynamic spectrum environment, by combining exploration and exploitation actions. This is required, for example, by routing protocols, which must identify the best path between CR source-destination nodes, while the quality of each path may dynamically change over time as a function of PU activity, intra-network CR interference, and so on [9].
- *Network-awareness.* RL allows to implement a spectrum-aware paradigm of communication. Many different factors, such as the radio resources and the channel heterogeneity affect the CRAHNs performance in a complex way. Instead of addressing a single factor at a time, a RL agent can observe all the factors as a state, receive an aggregate feedback (e.g. the cost of each transmission) and optimize a general goal as a whole, e.g. throughput [22].
- *Distributed implementation.* In most cases, RL techniques provide a simple yet effective modeling approach [2]. Moreover, multi-agent RL algorithms [5] can be deployed by each node of the network in a distributed way, introducing a limited network overhead.

At the same time, the main drawbacks of RL techniques over CRAHNs are:

- *Random fluctuations.* RL techniques may force a CR node to perform random actions as it learns about the environment, so that feedbacks about the cost of each state-action pair are collected. The benefits of exploration constitute a trade-off with the increased cost of the learning process, which may select suboptimal actions, and thus lead to temporary performance degradation.
- *Slow convergence.* Many RL techniques (specially Time Discounted methods [2]) guarantee convergence to the optimal policy only if each action is executed in each state an infinite number of times. This is clearly not realistic for wireless applications. However, we also highlight that convergence is not fundamental for CRAHNs protocols, due to the non-stationary characteristics of the network environment.

Many different RL algorithms have been proposed in the literature [2]. In some cases, the difficulty relies in identifying the algorithm which best applies to the CRAHNs problem. To this aim, in Section 4 we review the basic RL model and discuss the RL algorithms which are suitable for CRAHNs issues.

3   RL Techniques

In the RL model [2,12], an agent interacts with its environment over a potential infinite sequence of discrete time steps $t = 1, 2, 3, \ldots$. At each step, it observes the current environment, selects a possible action and receives a reward from the environment for that specific action. The goal of the agent is to decide the sequences of actions maximizing some cumulative measures of the rewards, over time. RL model is defined by a Markov Decision Process (MDP), consisting in:

- A discrete *set of states* S which constitute the environment.
- A discrete *set of actions* A.

- A *reward function* $R : S \times A \longrightarrow \Re$.
- A *state-distribution function* $T : S \times A \times S \longrightarrow [0, 1]$.

The environment is defined by a discrete set of states (i.e. S) and must be observable (or partially observable) by the RL agent. The reward function R specifies the expected instantaneous reward, as a function of the current state and of the action performed. For each tuple $< s, a, s' >$, the state-distribution function $T(s, a, s')$ gives the probability to transit from state s to state s' after executing action a. Additionally, the policy π defines the mapping between the states and actions, for each step t. The goal of the agent is to find the optimal policy, defined according to different reward models [2,12]. In the *infinite-horizon discount model*, the policy π attempts to maximize the long-run expected reward, but discounts the rewards received in the future, i.e.:

$$E(\sum_{t=0}^{\infty} \gamma^t r_t) \tag{1}$$

where $0 \leq \gamma \leq 1$ is a discount factor which determines the weight of future rewards. If $\gamma = 0$, the agent aims only at maximizing its immediate reward.

Most of the RL algorithms are based on the concept of state-value function (V) and state-action function (Q). The state value function $V^\pi(s)$ defines the expected reward when executing the policy π, from state s. Analogously, the state-action function $Q^\pi(a, s)$ gives the expected reward when the agent is in state s, executes action a and then follows the policy π. Several RL techniques proposed in the literature differ in the way $V^\pi(s)$ and $Q^\pi(a, s)$ functions are updated at each step, till the optimal policy π^* is found [2,12].

Most suitable RL techniques for CRAHNs are:

Model-based learning. These algorithms requires a model of the environment, i.e. the reward R and state-distribution T functions. For example, the Dyna architecture [15] uses experience to build a model of the environment, and through the model it adjusts the policy in use. It learns T and R by incrementing statistics after each transition from s to s' and averaging the reward $R(s, a)$. Model-based learning techniques have been applied for routing in wireless ad hoc networks [8], modelling the quality of each link as a stochastic process. Generally speaking, it might be difficult to learn the models of the environment in CRAHNs, due to the large number of parameters affecting the network performance.

Q-learning. Q-learning [23] is an on-line RL algorithm which attempts to estimate the optimal action-state function $Q(s, a)$, without requiring a model of the environment and a representation of the policy in use i.e. π. Let the agent be in state s, execute action a and then observe the reward r and the next state s'. Q-learning updates the Q function in this way:

$$Q(s, a) \rightarrow Q(s, a) + \alpha[r + \gamma max_{a'} Q(s', a') - Q(s, a)], \tag{2}$$

where γ is the discount factor discussed above and α is a parameter tuning the speed of learning. At each state s, the agent chooses the action a which maximizes the $Q(s, a)$ values (*exploitation*), or chooses randomly among the available actions (*exploration*). Q-learning can be easily implemented over distributed systems, with low overhead in terms of communication, computation and memory usage. As a result, Q-Learning has been applied to different problems over CRAHNs, e.g. PU sensing detection [3], spectrum selection [24] and routing [6]. The main drawback is the speed of learning, which depends on the accurate tuning of the γ and α parameters.

Dual RL. This algorithm is very similar to the Q-learning scheme, but it updates the $Q(s, a)$ values also considering the value of the previous state, instead of next state only [14]. Dual RL techniques have been applied to routing problems in CRAHNs, so that each time a packet is transmitted on a link the $Q(s, a)$ are updated at both transmitter and receivers nodes [22]. Dual RL enhances Q-learning in terms of speed of convergence, but it introduces some additional overheads for its implementation.

Multi-Agent Learning. These techniques extend classical RL algorithms, in a system of homogeneous agents which have system-wide optimization goals. Cooperative RL techniques attempt to coordinate the behavior of the agents, so that a coherent joint behavior is observed [5]. Many CRAHNs problems can be formulated as cooperative problems. For instance, CR users should distributively learn an optimal strategy to control the interference at the primary receivers, at maintain it under a given threshold [10]. The main drawbacks of this approach are: the additional overhead, required for the agent cooperation, and the complexity in implementation, which may also affect the converge of the learning process. At present, very few applications have been proposed for wireless systems [10].

4   RL Applications for CRAHNs

In this section, we review existing RL-applications from the viewpoint of higher level protocol implementations in CRAHNs: (*i*) routing (Section 4.1), (*ii*) link layer spectrum sensing (Section 4.2) and (*iii*) link layer spectrum decision (Section 4.3). For each domain, we analyze the RL-formulation, we shortly review the most significant RL-based protocols proposed in the literature and we discuss advantages and open issues.

4.1   Routing Protocols

Problem Formulation. In CRAHNs, routing protocols have the twofold goal of (*i*) discovering a path from a CR source to a CR destination node, by avoiding regions characterized by PUs activity, and of (*ii*) accounting the spectrum to be used on each intermediate link. Moreover, they should be able to cope with the dynamics of CRAHNs, e.g. mobility, PU interference, variable link quality. As a result, spectrum awareness and re-configurability are two important requirements for routing protocols over CRAHNs [16]. The routing process can be modeled as a RL task, in which the CR source node must learn the optimal

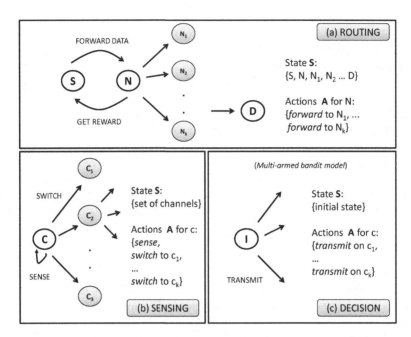

Fig. 1. The MDP process for a generic routing algorithm (a), spectrum sensing problem (b) and spectrum detection problem (c)

path toward the destination by a trial and error interaction [9]. For each data transmission, the CR node receives a reward which is an an estimate of the cost of forwarding, e.g. mean-access delay or amount of energy consumed. The MDP process for a generic routing protocol is depicted in Figure 1(a).

RL-based approaches. Q-routing [18] is a routing protocol for dynamically changing networks, which has been applied in wireless ad hoc networks [6]. It is an application of the Q-Learning scheme, where each node x:

- Has a *set of actions* A, which correspond to the set of neighbors of node x.
- Receives a *reward* r after forwarding a packet to a neighbor y, which is an estimation of the transmission delay between node x and y.
- Maintains a *table* of Q values for each destination d, where the entry $Q_d(y, d)$ is the *expected delivery time* to d using next-hop node y.

After forwarding a packet to node y with destination d, node x updates its Q-table entry in this way:

$$Q_d(x, y) = q_x + \delta + min_z Q_d(y, z) \qquad (3)$$

where q_x is the time spent by the packet in the queue of x, δ is the transmission delay and $min_z Q_d(y, z)$ is the best delivery time for node y and for destination d. In [6], Q-routing is evaluated for classical wireless ad hoc networks, and the Q-table is enlarged to take into account different parameters, e.g. network connectivity and residual energy of each node. In [21], the authors propose the LQ-routing protocol, which uses the conventional Q-routing approach, but also introduces the notion of route lifetime to represent the stability of routes connecting to the destination. SAMPLE [8] protocol models the routing process as a collaborative RL-task among the nodes of the network. The main features of the SAMPLE protocol are: (i) it keeps a statistical model of the quality of each link, based on the ratio of successful over attempted unicast transmissions, (ii) it uses a decay function, so that routes which are not advertised are gradually degraded and (iii) it exploits piggybacking techniques to disseminate Q-values inside the network. The authors of [22] propose two RL-based spectrum-aware routing protocols for CRAHNs. Here, the CR nodes store a table of Q-values that estimate the number of available channels on the routes, as a function of the PUs activity. The Q-values are updated after each successful transmission, using a Dual RL technique. Then, each CR node forwards a packet to the next-hop node which guarantees more available channels toward to the destination.

Discussion. All the Q-routing variants discussed so far are shown to improve the performance of classical ad hoc routing schemes (e.g. AODV, DSR, DSDV), in most of the evaluated scenarios. However, except for [8,22], they do not take into account spectrum considerations, which are fundamental for routing over CRAHNs. Moreover, none of the previous approach integrates channel and next-hop selection into the learning process.

4.2 Spectrum Sensing

Problem Formulation. In CRAHNs, each CR user should perform periodic sensing on the channel in use, to avoid collisions with PUs. Additionally, it must observe the available spectral resources in all the other bands, in order to detect spectrum holes and to switch to a new band, if necessary [1]. While sensing, a CR user can not use the channel for communicating with other nodes. Finding the optimal tradeoff between channel sensing and channel exploitation involves a learning process in which each node should determine the frequency and duration of sensing, on each channel. Spectral resource detection can be modeled as a RL-problem, through an MDP (Figure 1(b)). The available number of licensed bands constitute the set of states S of the MDP. At each step, the CR user can perform one of these actions: (i) transmit on the current band, (ii) sense the current or another band or (iii) switch to another band.

RL-based approaches. In [3], the authors solve the spectral detection problem discussed above by using an actor-critic RL approach [2]. After each action, a CR node receives a reward which is: the number of available subcarriers in case of transmission, 0 in case of sensing and a fixed penalty in case of switching. Using the reward, the CR node updates the state values e.g. $V(s)$, and computes the reliability of each state, which is then used by the actor to update the current policy π. Error-free PU detection is assumed by the authors of [3]. In [20], the Q-learning technique is used to detect the presence of PU on the spectrum in use by CR users, in order to reduce the occurrence of mis-detection and false detection events. In the implementation proposed in [20], each Q-value represents the signal strength detected during sensing on a given channel.

Discussion. The simulation results in [3] show that their proposed RL-scheme can quickly converge to the optimal solution in scenarios with stationary PU activity, but do not address the environments with dynamically changing availability of the spectrum resources.

4.3   Spectrum Decision

Problem Formulation. In CRAHN, each CR user should determine a channel where to transmit, given the twofold objective of (*i*) maximizing the overall performance for stable QoS provisioning and of (*ii*) mitigating the interference to PUs. The spectrum heterogeneity implies that different channels might be characterized by different properties (in terms of e.g. transmitting range, data-rate, Bit Error Rate) and varying activity patterns by PUs, over time. Spectrum decision can be modeled as a MDP process for each CR user i, as shown in Figure 1(c). The reward can be a local feedback of the node or a network-wide metric (e.g. total interference to PU receivers).

RL-based approaches. Q-learning based spectrum allocation has been extensively investigated for cellular networks [4,19]. In CRAHNs, the authors of [24] consider the RL-formulation discussed above, and assign rewards to the CR users after each data transmission. For each positive data packet transmission, there is a positive constant value of $+RW$, otherwise a negative constant value $-CT$ is incurred. In practice, the value of RW and CT should be the amount of revenue and cost that a network operator earns or incurs for each data successful transmission or failure [24]. In [11], the authors consider a network case composed by a set of transmitting-receiving pairs of nodes. At each step, the Signal-to-Noise Ratio (SNR) is computed at the receivers node. If the SNR value is higher than a given threshold, then the transmitter node increases its Q-value of a fixed weight factor, otherwise it applies a penalty and quits the current spectrum. In [17], an analytical modeling of dynamic spectrum allocation over CRAHNs is proposed. Simulation results show that Q-learning enhances a random spectrum allocation scheme, and its performance are comparable with those of the analytical model. In [10], the authors consider a secondary CR system based on the IEEE 802.22 standard, and apply RL techniques to learn how to control the aggregated interference at the PUs receivers. To this aim, the authors propose a Q-learning based distributed scheme. However, the overhead of the proposed solution is not shown in [10].

Discussion. All the Q-learning solution described so far are shown to provide adaptive and dynamic channel selection for CRAHNs. Performance results show that in some cases RL-based approaches guarantee higher performance than classical distributed channel selection scheme. However, none of the previous scheme take into account the PUs interference into the MDP process. Moreover, they do not provide an analytical modeling of the reward function, which is usually modeled through a scalar vector [11,24].

5   RL Case Study: Joint Spectrum and Power Allocation

In this section, we consider a case study of RL techniques for wireless ad hoc cognitive sensors networks. They are composed of small, resource constrained nodes, which are suited for monitoring, data gathering, and surveillance operations. In contrast to the classical sensor network, our proposed cognitive sensors can intelligently choose their spectrum for transmission, transmit power, and thereby support high bandwidth applications. This network model poses several challenges. Firstly, the frequency space may be large, composed of several dozens of channels. Moreover, the sensors are typically deployed in large densities, and their individual transmit powers directly decide the level of interference to several nodes in the neighborhood. Here, we show how the spectrum and power allocation problem can be modeled through an multi-agent RL model, so that each CR sensor (also called as agent here) locally adjusts its choice of spectrum, and its transmit power, subject to connectivity and interference constraints.

We assume time to be slotted, and at the start of each slot, the sensor senses the spectrum with perfect accuracy. If the spectrum is available, it goes ahead with the transmission. Now, this transmission may be successful, or it may result in a collision. Through receiver feedback, we allow the sender node to be informed if the collision was a result of intra-CR network interference, or due to simultaneous transmission by a neighboring PU. Based on the result of the transmission, an appropriate reward is assigned to the choice of the state, which in turn, determines future choices of spectrum and power. Considering the RL model described in Section 3, we define the *state* of an agent as the current spectrum and power value of its transmission. We therefore define the state of the system at time t, denoted s_t as:

$$s_t = (\vec{s_p}; \vec{p_w})_t \tag{4}$$

where $\vec{s_p}$ is a vector of spectrums and $\vec{p_w}$ is a vector of power values across all agents. Analogously, we define the set of action a_t at time t as:

$$a_t = \vec{k_t}; \tag{5}$$

where $\vec{k}$ is a vector of actions across all agents. Here k_i is the action of the i-th agent and $k_i = \{jump_{spectrum}; jump_{power}\}$, e.g. each agent can switch from its current spectrum to a new available spectrum, or switch from its current power value to another power value. After each transmission, a CR user receives a reward, which is used to adjust the current policy π. We consider the following different reward r values for different network conditions [13]:

1. *Interference between PU and Sensors*: When the licensed user and the sensor transmit concurrently in the same spectrum, in the same slot, the receiving sensor may experience a collision. Moreover, the PU receiver too may be unable to receive the PU transmission correctly, which is a serious degradation of performance, and must be avoided. Thus, we allocate a comparatively higher penalty P_{PU}, which is equal to -15 in our experiments.
2. *Intra-sensor network Collision*: If the collision is caused by simultaneous transmissions by multiple sensor nodes, then we apply a fixed penalty P_{COL}, equal to -5 in our experiments.
3. *Channel Induced Errors*: The inherent fluctuations in the channel quality, sudden drops in signal strength caused by fading, and noise characteristics result in channel induced bit-flips that may cause the packet to be dropped. We apply the same penalty P_{COL} of the previous discussed case here, thereby forcing the sender to switch to a more robust channel.
4. *Link Disconnection*: If the received power (P_{rx}^j) is less than the threshold of the receiver P_{rth} (here, assumed as -85 dBm), then all the packets are dropped. In such cases, the sender should quickly increase its choice of transmit power so that the link can be re-established. We address this case by applying a fixed penalties P_{LD}, which is equal to -20 in our experiments.
5. *Successful Transmission*: If none of the above conditions are observed to be true in the given transmission slot, then packet is successfully transmitted from the sender to receiver. Since the actual combination of spectrum/power produced a successful outcome, we encourage the agent to stay in the current state through a positive reward (e.g +5 in our experiments).

The learning algorithm is based on a revised version of the Q-learning algorithm described in Section 3. Details of our learning algorithm can be found in [13]. In this paper, we focus on the comparison between the RL-based approach with other classical spectrum and power selection schemes for a random topology CRAHN with 100 CR users. In the Random (RA) scheme, each CR user selects a random combination of spectrum and power in each slot. In the Dynamic Spectrum Assignment (DSA) scheme, each CR user chooses the less interfered spectrum in its 1-hop neighborhood, and switches to a new spectrum band in case of PU detection. Moreover, each CR user chooses the minimum power level, which provides network connectivity with the receiver node. Each CR user can switch among 10 available spectrum bands, where each band has different Bit Error Rate (BER) and transmitting range characteristics. The permissible power values for the CR users are uniformly distributed on 10 discrete levels between $0.5m - 4$ mW. We consider a CRAHN with 25 PUs, where each PU is randomly assigned one default channel in which it stays. We consider two network configurations: (*i*) *stationary* PU activity, i.e. each PU is always active on its band, and (*ii*) *dynamic* PU activity, i.e. each PU is active on its band with a given probability P_{active}. Fig 2(a) shows the average probability of successful transmission over simulation time, in the stationary case. The time scale on the *x-axis* is represented by epochs, each of which is composed of 50 time slots. From Fig. 2(a), we can see that the RL-based approach quickly converges after a learning phase, and provides higher performance than the non-RL schemes. Fig. 2(b) shows the average probability of successful transmission for the stationary case, as a function of the CR system load. The performance improvement of the RL-based scheme is even more consistent under higher saturation conditions. Fig 2(c) shows the average probability of successful transmission for the non-stationary case, where we vary the P_{active} parameter on the x-axis. In this case, the CR users should dynamically adapt their behavior based on the spectrum availability. Again, the RL-approach shows its suitability for operating in dynamically environment.

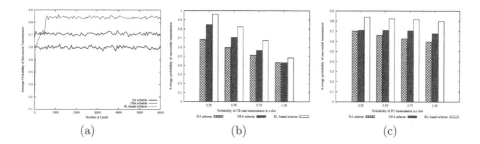

(a)   (b)   (c)

Fig. 2. The average probability of successful transmission for the stationary case is shown in Figure 2(a) and 2(b). The average probability of successful transmission as a function of the PU activity is shown in Figure 2(c).

6 Conclusions

In this paper, we addressed the application of Reinforcement Learning (RL) techniques for distributed network protocols in CRAHNs. We surveyed several RL techniques and their applications in three different CRAHNs domains, i.e. routing, spectrum sensing and spectrum decision. We found that in many cases RL-based schemes provide high adaptability to the varying spectrum conditions. However, only few protocols have been evaluated against classical schemes for CRAHNs. Moreover, few of them address joint optimization of cross-layer parameters. To this aim, we proposed our RL-framework for the joint selection of optimal spectrum and transmit power in CRAHNs. The proposed framework have been compared with other non-learning scheme. Simulation results show the performance improvement of the RL-based scheme under both stationary and dynamic spectrum environments.

References

1. Akyildiz, I., Lee, W.Y., Chowdhury, K.R.: CRAHNs: Cognitive Radio Ad Hoc Networks. Ad Hoc Networks Journal 7(5), 810–836 (2009)
2. Barto, A.G., Sutton, R.: Reinforcement Learning: An Introduction. MIT Press, Cambridge (1998)

3. Berhold, U., Fu, F., Van Der Schaar, M., Jondral, F.K.: Detection of Spectral Resources in Cognitive Radios Using Reinforcement Learning. In: Proc. of Dyspan'08, Chicago, pp. 1–5 (2008)

4. Bernardo, F., Augusti, R., Perez-Romero, J., Sallent, O.: Distributed Spectrum Management based on Reinforcement Learning. In: Proc. of CROWNCOM'09, Hannover (2009)

5. Busoniu, L., Babuska, R., De Schutter, B.: A Comprehensive Survey of Multi-Agent Reinforcement Learning. IEEE Transactions on Systems, Man, and Cybernetics 38(2), 156–172 (2008)

6. Chetret, D., Tham, C., Wong, L.: Reinforcement Learning and CMAC-based Adaptive Routing for MANETs. In: Proc. of ICON'04, pp. 540–544 (2004)

7. Clancy, C., Hecker, J., Stuntebeck, E., O'Shea, T.: Applications of Machine Learning to Cognitive Radio Networks. Wireless Communications 14(4), 47–52 (2007)

8. Dowling, J., Curran, E., Cunningham, R., Cahill, V.: Using Feedback in Collaborative Reinforcement Learning to Adaptively Optimize MANET Routing. IEEE Transactions on Systems, Man and Cybernetics 35(3), 360–372 (2005)

9. Forster, A.: Machine Learning Techniques Applied for Wireless Ad-Hoc Networks: Guide and Survey. In: Proc. of ISSNIP'07, Melbourne, pp. 367–370 (2007)

10. Galindo-Serrano, A., Giupponi, L.: Aggregated Interference Control for Cognitive Radio Networks Based on Multi-Agent Learning. In: Proc. of CROWNCOM'09, Hannover (2009)

11. Jiang, T., Grace, D., Liu, Y.: Performance of Cognitive Radio Reinforcement Spectrum Sharing Using Different Weighting Factors. In: Proc. of CHINACOM'08, Hangzhou, pp. 1195–1199 (2008)

12. Kaelbling, L.P., Littman, M.L., Moore, A.W.: Reinforcement Learning: A Survey. Journal of Artificial Intelligence Research 4(1), 237–285 (1996)

13. Wu, C., Chowdhury, K.R., Di Felice, M., Meleis, W.: Spectrum Management of Cognitive Radio Using Multi-agent Reinforcement Learning. To appear on Proc. of AAMAS'10, Toronto (2010)

14. Kumar, S., Miikkulainen, R.: Dual Reinforcement Q-Routing: An Online Adaptive Routing Algorithm. In: Proc. of Artificial Neural Networks in Engineering Conference, St. Louis, pp. 231–238 (1997)

15. Kuvayev, L., Sutton, R.: Model-based Reinforcement Learning with an approximate, Learned Model. In: Proc. of the Yale Workshop on Adaptive and Learning Systems, Yale, pp. 101–105 (1996)

16. Kyasanur, P., Vaidya, N.H.: Protocol Design Challenges for Multi-hop Dynamic Spectrum Access Networks. In: Proc. of DySPAN'05, Baltimore, pp. 645–648 (2005)

17. Lim, K.A., Komisarczuk, P., Teal, P.D.: Performance Analysis of Reinforcement Learning for Achieving Context-Awareness and Intelligence in Cognitive Radio Networks. In: Proc. of WLN'09, Zurich, pp. 11–35 (1999)

18. Litman, M., Boyan, J.: Packet routing in dynamically changing networks: a reinforcement learning approach. Advances in Neural Information Processing Systems 7(1), 671–678 (1994)

19. Nie, J., Haykin, S.: A Dynamic Channel Assignment Policy Through Q-Learning. IEEE Transactions on Neural Networks 10(1), 1443–1455 (1999)

20. Reddy, Y.B.: Detecting Primary Signals for Efficient Utilization of Spectrum Using Q-Learning. In: Proc. of ITNG'08, Las Vegas, pp. 360–365 (2008)

21. Tao, T., Tagashira, S., Fujita, S.: LQ-Routing Protocol for Mobile Ad Hoc Networks. In: Proc. of ICIS'05, Washington, pp. 441–446 (2005)
22. Wahab, B., Yang, Y., Fan, Z., Sooriyabandara, M.: Reinforcement Learning Based Spectrum-aware Routing in Multi-hop Cognitive Radio Networks. In: Proc. of CROWNCOM'09, Hannover (2009)
23. Watkins, C.: Learning from delayed rewards. PhD thesis, Cambridge, UK (1989)
24. Yau, K.-L.A., Komisarczuk, P., Teal, P.D.: A Context-aware and Intelligent Dynamic Channel Selection Scheme for Cognitive Radio Networks. In: Proc. of CROWNCOM'09, Hannover (2009)

Frequency Agility in IPv6-Based Wireless Personal Area Networks (6LoWPAN)
(Invited Paper)

Riccardo Tomasi[1], Hussein Khaleel[1,2], Federico Penna[1,2], Claudio Pastrone[1], Roberto Garello[2], and Maurizio Spirito[1]

[1] Istituto Superiore Mario Boella, Torino, Italy
{lastname}@ismb.it
[2] Politecnico di Torino, Dipartimento di Elettronica, Torino, Italy
{firstname.lastname}@polito.it

Abstract. This paper presents a demonstrator of a multi-hop 6LoW-PAN provided with frequency-agility extensions. A reference architecture is presented along with the basic components introduced to build a distributed spectrum sensing and interference resolution service in a multi-hop environment. Moreover, a frequency-agility management plane is proposed for the 6LoWPAN communication stack. The proposed solution is implemented in a small-scale network adopting TinyOS and an open-source implementation of 6LoWPAN protocol stack. The resulting demonstrator proves the capability of the proposed system to characterize the spectrum occupancy state in a multi-hop environment. In addition, it shows the ability of the network to reallocate to the best available channel in case a critical level of interference is detected on the current operating channel.

1   Introduction

An unprecedented growth of embedded short-range wireless devices operating in the Industrial, Scientific and Medical (ISM) bands is expected when the "Internet Of Things" [1] will become a reality. In order to make this paradigm practical with billions of devices deployed on the field, efficient spectrum sharing techniques and protocols must be defined and adopted.

Nowadays, the 2.4 GHz ISM band is already one of the most crowded parts of the spectrum. Numerous wireless systems – IEEE 802.11 Wireless Local Area Networks (WLANs), IEEE 802.15.4 Wireless Personal Area Networks (WPANs) [2], Bluetooth [3], etc. – operate in this band, causing potential coexistence problems that affect especially low-power devices.

Most of the above systems implement already some methods at PHY/MAC layer to cope with interference. For instance, Bluetooth implements a frequency hopping scheme: after transmitting or receiving a packet, the system hops to a new frequency according to a predefined pseudo-random sequence of channels. IEEE 802.15.4, which defines PHY and MAC layers of WPANs, makes

E. Osipov et al. (Eds.): WWIC 2010, LNCS 6074, pp. 146–157, 2010.
© Springer-Verlag Berlin Heidelberg 2010

use of Direct Sequence Spread Spectrum (DSSS) to increase the physical layer robustness. Additional techniques at higher layers of the protocol stack might be required to cope with interference. The widely adopted Zigbee standard [4], based on IEEE 802.15.4, relies on a particular device, named network manager, to gather network interference reports and to switch frequency if needed. To support such features the ZigBee standard defines protocol messages only and leaves the design of interference detection mechanisms and frequency agility policies to vendors.

Interference is expected to be a major issue also in the emerging IETF proposed standard known as 6LoWPAN (IPv6 over Low power Wireless Personal Area Networks) [5,6,7]. 6LoWPAN also adopts IEEE 802.15.4 and is foreseen to become a reference solution for the upcoming "Internet Of Things". In such types of large-scale networks, interference issues are still to be thoroughly addressed by the research community, and efficient, scalable and interoperable solutions have not been identified, yet.

In recent years, the problem of coexistence of heterogeneous networks in the ISM band has received significant attention from the scientific literature as well. Non-standard solutions to enable frequency-agile coexistence between IEEE 802.15.4 (WPAN) and IEEE 802.11 (Wi-Fi) networks have been proposed in [8,9,10]. In [11,12,13,14], methods based on the Cognitive Radio (CR) [15,16] have been presented that treat users with lower power and more vulnerable to interference (e.g., WPAN devices) as "secondary users", and Wi-Fi as the "primary" network. Efficient coexistence is thus enabled by implementation of *spectrum sensing* techniques in secondary devices, in order to identify time-frequency slots ("spectrum holes") left free by primary users.

The present work extends reference [14] and applies a similar CR-based frequency agility model to 6LoWPAN networks. Due to the expected wide diffusion of this technology in the next years, it is crucial to ensure to 6LoWPAN devices robustness and protection from interference in all operating conditions. In addition, this work considers spectrum sensing in *multi-hop* scenarios, where measurements collected by end-devices can be forwarded through one or more 6LoWPAN router nodes. Also, the network may be divided into multiple clusters, in charge of detecting interference in different regions. Spatially-diversified information on spectrum occupancy is then fused by a centralized network entity, and a global decision on the "best available channel" is made based on a suitable evaluation metric.

The remainder of the paper is organized as follows: in Sec. 2 a reference high-level design for frequency-agile 6LoWPANs is proposed; in Sec. 3 a proof-of-concept demonstrator is described; in Sec. 4 conclusions and future work are outlined.

2   Frequency Agile 6LoWPAN Design

This section proposes a possible reference architecture for a 6LoWPAN provided with Frequency Agility (FA) extensions. The purpose of this section is to specify such functionalities and outline their relationship with the 6LoWPAN stack and other relevant protocols.

FA extensions can be applied to different classes of LoWPANs (Low-power WPANs) as defined in [7]: ad-hoc LoWPANs, simple LoWPANs or to Extended LoWPANs (i.e. LoWPANs with multiple Edge Routers belonging to the same network domain and connected via a backbone link). The remaining of the paper is focused on the case of Simple LoWPANs, but the design can be easily extended to suit other LoWPAN classes.

2.1 Reference Scenario, Architecture and Definitions

In simple LoWPANs, Routers (R) and End-devices, also known as Hosts (H) form a multi-hop tree which is rooted at the Edge Router (E) node. R nodes can provide packet forwarding to other nodes, while H nodes can only assume the role of "leaf" nodes. All these nodes are provided with a 6LoWPAN communication stack enhanced with FA extensions (see reference architecture in Fig. 1.*i*).

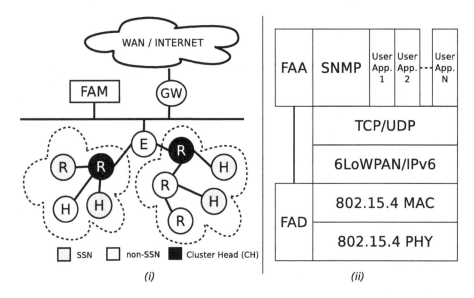

Fig. 1. Reference architecture *(i)* and proposed FA extensions to 6LoWPAN stack *(ii)*

All radio transceivers of the nodes within the LoWPAN are tuned on the same IEEE 802.15.4 channel, called "operating channel".

The current operating channel might suffer from interference generated by several external sources. In order to enable the LoWPAN to detect such interference and move to a less interfered channel, a number of nodes can be configured to operate as Spectrum-Sensing Nodes (SSNs). SSNs can be either specific nodes, installed for this purpose, or general-purpose nodes configured to dedicate some resources to detect interference. Non-SSNs nodes are LowPAN nodes equipped with FA capabilities but not participating to spectrum sensing. The role of each node can be changed at runtime in order to properly share the workload among the nodes of the network.

The key idea can be summarized as follows. SSNs can independently monitor different IEEE 802.15.4 channels for interference through an Energy Detection procedure and communicate the result of this operation to a central entity, called Frequency Agility Manager (FAM). The FAM can determine whether the conditions on the current operating channel are still acceptable or not. In the latter case the FAM forces the whole LoWPAN (both SSNs and non-SSNs) to move to a new channel with better interference conditions.

In order to extend the 6LoWPAN stack to include FA capabilities, two new modules are defined, namely the Frequency Agility Driver (FAD) and the Frequency Agility Agent (FAA) (Fig. 1.ii). The FAD is a low-level module, designed to provide a wrapper for local FA-related commands offered by the IEEE 802.15.4 stack. The FAD leverages on IEEE 802.15.4 functionalities for tasks such as Energy Detection or setting the operating channel of the local transceiver [2]. The FAA is a high-level module superseding the control of FA-related functionalities for the local node. The FAA is in charge of running FA routines and exposing the control of FA operations and configurable parameters to the FAM. Configurable parameters include, for example, how often and for how long the local node should perform Energy Detection.

Performing the aforementioned operation in a large-scale network, the use of a "flat" hierarchy would generate a large amount of many-to-one multi-hop traffic (from each SSN to the FAM and vice-versa), resulting in scalability problems. In light of this observation, to cope with large-scale LoWPANs it is thus assumed that the network can be partitioned in clusters and that a Cluster Head (CH) can be selected among the available R nodes within each cluster. The selection of a specific method for LoWPAN partitioning or CH Selection is outside the scope of this work (suitable methods are available in [17,18]).

Let M be the number of clusters in the network, N the total number of nodes in the network and N_m the number of nodes in cluster m. Clustering should enhance scalability by reducing FA-related traffic by an N_m factor in a LoWPAN-wide scale, moving part of the FA-related traffic to a more local cluster-wide scale. In up-link, clusters limit the traffic from SSNs to the FAM by aggregating FA information from spatially-close SSNs. In down-link, they limit traffic from the FAM to SSNs by delegating CHs to actually control nodes belonging to the cluster, when a command from the FAM is issued.

2.2   FA Model and Procedures

FA-related procedures are described in details in Fig. 2. All FA-related communications occur on the current operating channel, chosen by the FAM among the 16 available IEEE 802.15.4 channels. Such behavior is referred to as "in-band signaling".

We denote by $\mathcal{C}$ the available channel set (i.e., for IEEE 802.15.4, $\mathcal{C} = \{11, \ldots, 26\}$) and by $c_S \in \mathcal{C}$ the current operating channel.

Periodically, each SSN (i) performs Energy Detection on a certain subset of channels $\mathcal{C}_i \subseteq \mathcal{C}$, and then builds a quantized energy Probability Density Function (PDF) from the detected energy values[1]. SSNs can perform these operations by following the procedure described in [14].

Different channel subsets $\mathcal{C}_i$ are assigned by the CH to SSNs in its cluster, such that

$$\bigcup_{i=1}^{N_m} \mathcal{C}_i = \mathcal{C}$$

for each cluster m. In such way, a complete spectrum scan is performed by each cluster, while the sensing burden is distributed among different nodes and the timeliness of FA-information is maximized. Subset assignments are implemented as channel masks sent by the CH to each of the SSNs.

The CH then merges the energy PDFs received from the cluster SSNs and, periodically, transmits this data (i.e. an up-to-date map of the spectrum occupation for the considered cluster) to the FAM.

In addition, traffic within the cluster, including FA packets containing PDFs, can be exploited by the CH to assess packet loss rate through low-power channel quality estimation techniques (e.g. [19]). Such techniques, characterized by low computational cost and small protocol overhead, provide to the CH an additional channel reliability metric for each one-hop link within the cluster. It is important to observe that such techniques are necessarily "blind" with respect to the causes of packet loss, which might be either interference or e.g. low received power caused by high distance. Using such metrics, the CH is thus able to compute an aggregated, cluster-wide "average" packet loss indication.

The FAM collects the spectrum information received from different clusters and uses it to evaluate the spectrum occupancy state in the network. The following metrics are taken into account:

- *Outage probability* per channel [13]: the probability that the energy of the interfering signal exceeds a given threshold, representing the maximum energy of interference tolerable by WPANs for correct communication.
- *Periodogram*: the average Received Signal Strength Indication (RSSI) value per channel, computed as the statistical mean of the PDF.
- *Spectrogram*: a representation of the channel occupancy state in both time domain and frequency domain.

Among the above metrics, outage probability is chosen as the most representative means to characterize the spectrum state. Thus, the FAM aggregates the outage probability values related to each CH and uses them to select the best channel, c^*, through the following procedure:

---

[1] It is assumed that all nodes within a cluster are under the same spectrum conditions, for this reason all sensing metrics in this work are defined cluster-wise and not node-wise.

$$c^* = \arg\min_{c \in \mathcal{C}} \sum_{m=1}^{M} P_{\text{out},m}(c) \frac{N_m}{N} \tag{1}$$

$$\text{subject to: } P_{\text{out},m}(c) < P_{\max} \ \forall m \in \{1, \ldots, M\}$$

where $P_{\text{out},m}(c)$ is the outage probability of cluster m on channel c, and $P_{\max}$ is a constraint on outage probability that must be met by every single cluster. This constraint is introduced to avoid solutions that, despite being globally optimal, penalize too much a certain part of the network.

Based on the resulting aggregated information, the FAM is able to determine the interference conditions on the current operating channel. In fact, three different interference scenarios can occur:

- "Type 1 Interference": occurs if the expected number of FA messages is received at the FAM, but the spectrum sensing data indicate the presence of unacceptable interference.
- "Type 2 Local Interference": occurs when the aggregated packet loss rate within a specific CHs exceeds a given threshold.
- "Type 2 Global Interference": occurs when the reception rate of FA messages from CHs at the FAM is less than a given threshold;

Type 2 interference is introduced to cope with scenarios whose conditions are so poor to prevent transmission of data from SSNs to CHs or from CHs to the FAM. If one of these conditions is detected and remains persistent for a predefined time interval, the FAM initiates a *channel switch procedure* as illustrated in Fig. 2.

The FAM first selects a new "best" operating channel using Equation 1, then the FAM issues multiple *channel switch commands* (indicating the new operating channel) towards a target multicast address valid for the whole set of CHs. When CHs receive the channel switch command, they start a local procedure to force all nodes (both SSNs and non-SSNs) within the cluster to allocate to the new channel.

The channel switch procedure is completed within the cluster when either all nodes in the cluster confirm to the corresponding CH the reception of the channel switch command or the CH reaches a maximum number of attempts to deliver the channel switch command. Upon completion, CHs reallocate to the new channel and notify the FAM. Finally, the FAM forces also the E node to change its channel, thus concluding the channel switch procedure.

During the channel transition phase, different nodes and clusters might be tuned on different operating channels at the same time. The duration of such condition should be minimized because it can result in temporary network partition and consequent loss of packets. To this purpose, each node and each CH should be configured not to change its own operating channel immediately upon reception of the channel switch command. The actual transition should only occur after a specific guard time, configurable by the FAM.

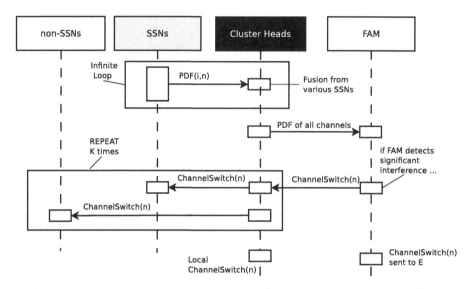

Fig. 2. Sequence diagrams: spectrum sensing and channel switch procedures

2.3 Implementation Aspects

A number of implementation aspects should be taken into account when realizing a Frequency-Agile LoWPAN according the the aforementioned design.

It is important to note that while SSNs are performing Energy Detection, they are temporarily not able to participate in the LoWPAN messages exchange, as their on-board transceiver cannot encode/decode radio packets while it is sampling the radio channel for interference. For this reason, it is recommended that only H nodes are configured as SSNs because they do not contribute to packet forwarding (like R nodes) or data gathering and merging (like CH nodes). It is possible though to configure R nodes as SSNs but care must be taken in managing the timing of the spectrum sensing cycles and the packet forwarding operations, which may require that an R node and all of its children are time-synchronized. For this reason an R node should be allowed to act as an SSN only when it performs a low duty-cycle spectrum sensing. Furthermore, in application scenarios where interference is particularly relevant, network administrators should consider the installation of additional SSNs specifically dedicated to provide a continuous spectrum sensing service.

Since FA is a network management issue, it should rely on standard management protocols, such as the Simple Network Management Protocol (SNMP) [20]. In such case, the FAM takes the role of SNMP manager, and FAAs take the role of SNMP agents. SNMP commands, namely "SET" and "GET", can be used by the FAM and CHs for all FA-related configurations and queries within the LoWPAN. Such procedures, however, would not be optimal if standard SNMP implementations are used, because of the high overhead introduced by continuous peer-to-peer SNMP polling. To this purpose, the use of a 6LoWPAN-adapted version of SNMP is suggested (such as [21]). Specifically, two 6LoWPAN-SNMP features are considered of interest. First, since many FA commands (such as channel switch) are directed to all nodes, multicast support is beneficial. Second, since the transmission of PDFs by each SSN is periodic, the use of a periodic GET should also be exploited to remove SNMP polling cycles. The use of SNMP commands such as TRAP or INFORM should also be investigated, for instance to let CHs notify instantly the FAM about harsh interference conditions.

FA-enabled LoWPANs are effective even when the number of SSNs is relatively small, provided that their overall spatial coverage is sufficient to cover the whole LoWPAN area (spatial diversity). Therefore, specific attention must be paid by LoWPAN designers/managers to the spatial distribution of SSNs.

3   Demonstration

In this section, a multihop 6LoWPAN-based frequency-agile demonstrator system is presented and its expedience is discussed. The purpose of such implementation is to demonstrate the feasibility of FA features within a simple 6LoWPAN deployment. The demonstrator implements the main features introduced in Sec. 2 to realize a distributed Energy Detection application that can provide spectrum awareness to the network itself or to other co-located networks. The demonstrator implements the main features of the system described in Sec. 2 as a proof of concept, while specific details (mostly discussed in Sec. 2.3) are left as future extensions.

The architecture of the demonstrator is depicted in Fig. 3. The demonstrator is made of two main components: the *Simple 6LoWPAN* and the *Control Center*. The Simple 6LoWPAN is an implementation of a realistic LoWPAN operating under interference that performs spectrum sensing and data transfer.

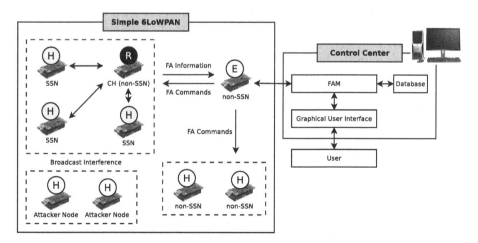

Fig. 3. Demonstrator architecture

The Control Center collects and processes the data from the Simple 6LoW-PAN, hosts the FAM, and provide figures about the Simple 6LoWPAN performance. In addition, the Control Center provides a Graphical User Interface (GUI) to visualize information about FA features and to control operations of the Simple 6LoWPAN. A detailed description of the demonstrator components is provided in the following sections.

3.1 Simple 6LoWPAN

The scenario under consideration involves SSNs and non-SSNs operating as described in Sec. 2. In addition, *Attacker Nodes* are introduced to emulate malicious devices. Such nodes periodically scan the available IEEE 802.15.4 channels looking for active 6LoWPANs and, upon finding a network, they generate (broadcast) interfering traffic on the corresponding channel for a predefined time interval. Such interference disrupts the 6LoWPAN operations and triggers the channel switch procedure.

All 6LoWPAN nodes are implemented on Crossbow TelosB [22] wireless sensor nodes, running TinyOS [23], and adopting the 6LoWPAN stack BLIP [24].

3.2 Control Center

The Control Center hosts the FAM functionalities and provides the user with a real-time GUI to visualize the spectrum occupancy state and configure the various operation parameters described in Sec. 3.1. The Control Center consists of the following subcomponents (see Fig. 3):

- The *FAM* (see Sec. 2) processes the FA data and obtains information about the spectrum occupancy state. The FAM uses this information to compute a number of assessment metrics describing the spectrum occupancy state and to keep track of the best available channel. If the FAM detects that the current operating channel is under critical level of interference, it generates a frequency change message to be sent to the 6LoWPAN nodes in order to reallocate to the best available channel. In addition, the FAM computes the amount of received data from non-SSNs during a predefined time window thus providing performance figures such as packet loss and throughput useful to observe the 6LoWPAN performance under different interference conditions.
- The *Database* collects and stores spectrum sensing data for time-based data processing, long-term statistics, or future reference.
- The *Graphical User Interface (GUI)* is a web-based application, which graphically represent spectrum occupancy state information regularly updated by the FAM, including PDFs, periogram, spectrogram, current/best channel and performance figures such as packet loss rate and throughput. The GUI also allows the user to manually set the parameters that control operations of each SSN. Furthermore, it offers an interface to manually assign the operating channel for the 6LoWPAN devices (excluding Attacker Nodes). Fig. 4

shows the GUI representation of the average outage probability per IEEE 802.15.4 channel. The figure indicates (based on the outage probability value) that the current operating channel (22) is under unacceptable level of interference, deliberately injected by an Attacker Node.

In the current setup, the Control Center is implemented onboard a Linux-based personal computer. The FAM is implemented on-board the Control Center for research and demonstration purposes, as it offers increased flexibility and computation power compared to a 6LoWPAN-based node. This kind of setup is suitable for Simple and Extended 6LoWPAN deployments, where infrastructure is available. In ad-hoc, infrastructure-less deployments, a 6LoWPAN based node could host the FAM, implementing a reduced set of its functionalities based on the computation/memory resources of the node.

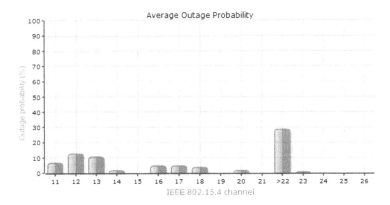

Fig. 4. GUI Snapshot: Average outage probability per IEEE 802.15.4 channel

4   Conclusions and Future Work

This work presents an approach to extend 6LoWPAN-based networks with FA features. The proposed approach suggests the introduction of two modules to the 6LoWPAN network stack, namely the FAD and the FAA, which perform the local FA-related operations of a 6LoWPAN node. The global FA network management is dealt by the FAM: a unique centralized entity in the 6LoWPAN that controls the FA functionalities of the whole network. Scalability issues are addressed through a cluster-based approach.

A proof of concept implementation of the proposed system is described, based on TelosB wireless sensor nodes running TinyOS and a personal computer running Linux. Based on a number of suitable spectrum evaluation metrics, the FAM detects the presence of interference introduced by Attacker Nodes and re-allocate the network to the best available channel. The user can monitor such process through presentation functionalities offered by the GUI.

Ongoing research activities are addressing integration of SNMP in the actual implementation and other improvements to make the system compliant with different scenarios. These improvements include, for instance, the definition of extensions to cope with Extended 6LoWPANs, or the implementation of a fully distributed FAM to enable autonomous operation in case of lack of infrastructure.

Acknowledgment. This work was inspired by the collaboration between ISMB and Politecnico di Torino within the FP7 Network of Excellence Newcom++ (contract no. 216715).

References

1. Vermesan, O., Harrison, M., et al.: Internet of Things Strategic Research Roadmap. Technical report, Cluster of European Research Projects on the Internet of Things (CERP-IoT), Brussels, Belgium (September 15, 2009)
2. IEEE: Ieee standard for information technology- telecommunications and information exchange between systems- local and metropolitan area networks- specific requirements part 15.4: Wireless medium access control (mac) and physical layer (phy) specifications for low-rate wireless personal area networks (wpans). IEEE Std 802.15.4-2006 (Revision of IEEE Std 802.15.4-2003) (2006)
3. Bluetooth SIG: Bluetooth technical specifications radio and baseband architecture (2009), http://www.bluetooth.combluetoothtechnologyworks
4. ZigBee Standards Organization: Zigbee specification. ZigBee Document 053474r17 (January 2008)
5. Kushalnagar, N., Montenegro, G., Schumacher, C.: IPv6 over Low-Power Wireless Personal Area Networks (6LoWPANs): Overview, Assumptions, Problem Statement, and Goals. RFC 4919 (Informational) (August 2007)
6. Montenegro, G., Kushalnagar, N., Hui, J., Culler, D.: Transmission of IPv6 Packets over IEEE 802.15.4 Networks. RFC 4944 (Proposed Standard) (September 2007)
7. Shelby, Z., Bormann, C.: 6LoWPAN: The Wireless Embedded Internet. Wiley Series on Communications Networking & Distributed Systems. Wiley, Chichester (2010)
8. Han, S., Lee, S., Lee, S.: Coexistence performance evaluation of ieee 802.15.4 under ieee 802.11b interference in fading channels. In: Proceeding of 18th IEEE International Symposium on Personal, Indoor and Mobile Radio Communications (PIMRC), Athens, Greece. IEEE, Los Alamitos (September 2007)
9. Yuan, W., Wang, X., Linnartz, J.: A coexistence model of ieee 802.15.4 and ieee 802.11b/g. In: Proceedings of the 14th IEEE Symposium on Communications and Vehicular Technology in the Benelux (SCVT 2007), Delft, Netherlands (November 2007)
10. Pollin, S., Tan, I., Hodge, B., Chun, C., Bahai, A.: Harmful coexistence between 802.15.4 and 802.11: A measurement-based study. In: Proceedings of 3rd International Conference on Cognitive Radio Oriented Wireless Networks and Communications (CROWNCOM2008), Singapore (May 2008)
11. Pollin, S., Ergen, M., Dejonghe, A., van der Perre, A., Catthoor, F., Moermann, I., Bahai, A.: Distributed cognitive coexistence of 802.15.4 with 802.11. In: Proceedings of 1st International Conference on Cognitive Radio Oriented Wireless Networks and Communications (CROWNCOM 2006), Mykonos Island, Greece (June 2006)

12. Penna, F., Pastrone, C., Spirito, M., Garello, R.: Measurement-based analysis of spectrum sensing in adaptive wsns under wi-fi and bluetooth interference. In: Proceedings of the IEEE 69th Vehicular Technology Conference (VTC), Barcelona, Spain (April 2009)
13. Khaleel, H., Pastrone, C., Penna, F., Spirito, M., Garello, R.: Impact of wi-fi traffic on the ieee 802.15.4 channels occupation in indoor environments. In: The 11th International Conference on Electromagnetics in Advanced Applications (ICEAA '09), Turin, Italy, September 2009. IEEE, Los Alamitos (2009)
14. Khaleel, H., Penna, F., Pastrone, C., Tomasi, R., Spirito, M.: Distributed spectrum sensing and channel selection in opportunistic wireless personal area networks. In: The Second ACM International Workshop on Mobile Opportunistic Networking (MobiOpp) 2010, Demo Session, Pisa, Italy. ACM, New York (February 2010)
15. Mitola, J., Maguire, G.Q.: Cognitive radios: making software radios more personal. IEEE Personal Communications 6(4) (September 1999)
16. Haykin, S.: Cognitive radio: brain-empowered wireless communications. IEEE Transactions on Communications 23(2), 201–220 (2005)
17. Handy, M., Haase, M., Timmermann, D.: Low energy adaptive clustering hierarchy with deterministic cluster-head selection. In: IEEE MWCN, pp. 368–372 (2002)
18. Xia, D., Vlajic, N.: Near-optimal node clustering in wireless sensor networks for environment monitoring. In: AINA '07: Proceedings of the 21st International Conference on Advanced Networking and Applications, Washington, DC, USA, pp. 632–641. IEEE Computer Society, Los Alamitos (2007)
19. Woo, A., Tong, T., Culler, D.: Taming the underlying challenges of reliable multihop routing in sensor networks. In: SenSys, pp. 14–27. ACM Press, New York (2003)
20. Harrington, D., Presuhn, R., Wijnen, B.: An Architecture for Describing Simple Network Management Protocol (SNMP) Management Frameworks. RFC 3411 (Standards Track) (December 2002)
21. Choi, H., Kim, N., Cha, H.: 6lowpan-snmp: Simple network management protocol for 6lowpan. In: 10th IEEE International Conference on High Performance Computing and Communications, pp. 305–313 (2009)
22. Crossbow: Telosb datasheet, http://www.xbow.com/products/product_pdf_files/wireless_pdf/telosb_datasheet.pdf
23. Levis, P., Madden, S., Gay, D.: TinyOS: An Operating System for Sensor Networks. In: Weber, W., Rabaey, J., Aarts, E. (eds.) Ambient Intelligence. Springer, Heidelberg (2004)
24. University of California at Berkeley: 6lowpan stack blip (2009), smote.cs.berkeley.edu:8000/tracenv/wiki/blip

Competitive Unlicensed Spectrum Sharing with Partial Information on Slow Fading Channels

Xiao Lei[1], K. Avrachenkov[2], L. Cottatellucci[1], and A. Garnaev[3]

[1] Eurecom, Mobile Communications, Sophia Antipolis, France
[2] Inria, Sophia Antipolis Cedex, France
[3] Saint Petersburg State University, Russia
laura.cottatellucci, lei.xiao@eurecom.fr,
K.Avrachenkov@sophia.inria.fr, agarnaev@rambler.ru

Abstract. We consider a slow fading multiuser environment with primary and secondary users. The secondary users have only partial knowledge of the channel and are subjected to transmitted power constraints by the primary users. Their communications are intrinsically affected by outage events. We propose and analyze two algorithms for joint rate and power allocation. In one algorithm, the secondary transmitters cooperate to maximizing a common utility function accounting for the total throughput of the network. In a second approach based on a game framework, the secondary users aim at maximizing selfishly their own utilities. The latter approach shows better fairness properties at the expenses of some global performance loss compared to the optimum cooperative approach.

1 Introduction

Spectrum sharing in cognitive radio [1] enables an efficient use of the scarce frequency spectrum by allowing the coexistence of licensed and unlicensed users in the same spectrum. In a typical scenario where independent systems do not cooperate and there is no centralized authority to handle the network access for secondary users, distributed algorithms to share the available resources play a key role. Game theory offers a natural framework to construct distributed algorithms. The literature in the field is copious and an exhaustive overview exceeds the scope of this work. The interested reader can refer to [2,3]. However, the spectrum allocation problem among secondary users has been neglected for the case of practical and theoretical interest when the channel is slow fading and the secondary users have only partial channel state information. In these conditions, the secondary users suffer from outage events and a certain level of information loss need to be tolerated. In this work we propose two algorithms, one based on game theory and the other on optimization for the joint power and rate allocation among secondary users. We analyze the characteristics of the game approach in terms of existence and multiplicity of the Nash equilibria

E. Osipov et al. (Eds.): WWIC 2010, LNCS 6074, pp. 158–169, 2010.
© Springer-Verlag Berlin Heidelberg 2010

in the extreme regimes of high and low noise plus interference from primary users. In the former case, a closed form expression for the Nash equilibrium is provided. In the latter case, criteria for the convergence of best response algorithms are discussed. The optimization approach is also analyzed in the two above mentioned regimes and closed form expressions for the resource allocation are provided.

Due to space constraints, the proofs of the theoretical results are omitted in this paper.

2   System Model

We consider a multiuser environment consisting of two secondary users and a primary user sharing the same time and frequency band but transmitting to independent receivers. The independent systems do not cooperate and no centralized authority is assumed to handle the network access for secondary users. The secondary users compete for the shared bandwidth constrained by a target quality of service for the primary user. We denote by $\mathcal{S}_*$ and $\mathcal{D}_*$ the transmitter and the receiver of the primary user while $\mathcal{S}_i$ and $\mathcal{D}_i$, for $i = 1, 2$ denote the source and the destination of the secondary users, respectively. Let $\mathcal{I} = \{*, 1, 2\}$. We denote by g_p, with $p \in \mathcal{I}$, the channel attenuation of the direct link $\mathcal{S}_p - \mathcal{D}_p$. The channel attenuations of the interfering links between transmitter $\mathcal{S}_p$ and receiver $\mathcal{D}_q$, with $p \neq q$ and $p, q \in \mathcal{I}$ are denoted by h_{pq}. The rate and the power of the signal transmitted by $\mathcal{S}_p$ are R_p and P_p, respectively. The primary system broadcasts the transmitted power on the signaling channel such that all the transmitters know it, or, alternatively, the transmitters estimate it. The channel is fading and each link fades independently with statistics known at the secondary sources and given by a probability density function $\Theta_{pq}(h_{pq})$, with $p, q \in \mathcal{I}$. We assume also that the fading is Rayleigh distributed and $\Theta_{H_{pq}}(h_{pq}) = \frac{1}{\sigma_{pq}^2}\exp(p_{pq}/\sigma_{pq}^2)$. The sources transmit Gaussian symbols and the received signals at the destinations are impaired by white additive Gaussian noise with variance N_0.

3   Problem Statement

We will consider the problem of joint power and rate allocation by the secondary sources under constraints on the quality of service of the primary communication in the case of block fading, i.e. varying channel which is constant in the timeframe of a codeword but independent and identically distributed from codeword to codeword.

We assume that all the receivers estimate their respective direct links g_p, $p \in \mathcal{I}$ and broadcast it on the signaling channel such that all the transmitters in the system know them. Furthermore, the secondary sources are supposed to track the interference link from the primary source and exchange this information with the other secondary users, i.e. transmitter $\mathcal{S}_i$, $i \in \{1, 2\}$ has knowledge of both h_{*1} and h_{*2}. Only statistical knowledge of the reverse link from a secondary transmitter to the primary user is available at the secondary users.

Because of the partial knowledge of the channel by the sources and the assumption of block fading, reliable communications, i.e. with error probability arbitrarily small, are not feasible and outage events may happen. If the source $p \in \mathcal{I}$ transmits at a certain rate with constant transmitted power P_p, an outage event happens if

$$R_p > \log\left(1 + \frac{P_p g_p}{N_0 + P_{q_1} h_{q_1 p} + P_{q_2} h_{q_2 p}}\right), \qquad p, q_1, q_2 = \mathcal{I} \text{ with } i \neq j, \quad (1)$$

and the outage probability of source p depends on the choice of R_p, P_p, P_{q_1} and P_{q_2}. We define the throughput as the average information that can be reliably received by the destination. The throughput is given by

$$T_p(P_p, R_p, P_{q_1}, P_{q_2}) = R_p \Pr\left\{R_p \leq \log\left(1 + \frac{P_p g_p}{N_0 + P_{q_1} h_{q_1 p} + P_{q_2} h_{q_2 p}}\right)\right\} \quad (2)$$

where $p, q_1, q_2 = \mathcal{I}$ with $p \neq q_1 \neq q_2$, , and $\Pr\{\mathcal{E}\}$ denotes the probability of the event $\mathcal{E}$. We assume that the metric to measure the performance loss of the primary user is the average interference $\sigma_{i*}^2 P_i + \sigma_{j*}^2 P_j$ and the secondary users pay a penalty proportional to the average interference caused to the primary communication.

We study joint power and rate allocation for the secondary communications by applying two different criteria. In the optimization approach the secondary transmitters cooperate to maximize a global utility function accounting for the total throughput of the secondary users and the costs due to the transmitted power and the interference caused to the primary user,

$$\begin{aligned} u(P_1, P_2, R_1, R_2) &= \sum_{i=1, i \neq j}^{2} \left(T_i(P_i, R_i, P_j, R_j) - C_i P_i - K_i \sigma_{i*}^2 P_i\right) \\ &= \sum_{i=1}^{2} \left(R_i F_i(t_i) - C_i P_i - K_i \sigma_{i*}^2 P_i\right). \end{aligned} \quad (3)$$

where $F_i(t_i) = 1 - exp\left(-\frac{t_i}{P_j \sigma_{ji}^2}\right)$, with $t_i = \frac{P_i g_i}{e^{R_i} - 1} - N_0 - P_* \sigma_{i*}^2$, and C_i and K_i are unit costs per transmitted power and per average generated interference, respectively. Note that the costs C_i and K_i can be interpreted as the Lagrangian multipliers of constraints on the maximum power and maximum average interference to the primary user. Then, the utility function (3) corresponds to the dual function (see e.g. [4]) of a constrained optimization problem with objective function 2.

Alternatively, we investigate the case as the secondary users are rational and selfish and allocate their rates and powers to maximize their own utility functions. The utility function of transmitter $i = 1, 2$ is given by

$$\begin{aligned} u_i(P_i, P_j) &= T_i(P_i, R_i, P_j, P_*) - C_i P_i - K_i(\sigma_{i*}^2 P_i + \sigma_{j*}^2 P_j) \\ &= R_i F_i(t_i) - C_i P_i - K_i(\sigma_{i*}^2 P_i + \sigma_{j*}^2 P_j) \qquad \text{with } i \neq j. \end{aligned} \quad (4)$$

4   Game-Based Resource Allocation

Power and rate allocation for the two secondary transmitters can be formulated as a game $\mathcal{G} = \{\mathcal{S}, \mathcal{U}, \mathcal{P}\}$, where $\mathcal{S}$ is the set of players (the two secondary transmitters), $\mathcal{U} = \{u_1, u_2\}$ is the set of the utility functions defined in (4), and $\mathcal{P}$ is the strategy set defined by $\mathcal{P} \equiv \{(P_1, R_1), (P_2, R_2) | P_1, P_2, R_1, R_2 > 0\}$. The power and rate allocation of the secondary transmitter is obtained as an equilibrium point of the system. When both transmitters aims at maximizing their utility function, on equilibrium point is the Nash equilibrium defined by the allocation strategy $(P_1^*, R_1^*, P_2^*, R_2^*)$ such that

$$u_1\left(P_1^*, R_1^*, P_2^*, R_2^*\right) \geq u_1\left(P_1, R_1, P_2^*, R_2^*\right) \quad \text{for} \quad \forall P_1, R_1 \in \mathbb{R}_{++}$$

$$u_2\left(P_1^*, R_1^*, P_2^*, R_2^*\right) \geq u_2\left(P_1^*, R_1^*, P_2, R_2\right) \quad \text{for} \quad \forall P_2, R_2 \in \mathbb{R}_{++}$$

where $\mathbb{R}_{++}$ denotes the set of positive reals.

Nash equilibria of the game $\mathcal{G}$ necessarily satisfy the following system of equations

$$\frac{\partial u_i}{\partial P_i} = \frac{R_i g_i}{(e^{R_i} - 1)P_j \sigma_{ji}^2} - C_i - K_i \sigma_{i*}^2 = 0$$

$$\frac{\partial u_i}{\partial R_i} = F_i(t_i) - \frac{R_i P_i g_i e^{R_i}}{\left(e^{R_i} - 1\right)^2} F_i'(t_i) = 0$$

or equivalently,

$$1 - \exp\left(-\frac{t_i}{P_j \sigma_{ji}^2}\right) = P_i\left(C_i + K_i \sigma_{i*}^2\right) \frac{e^{R_i}}{e^{R_i} - 1} \tag{5}$$

$$\frac{1}{P_j \sigma_{ji}^2} \exp\left(\frac{-t_i}{P_j \sigma_{ji}^2}\right) = \frac{\left(C_i + K_i \sigma_{i*}^2\right)\left(e^{R_i} - 1\right)}{R_i g_i} \tag{6}$$

From (5) and (6) we obtain

$$P_i \frac{e^{R_i}}{e^{R_i} - 1}\left(C_i + K_i \sigma_{i*}^2\right) + \frac{(e^{R_i} - 1)\sigma_{ji}^2(C_i + K_i \sigma_{i*}^2)}{R_i g_i} = 1 \tag{7}$$

which yields

$$P_i = \left(1 - \frac{(C_i + K_i \sigma_{i*}^2)P_j \sigma_{ji}^2}{R_i g_i}(e^{R_i} - 1)\right)\frac{(e^{R_i} - 1)}{(C_i + K_i \sigma_{i*}^2)e^{R_i}} \quad i = \{1, 2\}. \tag{8}$$

A solution of the 4-equation system (5)-(6) is a Nash equilibrium if it satisfies the conditions

$$\frac{\partial^2 u_i}{\partial R_i^2} < 0, \frac{\partial^2 u_i}{\partial P_i^2} < 0, H = \frac{\partial^2 u_i}{\partial R_i^2}\frac{\partial^2 u_i}{\partial P_i^2} - \left(\frac{\partial^2 u_i}{\partial P_i \partial R_i}\right)^2 > 0. \tag{9}$$

It is straightforward to verify that the utility function is not concave in R_i. Hence, the results of N-concave games cannot be applied here. Additionally,the analysis of the general case results complex. In order to get additional insights into the system behavior, we consider firstly the following extreme cases : (1) the interference from the primary user and the noise tend to zero, (*secondary-user interference limited regime*), (2) the noise is much higher than the transmitted power (*high noise regime*).

Secondary-User Interference Limited Regime – When $N_0 + P_* h_{*i}$ is negligible compared to the interference, the payoff function is still given by (4), with $t_i = \frac{P_i g_i}{e^{R_i} - 1}$.

Proposition 1. *When the interference from the primary user and the noise tend to zero, the Nash equilibrium of game $\mathcal{G}$ satisfy the system of equations*

$$x_1 = \kappa_2 f(x_2) \tag{10}$$
$$x_2 = \kappa_1 f(x_1)$$

where $x_i = \frac{g_i}{(C_i + \kappa_i \sigma_{i*}^2) P_j \sigma_{ji}^2}$, $\kappa_i = \frac{(C_i + K_i \sigma_{i*}^2) g_j}{(C_j + K_j \sigma_{j*}^2) \sigma_{ij}^2}$, $i, j \in 1, 2$, $i \neq j$ *and*

$$f(x) = \left(1 - \frac{e^{R(x)} - 1}{x R(x)}\right)^{-1} \left(1 - e^{-R(x)}\right)^{-1} \tag{11}$$

for $1 < x < \infty$. *In (11),* $R(x)$ *is the unique positive solution of the equation*

$$1 - \frac{xR}{e^R - 1} \exp\left(-\frac{x}{e^R} + \frac{e^R - 1}{Re^R}\right) = 0 \tag{12}$$

such that

$$-x + \frac{e^R - 1}{R} \neq 0. \tag{13}$$

Let (x_1^0, x_2^0) *be solutions of system (10). The corresponding Nash equilibrium is given by*

$$P_1 = \frac{g_2}{(C_2 + K_2 \sigma_{2*}^2) x_2^0 \sigma_{12}^2}, \quad R_1 = R(x_1^0),$$
$$P_2 = \frac{g_1}{(C_1 + K_1 \sigma_{1*}^2) x_1^0 \sigma_{21}^2}, \quad R_2 = R(x_2^0).$$

Remarks Note that the solution $\overline{R}(x)$ to

$$\frac{e^R - 1}{R} = x$$

is also a solution to (12). It is possible to verify that such a solution corresponds to a minimizer of the utility function. The solution $R(x_j)$ to (12) is the rate which maximizes the utility function corresponding to the transmit power of the other transmitter $P_i = \frac{g_j}{(C_j + K_j \sigma_{j*}^2) x_j \sigma_{ij}^2}$. It lies in the interval $\left(0, \overline{R}(x_j)\right)$ and we refer to it as the *best response in terms of rate* of player j to strategy P_i of player i. Similarly, $\kappa_j f(x_j)$ is the *best response in terms of power* of user i to the strategy P_i of its opponent.

The solution (x_1^0, x_2^0) to system (10) depends on the system parameters only through the constants κ_1 and κ_2. The existence and uniqueness of Nash equilibrium for the class of systems considered in Proposition I reduces to the analysis of the solution of system (10) and depends on the system via x_1 and x_2. The solution to equation (12) can be effectively approximated by $R(x) \approx 0.8 \log(x)$. Then, the function $f(x)$ is approximated by

$$f(x) \approx \left(1 - \frac{e^{0.8 \log(x)} - 1}{x 0.8 \log(x)}\right)^{-1} \left(1 - e^{-0.8 \log(x)}\right)^{-1}.$$

The following proposition provides sufficient conditions for the existence of a Nash equilibrium.

Proposition 2. *When the interference from the primary user and the noise tend to zero, a Nash equilibrium of the game $\mathcal{G}$ exists if*

$$(\kappa_1 - 1)(\kappa_2 - 1) > 0$$

with κ_i defined in Proposition 1.

General conditions for the uniqueness of the Nash equilibrium are difficult to determine analytically. Let us observe that in general a system with noise and interference from the primary source that tend to zero may have more than one Nash equilibrium. Let us consider the two systems corresponding to the two pairs of coefficients $\kappa_1^{(1)} = \kappa_2^{(1)} = 1.05$ and $\kappa_1^{(2)} = \kappa_2^{(2)} = 2$. The two curves $x_2 = \kappa_1^{(1)} f(x_1)$, for $i = \{1, 2\}$ cross each other in $x_1 = x_2$. Additionally, the curve $x_2 = \kappa_1^{(1)} f(x_1)$ has two asymptotics in $x_1 = 1$ and $x_2 = 1$. Then, by observing Figure 1 , it becomes apparent that the curves with $\kappa_1^{(1)} = \kappa_2^{(1)} = 1.05$ will cross again for high x_1 and x_2 values. In contrast, the curves with $\kappa_1^{(1)} = \kappa_2^{(1)} = 2$ will diverge from each other, and these crossing points correspond to Nash equilibria. It is worth noticing that for $x_1 \gg 1$, $x_2 \approx 1$, (and for $x_2 \gg 1$, $x_1 \approx 1$). Then, from a telecommunication point of view, it is necessary to question whether the model for $N_0 + P_* h_{*i} \to 0$ is still applicable. In fact, in such a case, $P_1 \ll \frac{g_1}{C_1 \sigma_{12}^2}$, but also $P_1 \gg N_0 + P_* h_{*1}$ has to be satisfied because of the system model assumptions. Typically, the additional Nash equilibria with some $x_i \approx 1$ are not interesting from a physical point of view since the system model assumptions are not satisfied.

By numerical simulations, we could observe that games with multiple Nash equilibria exist for a very restricted range of system parameters, more specifically for $1 \leq \kappa_i \leq 1.1$.

Proposition 1 suggests also an iterative algorithm for computing Nash equilibrium based on the best response. Choose an arbitrary point $x_1^{(0)}$ and compute the corresponding value $x_2^{(0)} = \kappa_1 f(x_1^{(0)})$. From a practical point of view, this is equivalent to choose arbitrarily the transmitted power $P_2^{(0)} = \frac{g_1}{\sigma_{21}^2 x_1^{(0)}(C_1 + \kappa_1 \sigma_{1*}^2)}$ for transmitter 2 and determine the power allocation for user 1 which maximizes its utility function. The optimum power allocation for user 1 is $P_1^{(0)} = \frac{g_2}{\sigma_{12}^2 x_2^{(0)}(C_2 + \kappa_2 \sigma_{2*}^2)}$. We shortly refer to $P_1^{(0)}$ as the best response of user 1 to user 2. Then, by using $x_2^{(0)}$ it is possible to compute $x_1^{(1)} = \kappa_2 f\left(x_2^{(0)}\right)$, the best response of user 2 to user 1. By iterating on the computation of the best responses of user 1 and user 2 we can obtain resource allocations closer and closer to the Nash equilibrium and converge to the Nash equilibrium. We refer to this algorithm as the best response algorithm.

The best response algorithm is very appealing for its simplicity. Nevertheless, its convergence is not guaranteed. This issue is illustrated in Figure 1. Let us consider the interference channel with $\kappa_1 = \kappa_2 = 1.05$ and the corresponding solid and dashed curves $x_2 = \kappa_1 f(x_1)$ and $x_1 = \kappa_2 f(x_2)$. The Nash equilibrium exists and is unique but the best response algorithm diverges from the Nash equilibrium even for choices of the initial point arbitrarily close to the Nash equilibrium but different from it. Numerical results show that if κ_1 and κ_2 are both greater than 1.2, the best response algorithm always converges to a Nash equilibrium.

Analytically, it is possible to prove the following Proposition.

Proposition 3. *For sufficiently large κ_1 and κ_2, the fixed point iterations*

$$\begin{cases} x_1^{(k+1)} = \kappa_2 f(x_2^{(k)}), \\ x_2^{(k+1)} = \kappa_1 f(x_1^{(k)}), \end{cases} \tag{14}$$

converge.

In fact, large values of κ_1 and κ_2 correspond to a realistic situation for system where the noise plus the interference from the primary source are negligible compared to the transmitted powers of the secondary users.

High noise regime – Let us turn to the case when noise is much higher than the transmitted power, $P_i g_i \ll N_0 + P_* h_{*i}$. The throughput can be approximated by

$$\begin{aligned} \overline{T}_i(P_i, R_i, P_j, P_*) &= R_i \Pr\left\{ R_i \leq \frac{P_i g_i}{N_0 + P_j h_{ji} + P_* h_{*i}} \right\} \\ &= R_i \Pr\left\{ h_{ji} \leq \frac{1}{P_j}\left(P_i \frac{g_i}{R_i} - N_0 - P_* h_{*i} \right) \right\} \end{aligned} \tag{15}$$

The utility function is given by

$$v_i = R_i \left(1 - \exp\left(-\frac{1}{P_j \sigma_{ji}^2 \left(P_i \frac{g_i}{R_i} - N_0 - P_* h_{*i} \right)} \right) \right) - C_i P_i - K_i(\sigma_{i*}^2 P_i + \sigma_{j*}^2 P_j)$$

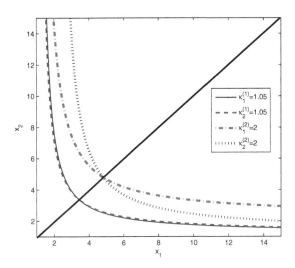

Fig. 1. Graphical investigation of convergence of the best response algorithm in the interference limited regime

for $i = 1, 2$. Correspondingly, we consider the game $\overline{\mathcal{G}} = \{\mathcal{S}, \mathcal{V}, \mathcal{P}\}$, where the set of players and policies coincide with the corresponding sets in $\mathcal{G}$ while the utility function set $\mathcal{V}$ consists of the functions (15). The joint rate and power allocation for selfish secondary transmitters is given by Nash equilibrium of game $\overline{\mathcal{G}}$. The following proposition states the conditions for the existence and uniqueness of a Nash equilibrium in $\overline{\mathcal{G}}$ and provides the equilibrium point.

Proposition 4. *Game $\overline{\mathcal{G}}$ admits a Nash equilibrium if and only if*

$$\frac{g_i}{C_i + K_i \sigma_{i*}^2} > N_0 + P_* h_{i*}, \quad i = 1, 2.$$

If the above conditions are satisfied, $\overline{\mathcal{G}}$ has a unique equilibrium $((R_i^*, P_i^*), (R_j^*, P_j^*))$ where P_i^* and P_j^* are the unique roots of the equations

$$\left(1 - \ln\left(\frac{Q_j P_i \sigma_{ij}^2}{g_j}\right)\right) P_i \sigma_{ij}^2 = \frac{g_j}{Q_j} - N_0 - h_{*i}$$

and

$$\left(1 - \ln\left(\frac{Q_i P_j \sigma_{ji}^2}{g_i}\right)\right) P_j \sigma_{ji}^2 = \frac{g_i}{Q_i} - N_0 - -h_{*j}$$

in the intervals $\left(0, \frac{g_j}{Q_j \sigma_{ij}^2}\right)$ and $(0, \frac{g_i}{Q_i \sigma_{ji}^2})$ respectively, being $Q_i = C_i + K_i \sigma_{i*}^2$. Also,

$$R_i = \frac{P_i g_i Q_i}{g_i - P_j \sigma_{ji}^2 Q_i} \quad \text{and} \quad R_j = \frac{P_j g_j Q_j}{g_j - P_i \sigma_{ij}^2 Q_j}.$$

General case – Let us consider now the general case, when the noise, the powers of interferences and the transmitted powers are of the same order of magnitude. A Nash equilibrium necessarily satisfies the system of equations (6) and (8). Substituting (8) in (6) yields

$$1 - \frac{x_i R_i}{e^{R_i} - 1} \exp\left(-\frac{x_i}{e^{R_i}} + \frac{e^{R_i} - 1}{R_i e^{R_i}} + n_i\right) = 0 \quad i = 1, 2 \tag{16}$$

with $n_i = \frac{N_0 + P_* h_{*i}}{P_j \sigma_{ji}^2}$. Equations (8) and (16) provide an equivalent system to be satisfied by Nash equilibrium. In order to determine a Nash equilibrium we can proceed as in the case of the secondary-interference limited regime. Observe that, in this case, (16) depends on the system parameters and the other player strategy not only via x_i but also via n_i. Then, the general analysis feasible for any communication system in the secondary interference limited regime is no longer possible and the existence and multiplicity of Nash equilibria should be studied independently for each communication system. In the following, we detail guidelines for this analysis.

From (16), it is possible to determine the best response in terms of rate of transmitter i to policy P_j of transmitter j. Conditions for the existence of such best response are detailed in the following statement.

Proposition 5. *Equation (16) admits positive roots if and only if*

$$1 - x_i e^{-x_i + 1 + n_i} > 0. \tag{17}$$

If (17) is satisfied, (16) admits a single positive root in the interval $(0, \log x_i)$, which corresponds to the best response in terms of rate to policy P_j of user j.

From the best responses in terms of rate, it is straightforward to determine the best response in terms of powers for the two players.

5   Optimum Joint Rate and Power Allocation

In this section, we study the joint rate and power allocation when both the secondary users cooperate to maximize the utility function.

In this case we assume that the strategy set is defined by[1]

$$\overline{\mathcal{P}} = \{(P_1, R_1), (P_2, R_2) | P_1, P_2, R_1, R_2 \geq 0\}.$$

We consider again the two extreme regimes when the noise and the interference generated by the primary user is very high and when it is very low. In both cases we show that the optimum resource allocation privileges a single secondary user transmission. The following two propositions state the results.

---

[1] Note that $\overline{\mathcal{P}}$ is the closure of the open strategy set $\mathcal{P}$ of game $\mathcal{G}$.

Proposition 6. *Let us assume that the noise plus the interference from the primary user are very high compared to the power transmitted by the secondary transmitter, or equivalently, $\frac{g_i}{C_i} > N_0 + P_* h_{*i}$ and $\frac{g_i}{C_i} \approx N_0 + P_* h_{*i}$, $i = 1, 2$. Then, if*

$$\log \frac{g_i}{C_i(N_0 + P_* h_{*i})} + C_i\left(N_0 + P_* h_{*i}\right) > \log \frac{g_j}{C_j(N_0 + P_* h_{*j})} + C_j\left(N_0 + P_* h_{*j}\right)$$

$$i, j = 1, 2 \quad i \neq j \quad (18)$$

transmitter i transmits at power $P_i = \frac{1}{g_i}\left(\frac{g_i}{C_i} - N_0 - P_* h_{*i}\right)$ and rate $R_i = \log\left(\frac{g_i}{C_i(N_0 + P_* h_{i*})}\right) \approx \frac{g_i}{C_i(N_0 + P_i)}$, and the transmitter j is silent, i.e. $P_j = R_j = 0$.

Similarly, for the noise and interference from the primary user negligible compared to the interference from the secondary user the following result holds.

Proposition 7. *Let us assume that the noise plus the interference from the primary user are very low while the potential interference from the secondary source could be substantially higher, i.e, $N_0 + P_* h_{*1} \to 0$ and $\frac{\sigma_{21}^2}{C_2} \gg 0$ for transmitter 1 and $N_0 + P_* h_{*2} \to 0$ and $\frac{\sigma_{12}^2}{C_1} \gg 0$ for transmitter 2. There does not exist an optimum allocation strategy for both $P_1, P_2 > 0$. If (18) is satisfied, transmitter i transmits at power and rate*

$$P_i = \frac{1}{g_i}\left(\frac{g_i}{C_i} - N_0 - P_* h_{*i}\right) \approx \frac{1}{C_i} \quad \text{and} \quad R_i = \log\left(\frac{g_i}{C_i(N_0 + P_* h_{*i})},\right)$$

respectively, while transmitter j stays silent.

Note that both under the conditions of Proposition 6 and 7, a decision on the optimum resource allocation would require knowledge of both h_{*1} and h_{*2} at both secondary transmitters. A distributed resource allocation approach requires an exchange of information between transmitter 1 and transmitter 2, which has been introduced in the system model.

Closed form resource allocation strategies for the general case are not available and numerical constrained optimization is necessary.

6   Numerical Result

In this section, we assess the performance of the proposed algorithms and compare them. The resource allocation has a complex dependency on several system parameters, e.g. noise, interference from the primary user, channel gains, costs. We first investigate the performance of the game based resource allocation on the system parameters. We consider a system with parameters $\sigma_{12}^2 = \sigma_{21}^2 = 0.1$ and $g_1 = g_2 = 1$. Figure 2 shows the throughput attained by the game based algorithm for increasing costs $Q_i = C_i + K_i \sigma_{i*}^2$ and $Q_i = Q_j$. As expected, in the general case, an increase of the costs implies a decrease of the achievable

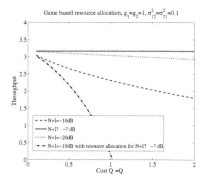

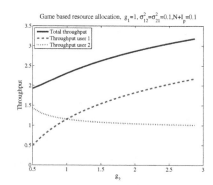

Fig. 2. Throughput attained by Nash equilibria versus costs $Q_1 = Q_2$ for different values of the noise plus interference from the primary user

Fig. 3. Throughput of the two secondary users and total throughput attained by Nash equilibria versus user 2 channel attenuation g_2

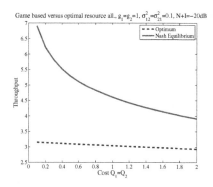

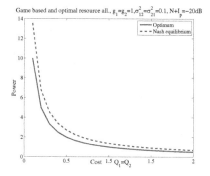

Fig. 4. Throughput versus costs $Q_1 = Q_2$. Comparison between the throughput attained by Nash equilibria or by optimum resource allocation

Fig. 5. Transmitted power versus costs $Q_1 = Q_2$. Comparison between the resources allocated by Nash equilibria or by optimum resource allocation.

throughput. The solid line in Figure 2 shows the throughput in the secondary interference limited regime. In this case the system performance is completely independent of the channel cost. At first glance, this bahaviour could appear surprising. However, it is a straightforward consequence of Proposition 1 when we observe that the best responses depend on the costs only via the ratio Q_1/Q_2. The dependency of the throughput on the costs becomes more and more relevant when $N + I_p$, the noise and the interference from the primary user, increases. Finally, the dashed dotted line in Figure 2 shows the degradation in terms of throughput, when the presence of $N + I_p$ is neglected in the resource allocation but $N + I_p = -10dB$. Figure 3 illustrates the dependency of the throughput on the channel attenuation g_2 of user 2 for the following set of parameters:

$\sigma_{12}^2 = \sigma_{21}^2 = 0.1$, $N + I_p = -10dB$, $Q_1 = Q_2 = 1$. For increasing values of g_2, the total throughput increases. In contrast, the throughput of user 1 decreases because of the increased interference of user 2 on user 1. Note that for game based resource allocation the users access simultaneously to the channel while the optimum resource allocation privileges a time sharing policy.

Figure 4 and 5 compare the game based resource allocation to the optimum one. They show the throughput and the power, respectively, as function of the costs. For very low values of $N + I_b$ and low costs, the optimum resource allocation outperforms significantly the game based approach at the expenses of fairness. In fact, the former assigns the spectrum to a single user. The performance loss at the Nash equilibrium decreases as the costs increases.

Acknowledgment

This work is supported by the ANR project Ecocells.

References

1. Mitola, J.: Cognitive radio for flexible mobile multimedia communication. In: Proc. IEEE Int. Workshop Mobile Multimedia Communcations (MoMuC), San Diego, CA, November 15-17, pp. 3–10 (1999)
2. Etkin, R., Parekh, A., Tse, D.: Spectrum sharing for unlicenced bands. IEEE J. Select. Areas Commun. 25(3), 517–528 (2007)
3. Scutari, G., Palomar, D.P.: MIMO cognitive radio: A game theretical approach. IEEE Trans. on Signal Processing 58(2), 761–780 (2010)
4. Boyd, S., Vandenberghe, L.: Convex optimization. Cambridge University Press, New York (2007)

Structure of Service Areas in
Wireless Communication Networks

Janne Riihijärvi and Petri Mähönen

Institute for Networked Systems, RWTH Aachen University
Kackertstrasse 9, D-52072 Aachen, Germany
{jar,pma}@inets.rwth-aachen.de

Abstract. In this paper we study the influence of the distribution of transmitter locations on the structure of service areas of individual transmitters. In order to obtain a general model, we approximate the collection of service areas by Voronoi diagrams generated by the transmitter locations. We give an overview of the key statistical characteristics of Voronoi cells, and how they can be computed efficiently. We then apply these techniques to both probabilistic node location models, as well as location data sets corresponding to different network types. The results indicate that the statistics of service areas under this approximation have strong dependency on the structure of the transmitter distribution, and that real networks tend to lead to highly different structures compared to commonly utilized node location models.

1 Introduction

Wireless networks are becoming increasingly heterogeneous in terms of usage and structure. In addition to carefully optimized and planned networks, such as cellular systems, unplanned deployments of, e.g., Wi-Fi access points are becoming more and more widespread. This increasing diversity is also creating the need for rethinking approaches towards the management of wireless networks. Cognitive Wireless Networks (CWNs) are an example of a promising approach in this domain, emphasizing awareness on the radio environment, self-organization and adaption of the network to prevailing conditions [1,2,3,4]. It has also been observed that many of the performance characteristics of the network are very sensitive to the actual distribution of the network nodes [5,6], resulting in proposals to consider network topology as key ingredient in design of resource management algorithms for CWNs [7]. Earlier work has mainly focussed on characteristics such as connectivity and inter-node interference in ad hoc and mesh networks, rather than cellular or broadcast networks. However, both ad hoc and mesh networks are still niche applications considering number of users and deployed networks.

In this paper we extend our earlier work on the influence of node location distributions on network structure to cover the cases of cellular and broadcast networks. More specifically, we focus on the influence of transmitter locations on the structure of *service areas* in such networks. The abstraction we employ for

E. Osipov et al. (Eds.): WWIC 2010, LNCS 6074, pp. 170–179, 2010.

determining this dependency is approximating service areas by the *Voronoi polygons* [8,9] generated by the transmitters. This corresponds to situations in which selection of the service node is made based on distance alone, or some monotonic function thereof, such as received signal strength in isotropic propagation conditions. We do not explicitly consider coverage range of different technologies in this paper, only focussing on the structure of the area that the transmitter would have to serve under these approximations. Such extensions are, however, rather straightforward to add into the methodology described below.

The rest of the paper is structured as follows. In Section 2 we describe the stochastic node location models we use in our study in addition to empirical data sets. In Section 3 we give an overview of the structure and characteristics of Voronoi diagrams, including some of the key statistics used to characterize sizes and shapes of individual Voronoi cells. We also discuss in some detail how to carry out reliable simulation studies on randomly generated Voronoi diagrams. In Section 4 we apply the described techniques to a number of data sets, and draw final conclusions in Section 5.

2   Stochastic Models of Transmitter Locations

We will discuss the different model of transmitter locations used in our study. In addition to experimental data sets consisting of transmitter locations for various wireless communications networks, we shall consider a number of stochastic location models with different characteristics. More precisely, we consider different *point processes*, resulting in collections $\{X_i\}_{i=1}^n$ of n indistinguishable locations in a region E. Both the individual locations $X_i \in E$ and the total number of points n are in general random, and for most cases have a complicated dependency structure. We shall introduce briefly some of the commonly used point processes appropriate for modeling different types of networks. For a more complete description of the theory and also applications in wireless communications domain we refer the reader to [10,11,12,13,14].

The simplest assumption is that all the X_i are uniformly distributed random variables on E. This results in the *binomial point process* if n is fixed, or the *Poisson point process* if n is a Poisson random variable with mean $\lambda|E|$, where $\lambda \in \mathbb{R}_+$ is called the *intensity* of the process, and $|E|$ is the area of E. As we shall see in the following section, the statistical properties of the service area model considered in this paper are well-known for transmitter locations resulting from a Poisson process, so we shall include this case as the comparison baseline. As new contributions we also study service areas for *clustered* and *regular* point processes as well. In order to provide the reader a better intuition of nature of such point processes, we show typical example realisations of them in Figure 1. Clustered distributions are often used to model unplanned network deployments, such as Wi-Fi access points being deployed by individual users, whereas regular distributions are often similar to planned network deployments in structure.

For the clustered case we assume that the locations are generated by the *Thomas point process* [15]. In the Thomas process *cluster centres* are first sampled from a Poisson point process of intensity κ. Then around each cluster centre,

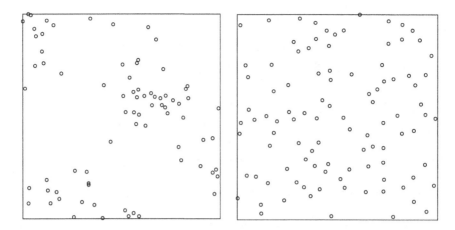

Fig. 1. Example realisations of a clustered point process (right panel) and a regular point process (left panel)

cluster members are generated, which form the actual point pattern. The locations of the cluster members are taken to follow symmetric bivariate normal distribution with the common variance σ^2 and mean located at the cluster centre. The number of cluster members for each cluster is Poisson distributed with parameter μ, resulting in mean number of $\kappa\mu$ points in total. The left panel in Figure 1 depicts a realisation of the Thomas process on unit square with $\kappa = 5$, $\sigma = 0.1$ and $\mu = 20$.

The regular point process considered in the following is the *Simple Sequential Inhibition (SSI) process*. The locations of the n individual points in the SSI process are sampled from the uniform distribution on E, but conditioned to be at least some minimum *hard-core distance* r apart from previously sampled locations. Parameter values $r = 0.04$ and $n = 100$ were used for generating the right panel of Figure 1.

3   Models and Statistics for Service Areas

The simplest model for a service area of a given transmitter or network interconnection point X_i is simply the region that consists of those points $y \in E$ that are closer to X_i than any other transmitter or interconnection point. Put formally, this leads to the definition of the service area of X_i as the *Voronoi polygon* or *Voronoi cell* of X_i as the closed set

$$V(X_i) \equiv \left\{ y \in \mathbb{R}^2 \,\middle|\, \|y - X_i\| \leq \|y - X_j\|, j \neq i \right\}. \qquad (1)$$

Considering then a collection of n locations or *generators* $\boldsymbol{X} = \{X_1, \ldots, X_n\}$, with $2 < n < \infty$, the set $\mathcal{V}(\boldsymbol{X}) \equiv \{V(X_1), \ldots, V(X_n)\}$ of all Voronoi polygons is the *Voronoi diagram* generated by $\boldsymbol{X}$. In practice we focus on some bounded

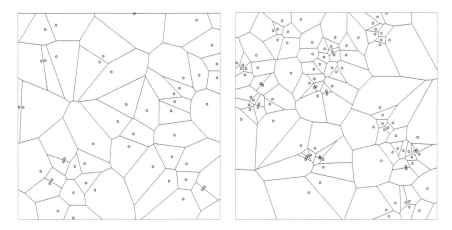

Fig. 2. Example realisations of a random Voronoi diagram with generators sampled from a Poisson point process (left) and from a Thomas point process (right)

region E, resulting in the *bounded Voronoi diagram* defined by $\mathcal{V}_{\cap E}(\boldsymbol{X}) \equiv \{V(X_1) \cap E, \ldots, V(X_n) \cap E\}$. The boundary $\partial V(X_i)$ of a Voronoi polygon consists of line segments, half-lines or infinite lines, all called *Voronoi edges*. A point shared by three or more Voronoi edges is called a *Voronoi vertex*.

It is intuitively clear that the structure of $\mathcal{V}(\boldsymbol{X})$ should depend heavily on that of $\boldsymbol{X}$. This effect is illustrated in Figure 2 where Voronoi diagrams with Poisson and Thomas generator processes are contrasted. Visually the clustered structure of the Thomas process would seem to increase the variance of cell sizes (that is, the areas of the Voronoi regions) quite substantially. To quantify such an observation we need to be able to reason about the statistics of a *typical cell* of a random Voronoi diagram. In case of the generators being a realisation of the Poisson point process (resulting in a *Poisson-Voronoi tessellation*) a number of analytical results are available. See, for example, [8,9] for an overview and further references. Unfortunately many of the expressions for the characteristics of the typical cell have defied analysis even in the Poisson-Voronoi case. Monte Carlo studies thus appear unavoidable, especially for determining the statistics of interest for random Voronoi diagrams with non-Poisson distribution of generators.

For numerically generating instances of typical cells of random Voronoi diagrams, Hinde and Miles have given in [16] an algorithm which is still serviceable today. The algorithm operates by sampling from the point process of the generators, and randomly selecting one point of the outcome to be the central point. Assuming stationarity, we then translate this central point to the centre of the simulation area by applying periodic boundary conditions, form the Voronoi diagram, and take the Voronoi polygon the central point is the generator for a realisation of the typical cell. The individual cells obtained this way over the course of multiple simulation runs represent faithfully the statistics of a single large realisation of the random Voronoi diagram. The specific advantage of this approach is the avoidance of edge effects (given that the average number of

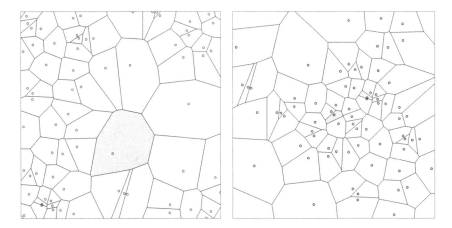

Fig. 3. Contrasting two methods for choosing typical cells. In the left the cell containing the origin is chosen introducing bias towards larger cells whereas on the right the method explained in the text is used.

generator points is high enough), which could significantly influence the results if averaging would be carried out over all the cells of a simulated instance. Alternative way of selecting the typical cell would be to select the Voronoi polygon that contains a randomly or deterministically selected point, such as the centre of the simulation area. However, prescriptions like this bias the results towards those of the larger cells, as those are more likely to be selected with this method compared to the approach of Hinde and Miles (see Figure 3 for illustration). For selected processes it is also possible to sample typical cells directly, without constructing a larger Voronoi diagram than necessary. See [9] for a discussion in the Poisson-Voronoi case.

We focus on three characteristics of a typical Voronoi cell, namely the area A, the number of neighbouring cells n, and the cell perimeter P. Instead of dealing with the area and the perimeter directly, we work with the *normalised area* $a \equiv \lambda A$ and *normalised perimeter* $p \equiv \sqrt{\lambda}P/4$, where λ is the intensity of the generator process. This way the exact density of the generators becomes immaterial, and we conveniently have $\mathbb{E}\{a\} = \mathbb{E}\{p\} = 1$. We are not only interested in the cell perimeter as an independent object of study but also use it to calculate the *form factor* $F \equiv 4\pi A/P^2$ of the typical cell. The form factor characterises the "roundness" of the cell, with the limits $F \to 1$ as the cell approaches a circular disc, and $F \to 0$ as the cell becomes more and more elongated.

4   Results

We shall first consider the case of the generators $\boldsymbol{X}$ arising from the three point processes introduced above. We applied the Hinde-Miles algorithm to generate 300 000 typical cells for each of the point processes studied, each individual

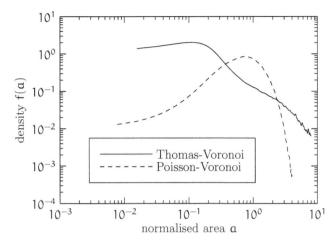

Fig. 4. Estimated probability densities of the normalised areas of typical Voronoi polygons for Thomas-Voronoi and Poisson-Voronoi diagrams

realisation containing on average 300 generator points and cells. For the Thomas case, parameter values used were $\kappa = 15$, $\sigma = 0.08$ and $\mu = 20$, and for the SSI process the hard-core radius was set to $r = 0.03$.

Figure 4 shows the comparison of the estimated densities of the normalized areas between the Poisson and Thomas cases. For the Poisson case the density is rather sharply peaked around the mean at $a = 1$, with very low values for both very small and very large ($a \gg 4$) cells. The behaviour of the normalized area is significantly different for Thomas-Voronoi case, as could be expected from the example that was shown in Figure 2. While much of the density is now concentrated on small values of a reflecting the clustered nature of N, a heavy tail falling off approximately as a power law is clearly visible.

Numerical characteristics of the measured distribution of normalised Voronoi cell areas are given in Table 1. The given values include the second, third and fourth moments as well as the standard deviation $\sigma(a)$ together with the *skewness* β_1 and the *kurtosis* β_2, defined by

$$\beta_1 \equiv \frac{1}{\sigma^3} \mathbb{E}\left\{(a - \langle a \rangle)^3\right\} \quad \text{and} \quad \beta_2 \equiv \frac{1}{\sigma^4} \mathbb{E}\left\{(a - \langle a \rangle)^4\right\} - 3, \qquad (2)$$

Table 1. Statistics of normalised Voronoi cell areas for various generator point processes

Process	Moments			σ	β_1	β_2
	$\mathbb{E}\left\{a^2\right\}$	$\mathbb{E}\left\{a^3\right\}$	$\mathbb{E}\left\{a^4\right\}$			
Poisson	1.2802	1.9946	3.6595	0.5294	1.0369	1.6179
Thomas	2.6560	15.411	155.12	1.2869	4.4307	35.799
SSI	1.1042	1.3426	1.7909	0.3228	0.8905	1.2164

Table 2. The empirical location data sets for which services areas were studied. The upper half corresponds to data sets available through the FCC licensing database, whereas lower half corresponds to Wi-Fi access point location data for different US cities.

Data set	Number of points
AM stations	4934
FM stations	15535
NTSC TV stations	8922
Digital TV stations	1056
Cellular sites	21115
Boston	77665
Los Angeles	421094
Manhattan	58861
San Francisco	47158
Seattle	146671

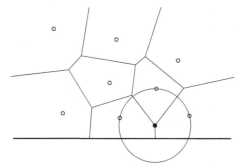

Fig. 5. A method for checking the presence of edge effects on a cell. If any of the circles centered at cell vertices intersecting three nearest generators intersects the edge of the area considered the cell should be rejected. (Figure adapted from [17].)

respectively. The values for the Poisson-Voronoi case can be contrasted to those given by Tanemura [17], as these are the most detailed simulations available. Even though our cell count is lower, very good correspondence can be observed. Also the comparison against analytically known results validates the simulations carried out to a good accuracy. For example, Gilbert has given in [18] an integral expression for $\mathbb{E}\left\{a^2\right\}$ that can be numerically evaluated to equal $1.2801760409\ldots$ (see, for example, [19] for details). This agrees very well with the value of 1.2802 given in the table.

We shall next consider the sizes of the service areas for scenarios in which the generators are obtained from empirical location data. We consider the ten data sets summarized in Table 2, consisting on both transmitters locations for

Table 3. Statistical characteristics of the Voronoi diagrams for the empirical generator data sets

Data set	Area				Neighbours		Form factor	
	$\mathbb{E}\{A\}$	$\mathbb{E}\{a^2\}$	$\mathbb{E}\{a^3\}$	$\sigma(a)$	$\mathbb{E}\{n\}$	$\sigma(n)$	$\mathbb{E}\{F\}$	$\sigma(F)$
AM transmitters	2.75×10^9	6.6768	146.66	2.3829	5.9649	1.5075	0.6677	0.1460
FM transmitters	1.08×10^9	9.1403	349.69	2.8532	5.9782	1.6453	0.6405	0.1598
TV (NTSC)	3.10×10^9	9.8078	763.02	2.9681	5.9737	1.7207	0.6179	0.1740
TV (Digital)	1.41×10^{10}	3.4373	22.841	1.5621	5.8758	1.7086	0.5892	0.1879
Cellular	7.35×10^8	43.600	19102	6.5270	5.9885	1.4794	0.6866	0.1300
Boston	33984.1	144.71	159795	11.988	5.9951	2.0002	0.5593	0.2006
Los Angeles	44163.9	733.88	3032228	27.072	5.9984	2.4184	0.4739	0.2238
Manhattan	2535.82	129.85	89901.82	11.351	5.9952	1.8478	0.6166	0.1769
San Francisco	8291.98	100.20	40976.72	9.9599	5.9939	2.0037	0.5737	0.1851
Seattle	191795	563.99	1170616	23.728	5.9989	2.0718	0.5356	0.2023

technologies often considered in the cognitive radio context, as well as Wi-Fi access point locations for a number of US cities. The data sets were obtained from the FCC licensing database, as well as from the WiGLE database maintained by the wardriving community [20]. One of the challenges in estimating the properties of the Voronoi diagrams generated by experimental location data is that the Hinde-Miles sampling technique can obviously no longer be applied. Thus statistical estimates must be carried out by considering a subset of the cells in the diagram, selected in a manner to mitigate the edge effects. An effective criteria for selecting the cells to be rejected given by Tanemura [17] is illustrated in Figure 5, and was incorporated into the estimation process.

Results for the empirical data sets are summarised in Table 3. In addition to statistics for the normalized area, the table includes statistics for the physical area of the cells, number of neighbouring cells (corresponding to the number of Voronoi edges of the cells) and the form factor. From the area statistics we can easily observe the high level of clustering and density fluctuations present in the Wi-Fi data sets compared to the broadcasting and cellular data sets. For the latter case, we can also see that the digital TV transmitter data set results in the most regular of the Voronoi diagrams, with relatively little variation in the sizes of the individual cells. This is typical for networks carefully deployed to optimize coverage. We can also see major variation in the shapes of the cells for different generator data sets. Broadcast networks and cellular networks tend to have rather symmetric cells, with little variation over the whole Voronoi diagram. The Wi-Fi networks on the other hand contain rather elongated cells, with very high variability in the shapes of the individual cells. It is also interesting to notice that for all network types the structure of the arising service areas is very different from the Poisson-Voronoi case, indicating that the simple Poisson point process model of transmitter locations might result in misleading results in relation to structure of service areas of the different node location models.

5 Conclusions

In this paper we studied the influence of the distribution of transmitter locations on the structure of service areas of the network. We approximated the service areas of the transmitters by their Voronoi polygons, and determined some of the key statistical characteristics of the arising Voronoi diagrams. In particular, we studied using synthetic and empirical data sets the influence of transmitter location distributions on the structure of the service areas in terms of the shapes and sizes of the resulting cells. The results indicate that the statistics of service areas under this approximation have strong dependency on the structure of the transmitter distribution, and that real networks tend to lead to significantly different structures compared to commonly utilized node location models. The results shown here can also be seen as a first step towards direct modeling of the structure of service areas. Such models would have a number of applications ranging from network optimization problems to studies in network economics. Refining the approach and studying these applications in more detail are core parts of our ongoing and future work.

Acknowledgment

The authors would like to thank RWTH Aachen University and the German Research Foundation (Deutsche Forschungsgemeinschaft, DFG) for providing financial support through the UMIC research centre. We would also like to thank the European Union for providing partial funding of this work through the ARAGORN and the FARAMIR projects.

References

1. Mitola, J.: Cognitive radio architecture: the engineering foundations of radio XML. Wiley-Interscience, Hoboken (2006)
2. Mitola, J.: Cognitive Radio: An Integrated Agent Architecture for Software Defined Radio. PhD thesis, KTH (Royal Institute of Technology) (2000)
3. Fette, B.: Cognitive radio technology. Newnes (2006)
4. Mähönen, P., Riihijärvi, J., Petrova, M., Shelby, Z.: Hop-by-Hop Toward Future Mobile Broadband IP. IEEE Communications Magazine 42(3), 138–146 (2004)
5. Riihijärvi, J., Petrova, M., Mähönen, P.: Influence of node location distributions on the structure of ad hoc and mesh networks. In: Proc. of IEEE Globecom 2008, New Orleans, USA (November 2008)
6. Ganti, R., Haenggi, M.: Interference and outage in clustered wireless ad hoc networks. Submitted to IEEE Trans. on Information Theory (2007)
7. Mähönen, P., Petrova, M., Riihijärvi, J.: Applications of topology information for cognitive radios and networks. In: Proceedings of IEEE DySPAN'07, Dublin, Ireland (April 2007)
8. Aurenhammer, F.: Voronoi diagrams—a survey of a fundamental geometric data structure. ACM Computing Surveys (CSUR) 23(3), 345–405 (1991)
9. Okabe, A., Boots, B., Sugihara, K., Chiu, S.: Spatial Tessellations: Concepts and Applications of Voronoi Diagrams, Probability and Statistics, 2nd edn. Wiley, Chichester (2000)
10. Stoyan, D., Kendall, W.S., Mecke, J.: Stochastic geometry and its applications. Wiley, Chichester (1995)
11. Riihijärvi, J., Mähönen, P.: Exploiting Spatial Statistics of Primary and Secondary Users towards Improved Cognitive Radio Networks. In: Proc. of International Conference on Cognitive Radio Oriented Wireless Networks and Communications (CROWNCOM), Singapore (May 2008)
12. Riihijärvi, J., Mähönen, P., Rübsamen, M.: Characterizing wireless networks by spatial correlations. IEEE Communications Letters 11(1), 37–39 (2007)
13. Ripley, B.: Spatial Statistics. John Wiley & Sons, Inc., Chichester (1981)
14. Cressie, N.: Statistics for spatial data. John Wiley & Sons, New York (1993)
15. Thomas, M.: A generalization of poisson's binomial limit for use in ecology. Biometrika 36, 18–25 (1949)
16. Hinde, A., Miles, R.: Monte carlo estimates of the distributions of the random polygons of the voronoi tessellation with respect to a poisson process. Journal of Statistical Computation and Simulation 10(3), 205–223 (1980)
17. Tanemura, M.: Statistical Distributions of Poisson Voronoi Cells in Two and Three Dimensions. Forma 18(4), 221–247 (2003)
18. Gilbert, E.: Random subdivisions of space into crystals. The Annals of Mathematical Statistics, 958–972 (1962)
19. Finch, S.: Poisson-Voronoi Tessellations (2005) (unpublished note)
20. WiGLE, http://www.wigle.net/

Quality of Experience Enforcement in Wireless Networks*

R. Serral-Gracià, M. Yannuzzi, E. Marin-Tordera, X. Masip-Bruin, and S. Sánchez

Advanced Network Architectures Lab, Technical University of Catalunya (UPC), Spain
{rserral,yannuzzi,eva,xmasip,sergio}@ac.upc.edu

Abstract. In this paper we present a Multimedia Wireless Management System, which can be used on-line to assess and guarantee the quality of multimedia traffic in a wireless network. The proposed platform uses both network and application layer metrics to build up a scalable quality assessment of multimedia traffic. Moreover, the system provides traffic provisioning capabilities by coordinating the network access and usage both from the wireless node and from the network access point. These two combined features permit our platform to guarantee a satisfactory multimedia user experience in wireless environments. We evaluate our proposal by issuing an experimental deployment in a testbed and performing a series of tests under different network situations to demonstrate the Quality of Experience guaranties of our system. The results show that the quality of video perceived by end-users is considerably improved compared to the typical wireless network.

Keywords: QoE, Wireless Network Management, Multi-layer.

1 Introduction

The massive market penetration of new mobile devices such as laptops, mobile phones, and netbooks, all with different Internet connection capabilities, encouraged the broad deployment and adoption of wireless technologies such as GPRS, Bluetooth, or Wireless LAN (WLAN) everywhere. In addition, the good performance/cost tradeoff of the latter favored the apparition of a vast number of hotspots offering Internet connectivity, e.g., at the city's airport, at the university campus, or even at the coffee shop next door, contributing to increase the user's effective on-line periods [1].

This "always connected" attitude acquired by the users has greatly affected the network usage patterns. Indeed, watching on-line TV programs, video-chatting with family or friends, or visiting video-streaming sites are now common practices. As a consequence, all this new multimedia traffic has introduced a series of network constraints in terms of latency and data transmission reliability, that network technologies must comply with in order to offer a competitive network connection. Despite of this, WLAN and other mobile technologies using a shared medium access, do not have mechanisms to guarantee such reliability.

---

* This work was partially funded by Spanish Ministry of Science and Innovation under contract TEC2009-07041, and the Catalan Government under contract 2009 SGR1508.

E. Osipov et al. (Eds.): WWIC 2010, LNCS 6074, pp. 180–191, 2010.

To overcome this limitation, in this paper we present a Multimedia Wireless Management System (MWMS), offering an on-line multimedia traffic quality monitoring and enforcing platform for wireless environments. Hence the contribution of this work is twofold:

1. First, we propose a multi-layer approach to on-line multimedia traffic quality assessment and enforcement, which combines application and networking data in order to guarantee higher priority for the multimedia flows in the wireless network.
2. And second, our solution uses a two-way approach, i.e., traffic control both from the network access point and from the end-node, to overcome the inherent unreliability of the wireless medium, hence guaranteeing the proper quality of multimedia flows.

Our system uses both network metrics such as used bandwidth and packet losses; and application metrics, namely, the Mean Opinion Score (MOS), in order to make informed management decisions. The main difference of our approach compared to other existing solutions [2] is that we use information from different layers, and combine them at both edges of the wireless network to provide a complete resource management platform.

We experimentally evaluate our proposal in our testbed by comparing the perceived user experience, i.e., Quality of Experience (QoE), between our platform and the generic case of unmanaged network resources. To do this comparison, we generate a video stream using a well-known multimedia streaming application under different network service degradation scenarios. The results show that the quality of the flows is properly maintained during the streaming when the network is managed by our MWMS, while the user perception is clearly degraded in the same conditions with an unmanaged network.

The rest of the paper is structured as follows, the next section details some related work about the requirements in order to design a QoE assessment and enforcement platform. In Sections 3 and 4 we describe our MWMS, and the policies used to perform the resource management. In Section 5, we detail the experimental testbed used and evaluate our platform. We continue in Section 6 with the analysis of the scalability of our solution, and finally in Section 7, we conclude and outline our future lines of research in this topic.

2 Related Work

A full-fledged Multimedia Wireless Management System must consider three important aspects in its design, *i)* it needs mechanisms to compute the QoE, *ii)* then it must consider the medium reliability, specially in wireless links, and finally *iii)* it requires mechanisms for resource reservation.

QoE sets the umbrella of techniques used for the subjective analysis of the end-user perception of a given service. This *subjectiveness*, can be made objective by means of well-known techniques, such as the MOS [3], combined with the E-Model [4] for voice transmission, or techniques such as [5] for video streams. This paper does not intend to propose a new method for computing the QoE, but rather to exploit existing techniques to receive feedback about the quality delivered to the user, so that we can dynamically manage the resources on the wireless network. In particular, in this work we compute the multimedia flow's QoE by using the technique detailed in [6], a solution which is able to estimate the perceived QoE from a single point of analysis by using frame loss and frame type information at the application layer.

Regarding the reliability of the wireless environment, in the case of WLAN, there are some efforts to provide Quality of Service (QoS) in the Wireless MultiMedia extensions (WMM), which in conjunction with the standardized medium access algorithm defined in 802.11e [7] can prioritize certain packets on the network. However, this standard even if based on a powerful medium access control, is insufficient to have higher level guaranties of proper multimedia quality, specially from the end-user perspective. Most of the contributions in quality assessment in wireless environments are based on low level mechanisms to provide QoS [2, 8], but neither considering user's perception nor application's specific constraints. Our MWMS, specifically uses QoE metrics as the control axis for the resource management.

Similarly to our approach, in [9] the authors propose a cross-layer QoE framework for HSDPA networks, the main difference with our approach is that they center the quality improvements by re-adapting the requirements of the applications for improving the MOS, while we improve the user perceived quality by prioritizing the Multimedia traffic.

Finally, the last identified challenge in our platform is the definition of the mechanisms to prioritize the traffic in the network. In this regard, there are several existing techniques both in commercial routers as in commodity operating systems (ACLs, firewalls, etc.), which permit to limit and control the up and downstream load of the wireless network. More specifically, in our work we use [10] as a solution that provides a very versatile mechanism, namely Traffic Control, to enable fine control of the upstream by priority queuing the packets matching a specific criteria, and the downstream, e.g., by delaying TCP's ACK packets.

3   Multimedia Wireless Management System

The Multimedia Wireless Management System (MWMS) presented in this paper is a multi-layer approach to on-line assessing and enforcing of the QoE in multimedia flows. MWMS proposes an efficient platform that combines information from different layers and provides a very fast and reliable traffic provisioning mechanism for multimedia flows in wireless environments.

The complete framework is presented in Figure 1. The MWMS is mainly composed of three different parts, first the Client Side, with two different tasks, to assess the user perceived QoE, and to manage the wireless link usage of the end-node, by locally detecting possible causes of service degradation. Second, the Network Side, which controls the access to the whole wireless network by relying on the multimedia flows' QoE as a metric. And third, the Server Side, which streams the media over the network. In this work we focus on the management system on the client and network sides, leaving the end-to-end QoE assessment and provisioning as an important part of our future work.

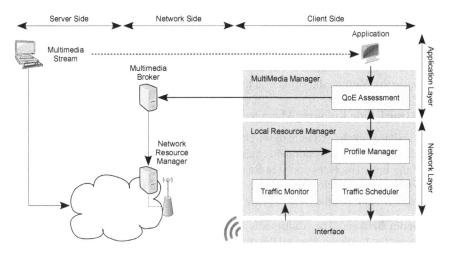

Fig. 1. The Multimedia Wireless Management System (MWMS)

3.1   Client Side Resource Management

QoE assessing of multimedia flows is not a trivial task, as it involves comparison of the original and received video frames using PSNR [5], which means that this mechanism cannot be used in a real-time assessment platform. However, this approach can be simplified by using approximations such as [6]. In this case, the best location to perform the user satisfaction assessment is within the destination multimedia application, where the most accurate information about the data delivered to the user can be gathered. To this end, we propose to directly adapt the end-user application in order to infer the delivered QoE, while giving feedback both to the Local Resource Manager (cross-layer vertical signaling) and to the Multimedia Broker (horizontal signaling). It is worth noticing that the application's adaptation only involves to inform the MWMS about the lost frames and their type in the video stream [6].

Local Resource Manager: The Local Resource Manager (LRM) performs the low level monitoring and measurement tasks of the wireless link in the local node. LRM is composed by three different entities, i.e., the Traffic Monitor, the Profile Manager and the Traffic Scheduler.

   The *Traffic Monitor* monitors in real-time the bandwidth and resource usage of the wireless node, periodically reporting its status to the Profile Manager. Then the *Profile Manager* computes the amount of raw resources required in terms of bandwidth, delay, jitter, and packet losses in order to optimize the resource reservation performed by the Traffic Scheduler. Such parameters are inferred from the effective requirements imposed by the Multimedia Manager. Finally, the *Traffic Scheduler* prioritizes the multimedia traffic over the rest of the wireless node traffic in case of service degradation.

MultiMedia Manager: The MultiMedia Manager (MMM) gathers quality information directly from the client application, it issues periodic queries about the experienced QoE, and receives information about the resource availability in the wireless node from the lower layers. The task of the MMM is twofold. On the one hand, if the service degradation is caused by other applications within the wireless node, the Multimedia Manager instructs the LRM to increase the priority of the multimedia flows. On the other hand, if the degradation is due to the wireless network, the MMM requests more resources to the Multimedia Broker on the Network Side.

3.2 Network Side Resource Management

Given the shared medium nature of wireless links, in order to provide service guaranties and a reliable resource allocation mechanism, the network must be controlled from both sides of the link. The Network Side Resource Management manages the resources in the downstream to the wireless node, and it is composed of two different parts, i.e., the *Multimedia Broker* and the *Network Resource Manager*.

Multimedia Broker: The Multimedia Broker (MB) is the entity within the network that receives the feedback from all the subscribed multimedia applications about the experienced user satisfaction in real-time. The MB interfaces with the Network Resource Manager in order to instruct whether more resources are needed, and as we detail in the next section, it bases the resource reservation decision depending on a preset acceptable QoE boundary. By design, the MB is independent of the underlying network, consequently it does not consider specific network metrics, but it only triggers resource reservations to the Network Resource Manager.

Network Resource Manager: The Network Resource Manager (NRM), analogously to the LRM, is responsible of guaranteeing that the multimedia traffic is received properly by the end-user. To this end, the NRM defines the different traffic profiles recognized by the system, and maps the input received by the MB to actual network parameters. Then, at the lower layer, it also controls the overall access to the wireless environment by scheduling the traffic within the wireless access point. With this two-way approach (i.e., client and network sides), the system can effectively guarantee the offered service to the user from both sides of the wireless network.

One important task of the network side resource management left as future work is the connection management and prioritization among the multimedia flows. This can be accomplished by a Connection Access Control (CAC) system, by introducing a business model with billing and accounting processes to define user categories, or by a combination of both alternatives.

4   Quality of Experience Assessment and Enforcement

After the introduction of the MWMS building blocks, this section is devoted to the description of the specific criteria used for reserving and releasing the mentioned resources. As outlined previously, MWMS defines two modes of resource allocation, local node resource management and network resource management.

4.1 Local Resource Management

The local resource management is driven by two different layers, first the low level resource allocation and second the high level QoE assessment.

The low level local resource allocation policy is based on the local's node resource usage monitoring and reservation as follows:

Definition 1. *Let* $\mathcal{U}_t \in [0,1]$ *be the used resources at time t in the input queue for the wireless node. Then* $\mathcal{U}_t$:

$$\mathcal{U}_t = R_t + \mathcal{B}_t \tag{1}$$

Where $R_t = \sum_{j=1}^{n} r_j$, with $R_t \in [0,1]$, are the ratio of resources needed for all the flows $r_{1..n}$ under surveillance by the system, and $\mathcal{B}_t$ is the usage of the rest of the incoming background traffic toward the node at time t. Then, if $\mathcal{U}_t > \Theta$, where Θ is the upper bound for a reliable wireless link usage, the system issues a reservation as instructed by the Profile Manager for the R_t resources. It is important to notice that R_t is easy to compute because the resource usage of multimedia flows is rather constant over time.

Similarly to the resource reservation, the resources are released when the link usage drops below θ, i.e., $\mathcal{U}_t < \theta$, where θ is the lower safety bound in the link usage to trigger the resource release, or when the multimedia flow finishes, as advertized by MMM. The pseudo-code to implement the whole LRM can be found in Algorithm 1. It is worth noticing, that measuring the link usage is a straight-forward task because it only involves to query the queue status of the interface, as provided by kernel data structures.

Algorithm 1. *LRM*

    Input: resources, $\mathcal{U}$, *forced* {*resources* : Amount of resources to manage by the system,
                $\mathcal{U}$: resource usage ratio, *forced* : whether to force the resource reservation}
    Output: success or failure
    if $\mathcal{U} > \Theta$ **then**
        trigger *resourceReservation(resources)*
5:     currentReservation $\leftarrow$ *resources* {global status update}
        return success
    end if
    if *forced* **then**
        if *resources* > currentReservation **then**
10:        trigger *resourceReservation(resources)*
           currentReservation $\leftarrow$ *resources*
           return success
        end if
        return failure
15: **end if**
    if $\mathcal{U} < \theta$ **then**
        trigger *resourceRelease(currentReservation)*
        currentReservation $\leftarrow$ 0
    end if
20: **return** success

To complement the LRM, both allocation and release of resources can also be triggered by the higher MMM layer. Hence, besides the strict low level resource usage, the system must also consider the user perception of the delivered multimedia traffic. Therefore, the MMM assesses the QoE of the received multimedia streams as described below (we refer interested readers to [6] for a throughout description of the MMM QoE assessment).

Let $\sigma \in [1,5]$ be the lower tolerable MOS threshold for a multimedia flow. Then, for any multimedia flow j under surveillance present on the system, if the quality of experience $q(t)$ at time t of any flow j is $q_j(t) \leq \sigma$, MMM will trigger a *local resource reservation* request (vertical multi-layer signaling) to the LRM. If the reservation is not successful, or if the quality continues below σ, despite the reservation, MMM will trigger a *network resource reservation* request (horizontal signaling). The pseudo-code implementing the MMM process is detailed in Algorithm 2.

Algorithm 2. *MMM*

    Input: MM flows {MM flows : multimedia flows subscribed on the system}
    for all *flow* $\in$ *MM flows* **do**
        qoe $\leftarrow$ *assessQoE(flow)*
        if *qoe* $< \sigma$ **then**
5:        *status* $\leftarrow$ *LRM(#MM flows, U, true)*
           if *status* $==$ failure **then**
             trigger *NetworkResourceReservation(#MM flows)*
           end if
           return
10:     **end if**
    end for

As it can be noted from Algorithms 1 and 2, the LRM keeps track of the current status of the reservation and reports whether the reservation is successful or not. This process can be invoked in two different ways, periodically, as a traffic monitor, or it can be invoked by the MMM in case the QoE is below σ (see line 5 in Algorithm 2).

4.2 Network Resource Management

Analogously to the local resource management, the network resource management is composed of two different parts, the low level resource reservation, performed by the NRM and the high level management performed by the MB. The interfaces between these two levels are similar to the one detailed in the LRM and the MMM (as detailed in Algorithms 1 and 2). However, a key difference is the fact that the MB needs to consider all the reservation requests of all the nodes in the wireless network, opposed to the single node approach of the local resource management. Analogously the NRM will prioritize the multimedia flows subscribed into the system towards all the wireless nodes.

The flow subscription is issued by the MMM, which gathers the properties of the flow and informs the MB about specific application constraints, in terms of frame losses and required bandwidth.

5   Experimental Evaluation

This section details the tests, the testbed used, and the evaluations performed to validate the MWMS. All the evaluations are focused on comparing the end-user's MOS obtained by running MWMS against a typical unmanaged network.

5.1   Tests and Testbed

The testbed used to perform the MWMS validation is illustrated in Figure 2. It is composed by the Multimedia Streaming Server (MSS), the Network Access Point (NAP) and the Wireless Node (WN). All three components are standard PC using the Linux Debian Operating system with traffic control capabilities to manage the resources. In the testbed the MB and the NRM are embedded within the NAP, while in the WN we set up the MMM and the LRM, together with the video streaming client. On its side, the video server is configured to stream using the RealTime Protocol (RTP), a high quality video[1] of 1024x576 pixels with a bit rate of 5.5Mbps for both audio and video. The streaming application used is VideoLan Client (VLC) [11].

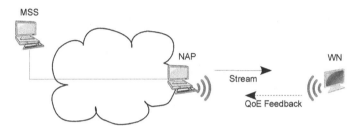

Fig. 2. Testbed main blocks

In order to test the MWMS we deployed our system as follows. We set up a high delay variation queue with limited capacity in order to produce a random amount of packet losses in the wireless network. In the WN we monitored the MOS of the traffic as described in Section 4, with a $\sigma = 3$ as advised in [5], $\Theta = 0.8$ and $\theta = 0.5$, and with an update interval of 1 second. Once the violation of QoE is assessed, the NRM configures a priority queue for the multimedia flows.

With the above methodology we simulate three different service degradation levels: *low*, *medium* and *high*. Finally, we run the same set of tests disabling our management system to compare the results in the same conditions.

5.2   MWMS Evaluation

The experimental evaluation of the proposed system is performed by running the tests specified previously. In our first study, we verify that the MWMS is able to provide better QoE during the whole test than the case with unmanaged network resources. To this end, in Figure 3 we show the Cumulative Density Function (CDF) of the obtained MOS over time, in the left we show the results for MWMS and in the right the case without any network management. For the sake of clarity, we transposed the CDFs, this way the X-Axis shows the normalized fraction of time where the quality of the video stream is below $q_j(t)$ (for all t in the test), while in the Y-Axis shows the instantaneous MOS for each test.

The figure highlights that MWMS easily outperforms the unmanaged case for all the tests, and independently of the level of service degradation the quality is very good

---

[1] The Elephant's Dream – http://www.elephantsdream.org

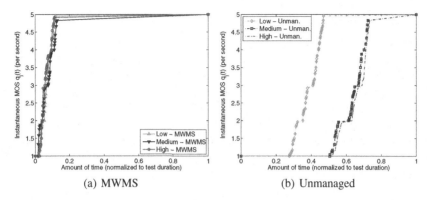

(a) MWMS   (b) Unmanaged

Fig. 3. Transposed Cumulative Density Function of the MOS per degradation level

most of the time. In particular we can see that in the case of MWMS only $\sim 6\%$ of the time the obtained MOS is below 3, while in the case of an unmanaged network it ranges from $\sim 35\%$ to $\sim 65\%$ of the time, i.e., around half of the streaming duration. Moreover, when MWMS is not present, between 30 and 50% of the time the quality reaches the lowest possible MOS value, i.e., 1, meaning that the video and audio are completely disrupted. Opposed to this, in the case of MWMS this value is around 1%, which roughly corresponds to the assessment and QoE enforcement setup time of the system.

It is worth noticing that the results for high and medium service degradation levels, the unmanaged network obtain similar results. The reason for that is the exponential degradation of the service in the presence of frame losses.

In order to analyze in more detail these results, in Table 1 we detail the numeric values in terms of quality. In the first column, we show the average MOS obtained for each one of the tests. As it can be noted, the quality is constant, around 4.75, when using MWMS, while it degrades in the case of an unmanaged network. In the second column we computed the 5th Percentile, which identifies the lower bounds in quality for the tests. As before, managing the system mostly avoids having low quality periods given the relatively high value of the percentile. The third and fourth columns in the table complement the above information by indicating the amount of service degradation periods, and the percentage of time with a degraded system, respectively. In particular, we can see that the degradation periods are fairly constant over the tests for the managed system, while they are much bigger when disabling the management. Since each period is equivalent to 1 second of streaming, we can notice that the amount of service degradation intervals are between ~ 8 and ~ 11 times higher when not using MWMS. Analogously, we can observe that in the worst case the percentage of time with service degradation with high degradation level is kept at 4.4% with MWMS, while it is ~ 15 times worse without our management solution.

In the results it can be noted that the MOS of the high degradation level with MWMS is better than the rest. This is caused by the fact that with high service degradation MWMS is able to react faster as the MOS decreases in less time and the degradation is more noticeable, activating the resource provisioning faster.

Another interesting study is the analysis of the duration of continuous service degradation periods. In Figure 4, we show the maximum and the average continuous duration

Table 1. Evaluation results: Columns 1 and 2 show MOS values for the different tests, Columns 3 and 4 the degradation periods

	Average	5th Prc.	# Degr	% Degr.
Low MWMS	4.74	2	38	5.9%
Low Unmanaged	3.45	1	243	37.8%
Medium MWMS	4.73	2.78	35	5.4%
Medium Unmanaged	2.44	1	409	64.7%
High MWMS	4.76	3	28	4.4%
High Unmanaged	2.38	1	427	66.5%

of the service degradation in the network for each test, the left figure shows the results for MWMS, while the case without management can be found on the right figure. As it can be observed, the least degradation period with MWMS is of 15 seconds, while it goes up to 94 seconds without MWMS. Regarding the average values, they are below five seconds with MWMS, raising up between 8 and 18 for the unmanaged system.

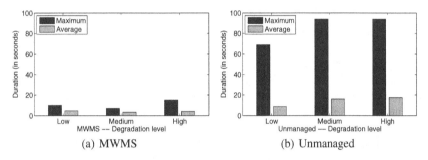

|(a) MWMS|(b) Unmanaged|

Fig. 4. Maximum and average continuous periods of service degradation

To finish our study, we further analyzed the causes of the degradation periods when using MWMS, and we observed that they were caused by external interferences of other nearby wireless networks, which cause burst of losses which are uncontrollable by our platform. However, even with these side effects, we claim that our system outperforms and delivers much better performance than an unmanaged network with a very simple yet effective platform.

6   Discussion

The final concern of any quality assessment and enforcement system is whether it is sufficiently scalable to be usable in a real deployment. In our case, MWMS is easily scalable given its inherently distributed design. In particular, each wireless node is in charge of locally monitoring the resources used, which only involves simple packet counting, and computing of instantaneous local bandwidth usage, while the application layer analyzes lost frames, which indeed is part of the multimedia decoding algorithm, and thus it is already performed on the system.

On the other hand, in the networking side, the NAP does not need to monitor the status of the network, since its functionality is limited to allocate resources when instructed. Such resource reservation is straight-forward because it only involves simple queue management, which is already present in most operating system's networking stack.

Added to the above, a wireless network has tight constraints in terms of available bandwidth and medium access; imposing hard limits in the maximum possible number of multimedia flows that can be served simultaneously. Therefore, depending on the used codec for the streaming and the required per flow bandwidth, a wireless system with 54Mbps can manage a very limited amount of simultaneous flows, e.g. less than 50 assuming 1Mbps streams[2], which is easily manageable with current queuing algorithms.

Finally, in terms of the bandwidth required to exchange the QoE information with the NAP, in MWMS the only feedback to the system is issued when a disruption is found, and given that the resources are released once the load of the system is reduced or the streaming has finished, it permits the system to greatly optimize the amount of required traffic, which is negligible compared with the existing network traffic.

7   Conclusions and Future Work

In this paper, we presented a Multimedia Wireless Management System (MWMS) which performs two different tasks. On the one hand, it is able to accurately assess the QoE of multimedia flows directly from application's data, and on the other hand, it guarantees the multimedia traffic quality by using low level resource management mechanisms. In addition, by directly acting over the access point of the network, the system is allowed to have a very tight control over the incoming traffic to the wireless network. This together with the QoE based feedback given from the wireless node, makes our MWMS a competitive solution for wireless network resource provisioning.

Given the versatility of our solution, we were able to evaluate its performance in a real environment under a different set of conditions, which prove that MWMS provides an effective QoE assessment and enforcement mechanism for multimedia streaming over wireless networks. Moreover, given the distributed and lightweight design of MWMS, the system can easily scale for managing a wireless network environment.

As an important part of our future work, one complementary part to complete the platform is the implementation of an admission control system in the wireless network in order to make a more fair use of the resources for all the nodes. This is to avoid the potential starvation of non-multimedia flows or the excess of resource reservation by some nodes in the wireless network.

Another line open for further research, is to develop an end-to-end mechanism, which combined with this local approach can guarantee the multimedia quality even in the case that the cause of the service degradation is not in the end-user network.

Finally, we plan to upgrade our platform by integrating support for the Wireless Multimedia extensions present in 802.11e, which can further improve the quality of multimedia flows.

---

[2] Given the overhead and the performance reduction caused by the MAC algorithms.

References

1. Rideout, V.J., Foehr, U.G., Roberts, D.F.: GENERATION M^2 Media in the Lives of 8- to 18-Year-Olds. A Kaiser Family Foundation Study (January 2010)
2. Lee, J., Liao, W., Chen, J.M., Lee, H.H.: A practical QoS solution to voice over IP in IEEE 802.11 WLANs. IEEE Communications Magazine 47(4), 111–117 (2009)
3. ITU-T Recommendation G.113: Transmission impairments due to speech processing (February 2001)
4. ITU-T Recommendation G.107: The E-model, a computational model for use in transmission planning (March 2005)
5. Klaue, J., Rathke, B., Wolisz, A.: EvalVid – A framework for video transmission and quality evaluation. In: Kemper, P., Sanders, W.H. (eds.) TOOLS 2003. LNCS, vol. 2794, pp. 255–272. Springer, Heidelberg (2003)
6. Serral-Gracià, R., et al.: Packet Loss based Quality of Experience of multimedia video flows. In: R. Rep. (2009),
   http://personals.ac.upc.edu/rserral/research/techreports/psnr_mos.pdf
7. IEEE Computer Society, IEEE Std 802.11e: Part 11: Wireless LAN Medium Access Control (MAC) and Physical Layer (PHY) specifications Amendment 8: Medium Access Control (MAC) Quality of Service Enhancements (November 2005)
8. Hock, D., Bayer, N., Pries, R., Siebert, M., Staehle, D., Rakocevic, V., Xu, B.: QoS provisioning in WLAN mesh networks using dynamic bandwidth control. In: European Wireless 2008, Prague, Czech Republic (June 2008)
9. Thakolsri, S., Khan, S., Steinbach, E., Kellerer, W.: QoE-Driven Cross-Layer Optimization for High Speed Downlink Packet Access. Journal of Communications 4(9), 669 (2009)
10. Linux Advanced Routing and Traffic Control, http://lartc.org/
11. Videolan media player, http://www.videolan.org/vlc

Anomaly-Based Intrusion Detection Algorithms for Wireless Networks*

Alexandros G. Fragkiadakis**, Vasilios A. Siris***, and Nikolaos Petroulakis

Institute of Computer Science, Foundation for Research and Technology - Hellas
(FORTH)
P.O. Box 1385, GR 711 10 Heraklion, Crete, Greece
{alfrag,vsiris,npetro}@ics.forth.gr

Abstract. In this paper we present and evaluate anomaly-based intrusion detection algorithms for detecting physical layer jamming attacks in wireless networks, by seeking changes in the statistical characteristics of the signal-to-noise ratio (SNR). Two types of algorithms are investigated: simple threshold algorithms and algorithms based on the cumulative sum change point detection procedure. The algorithms consider SNR-based metrics, which include the average SNR, minimum SNR, and max-minus-min SNR values in a short window. The algorithms are applied to measurements taken in two locations, one close and one far from the jammer, and evaluated in terms of the detection probability, false alarm rate, detection delay and their robustness to different detection threshold values. Our results show that the cumulative sum detection procedure can improve the detection probability and false alarm rate when measurements are taken far from the jammer, and can improve the robustness for different values of the detection threshold.

Keywords: Intrusion detection, signal-to-noise ratio, jamming, simple threshold algorithms, cumulative sum algorithms, performance evaluation.

1 Introduction

Due to their broadcast nature, wireless networks are more susceptible to attacks. Adversaries can exploit vulnerabilities in the physical and the medium access control layers [1,2,3,4,5], and heavily disrupt the communication between the network nodes. Attacks at the physical layer are usually referred to as jamming, and the corresponding adversaries (attackers) as jammers. A difficulty in detecting attacks at the physical layer is that channel impairments, which are not the result of attacks, can cause variations of the signal at a receiver.

---

* This work is supported in part by the European Commission in the 7th Framework Programme through project EU-MESH, ICT-215320, www.eu-mesh.eu
** Corresponding author.
*** V.A. Siris is also with the Department of Informatics at the Athens University of Economics and Business.

E. Osipov et al. (Eds.): WWIC 2010, LNCS 6074, pp. 192–203, 2010.

Intrusion detection involves the automated identification of unusual activity by collecting audit data, and comparing it with reference data. A primary assumption of intrusion detection is that a network's normal behavior is distinct from abnormal or intrusive behavior, which can be a result of a DoS (Denial-of-Service) attack. Various approaches to intrusion detection differ in the metrics (or measures/features) they consider, in addition to how and where these metrics are measured. Identifying the metrics to be monitored is important, because they affect the detection performance and the amount of monitored data can be particularly large, hence its collection can consume a significant amount of resources.

Intrusion detection procedures can be classified into three categories [6]: misuse (or signature-based) detection, anomaly detection, and protocol-based (or specification-based) detection. The three categories differ in the reference data that is used for detecting unusual activity: misuse detection considers signatures of unusual activity, anomaly detection considers a profile of normal behavior, and specification-based detection considers a set of constraints characterizing the normal behavior of a specific protocol or program.

In this paper we investigate anomaly-based intrusion detection algorithms. Unlike previous works, summarized in Sect. 2, that consider only very simple detection algorithms, a focus of this paper is to investigate and quantify when more intelligence in the detection algorithm can improve performance. In this direction, we consider both simple threshold detection algorithms and more advanced algorithms based on cumulative sum change point detection. The intrusion detection algorithms we consider seek changes in the signal-to-noise ratio (SNR) of received packets. In this work, we use a modified version of the madwifi driver[1] to perform SNR measurements. Our motivation for using SNR rather than some other metric (e.g., number of PHY errors) is that hardware radio interfaces and wireless device drivers typically provide values of the SNR for received packets.

The contributions of this paper are the following:

- We consider different metrics based on the SNR: average SNR, minimum SNR, and max-minus-min SNR.
- We investigate the performance of the algorithms in terms of the detection probability, false alarm rate, detection delay, and their robustness to different detection threshold values.
- We investigate the performance of the algorithms for measurements from an actual network, taken both close to and far from the jammer.
- We investigate the improvements of more intelligent algorithms, based on the cumulative sum (cusum) change point detection approach.

The rest of the paper is organized as follows. Related work is described in Sect. 2. The topology of the wireless testbed, the software used for collecting the SNR measurements, and the jamming model are presented in Sect. 3. The anomaly-based intrusion detection algorithms that we investigate are discussed in Sect. 4. The evaluation of the detection algorithms is presented in Sect. 5. Finally, conclusions and further work appear in Sect. 6.

---

[1] Madwifi project, http://www.madwifi.com

2   Related Work

This section presents a short overview of work related to intrusion detection in wireless networks. A key difference with this paper, which constitutes our main contribution, is that we investigate the performance improvements that can be achieved by cumulative sum change point detection algorithms, in terms of the detection probability, false alarm rate, detection delay, and robustness.

Different types of jammers have been defined in the literature. In [7], the authors describe four attack models: (*i*) a constant jammer that continuously emits RF signals without following any MAC protocol, (*ii*) a deceptive jammer that transmits normal packets, (*iii*) a random jammer that emits energy at random intervals followed by intervals of inactivity, and (*iv*) a reactive jammer that sends data only if it detects energy on the channel; this is the most effective jammer since it preserves energy, it can corrupt data with a higher probability, and is harder to detect. There are also jamming attacks at the MAC layer that try to exploit vulnerabilities in the RTC/CTS and NAV mechanisms [8]. In this paper, we consider a *periodic jammer* that periodically transmits packets, hence emits RF energy alternating between sleeping and jamming.

The authors in [9] describe several types of jammers and propose two types of detection algorithms that consider metrics such as the *packet delivery ratio*, the *bad packet ratio* and the *energy consumption amount*. The basic algorithm tries to detect jamming by using multiple if-else statements on the aforementioned metrics, while the advanced algorithm uses a distribution scheme where information is collected from neighboring nodes. The evaluation shows high detection rates, but trade-offs regarding the false alarm rate versus the detection probability or the detection delay are not presented. In [10], techniques that detect anomalies at all layers of a wireless sensor network are proposed. The authors show how the detection probability increases when the number of the nodes running the proposed procedure increases, but do not show the trade-off with the false alarm rate.

The authors of [11] show how the errors at the physical layer propagate up the network stack, and present a distributed anomaly detection system based on simple thresholds. A method for combining measurements using Pearson's Product Moment correlation coefficient is also presented. Several adversarial models are presented in [7], all focusing on RF jamming attacks. One of the proposed algorithms, applies *high order crossings*, a spectral discrimination mechanism that distinguishes normal scenarios from two types of the defined jammers. The authors introduce two detection algorithms, based on thresholds, that use signal strength and location information as a consistency check to avoid false alarms.

The authors of [8] presents a cross layer approach to detect jamming attacks. Jamming is performed at the physical layer by using RF signals, and at the MAC layer by targeting the RTS/CTS and NAV mechanisms of the IEEE 802.11 protocol. The authors of [5] consider the sequential probability ratio test, applied however to detect MAC-layer misbehavior. Finally, cusum algorithms have been used in several detection systems [5,12,13,14] but they focus on the MAC and upper layers, while we consider a metric (SNR) in the physical layer.

3 Measurement System and Experimental Setup

3.1 Network Topology

The topology of the network used to collect the SNR measurements is shown in Fig. 1. All nodes are equipped with Mini ITX boards, with 512 MB RAM and a 80 GB hard disk. They are also equipped with Atheros NMP 8602 802.11 a/b/g wireless cards, controlled by the Madwifi v 0.9.4 MAC driver, on Ubuntu Linux.

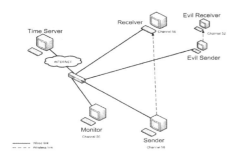

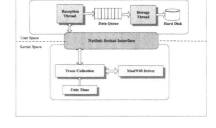

Fig. 1. Network layout

Fig. 2. Measurement module based on the Madwifi driver

UDP traffic is sent from the sender S to the receiver R at a constant rate of 18 Mbps. In addition to the receiver R, a monitor M also collects SNR measurements. Nodes S, M, and R all operate on channel 56. The network interface of monitor M is set to monitor mode, hence receives all packets sent on this channel. Jamming is performed by using two nodes, evil sender (ES) and evil receiver (ER); these two nodes operate on channel 52, which is adjacent to channel 56, hence produces interference. The solid lines in Fig. 1 represent a dedicated wired backbone for running the experiments. Finally, the time on all nodes is synchronized using the network time protocol (NTP) [15].

3.2 Collection of Measurements

Our modifications in the madwifi driver enabled the collection of SNR measurements in all the wireless nodes. The software collection module (Fig. 2) consists of several parts laying on both the kernel and user spaces of the Linux operating system. Data are collected through madwifi in kernel space and then asynchronously transmitted to user-space through the netlink socket interface. In user-space, the Reception Thread receives the data from kernel-space and stores them in a software first-in-first-out (FIFO) queue. The Storage Thread pulls out the data from the queue and stores them in the hard disk. The reason for the user-space functionality to be split into the above threads, connected through the queue, is to increase performance because the copy of the data from memory to the hard disk does not block the reception of the new data coming from the kernel-space. The Storage and Reception threads execute independently in the multi-threaded environment of Linux.

With the same software we are capable of collecting additional information for each packet, such as the long and short retry counters, the retry field of the MAC header, and the timestamps of the outgoing or the incoming packets; the timestamps are necessary to time align measurements at the jammer (evil sender in Fig. 1) and at the nodes where SNR measurements are collected: the receiver and the monitor. If the transmitted or received frame is a data frame, the software also records information such as MAC addresses, IP addresses, port numbers, etc.

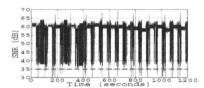

Fig. 3. Effect of jamming on SNR

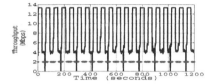

Fig. 4. Effect of jamming on throughput

3.3   Jamming Model

As indicated above, jamming is performed by an evil sender transmitting to an evil receiver on channel 52, which is adjacent with channel 56 on which the sender, receiver, and monitor operate, hence creates interference. The transmission power and rate of the evil sender is 13 dBm and 6 Mbps, respectively. The evil sender transmits data for 30 seconds, after which it remains inactive for 30 seconds. Figure 3 shows the impact of jamming on the SNR of the received packets. This figure shows that drops of the SNR value occur also in periods when there are no attacks. This is due to channel impairments but also to other sources of interference, since the network test-bed was located in a public area where people freely walked. Due to this behavior of the wireless channel, anomaly-based intrusion detection in wireless networks is challenging. Figure 4 shows the effect of jamming on UDP throughput.

4   Anomaly-Based Intrusion Detection Algorithms

We consider two types of algorithms: simple threshold algorithms and algorithms that implement a cumulative sum change point detection procedure. Both types can be applied to different metrics that are based on the SNR: average SNR, minimum SNR, and max-minus-min SNR. The values of these metrics are measured over a small time window.

4.1   Simple Threshold Algorithms

The simple threshold algorithms trigger an alarm when the metric that the algorithm considers deviates from its normal (expected) value by some amount. The normal value is given by the value of the metric, estimated in some long time interval, whereas the degree of deviation to signal an alarm is determined by the detection threshold.

The Simple Min algorithm. The metric used by this algorithm is the minimum value of the SNR in a small window K. An alarm is raised if the minimum value of the SNR deviates from the average value of the SNR, measured over a long window M. Let SNR_n be the SNR value for frame (sample) n. If N the number of samples, then for $n \in [M+1, N]$, the minimum SNR in the short window K is

$$SNR_{min}(n) = \min_{n-K+1 < i \leq n} SNR_i,$$

whereas the average SNR measured in window M is

$$\overline{SNR}(n) = \frac{\sum_{i=n-M+1}^{n} SNR_i}{M}.$$

An alarm is raised at the arrival of frame n if

$$\frac{\overline{SNR}(n)}{SNR_{min}(n)} \geq h, \tag{1}$$

where h is the detection threshold.

The Simple Max-Min algorithm. Rather than considering the minimum value of the SNR measured in a small window, this algorithm considers the maximum-minus-minimum values of the SNR measured in a small window. If D denotes the maximum-minimum value of the SNR, then

$$D(n) = \max_{n-K+1 < i \leq n} SNR_i - \min_{n-K+1 < i \leq n} SNR_i,$$

while the average value of D in the long window is

$$\bar{D}(n) = \frac{\sum_{i=n-M+1}^{n} D(i)}{M}.$$

An alarm is raised at the arrival of frame n if

$$D(n) - \bar{D}(n) \geq h. \tag{2}$$

The Simple Average algorithm. This algorithm compares the average value of the SNR in a short window, with the average value in a long window. If $\overline{SNR_{short}}(n) = \frac{\sum_{i=n-K+1}^{n} SNR_i}{K}$ is the average value of the SNR in a short window K, then an alarm is raised if

$$\frac{\overline{SNR}(n) - \overline{SNR_{short}}(n)}{\overline{SNR}(n)} \geq h, \tag{3}$$

where $\overline{SNR}$ is the average SNR in the long window.

4.2   Cumulative Sum (Cusum) Algorithms

Cusum algorithms belong to the category of change point detection algorithms, and were first introduced in [16]. These types of algorithms have been widely used in the literature, e.g. [5,12,13,14]. Let $\{x\}$ be an independent and identically distributed random variable, and assume there are two hypotheses: $H_0 : x = x_0$ and $H_1 : x = x_1$. H_0 is true when there is no attack, while H_1 is true when there is an attack. The probabilities of the above hypotheses are p_{θ_0} and p_{θ_1}, respectively. The statistical distribution of x has probability p_{θ_0} before a change occurs (i.e., before a jamming attack), and p_{θ_1} after the change has occurred. Cusum aims to detect this change based on the log-likelihood ratio of $k - i$ subsequent observations from x_i to x_k, given by the formula [17]: $S_k^j = \sum_{i=j}^{k} s_i$, where $s_i = \log \frac{p_{\theta_1}(x_i)}{p_{\theta_0}(x_i)}$ is the log-likelihood ratio for the observations from x_i to x_k. Generally, there are two main categories of cusum algorithms: parametric and non-parametric. For the parametric cusum, a model for $\{x\}$ is required, which is not easy to obtain in the area of the communication networks and especially for the SNR due to the volatile nature of wireless networks. For this reason, we consider non-parametric cusum algorithms where a model of $\{x\}$ is not required.

Cusum Min algorithm. The regression formula for the cusum min algorithm is given by

$$y_n = \begin{cases} y_{n-1} + Z_n - a & \text{if } y_n \geq 0 \\ 0 & \text{if } y_n < 0 \end{cases} \tag{4}$$

where $a > 0$ is a tuning parameter of the algorithm, and $Z_n = \frac{\overline{SNR}(n)}{SNR_{min}(n)}$. Note that y_n in (4) increases as $Z_n = \frac{\overline{SNR}(n)}{SNRmin(n)} > a$, i.e. as the minimum SNR value is smaller than the average SNR value by some amount which is determined by the value of a. In the experimental evaluation, we have considered $a = 0.7$.

An alarm is signaled when

$$y_n \geq h\,, \tag{5}$$

where h is the detection threshold.

Cusum Max-Min algorithm. This algorithm has the same regression formula as the cusum min algorithm, given by (4), however Z_n is now given by

$$Z_n = D(n) - \bar{D}(n)\,,$$

where $D(n)$ and $\bar{D}$ are the maximum-minus-minimum SNR in the short time window, and the average maximum-minus-minimum SNR estimated in the long time window. In the experimental evaluation, we have considered $a = 8$.

The alarm rule for the cusum max-min algorithm is identical to the rule for the cusum min algorithm, and is given by (5).

The Cusum Avg (average) algorithm. As above, this algorithm has the same regression formula as the cusum min algorithm, given by (4), however Z_n is now given by

$$Z_n = \frac{\overline{SNR}(n) - \overline{SNR_{short}}(n)}{\overline{SNR}(n)} .$$

In the experimental evaluation, we have considered $a = 0.8$.

The alarm rule for the cusum max-min algorithm is identical to the rule for the cusum min algorithm, and is given by (5).

5   Performance Evaluation

This section presents the performance evaluation of the proposed algorithms using the SNR measurements collected at the receiver and the monitor, Fig. 1. Observe in this figure that the receiver is close to the jammer, whereas the monitor is far from the jammer. As expected, our results show that the algorithms perform better when measurements at the receiver are considered, compared to when measurements at the monitor are considered. The attacks are launched with the transmission of periodic traffic from the evil sender in Fig. 1, and are depicted as orthogonal boxes in Fig. 3.

The performance of the algorithms is evaluated in terms of the detection probability DP, false alarm rate FAR, average detection delay DD, and the robustness to different detection threshold values. The detection probability is defined as the ratio of the detected attacks over the total number of the attacks. The false alarm rate is the ratio of the number of the false alarms over the total duration of the experiment in minutes. A false alarm occurs when an alarm is raised but there is no attack. Finally, the average detection delay is given by $DD = \frac{\sum_{i=1}^{k} [t_a(i) - t_s(i)]}{k}$, where k is the total number of the attacks, $t_a(i)$ is the first time an alarm is raised during the ith attack (more than one alarms can be raised during a single attack), and $t_s(i)$ is the time when the ith attack begins. The detection delay is measured in minutes.

The size of the sliding window used in the experiments is 1000 and 10, for the long and short windows respectively. Note that 1000 samples correspond to approximately 0.9 seconds, which is about one thirtieth of the attack duration (30 seconds).

5.1   DP and FAR Tradeoff

We begin by discussing the tradeoff between the detection probability DP and the false alarm rate FAR, Fig. 5. The various points shown in this graph correspond to different values of the detection threshold parameter. Observe in the top three subfigures in Fig. 5, which shows the results when measurements at the receiver are used for detection, that the performance of all three algorithms, and their cusum variants discussed in the previous section, is very good and close to the top-left corner which corresponds to 100% detection probability and zero false alarms/min for the false alarm rate. Hence, the tradeoff between detection probability versus false alarm rate is not influenced by the use of the cusum mechanism. This is not the case when detection is based on measurements at the monitor, which correspond to the bottom three figures in Fig. 5; observe that when detection is based on measurements taken at the monitor, which happens to be far from the jammer, the cusum mechanism can significantly improve the detection probability versus false alarm rate in the case of the *Max-Min* and *Min SNR* metrics. Finally, note that although for measurements at the receiver, the cusum mechanism does not improve the detection probability versus false alarm rate, as we will see in the following subsection, it does improve the robustness of the algorithms, where by robustness we mean that the performance of the algorithms remains relatively stable for small variations of the detection threshold.

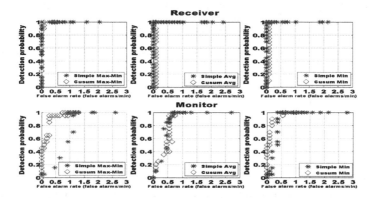

Fig. 5. Detection probability versus false alarm rate for the different algorithms when applied to measurements at the receiver and the monitor

5.2   Robustness and Detection Delay

Next, we discuss the robustness of the algorithms, by investigating how their performance, in terms of the detection probability and false alarm rate varies when the detection threshold changes. First, assume that M is defined as $M = \frac{1}{c+DP} + FAR$, $c > 0$, which combines the detection probability DP and false alarm rate FAR. We define that a detection algorithm is (relatively) robust if the detection threshold needs to change by more than 20% so that the metric M changes by more than 20%. Both these numbers and the specific form of function M are operator-dependent; the methodology we present to evaluate the robustness of the detection algorithms can be applied to any functions that combine the metrics DP, FAR. In the graphs shown below, the range of detection threshold values for which an algorithm is robust, is shown as a shaded area.

Max-Min algorithms. Figure 6 shows how the DP, FAR, and DD vary with the detection threshold. The values of DD are referred on the right vertical axis.

Also, in all subsequent figures, the values of FAR greater than one are not shown; these values appear for small values of the detection threshold located on the left part of each graph. Observe that the threshold values (21-22) where the *Simple Max-Min* algorithm achieves a high DP and low FAR are not inside the stable region. Hence, although for these values the *Simple Max-Min* algorithm achieves good performance in terms of the DP and FAR, its performance is sensitive to small changes of the detection threshold. On the other hand, the detection threshold (≈ 220) for which the *Cusum Max-Min* algorithm achieves high DP and low FAR is inside the stable region. Finally, observe that the detection delay for both the *Simple Max-Min* and *Cusum Max-Min* algorithms is less than 0.1 minutes, within threshold areas they achieve high performance.

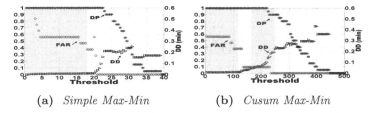

      (a) *Simple Max-Min*   (b) *Cusum Max-Min*

Fig. 6. DP, FAR, and DD for *Simple Max-Min* and *Cusum Max-Min*; measurements at the receiver

Min algorithms. Similar to the *Max-Min* algorithms, the *Cusum Min* algorithm achieves a high DP and low FAR for values of the detection threshold that are inside the stable region, which is not the case for the *Simple Min* algorithm, Fig. 7. The detection delay for the *Simple Min* algorithm is approximately 0.002 minutes, whereas for the *Cusum Min* the detection delay increases from 0.003 to 0.009 minutes, as the detection threshold increases.

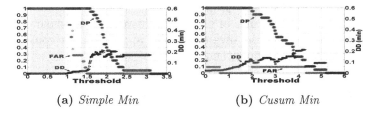

        (a) *Simple Min*   (b) *Cusum Min*

Fig. 7. DP, FAR, and DD for *Simple Min* and *Cusum Min*; measurements at the receiver

Avg algorithms. Fig. 8 shows the DP, FAR, and DD for the *Simple Avg* and *Cusum Avg* algorithms, as a function of the detection threshold. As with the *Max-Min* and *Min* algorithms, the cusum procedure improves the robustness of the algorithm. The detection delay for the *Simple Avg* algorithm is approximately 0.05 minutes, whereas for the *Cusum Avg* algorithm the delay varies from 0.05 to 0.1 minutes.

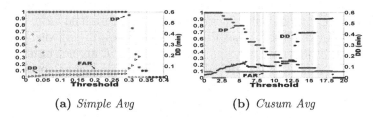

(a) *Simple Avg*   (b) *Cusum Avg*

Fig. 8. *DP*, *FAR*, and *DD* for *Simple Avg* and *Cusum Avg*; measurements at the receiver

All the above algorithms except the *Cusum Max-Min* can achieve perfect performance: 100% detection probability and zero false alarm rate.

6   Conclusions and Further Work

We have presented and evaluated algorithms for the detection of jamming attacks in IEEE 802.11 networks, based on actual measurements. The algorithms seek changes in the statistical characteristics of the collected SNR values and are of two types: simple threshold algorithms and cusum-type algorithms. The algorithms were evaluated in terms of the detection probability, false alarm rate, average detection delay and their robustness to different detection threshold values.

All algorithms have high performance when applied to measurements collected at a node close to the jammer. In the case of measurements collected at a node far from the jammer, the performance of the simple threshold algorithms deteriorates significantly; for such measurements the algorithms based on cumulative sum change point detection show higher performance in terms of the detection probability and false alarm rate. Even in the case of measurements taken close to the jammer, the cusum algorithms have higher robustness, i.e. they exhibit similar performance for a range of value of the detection threshold.

Ongoing work includes the investigation of approaches for combining measurements at different locations, and at different layers.

References

1. Bicacki, K., Tavli, B.: Denial-of-Service attacks and countermeasures in IEEE 802.11 wireless networks. In: Computer Standards and Interfaces. Elsevier, Amsterdam (September 2008)
2. Thuente, D., Newlin, B., Acharya, M.: Jamming Vulnerabilities of IEEE 802.11e. In: Proc. of MilCom 2007, pp. 1–7. IEEE, Los Alamitos (October 2007)
3. Wenyuan, X., Ke, M., Trappe, W., Yanyong, Z.: Jamming sensor networks: attack and defense strategies. IEEE Network, 41–47 (May 2006)
4. Hall, M., Silvennoinen, A., Haggman, S.: Effect of pulse jamming on IEEE 802.11 wireless LAN performance. In: Proc. of MilCom 2005, pp. 2301–2306. IEEE, Los Alamitos (October 2005)

5. Cardenas, A., Radosavac, S., Baras, J.: Evaluation of Detection Algorithms for MAC Layer Misbehavior: Theory and Experiments. To appear in IEEE/ACM Transactions on Networking (2009)
6. Mishra, A., Nadkarni, K., Patcha, A.: Intrusion Detection in Wireless Ad Hoc Networks. IEEE Wireless Communications, 48–60 (February 2004)
7. Xu, W., Trappe, W., Zhang, Y., Wood, T.: The Feasibility of Launching and Detecting Jamming Attacks in Wireless Networks. In: Proc. of ACM MobiHoc (May 2005)
8. Thamilarasu, M., Mishra, S., Sridhar, R.: A Cross-layer approach to detect jamming attacks in wireless ad hoc networks. In: Proc. of Milcom 2006, Washington DC, USA, October 2006, pp. 1–7 (2006)
9. Cakiroglou, M., Ozcerit, T.: Jamming detection mechanisms for wireless sensor networks. In: Proc. of 3rd Int. Conference on Scalable Information Systems, Napoli, Italy (June 2008)
10. Bhuse, V., Gupta, A.: Anomaly intrusion detection in wireless sensor networks. Journal of High Speed Networks, 33–51 (2006)
11. Sheth, A., Doerr, C., Grunwald, D., Han, R., Sicker, D.: MOJO: a distributed physical layer anomaly detection system for 802.11 WLANs. In: ACM MobiSys (2006)
12. Wang, H., Zhang, D., Shin, K.: Change-point monitoring for the detection of DoS attacks. In: Transactions on Dependable and Secure Computing. IEEE, Los Alamitos (2004)
13. Yan, G., Xiao, Z., Eidenbenz, S.: Catching instant messaging worms with change-point detection techniques. In: Proc. of the 1st Usenix Workshop on Large-Scale Exploits and Emergent Threats (April 2008)
14. Chen, Y., Hwang, K., Ku, W.: Distributed Change-Point Detection of DDoS Attacks: Experimental Results on DETER Testbed. In: Proc. of USENIX Security Symposium, Boston, USA (August 2007)
15. Ntp: the network time protocol, http://www.ntp.org
16. Page, E.S.: Continuous inspection schemes. Biometrika, 100–115 (1954)
17. Basseville, M., Nikiforov, I.V.: Detection of Abrupt Changes: Theory and Applications. Prentice-Hall, Englewood Cliffs (1993)

A Stable Linked Structure Flooding for Mobile Ad Hoc Networks with Fault Recovery

Tom Leclerc, Laurent Ciarletta, and André Schaff

LORIA - Campus Scientifique - BP 239 - 54506 Vandœuvre-les-Nancy Cedex
{tom.leclerc,laurent.ciarletta,andre.schaff}@loria.fr

Abstract. Efficient message dissemination in ad hoc networks can be fostered by exploiting stable (sub-)structures. By efficient we mean low network resource usage regarding reachability. In this paper we build a hierarchical protocol. We first create single-hop clusters among stable-connected devices. On top of those clusters, we further determine inter-cluster relays (ICR), finally providing an overall stable-connected structure. Our proposed stable linked structure flooding (SLSF) protocol efficiently disseminates data among stable nodes. Additional fault recovery mechanisms are employed to compensate for local intermittent node failures if needed. The experiments show that our approach increases flooding performances with a low bandwidth usage. Furthermore SLSF remains very efficient with or without the fault recovery mechanism that provides robustness.

1 Introduction

Mobile ad hoc networks are composed of a collection of devices that communicate with each other over a wireless medium [1]. Such a network can be formed spontaneously whenever devices are in transmission range. Potential applications of such networks can be found in traffic scenarios, environmental observations, ubiquitous Internet access, and in search and rescue scenarios as described in detail in [2]. However, since joining and leaving of nodes occurs dynamically, the network topology changes frequently. Our solution starts by building local groups of one-hop stable-connected devices in a self-organizing manner. Moreover, the approach we introduced in [3] aims at discovering stable connections between groups, thus creating bigger stable-linked network structures. We exploit the stable-linked structures within the network topology to streamline information exchange and to minimize the overhead. The local one-hop groups are built using the NLWCA clustering protocol [4]. As in WCPD [5] specific beacon formats are used to detect nearby stable-connected clusters. Furthermore, to create bigger stable-connected structures we present Inter-Cluster Relays (ICR). Finally, to add robustness, a fault recovery protocol is employed to compensate for local intermittent node failures. Fault recovery can be selectively enabled/disabled on per-packet basis.

The remainder of this paper is organized as follows. The next Section 2 sets the context and presents the related work for this paper. Section 3 describes the

E. Osipov et al. (Eds.): WWIC 2010, LNCS 6074, pp. 204–215, 2010.

building blocks of our SLSF protocol. In Section 4 we evaluate our approach and present the simulation results. We conclude our paper and present the future work in section 5.

2   Context and Related Work

2.1   NLWCA and WCPD

The Weighted Cluster-based Path Discovery protocol (WCPD) is designed to take advantage of the cluster topology built by the Node and Link Weighted Clustering Algorithm (NLWCA) in order to provide path discovery and broadcast mechanisms in mobile ad hoc networks.

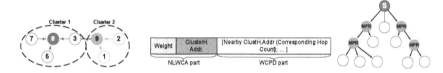

Fig. 1. Example of two clusters built by NLWCA   **Fig. 2.** NLWCA+WCPD Beacon   **Fig. 3.**   OLSR topology from one source

NLWCA organizes ad hoc networks in one-hop clusters (Figure 1) by using only information available locally. Each device elects exactly one device as its clusterhead (CH), i.e. the neighbor with the highest weight. So far, a topological chain can be formed by so called sub-head nodes. A sub-head is a node that elects a neighbor node as CH but at the same time is elected as CH by some other one-hop neighbor nodes. However, sub-heads can lead to more than three hops between a source CH and its nearby CHs which could lead to a complex communication protocol. To obtain strict one-hop clusters, thus simplifying the protocol, a rule was added to the original NLWCA algorithm: a node that already elected a foreign node as CH is not eligible to be elected by another node as CH. From a graph theory point of view, one-hop clusters form a dominating set.

The main goal of NLWCA is to avoid superfluous re-organization of the clusters, particularly when clusters cross each other. To achieve this, NLWCA assigns weights to the links between the own node and the network neighbor nodes. This weight is used to keep track of the connection stability to the one-hop network neighbors. When a link weight reaches a given stability threshold it is considered stable and the device is called stable neighbor device. The CH is elected only from the set of stable neighbors which avoids the re-organization of the topology when two clusters are crossing for a short period of time.

WCPD, on top of NLWCA, discovers nearby stable-connected clusters in a pro-active fashion. For the nearby CHs discovery algorithm, WCPD uses the beacon to detect devices in communication range. NLWCA and WCPD combined provide to each node, through the beacon (Figure 2), following information about each stable one-hop neighbor: its weight, its CH ID, the ID set of discovered CHs and their respective path length.

The WCPD broadcasting algorithm is simple: the broadcast source node sends the message to the CH, which stores the ID of the message and broadcasts it to the one-hop neighborhood. After that, it sends it to all nearby CHs by multi-hop unicast. The inter-cluster destination nodes repeat the procedure except that the message source clusters are omitted from further forwarding. Additionally, the information about the ID of the broadcast messages and their sources is stored for a given period of time to avoid superfluous re-sending of the message.

2.2   OLSR

The Optimized Link State Routing Protocol (OLSR) [6] is a well known routing protocol designed for ad hoc networks. It is a proactive protocol; hence it periodically exchanges topology information with other nodes of the network. One-hop neighborhood and two-hop neighborhood are discovered using Hello Messages (similar to beacons). The multipoint relay (MPR) nodes are calculated by selecting the smallest one-hop neighborhood set needed to reach every two-hop neighbor node. The topology control information is only forwarded by the nodes which are selected as MPR. Every node then has a routing table containing the shortest path to every node of the network. OLSR enables optimized flooding of the network by building a tree-like topology for every node from a source (Figure 3). Therefore, MPR selection constructs an optimal connected dominating set [7]. For this reason OLSR is our benchmark reference in Section 4.

2.3   Related Work

In ad hoc networks forwarding strategies should be employed to avoid broadcast storms (i.e. a message forwarded by all the nodes in the network). As depicted in [8], broadcast storms can be counter-measured using several schemes i.e. probabilistic, counter-based, distance-based, location-based and cluster-based. We use the latter scheme, cluster-based, since it is the only one based on network topology information. The cluster architecture we use solely relies on locally available information whereas [8] proposes a clustering technique where the CH is elected after an explicit message exchange among the neighbors.

The Zone Routing Protocol (ZRP)[9] combines proactive routing inside a zone using bordercast and on-demand routing outside. A node, sending a message, checks if the destination is in its zone, if not it bordercasts the message to its gateway nodes. Those nodes repeat the same process until the destination is reached. As every zone is centered on the current node the ZRP dissemination results in plain bordercasting a message ahead its destination. To route inside a zone, ZRP needs k-hop information (k>1), which results in scalability issues similar to OLSR.

In [10], the authors construct elected clusters based on beacon information which provides the number of neighbors and their stability represented by the number of beacons received. This approach is similar to NLWCA but does not rely on both a link weight and a node weight. Thus NLWCA has more flexibility in terms of cluster selection. Another similarity to our approach is the forwarding node selection (named gateway selection). The main differences is that our approach requires no message exchange except the payload broadcast itself for gateway selection. The comparison will not be further analyzed since to our knowledge the gateway selection process is insufficiently described.

Many ad hoc protocols use the selection of forwarding nodes to reduce redundant messages. In [11] and [12] broadcast relay gateways are selected with 2-hop knowledge. However we chose the already described OLSR protocol because of its popularity in ad hoc networks and Mesh networks, and also because it is the only one proved to optimize coverage of 2-hop nodes through MPRs [13]. MPRs build optimal connected dominating sets [7]. We take advantage of this property to build paths among the (not-connected) dominating sets built by the NLWCA clustering algorithm. Many other approaches that construct distributed connected dominating sets exist [14,15]. However, our goal is not to create connected dominating sets, but to disseminate information over the **stable** structure built by NLWCA, using ICRs between the CHs to optimize nearby-cluster-paths. Thus, as a result of our structure, we have connected dominating sets, but only between a CH and its nearby CHs.

3   SLSF

NLWCA and WCPD provide a stable-connected cluster architecture, however the broadcasting algorithm of WCPD needs many improvement on reachability performances compared to OLSR which performs very well on reachability but lacks in scalability and uses a lot of bandwidth [16]. Our SLSF (Stable Linked Structure Flooding) protocol replaces the inefficient broadcasting mechanism of WCPD with the ICR mechanism. SLSF combines the advantages of all the protocols NLWCA, WCPD and OLSR: scalability, stability, reachability, while keeping the drawbacks low (i.e. the bandwidth usage). SLSF forms a first level of hierarchy with a dominating set using NLWCA. Considering the dominant nodes of the underlying level (NLWCA), it forms an optimal connected dominating set with the ICR mechanism. The first level reduces the network to its dominant nodes and the second level insures shortest-path connectivity and minimal relay nodes among dominant nodes of the first level.

3.1   SLSF - Inter-cluster Relay

Multiple paths to reach a given CH requires choosing one path prior to another. We use a next-hop selection inspired by the MultiPoint Relay (MPR) mechanism of OLSR to select the forwarding neighbors. We name Inter-Cluster-Relays (ICR) the nodes selected as next-hop. The goal of ICR is to reach all nearby CHs with the minimal set of 1-hop neighbors while optimizing the hop-count. The ICR nodes are calculated by selecting the smallest one-hop neighborhood set (directly connected nodes) needed to reach every nearby CH. ICR selection remains straightforward because the possible inter-cluster configurations are restricted by the underlying one-hop cluster topology (examples on Figure 6).

SLSF, on top of NLWCA, discovers the nearby clusters (similar to WCPD) by reading the neighbor beacons. The improvement and novelty relies on the ICR selection which avoids superfluous network communication overhead without any additional message exchange. SLSF keeps the last beacon of every one-hop neighbor in cache. Hence every node has the following information locally available about each stable 1-hop neighbor: its weigth, its CH ID, the ID set of discovered CHs and their respective path length. ICR selection occurs as follows:

i. Select as ICR, neighbors that are the only one reaching a given nearby CH.
ii. Remove the now covered clusters from the list.
iii. Remove for every neighbor from the announced CH-list the entries with a worse hop count than the best one (i.e. keep only shortest path entries).
   1. Calculate the cluster reachability for every one-hop neighbor (i.e. number of foreign CHs the neighbor announces in its beacon).
   2. Select the neighbor with the best reachability.
   3. Else if equivalent: select the neighbor with the highest weight.
   4. Else if equivalent: select the node with the biggest IP address.
   5. Remove the now covered clusters from the list.
   6. While there is a not-covered CH, go back to 1.

3-hop Inter-cluster case. NLWCA builds one-hop clusters, thus it permits up to three hops (two slave nodes) between CHs. ICR selection with two hops (one slave node) between CHs (Figure 6b) is straight selection by the CH, however an additional hop (Figure 6d) requires additional attention.

A further hop involves an additional forward of the message to reach the nearby CH. For example on Figure 6d, the source CH2 designates a node as ICR (here the blue slave neighbor of CH2). The designated ICR has to make a choice between one of the two (orange) slaves of CH1. This choice is computed by using ICR selection using the list containing only 1 hop distant(from the blue slave: here the orange CH) clusterheads.

When to select ICR nodes? ICR selection is done based on events. Every time a change in the stable neighborhood that influences the ICR calculation occurs, the ICR selection is re-calculated. Thus broadcasting or forwarding a message using ICRs is immediate: replace the ICR set in the message with the one locally pre-calculated. Further detail on broadcasting in SLSF in section 3.2.

ICR: The big picture. To highlight the gain of ICR selection, Figure 4 shows an example with 5 clusters where the message source CH S sends a broadcast. The broadcast of S will have the format shown on figure 5.

On reception of this broadcast only nodes 1, 2 and 3 will forward the message, while the other neighboring nodes process the message silently. Note that node 1 selects 4 and 5 as ICR according to section 3.1 "3-hop Inter-cluster case".

We see that ICR selection reduces a lot the number of forwarding nodes. As an example, on Figure 4 there are 23 nodes in the network and only 10 nodes (including the CHs) are emitting to reach all the nodes in the network.

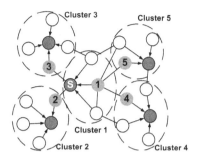

Fig. 5. Format of a broadcast message with payload

Fig. 4. ICR selection with 5 clusters

Fig. 6. Inter-cluster configuration examples where 1 and 2 are clusterheads

Every CH will emit the message once in order for their slave to receive it and if necessary include their local ICR selection for further forwarding in the network (see section 3.2). In comparison, there would be 15 nodes forwarding the message using OLSR. This is due to OLSR using only 2-hop information while SLSF uses 1-hop cluster information which represent information from up to 3-hops away. While 3-hop knowledge usually increases the amount of information to collect using clusters reduces drastically the nodes to keep track of for ICR selection.

3.2   SLSF - Broadcast

At this point, every communication occurs between one cluster and its nearby clusters. To enable communication with foreign clusters, we propose a simple broadcast mechanism. A more sophisticated foreign cluster-broadcast mechanism would be out of scope for this paper.

Our broadcast mechanism is simple now that we only need to deal at cluster level. A node willing to broadcast a message through the network will, unless it is its own CH, send it to its CH. The original message contains the source address, a corresponding sequence number and of course the payload data. The CH puts its own address as last crossed CH and adds a corresponding sequence number to the message. Finally it forwards it to all its nearby CHs using the ICR mechanism. On reception the nearby CHs replace the last crossed CH address with their own and replace the corresponding sequence number. The ICR (excluding from selection the cluster the message came from) set is also updated. To avoid superfluous re-sending of the message SLSF stores information about the ID of messages and their sources for a given period of time.

As an example, on Figure 7 the node 1 sends a message passing (as 1 is a slave) the message to CH9, which then uses the ICR mechanism for the dissemination. Note that node 7 is in the "3-hop inter-cluster case" (section 3.1). The message reaches all the nodes in the network following the path depicted on Figure 8.

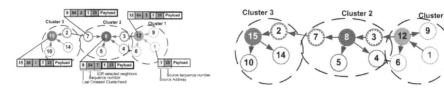

Fig. 7. Foreign-cluster broadcast - Format of a message sent from node 1

Fig. 8. Foreign-cluster broadcast - Path of a message sent from node 1

3.3   SLSF - Fault-Recovery

The goal of fault-recovery is to be able to transmit the message even if the ICR path fails without having the source to re-emit the message. To do so we propose two mechanisms, the first is the acknowledgement mechanism, enabling broadcasts to be acknowledged by nearby CHs and the second is the delayed transmission detecting transmission errors and handling them.

Acknowledgment mechanism. The following acknowledgement mechanism has two advantages. The first, for which it was actually designed, is permitting a delayed transmission to compensate local intermittent node failures. The second is classic acknowledgment of messages but only between adjacent CHs as opposed to acknowledgements from one end of the network to the other. The classic cluster-to-cluster acknowledgement is a consequence of the initial design. Further consideration of end-to-end acknowledgements would be out of scope for this paper but is an open interest for future work.

Our acknowledgement mechanism works using sequence numbers. Every node puts inside its beacon sequence numbers to acknowledge messages. However, only CHs acknowledge the messages while inter-cluster nodes forward merely the acknowledgement information coming from nearby CHs to their neighborhood. As consequence, beacons of CHs have a different format than inter-cluster node beacons. Following is an example illustrating how the acknowledgement mechanism works. Using Figure 1 as reference, we suppose node 9 sends a broadcast with sequence number N9. Nodes 1, 2 and 3 receive the message. Only node 3 will forward it to its neighborhood as it is designated ICR, since it is the only inter-cluster node. Node 1 and 2 process silently the message without forwarding it. CH8 receives the message from node 3, processes the messages, and puts in its beacon the acknowledged sequence number N9 for CH9. Beacon of CH8 contains now its weight, its CH-address (here its own), its nearby CHs with the corresponding hop count and the acknowledged sequence number. So, the SLSF beacon (Figure 9a) is only extended with one sequence number (Figure 9b).

Node 3 reads the CH8 beacon (Figure 9b) and includes in its beacon the new sequence number acknowledged by CH8 for the message source CH9. In order to reduce the beacon size for inter-cluster nodes, we compact acknowledgment information into the basic SLSF beacon by just adding sequence numbers in the right order and place. If we consider the basic SLSF beacon (Figure 10a) for the

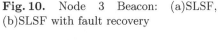

Fig. 9. CH8 Beacon: (a)SLSF, (b)SLSF with fault recovery

Fig. 10. Node 3 Beacon: (a)SLSF, (b)SLSF with fault recovery

Fig. 12. Node 3 SLSF beacon

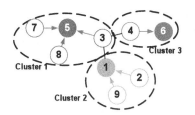

Fig. 11. Three clusters example

Fig. 13. Node 3 SLSF beacon with fault recovery

slave node 3 we integrate additionally inside the beacon the information that CH8 acknowledges sequence number N9 for CH9 and that CH9 acknowledges N8 for CH8 (Figure 10b). Note the inversion of the sequence numbers compared to the beacon of CH 8.

To really point out this inversion an example where three nearby clusters are inter-connected is necessary (Figure 11).In this example, node 3 is connected to three clusters. As a matter of fact, node 3 will forward any message exchange between those clusters. The beacon of node 3 has to contain all the acknowledgement information for the three CHs. The basic SLSF beacon of node 3 of Figure 11 is shown in Figure 12.

Node 3's beacon contains its own clusterhead, CH5, and two nearby CHs, CH1 and CH6, on 1 and 2 hop distance respectively. Now we consider we want the following information into that beacon, like for instance after some broadcasts were sent (Nx corresponds to the acknowledged sequence number):

CH1 acknowledges N5 for CH5 and N6 for CH 6 ⇔ CH1=[CH5/N5, CH6/N6]
CH5 acknowledges N1 for CH1 and N6 for CH 6 ⇔ CH5=[CH1/N1, CH6/N6]
CH6 acknowledges N5 for CH5 and N1 for CH 1 ⇔ CH6=[CH5/N5, CH1/N1]

The original SLSF beacon already contains the three CH-addresses (typically the IP addresses of the CHs); the own CH-address and two nearby CH-addresses. First sort all the acknowledgements CH-addresses in ascending order. For example CH6=[CH5/N5, CH1/N1] is sorted as CH6=[CH1/N1, CH5/N5]. For each CH-address in the beacon attach the corresponding sequence numbers and omit the superfluous CH-addresses inside the list, as shown on Figure 13. Doing so, putting in the right order the right sequence numbers, results in a new beacon with all the needed information just by adding the needed sequence numbers without additional addresses.

The constructed beacon (Figure 13) is received by the neighbors. For instance CH1 can reads in the beacon [N5,N6] and by ordering the announced CHs (CH1, CH5, CH6) and omitting itself (CH5, CH6) it can read that CH5 acknowledges N5 and CH6 acknowledges N6.

The presented acknowledgement mechanism permits acknowledgements between a cluster and its nearby clusters. While the acknowledgements of the CHs using beacons are straightforward, the inter-cluster beacons of the nodes are constructed using inversion and re-ordering to avoid redundant information inside the beacon and still enabling the source cluster to distinguish which cluster acknowledges which messages without any other message exchange than beacons.

Delayed transmission mechanism. The ICR selection enables the communication among nearby clusters in an optimized way. To keep the inter-cluster communication reliable in case the selected ICR path failed, we introduce a delayed transmission mechanism. Thus, we have an immediate communication path formed by the ICRs and we keep a backup, although delayed, path in case of failures.

Delayed transmission occurs as follows: If a broadcasted message is emitted from a source, all neighbor nodes NOT selected as ICR in the message will keep the message in cache and only in case of a failure transmit the message. While the ICR nodes forward the messages, the nodes pending for delayed transmission observe the neighboring beacons for acknowledgements of nearby CHs. On reception of a pending acknowledgement, the delayed transmission is aborted. If the pending time for delayed transmission times out, the message is broadcasted to all neighbors with the retransmitted flag set. Nodes that already received the message will discard it silently while others forward it immediately. The message arrives at destination in case of failure without re-emission of the message from the source. Thus, having only nodes that did not try forwarding the message yet, effectively (re)transmitting the message.

Following discusses the delay chosen for timeout to occur. If we consider the beacon-interval as bI, the number of nodes the message already passed through as hopCount and 4 the maximal number of hops for a message to go back and forth from the first slave to a cluster on (maximal) 2-hop distance. Then the transmission delay td is calculated as follows: $td = \left(\frac{4}{hopCount}\right) \times bI$. If the beacon-interval is 1 second and the hopcount is 1 then the transmission delay is set to 4 seconds. If the hopcount is 2 then the transmission delay is set to 2 seconds.

4   Simulation and Results

To evaluate the performances of our SLSF protocol, we implemented the three protocols (OLSR, NLWCA/WCPD and SLSF) on top of the JANE simulator [17] and performed several simulations. For those experiments we used the Restricted Random Way Point mobility model [18], whereby the devices move along defined streets on the map of Luxembourg City for 1000 seconds. For each device the speed was randomly varied between [0.5;1.5] units/s with a transmission range

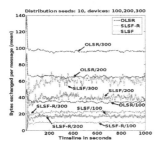 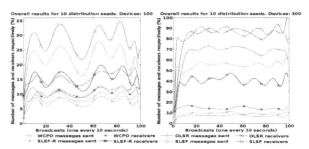

Fig. 14. Bandwidth used in order to build the topology for 100, 200 and 300 nodes

Fig. 15. Overall number of sent messages and node receivers for 100 and 300 nodes. (smoothed with a polynomial equation of the 16th grade for visibility sake).

of 25 units. For each experiment 10 different random distribution seeds were used in order to feature results from different topologies and movement setups. For the used mobile environment where nodes move with low (walking) speeds between 1.8 and 5.4 km/h the NLWCA link-stability threshold is set on 2 [4].

Simulations were done to determine the bandwidth used by the protocols in order to build the topologies and the information dissemination performance of broadcasting on top of the different topologies. Then we compared the efficiency of the protocols and finally made a static evaluation to compare information dissemination solely on MPR and ICR performances.

OLSR exchanges the sets of one-hop neighbor nodes with every node in communication range. Similar to OLSR, SLSF exchanges the list of the discovered nearby-CHs with the one-hop neighbor nodes. For our experiments we distinguished two different SLSF configurations. the first is SLSF without fault recovery referred as SLSF-R (minus fault recovery), thus only ICR selection with basic SLSF beacon (same format as the WCPD beacon, thus same bandwidth usage). The second is the full SLSF protocol with ICR selection and fault-recovery mechanism with added sequence numbers in the beacon. To find out the network load produced during this phase, the size of the exchanged data sets were tracked every second of the simulation: for OLSR the size of the one-hop neighbor sets, for SLSF-R and WCPD the size of the discovered CHs and for SLSF additionally to the discovered CHs the sequence numbers.

In order to monitor the information dissemination performance (Reachability) a node was chosen to broadcast a message every 10 seconds during different simulation runs. The number of sent messages (i.e. broadcasts and unicasts) during the dissemination and the number of reached network nodes were tracked.

As shown in Figure 14, OLSR uses a higher bandwidth in both sparser (100 nodes) and denser networks (300 nodes). This was expected since OLSR is exchanging the set of one-hop neighbors, while SLSF only exchanges the set of locally discovered nearby CHs which is a fractional amount of the total number of nodes. SLSF-R uses exactly the same bandwidth (80% less than OLSR) as WCPD since they share the same beacon structure. SLSF uses more bandwidth than SLSF-R, as sequence numbers were added to the beacon, but still uses about 40% less bandwidth than OLSR.

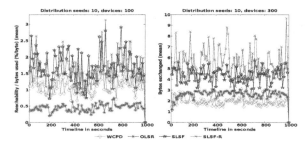
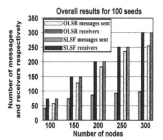

Fig. 16. Efficiency of Bandwidth usage for 100 and 300 nodes

Fig. 17. Static scenario with 100 to 300 nodes

The dissemination performance results (Figure 15, NOTE: periodicity in curves is induced by the smoothing) show that SLSF performs the best for all densities. For 300 nodes SLSF performs only slightly better than OLSR, but uses on average 10 to 15% less forwarders with 40% less bandwidth usage. WCPD performs the worst and uses accordingly lesser forwarding nodes. Whereas SLSF-R uses approximately the same amount of forwarders than WCPD, it reaches from 10% to 20% more nodes. This is the pure gain of ICR selection which optimizes the forwarding nodes.

Subsequently we calculated a "quality-cost" ratio extracted from the results of Figures 14 and 15. We calculated the percentage of nodes reached, divided by the bandwidth used. We see in Figure 16 that SLSF and SLSF-R are in average two to three times more efficient than OLSR. The poor performances of WCPD highlight the need for improvement that SLSF brings.

SLSF relies on stable structures built by NLWCA: only nodes considered as stable will receive the message. So finally, to compare the performances on equal levels, we experimented OLSR and SLSF in a static scenario where all nodes are considered stable connected. The experiments where done on a 300x300 units surface with 100 to 300 nodes randomly positioned using 100 different topology seeds. Again, the number of forwarding and receiving nodes using MPR and ICR selection where tracked. The results on Figure 17 show that SLSF outperforms OLSR in terms of ratio of forwarding nodes over receiving nodes. With increasing density on average with OLSR about 85% of the receivers are also forwarders, whereas in SLSF this amount decreases from 60% towards 30%.

5   Conclusion and Future Work

This paper proposes SLSF, a flooding protocol which selects Inter-Cluster Relays to optimize the communication among the stable-connected cluster architecture. To deal with intermittent message loss we added a fault recovery mechanism that can be selectively enabled on a per-packet basis.

The goal of the ICR (Inter-Cluster Relay) selection is to reach all nearby clusterheads with the minimal set of 1-hop neighbors while optimizing the hop-count. ICR selection on top of the stable-cluster architecture reduces substantially the number of forwarding nodes. Generally, SLSF performs well in high density networks while keeping the used bandwidth very low.

Currently we consider using SLSF as basis for Zerconf [19] (a service discovery protocol) in simulation and real world experiments.

As future work we plan to evaluate the performances using various mobility models and topology settings and also assess the results, in the context of the French National Research Project SARAH, deploying a large scale ad hoc network inside a museum.

References

1. Dousse, O., Thiran, P., Hasler, M.: Connectivity in ad-hoc and hybrid networks. In: IEEE Infocom 2002, pp. 1079–1088 (2002)
2. Paolo, S.: Topology control in wireless ad hoc and sensor networks. ACM Comput. Surv. 37(2) (2005)
3. Leclerc, T., Ciarletta, L., Schaff, A.: SLSF: stable linked structure flooding for mobile ad hoc networks. In: IEEE ISWPC, Palazzo Ducale, Modena, Italy (2010)
4. Andronache, A., Rothkugel, S.: Nlwca node and link weighted clustering algorithm for backbone-assisted mobile ad hoc networks. In: ICN '08. IEEE, Los Alamitos (2008)
5. Andronache, A., Rothkugel, S.: Hytrace backbone-assisted path discovery in hybrid networks. In: CTRQ '08, pp. 34–40. IEEE Computer Society, Los Alamitos (2008)
6. Optimized link state routing protocol (olsr), rfc3626 (2003)
7. Adjih, C., Jacquet, P., Viennot, L.: Computing connected dominated sets with multipoint relays. Research Report RR-4597, INRIA (2002)
8. Ni, S.Y., Tseng, Y.C., Chen, Y.S., Sheu, J.P.: The broadcast storm problem in a mobile ad hoc network. In: MobiCom '99. ACM Press, New York (1999)
9. Haas, Z.J., Pearlman, M.R., Samar, P.: The zone routing protocol (zrp) for ad hoc networks. Technical report (July 2002)
10. Foroozan, F., Tepe, K.: A high performance cluster-based broadcasting algorithm for wireless ad hoc networks based on a novel gateway selection approach. In: PE-WASUN '05, pp. 65–70. ACM, New York (2005)
11. Peng, W., Lu, X.: Ahbp: An efficient broadcast protocol for mobile ad hoc networks. Journal of Computer Science and Technology 16(2) (2001)
12. Lou, W., Wu, J.: Double-covered broadcast (dcb): a simple reliable broadcast algorithm in manets. In: INFOCOM 2004, vol. 3 (2004)
13. Jacquet, P., et al.: Performance analysis of OLSR multipoint relay flooding in two ad hoc wireless network models. RSRCP, Special issue on Mobility and Internet (2001)
14. Wu, J., Dai, F., Gao, M., Stojmenovic, I.: On calculating power-aware connected dominating sets for efficient routing in ad hoc wireless networks. IEEE/KICS Journal of Communications and Networks 4, 59–70 (2002)
15. Blum, J., Ding, M., Thaeler, A., Cheng, X.: Connected dominating set in sensor networks and manets. In: Du, D.-Z., Pardalos, P. (eds.) Handbook of Combinatorial Optimization, pp. 329–369. Kluwer Academic Publishers, Dordrecht (2004)
16. Leclerc, T., Ciarletta, L., Andronache, A., Rothkugel, S.: Olsr and wcpd as basis for service discovery in manets. In: UBICOMM '08. IEEE, Los Alamitos (2008)
17. Gorgen, D., Frey, H., Hiedels, C.: Jane-the java ad hoc network development environment. In: ANSS '07. IEEE Computer Society, Los Alamitos (2007)
18. Blažević, L., Giordano, S., Le Boudec, J.Y.: Self organized terminode routing. Cluster Computing 5(2) (2002)
19. Zeroconf: Zerconf, http://www.zeroconf.org/

Techniques for Measuring Quality of Experience

Fernando Kuipers[1], Robert Kooij[2],
Danny De Vleeschauwer[3], and Kjell Brunnström[4]

[1] Delft University of Technology, P.O. Box 5031, 2600 GA Delft, The Netherlands
F.A.Kuipers@tudelft.nl
[2] TNO, Brassersplein 2, 2612 CT, Delft, The Netherlands
robert.kooij@tno.nl
[3] Alcatel-Lucent Bell NV, Copernicuslaan 50, 2018 Antwerp, Belgium
danny.de_vleeschauwer@alcatel-lucent.com
[4] Netlab, Acreo AB, Kista, Sweden
Kjell.Brunnstrom@acreo.se

Abstract. Quality of Experience (QoE) relates to how users perceive the quality of an application. To capture such a subjective measure, either by subjective tests or via objective tools, is an art on its own. Given the importance of measuring users' satisfaction to service providers, research on QoE took flight in recent years. In this paper we present an overview of various techniques for measuring QoE, thereby mostly focusing on freely available tools and methodologies.

1 Introduction

In the 40 years of its existence, the Internet has gradually evolved from a small network where connectivity was key, to a large media-rich network in which the user is placed more and more central. Users do not only just consume content, but have also started actively producing content. Hand-in-hand with this evolution to a media-rich Internet, the user requirements have transcended requirements on connectivity and users now expect services to be delivered in par with their demands on quality. Research on how to measure user Quality of Experience (QoE) has consequently also blossomed in recent years. In the International Telecommunication Union (ITU) several standards related to QoE have been proposed or are under development. We refer to Takahashi et al. [18] for an overview of these standardization activities. According to the ITU-T Focus Group on IPTV (FG IPTV), *Quality of Experience (QoE) refers to the overall acceptability of an application or service, as perceived subjectively by the end-user.* QoE thereby includes the complete end-to-end system effects (client, terminal, network, services infrastructure, etc.), where overall acceptability may be influenced by user expectations and context. This definition explicitly refers to QoE as a subjective measure and properly measuring QoE should therefore involve tests with actual users, which is a time-consuming and costly process. For service and network providers it is preferable to have tools that objectively reflect within reasonable accuracy the subjective mean opinion score of users.

E. Osipov et al. (Eds.): WWIC 2010, LNCS 6074, pp. 216–227, 2010.

In this paper we present a set of techniques to measure QoE. The paper is not an exhaustive survey of the state-of-the-art in QoE, but instead provides a comprehensive palette of freely available tools and methods for conducting various QoE experiments. The remainder of the paper is organized as follows. In Section 2 we discuss the various parameters that affect QoE. The following three sections discuss measuring QoE for audio (Section 3), gaming (Section 4), and video (Section 5). Section 6 delves into the use of QoE in designing applications, and we conclude in Section 7.

2 QoE Framework

What makes QoE a somewhat elusive concept is that the parameters that define QoE may differ per service. For instance, zapping times play a role in television services, while in gaming it is not an issue. However, it is clear that QoE comprises more than just audio and video quality. We can classify the parameters that affect QoE into three groups:

1. The quality of the video/audio content at the source.
2. Quality of Service (QoS), which refers to the delivery of content over the network.
3. Human perception, which includes expectations, ambiance, etc.

The quality of the content relates to the kind of codec used, for instance MPEG-2 or MPEG-4, bit-rate, etc. The QoS parameters that affect the performance of streaming services most are bandwidth, delay, jitter, and packet loss.

The first two QoE categories are fairly easily quantified, while the latter one is not. Human perception is usually captured by a Mean Opinion Score (MOS), which reflects the appraisal of some test panel. The MOS is expressed on a five-point scale (ITU-T P.800), where $5 = excellent$, $4 = good$, $3 = fair$, $2 = poor$, $1 = bad$. The minimum threshold for acceptable quality corresponds to a MOS of 3.5.

In general, there are three possible methodologies for measuring QoE:

1. The no-reference model has no knowledge of the original stream or source file and tries to predict QoE by monitoring several QoS parameters in real-time.
2. The reduced-reference model has some limited knowledge of the original stream and tries to combine this with real-time measurements to reach a prediction on the QoE.
3. The full-reference model assumes full access to the reference video, possibly combined with the measurements conducted in a real-time environment.

The first model fits under the umbrella of the second, which on its turn can be brought under the third. The full-reference model therefore should be able to give the best accuracy, but it is a method that can only be applied if one has control over both end systems. A no-reference model can be more easily adopted, but might not always give accurate results. In the following section we will list both a no-reference and a full-reference model for capturing speech QoE.

3   QoE of Speech and Audio

The most prominent example of a no-reference model is the E-model (ITU-T Rec. G.107). It predicts the quality users experience during a voice conversation based on the end-device characteristics and the transport parameters. These characteristics and parameters are plugged into some functions internal to the E-model of which the coefficients were tuned based on subjective experiments. The E-model determines a rating R:

$$R = R_0 - I_s - I_d - I_e + A$$

where R_0 is the basic signal-to-noise ratio, I_s takes into account phenomena that occur simultaneously with the speech signal (like the loudness of the speech signal and the side-tone and quantization effects), I_d groups impairments associated with delay (such as, impairments due to echo and loss of interactivity), I_e accumulates the effects associated with special equipment (for example, the use of a low bit rate codec or packet loss), and A is an advantage factor (i.e., a decrease in R-rating a user is willing to tolerate because he or she has a certain advantage, e.g., being mobile).

While for traditional telephone conversations the factors R_0 and I_s were the most important, for packet-based networks (e.g., for VoIP applications), the terms I_d and I_e play the most prominent role (and A is considered to be just an additional budget in some mobile applications). Leaving out the advantage factor A and for end devices that are well tuned, $R_0 - I_s$ usually lies around 95. If echo is properly controlled (which we can safely assume in modern day applications), the term I_d remains practically constant for a one-way delay below 150 ms. If this delay (also termed interactivity bound) is exceeded, I_d increases (and R decreases) by about 1 point on the R-scale per 10 ms additional delay [10]. The term I_e includes the effect of using a low bit rate codec and the impact of packet loss. Each standard low bit rate codec has an associated I_e function that determines how much distortion the codec itself introduces and how much additional impairment is introduced by packet loss. It is not uncommon that a codec introduces 10 points of impairment on the R-scale and that per percent of packet loss an additional 5 points of impairment on the R-scale are introduced. The precise curves associated with various narrow-band codecs can be found in ITU-T Rec. G.107.

The rating R of the E-model can be translated to a MOS value as follows:

$$MOS = \begin{cases} 1 & R < 0 \\ 1 + 0.035R + (R - 60)(100 - R)\frac{7R}{10^6} & 0 \le R \le 100 \\ 4.5 & R > 100 \end{cases}$$

However, normally R is interpreted directly via the quality classes defined in ITU-T Rec. G.107. The current version of the E-model includes an extension to wideband codecs in an appendix, but this appendix is not normative yet. An alternative computational model is presented in Chen et al. [4], in which the user satisfaction is determined based solely on the parameters bit rate, jitter, and round-trip time.

An example of a full-reference model is the Perceptual Evaluation of Speech Quality (PESQ) model (ITU-T Rec. P.862). It assesses the listening-only quality of narrow-band speech encoded, packetized and sent over a (possibly packet-loss-prone) network. This model compares the original with the received signal and determines which differences result in annoying artifacts. For this purpose both signals need to be suitably aligned (which forms an integral part of the model). There is ongoing research on extending PESQ to wideband speech in Study Group 12 of the ITU-T.

While the listening quality for speech can be objectively measured by PESQ, the standard for objectively measuring audio QoE is called PEAQ (Perceptual Evaluation of Audio Quality). The PEAQ standard ITU-R BS.1387 was set in 1998 and was last updated in 2001. Like PESQ, PEAQ is a full-reference algorithm that analyzes the audio signal sample-by-sample after a temporal alignment of corresponding excerpts of reference and test signal. The algorithm takes perceptual properties of the human ear into account, integrating multiple model output variables into a single metric. PEAQ characterizes the perceived audio QoE, expressed as a MOS score, as subjects would do in a listening test according to ITU-R BS.1116. For educational use, there exists a free cross-platform program called Peaqb which accomplishes the same functions in a limited manner, as it has not been validated with the ITU data. PQevalAudio, another not validated implementation of the PEAQ basic model for educational use, is available from the TSP Lab of McGill University.

4   QoE of Interactive Gaming

In this section we consider the QoE of so-called First Person Shooter (FPS) games, because other types of online games, such as real-time strategy games and multiplayer role-playing games, pose less strict requirements with respect to network quality [7].

Many papers investigated the impact of delay, jitter, and packet loss on gameplay for FPS games, see for instance [1], [2], [22]. Most of these works focus on network performance metrics that game players can tolerate. Like the E-model for speech, Wattimena et al. [21] developed a G-model model for the prediction of the QoE of FPS games. Subjective tests were performed with FPS games such as Quake IV and later Quake III, Unreal Tournament, Counter Strike, and Halo. The finding was that the G-model produced a well-founded lower limit of gaming QoE.

In order to apply the G-model one first determines the round-trip time (RTT) of 10000 UDP packets that are send over the network. Define $PING$ as the average of all RTTs and $JITTER$ as the 99.9%-quantile of all RTT's minus the minimum RTT (ITU-T Rec. Y.1541).

We formulate the G-model as

$$MOS_{Gaming} = \max\left(4.33 - 3.08 \cdot 10^{-9}X^3 + 1.18 \cdot 10^{-5}X^2 - 1.15 \cdot 10^{-2}X, 1\right)$$

where the network impairment $X = \min\left(PING + 0.686 * JITTER, 650\right)$. This formulation is slightly different from [21], since we now use a standardized way of measuring $JITTER$.

According to [21] the correlation between the original G-model and the subjective data (of 33 test subjects) is very high (correlation coefficient $\rho = 0.98$). Note that, according to the G-model, FPS games are insensitive to packet loss.

5   QoE of Video

In this section, we discuss how to measure the QoE of streaming video services at the end user. Visually the most important factors for the video quality are: viewing distance, display size, resolution, brightness, contrast, sharpness, colorfulness, and naturalness. A distinction should be made between fidelity and quality, where fidelity stands for the closeness of the processed video to the original. For instance, for a low-quality original, a high-fidelity reproduction will still have low quality.

Visible distortions will most often lower the perceived quality. These may be introduced by lossy compression. The most widely used codecs use block-based Discrete-Cosine Transform (DCT) with motion compensation followed by quantization of the coefficients as a compression scheme, e.g. MPEG-2 and ITU-T H.264. The main distortion introduced by such codecs are: blockiness, blurring, color bleeding, ringing, DCT basis image effect, staircase effects on slanted lines, false edges, jagged motion, chrominance mismatch, mosquito noise, flickering, and aliasing.

For video containing audio the synchronization between video and audio is also an important perceptual factor.

Another source of errors occurs during transmission. The three most important transmission artefacts are packet loss, delay, and delay variations (jitter). The visual effect of lost information is highly dependent on the codec and on the type of information that is lost. Some errors might be concealed using error concealment strategies, whereas others have severe effects.

Finally, also channel zapping time can be identified as an important factor.

The perceived quality factors that are listed for streaming video also hold for video conferencing. In addition, due to its interactive nature, the same strict delay requirements as for VoIP hold. We shall address several of the above-mentioned components in the following subsections.

5.1   Visual Quality

Commonly used video quality metrics are:

- Peak-Signal-to-Noise-Ratio (PSNR) gives the ratio (in dB) between the signal power of the original signal versus the power of a reconstructed compressed signal. PSNR is usually derived via the mean squared error (MSE) between the two signals in relation to the maximum possible value of the luminance of the images. Although PSNR may not accurately reflect the QoE, as demonstrated in [9], it continues to be a popular method to evaluate the quality difference among videos.

- Video Quality Metric [17] (VQM) is a software tool developed by the Institute for Telecommunication Science (ITS) to objectively measure perceived video quality. It measures the perceptual effects of video impairments including blurring, jerky/unnatural motion, global noise, block distortion, and color distortion, and combines them into a single metric, by using a linear combination of these parameters. The Video Quality Experts Group[1] (VQEG) Phase II validation tests show that VQM has a high correlation with subjective video quality scores and as a result it has been adopted by ANSI (ANSI T1.801.03-2003), and by ITU-T (ITU-T J.144, and ITU-R BT.1683) along with three other metrics as standard for measuring video quality.
- Structural Similarity Index [19] (SSIM) uses a structural distortion based measurement approach. Structure and similarity in this context refer to samples of the signals having strong dependencies between each other, especially when they are close in space [20]. The rationale is that the human vision system is highly specialized in extracting structural information from the viewing field and it is not specialized in extracting the errors.

An important step in full- and reduced-reference video quality metrics to reach an accurate quality score is that the sampled videos need to be calibrated. The calibration consists of estimating and correcting the spatial and temporal shift of the processed video sequence with respect to the original video sequence. This is usually an integral part of the more sophisticated metrics, but it needs to be added separately to, for instance, PSNR to give sensible results.

The standard for video quality measurements by the ITU covers full-reference (ITU-T Rec. J.144 and ITU-R BT.1683) and reduced-reference (ITU-T Rec. J.249) methods for standard definition TV, as well as a full-reference (ITU-T Rec. J.247) and reduced-reference (ITU-T Rec. J.146) for multimedia. All these standards contain various metrics that have performed statistically equally well in evaluations performed by VQEG. However, there are currently no standards covering no-reference methods. A trend in recent years has been to propose so-called hybrid models that incorporate information from the bit stream as well as quality evaluation on the video itself. Although a good correlation with subjective quality can be reached, the disadvantage is that the models are tailored to a specific codec [5].

5.2 Audio-Video Synchronization

Audio-video synchronization refers to the relative timing of sound and image portions of a television program, or movie.

The ITU-R BT.1359-1 recommendation states that the tolerance from the point of capture to the viewer/listener shall be no more than 90 ms audio leading video to 185 ms audio lagging behind video.

---

[1] http://www.its.bldrdoc.gov/vqeg/

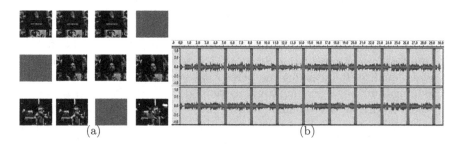

Fig. 1. (a) Video with red markers, and (b) accompanying audio with corresponding beep markers

Analyzing A/V synchronization can be done with an "artificially generated" video test sample (e.g., see Fig. 1). The test sample includes a video component and an audio component. The video component and the audio component both contain markers. The video marker displays between a first video state and a second video state, a red full screen image. Similarly, the audio waveform alternates between a first audio state and a second audio state, an audio "beep." The video and audio waveforms are temporally synchronized to transition from one state to another at the same time.

By comparing the audio and video tracks at the receiving end, any dissynchronization can be noticed. This approach was applied in [16] to test the A/V synchronization of four video conferencing applications. Also the audio delays among participants was measured by injecting in the video an artificial DTMF (dual-tone multi-frequency) tone. The audio was sent and recorded at one client. Other participants kept their speakers and microphones on, but did not produce extra audio. Based on the recorded audio tracks, the difference between the time the audio marker was sent from the client and the time the same audio marker was heard again at the client was extracted. The time difference is approximately twice the one-way audio delay plus the processing delay at a client.

5.3 Network QoS

As we have argued, QoE is determined by more than the QoS provided by the network. However, network or service providers only have control over their own equipment/network, and therefore it is important for them to know the relation between QoS and QoE. Accurately measuring QoS parameters like bandwidth and delay, is a research topic on its own, but fortunately QoE is an end-to-end measure that sees the network as a black box. This means that we can omit the details of the network and correlate the QoE of certain applications to (artificially introduced) artefacts like delay and packet losses. EvalVid [12] is a tool that facilitates just that. It can be used with the network simulator NS-2 to simulate the network environment and trace the video packets in different controlled communication conditions [11]. A video source file (usually in raw YUV format) is encoded into a compressed video file (either MPEG-4 or H.264). Then the compressed video file is time-stamped and transmitted via UDP packets over a real or simulated network to the receiver. By comparing the time-stamps of packets (and their type) at sender and receiver, frame loss and frame jitter can be computed. Also the PSNR can be returned by EvalVid. By precisely knowing and controlling the QoS parameters of the simulated environment, a correlation between QoE and QoS parameters could be established.

5.4 User Synchronization

While watching a football match it could be disturbing to hear the neighbors scream "GOAL" while you still are watching the pre-goal action. Such phenomena are referred to as user or peer lags. While watching the same channel, users' content might not be synchronized. Measuring the different "lag delays" can be done by using another artificial video displaying a timer. Each second (or at some other precision) a sequential number is shown. By using PlanetLab, or other similar platforms that give control over different geographically dispersed computers, one can set up several clients that are under full control. This approach has been applied in [15]. Unsynchronized users can especially affect the QoE when they are experienced in multi-party communications.

5.5 Start-Up and Zapping Time

One of the key elements of QoE of IPTV is how quickly users can change between TV channels, which is called channel zapping. Kooij et al. [13] conducted a number of subjective tests in order to get insight in the relation between QoE and zapping time. For the tests described in [13], during channel zapping, a black screen was visible which contained the number of the target channel. The test subjects (21 in total) could select one of the following five opinion scores: $5 = $ *excellent zapping quality*, $4 = $ *good zapping quality*, $3 = $ *fair zapping quality*, $2 = $ *poor zapping quality*, $1 = $ *bad zapping quality*.

The following model was proposed for the relation between zapping time (in seconds) and the QoE (expressed in MOS) of channel zapping:

$$MOS_{Zapping} = \max\left(\min\left(-1.02\ln(ZappingTime) + 2.65, 5\right), 1\right)$$

From this relation it was deduced that in order to guarantee a MOS of at least 3.5, we need to ascertain that zapping time < 430 ms.

The model presented in [13] was based on "lean forward" zapping, where test subjects were switching channels by clicking buttons with a mouse on a computer screen, and on fixed zapping times. Experiments reported in [14] include "lean backward" experiments, where the test subjects were sitting on a sofa with a remote control. For "lean backward" zapping the requirement for the zapping time could be relaxed to 670 ms. In [14] subjective experiments were also conducted with varying zapping times. The zapping time was uniformly distributed, with a variance bounded by the mean zapping time. In this case, to obtain a MOS rating of at least 3.5, the maximum allowed variance, and thus also the maximum allowed mean zapping delay, was 460 ms.

In [8] the QoE of channel zapping was assessed when, during zapping, advertisements are displayed, instead of a black screen. Based on Figure 2, we can conclude that:

- Users prefer advertisements only when the zapping time is sufficiently large.
- Short zapping times lead to insufficient time to view the advertisement. On the other hand, a long zapping time is also still not appreciated.

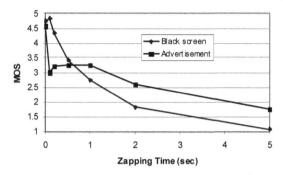

Fig. 2. MOS for "black screen" and "advertisement"

Analogous to the G-model for black screens, explained above, in [8] the following QoE model for advertisements was suggested:

$$MOS_{Ads} = \max\left(y_1, \min\left(y_2, y_3\right)\right)$$

where $y_1 = -15.8(ZappingTime) + 4.58$, $y_2 = 0.10\ln(ZappingTime) + 3.27$, and $y_3 = -0.93\ln(ZappingTime) + 3.27$.

In [15], with Wireshark and a small script that zaps from channel to channel, the zapping times of the P2PTV application SopCast have been measured. The used script simply starts a counter when a channel is clicked and it stops when enough data to be displayed has been fetched. The script was zapping among 20 popular and less popular channels. With an average zapping time of 50 seconds, SopCast faces an unacceptable delay. This delay was predominantly caused by the end systems (a SopCast buffer and a media player buffer needed to be filled) and by the process of finding peers to download content from. The actual network delay (QoS) was of minor influence.

6   Using QoE for Design

In this last section, we show how QoE models can be used when designing a system. Distributing television over a packet-based network will be our case study. First the quality with which the television signal will be transported needs to be determined (which can be assessed with models of Section 5.1). This desired quality impacts the required bit rate, which normally has to be chosen as low as possible. Given the desired quality, the required bit rate mainly depends on the interval between Intra frames (I-frames). I-frames can be decoded without making reference to other frames in the sequence, while Predicted frames (P-frames) and Bidirectionally predicted frames (B-frames) are encoded making reference to other frames. I-frames typically require 2 to 4 times more bits than P-frames for a difficult and easy scene respectively, while P-frames in turn usually require 3 times more information than B-frames. Spacing the I-frames further apart decreases the bit rate. Figure 3 shows the bit rate penalty to be paid by choosing a smaller interval between I-frames.

I-frames are anchor points in the sequence: the effect of a lost packet stops propagating at I-frames and a user can only tune in at these anchor points. The longest time a user has to wait to tune into a channel is equal to the interval between I-frames. Section 5.5 argued that in order to reach a MOS of 3.5 the zapping delay can be at most 460 ms. Figure 3 shows that for such a small interval between I-frames the bit rate penalty is high.

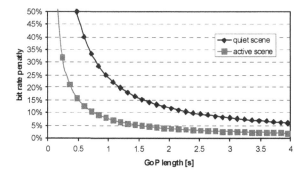

Fig. 3. Bit rate as a function of the interval between I-frames

In Degrande et al. [6] a system is discussed where the interval between I-frames is much larger than this 460 ms such that the bit rate penalty is small, while still maintaining a small zapping delay. For that purpose the most recent video information is kept in a circular buffer in the network. As soon as a user zaps to a channel, a recent I-frame is retrieved from that circular buffer and this allows the user to immediately tune in. However, since the user tunes in to an I-frame of the recent past (say an I-frame sent on the channel T seconds ago) he or she lags T s behind with respect to the current information that is sent over the channel. In order to catch up, the T s of video information needs to be burst to the user. This temporarily increases the bit rate for that user after a zap. The bursting rate has to be tuned such that this is not overwhelmingly large. However, the smaller the bursting rate is chosen, the longer the catch-up time is. Which of the two situations, 1) choosing a small interval between I-frames paying a high bit rate penalty, or 2) choosing a large interval between I-frames with a circular buffer to assist fast zapping and bursting to catch up, is best in terms of the required bit rate, depends on the frequency with which users are likely to change from one channel to the next.

7   Conclusions

In this paper we have provided an overview of some of existing techniques and tools for conducting Quality of Experience (QoE) measurements. QoE is a subjective measure, which makes quantifying it difficult. Consequently, one could find drawbacks to each of the presented techniques in this paper. On the other hand, these techniques are some of the most accessible ones and they do provide us with some insight into QoE, which could for instance already be used in the design of an application or the tuning of a network.

References

1. Armitage, G., Stewart, L.: Limitations of using Real-World, Public Servers to Estimate Jitter Tolerance Of First Person Shooter Games. In: Proc. of ACM SIGCHI ACE2004 Conference, Singapore (June 2004)
2. Beigbeder, T., Coughlan, R., Lusher, C., Plunkett, J., Agu, E., Claypool, M.: The Effect of Loss and Latency on User Performance in Unreal Tournament 2003®. In: Proc. of NetGames'04, Oregon, USA (2004)
3. Van den Branden Lambrecht, C.J., Verscheure, O.: Perceptual quality measure using a spatiotemporal model of the human visual system. In: Proc. of SPIE, vol. 2668, pp. 450–461 (1996)
4. Chen, K.-T., Huang, C.-Y., Huang, P., Lei, C.-L.: Quantifying Skype User Satisfaction. In: Proc. of SIGCOMM'06, Pisa, Italy, September 11-15 (2006)
5. Davis, A.G., Bayart, D., Hands, D.S.: Hybrid No-Reference Video Quality Prediction. In: Proc. of IEEE International Symposium on Broadband Multimedia Systems and Broadcasting (BMSB), Bilbao, Spain, May 13-15 (2009)
6. Degrande, N., Laevens, K., De Vleeschauwer, D., Sharpe, R.: Increasing the user perceived quality for IPTV services. IEEE Communications Magazine 46(2), 94–100 (2008)
7. Dick, M., Wellnitz, O., Wolf, L.: Analysis of factors affecting Players' Performance and Perception in Multiplayer Games. In: Proc. of NetGames'05, Hawthorne, NY, USA (2005)
8. Godana, B.E., Kooij, R.E., Ahmed, O.K.: Impact of Advertisements during Channel Zapping on Quality of Experience. In: Proc. of The Fifth International Conference on Networking and Services, ICNS 2009, Valencia, Spain, April 20-25 (2009)
9. Huynh-Thu, Q., Ghanbari, M.: Scope of validity of PSNR in image/video quality assessment. Electronics letters 44(13) (June 19, 2008)
10. Janssen, J., De Vleeschauwer, D., Büchli, M.J.C., Petit, G.H.: Assessing Voice Quality in Packet-Based Telephony. IEEE Internet Computing 6(3), 48–56 (2002)
11. Ke, C.-H., Shieh, C.-K., Hwang, W.-S., Ziviani, A.: An Evaluation Framework for More Realistic Simulations of MPEG Video Transmission. Journal of Information Science and Engineering 24, 425–440 (2008)
12. Klaue, J., Rathke, B., Wolisz, A.: EvalVid - A framework for video transmission and quality evaluation. In: Proc. of the International Conference on Modelling Techniques and Tools for Computer Performance Evaluation, pp. 255–272 (2003)
13. Kooij, R.E., Ahmed, O.K., Brunnström, K.: Perceived Quality of Channel Zapping. In: Proc. of the fifth IASTED International Conference on Comm. Systems and Networks, Palma de Mallorca, Spain, August 28-30, pp. 155–158 (2006)

14. Kooij, R.E., Nicolai, F., Ahmed, O.K., Brunnström, K.: Model validation of channel zapping quality. In: Proc. of Human Vision and Electronic Imaging Conf., January 19-22 (2009)
15. Lu, Y., Fallica, B., Kuipers, F.A., Kooij, R.E., Van Mieghem, P.: Assessing the Quality of Experience of SopCast. Int. J. Internet Protocol Technology 4(1), 11–23 (2009)
16. Lu, Y., Zhao, Y., Kuipers, F.A., Van Mieghem, P.: Measurement Study of Multi-party Video Conferencing. In: Proc. of IFIP Networking 2010, Chennai, India, May 10-14 (2010)
17. Pinson, M., Wolf, S.: A New Standardized Method for Objectively Measuring Video Quality. IEEE Transactions on Broadcasting 50(3) (September 2004)
18. Takahasi, A., Hands, D., Barriac, V.: Standardization Activities in the ITU for a QoE Assesment of IPTV. IEEE Communications Magazine, 78–84 (February 2008)
19. Wang, Z., Li, Q.: Video quality assessment using a statistical model of human visual speed perception. Journal of the Optical Society of America A 24(12), B61–B69 (2007)
20. Wang, Z., Bovik, A.C.: Mean squared error: love it or leave it? - A new look at signal fidelity measures. IEEE Signal Processing Magazine 26(1), 98–117 (2009)
21. Wattimena, F., Kooij, R.E., van Vugt, J.M., Ahmed, O.K.: Predicting the perceived quality of a First Person Shooter: the Quake IV G-model. In: Proc. of NetGames'06, Singapore, October 30-31 (2006)
22. Zander, S., Armitage, G.: Empirically Measuring the QoS Sensitivity of Interactive Online Game Players. In: Proc. of Australian Telecommunications Networks & Applications Conference 2004, Sydney, Australia (December 2004)

Fair Quality of Experience (QoE) Measurements Related with Networking Technologies

Isaias Martinez-Yelmo, Isaac Seoane, and Carmen Guerrero

Universidad Carlos III de Madrid.
Av. Universidad 30. 28911 Leganes (Madrid), Spain
{imyelmo,iseoane,guerrero}@it.uc3m.es

Abstract. This paper addresses the topic of Fair QoE measurements in networking. The research of new solutions in networking is oriented to improve the user experience. Any application or service can be improved and the deployment of new solutions is mandatory to get the user satisfaction. However, different solutions exist; thus, it is necessary to select the most suitable ones. Nevertheless, this selection is difficult to make since the QoE is subjective and the comparison among different technologies is not trivial. The aim of this paper is to give an overview on how to perform fair QoE measurements to facilitate the study and research of new networking solutions and paradigms. However, previously to address this problem, an overview about how networking affects to the QoE is provided.

1 Introduction

The first of all, it is necessary to define what QoE means. The concept of QoE can be applied to many topics; therefore, it is necessary to find a wide definition suitable for any field. An interesting, short and concise definition for QoE is: *Quality of Experience is a subjective measure of customer's experiences.* This definition summarizes the three key points related with QoE. The first one is the fact that QoE is based on *measurements*, which means some mechanisms are necessary to define what measurements are the most relevant and how they can be obtained. The second one is the subject that takes care of doing the measurements. This subject is the *customer/user* since it is the person who is paying for a service. This is a very interesting point because it does not matter how difficult is the implementation of a new feature from the user point of view, but the important is how useful are the improvements and benefits that users can experience from their perspective. Finally, it must be taken into account that these measurements are *subjective* and depend by in the own opinion of each individual person.

The concept of QoE has applicability in many research fields. In fact, the study of QoE is mandatory in any serious deployment related with new products, technologies or processes.

E. Osipov et al. (Eds.): WWIC 2010, LNCS 6074, pp. 228–239, 2010.

2   Evaluation of the QoE

Internet Service Providers (ISPs) use Quality of Service (QoS) parameters such as bandwidth, delay or jitter to guarantee their users a good service quality. Nowadays, the proliferation of multimedia content makes more important the provision of QoS if a good QoE wants to be provided to the final user. In addition to the classical networking configuration parameters, some advanced streaming techniques exist to minimize the end-to-end loss effects [1] and the links failures despite the guaranteed QoS [2] in the received streaming.

The reception quality with or without the improvements given by these solutions is measured using objective mathematical operations, comparing the original and the received stream, such as packet loss ratio and PSNR (Peak Signal to Noise Ratio). However, this approach has a lack of perceptual quality measurement that should take into account the perception and the understanding of the receiver. Better receiver experience cannot be measured only using good peak values or assuring low mean packet losses because the semantic losses of the received data are not included in these parameters.

At the same time as the multimedia applications spreading, several subjectivity measurement techniques have been studied to address opinion polls. Voice quality has been measured using opinion tests such as MOS (Mean Opinion Score), DRT (Diagnostic Rhyme Test) or DAM (Diagnostic Acceptability Test). This last one was designed to study the effect of voice transmission trough PSTN network and after that to evaluate voice codecs for digital communications.

MOS consists in a number from a simple five-division scale (ACR - Absolute Category Rating Method) [3] that summarizes how the result of a voice transmission or a playout is perceived by people during listening-opinion tests with some common sentences as reference. The numbers used for MOS graduation are illustrated in Table 1(b). The recommendations specify how to perform these tests or how to provide the information to the test subjects. They also explain how to prepare the reference set of a recording speech and the environmental conditions for the tests. All this methodology is specified by ITU-T in [3].

In addition, considering that the multimedia content have been increasing in requirements, some other recommendations has been developed due to the complexity of transcoding audio and video content and its perception by users [4, 5,6,7,8]. On the other hand, some evaluation tools for video quality measurement have appeared to automatize the opinion scoring [9, 10] to add subjectivity to the traditional frame-to-frame PSNR analysis. These tools, using the original stream as reference, map the opinion of thousand of tests previously made using MOS scoring to well known signal parameter changes to provide subjectivity to end-to-end system quality evaluation.

For statistical evaluation purposes inside the network itself, the Internet Engineering Task Force (IETF) has developed the Media Delivery Index (MDI) that gives an expected value for the video quality based on network parameters, independently of the encoding scheme. The MDI is described by two values: the delay factor (DF) and the media loss rate (MLR). The DF computes how many data units of time of data would need to be buffered to eliminate the jitter and

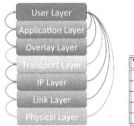

Value	Meaning
5	Perfect
4	Fair
3	Annoying
2	Very annoying
1	Impossible to communicate

(a) Networking Layers   (b) MOS score values

Fig. 1.

the MLR is the ratio between the lost and out of order packets and the received packets. Typical maximum acceptable values for MDI depend on the application. They can be 9-50ms for DF and from 0.004 on VoD to 0.0005 on HDTV for MLR [11].

3   Impact of Networking in QoE

The concept of *networking* is very wide, in continuous development, and it is always offering new features, advances and improvements. In fact, there are many topics, available technologies and application scenarios related with the networking topic. Thus, it is very difficult to explain how networking can affect the QoE. In order to address this explanation, we follow a layered approach very similar to the current TCP/IP model. Figure 1(a) is an example of this model.

3.1   Link Layer

The link layer plays a fundamental role in the user experience, especially in the last mile access. The link layer limits the maximum speed that can be transmitted in a link (Fast Ethernet[1]. In addition, it defines how the information is transported over the links and how the different terminals or computers can access to a link to transmit information.

However, not only these features are provided by the link layer; in addition, the link layer can support Quality of Service (QoS) parameters to prioritize some kind of traffic instead of other ones. This can also be done in Ethernet [12]. However, there are not only wired link layer technologies, there are also wireless ones. There is WiFi (802.11) with all its variations, especially the related ones with QoS (802.11e). On the other hand, WiMax (802.16) [13] is also available and can support QoS by default. Obviously, we cannot forget UMTS [14] that provides the wireless infrastructure for 3G networks.

All previous mentioned technologies (both wired and wireless) are mainly used for shared access, however there are other relevant technologies (usually for

---

[1] http://www.ieee802.org/3/

point-to-point communications) such as DSL[2] (Digital Subscriber Line) technologies or FTTH (Fiber To The Home) [15], which can also provide QoS.

Although link layer technologies have the same purpose, their speed, capacity, performance and behavior are completely different. Furthermore, their performance can vary depending on the scenario where these technologies are deployed and on any other external conditions. Therefore, it is necessary to describe with the higher accuracy the scenario and external conditions that would be used in a QoE measurement in order to assure the repeatability by other researchers and allow a fair comparison among different technologies. Usually, the most interesting studies about QoE are related with wireless technologies since they are frequently used by end users to retrieve the information from Internet. Some examples are [16], [17].

3.2   Network Layer

The network layer is only composed by IP (Internet Protocol [18]). The performance of IP depends on several factors. The first one is the path that packets must follow to reach the desired destination. This path depends on where the end points of a connection are attached, what ISPs give the connectivity to the customers and how the relationships among the different ISPs are. These relationships are usually based on peering and transit agreements among the different ISPs. In order to build correctly the routing tables in the routers of ISPs, BGP (Border Gateway Protocol [19]) is used. BGP manages the Autonomous Systems (ASs), which are a collection of connected IP routing prefixes under the control of one or more ISPs that present a common, clearly defined routing policy to the Internet. Therefore, the behavior of the Internet is based on how the ISPs establish their routing policies through BGP. This fact makes that many research activities related with IP are based on investigation these relationships among ASs and ISPs. There are many projects related with this topic, e.g. CAIDA[3] [20] or PingER[4] [21]. The results from these projects can be used to design and evaluate new proposals in scenarios closer to real conditions. If QoE measurements were considered using the information provided by these projects, the associated measurements would be more realistic and closer to the results in a real deployment.

On the other hand, other important factors affect IP. Originally, IP was designed considering only wired connections where the computers were always placed in the same location. However, with the introduction of wireless technologies and the accessibility to laptops or hand-held devices, the concepts of mobility and roaming arise. Therefore, it is necessary to adapt IP for mobile support: terminal mobility [22, 23], network mobility [24] and any other solutions such as multihoming [25, 26].

In any case, the connectivity among ISPs or the mobility affects delay, jitter and packet error probability and all these factors change the QoE perceived

---

[2] http://en.wikipedia.org/wiki/Digital_Subscriber_Line
[3] http://www.caida.org/
[4] http://www-iepm.slac.stanford.edu/pinger/

by customers. Thus, depending on the scenario and on the adopted technical solutions, the appreciated QoE would be different (e.g. [27, 28]).

3.3   Transport Layer

The transport layer also implies an important role in the QoE experimented by users. The predominant protocols are TCP (Transmission Control Protocol [29]) and UDP (User Datagram Protocol [30]). TCP plays an important role in best effort bulk transfers because it is a connection-oriented protocol and allows end-to-end flow congestion control. However, different congestion control mechanisms can be applied and they affect in a different way the QoE [31]. Besides TCP, other protocols have similar properties and should also be considered such as SCTP (Stream Control Transmission Protocol [32]) or DCCP (Datagram Congestion Control Protocol [33]). On the other hand, UDP is a connectionless protocol that usually is used for the transmission of real time information where it is not necessary flow control.

In this section, it is necessary to consider the peer-to-peer traffic that has been growing continuously these last years. A characteristic of peer-to-peer applications is that they need to open many connections (both UDP and TCP) to download the desired resources. These peer-to-peer flows have to compete with the other flows in the Internet. Thus, these last ones are affected negatively by the peer-to-peer traffic. A lot of UDP traffic affects negatively to TCP flows since less bandwidth is available for them. Furthermore, different flows competing for the available bandwidth also implies an underutilization of the total capacity. Therefore, it is necessary to study new mechanisms for the transmission of peer-to-peer traffic in such a way that the QoE experienced by the users of other applications would not be affected. The IETF Low Extra Delay Background Transport (LEDBAT[5]) Working Group (WG) is taking care about this problem in order to develop lower than best effort transport protocols that avoid to decrease the QoE appreciated in the rest of applications running on the Internet [34].

3.4   Overlay Layer

The overlay layer does not exist in the TCP/IP model. However, taking into account the evolution of peer-to-peer technologies, they have to be treated in a single section. A definition of an overlay network can be a computer network that is built on top of another network, usually an IP network. These networks are built at the application layer, but they are in most of the cases an intermediate piece of software that offers functionalities to the final application. Nowadays, the most common overlay networks are the peer-to-peer networks, which are being widely used for file-sharing (eMule[6] [35, 36], Bittorrent[7] [37]), streaming[8]

---

[5] http://www.ietf.org/dyn/wg/charter/ledbat-charter.html
[6] http://www.emule-project.net
[7] http://www.bittorrent.com/
[8] http://goalbit.sourceforge.net

and multimedia services (Skype[9] [38, 39]). This kind of applications is not only being considered for these purposes, but they are also being considered for the creation of CDNs (Content Distribution Networks). The adoption of peer-to-peer technologies is motivated by moving the traffic consumption of Content Providers (CPs) to their own costumers in order to reduce their payments to their ISPs. However, the peer-to-peer traffic has grown considerably in the last years, affecting users' QoE and overloading the links of ISPs. Some QoE papers related with video streaming and peer-to-peer are [40], [41].

It has been mentioned in the previous section how actions at the transport layer are being studied to reduce their impact. Additionally, actions at this level are also being taken into consideration. The IETF Application-Layer Traffic Optimization (ALTO[10]) WG is designing an Application-Layer Traffic Optimization service that will provide applications with information to perform better-than-random initial peer selection in order to reduce the traffic between ISPs [42]. This service will also help to improve and speed-up the overlay connections of the different peer-to-peer based application. Thus, the QoE experienced by users will improve unless content availability would be compromised (initial seeding). This fact is a remaining open issue.

3.5   Application Layer

There are many applications using networking services to work properly. These applications are the only thing that users can really appreciate and interact with. The average customer only takes care of starting an application and using it. In fact, the QoE experienced by customers would not be biased by all the complexity that exists under any application, they only consider if it works or not. An excellent example to consider is Skype [38]. Skype was originally a chat and VoIP service based on a peer-to-peer technology. Over the time, it has been improving its functionalities in order to get more and more customers. Nevertheless, the great success of Skype is not based on its functionalities, but on the fact that you install the software in any computer and network configuration and works without any complex configuration (install and use). This simplicity for the users is based on its extraordinary capabilities of crossing NATs and firewalls without reconfiguring any network equipment. Thus, in order to realize fair QoE measurements it is necessary to use the same networking conditions to compare different applications or use the most close conditions if different networking technologies are being compared. An example about QoE related with Skype is [43].

3.6   Cross-Layer Interactions

Although protocol design is usually based on a layered approach (for simplicity considerations), it must be taken into account that cross-layer interactions exist.

---

[9] http://www.skype.com
[10] http://www.ietf.org/dyn/wg/charter/alto-charter.html

These interactions can affect considerably the QoE experienced by customers. It is well known the effect of wireless technologies to the TCP throughput since losses in wireless link are misinterpreted by network congestion in TCP. Some efforts are being realized to minimize these cross-layer interactions (e.g. the IEEE 802.21[11] initiative). Thus, it is necessary to specify the conditions that have been adopted in any application or new networking technology since scenarios that seem to be quite similar can make obtain unexpected results. This fact can prevent the fair comparison of different solutions and lead to wrong conclusions. In the next paragraphs, we are going to detail a methodology in order to prevent this kind of situations. Some studies related with this topic and QoE are [44], [45]

4   Fair QoE Measurements in Networking

Taking into account the description given in the previous sections, we can appreciate the great number of variables that it is necessary to take into account when the QoE has to be evaluated. Therefore, it is necessary to follow a methodology that avoids unfair comparisons among different solutions, which would end in wrong conclusions.

Nowadays, the QoE is usually related with the Content Distribution across the Internet. Years ago, it was not considered the use of Internet for establishing voice or video calls and it was also not considered its usage for video broadcasting to a determined group of users. These new services are the focus of CPs and ISPs to get more profits from their networks. Therefore, it is necessary a mechanism to evaluate and compare VoIP and video services or new services such as CDNs.

The proposal that is going to be described in the next paragraphs has been developed inside the CONTENT NoE (see section 5 for further information). This proposal is motivated by the lack of well-defined metrics to compare and evaluate this kind of solutions. The idea is to define a Functional Benchmarking[12] (FBM) framework that facilitates fair comparisons among different proposals. This framework can be used for quantitative measurements such as Content Delivery or search efficiency (something important in CDNs) but also qualitative measurements related with QoE. The interesting point of this approach is the effort spent to normalize how to specify the experiments performed in order to allow a posterior fair comparison with all the research community.

4.1   Functional Benchmarking (FBM) Framework

The objective of this framework is to define a methodology that allows the evaluation and comparison of different solutions in a systematic and organized way. This approach tries to define a fair mechanism to compare different proposals. A comparison is said to be fair if the conditions that have been used in the different experiments are exactly the same. Therefore, the FBM is capable of defining all the external variables that affect an experiment in order to assure its posterior

---

[11] http://www.ieee802.org/21/

[12] http://heim.ifi.uio.no/~plageman/Site_3/Benchmarking.html

repeatability. This fact implies the definition of the environment, the workload that has been used to stress the system under evaluation and what information has been retrieved. Furthermore, it is necessary to specify precisely what metrics have been used to measure the different parameters. In the next paragraphs, we explain the different concepts in the FBM.

4.2   System Under Test (SUT)

This framework defines an entity named System under Test (SUT). This entity is formed by a set of functions that want to be evaluated using this methodology. An example could be the QoE experienced by a user with a mobile phone that is receiving a video stream under certain mobility conditions.

4.3   Input Parameters

These parameters define conditions used for the evaluation of the SUT. These conditions have a direct impact in the system that is being evaluated and they define the results that would be obtained. In this framework, the input parameters are divided in two different classes:

- **Environment.** It defines the computational and communication infrastructure as well as other relevant conditions for the assessment. The environment reflects the static conditions of the system under evaluation.
- **Workload.** It defines the parameters that are used to evaluate the SUT. The workload reflects the dynamic conditions of the system under evaluation.

The importance of this classification is to distinguish among the conditions that are imposed by the experiment itself (environment) and those conditions that stress the SUT (workload). For instance, the environment is related with the access technology used in the experiment, the OSs (Operative Systems) where the experiments are being executed or the selected peer-to-peer network for the development of an application. On the other hand, the workload is related with the background traffic in the different links, the number of entities participating in the experiment or the mobility pattern of the terminals that are being used in a certain testbed.

Following with the example presented in the definition of SUT, the environment would be any characteristic that belongs to the system under study. In that case, the mobile terminal could have a 3G connection with multihoming support. The workload would be external conditions to the system that affect to the perceived quality such as the concurrent users using the 3G cell.

4.4   Output Parameters

These parameters define the results obtained from the SUT when it has been tested under certain environment and workload. These parameters are also divided in two classes:

- **Performance.** The parameters in this class are related with the obtained efficiency in the SUT.
- **Cost.** This class if formed by those parameters that reflect the necessary resources used to achieve the obtained performance.

This classification helps to separate two different types of results that are usually considered. The results associated with the quality/performance of SUT and, on the other hand, the cost needed to achieve that quality/performance. A solution can obtain an exceptional performance t but it can consume too many resources, which is not desirable.

Again, if we consider the scenario in the definition of SUT, we can define the performance and cost parameters for that example. The performance associated to QoE would be the score given by users to the quality of the streamed videos. On the other hand, the cost would be the amount of traffic used to obtain that performance.

4.5   Using FBM

An example of using the FBM could be as follows: a new VoIP application based Chord Peer-to-Peer has to be analyzed on a wireless and mobile IP scenario.

The idea of using the FBM is to facilitate as much as possible the test environment to allow a fair comparison among different future proposals. The result of applying the FBM is shown in Table 1. This table indicates the different input parameters that must be specified to assure the repeatability of the experiments and the relevant output parameters that should be considered to compare the different proposals. The table is divided considering the different layers that have been mentioned previously. In addition, a user layer is included to introduce the QoE related measurements. In the considered example, a MOS score for the VoIP conversations should be provided by the users of the application using an environment and workload with the specific values that should be provided with each one of the parameters considered in table 1. In the proposed scenario, it must be taken into account the underlying network topology, background traffic, number of wireless stations competing for the channel access, etc. The quality of a VoIP conversation will not be the same when the scenario is composed by two stations belonging to the same wireless LAN rather than two wireless stations connected through several ASs. Therefore, it is necessary to specify this

Table 1. QoE measurements with FBM

Layer	Input		Output	
	Environment	Workload	Performance	Cost
User	screen size,light	-	MOS	-
Application	Codec	Load CPU, RAM	Decoding Time	CPU, RAM consumption
Overlay	Chord	N peers	Delay, hops	Bandwidth consumption
Transport	UDP	Concurrent flows	Packet Losses/Errors	Overhead
Network	Mobile IP,Topology	N handoffs,traffic	Packet Losses	N hops,Delay
Link	802.11	N stations,traffic	Availability,Retransmissions	Energy, Delay
Physical	Noise	N interferences	-	-

information. Furthermore, it must be taken into account the type of peer-to-peer network in order to allow the comparison with other topologies in the future.

5   Conclusions

This papers presents a short overview on how the QoE can be measured and how the different layers in a networking environment can influence in the perceived QoE. Furthermore, it presents different works related with QoE and the different layers in a networking environment. Finally, in order to facilitate a fair comparison among different research proposals, a Functional Benchmarking (FBM) Framework is defined to specify the necessary information to fairly compare different proposals (this framework is a joint research in the Content NoE). This framework establishes the definition of an environment and workload at the different layers that defines the state of the SUT. Furthermore, it specifies the output parameters that measure the efficiency and cost of the different proposals under evaluation. For each experiment must be defined with high precision any parameter to assure the complete repeatability of the experiments. The proposed framework helps to specify these parameters in an ordered and meaningful way.

Acknowledgments

We would like to acknowledge Marco Gramaglia for his comments. This work has been funded by the CONTENT NoE from the European Commission (FP6-2005-IST-41), by the Ministry of Science and Innovation under the CON- PARTE project (MEC, TEC2007-67966-C03-03/TCM), by T2C2 project grant (TIN2008-06739-C04-01) and by MEDIANET project (S2009/TIC-1468).

References

1. Chakareski, J., Han, S., Girod, B.: Layered coding vs. multiple descriptions for video streaming over multiple paths. Multimedia Systems 10(4), 275–285 (2005)
2. Begen, A.C., Altunbasak, Y., Ergun, O., Ammar, M.H.: Multi-path selection for multiple description video streaming over overlay networks. Signal Processing: Image Communication 20(1), 39–60 (2005)
3. ITU-T p.800 methods for subjective determination of transmission quality - series p: Telephone transmission quality; methods for objective and subjective assessment of quality. Technical report, ITU-T (August 1996)
4. Takahashi, A., Hands, D., Barriac, V.: Standardization activities in the ITU for a QoE assessmen of IPTV. IEEE Communications Magazine 46(2), 78–84 (2008)
5. ITU-T rec. p.910: Subjective video quality assessment methods for multimedia applications. Technical report, ITU-T (April 2008)
6. ITU-T rec. bt.500-12: Methodology for the subjective assessment of the quality of television pictures. Technical report, ITU-T (September 2009)
7. ITU-T rec. bt.710: Subjective assessment methods for image quality in high-definition television. Technical report, ITU-T (November 1998)

8. ITU-T rec. bt.1788: Methodology for the subjective assessment of video quality in multimedia applications. Technical report, ITU-T (January 2007)
9. Pinson, M., Wolf, S.: A new standardized method for objectively measuring video quality. IEEE Transactions on broadcasting 50(3), 312–322 (2004)
10. van den Branden Lambrecht, C., Verscheure, O.: Perceptual Quality Measure using a Spatio-Temporal Model of the Human Visual System. In: Proc. IST/SPIE Conference Digital Video and Compression: Algorithms and Technologies, vol. 2668 (1996)
11. IPTV QoE: Understanding and interpreting MDI values. Technical report, Agilent Technologies (2006)
12. IEEE: 802.1Q-2005. IEEE Standard for Local and Metropolitan Area Networks— Virtual Bridged Local Area Networks (2005)
13. IEEE: 802.16-2009. IEEE Standard for Local and metropolitan area networks Part 16: Air Interface for Broadband Wireless Access Systems (2009)
14. 3gpp: 3gpp Release 9 (December 2009)
15. Nowak, D., Murphy, J.: FTTH: The overview of existing technologies. In: SPIE Opto-Ireland 2005: Optoelectronics, Photonic Devices, and Optical Networks, Citeseer, vol. 5825, pp. 500–509 (2005)
16. Piamrat, K., Viho, C., Bonnin, J.M., Ksentini, A.: Quality of experience measurements for video streaming over wireless networks, pp. 1184–1189 (April 2009)
17. Piamrat, K., Ksentini, A., Bonnin, J.M., Viho, C.: Q-dram: Qoe-based dynamic rate adaptation mechanism for multicast in wireless networks, pp. 1–6 (December 30-April 2009)
18. Postel, J.: Internet Protocol. RFC 0791, Internet Engineering Task Force (September 1981)
19. Rekhter, Y., Li, T., Hares, S.: A Border Gateway Protocol 4 (BGP-4). RFC 4271, Internet Engineering Task Force (January 2006)
20. Claffy, K., Hyun, Y., Keys, K., Fomenkov, M., Krioukov, D.: Internet mapping: From art to science. In: CATCH '09: Proceedings of the 2009 Cybersecurity Applications & Technology Conference for Homeland Security, Washington, DC, USA, pp. 205–211. IEEE Computer Society, Los Alamitos (2009)
21. Cottrell, L., Satti, F., McKee, S., Kalim, U.: (icfa-scic) 2010 report. Technical report, International Committee for Future Accelerators - Standing Committee on Inter-Regional Connectivity (2010)
22. Perkins, C.: IP Mobility Support for IPv4. RFC 3344, Internet Engineering Task Force (August 2002)
23. Johnson, D., Perkins, C., Arkko, J.: Mobility Support in IPv6. RFC 3775, Internet Engineering Task Force (June 2004)
24. Devarapalli, V., Wakikawa, R., Petrescu, A., Thubert, P.: Network Mobility (NEMO) Basic Support Protocol. RFC 3963, Internet Engineering Task Force (January 2005)
25. Dhraief, A., Montavont, N.: Toward mobility and multihoming unification: the shim6 protocol: a case study. In: Wireless Communications and Networking Conference, WCNC 2008, pp. 2840–2845. IEEE, Los Alamitos (2008)
26. Bagnulo, M., Garcia-Martinez, A., Azcorra, A.: Ipv6 multihoming support in the mobile internet. IEEE Wireless Communications 14(5), 92–98 (2007)
27. Soto, I., Bernardos, C., Calderon, M., Banchs, A., Azcorra, A.: Nemo-enabled localized mobility support for internet access in automotive scenarios. IEEE Communications Magazine 47(5), 152–159 (2009)
28. Bernardo, F., Vucevic, N., Umbert, A., Lopez-Benitez, M.: Quality of experience evaluation under qos-aware mobility mechanisms, pp. 1–7 (June 2008)

29. Postel, J.: Transmission Control Protocol. RFC 0793, Internet Engineering Task Force (September 1981)
30. Postel, J.: User Datagram Protocol. RFC 0768, Internet Engineering Task Force (August 1980)
31. Trinh, T., Sonkoly, B., Molnár, S.: On the fairness characteristics of fast tcp. Annals of Telecommunications 65(1), 73–85 (2010)
32. Stewart, R.: Stream Control Transmission Protocol. RFC 4960 (Proposed Standard) (September 2007)
33. Kohler, E., Handley, M., Floyd, S.: Datagram Congestion Control Protocol (DCCP). RFC 4340 (Proposed Standard) Updated by RFCs 5595, 5596 (March 2006)
34. Shalunov, S.: datagram congestion control protocol, Internet Draf draft-ietf-ledbat-congestion-01.txt (March 2010)
35. Brunner, R., Biersack, E.: A performance evaluation of the Kad-protocol. Technical report, Corporate Communications Department. Institut Eurécom (2006)
36. Steiner, M., En Najjary, T., Biersack, E.W.: Analyzing peer behavior in KAD. Technical Report EURECOM+2358, Institut Eurecom, France (October 2007)
37. Erman, D., Ilie, D., Popescu, A.: Bittorrent session characteristics and models. Traffic Engineering, Performance Evaluation Studies and Tools for Heterogeneous Networks 61(84), 61
38. Baset, S.A., Schulzrinne, H.G.: An analysis of the skype peer-to-peer internet telephony protocol. In: INFOCOM 2006. 25th IEEE International Conference on Computer Communications. Proceedings, April 2006, pp. 1–11 (2006)
39. Rossi, D., Melia, M., Meo, M.: A detailed measurment of skype network traffic. In: IPTPS 2008 (2008)
40. Lu, Y., Fallica, B., Kuipers, F.A., Kooij, R.E., Mieghem, P.V.: Assessing the quality of experience of sopcast. Int. J. Internet Protoc. Technol. 4(1), 11–23 (2009)
41. da Silva, A., Rodriguez-Bocca, P., Rubino, G.: Optimal quality-of-experience design for a p2p multi-source video streaming, pp. 22–26 (May 2008)
42. Xie, H., Yang, Y.R., Krishnamurthy, A., Liu, Y.G., Silberschatz, A.: P4p: provider portal for applications. SIGCOMM Comput. Commun. Rev. 38(4), 351–362 (2008)
43. Huang, T.Y., Huang, P., Chen, K.T., Wang, P.J.: Can Skype be more satisfying? – a QoE-centric study of the FEC mechanism in the internet-scale VoIP system. IEEE Network (2010)
44. Tsagkaropoulos, M., Politis, I., Dagiuklas, T., Kotsopoulos, S.: Enhanced vertical handover based on 802.21 framework for real-time video streaming. In: Mobimedia '09: Proceedings of the 5th International ICST Mobile Multimedia Communications Conference, pp. 1–6. ICST, Brussels (2009)
45. Andersson, K., Granlund, D., Ahlund, C.: M4: multimedia mobility manager: a seamless mobility management architecture supporting multimedia applications. In: MUM '07: Proceedings of the 6th international conference on Mobile and ubiquitous multimedia, pp. 6–13. ACM, New York (2007)

QoE-Oriented Performance Evaluation of Video Streaming over WiMAX

Daniele Migliorini, Enzo Mingozzi, and Carlo Vallati

Dipartimento di Ingegneria dell'Informazione
University of Pisa, Italy
{d.migliorini,e.mingozzi,c.vallati}@iet.unipi.it

Abstract. Mobile broadband wireless networks, such as WiMAX, have
been developed over the last years in order to support wireless access to
real-time multimedia applications like Voice over IP or Video on Demand.
To this aim, these networks are designed to provide guarantees in terms
of network-related QoS parameters, like loss, delay, or jitter. However,
the assessment of the performance of multimedia applications requires to
take into account also the Quality of Experience (QoE), which is related
to the quality of the service as it is perceived by the user, and is better
measured by different metrics, like MOS or PSNR. In this paper, we
first describe the simulation framework we developed to assess the QoE
of video streaming over WiMAX. The framework integrates a WiMAX
simulator based on ns-2 with tools for analyzing H.264/SVC compressed
video, and allows to estimate the PSNR of actual videos whose streaming
is simulated over WiMAX by means of ns-2. Based on this framework,
we carry out a performance evaluation by considering videos encoded
with different H.264/SVC scalability options and under realistic network
conditions.

Keywords: IEEE 802.16, WiMAX, H.264, Scalable Video Coding,
Simulation.

1 Introduction

Over the last twenty years, a noticeable effort has been made in the development of new standard video coding schemes, aimed at continuously improving
the efficiency of coding in terms of both increasing the compression ratio and
reducing video quality degradation. Two notable examples are the MPEG-4 [1]
and the H.264/AVC [2] standards, which have proved to be so effective to enable
video streaming over the Internet. On the other hand, mobile broadband wireless access systems, like the IEEE 802.16/WiMAX [3] and the 3GPP Long Term
Evolution (LTE) [4], have evolved in the direction of increasing the available
capacity per user, thus opening the perspective of provisioning video streaming
services also over the wireless access trunk of the network. However, the delivery of video over wireless networks poses additional challenges. In fact, wireless
links, especially in a mobile environment, are characterized by high bit error

E. Osipov et al. (Eds.): WWIC 2010, LNCS 6074, pp. 240–251, 2010.

rates and time-varying capacities due to fading channel effects, which both may cause data losses up to values that traditional coding schemes were not designed to manage.

In order to deal with such issues, scalable video coding (SVC) has been recently introduced in the H.264 standard [5]. The rationale behind SVC is to encode a high-quality video into a set of subset bitstreams that can be decoded independently to achieve the desired level of quality of the decoded video: the more the bitstreams used for decoding, the higher the quality. The actual number of bitstreams can be chosen, for example, depending on the network conditions, or the computational capabilities of the terminal device. Scalability can be realized by leveraging on the image quality, the frame size, the frame rate, or a combination of them. This flexibility can also improve the error resiliency of the streamed video. In fact, during high loss phases, an SVC-encoded video can trade off quality for uninterrupted video playout.

In addition, it has been recognized that usual Quality of Service (QoS) performance metrics, such as the end-to-end latency or the packet loss, are not able to measure the overall quality of service as it is perceived by human, especially in the case of multimedia communication. To this aim, Quality of Experience (QoE) has been defined as the overall acceptability of an application or service, as perceived subjectively by end-users. Although correlated to QoS, QoE can be better assessed by more sophisticated metrics, which can be either subjective, like the Mean Opinion Score (MOS) [6], or objective ones, like the PSNR [7].

The main contribution of this work is a comprehensive simulation framework to assess the QoE of video streaming over Mobile WiMAX. The framework currently integrates the well-known packet-based ns-2 network simulator with external tools for analyzing H.264/SVC encoded video, and allows to estimate the PSNR of any video whose streaming is simulated over a WiMAX network by means of ns-2. The framework is in fact sufficiently general to be easily adapted to integrate any packet network simulator taking workload traces as input. To demonstrate the capabilities of this framework, we then carry out a QoE-oriented performance evaluation of video streaming with different H.264/SVC encoding options under realistic network conditions.

The rest of the paper is organized as follows. In Sects. 2 and 3 we briefly introduce H.264/SVC video coding and WiMAX, respectively. Sect. 4 provides a description of the simulation framework, while Sect. 5 includes the numerical results of the performance evaluation. In Sect. 6 we finally draw some conclusions.

2   H.264 Scalable Video Coding

An H.264 encoded video stream consists of successive GOPs (Group Of Pictures) including a number of I-, P- and B-frames, respectively. More specifically, each GOP begins with an I-frame (Intra-coded picture), which is a reference picture representing a fixed image and is coded independently of the other pictures in the GOP, thus not requiring any additional information to be reconstructed.

The size of an I-frame is usually larger than any other type of frame. P-frames (Predictive pictures) are coded based on prior I- or P-frames within a GOP and contain motion-compensated difference information. Finally, B-frames (Bidirectional predictive pictures) include difference information from the preceding and following I- or P-frame within a GOP.

For the purpose of encoded video streaming over a communication network, the H.264 standard defines a functional entity called NAL (Network Abstraction Layer) which is responsible for formatting the compressed bitstream produced by the VCL (Video Coding Layer) into data sequences easily manageable by the network. This process creates AUs (Access Units), each one corresponds to a decoded picture in a GOP. An AU is formed by a sequence of NALUs (Network Abstraction Layer Units), which can be of two types: Non-VCL and VCL. The VCL NAL units contain the encoded data of the picture, partially or entirely, while the non-VCL NAL units contain any associated additional information such as parameter and sequence sets.

The H.264/SVC introduces the possibility of encoding a video into a bitstream which contains one or more subset bitstreams (layers) that can themselves be decoded independently to achieve the desired level of quality of the decoded video. The video scalability is obtained through the selection of one or more subset bitstreams and discarding unnecessary information. In particular, several types/levels of scalability are defined and applied either in isolation, or combined together. In the following, we briefly summarize only two of them, namely the temporal scalability and the Signal-to-Noise Ratio (SNR) scalability, respectively, which are those used in the simulation framework. We refer the reader to [5] for further details.

With the *temporal scalability*, the same video stream is encoded into different layers corresponding to different temporal resolutions or frame rates. The quality of the decoded video depends on the number of layers used for actual decoding: the larger this number, the higher the resulting sample rate. In particular, a different Temporal ID (TID) is assigned to each different temporal layer. TID zero is assigned to the base layer with the lower frame rate. Each additional enhancement layer is coded depending on the information provided by the previous layer. It follows that, on one hand, the decoder is free to scale the frame rate by simply choosing a preferred TID and discarding all NALUs with a greater TID value. On the other hand, this also implies that, if a NALU with a given TID is lost or corrupted by the network, the decoder will be prevented from up-sampling the frame rate based on the corresponding layer and all subsequent ones.

With the *SNR scalability* all layers share a common frame rate and picture size, but provide distinct visual qualities because they are associated to different quantization parameters. In H.264/SVC we can obtain SNR scalability resorting to two kinds of strategies called CGS (Coarse Grain Scalability) and MGS (Medium Grain Scalability); in this work we focus only on the latter because it provides more flexibility of bit stream adaptation and error robustness. In MGS, the sub-layers provide successive refinements in the accuracy of transform coefficients, allowing the application to select the desired decoding quality by processing only the appropriate subset streams; this is implemented by assigning a different Quality ID (QID) to each layer, the first one being the base layer which corresponds to the lower bit rate (QID=0). From the network perspective, NAL units belonging to any enhancement layer can be discarded while still allowing picture decoding, at the cost of a degraded resulting image quality (SNR), thus achieving packet-based quality scalability.

3   IEEE 802.16/WiMAX

In this section we briefly introduce those aspects of IEEE 802.16 which are specifically relevant to this work. For a comprehensive description of the system, we refer the reader to the standard [3]. IEEE 802.16 is a point-to-multipoint broadband wireless access system, where a Base Station (BS) centrally coordinates the downlink and uplink transmissions to and from a number of Mobile Stations (MSs). The designated PHY layer for mobile operation is based on Orthogonal Frequency Division Multiple Access (OFDMA). In order to exploit multi-user and time diversity, adaptive modulation and coding is used. In particular, a set of different Modulation and Coding Schemes (MCSs) is defined: the more robust the MCS, the smaller the number of bits that are conveyed per OFDMA slot.

The MAC layer is connection-oriented. Each uni-directional connection is uniquely identified by a connection id (CID). The transmission of variable-length packets is supported by means of a convergence layer. One or more MAC Service Data Units (SDUs) can then be encapsulated into a single MAC Protocol Data Unit (PDU). Error detection and correction is implemented by means of Hybrid Automatic Repeat Request (H-ARQ). For H-ARQ enabled connections, MAC PDUs are concatenated into an H-ARQ sub-burst, which is appended a Cyclic Redundancy Check (CRC) trailer, encoded and transmitted over the air. The correct/incorrect decoding of an H-ARQ sub-burst is indicated by the recipient MS by means of a dedicated logical sub-channel in uplink. Failed H-ARQ sub-bursts can be re-transmitted by the BS up to a maximum number of times.

A key feature of the IEEE 802.16 MAC is Quality of Service (QoS) support by means of five different classes of service, representing both real-time and non-real-time requirements [8][9]. Each connection has its own set of associated QoS parameters. Advanced scheduling is implemented at the BS in order to ensure that QoS requirements of all connections are met.

4   The Simulation Framework

The goal of the proposed framework is to assess the QoE of video streaming over a packet network by means of simulation. Any network simulator can be in principle integrated into the framework, provided that: (*i*) it takes a trace-based workload as input, and (*ii*) it produces a packet trace as output, as a result of the simulation. The framework can be easily adapted to accommodate any specific trace format defined by the integrated simulator. In this case study, we used an

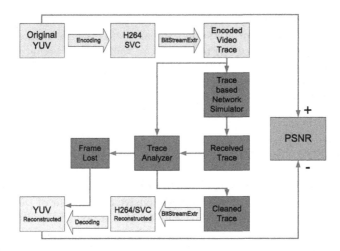

Fig. 1. Workflow of the evaluation framework

implementation of WiMAX over the well-known ns-2 simulator. We will refer in the following to this specific instance of the framework for the purpose of illustrating its operation. Fig. 1 represents the workflow of the evaluation process. The latter consists of four phases: encoding, simulation/post processing, decoding and data analysis. In the encoding phase, the original uncompressed video is encoded according to H.264/SVC, and a corresponding trace file is produced. After simulation, the output is post-processed in order to allow for the next operation, which is the decoding of the distorted video stream, as it was received by the end user as a result of the simulation. Finally, the PSNR is evaluated by comparing the original uncompressed and compressed videos with the distorted one. In the following, the different phases are further detailed.

4.1   Encoding

The source of the process is the original uncompressed raw video in the YUV color space. In this phase, the video is encoded using the H.264/SVC coding scheme. The encoding process is performed using the JSVM tool, the reference open source implementation of the H.264/SVC standard [10]. In particular, the JSVM tool `H264EncoderStatic` allows to encode a YUV video by configuring all the relevant H.264/SVC encoding settings, thereby including the type of scalability to be used, and the number of layers that will compose the output stream. The encoded video is not directly provided to the network simulator, but a corresponding trace file is rather produced. The latter is extracted from the H.264/SVC encoded video by means of the `BitStreamExtractor` JSVM tool, and includes a different entry for each packet of the NALU sequence. Among other parameters, the entry specifies the size of the packet, which is needed for the purpose of simulation, and the TID, the QID, and the packet type, which are needed instead during the decoding phase.

4.2 Simulation and Post-processing

The core of the framework is the WiMAX simulator. For each MS, it takes as input a video packet trace file, and provides as output a corresponding trace file of packets received by the MS as a result of the simulation. The output trace has the same format as the input trace (one entry per each NALU) with, in addition, the corresponding latency of transmission experienced in the network. If a packet is lost, the corresponding entry does not appear in the output.

As already mentioned, the output trace file needs further processing before being used for decoding the corresponding received video stream. In fact, the WiMAX simulator does not implement any playout buffer mechanism at the MS. Therefore, we implemented a tool, named `traceAnalyzer`, which simulates a simple constant-delay playout buffer at the MS, and additionally discards from the trace all the packets that arrived later (according to the trace records) than their corresponding playout deadline. More sophisticated playout buffer management algorithms can be implemented in `traceAnalyzer` to take into account more realistic scenarios.

Moreover, we have to deal with some issues related with the reliability of the current implementation of the H.264/SVC JSVM decoder. In fact, the JSVM decoder is not designed to recover from the loss of any packet in the NALU sequence. More specifically, it stops the decoding process if either a non-discardable packet (i.e., one including an I-frame) is missing, or if a packet with unmatched layer dependencies is found. On the other hand, both cases are typical when the video is transmitted over lossy wireless links of a mobile broadband system like WiMAX. In order to overcome the above limitations and be able to complete the decoding process, the `traceAnalyzer` tool restores the missing non-discardable packets in the output trace, and discards instead all the packets with unmatched layer dependencies within each NALU. The latter operation does not change the resulting quality of the video received and played at the MS, since the additionally discarded packets would have not be taken into consideration for decoding in any case, as explained in Sect. 2. On the other hand, by restoring missing non-discardable packets, we artificially improve the quality of reconstructed video at the MS, since the actually missed packet would in general cause the loss of the whole GOP it belongs to. This will be appropriately managed after decoding, as it will be explained in the following.

The `traceAnalyzer` tool provides then as output two different files: the post-processed trace file, and the list of GOPs that were improperly restored.

4.3 Decoding

The post-processed trace file is now ready to be used for decoding. First, the `BitStreamExtractor` tool is used to reconstruct the H.264/SVC stream starting from the post-processed trace and the original encoded video. The result is the encoded video as it was received by the MS as a result of the simulation. The obtained H.264/SVC distorted video can then be decoded into a YUV raw file by means of the JSVM `H264DecoderStatic` tool. Because of the post-processing done in the previous phase, the latter will always succeed in decoding the whole stream. However, the resulting YUV uncompressed stream is different from that played out at the MS for two reasons: (i) static decoding skips lost frames without considering a replacement for them, and (ii) entire GOPs that were actually lost are instead included because of post-processing treatment of non-discardable packets. To deal with the second issue, all GOPs that were incorrectly restored are now discarded from the uncompressed stream, based on the complementary information provided by `traceAnalyzer`. Then, to manage missing frames, because of both the first issue above or as a result of GOP elimination, the YUV video is further modified by adding, for each missing frame, a copy of the immediately previous one, thus implementing the freeze effect typical of a real decoder. The outcome of this phase is the raw video stream that would have been played out on the MS terminal, as a result of a given simulation run.

4.4   Data Analysis

To evaluate the quality perceived by the end user, a comparison between the distorted and the original raw video can now be performed. Several objective image and video distortion/quality metrics have been defined in the literature [7]. In this work, we adopt the most commonly used one, i.e., the peak signal-to-noise ratio (PSNR). The PSNR is widely used because it is simple to calculate and has clear physical meanings. It is defined as:

$$PSNR = 20log_{10}\left(\frac{MAX_I}{\sqrt{MSE}}\right) \qquad (1)$$

where

$$MSE = \frac{1}{mn}\sum_{i=0}^{m-1}\sum_{j=0}^{n-1}[I(i,j) - K(i,j)]^2 \qquad (2)$$

MAX_I is the maximum possible pixel value of the image. When the pixels are represented using 8 bits per sample, this is 255. It is easy to understand, however, that any other objective metric based on the comparison of the original and the distorted uncompressed streams are allowed by the framework. Moreover, since the actual distorted stream is fully available, also the evaluation of subjective metrics, such as the Mean Opinion Score (MOS), is enabled.

5   Performance Evaluation

We consider a single IEEE 802.16 cell with a variable number of MSs. In order to have a realistic characterization of the system, we consider time-varying channel conditions. In particular, channel state is modeled by means of a Discrete-Time Markov Chain according to [11]. The time unit of the DTMC is the frame, and each state represents a different channel response, with a corresponding MCS to be used for transmission in order to ensure a maximum target bit error rate. Moreover, to represent two different operating conditions, the DTMC may have either 4 or 8 states. In the former case, only the less efficient MCSs are

Table 1. WiMAX system parameters

Name	Value	Name	Value
Duplex mode	TDD	Average sojourn time $(1/\alpha)$	200 frames
DL Sub-channelization	PUSC		
OFDM symbols per frame	47	MCSs, *bad* channel conditions	QPSK1/2, QPSK3/4, 16QAM1/2, 16QAM3/4
Frame duration	5 ms		
LLC maximum segment size	100 bytes		
Packet Scheduler	Proportional Fair	Additional MCSs, *good* channel conditions	64QAM1/2, 64QAM2/3, 64QAM3/4, 64QAM5/6

Table 2. Video parameters

Original YUV file		H.264/SVC SNR scalability	
Size	21.75 MBytes	Size	15.45 MBytes
Frame per second	25	Layering	Dual Layer coding
Duration	600 seconds	Type of scalability	MGS
H.264/SVC Temporal scalability		Quantization	45 first layer, 35 second layer
Size	20.61 Mbytes		
Layering	Single Layer coding	Number of MGS sublayer	3
Quantization	45		
B-Frames	Yes	B-Frames	Yes
GOP size	16 Frames	GOP size	16 Frames

considered in order to model *bad* channel conditions. In the latter case, also the most efficient ones are considered to model *good* channel conditions. All states have the same average sojourn time equal to $1/\alpha$. To recover from packet losses, H-ARQ with chase-combining is used for each connection. Table 1 summarizes the values used for the most relevant WiMAX system parameters.

The original video file used for the analysis is extracted from a Video DVD with title "Tokyo Olympiad" [12]. This video has been H.264/SVC encoded with either temporal scalability or SNR scalability. All the relevant video related parameters are reported in Table 2. The same video is streamed to all the MSs. However, trace start times for different MSs are 7s apart of each other, to avoid peak rate synchronization. The constant playout delay is set to 2s.

In the following, we consider two scenarios with low (12 MSs) and high (20 MSs) load, respectively. In both cases, half of the MSs have bad channel conditions and the other half have good ones. For each scenario, we consider two possible values for the maximum number of H-ARQ sub-burst retransmissions (1 and 3, respectively) in order to analyze the impact of packet error recovery on video quality. For each combination of parameters, we ran 10 independent replications of the simulation experiment in order to estimate the average and 95% confidence interval for each metric of interest.

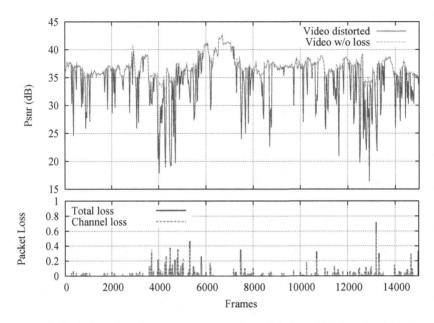

Fig. 2. PSNR and packet loss over time, SNR scalability, 20 MSs, 3 H-ARQ max retransmissions

5.1   Simulation Results

We consider first a scenario with 20 users (i.e., high load) and a maximum number of 3 retransmissions. In the top graph of Fig. 2 it is reported the PSNR of each frame of the video stream over time, both after H.264/SVC with SNR scalability encoding (referred to as "Video w/o loss"), and subsequent distortion due to network and playout buffer losses (referred to as "Video distorted"). On the other hand, In the bottom graph of Fig. 2, it is reported the normalized packet loss per frame of distorted video, due to both network and playout buffer losses ("Total loss") and to network losses only ("Channel loss"). The two graphs are aligned to capture the dependence of PSNR on losses due to transmission over a network. Results reported refer to an MS with good channel conditions. As can be seen from Fig. 2, even the loss of few consecutive packets leads to deep negative PSNR peaks with SNR scalability. However, such peaks have short duration, even when the packet loss is high and persistent. As a matter of fact, PSNR tends to return to its reference value (i.e., that one due to compression only). Moreover, most of the losses are due to the network, and only a few happen in the playout buffer.

Fig. 3 reports the results for the same scenario as that of Fig. 2, but with H.264/SVC with temporal scalability encoding. With this type of scalability, the loss of few sporadic packets seems to lead to a negligible PSNR degradation. However, in general packet loss is quite high and persistent, leading to stable low values of the PSNR. Moreover, it can be noted that the channel and total loss are almost always different, meaning that not only many packets are lost because of

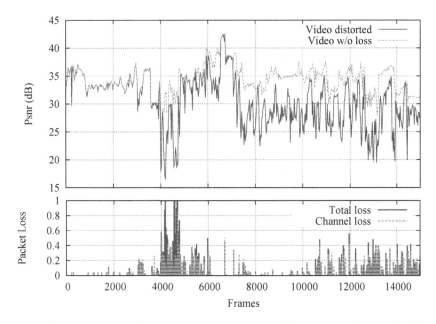

Fig. 3. PSNR and packet loss over time, temporal scalability, 20 MSs, 3 H-ARQ max retransmissions

the wireless channel, but also many of those that get to the MS arrived too late to be decoded and played out. This provides a hint for devising, at list in this case, a smart scheduling operation at the BS, in order to avoid wasting capacity by transmitting those packets whose transmission has been already delayed beyond their respective playout deadlines.

By comparing Figs. 2 and 3, we can see that the total packet loss is much higher with the temporal scalability than with the SNR scalability. This can be explained by considering that the throughput required by the former is higher than that of the latter, as confirmed by the different size of the encoded video files (see Tab. 2). Therefore, for the same number of users, the resulting load on the network is different and much higher with the temporal scalability, meaning that packets will experience a higher transmission delay, and will more likely miss their playout deadlines. We can also observe, by comparing Figs. 2 and 3, that very much different PSNR values result in the two cases because of few consecutive losses. This behaviour can be in particular observed during the first 4000 frames, and can be explained by considering the nature of the video. In fact, during the first seconds the scene is a slow-motion of a road race. Frames are therefore strongly correlated to each other. For this reason, the temporal scalability ensures a negligible quality degradation, because packet losses will eventually cause a down-sampling of the frame rate, which however does not impact on the PSNR since frames are changing slowly over time. On the other hand, with SNR scalability packet losses directly impact on the quality of decoded frames, which implies lower PSNR values in any case.

Table 3. Average PSNR with confidence interval, and PSNR degradation due to losses for all the considered scenarios

MSs, #rtx, Channel	TEMPORAL W/o loss: 34.34 dB			SNR W/o loss: 36.93 dB		
	dB	C. I.	%	dB	C. I.	%
12 MSs, 1 rtx, Good	32.68	0.496	4.86	31.15	0.161	15.65
12 MSs, 3 rtx, Good	34.22	0.032	0.38	35.86	0.112	2.90
12 MSs, 1 rtx, Bad	33.04	0.059	3.80	31.75	0.161	14.04
12 MSs, 3 rtx, Bad	34.21	0.018	0.41	36.15	0.045	2.13
20 MSs, 1 rtx, Good	30.59	1.143	10.92	30.39	0.437	17.71
20 MSs, 3 rtx, Good	30.54	0.999	11.09	35.07	0.079	5.04
20 MSs, 1 rtx, Bad	28.62	0.875	16.69	30.76	0.486	16.70
20 MSs, 3 rtx, Bad	24.28	0.592	29.30	32.62	0.873	11.68

Finally, we summarize in Table 3 the numerical results obtained for all the scenarios resulting from the different combinations of values of the number of MSs, the number of H-ARQ retransmissions, and the channel conditions, for both the SNR and the temporal scalability options. For each scenario, we report the PSNR of distorted video, averaged over its whole duration, along with the corresponding confidence interval. Moreover, we also report the relative decrease of the PSNR with respect to that calculated right after encoding (i.e., the reference one), which is also reported on top of the corresponding columns.

From Table 3 we can see that SNR scalability outperforms the temporal scalability in terms of average PSNR in almost all considered scenarios, even though we know from Fig. 2 that this is achieved with a higher variability over time with respect to temporal scalability. However, we also notice that its reference PSNR value is higher than that of temporal scalability. Therefore, at low loads, the video quality degradation is relatively higher for SNR than for temporal scalability. On the other hand, at high loads (20 MSs, 3 rtx), because of the different compression efficiency, the temporal scalability suffers from early congestion and therefore performs considerably worse.

As for the number of H-ARQ retransmissions, we can see that a higher number of retransmissions is always beneficial for SNR scalability, since it allows to reduce packet losses due to channel errors. On the other hand, for temporal scalability this is true only at low loads. In fact, at high loads, the increased number of retransmissions consumes additional capacity, which contributes to further overload the network. Finally, we can observe that at low loads there is basically no difference, in terms of average PSNR, between MSs with good and bad channel conditions, respectively. This is because there is sufficiently available capacity to accommodate the (re)transmissions with less efficient MCSs. On the other hand, at high loads this is no more true, and the performance becomes soon much worse.

6   Conclusions

In this paper we have described a simulation framework that allows to evaluate the PSNR of an actual video whose streaming is simulated over WiMAX by means of a packet based simulator. The framework works by constructing a packet trace from a real H.264/SVC encoded video. The trace is provided as input to the simulator, and then the simulation output is processed in order to produce the resulting decoded video stream, as if it were actually transmitted on the real network. Moreover, we used the framework to evaluate the performance of two different scalability encoding options of H.264/SVC, under realistic network configuration. The numerical results allowed to compare the two scalability options in terms of PSNR, as a function of a number of factors, such as the number of MSs, the number of H-ARQ retransmissions and the channel conditions.

References

1. ISO/IEC/JTC1/SC29/WG11, Overview of the MPEG-4 Standard (July 2000)
2. Wiegand, T., Sullivan, G.J., Bjontegaard, G., Luthra, A.: Overview of the h.264/avc video coding standard. IEEE Transactions on Circuits and Systems for Video Technology 13(7), 560–576 (2003)
3. IEEE 802.16-2009: IEEE Standard for Local and metropolitan area networks Part 16: Air Interface for Broadband Wireless Access Systems (May 2009)
4. 3GPP LTE Homepage,
   http://www.3gpp.org/ftp/Specs/html-info/36-series.htm
5. Reichel, J., Schwarz, H., Wien, M.: Joint scalable video model JSVM-5. JVT-R202 (Output Document from Joint Video Team (JVT) of ISO/IEC MPEG and ITU-T VCEG) (January 2006)
6. ITU-T Recommendation P.910. Subjective video quality assessment methods for multimedia applications (September 1999)
7. Wang, Y.: Survey of Objective Video Quality Measurements. Tech. report, Worcester Polytechnic Institute (June 2006)
8. Cicconetti, C., Eklund, C., Lenzini, L., Mingozzi, E.: Quality of Service Support in IEEE 802.16 Networks. IEEE Network 20, 50–55 (2006)
9. Cicconetti, C., Erta, A., Lenzini, L., Mingozzi, E.: Performance Evaluation of the IEEE 802.16 MAC for QoS Support. IEEE Trans. Mobile Comput. 6, 26–38 (2007)
10. The JSVM project home page,
    http://ip.hhi.de/imagecom_G1/savce/downloads/
    SVC-Reference-Software.htm
11. Liu, X., Sridharan, A., Machiraju, S., Seshadri, M., Zang, H.: Experiences in a 3G Network: Interplay between the Wireless Channel and Applications. In: Proc. ACM Mobicom'08, San Francisco, CA, September 14-19 (2008)
12. Wikipedia, Tokio Olympiad definition,
    http://en.wikipedia.org/wiki/Tokyo_Olympiad

An Overview of Quality of Experience Measurement Challenges for Video Applications in IP Networks[*]

R. Serral-Gracià[1], E. Cerqueira[2,3], M. Curado[3],
M. Yannuzzi[1], E. Monteiro[3], and X. Masip-Bruin[1]

[1] Advanced Network Architectures Lab, Technical University of Catalunya (UPC),
Jordi Girona 1-3, 08028 Barcelona - Spain
[2] Faculty of Computer Engineering, Federal University of Para,
Rua Augusto Corrêa, 01, CEP 66075-110, Belém - Brazil
[3] Department of Informatics Engineering, University of Coimbra,
Polo II, Pinhal de Marrocos, 3030-290 Coimbra - Portugal
{rserral,yannuzzi,xmasip}@ac.upc.edu, cerqueira@ufpa.br,
{marilia,edmundo}@dei.uc.pt

Abstract. The increase in multimedia content on the Internet has created a renewed interest in quality assessment. There is however a main difference from the traditional quality assessment approaches, as now, the focus relies on the user perceived quality, opposed to the network centered approach classically proposed. In this paper we overview the most relevant challenges to perform Quality of Experience (QoE) assessment in IP networks and highlight the particular considerations necessary when compared to alternative mechanisms, already deployed, such as Quality of Service (QoS). To assist on the handling of such challenges we first discuss the different approaches to Quality of Experience assessment along with the most relevant QoE metrics, and then we discuss how they are used to provide objective results about user satisfaction.

Keywords: QoE, Measurements, Challenges.

1 Introduction

In the past years Traffic Monitoring and Measurement has been the focus of active research within the networking community. In particular, one important topic in the area has been the network performance analysis [1, 2], which is centered in developing mechanisms for efficient Quality of Service (QoS) and Service Level Agreement (SLA) assessment in the network [3, 4]. QoS assessment addresses the different challenges associated with the accurate computation and estimation (most of the time) of network level metrics, such as, One-Way Delay, Jitter, or Packet Losses. Until recently, most approaches were network oriented and only considered the SLA among network operators and big content providers. This monitoring and measurement methodology has become insufficient as new types of content have emerged on the Internet. As a

---

[*] This work was partially funded by Spanish Ministry of Science and Innovation under contract TEC2009-07041, the Catalan Government under contract 2009 SGR1508, and CNPq(476202/2009-4)/FAPESPA(5183.UNI319.4107.07072009)).

E. Osipov et al. (Eds.): WWIC 2010, LNCS 6074, pp. 252–263, 2010.

consequence, in the recent years the multimedia content consumed by the users has dramatically increased, users are constantly downloading video streams, using video-conferencing applications, or even broadcasting their own video streams to the Internet, which, given the sensitivity of such traffic in terms of delay and packet loss, imposes tighter constraints on the end-user network and applications for a reliable content delivery, opposed to the inter-domain agreements of classic SLA. Therefore, the interest of Content Providers and Network Operators on offering a successful multimedia experience to the users becomes more important than just considering specific network performance parameters. This evolution offers new business models where the relevant factor, and the source of revenue, is not the network or even the content by itself, but rather the degree of satisfaction achieved by the customers who are paying for the service. Therefore, as a side effect, a renewed interest has appeared in operators and content providers to search for mechanisms capable of assessing such user satisfaction through Quality of Experience (QoE) techniques. These techniques can be exploited in order to offer Autonomic Network Management (ANM) capabilities to their networks, e.g., by automating the resource reservation and the traffic engineering through user satisfaction aware metrics.

In the scenario described, QoE assessment requires the definition of a new set of metrics, which must be able to objectively assess the end-user satisfaction. However, in practice, this is a challenging issue because the evaluation involves a number of subjective factors, usually not related to the network performance, e.g., the mood of the user, or the responsiveness of the system, opposed to the classical QoS assessment platforms, which are mostly network centered.

To better understand the new challenges of QoE assessment in multimedia applications, in this paper we overview the different approaches currently available for the QoE evaluation of the delivered multimedia experience, and as an use-case, we highlight the main issues that must be solved in IPTV scenarios.

The rest of the paper is organized as follows, in the next section we overview the different techniques for QoS assessment, addressing specifically the most useful for the QoE environment. In Section 3, we highlight the different approaches for QoE Measurement, which leads to the introduction of the specific metrics used in this environment in Section 4. We continue our dissertation in Section 5 by highlighting the different challenges we must face when designing a complete QoE assessment platform. Next we detail, as an use case, the issues found in the QoE assessment in an IPTV network, and finally in Section 7 we conclude with a summary of our contribution.

2   Background

This section discuses metrics and techniques historically used as a starting point for objective network quality assessment. In particular, metrics used in the QoS area which are the basis for some aspects of QoE assessment are described.

The efficient assessment of real-time multimedia applications, such as video streaming, mobile IPTV, urban monitoring cameras and other kinds of audio and video applications, is a key requirement to the success of all-IP networks. The quality level control of multimedia services aims to maximize the user's satisfaction and the usage of network resources, as well as, to keep and attract customers, while increasing the profits of network providers.

Differently from traditional applications, such as Web browsing and File Transfer Protocol (FTP), where the quality of network delivery is not critical, given that these applications are elastic and can tolerate certain amount of network impairments, multimedia services need the content delivery with low impact on the voice and video quality levels perceived by users. However, due to the nature of IP-based networks, various types of network impairments occur along the communication paths, which need to be measured and managed.

Most Quality of Service (QoS) assessment techniques are based on network measurements to control the quality level of applications in wired and wireless systems [5]. Existing QoS metrics, such as packet loss rate, packet delay rate, packet jitter rate and throughput, are typically used to indicate the impact on the video quality level from the network's point of view, but do not reflect the user's perception. Consequently, these QoS parameters fail in capturing subjective aspects associated with human experience. These network layer objective metrics are defined as follows:

- *One Way Delay*: the amount of time from the packet generation until its reception at the destination [6]. Reasonable values for this metric range from milliseconds for Real-Time Interactive (RTI) traffic to minutes in some Video on Demand (VoD) scenarios, such as Peer-to-Peer TV (P2PTV).
- *Packet Loss*: a packet loss is a packet generated in a node, but which does not reach its destination due to network issues [7]. Packet loss is the first cause of QoS and QoE disruption, since if a packet is lost, and not retransmitted on time it will get discarded, consequently producing video or audio disruptions. In real-time scenarios packet losses can be caused by buffer underruns or by network malfunction.
- *Jitter*: after packet loss, jitter is the second cause of service disruption. Jitter is defined as the variation in delay of consecutive packets in the stream [8]. If there is high jitter in the network it can cause buffer underruns, and therefore packet losses in the communication. Jitter is smoothed in the application layer with the de-jitter buffers, which increase delay, but reduce quality degradation.

In order overcome the limitations of current QoS-aware measurement schemes regarding subjective aspects related to human perception and to enable more accurate assessment of the quality experienced by users, Quality of Experience techniques have been introduced [9, 10]. QoE measurement operations in wired and wireless system can be used as an indicator of how a networking environment meets the end-user needs. Existing quality metrics aim to meet wider expectations by providing a good correlation with subjective ratings, cross-content, cross-distortion accuracy, and low computational complexity in order to enable in-service applications.

3   QoE Measurement Approaches

Two main QoE assessment approaches are receiving an important attention from industry research groups, commonly referred as Content Inspection/Artifact-based Measurement and Network-based Measurement. The former operates in the decoded content and can be configured to calculate the application quality level by using QoE metrics that range from simple pixel-to-pixel comparison schemes to sophisticated Human Visual System (HVS)-based frame-level artifacts analysis [11]. While the latter aims to predict the multimedia quality level based on information gathered from packet and network conditions without accessing the decoded video [12].

Objective and subjective content inspection measurement approaches are used to find distortions that can be introduced at any stage in the end-to-end multimedia delivery system, such as coding/decoding or network congestion. Existing objective video quality assessment models have been developed to estimate/predict the quality level of multimedia services by using QoE metrics that approximate results of subjective quality assessment [13]. QoE subjective measurements assess how audio and/or video streams are perceived by users [14], i.e., what is their opinion on the quality of particular audio/video sequences, as described in ITU-T recommendation BT 500 [12].

Content inspection measurement solutions can be assessed with No-Reference (NR), Reduced-Reference (RR) or Full-Reference (FR) approaches. The FR method accesses the original and received content in the evaluation process. The RR uses an alternative channel between senders and receivers to transmit the parameters of the delivered content in a reduced way or use watermarking schemes, while the NR approach assesses the content quality level without any knowledge of the original material.

Due to the time and processing demands, as well as feasibility issues of content-based assessments, multimedia quality prediction mechanisms can be used. These schemes predict the quality level that a specific content will have after the encoding process, based on the encoding parameters, packet inspections, and network conditions. Further processing of the original data is not required, minimizing this way the associated complexity and resource consumption. Opposed to this, network-based approaches verify all transmitted packets related with the application, the main issue is that such approaches need to perform deep-packet inspection. Additionally, they need to gather information about the current network conditions, such as packet loss rate and packet one way delay, to be used in the predictive process. The final quality level assessment decision can be taken based on previous information together with information about the multimedia characteristics, such as frame-rate, Group of Picture (GoP), frame type and dependence only available at application level.

Hybrid Content Inspection and Network Measurement approaches have also been proposed [15]. The main reason for the development of this kind of scheme is to allow network operators to combine the benefits of the two previous approaches and adjust performance, complexity and feasibility, as well as operational cost issues according to different needs, multimedia content type, networks and equipments.

4   Metrics

A metric is defined as *"a system of related measures that facilitates the quantification of some particular characteristic"*[1], and as such it implies a well defined and measurable component. However, when defining metrics for QoE assessment there are many

---

[1] http://www.dictionary.net/metric

subjective factors which might bias the user satisfaction towards a service, hence increasing the complexity of computing objective metrics. As a consequence, there are notable research efforts in objectifying such factors in order to have a measurable value of the user satisfaction in general.

The Mean Opinion Score (MOS) is metric typically used in QoE scenarios as we will detail later in this section. There is however, a main drawback of using this metric alone, because it only considers video and audio quality, ignoring other important aspects such as application responsiveness or degree of interactivity, which are also relevant for a complete QoE assessment framework.

Many alternatives have been proposed regarding classification schemes of mechanisms for video assessment [16]. Going beyond those approaches, we propose a more generic classification, which considers not only the video quality assessment methods but also other classes of metrics not directly related to perceived video quality. The two different types of metrics are, *i)* direct metrics, and *ii)* indirect metrics. The direct metrics are those which directly affect the perceived quality of the multimedia flows, while indirect metrics refer to other factors such as response time, or degree of interactivity, that impact on the service usability, but do not affect directly to the multimedia traffic. Both direct and indirect metrics have different relative importance depending on the service, and they affect the perceived experience in the delivered service in different ways.

4.1 Direct Metrics

Direct metrics consider factors that directly affect the user perception of the multimedia experience, i.e., received audio and video quality. Direct metrics are obtained from various types of data (potentially at different layers), such as delay variations or packet (frame) losses related with network performance, and codec information as determined by the application.

There is a broad diversity of direct metrics, it is not the goal of this work to provide a full list, but instead we refer to the most relevant metrics in the area of video quality assessment. For a more detailed list the reader is referred to [15, 16].

- *Peak Signal to Noise Ratio* (PSNR): it is a basic, yet important metric that assesses the similarity between two different images. It uses the Full Reference QoE measurement approach described above. PSNR computes the Mean Square Error (MSE) of each pixel between the original and received images, represented in dB. Images with more similarity will result in higher PSNR values.
- *Structural Similarity* (SSIM): the main drawback of PSNR is that it does not consider how human perception works, hence in some cases it cannot detect some human perceptible video disruptions. To address this shortcoming, SSIM combines luminance, contrast, and structural similarity of the images to compare the correlation between the original image and the received one. Similarly to PSNR, SSIM is also based on the Full Reference scheme.
- *Video Quality Metric* (VQM): improving the approaches described above, VQM detects human perceivable artifacts on the images, by considering blurring, global noise, and block and color distortions. This metric also uses the original video, hence using the Full Reference QoE measurement approach.

- *Mean Opinion Score* (MOS): MOS was originally devised for audio streams, it combines delays, perceived jitter at application layer, codec used for the communication, and packet losses—also at application layer. In the area of video QoE assessment can be considered as a meta-metric given that it considers values from other metrics to generate the final computed user perception. The most used extension of MOS was proposed in [17] where the authors propose a mapping between PSNR and MOS.

All the above direct metrics have the main issue that they require the presence of the original video frames in order to compare and assess the user perceived QoE. On the other hand, when there are no reference points of analysis, the solutions require low level performance information about frame losses, delays, and jitter, using the NR and RR models above, as we found in the Moving Pictures Quality Metric (MPQM) model—with its particular implementation V-Factor—in the context of IPTV traffic [18]. Whilst MPQM results are less accurate than the ones obtained with the previous approaches, it is usable in more scenarios, in particular when performing real-time assessment or in environments where the source video is not available.

4.2 Indirect Metrics

Indirect metrics consider properties that affect the multimedia experience, but that are not directly related to the quality of the multimedia content, such as artifacts that might cause undesirable side effects that affect the final user perception of the service. It is worth noticing that indirect metrics have not been studied in detail in the networking area, where the focus has been clearly centered in the network performance and in direct metrics assessment. Nevertheless, as the multimedia applications continue to expand, this research area will become more appealing in the near future.

Given their nature, indirect metrics are closely related with the type of delivered service, and in general they require access to application or run-time information since they depend on user actions such as pressing the "play button". In this work, we describe the most relevant indirect metrics for the assessment of video applications.

- *Start-up time*: this metric defines the time span since the user queries the system about a specific content until he/she receives it. A classic example of this is the waiting time experienced by an user from the time he/she clicks on a video link until the video is actually reproduced on the user's screen.
- *Response time*: this metric is an extension of the start-up time. It is defined as the time span since the user issues a command or performs an action until it is acknowledged by the system and an answer arrives at the user, e.g., when the user pauses a video. In video-conferencing this metric is interpreted as interactivity degree, which determines the fluency of a conversation among the conference participants.
- *Delivery Synchronization*: when several users are using a service, the content should be received at the same time by all the participants. This is critical in on-line gaming where the users need to react fast to the actions of others.
- *Freshness*: this metric specifies the time span from content generation until its reception by the user. It is specially important in live video streaming, where the users

want the content as fast as possible (e.g., to celebrate a goal in a football match). This metric greatly affects applications performing live streaming in P2P networks (P2PTV).

- *Blocking:* this metric is closely related the direct metrics because it models the jerkiness of the video, normally caused by empty buffers on the receiver.

As it can be observed, all the above indirect metrics are related in one way or another with the computation of time intervals. The issue of time interval computation has been broadly studied in the QoS and performance analysis fields [1], which involves high precision time synchronization techniques between the end-points. Luckily, in the area of QoE, such sub-millisecond accuracy is not required, since in most scenarios, human perception has resolutions which range from tens to hundreds of milliseconds, which is fairly easy to accomplish with state-of-the-art hardware.

5   Challenges

When designing a QoE assessment platform many factors must be considered. In this paper we focus our the discussion on highlighting the main concerns found in such designs in the area of multimedia applications.

It is not our goal to propose an integrated solution for QoE assessment, but rather to identify the main issues from two different viewpoints, namely, issues related with data acquisition, and issues related with results analysis and interpretation.

5.1   Data Acquisition

Any measurement platform, whether it is aimed at QoS or QoE assessment needs to collect data. Classically in QoS environments such traffic collection involved computationally intensive operations coping with huge amounts of data in high speed links which forced sampling [4] or data aggregation schemes to provide some means of scalability. Contrary to this, in the case of QoE environments, since we are coping with user perception, we cannot use backbone equipment to measure network performance, because the traffic collection must be issued as close to the end-user as possible to have an accurate estimate of the user's perception. This has the advantage that the amount of data to process is greatly reduced at the user end-point. But, despite of this, if the application does not have any integrated measurement techniques, it greatly complicates the traffic analysis, given that application dependent data is necessary. On top of that, when using handheld mobile devices, in general the computational constraints and battery life can impose important issues to perform such assessment.

When acquiring the information in order to assess the QoE level, we have to answer three different questions, *i) Which* information do we have to acquire?, *ii) Where* do we have to collect it?, and *iii) How* do we perform the acquisition?. The *Which* is determined by the metric selection, while the *Where* and the *How* determine the accuracy we will obtain. These issues are further detailed in the next sub-sections.

Metric selection: The context in which the collection is performed will determine the metrics that can be computed and the QoE measurement approach that can be used, i.e., FR, NR, RR. Moreover, this selection will have critical impact on the assessment accuracy.

Normally, when working on real-time QoE assessment platforms the original transmitted data is not available. This implies that Reduced Reference or Non Reference techniques must be used, and thus accuracy will be bounded, specially when Non Reference is used. On the contrary, Full Reference techniques guaranty more accurate results, but with the limitation of not being usable in real-time environments.

Another aspect regarding the accuracy is related on whether we have access to application dependent information. The critical issue in this case is *Where* to perform the assessment, e.g., in the end-user application, at IP layer in the end-user host, or in the egress router. Choosing the location *Where* to perform the analysis will determine *How* the data acquisition must be performed. As an example, QoS solutions classically use the egress router of the network to perform the traffic analysis. At this point, gathering application dependent data is challenging, specially regarding the computational demands of deep packet inspection, and the broad range of applications and configurations existing nowadays. When the acquisition is done locally at the end user's premises (e.g., in the set-top box in IPTV environments), more application dependent information is available, such as used codec, which greatly improve the computed QoE accuracy. Finally, if the gathering is performed by the end-user's application, we have access to user's important data, such as, user perceived delays and losses, and status of the de-jitter buffers, which help further increasing the accuracy of the user perceived QoE.

5.2 Results Analysis

Selecting the proper metrics, and performing an accurate metric computation is only the first step to a successful QoE assessment. The next step is to decide whether the user is satisfied or not. In general, it is broadly accepted that the lower threshold for a successful experience of a video transmission is a MOS value of 3. Nevertheless, as we have highlighted in Section 4, MOS is derived from other metrics, which in some cases do not consider all the necessary factors for a complete assessment. On top of that, depending on the type of the offered service some metrics—specially indirect metrics—have radically different constraints.

To illustrate this point let's consider three different types of service, namely, Real-Time Interactive (RTI), Video on Demand (VoD), and Live Streaming (LS). On-line gaming platforms and video-conferencing are examples of RTI applications, while generic video streaming applications belong to the VoD category, where the streamed content is not live, but stored in a particular location and then it is reproduced. Finally, streaming applications fall in the LS category, where live content, such as sport events, is streamed to the end user.

Table 1 details the effects of direct and indirect metrics on the different categories of applications identified above. It can be observed in the table that each metric affects each application category in different ways. We grouped the direct metrics together

Table 1. Metric effect on the different application categories

Metric	RTI	VoD	LS
Direct Metrics	High	Medium	High
Start-up	High	Medium	High
Response time	High	Medium	Low
Delivery Synchronization	High	Low	High
Freshness	High	Low	High
Blocking	High	High	High

because all assess the image quality, differing only on the methodology and accuracy but not on the effects depending on the service category.

In the table we can notice that RTI applications are very sensible to all the different metrics, both direct and indirect, since interactivity forces the use of small de-jitter buffers and, due to required small lags in the communication, using retransmissions is not feasible. Another important point to consider is the Delivery Synchronization, when several (more than two) users are sharing a video-conference. If the reception of the audio and video is not synchronized among the interlocutors, it will add unnecessary noise to the conversation, e.g., when one participant is responding to a statement, while some of the others are still listening to the previous sentence.

In the case of VoD applications, the constraints are more relaxed, specially for the indirect metrics. Since Delivery Synchronization and Freshness have little or no interest in this case, as the user selects the content to view individually and is not interested on its age or if anyone else is also receiving it. Regarding the start-up time, it determines the waiting time until the video starts at the destination. High values in this metric can be annoying, but users can cope with lags up to several seconds without much concern. The effects are similar for the Response Time, since in this case, when a user, e.g., wants to fast-forward a video, normally a small lag in the action is acceptable. As expected, the direct metrics have a relevant impact in VoD. But depending on the transmission protocol, the frame losses can be greatly avoided by retransmissions given the large de-jitter buffers used by these applications.

Finally regarding LS, this type of service has tighter constraints than VoD, but looser than RTI. In such environments, the content should arrive as fast as possible to its destination, because the user wants the contents in "real-time", and if the start-up takes too long, or the content is not "fresh" compared to other sources, the user can decide to switch to other means of broadcasting, e.g., digital TV, satellite, and thus the revenue of the provider will decrease. Another relevant metric in this type of service is the Delivery Synchronization. For instance, if someone is watching a sport event, and is receiving the contents delayed relatively to other sources, the user is most likely to switch to this other delivery system to have more up-to-date content. On the contrary, the Response Time has low relevance in this case, because, in general, in such live events the actions the user can perform are very limited (i.e., stop the playback).

It can be noted that regardless the application category, all metrics are affected equally by the *Blocking*, this is caused because, even with large buffers, a multimedia stream must be played smoothly on the end-user premises for a proper QoE.

6   Use-Case: IPTV

The use of IPTV services has been growing up in the recent years, and the user perceived quality is the most important feedback parameter for providers. Recent studies have shown that 84 percent of IPTV providers think video quality monitoring is critical or very important for the success of the business.

Unlike QoS assessment operations that are performed along the communication paths, QoE measurements in IPTV scenarios involve coding/decoding processes, analysis of the transmission links and user perspective, as presented in Fig. 1.

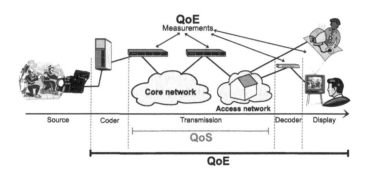

Fig. 1. Applications of Objectives Quality Assessment Model in IPTV

In fixed and mobile IPTV systems, most of the technical challenges are related with terminal capabilities, wireless/wired links, business, mobility issues and QoS and QoE control. In order to simplify the explanation of this use case, only QoS and QoE measurements will be explored. It is assumed the delivery of a MPEG-4 AVC/H.264 High Definition video over Digital Subscriber Link (DSL) IPTV access networks, commonly used in North American and other countries. The GOP length is 32 frames with IBBBP structure to allow a high quality, and the packets are transported over RTP/UDP/IP.

In the first example, Network-based Measurement is configured in the system to assess the quality level of the IPTV service. A centralized assessment mechanism (distributed schemes could also be used) is placed in the access network to predict the video quality level based on information about packet header, packet payload information and network conditions, without decoding the ongoing video content.

The mechanism verifies all packets being delivered associated with the IPTV service, by accessing the packet beyond layer 2 information and collecting data about the frame type, frame dependency, GOP, transport protocol, content characteristics, packet loss rate, packet delay rate and packet jitter. Together with utility function models [19] for IPTV applications, this mechanism maps network-content based information into user utility function and presents a final score about the quality level of the delivered application. For instance, if an *I* frame was lost and due to the application frame-dependency, it will result in 14 impaired frames and low quality video sequence will be received.

Unlike the previous approach, the Content Inspection/Artifact-based Measurement scheme studies the decoded video by using objective metrics. The assessment can be done in network edges, in the set-top box, or even in user's terminals. To provide real-time measurements, Non Reference metrics are used to define the IPTV quality level, such as blockiness, blur, flickering and noise. In this example, the blockiness is configured as an objective metric and each blocking artifact has at least one visible corner. After decoding the video, the mechanism measures the absolute difference of pixels luminance (intra-pairs and inter-pairs) and outputs a ratio between the sum of pixel intra- and inter-pairs difference as a quality score. Based on utility function and blockiness values, a final result is contained to inform the quality level of the IPTV service.

7   Conclusions

In this paper we overviewed the different challenges found in the design of QoE assessment platforms. The study focused on the case of video delivery over the network. As we observed, the first step to have a full-fledged QoE assessment mechanism is to decide which are the most suitable metrics for the quality assessment. To ease the selection the metrics were separated into two different categories, direct and indirect. Direct metrics have been the most studied, these type of metric require specific information about the delay variation and the packet/frame losses in order to assess the quality of the received image from the network point of view. As we pointed out, depending on the amount of available information, three different models can be used, namely, Full-Reference, Reduced- Reference and No-Reference, each one with different requirements and levels of accuracy.

The main challenges concerning data acquisition and results analysis were identified. Regarding data acquisition, we have discussed that three questions must be answered prior to the design of the assessment framework, namely, *Which*, *Where* and *How*. The answer to these questions will determine the different capabilities that will be deployed in the assessment system.

Finally, and as a use case we discussed about a broadly used service, i.e., IPTV, where we detailed the different steps and requirements that must be met in order to deploy a sound QoE assessment platform for such a service.

References

1. Crovella, M., Krishnamurthy, B.: Internet Measurement. Infrastructure, Traffic, and Applications. John Wiley & Sons, Ltd., Chichester (2006)
2. Serral-Gracià, R., Barlet-Ros, P., Domingo-Pascual, J.: Coping with Distributed Monitoring of QoS-enabled Heterogeneous Networks. In: 4th International Telecommunication Networking Workshop on QoS in Multiservice IP Networks, Venice, Italy, February 2008, pp. 142–147 (2008)
3. Serral-Gracià, R., Labit, Y., Domingo-Pascual, J., Owezarski, P.: Towards End-to-End SLA Assessment. In: INFOCOM 2009. The 28th Conference on Computer Communications, pp. 2581–2585. IEEE, Los Alamitos (2009)

4. Sommers, J., Barford, P., Duffeld, N.G., Ron, A.: Accurate and Efficient SLA Compliance Monitoring. In: Proceedings of ACM SIGCOMM, Kyoto, Japan, August 2007, pp. 109–120 (2007)
5. Jian-ren, Y., Rui-min, H., Jun, C., Jian-bo, Z.: A Service-Oriented Framework of Distributed QoS Measurement Based on Multi-Agent for Overlay Network, pp. 158–162 (February 2009)
6. Almes, G., Kalidindi, S., Zekauskas, M.: A One-way Delay Metric for IPPM. RFC 2679 (September 1999)
7. Almes, G., Kalidindi, S., Zekauskas, M.: A One-way Packet Loss Metric for IPPM. RFC 2680 (September 1999)
8. Demichelis, C., Chimento, P.: IP Packet Delay Variation Metric for IP Performance Metrics (IPPM). RFC 3393 (November 2002)
9. Piamrat, K., Viho, C., Bonnin, J.M., Ksentini, A.: Quality of Experience Measurements for Video Streaming over Wireless Networks, pp. 1184–1189 (April 2009)
10. Wang, B., Wen, X., Yong, S., Wei, Z.: A New Approach Measuring Users' QoE in the IPTV, pp. 453–456 (May 2009)
11. Romaniak, P.: Towards Realization of a Framework for Integrated Video Quality of Experience Assessment, pp. 1–2 (April 2009)
12. Lin, T.L., Kanumuri, S., Zhi, Y., Poole, D., Cosman, P.C., Reibman, A.R.: A Versatile Model for Packet Loss Visibility and its Application to Packet Prioritization. IEEE Transactions on Image Processing 19(3), 722–735 (2010)
13. He, Y., Huang, T.: Objective quality definition of scalable video coding and its application for optimal streaming of FGS-coded videos. Computer Communications 32(1), 34–40 (2009)
14. Janowski, L., Papir, Z.: Modeling subjective tests of quality of experience with a Generalized Linear Model, pp. 35–40 (July 2009)
15. Romaniak, P., Mu, M., Mauthe, A., D'Antonio, S., Leszczuk, M.: Framework for the Integrated Video Quality Assessment. In: 18th ITC Specialist Seminar on Quality of Experience, Blekinge Institute of Technology, Karlskrona, Sweden (May 2008)
16. Cerqueira, E., Janowski, L., Leszczuk, M., Papir, Z., Romaniak, P.: Video Artifacts Assessment for Live Mobile Streaming Applications. In: Mauthe, A., Zeadally, S., Cerqueira, E., Curado, M. (eds.) FMN 2009. LNCS, vol. 5630, pp. 242–247. Springer, Heidelberg (2009)
17. Klaue, J., Rathke, B., Wolisz, A.: EvalVid - A Framework for Video Transmission and Quality Evaluation. In: Proceedings of the 13th International Conference on Modelling Techniques and Tools for Computer Performance Evaluation, pp. 255–272 (2003)
18. Cognet, Y.: Measuring IPTV QoS performance at the box (2006), http://www.videsignline.com/
19. Mu, M., Mauthe, A., Garcia, F.: A Utility-Based QoS Model for Emerging Multimedia Applications. In: The Second International Conference on Next Generation Mobile Applications, Services and Technologies NGMAST, Cardiff, UK, pp. 521–528. IEEE Computer Society, Los Alamitos (2008)

QoE Model Driven for Network Services

Hai Anh Tran and Abdelhamid Mellouk

Network and Telecom Dept & LiSSi Laboratory
University of Paris-Est Creteil (UPEC)
122 rue Paul Armangot 94400, Vitry sur Seine, France
{hai-anh.tran,mellouk}@u-pec.fr

Abstract. Actually, wealthy network services such as Internet protocol television (IPTV) and Voice over IP (VoIP) are expected to become more pervasive over the Next Generation Network (NGN). In order to serve this purpose, the quality of these services should be evaluated subjectively by users. This is referred to as the quality of experience (QoE). However, there are many issues that may impact user's perception in many different ways. This paper surveys the QoE models and systems for existing and future network services.

Keywords: Quality of Service (QoS), Quality of Experience (QoE), network services, user satisfaction, service billing.

1 Introduction

The theory of quality of experience (QoE) has become commonly used to represent user perception. For evaluating network service, one has to measure, monitor, quantify and analyze the QoE in order to characterize, evaluate and manage services offered over this network. In fact, the network provider's aim is to provide a good user experience at minimal network resource usage. It is important from the network operator to be aware of the degree of influence of each network's factor on the user perception.

For users, also for operators and Internet service providers, the end-to-end quality is one of the major factors to be achieved. Actually the new term of QoE has been introduced to make end-to-end QoS more clearly captures the experience of the users. Even if it is linked to the concept of QoS, which attempts to objectively measure the service delivered, QoE also takes in account the needs and the desires of the subscribers when using network services. For example an operator may provide reliable data services, and have a high QoS, but the users may still be dissatisfied with the content causing a low QoE. In this field, several new developments have occurred. QoS now includes a wide range of services, involving wider bandwidth for audio and speech, new multimedia services such as IPTV.

In the recent years, there are many researches, proposals that are made in order to measure, evaluate, and improve QoE in networks. Definition of new performance parameters and values, new assessment methodologies and new quality prediction models are needed. This survey aimed to make a synthesis of these researches in grouping them into different classes.

E. Osipov et al. (Eds.): WWIC 2010, LNCS 6074, pp. 264–277, 2010.
© Springer-Verlag Berlin Heidelberg 2010

The survey is structured as follows. In section 2, we explain the importance of QoE in network services. We talk about QoE metrics in section 3. In section 4, we show briefly some QoE models in current network services. In section 5, we present the major aspects which impact QoE performances. In the last section, we focused on end-to-end QoE, especially on our preliminary work based on QoE routing policies. In section 6, we make some concluding remarks and highlight some future areas of work.

2 QoS/QoE Relationship

Regarding terminal users, operators and Internet service providers, QoE has been introduced to make end-to-end QoS based on the experience of the users. Even if it is linked to the concept of QoS, which attempts to objectively measure the service delivered, QoE also takes in account the needs and the desires of the subscribers when using network services. QoS is merely about metrics: packet delay, loss and jitter. Certainly delay and loss are critical because of a recent increased boom in the use of conferencing applications: videoconferencing, internal/external webinars/webcasts, etc. But QoS is just the first step. QoE is more about what happens in the customer's psyche. Good metrics mean nothing if a subscriber to a service is having a problem that is getting him or her angry enough to switch service providers, thus adding to "churn". So one uses QoE assess to prevent churn problem. Network providers that provide good QoE has a significant competitive advantage, while providers that ignore the importance of QoE may suffer unnecessary costs, lost revenue and diminished market perception. A statistics of Soldani and al. [1] firms that around 82% of customer defections (churning) are due to frustration over the product or service and the inability of the provider/operator to deal with this effectively. More seriously, this is a chain reaction, for example 1 frustrated customer will tell 13 other people about their bad experience. An operator cannot afford to wait for customer complaints to assess the level of its service quality. Statistics have shown that for every person who calls with a problem, there are another 29 who will never call. About 90% of customers will not complain before defecting – they will simply leave (churn) once they become unsatisfied. This churn directly affects the profitability and image of the operator, especially if it happens in the early stage of their induction. So, the only way to overcome in this situation is to devise a strategy to manage and improve QoE.

Although QoE is very subjective in nature, it is very important that a strategy is devised to measure it as realistically as possible. The ability to measure QoE will give the operator some sense of the contribution of the network's performance to the overall level of customer satisfaction in terms of reliability, availability, scalability, speed, accuracy and efficiency.

For example, in VoIP services (key services in Next Generation Networks), in order to attract customers, the quality of delivery for VoIP needs to be measured and optimized to ensure QoS and QoE support to users in future multimedia networking systems. Due to the limitations of traditional QoS solutions regarding voice-awareness and human perception, QoE assessment approaches have been introduced to estimate the quality level of VoIP services from the user point of view. The result of an assessment solution can be used for both clients (to know the real quality of the subscribed services) and providers (future network management and optimization procedures such as resource reservation, mobility prediction and QoE routing, as well as for pricing schemes).

3 QoE Metrics

One has to measure QoE even it is subjective in nature. Therefore a strategy has to be created to measure QoE as realistically as possible. In fact, a top-down approach can be used for QoE measurement: firstly one has to know the factors contributing to user perception. Secondly one applies that knowledge to construct operating requirements. Finally one has to devise a methodology to measure these factors constantly and improve them as when needed.

When identifying QoE metrics, there will be as many different expectations as there are users, but most of these expectations can be grouped under two main categories: *reliability* and *quality* [1]. In network service, the *reliability* dimension has some Key Performance Indicators (KPI) as follow:

- Service availability (anywhere)
- Service accessibility (anytime)
- Service access time (service setup time)
- Continuity of service connection (service retainability)

With regard to *quality*, it refers to the quality of the service and application software features, KPIs are:

- Quality of session
- Bit rate
- Bit rate variation
- Active session throughput
- System responsiveness
- End-to-end delay
- Delay variation

The KPIs are measured for each service (or a mix of service). Using these values of KPIs, we calculate an estimate of the score of each service. These scores are compared to "QoE targets" set in advance for each KPI.

The value of each of these metrics would translate to different level of impact on the actual QoE. Some will be totally irrelevant in one case while being the most important in another. It all depends on the type of service application being run by the user. For example, voice and videoconferencing calls are the two most popular service applications, they needs certain characteristics: they preserve the time relation (variation) between information entities of the stream to minimize delay variation. They are relatively insensitive to packet loss. Guaranteed resource allocation without retransmissions and real time traffic are important characteristics too. In applications like Web and WAP browsing, remote server access (Telnet) and interactive gaming, we have to consider the characteristics such as: Request–response pattern of use, Preserve payload content, transmission delay, dynamic resource allocation, best-effort traffic.

The second way to classify QoE metrics and evaluation procedures can be divided into quantitative (objective) and qualitative (subjective) sets. Subjective methods are conducted to obtain information on the quality of multimedia services based on systems of human opinion score, while objective methods are used to estimate the performance of multimedia systems using models that approximate results of subjective quality evaluation. In other words, the QoE metrics can be classified according to their objectivity and range of quantitative to qualitative. In addition, objective measures of QoE can be classified based on the amount of reference information available during the assessment process of quality of service multimedia, such as Full Reference (FR), Reduced Reference (RR) and No Reference (NR). For example in comparison of video signals, we can find:

- *Full Reference*: the degraded signal is compared pixel by pixel with the original signal. It is a very detailed comparison, which requires considerable computing resources.
- *No Reference*: a video analysis (stream) on receipt without comparing the original signal. These methods are very small, making them very suitable for analysis in real time. However, KPIs output is low, especially compared to methods "Full Reference".
- *Reduced Reference*: is a compromise between the two previous types.

Subjective parameters assess how audio and video data are collected by users, namely, what is their opinion about the quality of sequences of audio / video. A very popular example of a qualitative metrics (subjective), called a Mean Opinion Score (MOS), was standardized first by the International Telecommunication Union (ITU). With this metric, the system quality is assessed subjectively by users in a five-point scale, where "five" is the best and "one" is the worst. Concretely, these five-point scales are: *Poor, Fair Good, Very Good* and *Excellent*. The MOS is used especially in subjective tests of audio listening, where a number of people express the quality of the audio. This type of testing is time consuming, tedious, costs money and is not particularly applicable in a production environment. Therefore, it is impossible to use the results (MOS measures) to adjust the parameters of the network or service to maintain the MOS (QoE). Therefore we need objective methods that estimate the MOS score and that can run in real time so that scores is returned to the network and service providers to maintain the best QoE in real-time.

Another example of a qualitative metric is *R-factor*, which can be used in a manner similar to MOS. *R-factor* is used for subjective evaluation of speech quality in voice transmission systems.

4   QoE Models

Recently, several QoE models have been proposed in literature. In [14], Y. Gong and al. proposed a pentagram model for measuring QoE. This model consists of five factors: integrality, retainability, availability, usability, and instantaneousness. The authors defined a model of experience taking into account these factors in quality evaluations. They have applied this model to measure experience of a VoIP service.

Firstly authors showed QoE Key performance indicators and the most important measures:

- *Service integrality* (delay, jitter, and packet loss ratio) (*parameter a in (1)*)
- *Service retainability* (Service interruption ratio) (*parameter b in (1)*)
- *Service availability* (The success ratio of user access service) (*parameter c in (1)*)
- *Service usability* (Service usability) (*parameter d in (1)*)
- *Service instantaneousness* (The response time(s) of establish and access service) (*parameter e in (1)*)

Since each factor is determined, QoE can be computed:

$$QoE = \frac{1}{2}\sin(\lambda)(ab + bc + cd + de + ea) \tag{1}$$

Where: λ represents the 72-degree angle between the two sides in the QoE pentagram model.

This model facilitated QoE measurement during a service use process. The purpose of authors is to improve and represent new ways to evaluating and measuring perception of VoIP services.

H. Kim and al. [15] proposed an another approach for the objective QoE measurement through the QoS parameter. In this paper, the QoS and QoE correlation model is described and the QoE evaluation method using QoS parameter in the converged network environment is studied. Authors outlined some QoE evaluation method such as: opinion rating (MOS) based on customer's satisfaction, PSQM (Perceptual Speech Quality Measure), PESQ (Perceptual Evaluation of Speech Quality) and E-Model. They described the QoS-QoE correlation model with a QoE measurement scheme using the QoS parameters (such as delay, delay variation, and information loss):

$$QoS = F(D, J, L, E, B, S) \tag{2}$$

$$QoE(QoS) = K\left\{\frac{\left(e^{QoS-\alpha} + e^{-QoS+\alpha}\right)}{\left(e^{QoS-\alpha} + e^{-QoS+\alpha} + \beta\right)} + 1\right\} \tag{3}$$

Where: α is the QoS quality class of the network level, β is determined according the class of service and K is the coefficient regarding the satisfaction about the use service.

The QoE class measured by the QoS quality parameter of a network-level is mapped like MOS. So, by using the quality of service information measured in a network level, authors explain the proposed QoS-QoE correlation model for the objective QoE.

In [16], S. Moebs balances the constraints imposed by QoS restrictions with the requirements of flow and learning in order to produce the highest possible QoE for the learner using an adaptive multimedia system. Authors presented an adaptive multimedia e-learning systems based on a basic architecture that consists of a user model, a domain model and an adaptation model. The domain model represents the concept of the subject domain and it usually describes these concept structures as concept maps, semantic networks or concept graphs. The user model represents general characteristics of the user such as location, preferences for devices, previous knowledge, knowledge state or learning goals. The adaptation model connects the two previously outlined models, using adaptation rules. This relationship is represented by the function from equation:

$$QoE = f(QoL(QoS), QoF(QoS)) \tag{4}$$

QoS is based on packet loss, delay and jitter in background application like video, audio and data. QoL is based on the user model aspects feedback, a clear set of learning goals, interaction, the balance of skill and challenges in learning, learning styles, assessment of the previous knowledge and the domain model. QoF is based on feedback, a clear set of goals for using the website, interaction, the balance of skill and challenges, which include use of technology and emotions.

A. Hamam and al. [17] proposed a taxonomy for measuring the QoE of a haptic user interface applications. This taxonomy is modeled using a mathematical model where QoE is computed as the weighted linear combination of the QoS and User Experience for a particular haptic user interface:

$$QoE = \zeta \times QoS + (1 - \zeta) \times UE \tag{5}$$

If the quality factors are restricted between 0 and 1, then the overall quality of experience will also have a value between 0 and 1. To achieve this condition, the sum of constant coefficients must be equal to 1.

The proposed model is evaluated using two HUI-based applications: the haptic learning system and the haptic enabled UML CASE tool.

5   Strategies for QoE Systems

This section will present which aspects should be considered in order to build a global system based on QoS/QoE measurement.

5.1   QoE Measuring, Monitoring and Performance Improvement Strategies for Network Services

It has become very meaningful for an operator to measure the QoE of its network and customers accurately with the development of mobile services. The measurements can be used in order to analyze problematic cases and improve the performance of the network. The competence to measure QoE will help the operator to collect the contribution of network performance to the overall level of customer satisfaction.

5.1.1   QoE Monitoring System in UMTS Cellular Systems

The architecture proposed in [1] consists of three layers: Network elements, Element management layer and Network management layer. In the first layer, *Network elements*, the network element is used to collect performance measures, usage data and generate alarms. The second layer, *Element management layer,* is responsible for aggregating and transferring collected QoE and QoS performance measurements and generated alarms/events. This layer consists of two functions: *performance management* and *fault management*. The third layer, *Network management layer (NML)*, is responsible for the collection and processing of performance, fault and usage data. This layer provides the following functions: a) Service quality management (SQM): this is responsible for the overall quality of a service as it interacts with other functional areas to access monitored information; b) Customer QoS management (CQM): this includes monitoring, managing and reporting the QoS customers. Authors have constructed a QoE monitoring framework with two practical approaches to measuring QoE in mobile networks: *Service level approach using statistical samples* and *Network management system approach using QoS parameters*. With the *service level approach using statistical samples*, the main idea of this approach is statistical sampling and taking the most accurate measurements according to that sample. In this approach, most measured performance indicators are at application level, providing the real end-user perspective. Furthermore, in the *network management system approach using QoS parameters*, hard QoS performance metrics from various parts of the network are mapped onto user-perceptible QoE performance targets.

5.1.2 QoS/QoE Measurement System Cellular Phone for Next Generation Network (NGN)

Guaranteed quality end-to-end must be supplied by services provided in NGN. As the fluctuation of network conditions is large in Fixed Mobile Convergence (FMC), a novel approach where a network node and a mobile terminal such as a cellular phone cooperate with each other to control the service quality is essential. S. Uemura and al. [9] present a QoS/QoE measurement system implemented on a cellular phone.

The cooperation between mobile terminal such as a cellular phone and the network node is needed (Fig. 1), in order to maintain end-to-end service quality.

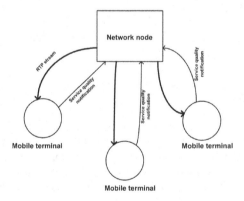

Fig. 1. Cooperation between the network node and the mobile terminal

The mobile terminal measures the service quality and sends the result to the network node. On the other hand, the network node plays implements resource or admission control based on this service quality.

This system consists of SIP, RTP and QoS/QoE measurement components. In this system, one establishes a VoIP session based on Session Initiation Protocol (SIP) and Session Description Protocol (SDP).

After the establishment of the VoIP session, the voice captured by the microphone is digitized and packetized. Then the digitized voice packets are sent by using Real-Time Transport Protocol (RTP). RTP Control Protocol (RTCP) is implemented in this system. RTCP is an accompanying protocol to feedback the network conditions from the RTP receiver to the RTP sender. From the feedback report sent by the RTP receiver, the RTP sender can know the network conditions such as the packet loss ratio, jitter, and delay. A QoS/QoE measurement component computes the QoS metrics and the QoE metrics by using RTCP and RTCP XR feedback reports. In the same way, the R factor [10], MOS-LQ (MOS Listening Quality) and MOS-CQ (MOS Conversational Quality) are also calculated. The R factor can be calculated by using about 20 QoS metrics such as packet loss rate and delay, and is expressed as a scalar in the range of 0 to 100. MOS-LQ and MOS-CQ are expressed as a scalar in the range of 1 to 5.

Authors proposed an estimation method that can calculate MOS-LQ simply using a set of QoS metrics. The metrics that are likely to affect the speech quality are calculated. Based on these metrics and the partial regression coefficients, the estimated MOS-LQ can be obtained as follows:

$$\text{MOS-LQ} = \alpha_1*\text{loss\_rate} + \alpha_2*\text{burst\_duration} + \alpha_3*\text{gap\_duration} + \\ \alpha_4*\text{burst\_density} + \alpha_5*\text{gap\_density} + \alpha_6*\text{R\_factor} + \alpha_7 \tag{6}$$

where α_i (i=1..7) is a partial regression coefficient for each metric.

5.2 Modeling of User Satisfaction

A number of investigations in network quality improvement have approached the definition of user satisfaction. The focus is primarily on the attributes of the system with attention paid to the attributes of the user or of the context in which network usage occurs.

For this, K. Engelbrecht and al. [2] present a new approach to predicting judgments model, using Hidden Markov Models (HMMs). The user's opinion is considered as a continuous process evolving over time. An HMM reproduces a sequence of events as a sequence of states, in which each state emits certain symbols with some probability. In fact, the transitions between states are probabilistic. The model consists of a set of state symbols, a set of emission symbols, the probabilities for the initial state, the state transition matrix, and the emission matrix. The transition matrix contains the probabilities for transitions from each state to each other state or itself. The emission matrix contains the probabilities for each emission symbol to occur at each state. While the sequence of emissions can be observed, the state sequence is hidden. However, given an emission sequence, standard algorithms defined for the HMM allow to calculate the probability of each state at each point in the sequence. The probability for the model to be in a state is dependent on the previous state and the emissions observed at the current state. Authors gave a model where the user judgment can either be "bad" or "good". Each judgment has a probabilistic relation to the current events in the dialog.

5.3   User Mobility in QoE

In next generation wireless networks, the all-IP paradigm is a promising solution that contributes benefits by providing IP-based transport through the radio and core network parts. In fact, this concept requires a precise management of user's mobility.

F. Bernardo and al. [5] propose mechanisms in order to evaluate the QoE that users perceive when the different QoS-aware mobility management strategies are applied. In their work, the authors utilize a testbed that enables the possibility of measuring the QoE of the user that would use those applications in a real heterogeneous wireless access network

The testbed reproduces a Beyond 3G heterogeneous radio access network that includes three Radio Access Networks (RANs): UTRAN, GERAN, and WLAN interfacing a common Core Network (CN), which is based is based on DiffServ/MPLS.

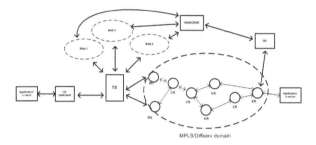

Fig. 2. Testbed functional architecture

A Traffic Switch (TS) establishes different interconnection configurations between the User Equipment (UE) and the Ingress Routers (IRs) in the CN depending on the RAN the User Under Test (UUT) is currently connected to. The e2e QoS management architecture is composed of the QoSClient, the Bandwidth Broker (BB), and the Wireless QoS Broker (WQB). Mobility Management (MM) is supported in the testbed by 3 entities, namely the Mobile Node (MN), the Access Router (AR) installed in each IR and the Anchor Point (ANP) located in Egress Router (ER). The MN resides in the UE machine and is the entity that triggers the MPLS tunnel switching.

In the testbed, there are different handover types that are executed as the UUT moves along the scenario. The first type is *Horizontal Handover (HHO)*, in this mechanism; handover is realized between base stations of the same RAN, called intra-RAN handover. The second type is *Intra-IR Vertical Handover (VHO)* where the handover is performed between base stations of different RANs attached to the same ingress router of the CN. All packets sent to the old RAN during the execution of the VHO are eliminated by default once the VHO is executed, but one can forward those packets to the new RAN during the VHO. *Inter-IR Vertical Handover* is the third handover type. In this type, MM plays a crucial role with an IR change. On the core network side, the data information of the UUT is encapsulated into MPLS tunnels from the ER to one of the IRs for downlink and for uplink. Further, on the radio domain, the TS filters the UUT's data packets in the UE interface (uplink) or IR interfaces (downlink) to pass them to the appropriate RAN.

In order to avoid packet loss and a significant QoS degradation for the final user, an advanced MM procedure called *handover preparation* is also implemented in the testbed. This procedure establishes prior to a VHO an Inter-IR tunnel (between IRs) to minimize packet loss during the VHO execution. After different handover types tested, the QoE of the UUT is depicted in different MOS values of different handover types considered in this paper. The authors use a fullreference model-based objective metric for the QoS evaluation. A satisfaction level measurement is given by the QoS evaluation method. This metric expresses the subjective score that human given to the experiment.

5.4 Network Resource Utilization and Management in QoE

Well managing the use of network resource is a good way to handle and maintain the system quality, so it is also a significant impact on end user perception. Indeed, there were many systems that take into account this feature.

An example for this is a network resource management system [6] for *Resource and Admission Control Functions (RACF)* that can be operated based on the end-user QoE. The Policy Enforcement Functional Entity (PE-FE) in the network node provides a function of the rate limiting and bandwidth allocation according to an instruction of RACF. A concept of Network Resource Management system (NetRM) is constructed to provide service-oriented network services via Web services interface (WSI). NetRM decides to allocate and control the appropriate end-to-end network resources to meet the service requirements (the end-user QoE and the QoS metrics). It includes also resource control functions related to Policy Decision Functional Entity (PD-FE) and Transport Resource Control Functional Entity (TRC-FE) in RACF. The network resource management architecture is depicted in Fig. 3. NetRM provides guaranteed and scheduled network services to network service clients. Using a Web application server (Web AS), Web service module of NetRM handles service messaging. A mediation module assigns appropriate resources using optimized-path discovery and scheduling functions. The information about reservations and network resources is dynamically managed by a transaction and a resource database.

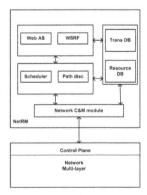

Fig. 3. Network resource management architecture

For the maintenance of the QoE, the network resource management function should be supported in each access network and it should be utilized when the communication service is going to be set up to allocate required bandwidth or offer a certain service class.

5.5 Billing and Pricing in QoE

We consider here QoE requirements regarding Service Billing for IPTV Service. In fact, QoE is used also as a measure of how well an IPTV service satisfies the customers' expectation. Service billing has a strong relation with the customers' expectation for a service quality. In [13], authors give an example where a service has a long channel zapping delay. An IPTV customer who subscribes basic class accepts this channel zapping time. On the other side, for the premium IPTV customer who pays more expensive service charge may be dissatisfied. Even if the channel zapping times that two customers experienced are numerically the same, the satisfaction levels of two customers may quite different. Since customers tend to expect a better service quality as the service charge increases, the customers' evaluation for the service strongly depends on its service billing.

As an example of QoE metric with service billing, authors propose *End-users' Utility*, which is a relative satisfaction level for a service quality. An another metric is *Service Quality Metric* (T_s) for IPTV, e.g., Channel zapping delay, Control command response time, STB startup time, Picture quality, etc. The third metric is *Service Billing* (B_s) that is the service charge for a service S. Finally U_s can be defined as: $U_s = \mathrm{f}\,(T_s, B_s)$. In this formula, f is a weight function that transforms the absolute service quality metric, T_s, with service billing as a relative end-users' utility value U_s. Therefore, even if two customers have identical service quality metrics, i.e., two customers' channel zapping delays are the same, their satisfaction levels (U_s) can be different. It is because each customer may pay a different service charge. The weight function depends on the types of services, the types of customers and the policies of service billing.

5.6 Optimization for End-to-End QoE

Actually, multimedia services are being accessed via fixed and mobile networks. These services are typically much more sensitive to packet loss, delay and congestion than traditional services. In particular, multimedia data is often time critical and, as a result, network issues are not well tolerated and significantly deteriorate the user's Quality of Experience (QoE). Therefore, measurement and optimization of QoE are more and more necessary. In this section, we present a proposition concerning this purpose and our idea of integration of QoE measurement in an adaptive and evolutionary system.

5.6.1 Adaptive Mechanism for Video Distribution Network

In order to increase video quality as perceived by end users, multipath video streaming in Video Distribution Network (VDN) is properly a solution. M. Ghareeb and al. [8] propose an adaptive mechanism for maximize the video quality at the client. In this model, the QoE is measured using Pseudo-Subjective Quality Assessment (PSQA) tool.

After receiving a client demand, the video server chooses an initial strategy and an initial scheme to start the video streaming. Then, client uses PSQA to evaluate the QoE of the received video in real time and send this feedback to server. After examining this feedback, the video server will decide to keep or to change its strategy. With this adaptative mechanism, all is done dynamically and in real time.

MPEG represents the video in consecutive GOPs (group of pictures), each contains three types of frames: an intra-frame (I-frames), forward predicted frames (P-frames), and bi-directional predicted frames (B-frames). Among them, the type I-frame is the most important. In [8], authors developed a solution based on frame type to split the video into separated sub-flows. One uses two different strategies: (a) (I‖P‖B strategy) that splits the video into three separated subflows, and then it sends I,P,B frames successively over the three best paths(the I frame is send in the best path); (b) (IP‖B strategy) that puts I and P frames in the same sub-flow and B-frames in second one. Here, the sub-flow with IP-frames is the one that will be sent over the best path, and B-frames will be sent over the second best path.

The VDN node calculates the best paths based on the available bandwidth of the overlay links from the node to its neighbors. The main objective of this method is to keep a high quality of the perceived video at the end-user. The algorithm is described as follows (Fig. 4):

- First, the client requests a video stream with certain level of quality.
- The server chooses the MOS threshold according to this level. It starts streaming the requested video using an initial strategy.
- Then, client uses PSQA tool to evaluate the QoE of the streams and periodically sends back the MOS evaluations to the server.
- At the server side, if this MOS value equals or exceeds the specified threshold, the server will continue to use the same initial strategy and scheme. If MOS value is less than the threshold, the algorithm recalculates the available bandwidth of all the paths from the server to the client.

Fig. 4. Video streaming process over VDN

One of two cases will take place: (a) best path has changed, so the algorithm dynamically reacts to change the scheme with keeping the same old strategy; (b) best path does not change, video server directly changes the streaming strategy, keeping the same old path-scheme.

5.6.2 Adaptive AS Routing Based on QoE

Another idea to take into account end-to-end QoE consist to develop adaptive mechanisms that can retrieve the information from their environment (Quality of Experience: QoE) and adapt to initiate actions. These actions should be executed in response

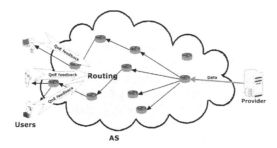

Fig. 5. QoE Routing System

to unforeseen or unwanted events as an unsatisfactory QoS, a negative feedback or malfunctioning network elements.

Concretely, the system integrate the QoE measurement in an evolutionary routing system (intra-AS or inter-AS) in order to improve the user perception based on the choose of the "best optimal QoE paths". So in that way, the routing process is build according to the improvement of QoE parameters. The system is based on adaptive algorithms that simultaneously process an observation and learn to perform better. Such adaptive algorithms are very useful in tracking a phenomenon that evolves over time. To realize this purpose, QoE evaluation of the end user must be made in current conditions:

- The QoE evaluation must be realized in real time,
- The network is "alive" (whose behavior varies based on multiple criteria),
- This evaluation must be Realistic (representative of the overall end-to-end service).

6   Conclusion

Nowadays the new network services, such as VoIP, video on demand, IPTV, become increasingly numerous. Thus improving the quality of the offered services as perceived by the users, referred to as the quality of experience (QoE), becomes very important to network service providers. In this survey, we have tried to show many issues that may impact user's perception in many different ways, such as the method of measuring QoE, modeling of user satisfaction, as well as the impact of user mobility and network resource utilization.

Extensions to the framework for using these techniques across hybrid networks to achieve end-to-end QoE needs to be investigated particularly for large-scale networks. Our work in progress is to define a global routing system based on QoE terminal feedbacks using adaptive and evolutionary approaches.

References

[1] Soldani, D., Li, M., Cuny, R.: QoS and QoE Management in UMTS Cellular Systems. Wiley, New York (2006)
[2] Engelbrecht, K.-P., Gödde, F., Hartard, F., Ketabdar, H., Möller, S.: Modeling User Satisfaction with Hidden Markov Models. In: Proc. of Sigdial (2009)

[3] Sugianto, L.-F., Tojib, D.R.: Modeling User Satisfaction With an Employee Portal. International Journal of Business and Information (2006)

[4] Latréa, S., Simoens, P., De Vleeschauwer, B., Van de Meerssche, W., De Turck, F., Dhoedt, B., Demeester, P., Van den Bergheb, S., de Lumley, E.G.: An autonomic architecture for optimizing QoE in multimedia access networks. In: Computer Networks, Elsevier, Amsterdam (2009)

[5] Bernardo, F., Vučević, N., Umbert, A., López-Benítez, M.: Quality of Experience Evaluation under QoS-aware Mobility Mechanisms. In: European Wireless Conference (2008)

[6] Yamada, H., Fukumoto, N., Isomura, M., Uemura, S., Hayashi, M.: A QoE based service control scheme for RACF in IP-based FMC networks. In: E- Commerce Technology and the 4th IEEE International Conference on Enterprise Computing (2007)

[7] EMPIRIX test group, Assuring QoE on Next Generation Networks, White Paper by Empririx (2009)

[8] Majd, G., Cesar, V., Adlen, K.: An Adaptive Mechanism For Multipath Video Streaming Over Video Distribution Network (VDN). In: First International Conference on Advances in Multimedia (2009)

[9] Uemura, S., Fukumoto, N., Yamada, H., Nakamura, H.: QoS/QoE measurement system implemented on cellular phone for NGN. In: IEEE Consumer Communication and Networking Conference (2008)

[10] ITU-T Recommendation G.107, The E-model, a computational model for use in transmission planning in International Telecommunication Union (May 2003)

[11] Ciubotaru, B., Muntean, G.–M.: SASHA - A Quality-Oriented Handover Algorithm for Multimedia Content Delivery to Mobile Users. IEEE Transactions on Broadcasting, Special Issue on IPTV in Multimedia Broadcasting (2009)

[12] Agboma, F., Liotta, A.: QoE-aware QoS Management. In: The 6th International Conference on Advances in Mobile Computing and Multimedia (2008)

[13] ITU-T Recommendation, QoE requirements in consideration of Service Billing for IPTV Service, UIT-T FG IPTV (2006)

[14] Goong, Y., Yang, F., Huang, L., Su, S.: Model-Based Approach to Measuring Quality of Experience. In: First International Conference on Emerging Network Intelligence (2009)

[15] Kim, H.J., Lee, D.H., Lee, J.M., Lee, K.H., Lyu, W., Choi, S.G.: The QoE Evaluation Method through the QoS-QoE Correlation Model. In: Fourth International Conference on Networked Computing and Advanced Information Management (2008)

[16] Moebs, S.: A Learner, is a Learner, is a User, is a Customer - QoS-based Experience-aware Adaptation. In: 16th ACM International Conference on Multimedia (2008)

[17] Hamam, A., Eid, M., Saddik, A.E., Georganas, N.D.: A quality of experience model for haptic user interfaces. In: Ambi-Sys Workshop on haptic user interfaces in ambient media systems (2008)

Multivariate Fairly Normal Traffic Model for Aggregate Load in Large-Scale Data Networks

F. Mata, J.L. García-Dorado, and J. Aracil

High Performance Computing and Networking Group, UAM, Spain
{felipe.mata,jl.garcia,javier.aracil}@uam.es
http://www.hpcn.es

Abstract. Traffic models are crucial for network planning, design, performance evaluation and optimization. However, it is first necessary to assess the validity of the newly proposed models. In this paper we present the validation of a multivariate fairly normal model for aggregate traffic that exploits the well-known day-night traffic pattern, which was first assumed and applied in a former work to detect changes in the Internet links' load on-line. The validation process entails several normality analytical and graphical tests which are applied to real network traffic measurements, on attempts to assess fairly normality both in the marginal and joint distributions of the multivariate model. The results of the normality tests provide evidence that our design is adequate to model aggregate traffic accurately capturing the day-night traffic pattern.

1 Introduction

Network traffic models are broadly used in conjunction with network measurements (Section 2). Such models allow to evaluate the performance of telecommunication networks, perform capacity planning and establish congestion control policies, among other tasks. However, in order to obtain accurate results the models require goodness-of-fit to real network measurements, small number of parameters, computationally feasible parameter estimators and analytical tractability. Therefore, such properties must be validated when designing a new network traffic model. Among these properties, the most challenging to validate is the goodness-of-fit of the proposed model to real network measurements. We perform such validation in this work, where the goodness-of-fit of a multivariate fairly Gaussian model first introduced in [13] is assessed. Once the goodness-of-fit is validated, proving that the model is tractable and its parameters are computationally feasible to estimate is straightforward, given the vast literature available for multivariate Gaussian models (e.g. [24]).

The day-night pattern of traffic is a well-known phenomenon in the Internet [23]. Such pattern (with minor differences) was also observed in our datasets (described in Section 3). Therefore, we performed an in-depth analysis of the day-night pattern exhibited in our measurements in Section 4. The invariance of the pattern motivated us to use a multivariate model (Section 5) in order to properly capture its peaks and off-peaks, and the assumption of normality was

E. Osipov et al. (Eds.): WWIC 2010, LNCS 6074, pp. 278–289, 2010.

based on former studies [8,15]. We preprocessed our dataset according to the proposed model and applied statistically sound normality tests (Section 6) in order to assess the model's validity. The results of such validation are presented in Section 7. Finally, a discussion of the results is presented in Section 8, which concludes the paper.

2   Related Work

The traffic modeling literature offers a great variety of works that have presented network traffic models, which can be classified depending on the modeling target. In this light, there are studies that either model and parametrize specific applications and services (such as P2P [4] or VoIP [3]) or instead focus on a particular network protocol (for instance TCP [18,1,20]). Such characterizations differ from ours because we do not focus on an specific kind of traffic, but instead model the aggregate traffic traversing a link. In an early stage, Poisson processes were used to model the process of connection arrivals without making a distinction between network protocols or applications. However, Poisson processes for modeling the Internet packet inter-arrivals seems to be no longer valid [21], and the research community have moved to statistically self-similar processes that exhibit Long-Range Dependence (LRD) to model traffic aggregates [9].

Self-similar models features are dominant in short timescales of traffic (seconds), however, the network manager usually works with the time series of aggregate traffic per day or week, in larger time intervals (five minutes). If the aggregate traffic grows beyond a given threshold (say 80% of the link capacity [16]) then the network manager will consider a possible capacity upgrade. Precisely, we wish to determine if a link remains (statistically) stable or if it shows a different (possibly growing) behavior. In the latter case, the network manager will take action. Note that the vast majority of traffic models in the literature assume stationarity (e.g. all self-similar models). Nevertheless, traffic is strongly non-stationary in a real network. Indeed, non-stationarity is what matters most for capacity planning purposes, because capacity upgrades are only justified when the link's load shows statistically significant changes (not just ocassional peaks). This, in addition to the well-known shortcommings in the self-similar processes' parameter estimation [7], have given raise to more manageable traffic models, which make use of well-known distributions such as the Gaussian [8,15] and Gamma [14,11] distributions to model at larger timescales. The difference between these approaches and our contribution is that we, instead of modeling several realizations of a day with the same distribution, model each day as a realization of a multivariate sample, thus considering constant the distribution for measurements obtained for the same interval of a small set of consecutive days (after which non-stationarity is exhibited in terms of changes in the parameters values). This allows us to accurately capture the well-known daily traffic pattern [23] and apply its exhibited invariance, i.e. the fact that the shape of the pattern is similar between different days (Section 4). In this light, another work dealing with the daily traffic pattern is that of Papagiannaki et al. [19]. In such study, the authors apply wavelet multiresolution analysis to identify the long-term trend that is later modeled with an autoregressive integrated moving average time series model. The difference with our model, in addition to the model itself, is the application that is given to the model. They use the time series model to predict when the links' capacity should be upgraded, whereas we apply our model to detect sustained statistical significant changes in the load [13] that may lead a network manager to consider capacity upgrades.

3   Description of the Measurement Dataset

The data used in this study are MRTG [17] records of different links within the Spanish National Research and Education Network (NREN) RedIRIS[1]. There are MRTG records for the traffic traversing the incoming and outgoing interfaces of several Points of Presence (POPs) and the access routers of some universities within the RedIRIS network. We denote as incoming the traffic from the Internet to the campus, and as outgoing the traffic from the campus to the Internet. In total, there are measurements for 23 different network devices that we treat as different links. The MRTG records are extracted with a granularity of 5 minutes, i.e. every five minutes a new record is output. Each record has five different values. The first one is the UNIX time of the measurements, that will be used in the preprocessing step described in Section 5. The next ones are the average and maximum transfer rates, in bytes per second since the last record, for both interfaces. With this time granularity, we have 288 records per day and direction. Our measurements span from the 6th of February 2007 to the 10th of March of 2009, which leads to more than 750 days worth of data per link.

4   Analysis of the RedIRIS Day-Night Traffic Pattern

In this section we analyze the MRTG measurements described in the previous section, and plot the values of selected days, in order to better understand the behavior of the daily and weekly patterns in the RedIRIS network. In order to make the measurements of different days comparable, we plot utilization (i.e. absolute rate divided by the capacity of the link) values, which are dimensionless. We first graphed the same day of the week for different weeks, in hopes that the day-night pattern is repeated for the same day of the week through different weeks. This intuition was confirmed by the results of the working days, from which the peak and off-peak pattern is very similar to the one described in [23] (note that the differences are due to the kind of users on the network). However, this pattern is not exhibited by the traffic during non-working days. The utilization during these days is nearly flat, and its value is essentially the same during night-hours of working-days, which lead us to think that this traffic may be due to applications that are left running without user supervision (e.g. Skype [2] when it becomes a supernode). This differences are shown in Fig. 1,

---

[1] http://www.rediris.es/rediris/index.en.html

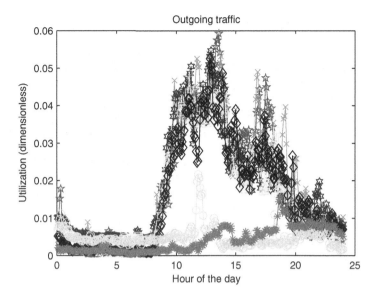

Fig. 1. Time Series representation of the utilization of a RedIRIS link for a whole week

where the working days (the top five time series) have close similar daily pattern, which clearly differs from the holidays pattern (the bottom two time series). It can also be observed that there are some days which show traffic burst. This could be due to measurement errors, or outliers at the 5 minute granularity of the measurements. Therefore, an averaging process is encouraged in order to reduce the impact of these outliers. In addition to this, it can be observed that the utilization values are always under 10%. Therefore, the links are never congested, which means that there are not inaccuracies due to *clipping* of traffic peaks reaching link's capacity. This hypothesis of *free traffic* makes our model to be unbieased because we do not encounter with the restriction that is introduced by reaching the maximum value of the link's capacity.

5   Description of the Multivariate Fairly Normal Model

This section describes the multivariate model for network traffic, which was first introduced in [13]. This model takes into account the day-night traffic pattern observed in the previous section, as follows. As the day-night pattern of working days looks similar from one day to another, both in shape and values, we decided to use a multivariate distribution to model the samples obtained from the MRTG records for each day (remember that each day corresponds to 288 samples per direction with the 5 minutes MRTG measurements granularity). Therefore, the realizations during different days at the same time can be considered to follow the same (unknown) distribution. However, a 288-variate distribution is not an adequate model, because its high dimensionality makes it difficult to work with.

In order to make the model more manageable, we averaged the MRTG values into 16 disjoint intervals of 90 minutes. The reasons to choose such averaging period are manifold: first, chances are that data is missing in the five minutes timescale, which are reduced using 90 minutes intervals; second, the different measurement points may not be perfectly synchronized. A timescale of 90 minutes is coarse enough to circumvent this problem [19]; third, the averaging process reduce the impact of outliers and measurement errors in the results; last, but not the least, the assumption of normality for Internet traffic holds when there is enough temporal aggregation of the measurements [8,15]. Thus, in addition to simplifying the model, we obtain a reasonable distribution for the averaged samples.

However, as we have seen in the previous section, this model cannot be applied to working days and weekends at the same time, because their day-night pattern strongly differs. Therefore, we focus on working days, as their day-night pattern is of higher interest for traffic engineering tasks, and remove weekends from our sample. In addition, we remove outliers. Therefore, the following days are removed from the sample:

- Days for which at least one of the 90 minutes intervals have no measurements. If so, we have no value for this period, and the day-sample will have missing values.
- Summer & Christmas Holidays. During summer and Christmas holidays the pattern of usage of the network resources is comparable to the weekends pattern. Therefore, we also remove these days from the data. Summer holidays are considered from the 1st of July to the 30th of August. Christmas holidays are considered from 22th of December to 7th of January.
- National & Regional Holidays. The national holidays are removed from the data for all the links because all companies and universities are closed. For Regional Holidays, we only remove traffic from the affected region links.
- Exam periods. As we are mainly using traffic from universities, exam periods can affect the traffic patterns, because students do not use the network as much as when they have no exams.

After the preprocessing step, the data set contains more than 300 samples per link and direction, and each of them represents a day worth of traffic that we model with a p-variate normal distribution, where $p = 16$. Note that this preprocessing step can be done in an on-line fashion because these days are known in advance. Finally, Table 1 shows the vector component (out of the 16 components in the 16-variate normal random variable) and the corresponding time period.

6   Methodology

In order to validate the model, we have performed several verifications of the normality assumption for the 16 variables of our model. Therefore, we have applied several univariate normality tests. In addition to this, we have tested for multivariate normality. This is necessary because the fact that several variables have

Table 1. Equivalence in time of the variables

Number of the variable	Time interval	Number of the variable	Time interval
1	00.00-01:30	9	12:00-13:30
2	01:30-03:00	10	13:30-15:00
3	03.00-04:30	11	15:00-16:30
4	04:30-06:00	12	16:30-18:00
5	06.00-07:30	13	18:00-19:30
6	07:30-09:00	14	19:30-21:00
7	09.00-10:30	15	21:00-22:30
8	10:30-12:00	16	22:30-00:00

univariate normal distributions does not imply that they jointly have normal distribution [6]. In what follows, we briefly describe the normality tests applied for both univariate marginals and the joint multivariate distributions.

We have applied two statistical tests that are available in the statistic toolbox of Matlab for testing univariate normality. These tests are Lilliefors and the Jarque-Bera (JB) tests. The Lilliefors test is an enhancement of the Kolmogorov-Smirnov test for testing normality when the parameters are estimated from the sample. Precisely, Lilliefors [10] computed the distribution of the KS statistic under this situation, tabulating it [22]. Therefore, Lilliefors test is useful to detect deviations from normality regarding the localization and scale parameters. On the contrary, the JB test [5] tests the deviation from normality using the skewness and kurtosis of the sample, whose sample statistic follows a χ^2 distribution with two degrees of freedom under the null hypothesis of normality.

In addition to the analytical tests, we also assessed the normality of the dataset by means of graphics. The most accepted graphical test for any kind of distribution is the Quantile-Quantile (Q-Q) plot [25]. In a Q-Q plot, the percentiles of one distribution (the sample) are depicted as a function of the percentiles of the other distribution (the distribution of reference). If the graphed values form a straight line (small deviations in the tails are accepted), the null hypothesis that the sample comes from the hypothesized distribution cannot be rejected. These plots are useful both for testing univariate and multivariate normality. In univariate normality, the parameters of the reference distribution are estimated from the data, whereas in the p-variate case, the Mahalanobis distances [12] given by equation (1) are computed (where $\bar{x}$ and $\mathbf{S}$ are, respectively, the sample mean and sample covariance matrix, whereas $x_j, j \in 1, \ldots, N$ are the population samples), and are plotted against a χ^2 distribution with p degrees of freedom as reference distribution. This latter plots are commonly referred as χ^2 plots [6].

$$D_j^2 = (x_j - \bar{x})^t \mathbf{S}^{-1} (x_j - \bar{x}) \tag{1}$$

We have not applied analytical multivariate normality tests to our dataset because testing for multivariate normality analytically is very challenging. There are few analytical procedures for testing multivariate normality and usually the results are obtained through simulations and approximations. Therefore, we only assess multivariate normality graphically.

7   Validation of the Model Results

This section is devoted to present the results of the test described in Section 6 when applied to the dataset of Section 3. Such dataset is preprocessed according to the network model introduced in Section 5. The normality tests are divided into univariate normality tests, where we apply the analytical tests and Q-Q plots described in the former section to each component of the multivariate random variable, and multivariate normality test, where we graph the χ^2 plots of the Mahalanobis distances.

7.1   Univariate Normality Tests

We applied the analytical tests of Section 6 independently to samples of the outgoing and incoming directions. Therefore, it is not necessary to apply corrections for the significances of the test (like the Bonferroni correction). First of all, we tested the overall dataset for univariate normality. The conclusion was that the null hypothesis of normality must be rejected for both directions in all the observed links. This does not necessarily mean that the normality assumption is not valid. The normality hypothesis can be rejected in this case because there are variations with time in the distribution parameters (i.e. non-stationarity). To

Table 2. Percentage of rejections of the normality assumption per variable in the incoming/outgoing direction

Number of the variable	Lilliefors Test	JB Test
1	18.42/18.57	16.78/20.52
2	26.64/22.80	20.07/21.17
3	30.26/23.13	21.71/21.50
4	31.25/25.73	23.36/24.76
5	30.26/23.45	24.67/28.01
6	21.05/17.26	21.05/20.52
7	18.75/11.73	18.09/18.24
8	15.46/18.24	19.08/20.52
9	17.76/16.94	18.75/23.45
10	18.42/19.22	21.38/22.48
11	17.76/15.96	12.5/15.64
12	16.78/15.64	13.49/12.70
13	18.09/18.24	13.49/14.98
14	16.12/16.61	16.45/14.98
15	19.08/21.50	15.79/22.15
16	15.13/23.13	16.45/25.73

circumvent this possibility, we divided the whole dataset into non-overlapping subsets of 20 contiguous samples (one sample per day), and perform the normality tests to these day-samples. The duration of these subsets is considered sufficiently large to perform the normality tests but smaller enough to avoid significant changes in the distribution parameters. In total, we performed more than 300 normality tests per direction (taking into account the samples of all the links). The percentages of rejections, under the assumption of normality with a confidence level $\alpha = 0.01$, for each vector component are presented in Table 2, where the first column reflects the number of the variable and the second and third column present the results for the Lilliefors and the JB tests, respectively. We have used the convention of incoming/outgoing to present the results of both directions in the same table.

As can be seen in the table, the results for the Lilliefors and JB tests are quite similar for all the variables, and the maximum value is near 30%, which means that for such variable, 30% of the times the null hypothesis of normality was rejected. As we are dealing with real world measurements, it is typical to have deviations from normality, which are detected by the normality tests. Therefore, a rate of non-rejection larger than 70% is enough to assume the fairly Gaussian assumption.

The results for the visual assessment of normality are presented in Fig. 2 and Fig. 3 for two different variables representing different directions of the same link, where the normality assumption is doubtless exhibited, because nearly all the points of such Q-Q plots are aligned in a straight line except for a small number of them in the tails. We have selected such Q-Q plots as we have found them to be representative of the obtained results.

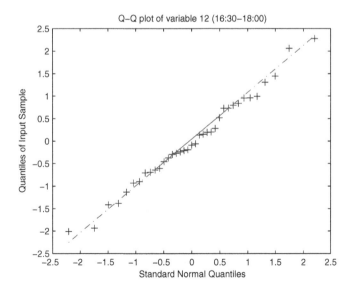

Fig. 2. Q-Q plot for variable 12 in the incoming direction

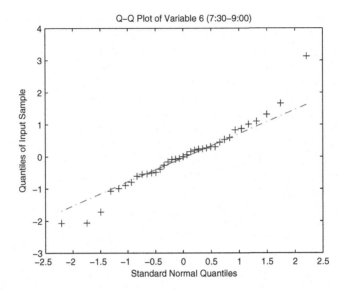

Fig. 3. Q-Q plot for variable 6 in the outgoing direction

7.2   Multivariate Normality Tests

Figure 4 and Fig. 5 present the χ^2 plots for the incoming and outgoing directions, respectively, of the same link. Again, the criteria used to select such plots is their representativeness of the results.

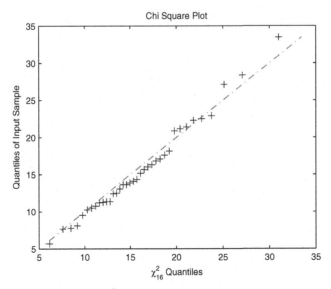

Fig. 4. χ^2 plot for the incoming direction

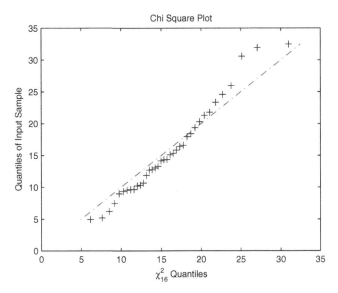

Fig. 5. χ^2 plot for the outgoing direction

These plots evidence that also multivariate normality can be assumed from the samples of the model. However, we see that the normality assumption is stronger in the incoming direction. This is reasonable, because the amount of traffic in the incoming direction is larger and, consequently, the larger aggregation of traffic in the incoming direction, the stronger the normality assumption.

8   Summary and Conclusions

In this paper we have used a multivariate normal distribution to model the daily traffic pattern. We have used 16 dimensions (i.e. time intervals) for our multivariate distribution because this is a good compromise between simplicity and level of detail. The multidimensional nature of the model keeps track of the well-known traffic daily pattern [23]. On the one hand, previous studies have reported on the fairly Gaussian nature of the marginal distribution [15,8]. Then, we have performed an exhaustive validation of the model, testing for the multivariate normality assumption. However, testing for multivariate normality is not straightforward, and several procedures must be followed. First, univariate normality for all the dimensions should be tested independently. As these tests are applied to independent samples, there is no need to apply corrections for the significances of the test (like the Bonferroni correction). We have performed two different analytical tests for normality, and also assessed it by graphical methods. Once the univariate fairly normality assumption is verified (see Table 2) it is necessary to test for joint normality, because the univariate normality does not imply joint multivariate normality. Therefore, we computed the Mahalanobis distances for the samples and performed χ^2 plots, that confirmed the fairly multivariate normality assumption. As a result, we have presented a fairly multivariate normal model whose validity has been assessed with rigorous and well-known statistical tests.

Acknowledgments. The authors would like to thank the support of the Spanish Ministerio de Ciencia e Innovación (MICINN) to this study, under project DIOR (S-0505/TIC/000251) and the FPU fellowship program that has partially funded this research work.

References

1. Abendroth, D., Berg, H.v.d., Mandjes, M.: A versatile model for TCP bandwidth sharing in networks with heterogeneous users. AEU - International Journal of Electronics and Communications 60(4), 267–278 (2006)
2. Bonfiglio, D., Mellia, M., Meo, M., Rossi, D.: Detailed Analysis of Skype Traffic. IEEE Transactions on Multimedia 11(1), 117–127 (2009)
3. Dang, T.D., Sonkoly, B., Molnar, S.: Fractal analysis and modeling of VoIP traffic. In: Telecommunications Network Strategy and Planning Symposium, pp. 123–130 (June 2004)
4. Gummadi, K.P., Dunn, R.J., Saroiu, S., Gribble, S.D., Levy, H.M., Zahorjan, J.: Measurement, modeling, and analysis of a peer-to-peer file-sharing workload. In: ACM Symposium on Operating Systems Principles, pp. 314–329 (2003)
5. Jarque, C.M., Bera, A.K.: Efficient tests for normality, homoscedasticity and serial independence of regression residuals. Economics Letters 6(3), 255–259 (1980)
6. Johnson, R.A., Wichern, D.W.: Applied multivariate statistical analysis. Prentice-Hall International Editions (1992)
7. Karagiannis, T., Molle, M., Faloutsos, M.: Long-range dependence ten years of Internet traffic modeling. IEEE Internet Computing 8(5), 57–64 (2004)
8. Kilpi, J., Norros, I.: Testing the Gaussian approximation of aggregate traffic. In: ACM SIGCOMM Workshop on Internet Measurment, pp. 49–61 (2002)
9. Leland, W.E., Taqqu, M.S., Willinger, W., Wilson, D.V.: On the self-similar nature of Ethernet traffic (extended version). IEEE/ACM Transactions on Networking 2(1), 1–15 (1994)
10. Lilliefors, H.W.: On the Kolmogorov-Smirnov test for normality with mean and variance unknown. Journal of the American Statistical Association 62(318), 399–402 (1967)
11. Liu, Z., Almhana, J., Choulakian, V., McGorman, R.: Traffic modeling with gamma mixtures and dynamical bandwidth provisioning. In: Communication Networks and Services Research Conference, pp. 8–130 (May 2006)
12. Mahalanobis, P.C.: On the generalized distance in statistics. In: Proceedings of the National Institute of Science, vol. 12, p. 49 (1936)
13. Mata, F., Aracil, J., García-Dorado, J.L.: Automated Detection of Load Changes in Large-Scale Networks. In: International Workshop on Traffic Monitoring and Analysis, pp. 34–41 (May 2009)
14. McGorman, R., Almhana, J., Choulakian, V., Liu, Z.: Empirical bandwidth provisioning models for high speed Internet traffic. In: Communication Networks and Services Research Conference, pp. 8–195 (May 2006)

15. van de Meent, R., Mandjes, M., Pras, A.: Gaussian traffic everywhere? In: IEEE International Conference on Communications, vol. 2, pp. 573–578 (June 2006)
16. Nucci, A., Papagiannaki, K.: Design, Measurement and Management of Large-Scale IP Networks. Cambridge University Press, Cambridge (2008)
17. Oetiker, T., Rand, D.: MRTG: The Multi Router Traffic Grapher. In: USENIX Conference on System Administration, pp. 141–148 (1998)
18. Padhye, J., Firoiu, V., Towsley, D.F., Kurose, J.F.: Modeling TCP Reno performance: a simple model and its empirical validation. IEEE/ACM Transactions on Networking 8(2), 133–145 (2000)
19. Papagiannaki, K., Taft, N., Zhang, Z.L., Diot, C.: Long-term forecasting of Internet backbone traffic. IEEE Transactions on Neural Networks 16(5), 1110–1124 (2005)
20. Paxson, V.: Empirically derived analytic models of wide-area TCP connections. IEEE/ACM Transactions on Networking 2(4), 316–336 (1994)
21. Paxson, V., Floyd, S.: Wide area traffic: the failure of Poisson modeling. IEEE/ACM Transactions on Networking 3(3), 226–244 (1995)
22. Sheskin, D.: Handbook of parametric and nonparametric statistical procedures. CRC Press, Boca Raton (2004)
23. Thompson, K., Miller, G.J., Wilder, R.: Wide-area Internet traffic patterns and characteristics. IEEE Network 11(6), 10–23 (1997)
24. Tong, Y.L.: Multivariate normal distribution. Springer, Heidelberg (1990)
25. Wilk, M.B., Gnanadesikan, R.: Probability plotting methods for the analysis for the analysis of data. Biometrika 55(1), 1 (1968)

Live Traffic Monitoring with Tstat: Capabilities and Experiences

A. Finamore[1], M. Mellia[1], M. Meo[1], M.M. Munafò[1], and D. Rossi[2]

[1] Politecnico di Torino
lastname@tlc.polito.it
[2] TELECOM ParisTech
dario.rossi@enst.fr

Abstract. Network monitoring has always played a key role in understanding telecommunication networks since the pioneering time of the Internet. Today, monitoring traffic has become a key element to characterize network usage and users' activities, to understand how complex applications work, to identify anomalous or malicious behaviors, etc. In this paper we present our experience in engineering and deploying Tstat, a passive monitoring tool that has been developed in the past ten years. Started as a scalable tool to continuously monitor packets that flow on a link, Tstat has evolved into a complex application that gives to network researchers and operators the possibility to derive extended and complex measurements. Tstat offers the capability to track traffic flows, it integrates advanced behavioral classifiers that identify the application that has generated a flow, and automatically derives performance indexes that allow to easily characterize both network usage and users' activity. After describing Tstat capabilities and internal design, in this paper we present some examples of measurements collected deploying Tstat at the edge of our campus network for the past years.

1 Introduction

The importance of traffic monitoring and analysis has always played a key role in understanding telecommunication networks. Since the early days of the Internet, several methodologies and tools have been engineered to perform traffic monitoring, to detect problems and to understand the network behavior and users' usage. Due to the availability of cheap, high-performing PCs and network interfaces, and driven by the explosive growth of the Internet, nowadays traffic monitoring is considered a crucial component of the network and a lot of advanced tools and methodologies are available to "monitor the Internet".

At a very high level, there exist two antagonist approaches to traffic measurement: *passive* and *active*. The *active* approach aims at interfering with a network to induce a measurable effect. For example, active approaches inject ad-hoc probe traffic or modify the network state, e.g., enforcing artificial network conditions. Active approaches induce a cause-effect relationship between the network and the traffic, triggering a measurable effect which is the goal of the

E. Osipov et al. (Eds.): WWIC 2010, LNCS 6074, pp. 290–301, 2010.

measurement itself. Active approaches are the core for a number of tasks such as operation and management (e.g., ICMP), network tomography (e.g., traceroute), delay and capacity measurement (e.g., ping, capprobe[1], pathchar[2]), controlled empirical studies (e.g., netem, dummynet[3]). In the *passive* approach the traffic exchanged on the network is merely observed as to infer some of its root properties, but taking care not to interfere with the observation. In this case, a passive "sniffer" is used to observe normal traffic; for example, at the physical-level this is done by means of passive optical splitter, at higher layers by means of replication of layer-2 frames. Copies of the traffic are then sent to an "analyzer machine" for processing. Passive monitoring applications are diverse and range from user characterization to intrusion detection, from traffic classification to policing, just to mention a few.

Over the years, several tools have been engineered to passively analyze traffic, each of which has some type of specialization. Wireshark[4], for instance, is a well-known protocol analyzer with several advanced analysis capabilities, which allow the user to interact with the collected packets through a GUI interface. Other tools like Snort[5], an intrusion detection system, or CoralReef[6], an advanced classification tool, are designed to work in real time and minimize the human interaction.

Tstat [7] is one of such passive analysis tools, developed in the past ten years by the Politecnico di Torino networking research group, and nowadays used by several researchers and network operator worldwide. Tstat started as evolution of TCPTRACE[8], which originally allowed to track single TCP flows and offered the user detailed statistics about each flow. After years of development, Tstat is now a scalable application that gives network researchers and operators the ability to derive an extended set of advanced measurements, focusing on an IP network. Tstat offers live and scalable traffic monitoring up to Gbps on off-the-shelf hardware. It implements traffic classification capabilities, including advanced behavioral classifiers, while presenting advanced performance characterization of both network usage and users' activities. In this paper, we report on the Tstat architecture and functionalities, illustrating through several examples its capabilities.

2 Tstat Features

Tstat is a traffic analyzer tool with a very flexible design: it consists of different modules that produce a wide set of statistics in different formats. Tstat is highly configurable at runtime, so that many features can be activated and deactivated on the fly, without interrupting the program. In the following, we first overview Tstat architecture, we then present its capabilities.

2.1 Data Structures and Workflow

Tstat is an IP network passive sniffer that processes packet-level traffic to produce both per packet and per flow statistics. The basic entity in Tstat is a

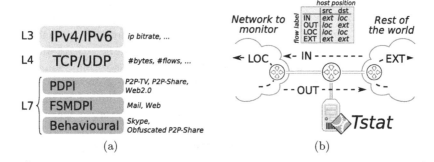

Fig. 1. Tstat modules (a) and monitoring probe setup (b)

flows, i.e., a single communication considering all IP packets having the same tuple $flow_{ID} = (ipProtoType, ipSrcAddr, srcPort, ipDstAddr, dstPort)$. Since services in the Internet typically require bidirectional conversations, *connections* are defined by grouping together the two flows going in opposite directions, i.e., in which src and dst addresses are exchanged. Connections are identified and tracked for both TCP and UDP traffic. Tstat discriminates client-to-server and server-to-client flows, where the client is conventionally identified as the sender of the first packet seen of the connection. Flow end is detected due to either proper connection tear-down (possible only in the TCP case), or a flow inactivity timeout (i.e., in case no new packet is seen for a connection for more than 120 seconds).

A common data structure is used to store some basic connections information, like the connection id, the total number of packets and bytes seen up to a given time, the timestamp of the first and last packet. Given a connection, two independent data structures collect statistics for each direction while advanced information related to a specific transport-layer (e.g., TCP, UDP, RTP), or to the application-layer (e.g., BitTorrent, Skype, ...), are grouped in specific structures linked to the flow data structures.

Since flow and connection structures must be accessed and updated for each packet, pointers to the structures are stored in two hash-tables, one for TCP and one for UDP connections. A simple hash function $hash(flow_{ID}) = (ipSrcAddr + srcPort + ipdstAddr + dstPort) \ mod \ N$ is used, being N the number of entries of the hash-table. Collisions are handled using a linked list.

Fig. 1(a) reports a simplified version of the analysis steps performed on each packet. After layer-2 (L2) framing de-encapsulation which is not subject of statistics, Tstat processes the L3 (network-layer) header: since Tstat is explicitly designed to process only IPv4 and IPv6 packets, possible non-IP packets are immediately discarded. Given the datagram service offered by IP networks, at the L3 only some per-datagram statistics are collected, like bitrate, packet length, etc.

The control is then handed over to the L4 (transport-layer) analysis. For both TCP and UDP, Tstat maintains a set of common statistics generally applicable (like the volume expressed in terms of bytes, packets or flows) and performs further analysis like the identification of duplicated packets. For a TCP segment, further statistics are computed, like congestion window size, number of retransmissions [9], interrupted flows [10], etc.

At the L7 (application-layer), the main goal is to classify the traffic. A set of classification engines are triggered to identify which application has generated the flow under analysis. More in details, Tstat implements three different engines, based on different technologies:

Pure Deep Packet Inspection (PDPI): each application is uniquely identified by an expression of L7 payload bytes, called *signatures*. All the applications signatures are collected in a dictionary, defining a set of classification rules. Using a *pattern matching* approach, the signatures are then checked against the current payload until either a match is found, or all the signatures have been tested. In the first case, the flow is labeled according to the application associated to the rule that has matched, while in the second case the flow is labeled as "unknown". This approach is used to identify *Web 2.0* (Megaupload, RapidShare, YouTube, Vimeo, Facebook, Flickr), *P2P-TV* (PPLive, TvAnts, Sopcast), and *P2P-file-sharing* (Bittorrent, eMule, Kad, DC++, Gnutella) partially derived from *IPP2P*[11].

Finite State Machine Deep Packet Inspection (FSMDPI): the mechanism is similar to PDPI but involves the inspection of more than one packet of a flow. Finite State Machines (FSM) are used to verify the application protocol so that, to have a positive match, a specific sequence of matching rules have to be triggered. For example, if the first packet contains 'GET http://' and response carries 'HTTP/1.0 OK', the flow can be considered as HTTP. Using this approach, Tstat identifies *Mail* (IMAP, POP3, SMTP), *Chat* (MSN, XMPP/Jabber, Yahoo), *Web* (HTTP), *Encripted traffic* (SSL/TLS, SSH) and *VoIP* (RTP/RTCP).

Behavioral: given that the previous classifiers are based on payload inspection, in many cases they fail to correctly classify applications which rely on encryption mechanisms to protect the payload. In this case, behavioral classifiers can be used. They exploit *statical properties* like the packet size or inter arrival time to distinguish among applications. Using this approach, Tstat identifies *Skype* [12] and *Obfuscated P2P-file-sharing* (BitTorrent, eMule) traffic as well.

All these techniques are designed to work even if the complete packet payload is not available due to privacy or disk space concerns.

Once the traffic has been classified, further analysis can be carried out by application-specific plugins. For instance, once an RTP flow has been recognized, specific VoIP metrics are computed, like packet loss probability, loss burst length, jitter, etc.

Computational complexity of the above operations has been extensively analyzed in [13,14], showing that with off-the-shelf hardware it is possible to process several Gbps with no particular problems.

2.2   Input

Tstat offers the capability to both (i) monitor in real time operational networks and (ii) offline analyze packet level traces. In the first case, the software runs on a *probe*, i.e., a dedicated PC that "sniffs" traffic flowing on an operative link, as shown in Fig. 1(b). In this context, Tstat processes data packets that are captured in real time from a network interface. The standard *libpcap* library is supported to capture packets from standard Ethernet cards, but dedicated hi-end capture devices such as Endace DAG [15] or AITIA S1GED [16] cards are also supported. When used to process already captured packet level traces, Tstat reads from data files that store the packet level trace. This allows to inspect specific traffic for post-mortem analysis, to develop more complex statistical analysis for advanced performance evaluation (e.g., testing several algorithms, or checking the impact of some parameter over the same trace multiple times). A variety of dump file formats are supported, like pcap, erf, etherpeek, snoop, ns2 and netmetrix, and files can also be provided in compressed form, derived from 7zip, gzip and bzip.

Finally, it is also possible to compile Tstat as a *library*, called *libTstat*, so that its analysis capabilities can be easily linked to other traffic analysis tools. In this case, Tstat runs as a "plugin" of the other application and a simple API is used to pass packets to Tstat. In this case Tstat no longer has control on the measurement interface and the main application is free to tune the amount of payload handed over to Tstat or to filter out some packets, or to anonymize IP addresses and ports for privacy purposes. In our experience, this approach has revealed very successful, facilitating the integration of Tstat with the monitoring tools that operators may already have developed. For example, Tstat has been successfully integrated into TIE, a analysis tool developed by the university Federico II di Napoli, and METAWIN.

When characterizing a network, such as a campus LAN or an ISP Point-of-Presence (PoP), as reported in Fig. 1(b), it is often very useful to distinguish the traffic transmitted by "local" hosts from traffic sent by "external" hosts. By simply providing a set of IP network addresses used by local hosts, Tstat label flows according to theirs source. Four cases are possible:

- *incoming* traffic (in), if the source is external and the destination is local;
- *outgoing* traffic (out), if the source is local and the destination is external;
- *local* traffic (loc), if both source and destination are local;
- *external* traffic (ext), if both source and destination are external;

If the set of local network addresses is not provided, Tstat labels all the flows as local. Since the external flows contain traffic which does not involve the local network, statistics are collected only for the first three directions. Tstat allows to configure different sets of statistics for different classes, e.g. collect the incoming bitrate and the outgoing number of flows.

2.3   Output

Output statistics are reported in different formats, providing different levels of information:

Connection Logs: A set of text files which provide detailed information for each monitored connection. Each log is arranged as a simple table where each column is associated to a specific information while each line contains statistics related to the two flows of a connection. Tstat generates several different log files: UDP log, which collects all statistics related to UDP connections; multimedia log, which collects statistics for RTP/RTCP traffic; Skype and chat log, which collects statistics about Skype and Chat services; finally, TCP log, which collects statistics related to TCP traffic, and is split into two separate logs, discriminating "complete" connections (i.e., TCP connections properly started by a three-way handshake) from "incomplete" connections (i.e., TCP connections with partial three-way-handshake, due to routing asymmetry, packet loss, or malicious traffic, like port-scan). When a connection is closed, a line in the corresponding log is added.

Histograms: A set of histograms are used to collect empirical frequency distributions of parameters such as IP packet length, number of times a L4 port has been used in a flow, probability of an interrupted TCP flow, per-protocols bitrates, or number of flows active in a time slot. For each measured metric, the corresponding histogram is stored on separate file, using a two column table reporting the indication of the bins and the number of samples observed in that bin. Histograms can be generated periodically, i.e., every 5 minutes by default the current histogram is flushed to disk and a new collection starts, or a unique histogram for each feature can be saved at the end of the analysis.

Round Robin Database (RRD): A Round Robin Database (RRD)[17] is created for continuous monitoring a given statistics. RRD has been designed as a scalable mechanism to store historical data, by aggregating them with different granularity: newer samples are stored with higher frequencies, while oldest data are averaged in coarser time scales. This dramatically reduces the requirements in terms of disk space and, thanks to the tools provided by the RRD technology, it is possible to easily inspect the results. Indeed, it is possible to associate each Tstat probe to a website template using a simple *CGI* interface to query the RRD database [18], and obtain plots of historical measurements.

Packet traces: At the end of the packet analysis, it is possible to dump it into pcap traces. The traffic can be saved in an aggregated IP trace but it is also possible to separate TCP from UDP. Moreover, by exploiting its classification capabilities, Tstat can also split the UDP traffic according to the application layer. For example, RTP connections can be saved on a different file with respect to eMule without the need for processing the original traffic more than once.

The chosen output configuration anyway is very flexible thanks to the *runtime* engine. With this module in fact is possible to change the output configuration

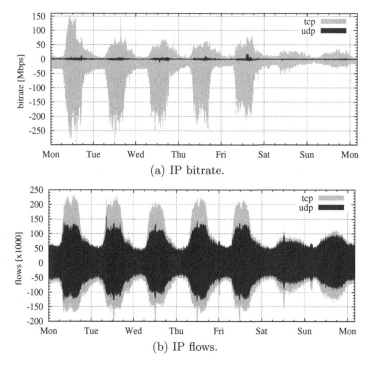

(a) IP bitrate.

(b) IP flows.

Fig. 2. One week of outgoing(+) and incoming(-) traffic volume

at runtime i.e. without the need to restart the program. In this way, is possible to configure a Tstat probe with a base configuration while specific statistics can be enable/disabled when needed.

3   Gallery of Tstat Capabilities

3.1   Campus Network

Politecnico di Torino institution is the second largest technical University in Italy, with about 1800 staff members and 28,000 students. The campus network is connected to the GARR [19] network, the Italian and European research network, with a 1 Gbps link. It is subdivided in more than 14 subnetworks, with approximatively 9,000 PCs and 50 servers accessing the network during a typical working day.

The Politecnico network has been constantly monitored using a Tstat probe since 2000. The probe runs on common PC hardware, i.e., dual core Intel Xeon 2.40GHz, 1 Gbyte of RAM and a simple Intel based Ethernet card. Linux is used as OS. The probe is configured to use the *runtime* engine. RRD are continuously collected and can also publicly browsed through the Web interface provided in the Tstat website [18].

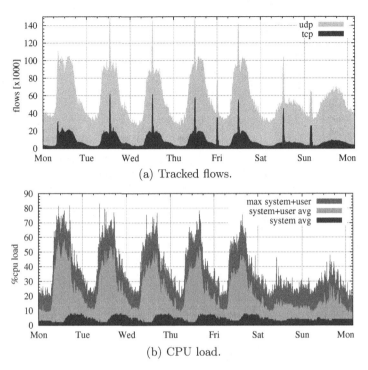

(a) Tracked flows.

(b) CPU load.

Fig. 3. One week of load sustained by the probe

3.2 RRD Examples

In this section, we report some examples of RRD graphs that can be obtained using a Tstat probe. Results reported cover a period of time between January 2009 to March 2010. One week of traffic, the first of February 2010, has also been chosen and analyzed as representative of the traffic of the campus network.

The plots show the variation over time of given measures in the considered periods, and each point corresponds to a 5 minute time-window. Positive and negative y-axis values (when they both are present) are used to distinguish outgoing and incoming traffic directions, respectively. Curves are stacked, so that the measures are breakdown in classes each associated to a different colour.

Traffic volumes. Fig. 2 reports the bitrate and the number of new connections over a one week time period. As expected, we observe that the traffic is highly asymmetric in terms of bitrate, e.g., in normal condition, the incoming traffic volume is 4-5 times larger than the outgoing traffic. The difference in terms of connections is only about 25% of the total. This is due to the intrinsic characteristics of our campus network, where most of the users require information to the outside world, i.e., they open outgoing connections that produce incoming volume. It can be seen that traffic volume evolution follows a well known day/night pattern, with extremely low values during nights and week-end days: a sustained

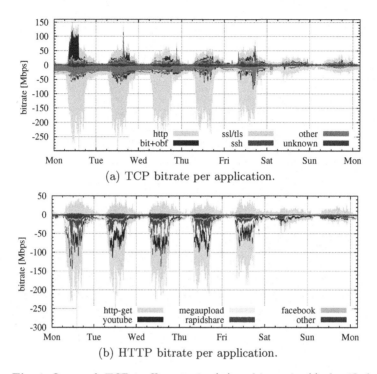

(a) TCP bitrate per application.

(b) HTTP bitrate per application.

Fig. 4. One week TCP traffic outgoing(+) and incoming(-) classified

activity is present between 8am and 6pm (i.e., during office hours), with a drop around 12am corresponding to lunch time. Similarly, during the week end traffic is much smaller given fewer users are in the University premises.

By comparing Fig. 2(a) with Fig. 2(b), we can see that TCP accounts for more than 90% of the traffic volume, but UDP accounts for a very significant amount of connections. Indeed, UDP represents nearly half of the connections during the day, and practically all of the connections during the night. This higher number of UDP connections is due to the connectionless service of UDP, that is used by applications such as DNS which exchange very little amount of traffic. Later on, we will focus more deeply on traffic classification.

As a last example, Fig. 3(a) reports the number of TCP and UDP connections Tstat tracked. Since connections are bidirectional, we do not distinguish incoming and outgoing flows. As expected, the number of connections follows the daily pattern already noticed in Fig. 2(a) and Fig. 2(b). Interestingly, some very regularly spaced peaks in the number of TCP connections are present, possibly corresponding to some experiments, network or port-scan activities.

Finally, Fig. 3(b) reports the average CPU load of the probe machine, separately showing the system space CPU time and the user space CPU time, i.e., the time spent in kernel mode by OS calls, and the time spent in running Tstat. Measurements refer to the average CPU utilization in a time window of 5 minutes. To identify critical situations, the total maximum CPU load sustained in

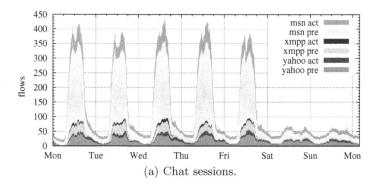

(a) Chat sessions.

Fig. 5. One week chat session classified

the 5 min time window is shown. The maximum load always smaller than 100% confirms that the Politecnico di Torino Tstat probe was able to process an aggregate amount of traffic of up to 400 Mbps, composed by more than 2,000 new connections per second using common hardware. Based on our experience [13], the major bottleneck of the probe is due to the Ethernet NIC communications, which, not being optimized for packet capturing, can overload the PC system bus by generating too many IRQ per seconds. The use of dedicated traffic capturing devices like [15,16] solves this problem.

Traffic classification. As briefly described in the previous section, Tstat offers advanced traffic classification capabilities. Fig. 4, Fig. 5 and Fig. 6 report some examples of such capability. Fig. 4(a) starts showing the TCP traffic volume breakdown per application. Among all the protocols identified by Tstat, we select the topmost 4 applications, namely: HTTP, SSL/TSL, SSH and BitTorrent (both plain and obfuscated). Other correctly classified protocols are aggregated in the "other" class, while unclassified traffic is labeled as "unknown". As always, outgoing/incoming traffic is reported using positive/negative values. Results shows, that the large majority of incoming traffic volume is due to HTTP traffic, with a small fraction of SSH traffic, and little Bittorrent traffic. Indeed, the campus network traffic is regulated by a firewall which limits the possible protocols; for example, it blocks eMule traffic which is very common in other scenarios. Considering outgoing traffic, HTTP traffic represents only half of the total volume, which is due to Web service asymmetry. On the 1st day, it is however possible to see an "abnormal" activity, represented by some local Bit-Torrent client that was transmitting a lot of data, possibly seeding some content. Some other strange activities are also present. For example, there is a moderate constant and large amount of unclassified traffic which is due to the PlanetLab nodes present in the campus network that were likely conducting experiments using some unknown protocol.

Given the predominance of HTTP traffic, it is interesting to observe which application is actually used to generate traffic. Fig. 4(b) reports the breakdown

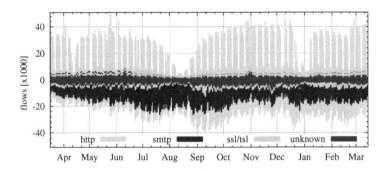

Fig. 6. One year of TCP flows classified

of the HTTP volume of traffic per application. It shows that popular streaming services, like YouTube, or social networks, like Facebook, generate about 30% of HTTP traffic. More interestingly, about 30% of the incoming volume is due file hosting services (like Megaupload or RapidShare), which are becoming alternatives for downloading contents when P2P file sharing applications are not available or strictly regulated as in our campus network.

We now focus on chat services, to show another capability of Tstat. Fig. 5 shows users chatting habits during the week. It considers Windows Live Messenger (MSN), XMPP based chat services (like Google Talk) and the proprietary Yahoo Messenger. Chat traffic is further classified as *presence* and *activity*, respectively referring to traffic generated by the client to simply use the service, and actual chat sessions generated by the user. Besides showing the different popularity of the three chat services, Fig. 5 shows that the number of users logged, but inactive, is much larger than the number of users that actually have ongoing chat sessions. This is especially evident for MSN, which is by far the most popular chat service in the campus network.

Finally, Fig. 6 reports the number of TCP connections seen every 5 minutes, averaged over a one day log interval. The plot covers a period of time starting from April '09 to March '10. As already observed for Fig. 2(b), the number of outgoing flows is higher than the incoming one (reported using negative values on the y-axis, as usual). The year-long plot allows to appreciate the weekly periodicity of traffic, with weekend days showing much less activity. The summer and Christmas periods show also a clear drop in traffic, being those a typical vacation period. Finally, as already noticed, the large majority of traffic is due to HTTP based services in our network. In more depth, more than the 50% of the incoming connections are due to SMTP traffic, i.e., emails received by the campus mail server. For the large part, this traffic corresponds to spam messages that the network has to carry, which is later on tagged as SPAM by the email server. The amount of email connections received on average is indeed equal to more than 20,000 every 5 minutes, and it is not correlated to user activity, e.g., during the summer the volume of SMTP connections is constantly high despite a few users only are presents.

4   Conclusions

This paper reported our experience with the use of Tstat in live traffic monitoring of operational networks: Tstat capabilities have been quickly described and, as an example, practically used in our campus network.

Started as a scalable flow-level logger, Tstat capabilities evolved toward upper layer analysis and classification capabilities. The flexible input/output interface makes it worth using for researchers (with a great deal of information available for post-processing) but also simple to deploy and use as-is (with a nice browsable Web interface). Among other interesting features of Tstat, we point out its high configurability, possibly at runtime. Moreover, Tstat is also extensible by writing new specified plugins. Finally, Tstat can also be embedded in current monitoring applications and infrastructures, for which it can run as a plugin.

References

1. Kapoor, R., Chen, L.-J., Lao, L., Gerla, M., Sanadidi, M.Y.: CapProbe: A Simple and Accurate Capacity Estimation Technique. In: ACM SIGCOMM'04, Portland, USA (2004)
2. Downey, A.B.: Using pathchar to estimate Internet link characteristics. ACM SIG-COMM Computer Communication Review (1999)
3. Rizzo, L.: Dummynet: a simple approach to the evaluation of network protocols. ACM Computer Communication Review (January 1997)
4. Wireshark Homepage, http://www.wireshark.org/
5. Roesch, M.: Snort - Lightweight Intrusion Detection for Networks. In: 13th USENIX LISA Conference (1999)
6. Moore, D., Keys, K., Koga, R., Lagache, E., Claffy, K.: The CoralReef Software Suite as a Tool for System and Network Administrators. In: 15th USENIX Conference on System Administration, San Diego, CA (December 2001)
7. TSTAT Homepage, http://tstat.tlc.polito.it
8. TCPTrace Homepage, http://www.tcptrace.org
9. Mellia, M., Meo, M., Muscariello, L., Rossi, D.: Passive analysis of TCP anomalies. Elsevier Computer Networks 52(14) (October 2008)
10. Rossi, D., Casetti, C., Mellia, M.: User Patience and the Web: a Hands-on Investigation. In: IEEE Globecom'03, San Francisco, CA, USA (December 2003)
11. IPP2P Homepage, http://www.ipp2p.org
12. Bonfiglio, D., Mellia, M., Meo, M., Rossi, D., Tofanelli, P.: Revealing Skype Traffic: When Randomness Plays with You. ACM SIGCOMM Computer Communication Review 37(4), 37–48 (2007)
13. Rossi, D., Mellia, M.: Real-Time TCP/IP Analysis with Common Hardware. In: IEEE International Conference of Communication (ICC'06), Istanbul, Turkey (June 2006)
14. Rossi, D., Valenti, S., Veglia, P., Bonfiglio, D., Mellia, M., Meo, M.: Pictures from the Skype. ACM Performance Evaluation Review (PER) 36(2), 83–86 (2008)
15. Endace Homepage, http://www.endace.com
16. AITIA Homepage, http://www.aitia.ai
17. RRDtool Homepage, http://oss.oetiker.ch/rrdtool/
18. TSTAT RRD Web interface, http://tstat.tlc.polito.it/web.shtml
19. GARR Homepage, http://www.garr.it/reteGARR/index.php

Integrated Measurement and Analysis
of Peer-to-Peer Traffic

N.M. Markovich[1], A. Biernacki[2], P. Eittenberger[2], and U.R. Krieger[2,*]

[1] Institute of Control Sciences, Russian Academy of Sciences, Moscow
[2] WIAI, Otto-Friedrich Universität, D-96045 Bamberg, Germany
`udo.krieger@ieee.org`

Abstract. We present a comprehensive traffic measurement and analysis concept to cope with the rapid deployment of peer-to-peer multimedia applications and their overlay structures. It integrates four orthogonal dimensions: traffic measurements at the packet layer, data extraction, flow analysis and inspection of peer-to-peer overlays based on a hierarchical multi-layer modeling concept, a characterization of overlay structures by techniques and metrics of complex networks, and a statistical characterization of peer-to-peer traffic features.

Keywords: Traffic measurements, peer-to-peer overlay, peer-to-peer traffic characterization, IPTV, SopCast.

1 Introduction

Currently, the rapid development of new multimedia services including VoIP, video streaming and video on demand as well as IPTV and the integration of triple play into the service portfolios of network operators indicate an evolutionary path towards next generation networking. The dissemination of multimedia content can be performed by diverse communication channels according to different paradigms including broadcast, multicast, unicast or peer-to-peer communication patterns (see Fig. 1). While network operators and content providers have advocated in favour of multicast architectures adopting the technology of content distribution network providers, peer-to-peer technology has gained an increasing attention in recent years.

Peer-to-peer (P2P) overlay networks are used with growing intensity to implement the content dissemination and control planes of many new portals and their multimedia service components like GoalBit, Zattoo, PPLive, SopCast, Voddler or Skype (see, e.g., [1], [8], [12], [13]). The availability of DSL-based high speed access to the Internet in residential networks and powerful stationary and mobile terminals have fertilized the rollout of these service platforms and will intensify the demand in the next years.

To respond to this rapid deployment of P2P overlay structures, we have developed a comprehensive P2P traffic measurement, modeling and teletraffic analysis

---

* The authors acknowledge the support by the projects BMBF MDA08/015 and COST IC0703.

E. Osipov et al. (Eds.): WWIC 2010, LNCS 6074, pp. 302–314, 2010.

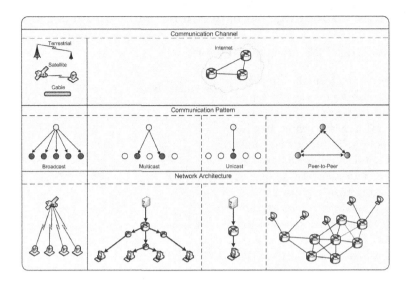

Fig. 1. Network architectures supporting multimedia content distribution

concept. It integrates four orthogonal dimensions to cope with the analysis of P2P structures and P2P traffic characterization: (1) traffic measurements at the packet layer combining passive and active monitoring techniques, (2) data extraction, analysis and inspection of P2P overlays based on a hierarchical multi-layer modeling concept, (3) a characterization of the overlay structure by techniques and metrics of complex networks, and (4) teletraffic modeling based on a statistical characterization of P2P traffic features. It incorporates the analysis and estimation of the bivariate distribution $\mathbb{P}\{X_i \leq x, Y_i \leq y\}$ of packet inter-arrival times X_i and packet lengths Y_i extracted from corresponding flow data $\{(X_1, Y_1), ..., (X_n, Y_n)\}$ of collected i.i.d samples.

In recent years numerous measurement studies of different VoIP and P2PTV applications have been performed, e.g. by Ciullo et al. [3], Hei et al. [5], Liu et al. [9], Silverston et al. [14], and Tang et al. [15] among others. We have also recorded a moderate number of traces of prototypical streaming applications in 2007 and 2009 and performed a statistical analysis of the peer-to-peer transport services (cf. [4], [8], [10]). In this paper we present our P2P modeling approach and an integrated measurement and teletraffic analysis concept. Based on a measurement study in a home environment we further discuss some characteristic traffic features arising from a SopCast session. The data analysis illustrates the features of our approach, partly validates former findings and provides new teletraffic models of the transport service applied by SopCast.

The rest of the paper is organized as follows. In Section 2 we provide an overview of the modeling and measurement concept and its integration into the tool Atheris. In Section 3 the data analysis and modeling of typical P2PTV packet traffic arising from a SopCast session is discussed. Finally, some conclusions are drawn.

2   A P2P Modeling, Measurement and Analysis Concept

2.1   Modeling P2P Overlay Networks

Peer-to-peer multimedia applications establish an overlay on top of the packet-switched TCP/IP transport network based on a tree or mesh topology. Then they normally apply a pull mechanism to distribute the video content among all peers looking to a certain live TV channel or recorded video stream. The latter is described by an object space $\mathcal{O} = \{O_1, \ldots, O_m\}$.

From a logical perspective, this approach generates a multi-tier peer-to-peer architecture of the streaming infrastructure where the overlay network is mapped by a dissemination topology of the replicated streamed video data onto the used transport infrastructure derived from the TCP/IP protocol suite (see Fig. 2).

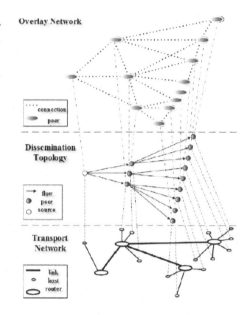

Fig. 2. Multi-tier peer-to-peer architecture of a content dissemination infrastructure

Inspired by the approach of Tang et al. [15], we can describe this hierarchical multi-layer infrastructure to analyze the P2P overlay structure, to describe the P2P traffic relations, and to perform a traffic characterization as well as the interactive investigation of corresponding traffic flows during P2P sessions. It covers the observed parts of the overlay structure by means of an undirected *neighborhood graph* $G_N = (V_N, E_N)$ among an object specific, time dependent peer population $\mathcal{P}^{(O_i)}(t) = \{p_1(t), \ldots, p_{n(t)}(t)\} \subset \mathcal{U}$ within a finite universe $\mathcal{U}$, see Fig. 2. The engaged peers form an overlay structure of common interest called *neighborhood community* (cf. [15]). It dynamically evolves in time since peers may join or leave this community of common interest related to an object O_j, e.g. due to channel hopping. The exchange of content data is described by a directed *dissemination flow graph* $G_V = (V_V, E_V, f, c)$, $V_V \subseteq V_N$, among pairs (p_i, p_j) of peers derived from a dissemination topology (V_V, E_V) (cf. [15]). $e = (p_i, p_j) \in E_V$ means that a flow $\phi(e)$ of requested video chunk sequences called *micro-flows* is transferred from peer p_i to p_j on request of p_j, see Fig. 3. In our single-site monitoring approach p_j represents a home peer. Further, we can study the feeding relations of this home peer as source (see Fig. 2). G_V includes a capacity function $c : V_V \times V_V \longrightarrow \mathbb{R}_0^+$ and a flow function $f : V_V \times V_V \times T \longrightarrow \mathbb{R}_0^+$ which assigns to each flow $\phi(p_i, p_j)$ from p_i to p_j its intensity as flow rate $f(p_i, p_j, t) \geq 0$ and an attribute $t \in T = \{t_1, \ldots, t_h\}$

determining the flow type. Thus we can distinguish between different kinds of control and content flows.

Finally, the underlying TCP/UDP-IP transport network connecting the peers p_i, p_j by flow paths $p = w(p_i, p_j) = (e_1, \ldots, e_{n_p})$ along capacity constrained links (e_k, c_k) is taken into account(see Fig. 2).

The capacity function c of a link in the overlay network is determined by the bottle-neck capacity of the underlying path $w(p_i, p_j)$ in the router network and normally unknown. Thus, one has to measure it by appropriate bandwidth estimation techniques and to de-termine the length (i.e. hop count) $L[w(p_i, p_j)]$ and round trip delay $R[w(p_i, p_j)]$ of the route in the transport network by path-pinging the corresponding hosts of the peers. To get c for both directions, it is necessary to implement a measurement instrumentation in the peers

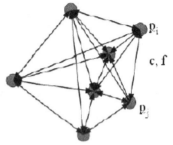

Fig. 3.   Flow   dissemination graph of a P2P model

feeding the home peer demanding an expensive instrumentation of the complete infrastructure, for instance, by PlanetLab experiments which is out of scope.

In 2007 and during the second quarter of 2009 we have performed measure-ment studies to collect representative traces of Joost, Zattoo, PPLive and Sop-Cast sessions covering both a wired and a wireless access to the Internet. The used test bed of the latter campaign has been developed to study the basic oper-ation of the P2PTV streaming system SopCast in the typical home environment of a German customer (cf. [4]). Traces with volumes of 136 to 138 MB arising from live-streamed soccer matches during SopCast sessions of approximately 30 minutes have been gathered at the portable host of the SopCast client. In our further illustrations we will use the corresponding packet flows extracted from this traces.

In summary, the modeling approach of an overlay structure yields a hierarchi-cal aggregated flow model of superimposed micro-flows in upward and downward direction to a home peer. Using the monitored data, it allows us to describe the exchange of chunk sequences among the peers by appropriate teletraffic models.

2.2   Determination of the P2P Flow Graph

In our measurement concept we have combined a passive single point monitoring of a P2P overlay network at a selected *home peer* p_1 with the active probing of the connections $\{p_1, p_j\} \in E_N$ to this observed peer p_1 in a time interval $[0, t]$. To identify the flow graph from the perspective of this single monitoring site, we apply trace routing at the IP layer of the transport paths $p = (e_1, \ldots, e_{n_p})$ starting from (or leading to) p_1. Further, we are able to estimate dynamically the available bandwidth $c = \min\{c_i \mid e_i, i = 1, \ldots, n_p\}$ of the path p along its constituting links e_i with the inferred (uplink) capacities c_i.

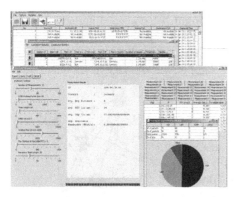

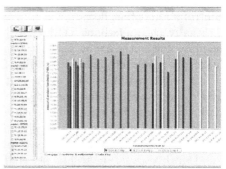

Fig. 4. Path probing   **Fig. 5.** Visualization of a bandwidth estimate

Since an end-to-end monitoring approach with two active probing and evaluating points is not available for bandwidth estimation, we have integrated the sender based approach implemented by the tool *Pathneck* (cf. [6]).

The individual flows of multimedia content feeding the home peer or fed by the latter have to be identified in the collected traces by post-processing steps. For this purpose, the flows can be specified as sequence of related IP packets determined by the conventional 5-tuples (A_s, P_s, A_d, P_d, pr) of the source and destination addresses A_s, A_d, the corresponding ports P_s, P_d and the related protocol identifier pr. They characterize the endpoints of a TCP or UDP transport connection along a path p, segment and assemble the packet sequences into flows based on various timeout methods, e.g. a fixed elapsed time determining flow expiration. Within a set of traces we have to derive the latter structures. We can, for instance, apply the corresponding C and Perl functions like *crl_flow* of the flows stack software implemented by the universal CAIDA suite *CoralReef* for passive Internet traffic monitors (cf. [7]). It offers the capability to determine the flow length, FlowType and CounterType of the packet streams in time intervals of predefined fixed length and to store it into Tables as well as to get access to the data and process them efficiently (cf. [7]). By appropriate filtering a flow analysis generates lists of detected flows within a P2P session of a home peer including the packet and volume statistics of each flow. Further, we can calculate the instantaneous traffic rates $\lambda_{j,i}(t) = \lim_{\Delta t \to 0} \frac{1}{\Delta t} \mathbb{P}\{N_{j,i}(t + \Delta t) - N_{j,i}(t) = 1 \mid N_{j,i}(t), \sigma(t)\}$ that are related to the packet counting process $N_{j,i}(t)$ of a flow $\phi(p_j, p_i)$ by the ratio of the observed number of packets in a finite interval of length $\Delta t > 0$ (based on the past history $\sigma(t)$ of the packet arrivals in $[0, t]$). Additionally, a flow selection arising from a set of most active peers by Table operations, flow aggregation into superimposed streams to a home peer, the construction of an IP-matrix table or the mapping of addresses to countries are possible, too (cf. [7]). This functionality has been provided by a virtual machine encapsulating the corresponding functions of CoralReef.

We have further integrated into our concept the capability to investigate flows within peer-to-peer sessions by adequate inspection techniques using empirical statistical characteristics like histograms (see Figs. 4, 5). We are also able to analyze the geographical distribution of the peer population feeding a monitored home peer.

2.3 Integration of Measurement and Analysis by the Tool Atheris

The concept has been used to develop the new versatile, extensible JAVA measurement and analysis tool Atheris based on a modular object-oriented software design. It has been implemented both for a Linux and Windows OS (see Fig. 6). The Linux version is built on top of libpcap and its Java wrapper Jpcap and integrates an adjusted C version of the bandwidth estimation tool Pathneck. The Windows version relies on WinPcap, Jpcap, and a Java based implementation of the bandwidth estimation system.

The major advantage of Atheris arises form the possibility to simultaneously monitor and analyze in an on-line manner P2P applications and to probe the dissemination paths p to a home peer. One key analysis feature concerns the capability to estimate the available bandwidth c of specific paths p and to inspect interactively selected traffic flows $\phi(p_j, p_i, t)$ of a certain type t.

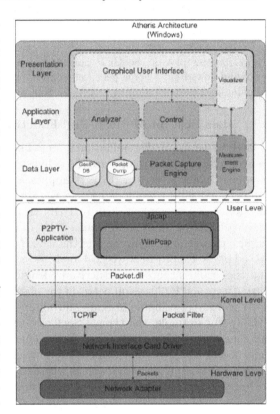

Fig. 6. Design of Atheris

3 Analysis and Teletraffic Modeling of P2P Flows

We show in the following section that single site observations in peer-to-peer networks can already reveal many details about the operational characteristics of a dissemination system despite all limitations of this approach (cf. [4], [15]).

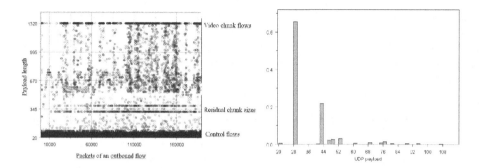

Fig. 7. Scatter plot of the UDP payload (in bytes) of frames of the superimposed outbound flows from a home peer (left) and a histogram of the UDP payload of all its signaling packets (right) during a typical SopCast session

3.1   Identification of Mesh-Pull Functions

A modern mesh-pull dissemination system like SopCast establishes a dense peer-to-peer mesh network to operate the delivery of the multimedia content in terms of smaller chunks (cf. [4], [15]). It applies a pull mechanism to distribute the content among all peers looking to a certain live TV channel or recorded video stream. SopCast employs mainly UDP as transport protocol to perform the topology discovery and maintenance tasks of the peer-to-peer mechanism as well as the control and delivery tasks of the video content dissemination among the involved peers. Empirical statistical analysis based on scatter plots and histograms and the visual inspection of the frame lengths of the packet flows instantiated during a typical P2P session between the observed client and the communicating peers can reveal valuable insights on the functioning of a mesh-pull system (see Fig. 7). For example, the typical SopCast session data depicted in Fig. 7 show the characteristic footprints of the frame length at 62, 70, 84, 88, 90, 94 bytes for control and 1362 bytes for content flows with a UDP payload of 20, 28, 42, 46, 48, 52 and 1320 bytes in agreement with [15]. A flow-based analysis is required to study the intrinsic structure of typical flows (cf. [4]).

3.2   Hierarchical Structure of a P2P Session

Overlay networks normally embed a home peer requesting a video stream into a dense mesh of feeding peers to guarantee a reliable and timely supply of chunk sequences to the streaming engine of a host. For instance, our analysis has revealed that SopCast clients are typically connected to up to thousand different peers during the lifetime of a session Therefore, it is necessary to investigate the preference relationship among the peer flows to understand the inherent hierarchical structure of the mesh-pull topology. One can use as metric the number of transferred packets of all active flows or those feeding the home peer, and the intensity or the volume of these flows depicted on a logarithmic scale.

The first criterion, for example, is simple to monitor and allows us to distinguish three local levels of peers associated with a home peer $p_1 \in V_V$ during

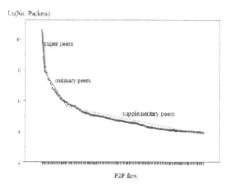

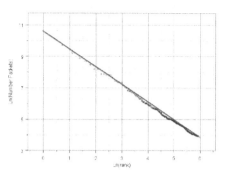

Fig. 8. Classification of peer relations based on flows feeding a home peer

Fig. 9. Rank-frequency plot of flows feeding a home peer

a session, namely his individual *super peers*, *ordinary peers* and *supplementary peers* (see Fig. 8). The investigation of the transferred accumulated volumes among the peers of the flow graph G_V, in particular the number of packets and the byte volumes flowing inbound and outbound to a home peer reveal the hierarchical structure of the overlay. In our SopCast session example it is illustrated by a home peer p_1 at 10.59.1.106 whose inbound traffic is generated by $n = 375$ superimposed flows from distinct feeders p_i.

If we arrange the n flows according to the number of exchanged packets on a logarithmic scale, we can realize the hierarchy of the peer classes. Interpreting the relative number of transferred packets as frequency f_i to select a feeder p_i, we can model the ranked selection process by a versatile heavy-tailed distribution of a random variable (r.v.) Y on the integers $\mathbb{N}$. It should obey a distribution function (df) of a generalized Zipf type. We may choose, for instance, a special case of the zero-truncated *Lerch distribution* with probability mass function (pmf)

$$p_k = \mathbb{P}\{Y = k\} = C \cdot \frac{p^k}{(a + k)^\alpha} , \qquad k \in \mathbb{N}, \tag{1}$$

the parameters $a > -1$, $p \in (-1, 1]$, and the tail coefficient $\alpha \in \mathbb{R}$. The normalization constant $C = [p\Phi(p, a + 1, \alpha)]^{-1}$ is defined in terms of the Lerch' transcendent $\Phi(p, a, \alpha) = \sum_{k=0}^\infty p^k \cdot (a + k)^{-\alpha}$, (cf. [2], [16]). Selecting the parametrization $p = 1, a \geq 0, \alpha > 1$, we get the Zipf-Mandelbrot df $\mathbb{P}\{Y = k\} = C \cdot (a + k)^{-\alpha}$, $k \in \mathbb{N}, C^{-1} = \Phi(1, a + 1, \alpha)$ and with the restriction $a = 0$ the well-known Zipf law

$$\mathbb{P}\{Y = k\} = C \cdot \frac{1}{k^\alpha} , \quad k \in \mathbb{N}, \quad C^{-1} = \Phi(1, 1, \alpha). \tag{2}$$

If we plot the rank-frequency relationship of the relative number f_i of packets of all inbound flows $\phi(p_i, p_1)$ transferred from a peer p_i to the home peer p_1 on a log-log scale, we can identify in this case (2) a linear relation between $\ln f_i$ and $\ln i$ of the related ranks i of the feeders p_i, see Fig. 9. Thus, a pmf of Zipf type

(2) adequately describes the local hierarchical peer structure seen by the home peer in our SopCast session.

If we interpret the transferred number of packets of a flow $\phi(p_i, p_1)$ as realization x_i of an equivalent income $X_i \in \mathbb{R}$ of the feeding peer $p_i, i \in \{1, \ldots, n\}$, we can represent the P2P model of a session by a corresponding heavy-tailed physical model of Pareto type with a r.v. X and its sample $\{X_1, \ldots, X_n\}$ (cf. [11]). We denote the distribution function of this Pareto model associated with the Zipf ranking law by

$$F(x) = \int_{x_0}^{\infty} f(x)dx = \mathbb{P}\{X \le x\} = 1 - Cx^{-\beta} = 1 - \left(\frac{x}{x_0}\right)^{-\beta} \tag{3}$$

with $x \ge x_0$ and tail index $\beta = 1/\alpha$.

The corresponding $1 - p$ quantile function of this Pareto model $x_p = F^{-1}(x_0, p, \beta) = \left(\frac{p}{C}\right)^{-1/\beta} = x_0 \cdot p^{-1/\beta}$ can be used to define the local classes of the feeding peers. Taking, e.g., the 2.5% or 5% and 10% or 20% levels for p, their quantiles $x_{0.025}, x_{0.5}, x_{0.1}, x_{0.2}$ specify the break points of the local classes of super peers, ordinary and supplementary peers associated with a home peer.

Using the transferred numbers of packets $x_1 \ge x_2 \ldots \ge x_n$ of the flows or approximating the pmf $p_i = \mathbb{P}\{Y = i\}$ by the empirical values $\{f_i, i = 1, \ldots, n\}$ of the n flows, we can estimate the tail index β by Hill's estimate

$$\widehat{\beta} = \left[\frac{1}{n-1}\left(\sum_{k=1}^{n-1} \ln(\frac{x_i}{x_n})\right)\right]^{-1} = \left[\frac{1}{n-1}\sum_{k=1}^{n-1}\ln(x_i) - \ln(x_n)\right]^{-1}$$

or in terms of Newman's estimate [11] $\widehat{\alpha} = \frac{1}{n}\sum_{k=1}^{n}\ln(\frac{f_i}{f_{\min}})$ where $f_{\min} = f_n$ represents the minimal measured value (cf. [11]).

In our Sopcast example it follows $x_0 = 51$, $\beta = 1.2 > 1$ and, thus, the mean $\mathbb{E}(X) = \beta x_0/(\beta - 1) = 306$ exists. Based on this Pareto model (3) of the peer preference relation the median is determined by $x_{1/2} = 51 \cdot 2^{1/\beta} = 90.87$.

Applying the size-weighted df

$$W(x_p) = \frac{\int_{x_p}^{\infty} xf(x)dx}{\int_{x_0}^{\infty} xf(x)dx} = (\frac{x_p}{x_0})^{-(\beta-1)}, \tag{4}$$

size-count disparity issues can be studied. It means that the fraction of those packets sent by the most active part of the peers p_i is specified in terms of (4) by the ratio of the packet load of the fraction of flows exceeding level x_p to the total packet load. Hence, the most active $p \cdot 100$ % of the flows determine the fraction $W(x_p)$ of the sent packets by means of the $1 - p$th quantile x_p, i.e. $1 - F(x_p) = p \in (0, 1)$, in terms of $W(x_p) = p^{(\beta-1)/\beta}$, related to the Lorenz curve (cf. [11]).

In our SopCast example we get $W(x_{0.5}) = 2^{-(\beta-1)/\beta} = 0.89$. It means that 89 % of the mean packet load are sent by the 188 most active flows. For the top 10 flows we get $p = 10/375 = 0.0266$ and $W(x_{0.0266}) = 0.0266^{0.2/1.2} = 0.546$, i.e more than half of the packets are sent by the top 10 flows. The top 20% of

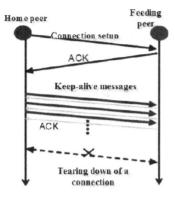

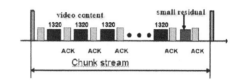

Fig. 10. SopCast connection setup

Fig. 11. Chunk stream of video content (see also [15])

the flows, i.e. 75 out of 375, achieve an activity ratio of $W_{x_{0.2}} = 0.76$ of the issued packets which confirms the 80/20 rule of heavy-tailed modeling (cf. [11]). In summary, we see that the first group with around 2.6 % of the flows provides a bit more than 54 % of the number of packets exchanged with the home peer and consists of less than 11 peers with high upload capacity, the second group of the top 20% of the flows excluding top 10 offers additionally 22 % of the packet load and the third group the residual less than 24 %. (see Fig. 8).

3.3   Teletraffic Analysis of a Dominant Packet Flow

One can study the UDP flows during a P2PTV session from the perspective of the initiating home peer p_1. The investigations confirm that first several control flows

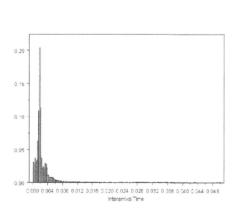

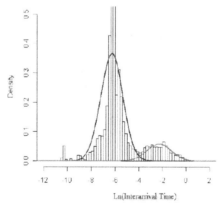

Fig. 12. Packet inter-arrival times arising from the downward flow of a dominant super peer

Fig. 13. Approximation of the packet inter-arrival times on a logarithmic scale

are instantiated for the initial opening of several connections to the ordinary and super peers indicated during registration in the downloaded peer list (see Fig. 10, cf. [15]). After the establishment of the neighborhood graph the communication on the flow graph is started implying the simultaneous existence of several flows $\phi(p_j, p_1)$. The latter are used to exchange video chunks between the monitored home peer p_1 and its neighbors p_j. Each flow consists of multiple consecutive packet sequences, i.e. micro-flows, and comprises a pair of a video chunk request on the uplink and the requested chunk packets on the downlink (cf. [4]). These pairs can be identified by a request packet with a frame length of 88 bytes which decomposes the incoming flow of a certain peer p_j into several chunk sequences (cf. [15]). They are answered by video contents with a maximal frame packet length of 1362 byte, i.e. 1320 bytes UDP payload, and acknowledged by p_1 with packets of 28 byte UDP payload, see Fig. 11. We suspect that the latter message applies a TCP semantics calling the next requested video block and acknowledges all correctly received previous ones. Exchanged between the feeding peers p_j and p_1, these flows create the superimposed inbound flow to the home peer p_1.

If we look into the downward flows and sort them according to their contribution we can recognize a dominant super peer at the IP address 150.237.180.164. The analysis of its packet inter-arrival times at the normal scale does not provide much structure whereas a logarithmic transformation can reveal its compositional character (see. Figs. 12, 13). If one disregards the small correlation up to lags 100 among the packets (see. Fig. 14), one can approximate the inter-arrival time of such a dominant downward flow by a recurrent stream whose packet inter-arrival time follows a mixture of two log-normal distributions (see. Fig. 13). It enables the development of appropriate simple teletraffic models of P2P traffic at the IP packet level by renewal

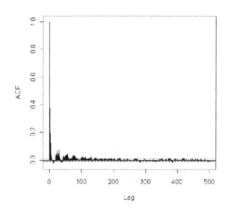

Fig. 14. ACF of packet inter-arrival times arising from the downward flow of a dominant super peer

streams with independently marked packet lengths that are derived from the histogram estimates of the IP datagram length with an 80% atom at 1348 bytes and several atoms of the control packets determined by a histogram estimate (see Fig. 7).

4   Conclusions

Responding to the rapid deployment of multimedia applications provided by peer-to-peer overlay structures, we have presented a comprehensive concept integrating modeling, measurement, and teletraffic analysis of peer-to-peer traffic flows at the packet and session levels. A first version of this concept has been implemented in the JAVA tool Atheris on Windows and LINUX operating systems. It incorporates passive and active measurements at a single point in the overlay network. The data analysis focuses on the identification, data extraction and inspection of flows upward and downward to an observed home peer applying corresponding functions of CoralReef. We have illustrated the latter concept by traffic characteristics of individual streams issued by feeding peers in a SopCast overlay network.

We are convinced that our integrated monitoring and analysis approach can provide a deeper insight into the dynamics of P2P multimedia applications and support the rapid development of appropriate teletraffic models at the packet and session levels as well as at the structural level of the overlay.

References

1. Ali, S., Mathur, A., Zhang, H.: Measurement of commercial peer-to-peer live video streaming. In: Proc. of ICST Workshop on Recent Advances in Peer-to-Peer Streaming, Waterloo, Canada (2006)
2. Aksenov, S.V., Savageau, M.A.: Some properties of the Lerch family of discrete distributions. University of Michigan, Ann Arbor (February 2008)
3. Ciullo, D., et al.: Understanding P2P-TV systems through real measurements. In: Proc. GLOBECOM 2008, pp. 2297–2302. IEEE Computer Society, Los Alamitos (2008)
4. Eittenberger, P., Krieger, U.R., Markovich, N.M.: Measurement and Analysis of Live-Streamed P2PTV Traffic. In: Czachórski, T. (ed.) Performance Modelling and Evaluation of Heterogeneous Networks, Proc. HET-NETs 2010, Zakopane, Poland, January 14-16 (2010)
5. Hei, X., Liang, C., Liang, J., Liu, Y., Ross, K.W.: A measurement study of a largescale P2P IPTV system. IEEE Tran. on Multimedia 9(8), 1672–1687 (2007)
6. Hu, N., Steenkiste, P.: Evaluation and Characterization of Available Bandwidth Probing Techniques. IEEE Journal on Selected Areas in Communications 21, 879–894 (2003)
7. Keys, K., et al.: The Architecture of CoralReef: An Internet Traffic Monitoring Software Suite. Coral Reef Documentation, CAIDA (2001),
   http://www.caida.org/tools/measurement/coralreef/doc/doc/index.html
8. Krieger, U.R., Schweßinger, R.: Analysis and Quality Assessment of Peer-to-Peer IPTV Systems. In: Proc. 12th Annual IEEE International Symposium on Consumer Electronics (ISCE2008), Algarve, Portugal, April 14-16 (2008)
9. Liu, F., Li, Z.: A Measurement and Modeling Study of P2P IPTV Applications. In: Proc. of the 2008 International Conference on Computational Intelligence and Security, vol. 1, pp. 114–119 (2008)
10. Markovich, N.M., Krieger, U.R.: Statistical Analysis and Modeling of Skype VoIP Flows. Special Issue Heterogeneous Networks: Traffic Engineering and Performance Evaluation, Computer Communications (submitted)
11. Newman, M.E.J.: Power laws, Pareto distributions and Zipf's law. Contemporary Physics 46, 323–351 (2005)
12. Peltotalo, J., et al.: Peer-to-peer streaming technology survey. In: Proc. of the Seventh International Conference on Networking ICN '08, pp. 342–350. IEEE Computer Society, Washington (2008)

13. Sentinelli, A., Marfia, G., Gerla, M., Kleinrock, L., Tewari, L.: Will IPTV ride the peer-to-peer stream? IEEE Communications Magazine 45(6), 86–92 (2007)
14. Silverston, T., et al.: Traffic analysis of peer-to-peer IPTV communities. Computer Networks 53(4), 470–484 (2009)
15. Tang, S., Lu, Y., Hernández, J.M., Kuipers, F.A., Van Mieghem, P.: Topology dynamics in a P2PTV network. In: Fratta, L., Schulzrinne, H., Takahashi, Y., Spaniol, O. (eds.) IFIP-TC 6. LNCS, vol. 5550, pp. 326–337. Springer, Heidelberg (2009)
16. Zörnig, P., Altmann, G.: Unified representation of Zipf distributions. Computational Statistics & Data Analysis 19, 461–473 (1995)

An Experimental Evaluation of Packet-Level Measurements of Hidden Traffic Load

José Núñez-Martínez[1], Marc Portoles-Comeras[1], Albert Cabellos-Aparicio[2],
Daniel López-Rovira[2], Josep Mangues-Bafalluy[1], and Jordi Domingo-Pascual[2]

[1] Centre Tecnològic de Telecomunicacions de Catalunya
Castelldefels (Barcelona), Spain
[2] Universitat Politècnica de Catalunya
Departament d'Arquitectura de Computadors
Barcelona, Spain

Abstract. Hidden traffic interference has been identified as an important source of network instabilities in dense wireless network deployments. This paper follows recent research results that relate packet loss and hidden traffic interference and explores, through extensive experimentation, the possibility to infer hidden traffic load using loss measurements in practical WLAN deployments. Furthermore, we present a preliminary tool able to provide online estimates of the hidden traffic load combining active and passive measurements.

Keywords: Wireless, Measurements, Hidden traffic, Experimental.

1 Introduction

WLAN deployments have spread at an unprecedented pace during the last years. The high availability of off-the-shelf hardware and software solutions and the configuration flexibility that they offer have driven the use of IEEE 802.11 devices in multiple and varied scenarios.

However, as a side consequence of this success, it is common to find multiple wireless devices or WLAN deployments coexisting in shared spaces. As a result, the interference between WLAN transmissions has been identified as an important source of unexpected problems in wireless networks. This has been specially remarked and studied in the context of wireless mesh networks (e.g. [1],[2]) where it highly increases the complexity of tasks such as routing (e.g. [4], [5]). However, the undesirable effects of interference also extend to traditional WLAN access networks, specially in dense urban areas or offices, where it has fostered the development of strategies for channel and power allocations (e.g. [3]).

This paper focuses on the measurement of hidden traffic interference from a packet level perspective. We consider as hidden interference those transmissions that are not considered (i.e. sensed) harmful from a sender-side perspective when transmitting a packet, but that lead to losing this packet at the receiving side

E. Osipov et al. (Eds.): WWIC 2010, LNCS 6074, pp. 315–326, 2010.

of the communication. Note here that the study does not restrict to a particular interference model [8], but considers the measurement of hidden interfering transmissions from a generic perspective.

More specifically, the paper studies the inter-relation that exists between packet losses and the presence of hidden transmission and takes base in our previous work [9]. In [9] we used renewal theory arguments to show how the losses of a probing packet sequence can be used to measure (infer) the actual hidden traffic load affecting the communication between a pair of nodes. We provided expressions of the bias that such a measure presents and suggested methods to avoid it.

In this paper we extend our previous work and we present extensive experiments validating the assumptions taken in a wide range of scenarios. Our experiments confirm that loss samples are biased measurements of hidden traffic, and that this bias can be quite large, eventually. The experiments serve also to analyze the use of simple estimators to measure hidden traffic in practical scenarios. Finally the paper presents a preliminary tool to gather online measurements of hidden traffic load.

The results of this study provide fundamental insights to understand some of the results obtained in related literature (e.g. [1], [6]). From a use case perspective, the approach presented here can be used to model the effects of hidden traffic interference on those routing metrics that rely on active probing of wireless channels [2] (e.g. ETX and ETT), and to tune WLAN optimization strategies that rely on loss characterization [7].

2   The Interrelation between Probing Losses and Hidden Traffic Load

The study presented in [9] reveals how packet losses constitute, in fact, biased samples of hidden traffic load. Let us denote as $U(t)$ the process describing the *busy/idle* state of a wireless channel. If this channel utilization is hidden to a probing station, that sends probing packets at instants $\{T_n\}$, the *successful/lost* transmissions of these probing packets constitutes a sample of the hidden traffic load such that,

$$U_n = U(T_n) = \begin{cases} 1 & \text{probe packet n is lost} \\ 0 & \text{probe packet n is received} \end{cases} \tag{1}$$

Taking the long term hidden traffic utilization as $u_r = \lim_{t \to \infty} P[U(t) = 1]$, and assuming that the sequence of probing arrivals $\{T_n\}$ follows a Poisson distribution, the study in [9] reveals how the limiting average of the probability of losing a packet is biased with respect to the channel utilization. This can be expressed as

$$\lim_{n \to \infty} P[U_n = 1] = u_r + \varepsilon(T_p), \tag{2}$$

where $\varepsilon(T_p)$ is the bias term and depends on T_p, the time that it takes to transmit the probing packets over the air.

2.1 Building Loss Based Estimators of Hidden Traffic Load

The previous results provide fundamental insights that can be used to develop packet probing based estimators of the hidden channel utilization. Here we review two basic approaches that help illustrating the impact of the bias term.

Following the definitions in the paper, a sample-mean estimator of the hidden traffic utilization based on the losses of a Poisson sequence, can be defined as

$$\widehat{u}_s(T_p) = \frac{1}{N} \sum_{i=0}^{N-1} U_i = u_r + \varepsilon(T_p) + w, \tag{3}$$

where N samples are used for the estimation and where w denotes the noise associated to the measure (assumed with a zero mean and independent of the hidden traffic). As it can be seen the sample mean constitutes, in fact, a biased estimator of the hidden traffic utilization.

Another important result of [9] is that it shows that when T_p is sufficiently small, $\varepsilon(T_p)$ can be modeled as being linear with respect to T_p. As a consequence, the following proposed estimator uses two different probing sizes $T_p^1 > T_p^2$ to obtain a (linear approximation) based unbiased estimation of the utilization,

$$\widehat{u_r}(T_p^1, T_p^2) = \frac{\widehat{u}_s(T_p^2)T_p^1 - \widehat{u}_s(T_p^1)T_p^2}{T_p^1 - T_p^2}. \tag{4}$$

Next sections provide extensive experimental results validating, in practical cases, the statements of this section.

3 Experimentation Setup

This section describes the methodology employed to carry out experiments. Precisely, we have used a controlled experimentation platform called EXTREME Testbed®[13] and a sniffer attached to a real operational WLAN network.

3.1 Experimentation Platform

All the experiments were carried out using the EXTREME Testbed ® [13] deployed at CTTC. This is a multi-purpose networking experimental platform featuring high automation capabilities that support automatic execution of the experiments, data collection and data processing.

The EXTREME testbed is composed of a cluster of computer nodes. All these nodes are Pentium 4 PCs with a 3GHz processor, 512MB of RAM memory, and running Linux with kernel 2.6.27. Every node can be equipped with up to two wireless Network Interface Cards (NICs). The type of wireless NIC employed for the experiments is the LevelOne WNC-0300, which is based on the Atheros 11b/g chipset. The automated experiment setup in EXTREME makes an extensive use of the wireless extensions API [14] to configure and control wireless devices. Specifically, the Madwifi driver [10] supports this API and controls LevelOne cards.

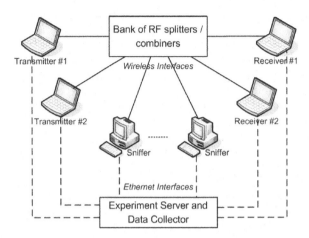

Fig. 1. Setup of EXTREME Testbed Ⓡ

Since the main objective of this study is devoted to study interference due to hidden nodes, the testbed setup was designed as to minimize the effects of channel propagation on the measurements. To this aim, all the communications between wireless devices are done through coaxial wires, and all wireless devices are connected to a central bank of splitters and combiners (see Figure 1). This bank of splitters replicates with very low attenuation (in comparison to open-air propagation) all signal inputs in each of its ports to the rest of ports. The bank of splitters and combiners is composed of minicircuit ZX10-4-27 splitters (with 4 ports) and minicircuit ZFSC-2-10G splitters (with 2 ports).

3.2 Traces from a Campus Network

We have also gathered data from a production WLAN AP belonging to a real university campus network. The traffic has been collected using a Linux box (PIV-2GB RAM) equipped with an Atheros card running MadWifi drivers [10] in monitor mode. In particular, we have collected traffic in the following scenarios[1]:

- *Filetransfer_far:* In this scenario, a contending machine was setup to download a large file from a remote server located at many hops from the campus network.
- *Filetransfer_close:* This scenario mimics the previous one, but the remote server was located in the same autonomous system than the campus network.
- *P2P:* In this scenario, the contending node was running a popular P2P application (BitTorrent).
- *Contending_n:* In this final scenario, we setup n contending nodes (ranging from 1 to 4) running a wide set of applications (filetransfer, e-mail clients, P2P...). This setup reproduces a WLAN link under heavy load.

---

[1] The traces used can be downloaded from [11].

4   Experiment Observations to Validate the Model

This section validates some of the statements presented in the previous section and in [9]. First we validate, in a controlled environment, the inter-relation between loss and hidden traffic. Second, we use measurements gathered in an operational campus network to show that the renewal theory assumptions taken in [9] correctly model practical wireless channel utilization. Third, we provide some results that relax the requirement to use Poisson probing in order to gather accurate measurements.

4.1   Validation in a Controlled Environment

We have used the EXTREME platform (see subsection 3.1) to study the inter-relation between packet loss and hidden traffic load in the absence of propagation losses.

Figure 2 reports the measurements of hidden traffic load, for different rates of hidden traffic, when using the sample mean and the estimation based on linear interpolation. The figure has been generated using more than 15k loss samples for each measurement point. To gather these measurements we have used a probing sequence with packets of 128 bytes in the sample mean case, and an additional sequence with packets of 64bytes in the linear approximation case. Hidden traffic is sent at a phy rate of 12Mbps, with Poisson distribution. Probing packets are sent at 6Mbps with Poisson distribution and broadcast.

As it can be seen, first, the sample mean provides biased estimates of the actual hidden traffic load. Second, when using the packet sizes we have chosen, the linear approximation of the bias is consistent and provides accurate estimates of the utilization using the linear approximation.

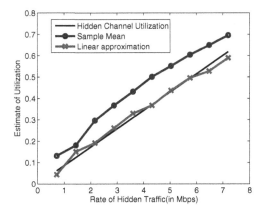

Fig. 2. Measurements of utilization using probing losses in a controlled environment

4.2   Validation of the Model Assumptions on WLAN Traffic

The purpose of this subsection is to validate some of the assumptions taken in section 2 and to analyze the accuracy of the proposed estimators using the datasets described in subsection 3.2, that have been collected in an operational campus network. Specifically, we are interested in obtaining realistic figures of the distributions of *busy/idle* states of channel occupancy in operational networks. We take the downlink traffic transmitted through the monitored AP as hidden to an eventual monitoring node and study whether the assumptions hold in such a case. Using the datasets we measure the actual traffic load and the measure that would be obtained using loss samples from an eventual probing sequence with mean inter-arrival time of 100ms.

Figures 3 and 4 show the results of these experiments. Please note that for readability we do not show all the results, the interested reader can find the remaining ones in [11]. Left plots show the accuracy of the sample-mean estimators (eq. 3) while right plots show the accuracy of the linear approximation proposed to obtain unbiased measurements (eq. 4).

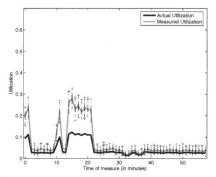
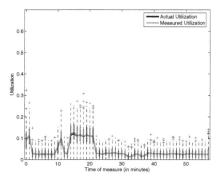

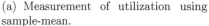

(a) Measurement of utilization using sample-mean.

(b) Measurement of utilization using un-biased estimator.

Fig. 3. Comparison of the accuracy of sample-mean vs unbiased estimator (filetransfer_far scenario)

From the figures we can see that all the experiments validate our analytical model, and show the large bias incurred by sample-mean based estimators. This bias is present in all the cases and may grow up to 50% in some scenarios. Concerning the linear approximation (right side of the plots) the experiments shows that it performs remarkably well. This also confirms that the linear assumption taken holds with a wide range of traffic profiles and with different amounts of contending (hidden) stations. It is worth noting here that the plots also reveal the higher variance of the (approximately) unbiased estimator in comparison to the pure sample-mean measure.

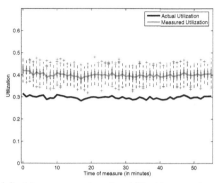 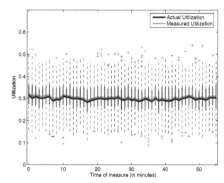

(a) Measurement of utilization using sample-mean.

(b) Measurement of utilization using unbiased estimator.

Fig. 4. Comparison of the accuracy of sample-mean vs unbiased estimator (contending_3 scenario)

4.3 Do We Really Need to Use Poisson Sequences?

One of the main assumptions taken in section 2 and used throughout the validation study is the use of Poisson probing sequence to sample channel use. The PASTA property associated to Poisson sequences guarantees the convergence of some of the findings and the accuracy of the estimators proposed. The objective of this section is to relax this assumption and show that channel utilization presents mixing properties [15] that allow using alternative probing patterns. Relaxing the Poisson assumption is useful in practice, as we will see in the next section, as it allows using, for example, *periodic* beacon broadcasts to get samples of hidden traffic utilization.

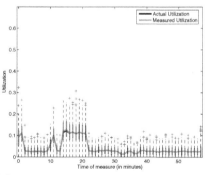 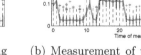

(a) Measurement of utilization using poisson probing (unbiased estimator).

(b) Measurement of utilization using periodic probing (unbiased estimator).

Fig. 5. Comparison of the accuracy of periodic vs. poisson probing (filetransfer_far scenario)

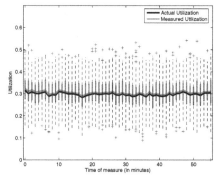
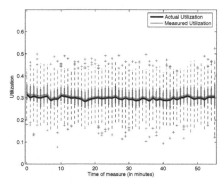

(a) Measurement of utilization using poisson probing (unbiased estimator).

(b) Measurement of utilization using periodic probing (unbiased estimator).

Fig. 6. Comparison of the accuracy of periodic vs. poisson probing (contending_4 scenario)

The hypothesis here is that although the sampling process is not poisson, the underlying traffic is mixing enough, and will produce similar results. For this we have repeated the experiments of the previous section but instead of using poisson probing, we use periodic probing. In particular each plots shows, in each case the accuracy of the proposed estimator using poisson probing (left) and periodic probing (right).

Figures 5 and 6 show the results for this experiment. Again, we only present the plots of the same scenarios than in the previous subsection, the interested reader can find the remaining ones in [11]. The results show that, for all the scenarios, the accuracy of the unbiased estimator is not affected by periodic probing and in fact, shows similar accuracy than when using poisson probing.

5   Design Options to Build a Tool to Measure Hidden Traffic Load

This section presents some preliminary observations on the design options to the design of a tool to obtain online measurements of hidden traffic load in practical scenarios.

5.1   Periodic Samples Using Beacon Frames

Beacon frames can be considered as periodic samples of the wireless channel. Indeed, in a vast majority of cases, Access Points send beacons with a periodic interval that comes in the TBTT field. As argued above in section the periodic nature of beacon broadcasts does not prevent their use, in a practical scenario, to gather samples of hidden traffic load. Note that the authors of [12] suggested previously the use of the TBTT field to gather information from beacon measurements.

We have implemented a tool that keeps track of the TBTT field in order to determine how many beacons might have been lost between two successive reception of beacon frames. However, as figure 7 reveals, beacon losses have to be handled with care, as APs are prone to reconfiguration procedures that may be easily mistook with periods of high traffic occupancy.

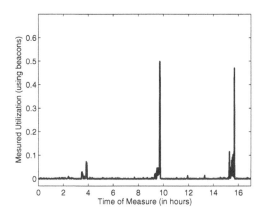

Fig. 7. Measurements of the beacon frame losses during night hours

5.2   Getting Samples Using Retry Counts

In order to obtain unbiased measurements of hidden traffic utilization we need packets of different sizes (and sufficiently small) that sample the occupancy of the wireless medium. However, generating broadcast frames without proper control of the WLAN network is generally a difficult task.

The solution that we investigate here takes advantage of the retry field present in the IEEE 802.11 packet header. In this case we propose the use of unicast packets as indicators of the presence of hidden traffic. The basic idea consists in that (1) a remote station sends packets of two different sizes to the monitoring stations. (2) the monitoring station determines how many packets are not successfully transmitted at their first attempt (i.e., they have their retry field to 1). Then, the packets with the retry field equal to 1 are used as indicators of frame losses, and thus, of hidden channel use.

Figure 8 shows the efficacy of using this method in a controlled environment. The figure plots the number of 128-byte packets that have not been successfully transmitted at their first attempt (sample mean) and a linear approximation of the hidden utilization using a second sequence of 64-byte long packets. As it can be seen the approach is accurate.

Figure 9 shows the results of applying retry based measurements to gather unbiased measurements of hidden traffic load in an operational environment.

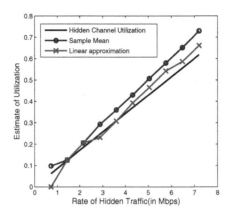

Fig. 8. Retry based measurements of hidden traffic in a controlled environment

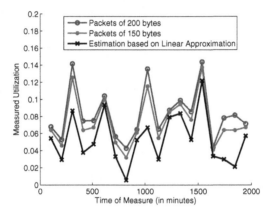

Fig. 9. Retry based measurements of hidden traffic in an operational network

5.3   Issues to Implement the Tool in Practice

There are a number of issues that difficult the implementation of a practical tool to measure the present of hidden traffic transmissions.

First, the solution to use unicast frames and retry counts suffers largely from adaptive mechanisms implemented in commercial WLANs. As an example, rate adaptation algorithms and variable retransmission strategies prevent the possibility to use a single value for T_p to be used in the estimation.

Second, channel propagation errors constitute an important source of distortion to the mechanisms introduced here. In many cases, channel propagation errors are more important than hidden transmissions which results in the impossibility to gather reliable measurements of hidden traffic load. A typical solution is to use low rate modulations to transmit probing packets in order to increase their reliability.

Finally, beacons present the desirable properties of being short and transmitted at a sufficiently low rate so that the impact of channel propagation is low. However, without having a certain level of control of a WLAN network, it is difficult to introduce additional broadcast transmissions to build unbiased estimators.

6   Conclusions

Hidden traffic interference has been identified as an important source of network instabilities in dense wireless network deployments. This paper explores the possibility to infer hidden traffic load using loss measurements in practical WLAN deployments. It takes base on [9], where we proposed an unbiased estimator for the hidden load interference. At present, existing estimators account for the hidden load computing the ratio of lost packets from a sequence of periodic probing and using a pure sample-mean estimator. In [9], we proposed an approximately unbiased estimator based on poisson sampling.

In this paper we have validated through extensive experimentation the validity of the assumptions taken in [9] along with the accuracy. The validation has been carried out both in a controled testbed (EXTREME® [13]) and using a dataset collected in an operational campus network. The results confirm the assumptions and show that the proposed estimator performs remarkably well. Further, the results also show that the proposed estimator can also operate when we sample the path using a periodic probing process, instead of a poisson one. This hypothesis has helped us to design a tool able to provide online estimates of the hidden traffic load combining active and passive measurements.

Acknowledgments. This work has been partially funded by the Spanish Ministry of Science and Innovation under grant number TEC2008-06826/TEC (project ARTICO), and by the Catalan Regional Government under grants 2009SGR-1140 and 2009SGR-940.

References

1. Padhye, J., Agarwal, S., Padmanabhan, V., Qiu, L., Rao, A., Zill, B.: Estimation of Link Interference in Static Multi-hop Wireless Networks. In: ACM/USENIX Internet Measurement Conference, IMC (2005)
2. Li, Y., Qiu, L., Zhang, Y., Mahajan, R., Zhong, Z., Deshpande, G., Rozner, E.: Effects of Interference on Wireless Mesh Networks: Pathologies and a Preliminary Solution. In: HotNets (2007)
3. Kauffmann, B., Baccelli, F., Chaintreau, A., Mhatre, V., Papagiannaki, K., Diot, C.: Measurement-Based Self Organization of Interfering 802.11 Wireless Access Networks. In: IEEE INFOCOM (2007)
4. Subramanian, A.P., Buddkihot, M.M., Miller, S.: Interference Aware Routing in Multi-Radio Wireless Mesh Networks. In: Proc. of IEEE WiMesh (2006)
5. Nuñez-Martinez, J., Mangues-Bafalluy, J.: A Survey on Routing Protocols that really Exploit Wireless Mesh Networks. Proc. of Journal of Communications (2010)

6. Ahmed, N., Ismail, U., Keshav, S., Papagiannaki, K.: Online estimation of RF interference. In: CoNEXT (2008)
7. Acharya, P., Sharma, A., Belding, E., Almeroth, K., Papagiannaki, K.: Rate Adaptation in Congested Wireless Networks through Real-Time Measurements. To appear in IEEE Transactions on Mobile Computing
8. Takai, M., Martin, J., Bagrodia, R.: Effects of wireless physical layer modeling in mobile ad hoc networks. In: MobiHoc (2001)
9. Portoles-Comeras, M., Sole, M., Nuez-Martinez, J., Cabellos-Aparicio, A., Mangues-Bafalluy, J., Domingo-Pascual, J.: Packet level measurement of hidden traffic interference in WLAN networks (2010) (submitted for publication)
10. MadWifi drivers, `http://madwifi.org`
11. WLAN Measurements, dataset and Technial report,
    `http://personals.ac.upc.edu/acabello/WLAN\_measurements/`
12. Vasudevan, S., Papagiannaki, K., Diot, C., Kurose, J., Towsley, D.: Facilitating access point selection in IEEE 802.11 wireless networks. In: Proceedings of the ACM SIGCOMM Internet Measurement Conference (IMC'05), p. 26 (2005)
13. EXTREME Testbed ® - System level testbed featuring IP mobility, CTTC,
    `http://www.cttc.es/en/projects/testbeds/project/EXTREME.jsp`
14. Wireless Extensions for linux,
    `http://www.hpl.hp.com/personal/JeanTourrilhes/Linux/`
15. Baccelli, F., Machiraju, S., Veitch, D., Bolot, J.: The Role of PASTA in Network Measurement. IEEE/ACM Transactions on Networking 17(4), 1340–1353 (2009)

0day Anomaly Detection Made Possible Thanks to Machine Learning

Philippe Owezarski, Johan Mazel, and Yann Labit

[1] CNRS; LAAS; 7 Avenue du colonel Roche, F-31077 Toulouse, France
[2] Université de Toulouse; UPS, INSA, INP, ISAE; LAAS; F-31077 Toulouse, France

Abstract. This paper proposes new cognitive algorithms and mechanisms for detecting 0day attacks targeting the Internet and its communication performances and behavior. For this purpose, this work relies on the use of machine learning techniques able to issue autonomously traffic models and new attack signatures when new attacks are detected, characterized and classified as such. The ultimate goal deals with being able to instantaneously deploy new defense strategies when a new 0day attack is encountered, thanks to an autonomous cognitive system. The algorithms and mechanisms are validated through extensive experiments taking advantage of real traffic traces captured on the Renater network as well as on a WIDE transpacific link between Japan and the USA.

Keywords: 0day anomaly detection, machine learning.

1 Introduction

Security in the Internet is a very important and strategic problem which raised and still raises significant research and engineering effort, but need to be continuously addressed. The main reason is that the threat in the Internet is moving fast: new kinds of attacks, worms, viruses appear almost every day, they use more and more advanced spreading and corruption strategies, and act so as to remain very hardly detectable. One of the problems then stands in detecting the new attacks (also called 0day - or 0d for short - attacks) the first time they are perpetrated. Current systems are unable of detecting such 0d attacks. When they are first observed, engineers first need to analyze them before searching for a detection and defense strategy, implement it, and finally deploy it. This is a reactive process which lets the network vulnerable for a too long period.

In this paper, we present our first work on designing new cognitive strategies and algorithms for detecting 0day attacks in the Internet. The idea is to design autonomous cognitive systems able to increase autonomously their knowledge database on attacks. As the object under concern in our research is the Internet, we will specifically focus on volume based DoS (Denial of Service) attacks which aim at decreasing network QoS (Quality of Service) and performance level by denying the access to network resources for legitimate users. In networking, such DoS attacks are part of a broader family of unwanted events called traffic

E. Osipov et al. (Eds.): WWIC 2010, LNCS 6074, pp. 327–338, 2010.

anomalies. We then aim at designing a new cognitive system which is able to autonomously classify anomalies in different categories. The idea is then to give the cognitive system the capability to analyze the anomaly for discovering whether it is legitimate or not, but also to autonomously extend the attack signature database of the related anomaly detection system (ADS) if the new encountered anomaly is classified by the system as an unknown attack. For this purpose, our algorithm relies on the use of machine learning techniques for autonomously issuing models of normal traffic, as well as attack signatures when attacks are encountered for the first time. This signature is then prone to be integrated in an associated defense system (whose description is out of the scope of this paper). This approach allows a significant reduction of the time the network is not protected against a new attack as it takes a short time to issue a new detection signature for classical IDS (Intrusion Detection System) or IPS (Intrusion Protection System) which can be immediately and automatically deployed.

The paper is organized as follows. Section 2 provides an overview on related work. Section 3 presents how the new detection and classification cognitive algorithm works, and justifies our choice of using unsupervised machine learning techniques. In Section 4, the validation data and methodology are presented, as well as the evaluation results. Section 5 then concludes the paper.

2   Related Work

There is now a large literature on the detection of network traffic anomalies. Most of the approaches analyze statistical variations of traffic volume (i.e. number of packets, bytes or new flows), traffic attributes (i.e. IP addresses and ports) distributions, or both, on a temporal or spatial manner. The anomalies can be observed from single links or network-wide data. Standard references include [3] [1] [9] [11], with some notable recent work as [13] [5] [4] [16]. Dimensionality reduction of aggregated traffic data has also received recent attention, and techniques like sketches [9] [13] [5] and principal components analysis [11] are very promising for online anomaly detection. Sketches based algorithms can detect low intensity anomalies and can identify the anomalous IP flows (something that might not be possible with techniques that operate only on the aggregated traffic or on origin-destination flows).

In this work, we base our research on the anomaly detection approach presented in [7]. It presents a two steps anomaly detection and classification algorithm that will be presented in section 3.1.

Some work has tried to apply machine learning techniques to anomaly or intrusion detection. Kuang and Zulkernine [10] used a modified KNN algorithm called CSI-KNN for Combined Strangeness and Isolation measure K-Nearest Neighbors. They perform supervised learning on the KDD dataset [8]. They use the feature provided by the dataset to generate two values (strangeness and isolation). These values are then processed to generate a graded confidence over the classification. Some papers push forward the use of machine learning with the goal of classifying automatically the traffic [12] or to discover new anomalies [6].

In [12], Lakhina et al. use clustering on the entropy of several parameters (IP addresses and ports). This approach groups anomalies with similar characteristics, but does not distinguish between different types of anomalies. Network operators still need to manually check each anomaly, but, if enough pre-labeled anomalies are part of a given cluster, they have a better way to prioritize between clusters than if no classification is done. In [6], Eskin et al. use unsupervised learning to detect new intrusions inside the KDD dataset. However, it remains a work mainly oriented on intrusion detection and it does not consider network anomalies. The authors even consider their work as inoperant in the case of Syn flood DDoS anomalies.

3   Application of Machine Learning to 0day Anomaly Detection

3.1   Two Steps Approach

Because of the limits of both the profile and signature based approaches for detecting attacks and anomalies, a new trend deals with combining both of them in a two steps approach. In general, the flow of alarms provided by a signature based IDS is analyzed with a profile based method in order to detect anomalies in the alarm flow. Performance of such an approach is very low [17]. We therefore argue that it is necessary to combine both detection techniques in a two steps approach. But we do think that the right approach deals with first using the profile based technique in order to detect traffic profile anomalies. In that case, the detection thresholds are set with very pessimistic values in order to avoid false negatives. Then, we apply a signature based detection technique which has also the capability of classifying the anomalies. It then helps to eliminate false positives, but also, by classifying the detected anomalies, to identify the kind of anomaly as well as the intension behind the anomaly (legitimate or malicious).

This paper then relies on our NADA [7] anomaly detection tool which has been designed following this two steps approach principle. The criterias used for the detection step are very simple and rough: it computes the number of packets, the number of bytes and the number of SYN packets. It monitors the evolution of these criterias and if a significant change is discovered, it raises an alarm. When it is the case, the network traffic is then deeper analyzed and several attributes are built from, either the detection step, either some indices built on network packets fields. All these attributes are then used by the classification system. This system uses a set of signatures that use attributes directly linked to the packet headers and are thus easily understood by network operators. This is one of the key features of this system.

These signatures have been built through expert knowledge in the domain of network traffic anomalies. Therefore, human intervention is required for the creation and tuning of the signatures. The purpose of our method is to create these signatures automatically in order to build a system that would be able to work autonomously. In order to achieve this goal, we are using machine learning.

3.2   Representations of Traffic

In all the previous work that we are aware of [12,6], two possible representations of network traffic through unsupervised learning have been considered. In the first representation, the network traffic is represented by several classes and each class is associated with a part of the network traffic. This situation is shown in figure 1 (a) (each cluster represents a part of the network traffic (legitimate or anomalous) and in figure 1 (c) (each curve represents a class of traffic). In the other representation, each class is a part of the normal traffic and any isolated point (or outlier) is considered anomalous. In figure 1 (d), the gaussian curve is the normal traffic and any point located too far from this curve is anomalous. In figure 1 (b), one cluster represents the normal traffic and each outlier represents an anomaly (here, the isolated dots).

Fig. 1. Model with clusters (a), Model with one cluster and outliers (b), Model with one class (c), Model with two class (d)

3.3   Choice of Machine Learning Techniques

Supervised/semi-supervised learning presents limitations because their use implies that we have labelled data at our disposal, i.e., in this case, traces for which we know that, at a certain time and for a certain duration, an anomaly has occurred. This, of course, implies that the considered anomalies are known and characterized, what is completely opposed to the goal addressed in this paper: real-time discovery of *0day anomalies*.

Unsupervised learning does not present this limitation. In fact, its purpose is precisely to find structure inside unknown data. Therefore, unsupervised learning appears as the technique to use.

Among the unsupervised techniques, we need one able to identify all the classes of traffic and that can keep some understandable attributes. We will only consider dimensional reduction, density estimation and clustering as they appear as the three most represented techniques in the literature.

- Dimensional reduction
  The principle of dimensional reduction deals with projecting the data from a vector space of high dimensions to a vector space of low dimensions. In our case, it means that we would end up with a vector space with a basis built on vectors that would have no physical/concrete meaning. One of our goal being to keep some understandable attributes in order to have easy to understand and meaningful signatures (i.e. for expressing anomaly characteristics), the dimensional reduction is in clear contradiction with our requirements.

— Density estimation

Density estimation is a family of methods for "one-class" problems. Its objective is to estimate the distribution of a set of observations and then predict whether or not a new observation should be considered as an outlier or a "normal" member of the single class. Density estimation is an efficient technique to detect outliers if the normal traffic is a single class and anomalies are only outliers. On the other hand, density estimation is inoperant if it has to consider several classes or if some anomalies are represented as classes. We cannot guarantee any of these conditions, therefore, density estimation is not suited to our case as global traffic can consist of several traffic classes.

— Clustering

Cluster analysis or clustering is the assignment of a set of observations into subsets (called clusters) so that observations in the same cluster are similar under some chosen criterias.

Clustering does not have any of the limitations listed above: it keeps all the attributes in a clear and intelligible form and it can consider and analyze them without any limitation on the number of classes (in our case, the number of classes of traffic including both normal and anomalous ones). Based on our first experiences, we selected the clustering technique as it appears as the most adapted and promising form of unsupervised learning for our problem.

3.4   Discovering Unknown New Anomalies with Machine Learning

In the previous subsection, we established two facts. First, it is possible to represent the traffic inside a vector space built on attributes. Second, unsupervised learning is able to extract the structure of a dataset from its representation in a vector space.

The interest of the extracted structure is directly linked to the pertinence of the considered vector space, i.e. the considered attributes. In our case, this pertinence is also related to the choice of two parameters: first, the aggregation metric used to structure the vector space during the traffic processing which determines how the group of packets are built, and second, the attributes built from the aggregated traffic.

Signatures are most of the times using different attributes. This implies that for trying to find these new signatures from scratch, it is needed to search for new previously unused attributes. Therefore, the discovery of new types of anomaly seems to be heavily linked to the discovery of new pertinent attributes.

The method that we intend to use to find new anomaly signatures is to look for anomalous representations (i.e. clusters or outliers) in the representation of the network traffic inside new attributes. In order to do so, we intend to generate new attributes, systematically try to find anomaly representations to assess the presence of a new anomaly, and if it is the case, build the corresponding new signature.

The problem of creating new pertinent signatures can then be split into three tasks: first, process the network traffic, second, generate new attributes, and third, search for new anomalies inside combinations of generated attributes.

Traffic aggregation and processing. Aggregation of traffic is the first part of traffic data processing. It is an important function because it allows us to change the point of view on the network traffic by changing the aggregation criteria. In fact, by aggregating the traffic according to the destination address of the network traffic with a certain network mask, one aggregate traffic destined to a restrained number of destinations hosts. One can then find anomalies that are impacting a small number of destination addresses (in some case targets of attacks) no matter how many sources are involved. This enables us to target anomalous traffic such as DDoS (Distributed Denial of Service) attacks. Corollary, for searching anomalies having a few number of sources and paying attention to the number of destinations, i.e. network scan or SYN port scan for instance, aggregation through the source IP address is the aggregation criteria to use. Similarly, it is also needed to target anomalies linked to the port number. The port number can then be used as an important aggregation parameter.

Attribute generation

- Create new attribute
  Currently, considered attributes are built on the distribution of the values of fields of packet headers. Some attributes are even built from values obtained over two different packet fields. We generalize this construction by using two steps. First, process values over the distributions of values of packet fields of the layers network and transport of the OSI model (IP address, TCP/UDP ports source/destination, flags, ...). The operators used on the distributions will be simple: number of different elements, proportion of the biggest element over the total, ... Second, sweep all possible combinations of one or two elements of the previously generated values. Once the combinations are obtained, we generate the attribute. If the combination contain one value, then the value is turned into an attribute. If the combination contain two values, then, we process the ratio of the first value over the second. At the end, we obtain a set of attributes built over the packet headers.

  However, it is obvious that such a variety of possible combinations applied to a big number of packet fields will generate a huge amount of possible combinations. The next issue will be to eliminate the attributes that seem to be of less interest.
- Attribute interest assessment
  If we want to extract clusters/outliers from the data spaces, we will need attributes that have a quantity of information as significant as possible. If all the values of the parts of the traffic for the considered attribute are close from a certain value, the search for network classes or outliers inside this restricted space will be very complex and unreliable. Therefore, a first elimination of the attribute with poor interest seems relevant. Entropy is

the mathematical tool that will be used for the evaluation of the quantity of information contained in the considered attributes.

Anomaly search. After the attribute generation step, our algorithm have several attributes built on the packet fields. The next step is now to apply unsupervised learning in order to find new anomalies.

We intend to sweep all possible combinations of the previously generated attributes and search for anomalies inside each combination. As previously said, each combination of attributes can be used to build a vector space with a basis constituted of the attributes selected. Therefore, we search for the presence of an anomaly inside the chosen vector space.

There are two steps in the search for anomaly: first, characterization of the traffic in the chosen vector space, and then application of unsupervised learning according to the result of the first substep. These two steps will be repeated on each vector space and on each combinations of attributes.

– Characterization of the traffic in the chosen vector space
  In order to find a new anomaly, we try to find a pertinent representation of a 0day anomaly in a new vector space built from new attributes. This representation may be either a cluster or an outlier.

  For this anomaly detection step, we apply a clustering technique on the traffic. The result of this step gives us the structure of the network traffic.

  At this point, two cases arise. First, we obtain one cluster. By doing the assumption that the normal traffic is much more important in volume than the anomalous one, we deduce that the normal traffic is composed of the only found cluster. Therefore, in this case, anomaly detection will be using outlier detection.

  Second, we obtain several clusters: this means that the traffic is composed of several classes. However, nothing guarantees that one of these clusters is not actually an anomaly. This step will then require human intervention to manually identify the clusters between genuine and anomalous network traffic. As far as our statistical study have advanced (cf. 4.3), this case seems to be rare. Therefore, human intervention seems not to be needed. However, our study being statistical, we cannot guarantee that this case is totally irrelevant.

– Search for anomalies
  According to the results of the characterization of the network traffic, we use the appropriated unsupervised learning technique to search for a 0day anomaly and its associated signature. Several situations are possible. If all clusters belong to legitimate traffic, outlier detection will be applied in order to search for anomalies. If there are some anomalous clusters, we will still apply outlier detection because there might be other anomalies (represented as outlier) than the ones in the clusters. At this point, we are able to identify the legitimate and the anomalous network traffic and know wether there is a new anomaly inside the considered vector space or not.

If it is the case, the matter of building the new signature is simple. In fact, once the anomalousness of each cluster and the presence of outliers is assessed, a convex or concave hull is drawn at half-distance between the normal representation(s) of traffic and the anomalous one(s). To obtain the updated signatures in terms of thresholds on a specific attribute, the hull is projected onto each axis of the vector space. In order to improve the system, we also could keep the hull and use it as a unique multi-dimensional threshold.

4   Validation

4.1   Data

A proper statistical validation of anomaly detection procedures requires the use of data with known, documented anomalies which can serve as the ground truth. Data might be collected from a real network and labelled afterwards by expert network operators. This would generate a dataset with known real anomalies (i.e. anomalies that happened on the wild), but might be prone to human errors (i.e. network operators might manually misclassify an anomaly), and does not permit control over the anomalies' characteristics (e.g. their intensity). Generating such datasets is expensive and currently very few are publicly available. The other way to generate labelled data is to artificially produce anomalies in real or simulated networks. With this approach, anomalies can be fully documented and are not subject to misinterpretations. Characteristics of the anomalies can also be controlled (i.e. varying its intensity, duration, etc.) to permit evaluation under different settings. The drawback is that the anomalies might not be too representative of current occurrences. We use both types of datasets to validate our algorithm: the METROSEC project [15] traces with artificially created anomalies and the MAWI traffic repository [14] with anomalies seen in the wild.

The first part of the traces used during our experiments comes from the MAWI dataset. It is composed of 15 minutes packets traces collected daily at 2PM from a Japanese network called WIDE since 1999 to present. These traces are provided publicly after being anonymized and stripped of their payload data. These traces are undocumented, but the authors of [5] started to label anomalies found in this database (http://www.manaworld.org/wide/anomalies/). Traces used are from samplepoint-B which is a trans-Pacific link between Japan and the United States. Traffic on this link is mostly exchanged between Japanese universities and commercial ISPs and consistently contain anomalies [2].

The second part comes from the METROSEC project. These traces consist of real traffic collected on the French National Research and Education Network (RENATER) with simulated attacks performed using real DDoS attack tools. This dataset was created in the context of the METROSEC research project. Traces contain anomalies that range from very low intensity (i.e. less than 4% of normal traffic volume) to very high (i.e. more than 80%). The traces are fully documented with start and ending time of capture and attack, intensity, type and number of bots (i.e. attacking sources) of the attacks.

4.2   Methodology

We want to demonstrate that our system is able to find an unknown anomaly inside network traffic. The unknown aspect is to be considered from the point of view of the detection system: it means that the system has no a priori knowledge over this kind of anomaly.

In order to validate our approach, we plan to use an incremental implementation and validation of our algorithm. It will allow us to validate each part of our algorithm separately. The validation will then consist of two steps:

– First, we want to detect an anomaly, unknown by the system, inside a trace where we know that the anomaly is present, and build its signature. The only parameters given to the algorithm will be the attributes (and thus the vector space) that will be used to find the anomaly. This implies that we skip the steps of our algorithm related to attribute generation and attribute selection. Then, we apply our algorithm and search for an anomaly using only the attributes related to the targeted anomaly. Therefore, by looking at the right attributes inside a documented tracefile which contains the anomaly that will fit these chosen attributes, we are supposed to find it. We also extend this work to several types of anomalies with their appropriate attributes.
– Second, we want to validate the global behavior of our algorithm. In order to do so, we use a documented trace file with a known anomaly inside. We do not proceed to any restriction over the used attributes and use instead the attribute generation and attribute selection steps of our algorithm. The validation of this step will be the finding of (at least) the documented anomaly and maybe other undocumented anomalies.

4.3   Experimentations

We chose to focus ourselves on the detection of TCP SYN DDoS as if it was an unknown attack, i.e. without any prior knowledge other than the attributes used for its signature, in this case: #respdest (number of responsible destinations), spprop (ratio of the number of SYN to the number of packets), oneportpred (occurence of main port over every other ports) and #rpkt/#rdstport (ratio of the number of packets to responsible destination ports). In order to apply our method, we use the parameters that fit this type of anomaly. The aggregation parameter used is the destination since we want to target an anomaly with several sources and only one destination. The attributes used to build the vector space are the ones related to this type anomaly cited above (#respdest, spprop, oneportpred and #rpkt/#rdstport). The next part explains the results of our investigations about the structure of the traffic in this restricted vector space, and then, the result of the anomaly search.

Characterization of network traffic. We proceed to the analysis of the traffic on the TCP SYN Flood DDoS attributes. In order to do this, we study several traces from the datasets cited in 4.1. We use 64 traces from the MAWI dataset. We also use one trace from Metrosec which has not any provoked anomaly inside.

We observe manually the data in the vector space considered. In order to do so, we generated two 3D images to be able to cover all the attributes of the chosen vector space and this, for all the traces. In the first image, the attributes used were spprop, oneportpred and #rpkt/#rdstport, in the second, we used #respdest, spprop and oneportpred. Then, we analyze them by hand.

It appears that for all images of the first type, the network traffic is composed of only one cluster. A good example is provided by figures 2 (a) and (b). The images of the second type are generally composed of only one class. The data often presents more noise than for the first attributes (cf figure 2 (c)). Some clusters arise, as in figure 2 (d), but as far as we now, they are directly related to scan events (network scans or port scans or both at the same time).

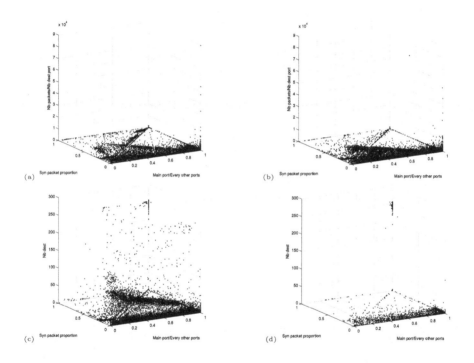

Fig. 2. Traffic representation for *spprop*, *oneportpred* and *#rpkt/#rdstport* (curves a et b) and *spprop*, *oneportpred* and *#respdest* (curves c et d)

However, considering the whole set of generated images, we can consider that the traffic is statistically composed of one class in the considered vector space.

0day anomaly search. As the traffic is generally composed of only one main class, the technique used to find a 0day anomaly in the vector space is outlier detection. We use a documented trace from the Metrosec project where a TCP SYN Flood DDoS has been produced and captured. We extracted a segment of

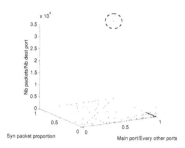

Fig. 3. Network traffic with a TCP SYN DDoS occuring

the original trace situated in the middle of the attack. We worked on part of the trace in order to reproduce the behavior of an online system that would operate on a finite windows of time. We then apply an outlier detection algorithm.

Our anomaly detection system is able to detect the outlier corresponding to the attack. This outlier corresponds to the first attack. Figure 3 shows the data space representation of the traffic inside three of the four attributes used for the outlier detection. It clearly appears that the point that represents the anomaly is on the top corner of the figure, while the normal traffic appears on the horizontal bottom plan. The generated signature will then be the one on equation 1.

$$\#rpkt/\#rdstport > 15000 \tag{1}$$

5 Conclusion

We propose a complete method to detect 0day network traffic anomalies and corresponding signatures through the use of machine learning. This method uses an automatic generation of attributes in order to generate semantically interesting attributes. Machine learning is then applied to several combinations of these attributes. At the end, our algorithm is able to find an anomaly it did not know before which could have been a 0day attack. It was then able to build the related signature automatically which can be integrated in security devices as IDS, IPS, firewalls, ... It was illustrated in this paper by a TCP SYN DDoS attack which was unknown from the system before it encounters it for the first time.

Acknowledgment. This work is achieved in the framework of the European ECODE project, granted and funded by the European Commission's ICT program under reference FP7-ICT-2007-2/223936.

References

1. Barford, P., Kline, J., Plonka, D., Ron, A.: A signal analysis of network traffic anomalies. In: IMW '02: Proceedings of the 2nd ACM SIGCOMM Workshop on Internet measurement, pp. 71–82. ACM, New York (2002)

2. Borgnat, P., Dewaele, G., Fukuda, K., Abry, P., Cho, K.: Seven years and one day: Sketching the evolution of internet traffic. In: INFOCOM 2009, pp. 711–719. IEEE, Los Alamitos (April 2009)
3. Brutlag, J.D.: Aberrant behavior detection in time series for network monitoring. In: LISA '00: Proceedings of the 14th USENIX conference on System administration, Berkeley, CA, USA, pp. 139–146. USENIX Association (2000)
4. Chhabra, P., Scott, C., Kolaczyk, E.D., Crovella, M.: Distributed spatial anomaly detection. In: INFOCOM 2008. The 27th Conference on Computer Communications, pp. 1705–1713. IEEE, Los Alamitos (April 2008)
5. Dewaele, G., Fukuda, K., Borgnat, P., Abry, P., Cho, K.: Extracting hidden anomalies using sketch and non gaussian multiresolution statistical detection procedures. In: LSAD '07: Proceedings of the 2007 workshop on Large scale attack defense, pp. 145–152. ACM, New York (2007)
6. Eskin, E., Arnold, A., Prerau, M., Portnoy, L., Stolfo, S.: A geometric framework for unsupervised anomaly detection: Detecting intrusions in unlabeled data. In: Applications of Data Mining in Computer Security. Kluwer, Dordrecht (2002)
7. Fernandes, G., Owezarski, P.: Automated classification of network traffic anomalies. In: 5th International ICST conference on Security and Privacy in Communication networks (SecureComm 2009), Athens Greece (September 2009)
8. KDD99. Kdd99 cup dataset (1999), http://kdd.ics.uci.edu/databases/kddcup99/kddcup99.html
9. Krishnamurthy, B., Sen, S., Zhang, Y., Chen, Y.: Sketch-based change detection: methods, evaluation, and applications. In: IMC '03: Proceedings of the 3rd ACM SIGCOMM conference on Internet measurement, pp. 234–247. ACM, New York (2003)
10. Kuang, L., Zulkernine, M.: An anomaly intrusion detection method using the csi-knn algorithm. In: SAC '08: Proceedings of the 2008 ACM symposium on Applied computing, pp. 921–926. ACM, New York (2008)
11. Lakhina, A., Crovella, M., Diot, C.: Diagnosing network-wide traffic anomalies. In: SIGCOMM '04: Proceedings of the 2004 conference on Applications, technologies, architectures, and protocols for computer communications, pp. 219–230. ACM, New York (2004)
12. Lakhina, A., Crovella, M., Diot, C.: Mining anomalies using traffic feature distributions. SIGCOMM Comput. Commun. Rev. 35(4), 217–228 (2005)
13. Li, X., Bian, F., Crovella, M., Diot, C., Govindan, R., Iannaccone, G., Lakhina, A.: Detection and identification of network anomalies using sketch subspaces. In: IMC '06: Proceedings of the 6th ACM SIGCOMM conference on Internet measurement, pp. 147–152. ACM, New York (2006)
14. MAWI. Mawi dataset, http://mawi.wide.ad.jp/
15. METROSEC. Metrosec dataset, http://www.laas.fr/METROSEC
16. Scherrer, A., Larrieu, N., Owezarski, P., Borgnat, P., Abry, P.: Non-gaussian and long memory statistical characterizations for internet traffic with anomalies. IEEE Trans. Dependable Secur. Comput. 4(1), 56–70 (2007)
17. Viinikka, J., Debar, H., Ludovic, M., Sguier, R.: Time series modeling for ids alert management. In: Proceedings of the ACM Symposium on InformAtion, Computer and Communications Security (AsiaCCS) (March 2006)

A Comparative Analysis of the Perceived Quality of VoIP under Various Wireless Network Conditions

Ilias Tsompanidis, Georgios Fortetsanakis,
Toni Hirvonen, and Maria Papadopouli*

Department of Computer Science, University of Crete &
Institute of Computer Science, Foundation for Research and Technology - Hellas
N. Plastira 100, Vassilika Vouton, GR-700 13 Heraklion, Greece

Abstract. This paper performs a comparative analysis of the perceived quality of (unidirectional, non-interactive) VoIP calls under various wireless network conditions (e.g., handover, high traffic demand). It employs the PESQ tool, E-model and auditory tests to evaluate the impact of these network conditions on the perceived quality of VoIP calls. It also reveals the inability of PESQ and E-model to capture the quality of user experience. Furthermore, it shows that the network condition and the evaluation method exhibit statistically significant differences in terms of their reported opinion score values. Finally, the paper highlights the benefits of the packet loss concealment of the AMR 12.2kb/s and the QoS mechanisms under these network conditions.

1   Introduction

Wireless networks often experience "periods of severe impairment" (PSIs), characterised by significant packet losses in either or both directions between the wireless Access Points (APs) and wireless hosts, increased TCP-level retransmissions, rate reduction, throughput reduction, increased jitter, and roaming effects. A PSI can last for several seconds to the point that it can be viewed as an outage. The frequency and intensity of PSI events in modern home and enterprize wireless networks is not well understood. Very few studies analyze the impact of PSI events on the quality of user experience. The throughput, jitter, latency, and packet loss, have been used to quantify network performance and various studies have shown their performance under different network conditions (e.g., handoff, contention, and congestion). Some important observations have been made in the context of wireless networks: (a) handovers result to packet losses (e.g., [1,2]), (b) queue overflows at APs lead to poor VoIP quality (e.g., [3]), and (c) average delay does not capture well the VoIP quality because of the burstiness of packet losses (e.g., [4]). For various applications, a maximum tolerable end-to-end network delay has been estimated (e.g., about 150ms for

---

* Contact author: Maria Papadopouli (mgp@ics.forth.gr)

E. Osipov et al. (Eds.): WWIC 2010, LNCS 6074, pp. 339–350, 2010.

VoIP applications [5,6]). Could such crude statistics accurately denote the quality of experience? There is evidence that depending on the temporal statistical characteristics of the packet losses and delays during a call, the impact on the user experience varies. However, there are a few comparative analysis studies of the impact of various network conditions on the perceived quality of experience.

Our attention has shifted from MAC- and network-based metrics to *application-based, objective and subjective user-perception metrics*. Specifically, our recent work [7] employed the E-model [8] and PESQ tool [9], aiming to quantify the VoIP quality under various wireless network conditions, namely, during a handover and under different background traffic conditions (normal and heavy traffic load/saturation conditions) at an AP. For each scenario/network condition, empirical-based measurements were collected from a real-life testbed. The analysis showed that both the network condition and codec type (G.711 vs. AMR 6.7kb/s vs. AMR 12.2kb/s), as well as their interaction, have a significant impact on the quality of user experience values. A comparative analysis of the E-model and PESQ with the Student's T-test reported significant differences between the estimations of these two models, which further motivated the need for more accurate user perception metrics. This paper builds on that work, extending it with *auditory (subjective listening) tests* and an analysis of the impact of QoS mechanisms on the perceived quality of VoIP. The main contribution of this paper is a methodology for evaluating the impact of different network conditions on the perceived quality of VoIP, which can be further extended to other applications and network environments. Specifically, it analyzes and discusses the following issues:

- the impact of network condition (handover, heavy TCP traffic, heavy UDP traffic), codecs, and QoS mechanisms on quality of user experience,
- the use of the E-model, PESQ tool, and auditory tests to estimate the quality of user experience.

For each scenario/network condition, empirical-based measurements were collected from a real-life testbed and listening tests were also conducted using VoIP recordings that correspond to these network conditions. The *impact* and *significance* of network conditions and evaluation metric (subjective tests, E-model, PESQ) on the estimated quality of user experience is identified using ANOVA. The rest of the paper is organized as follows: Section 2 outlines the related work. Section 3 describes our testbed, the different network conditions and discusses the analysis results. Finally, Section 4 presents our main conclusions and future work plans.

2   Related Work

While there have been several studies discussing the network statistics under different conditions, most of them focus on the impact of these conditions on the aggregate throughput and capacity. The IEEE802.11 handover has been analyzed and various improvements have been proposed. For example, Forte *et al.* [10] analyzed the various delays involved in the handoff/reassociation process in an experimental testbed and the impact of the handoff on a SIP call.

They reduced this overhead by enabling the wireless device to acquire a temporal address. SyncScan [11] reduces the network unavailability during an AP handoff by enabling the client to synchronize the scanning phase with the APs' beacons. Pentikousis *et al.* [12] measured the capacity of a WiMAX testbed in terms of VoIP calls. Ganguly *et al.* [13] evaluated various packet aggregation, header compression, adaptive routing, and fast handoff techniques. Anjum *et al.* [14] performed an experimental study of the VoIP in WLAN, quantifying the VoIP capacity under light and heavy traffic load, and the practical benefits of implementing backoff control and priority queuing at the AP. Finally, Shin *et al.* [6] performed empirical-based measurements and simulations to estimate the capacity of an 802.11 network in terms of number of VoIP calls and analyzed the impact of the preamble size, ARF algorithm, RSSI, packet loss, and scanning. They used as criterion for the quality of calls that the end-to-end delay should not exceed 150 ms and the packet loss probability should be 3% or less. In the context of Mobisense project, Deutsche Telecom Lab has developed a Next Generation Network (NGN) testbed and implemented a system that enables seamless codec changes to improve the quality during handovers [15]. They performed subjective tests to quantify the degradation in user perceived quality for various types of network changes, namely handovers between various types of networks and changeovers between various codecs [16]. An analysis of the E-model and PESQ quality estimation tools was also performed in the context of the NGN testbed [17] and an enhancement of the E-Model by adding a bandwidth switching impairment factor was proposed [18]. Chen *et al.* [19] analyzed the user satisfaction in Skype, employing the call duration as the quality benchmark. Hoene *et al.* [20] evaluated the call quality in adaptive VoIP applications and codecs and showed that high-compression codecs (with relatively low voice quality) may behave better than top-quality codecs under packet losses and limited available bandwidth. Markopoulou *et al.* [21] focused on ISP network problems and showed that ISP networks suffer from PSIs affecting the real-time applications.

3   Performance Analysis

3.1   Network Conditions, Scenarios, and Testbeds

We distinguish several network conditions that result in PSIs and form the following scenarios:

- **handover:** no background traffic, user mobility and client handover between wireless APs
- **heavy UDP traffic:** no user mobility, UDP flows saturating the wireless LAN
- **heavy TCP traffic:** no user mobility, TCP flows, generated by a BitTorrent client, saturating the wireless LAN

We setup two control testbeds, namely the *handover testbed* (in which a user, performing a VoIP call, roams in the premises of FORTH) and the *background traffic*

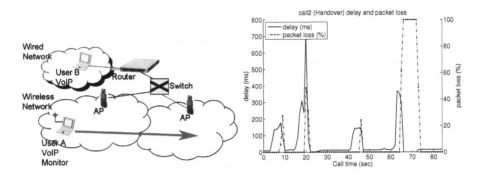

Fig. 1. Handover scenario: User A moves to the coverage area of a different AP while (s)he participates in a VoIP call with user B

testbed (in which background traffic that corresponds to the last two scenarios is generated). A recording of a female voice around 1:30 minutes long (source file) was "replayed" under the aforementioned network conditions. In each testbed, we emulated the corresponding conditions (background traffic/user mobility) of each scenario, "replayed" the source file, and collected the traces at the wireless VoIP client for analysis. Specifically, we analyzed the impact of each condition on the perceived user experience of the VoIP call. Note that these VoIP calls are essentially unidirectional (streaming-like and non-interactive). The network adapter of the wireless VoIP client captures packets in promiscuous mode with IEEE802.11+Radiotap pseudo-header provided by libpcap, using tcpdump with the appropriate settings. This header contains the RSSI value for each packet, the data rate, and the operating channel. The VoIP clients used H323 software with an G.711 codec (64kb/s).

The handover testbed includes one VoIP client connected via FastEthernet and one VoIP client connected via IEEE802.11 to the ICS-FORTH infrastructure network. A user holding a wireless laptop (User A) roams in the premises of ICS-FORTH. While moving, the wireless client slowly walks out of range of the AP and a handover is performed. As empirical studies have shown, handoff between APs in wireless LANs can consume from one to multiple seconds, as associations and bindings at various layers need to be re-established. Such delays include the acquisition of a new IP address, duplicate address detection, the reestablishment of secure association, discovery of available APs. The overhead of scanning for nearby APs can be of 250ms (e.g., [22,11]), far longer than what can be tolerated by VoIP applications. The active scanning in the handoff process of the IEEE802.11 is the primary contributor to the overall handoff latency and can affect the quality of service for many applications. The background traffic testbed includes a VoIP client connected via IEEE802.11, a VoIP client connected via FastEthernet, four wireless nodes connected via IEEE802.11 and one node connected via FastEthernet. The four wireless nodes produce the background traffic according to the predefined scenarios. All wireless nodes are connected to a single AP.

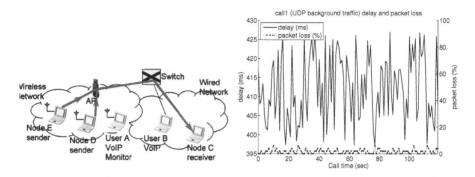

Fig. 2. Heavy UDP traffic scenario: each of the nodes D, E, F and G transmit 2Mb/s UDP traffic towards node C (nodes F and G are not shown)

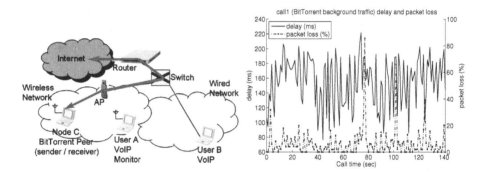

Fig. 3. Heavy TCP traffic scenario: Node C exchanges BitTorrent traffic with Internet peers (both uplink and downlink traffic)

The *heavy UDP traffic* scenario focuses on the quality of VoIP under congestion caused by a large amount of traffic load generated by a small number of flows, overloading the AP. Each of the four wireless nodes sends packets of 1500 bytes of UDP traffic to a wired node at a 2Mb/s data rate (a total of 8Mb/s). The AP operates in IEEE802.11b and the aggregate traffic exceeds the theoretical maximum throughput of an IEEE802.11 network (approximately 6Mb/s [23]). The two VoIP clients initiate a call under these conditions. These scenarios exhibit phenomena of congestion of the wireless channel and continuous contention of the wireless nodes.

In the *heavy TCP traffic* scenario, the background traffic is generated by one wireless node running a BitTorrent client, downloading three highly seeded files (while the VoIP call takes place). The BitTorrent protocol splits the files into small chunks and simultaneously downloads and uploads the shared chunks. In general, the number of generated flows in BitTorrent is high, often causing low-end routers to run out of memory and CPU. As in the previous scenarios, the AP operates in IEEE802.11b mode. The BitTorrent protocol introduces a high number of small TCP flows in both uplink and downlink directions, contending for the medium. This behavior puts stress on the queue, CPU and memory of APs.

3.2   Measurements and Evaluation

We performed a number of VoIP calls for each of the aforementioned scenarios (as shown in Figures 1, 2, and 3, user A initiates VoIP calls with user B), and collected the VoIP traces for analysis. Specifically, we measured the end-to-end delay and packet loss of the VoIP flow under the different network conditions, namely, handover, heavy UDP traffic, and heavy TCP traffic at the application layer. To measure the performance of a VoIP call, we used subjective and objective tests. The objective tests include the E-model and PESQ tool that report a Mean Opinion Score (MOS) value. In both studies, the same VoIP calls were used. For the auditory tests, a recording of a female voice of around 1:30 minutes long (source file) was "replayed" under the aforementioned network conditions. The received files (recorded at the wireless VoIP receiver of the testbed), each corresponding to a network condition, were used in the subjective study. The corresponding opinion scores reported by ten subjects that listened to these files were analyzed.

The E-model depends on various factors, such as voice loudness, background noise, equipment impairment, packetization distortion, codec robustness under various packet loss and end-to-end delays and impairments introduced by the packet loss and end-to-end delays and produces an *R-factor*, a rating that estimates the voice quality [8]: $R = R_o - I_s - I_d - I_{e-eff} + A$. The term R_o accounts for the basic signal-to-noise ratio the user receives and takes into consideration the loudness of the voice, the noise introduced by the circuit and by background sources. The term I_s represents voice specific impairments, such as too loud speech level, non-optimum sidetone and quantization noise, while the term I_d represents the impairments introduced by delay and echo effects. The term I_{e-eff} is the equipment impairment factor, which corresponds to impairments due to low bit-rate codecs and packet losses (i.e., percentage of packet losses and their burstiness index $BurstR$). Finally, the term A is an "advantage factor" that takes into consideration the user's expectation of potential glitches. All these factors have been extensively analyzed in ITU-T's G.107 recommendation (E-model). All E-model parameters are set to their default values, except for B_{pl} which is set to 25.1 (as G.113 recommends for G.711). The ITU-T provides an R-to-MOS conversion formula.

To extend our assessment with additional quality metrics, we also employ the PESQ test. As mentioned earlier, the E-model takes into account both delay and packet losses, while the PESQ focuses on packet loss effects, which were more significant than delays. PESQ gives the estimated perceptual difference between two audio signals, with the limitations that the samples must be temporarily synchronized and of 6 s to 20 s duration. The former requirement proved to be difficult when comparing recordings, so we opted to employ only the effects of packet loss and disregard any delay. The packet loss data from different scenarios was used with each of the three codecs (G.711 64kb/s, AMR 6.7kb/s, and AMR

12.2kb/s). Specifically, we first employed the collected packet traces (of the VoIP calls) with the packet loss information and encoded an audio signal based on each codec. We repeated the encoding using the same packet trace but without considering any packet loss to construct a *baseline audio signal*. Then, the PESQ tool estimated the MOS by comparing these two audio signals for each codec. Note that in this analysis, PESQ does *not consider any delay* information. In the case of G.711 codec, the packet loss locations were simply removed from the pulse-code modulation (PCM) audio, whereas in the case of AMR codecs, the lost packets were indicated by manipulating the bad frame bit of the packet headers in the encoded bitstream. In all cases, the PESQ test was performed between the coded audio *without* and *with* simulated packet losses in 10 s frames with 1 s "step size" (sliding window) for the entire call duration. The metric for a call was the average of all MOS values, each corresponding to a 10 s frame of that call.

We observed two types of handover, namely the *fast handover* and the *handover with deauthentication* (that lasts longer). Calls with *fast handovers* are characterized by minor packet losses and delays, resulting in close to excellent quality. Within a handover, the client initiates an active AP discovery during which packets are queued up. On the other hand, if a handover with deauthentication occurs, the inter-AP protocol will not handle the pending packets (at the old AP). In this case, the error rate and unacknowledged retransmissions will increase, and as a result, the degradation of MOS will become more prominent.

In the VoIP under heavy UDP traffic scenario (e.g., Figure 2), the MOS deteriorates due to the high packet delays. In this scenario, the very large delays are due to the presence of heavy background traffic resulting in an arrival rate higher than the 'service' rate at the AP (also observed in other studies, e.g., [24]). Indeed, a saturated network with full buffers will increase the mean delay values, trying to deliver all packets and occasionally dropping packets from the queue when a timeout occurs. The E-model reports a mediocre quality for these VoIP calls while PESQ results in a relatively good performance. The subjects in the auditory tests also report a reasonably high opinion score value. This is due to the "unidirectional" (and non-interactive) nature of these VoIP tests. In general, this scenario highlights the need for a prioritization scheme for different traffic classes, such as IEEE802.11e (also indicated in other studies, e.g., [3]).

In the VoIP under heavy TCP traffic scenario, the calls suffer from relatively high packet losses and delays. Although packet delays exceed the 150ms threshold, the overall voice quality is acceptable, consistently across E-model, PESQ, and subjective tests (in disagreement with the "rule-of-thumb") [7]. The nature of the BitTorrent protocol can explain this behavior: a BitTorrent client initiates many flows, with small payload sizes. Each flow tries to expand its TCP window, up to the point that packet losses occur, triggering the TCP congestion control which will drop the throughput of that flow. Other flows active at that time will also manifest this behavior. Since the number of flows at any given time is large, this phenomenon is repeated frequently, causing severe performance degradation (e.g., packet drops at the AP). In some calls, the large number of flows initiated by the BitTorrent client saturates the wireless LAN.

A preliminary analysis of VoIP calls shows a prominent discrepancy between the E-model MOS and PESQ MOS. In addition, it illustrates that not all the network conditions impact the MOS in the same manner [7]. We statistically analyzed the impact of the different codecs and scenarios on the user perception metrics. To investigate which parameters have a dominant impact on MOS, a two-way ANOVA was performed. The PESQ MOS was used as the user perception metric. Dependent variable is the average PESQ MOS value of each call, and the independent variables are the scenario and codec type. ANOVA indicates that *scenario* and *codec* type, as well as their interaction, have a *significant effect* on the PESQ MOS values. Furthermore, a multiple comparison test with Tukey's HSD criterion reveals the following: The handover exhibits higher MOS values than all other scenarios. The heavy TCP traffic performs similarly (in terms of MOS) as the heavy UDP traffic. The performance of AMR 6.7kb/s is similar to the performance of G.711 64kb/s (lower data rate vs. concealment tradeoff). The AMR 12.2kb/s performs *significantly better* (higher MOS) than G.711 64kb/s and AMR 6.7kb/s. The level of significance in all tests was set to 0.05. The AMR 12.2kb/s more sophisticated packet loss concealment justifies its better performance. The similar performance of AMR 6.7 kb/s and G.711—significantly lower than the performance of AMR 12.2kb/s—highlights the benefits of the packet loss concealment of the AMR 12.2kb/s under these network conditions. Note that the PESQ MOS of each call is the *average* of the values that correspond to all 10 s frame of the call.

To investigate if there are significant differences between the measurements of E-model and PESQ, we employed the Student's T-test. Specifically, we compared the average call MOS values of the G.711 codec across all scenarios. The test indicates *statistically highly significant* ($p < 0.01$) differences between the estimations of the two models. Especially, under heavy packet loss, E-model reports lower MOS values than PESQ. Finally, as the AMR codec tests show, in the context of heavy losses, it is beneficial to increase the codec bit-rate. A detailed discussion can be found in [7]. The statistically significant differences between the estimations of the PESQ tool and E-model motivated the need for auditory tests. Ten members of the FORTH-ICS, of age between 22-35 years old, without any hearing impairments, participated in an auditory test study. Specifically, for this study, we selected three calls, each corresponding to a network condition. The subjects listened to these three calls and reported an opinion score for each of them.

To investigate if there are significant differences between the measurements of E-model, PESQ and subjective tests, we again employed the ANOVA and Tukey's HSD test. The G.711 codec was used in all the calls. The test indicates statistically significant differences based on the evaluation method (criterion), scenario and their interplay (scenario and criterion). From the ANOVA and Tukey's HSD test results (Figure 4), we conclude that the heavy UDP is significantly different from the heavy TCP for each criterion. The heavy TCP is

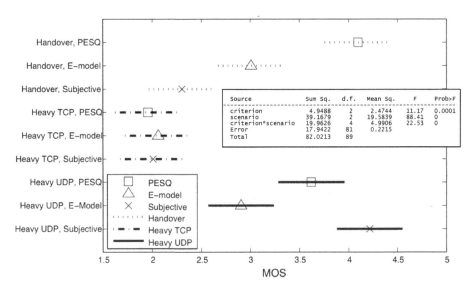

Fig. 4. Comparative statistical analysis of the impact of criterion (PESQ, E-model, and subjective tests) and scenario on MOS using the Tukey's HSD test. The corresponding ANOVA report is in the inset figure.

significantly different from the handover for the E-model and PESQ, respectively. Interestingly, in the case of handover, the three evaluation methods have significant differences from each other, while in heavy TCP, there are no significant differences. The comparison of the E-model and PESQ with the subjective tests reveals several weaknesses and distinct characteristics of these two metrics. For example, after the subjective tests, some users commented that the long pauses of the handover scenario had a strong negative impact on their experience. Due to its averaging, PESQ "masks" the negative impact of the intervals that correspond to the long pauses of the handover. On the other hand, although the E-model (using the packet loss burst ratio) deviates less from the subjective tests than PESQ, it still cannot capture accurately the effect of these long pauses. Moreover, the E-model considering the large delay may underestimate the performance (e.g., in the heavy UDP traffic scenario), while the lack of interactivity may mask its impact in the subjective tests. We plan to investigate the impact of the relative position and duration of long pauses on the perceived quality.

In the above measurements, there was no QoS mechanism enabled. To understand the impact of QoS, we enabled IEEE802.11e and WiFi Multimedia (WMM) on the Cisco APs and Class-based Weighted Fair Queuing on the Cisco router and repeated the empirical study. In this QoS-enabled empirical study, we only consider the G.711 codec. Note that the two VoIP experiments used in the subjective study in the context of handover are different. However the mobile user participating in the experiment followed the same path in the premise of the ICS-FORTH. In the handover scenario without QoS, we had observed

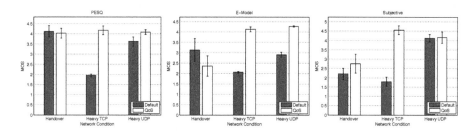

Fig. 5. Impact of QoS on MOS values of the VoIP calls, for different network conditions (all with G.711 codec). The default corresponds to the testbed without QoS. (95% confidence interval).

the presence of *handovers with deauthentication* that cause long pauses (6s or more) during a call. In these cases, the AP deauthenticates the client by sending *Previous authentication no longer valid* messages. According to the AP manufacturer [25], such deauthentication occurs when the error rates and the number of unacknowledged retransmissions reach an AP-specific threshold. When we repeated the experiment with QoS enabled, the presence of such handovers was even more prominent. Interestingly, the majority of the handovers lasted for 6s or more, because the AP was deauthenticating the client during the scanning phase. We speculate that a QoS-enabled AP attempts to transmit a larger number of high-priority frames during the client's scanning phase than a QoS-agnostic AP, reaching the aforementioned deauthentication threshold faster. We plan to investigate further this behavior. However, regardless of the causes for deauthentication, such long pauses severely impact the user perceived quality.

As expected, the QoS mechanisms improve the user experience of VoIP calls under all network conditions. Specifically, the QoS mechanisms improve the performance of VoIP calls under heavy UDP traffic. Especially, in the case of the E-model, their benefits are noticeable (as shown in Figure 5). In the case of heavy TCP traffic, the improvement is even more prominent, exceeding 100%. In the above QoS-enabled performance analysis, the G.711 64kb/s codec was used. In the context of a QoS-enabled emulation testbed, we also analyzed the performance of AMR 12.2kb/s and AMR 6.7kb/s. In the case of heavy UDP traffic and heavy TCP traffic, the user perceived quality using AMR 12.2kb/s is excellent, while the AMR 6.7kb/s performs close to G.711. In handover, the PESQ performs consistently higher than the subjective tests and E-model. However, this is an "overestimation" of the MOS due to the averaging that we perform by taking into consideration all the MOS values that correspond to individual 10s frames. A different approach in estimating the MOS value of a VoIP call using PESQ could potentially improve its estimation.

4   Conclusion and Future Work

The paper discusses situations in which common "rule-of-thumb" metrics cannot reflect the user-perceived quality. A comparative evaluation of the quality of

VoIP calls using PESQ, E-model, and subjective tests demonstrates the need of more accurate metrics, tailored to the specific requirements of the application at hand. In the context of VoIP calls, our analysis reveals the inability of PESQ and E-model to capture the user experience under specific network conditions. It also shows that the impact of network conditions, codecs, and their interplay on the perceived quality of experience varies. The analysis highlights the benefits of the packet loss concealment of the AMR 12.2kb/s and the QoS mechanisms under these network conditions. However, our experiments also indicate instances of deauthentication during handovers, resulting in severe performance degradation. As shown in this paper, not all network conditions impact the quality of VoIP applications in the same manner. Understanding which conditions cause severe impairment in the VoIP application, and which cross-layer measurements can be used to predict such impairment, is important in the design of adaptation mechanisms.

Acknowledgments. The authors would like to thank Henning Schulzrinne and Alexander Raake for providing valuable feedback on this work and Magda Chatzaki for her help in setting the QoS-enabled testbed.

References

1. Pack, S., Choi, J., Kwon, T., Choi, Y.: Fast handoff support in IEEE802.11 wireless networks. IEEE Communications Surveys and Tutorials 9(1), 2–12 (2007)
2. Wu, H., Tan, K., Zhang, Y., Zhang, Q.: Proactive scan: Fast handoff with smart triggers for 802.11 wireless LAN. In: IEEE INFOCOM, Anchorage, Alaska (2007)
3. Sunghyun, C., Javier, P., Sai, S., Stefan, M.N.: IEEE802.11e contention-based channel access (edcf) performance evaluation. In: IEEE International Conference on Communications, Anchorage, Alaska (2003)
4. Clark, A.: Extensions to the E-model to incorporate the effects of time varying packet loss and recency. T1A1.1/2001-037 (2001)
5. ITU: ITU-T recommendation G.113: Transmission impairments due to speech processing (2007)
6. Shin, S., Schulzrinne, H.: Experimental measurement of the capacity for VoIP traffic in IEEE802.11 WLANs. In: IEEE INFOCOM, Anchorage, AK, USA (2007)
7. Tsompanidis, I., Fortetsanakis, G., Hirvonen, T., Papadopouli, M.: Analyzing the impact of various wireless network conditions on the perceived quality of VoIP. In: IEEE LANMAN, New Jersey, USA (2010)
8. ITU: ITU-T recommendation G.107: The E-model, a computational model for use in transmission planning (2005)
9. ITU: ITU-T recommendation P.862: Perceptual evaluation of speech quality PESQ: An objective method for end-to-end speech quality assessment of narrow-band telephone networks and speech codecs (2001)
10. Forte, A., Shin, S., Schulzrinne, H.: Improving layer-3 handoff delay in IEEE802.11 wireless networks. In: ICST WICON, Boston, Massachusetts (2006)
11. Ramani, I., Savage, S.: Syncscan: practical fast handoff for 802.11 infrastructure networks. In: IEEE INFOCOM, Miami, FL, USA, vol. 1, pp. 675–684 (2005)

12. Pentikousis, K., Piri, E., Pinola, J., Fitzek, F., Nissil, T., Harjula, I.: Empirical evaluation of VoIP aggregation over a fixed WiMAX testbed. In: ICST TRIDENTCOM, Austria (2008)
13. Ganguly, S., Navda, V., Kim, K., Kashyap, A., Niculescu, D., Izmailov, R., Hong, S., Das, S.R.: Performance optimizations for deploying VoIP services in mesh networks. IEEE Journal of Selected Areas of Communications 24(11), 2147–2158 (2006)
14. Anjum, F., Elaoud, M., Famolari, D., Ghosh, A., Vaidyanathan, R.: Voice performance in WLAN networks - an experimental study. In: IEEE GLOBECOM, San Francisco (2003)
15. Vidales, P., Kirschnick, N., Lewcio, B., Steuer, F., Wältermann, M., Möller, S.: Mobisense testbed: Merging user perception and network performance. In: ICST TRIDENTCOM, Innsbruck, Austria (2008)
16. Möller, S., Wältermann, M., Lewcio, B., Kirschnick, N., Vidales, P.: Speech quality while roaming in next generation networks. In: IEEE International Conference on Communications, Dresden, Germany (2009)
17. Lewcio, B., Wältermann, M., Vidales, P., Raake, A., Möller, S.: Performance of instrumental speech quality measures for next generation wireless networks. In: IEEE International Conference on Acoustics, Rotterdam (2009)
18. Lewcio, B., Wältermann, M., Möller, S., Vidales, P.: E-model supported switching between narrowband and wideband speech quality. In: First International Workshop on Quality of Multimedia Experience (QoMex), San Diego (2009)
19. Chen, K.T., Huang, C.Y., Huang, P., Lei, C.L.: Quantifying skype user satisfaction. In: ACM SIGCOMM, Pisa, Italy (2006)
20. Hoene, C., Karl, H., Wolisz, A.: A perceptual quality model intended for adaptive voip applications. International Journal of Communication Systems 19(3), 299–316 (2006)
21. Markopoulou, A., Tobagi, F., Karam, M.: Assessment of VoIP quality over internet backbones. In: IEEE INFOCOM, New York, NY, USA, vol. 1, pp. 150–159 (2002)
22. Velayos, H., Karlsson, G.: Techniques to reduce IEEE802.11b MAC layer handover time. In: IEEE International conference on communications, Paris (2004)
23. Jun, J., Peddabachagari, P., Sichitiu, M.: Theoretical maximum throughput of IEEE802.11 and its applications. In: IEEE NCA, Cambridge, MA, USA, pp. 249–256 (2003)
24. Wang, S.C., Helmy, A.: Performance limits and analysis of contention-based IEEE802.11 MAC. In: IEEE LCN, Tampa, Florida, U.S.A. (2006)
25. Cisco Systems: Troubleshooting problems affecting radio frequency communication (2009)

Optimization of Service Discovery in Wireless Sensor Networks

Ayon Chakraborty[1], Kaushik Lahiri[2], Subhajit Mandal[1], Deepankar Patra[1],
Mrinal K. Naskar[3], and Amitava Mukherjee[2]

[1] Dept. of CSE, Jadavpur University, Kolkata 700032, India
[2] IBM India Pvt. Ltd., Kolkata 700091, India
[3] Dept. of ETCE, Jadavpur University, Kolkata 700032, India
{jucse.ayon,msubhajitju,deepankarbcse}@gmail.com,
{lkaushik,amitava.mukherjee}@in.ibm.com,
mrinalnaskar@yahoo.co.in

Abstract. With the advancement of ubiquitous computing, new types of Wireless sensor networks (WSNs) have emerged where sensors perform their tasks even as their surrounding network neighborhood changes, nodes terminate unexpectedly and signal strengths vary dynamically. In such scenarios, it is very important to use efficient service discovery algorithms adapt dynamically network changes. In this paper, we present a two level hierarchy for efficient service discovery. First, Proximal Neighborhood Discovery is prerequisite for service discovery followed by Optimal Service Discovery (OSD) which is based on the set of peers that a node should choose in order to utilize its requirements, instead of implementing all its required services itself. We present OSD algorithm, as a new approach in searching for the efficient service providers to obtain required services. We implement the proposed scheme in nesC and perform simulations using the interference-model in TOSSIM. The results show appreciable improvements over conventional approaches.

Keywords: WSN, Service Discovery, PSO, Simulated Annealing, nesC, TOSSIM.

1 Introduction

WSNs consist of spatially distributed collections of small, smart and cheap, sensing and computing devices. In a traditional WSN, sensors are deployed in a specific geographical location and are required to send data to a sink. Some typical applications are habitat monitoring and military reconnaissance. Since these carry out simple tasks of remote sensing, they do not need a specific service discovery model, as routing data to the sink itself is sufficient to provide the required "service".

With the emergence of pervasive computing, users have gradually become surrounded by a variety of smart wireless computing devices. The ultimate goal is to realize a true ubiquitous computing paradigm where such devices weave themselves into the fabric of our everyday life by providing various different services and become invisible, as revealed by Weiser [1]. In order to realize this, we need many sensors,

E. Osipov et al. (Eds.): WWIC 2010, LNCS 6074, pp. 351–362, 2010.
© Springer-Verlag Berlin Heidelberg 2010

non-sensor smart devices and human beings moving and collaborating with each other. Together they perform multiple tasks like interfacing, querying, routing, and data acquisition.

An example is a medical application. Here, for detecting a patient's movement patterns, multiple sensors collaborate and exchange measurements perceived by light sensors and send this data to a processor sensor. This processor also receives signals from heartbeat and blood pressure monitoring devices implanted into the patient's body. It combines and digitally processes all the signals received over a period of time and sends this to the nearest available analyzer sensor. The analyzer sensor takes help from a rule server sensor to quickly find patterns in the combined data that provide vital clues to the patent's health. It then routes only the analyzed summary data to a transmitter which further compresses it and securely sends it over the internet to a medical hub. The hub takes immediate action if necessary (e.g. notifying a doctor or ambulance) or simply stores the data in the patient's medical history for future analysis and action.

In the scenario just described, some sensors and devices are worn by the patient on his or her body and others are scattered around the patient's neighborhood (e.g. in the rooms of his/her home). There are two implications: 1) the relative positional coordinates of the sensors keep changing as the patient moves. 2) The set of collaborating sensors changes, as the most convenient and nearby sensors are used for quick analysis and transmission of data.

We can look upon the sensors as each providing some services of its own (service provider) and using some services provided by others (service consumer). From the point of view of a single sensor, it operates within a service neighborhood where it has to constantly collaborate with the neighbors to send service packets (where it is the service provider) and receive service packets (where it is consumer). Because of the implications described before, the neighbors keep changing their positions and their identities also change. Whenever such changes occur, each sensor has to rediscover the set of neighbors with whom it can collaborate most effectively (considering distance and packet loss) and who can also provide the set of services it requires. These changes can happen very frequently, e.g. as the patient moves about. As a result, we need extremely efficient and dynamic service discovery protocols.

Service discovery protocols for wireless networks [8] have been a sizzling subject for researchers over the past few years. These should allow devices to automatically detect useful services offered by other devices on a network along with their service attributes which help in determining their appropriateness in a given context. It also allows devices to advertise their own capabilities to the rest of the network. A few well known service discovery protocols are SLP, Sun Micro system's Jini and Microsoft's UPnP (Universal Plug and Play). However these protocols are not suited for ubiquitous environments which are dynamic, distributed and have energy constrained sensors. For such environments, highly efficient service discovery protocols are required which can adapt to the changing network topology. Such protocols should be able to quickly discover service providers in a dynamically changing network and also, more importantly, discover those providers which can provide the required services most efficiently, which is critical in a ubiquitous environment consisting of small sensor devices.

In this paper, we present a two level hierarchical approach for efficient service discovery. First, there is Proximal Neighborhood Discovery (PND) which a prerequisite for service discovery followed by the Optimal Service Discovery (OSD). Our algorithm is a based on modern heuristic techniques like Particle Swarm Optimization [2][3] and Simulated Annealing [4]. This algorithm finds out an optimal set of service providers from a potential set of sensors identified earlier by PND. It uses optimization parameters such as the distance of the provider and whether it is able to provide the required services. The main criteria used for choosing the parameters are 1) minimizing the use of communication power (e.g. by minimizing number of packet exchanges required) and 2) maximizing the packet reception probability (e.g. by using providers which have the best communication links with the consumer). Our results show appreciable improvements over conventional approaches, not only in terms of energy efficiency, but also minimizing packet loss.

We implemented our proposed algorithm using the nesC [5] programming language running on the TinyOS [6] software platform. Simulations were conducted using the TOSSIM [7] environment. The implementation of OSD in nesC not only shows the coding feasibility of the scheme, but also verifies that it can be run on real motes like MicaZ or Mica2. An interference model provided by the TOSSIM environment to simulate the unreliable wireless links is used for studying the successful packet delivery rates which made our simulation much more realistic.

The rest of the paper is organized as follows: Sections 2 introduces the rationale behind choosing the neighborhood and Service Discovery algorithms; Sections 3 and 4 elaborate on the working of the algorithms themselves; Section 5 discusses the implementation and compares the results obtained using our algorithm and other existing algorithms. We conclude in Section 6.

2 Rationale for Neighborhood and Service Discovery

As described in the introductory example, the network of sensors surrounding a particular sensor can change their positions quite frequently, e.g. as the patient embedded with a sensor enters or leaves a room. Whenever this happens, each sensor must quickly discover the new set of sensors surrounding it, i.e., its new neighbors. Discovering neighboring nodes (referred to as neighborhood discovery from now on) is a critical requirement for effective inter-node collaboration - inter-communication, routing and cluster formation.

Neighborhood discovery determines if direct single-hop radio communication is possible between two nodes. If the inter-node distance between the communicating nodes is greater than a certain threshold, then there is very high probability of packet loss due to larger interference and weaker signal strength. Although this situation can be partially improved by sending redundant packets or applying higher signal strength, these would drain out the resources (e.g. battery power) of the already energy-constrained sensor. Therefore it is critical to identify the right set of *neighbor* nodes (nodes with which a particular node can directly communicate by sending packets) with whom the best communication links can be established. This set of nodes can be termed as the *neighborhood* of the particular node.

Once each sensor has discovered its neighborhood, the network of sensors needs to collaborate and intercommunicate to achieve a set of objectives. When collaborating, each node acts as 1) a service provider by implementing a set of services itself and also 2) a service consumer where it depends on its neighbor nodes from whom it obtains a set of required services. In order to do this in the best possible manner, it is required that each service consumer node identifies the *optimal set of service providers* that can provide their required services. This optimal set can depend on several factors like the quality of connection with the providers, the number of bundled services that can be obtained from the same provider and the similarity of the service desired to the service provided. Considering all these factors and coming up with an optimal set of providers is the purpose of Optimal Service Discovery. Note that this optimal set should be arrived at in the fastest possible time. In fact, if there is a trade-off between the time taken for coming up with the solution and the quality of the solution itself, a higher priority should be given to a timely solution.

3   Proximal Neighborhood Discovery Algorithm

Proximal neighborhood discovery is the process by which a particular sensor discovers its neighboring nodes with which it has the best connectivity. The idea behind the discovery algorithm is simple.

- *Initialization:* The foreign node n_0 (which enters into the network) broadcasts neighborhood request beacons periodically for $t_{MAX\_BEACONS}$ times. These beacon messages consist of the id of the transmitting node n_0. The idea behind multiple broadcasts is to account for unpredictable packet loss.
- *Acknowledgement:* Whenever any node n_i receives a broadcast beacon from n_0, it replies back with an acknowledgement message containing its own id. Once n_0 receives back acknowledgement from n_i, it compares the received signal strength indication (RSSI) [13], S_i of the received acknowledgement message with a threshold value $S_{RSSI\_Threshold}$.
- If $S_i > S_{RSSI\_Threshold}$, it decides that n_i is a neighbor and adds it to the proximal neighborhood table t_{pn}. The threshold value of the signal strength is determined by factors such as the transmitting power of the node, the type of application and the physical environment in the network.

The discovery process is started immediately when the node enters a new network. Thereafter, for a particular node, inter-node communication is restricted to only those nodes that are in its proximal neighborhood table. As time passes, some nodes may leave the network or may drain out, or they might go out of range, also new nodes may join the network. Given the dynamical nature of the sensor networks and their topologies, nodes need to update themselves frequently about their neighbors by refreshing their local proximal neighborhood tables.

4   Optimal Service Provider Discovery Algorithm

As a pre-requisite for service discovery, a node first needs to know about its neighbors as described in Section 3. As a first step in service discovery, it needs to identify those neighbors that are capable for providing it with the services it needs. In a service-rich environment more than one neighbor can provide each of the services that it needs. So the outcome of the first step can potentially be a large set of nodes. Therefore, as a second step in discovery, it needs to intelligently choose only those few service providers that are 1) necessary and sufficient for it to get all its required services and 2) able to provide the services most efficiently. Efficient service providers are chosen based on:

1. Distance of the provider (nearer the better)
2. The number of services provided by a single node (more the better)
3. Appropriateness of the provided services. Appropriateness of a service depends on how closely the consumer's requested service matches the provider's provided service. This is required as very often the services are similar but do not match exactly.

The last step above is an optimization problem where, out of a set of available providers, the most efficient subset of providers must be identified.

The total set of neighbors have been already discovered (as in Section 3) and stored in the proximal neighborhood table t_{pn} as mentioned earlier. The initiator node n_0 starts by sending a service discovery beacon to each neighboring node n_i in table t_{pn}. These beacon messages consist of the id of the transmitting node n_0 and the set of services $S = \{S_{01} \dots S_{0n}\}$ required by it. One a neighboring node gets this beacon, it checks if it can provide any of the services and replies by sending an acknowledgement message. After the initiator has waited for a sufficient period of time by which it was expecting to receive all acknowledgement messages, it prepares the Service Discovery Table.

As an input to the optimization problem, we have the Service Discovery Table, which is a relation from the set of services (S) to the set of service providers (SP). This is the set of all capable providers from which we need to identify the optimal subset of most efficient providers.

4.1 OSD Algorithm Based on Particle Swarm Optimization

I) Problem Formulation: If the total number of required services is n, the solution space U can be said to be a collection of *arrangements* C, each of the form $\{SP_1, SP_2, .., SP_n\}$, where SP_i denotes the service provider selected for providing the ith service in the particular arrangement. Let Q_i be the set of *all* providers capable of providing the ith service. Thus, $\bigcup_{i=1}^{n} Q_i$ = SP which is nothing but the total set of service providers and U = $\{(SP_1, SP_2, .., SP_n) \mid SP_i \in SP$ for each $i\}$. Our problem is to find the optimal arrangement C from our solution space U, i.e., the optimal way to assign service providers for each of n services that are desired by a service consumer sensor.

In order to solve this optimization problem, we start based on the idea of Particle Swarm Optimization (PSO) [2] and then apply to it the principle of Simulated Annealing (SA) [10], in order to arrive at an optimal solution in a short time. Using this idea, an arrangement C_i denotes the ith *particle* in an n-dimensional system where each dimension represents a particular service. One restriction is that the *velocity* of a particle (the number of values it can have, i.e. the number of service providers that can be assigned) along a particular dimension (service) is finite and restricted to a set of possible values, that is, the ith dimension of the particle has a domain restricted to set Q_i. We call the set Q_i the *velocity space* along a particular dimension i. If the velocity restriction is not adhered to, the arrangement would not be valid.

II) Formulation of the Energy Function: While formulating the energy function or cost function, we used two important thumb rules. First, the service consumer sensor should obtain as many services as it can get from a single provider, i.e., look for bundled services. This would make it possible for the single provider to combine more than one service (e.g. information on a patient) on the same packet, thereby reducing the overall number of data packets that need to be sent. Second, the service providing nodes should be as closer as possible. This is important because the signal strength between communicating nodes decreases quickly with the distance apart which means that either more energy or greater number of packets are needed to successfully send data.

Mathematically, the first goal is to minimize the 'average distance of a service' for a particular service provider node and the second goal is to minimize the sum of the service distances for all the service providers. With this goal, we formulate the energy function required for simulated annealing. For a particular arrangement C_i the energy function f(i) can be stated as,

$$f(i) = \sum_{i=1}^{\eta(sp)} d(i) / \gamma(i) \tag{1}$$

where, d(i) is the distance of the service provider with id number i, and $\gamma(i)$ is the number of services (bundled service) provided by that particular provider.

Note that a nearer service provider implies a smaller d(i) and a bundled service implies a larger $\gamma(i)$. As the ratio of d(i) and $\gamma(i)$ decreases, the arrangement C_i of service providers becomes more and more favorable. This is what we wanted to achieve in the first place. So equation (1) is a suitably formulated energy function.

As discussed before, any arrangement C_i can be looked upon as a particle in an n-dimensional space. When a particle updates its position from C_{old} to C_{new}, the energy gained is given by: $\Delta f = f(C_{new}) - f(C_{old})$. This is same as ΔE, *the energy difference* between the two states, which is an important parameter in SA.

III) Iterative approach to the solution based on SA: We start from an initial solution, which can be any valid arrangement and calculate its energy value. At the next step and then each subsequent step, we change the current solution to another valid solution and recalculate the energy value. We accept or reject the new solution based on a probability determined by the following *probability function* P:

$$\begin{aligned} P &= 1 & \text{if} \quad \Delta E \leq 0 \\ &= e^{(\frac{-\Delta f}{\theta})} & \text{if} \quad \Delta E > 0 \end{aligned} \tag{2}$$

Here, Θ is a variable control parameter, called the *annealing temperature*, which is initially at a high value, but gradually decreases based on a *cooling schedule*, described in section 4.

If ΔE is negative (or zero), implying lower (or same) energy value of the new solution, it is always accepted, as P=1.

If ΔE is positive and P > random (0, 1), i.e., P is greater than a random number between 0 and 1, the new solution is accepted else it is rejected.

This second decision is of utmost importance, as we accept even higher energy value solutions with a certain probability, depending on the annealing temperature Θ. This ensures that our algorithm is not stuck at a local minimal value, which implies a sub-optimal solution. We proceed in this way, iteratively towards our ultimate solution till the annealing temperature has cooled down to its desired final value.

IV) Cooling Schedule: An important control parameter in equation (2) is Θ, called the *annealing temperature*; a parameter which is decremented, every time the system of particles approaches a better solution (or a low energy state). If Θ_i be the *initial temperature* and Θ_f be the *final temperature*, and t is the cooling time, then the designed *cooling schedule* is given by: $\Theta(t) = \Theta_f + (\Theta_i - \Theta_f)*\alpha^t$. Here α is the rate of cooling, usually $(0.7 \leq \alpha < 1.0)$ and t is the cooling time which in our case is the number of iterations. While the SA algorithm incorporates the concept of probability through the Metropolis acceptance rule [10], it can be slow. So in our proposed algorithm, we also utilize the fast optimal search capability of PSO.

V) Proposed algorithm based on PSO
Input: A set of N services and the set of Service providers pertaining to each instance of a service.

Step 1: Initialization: At first, a swarm of m particles C_1, C_2,....,C_m is initialized randomly:.

Here, a particle $C_i = \{SP_1^i, SP_2^i,..., SP_n^i \}$ is an arrangement of service providers where SP_k^i is the service provider which provides the kth service in the ith particle (arrangement) C_i. Here the number of services desired by the consumer is n.

The parameters Θ_i (initial temperature), Θ_f (final temperature), α (cooling rate) are initialized. A higher Θ_i gives a better result, but there is also a trade-off as this implies a larger number of iterations.

Step 2: Finding a local best solution: For each of the m particles, the next local best solution is found, at a particular temperature Θ, as described in section 3. This is done by randomly selecting a member from the velocity space along a random dimension less than or equal to N. This means that any one of the N service providers is chosen randomly and replaced by another valid service provider, which also is chosen randomly. The new solution C_{new} probabilistically replaces the old solution based on the probability function described earlier in equation (2). The updated solution is referred to as C_{ilbest} or the local best.

Step 3: Updating the pbest and gbest values: For each particle, C_{ilbest} obtained in step 2 is compared to the *historically obtained best solution for that particle* C_{ipbest}. C_{ipbest} is updated by C_{ilbest} according to the following rule:

C_{ipbest} = C_{ilbest} if $f(C_{ilbest}) - f(C_{ipbest}) < 0$
        = C_{ipbest} if $f(C_{ilbest}) - f(C_{ipbest}) \geq 0$

Now, comparing the all the C_{ipbest} values, C_{gbest} (the historically obtained best solution *globally across all particles*) is updated by that C_{ipbest} which has the minimum energy state i.e. the minimum value of $f(C_{ipbest})$ among all particles.

Step 4: Finding new solution based on crossover: Based on the global knowledge of the swarm each particle forms a new solution from its local best (C_{ipbest}) by crossing a part of it with the global best (C_{gbest}). For example, say, $C_{ipbest} = \{1,5,\mathbf{2,3,2},1\}$ and $C_{gbest} = \{1,3,\mathbf{1,4,3},3\}$. The portion $\{1,4,3\}$ is randomly chosen from C_{gbest} and inserted in the same position in C_{ipbest} to obtain C_{inew}. Thus C_{inew} becomes $\{1,5,\mathbf{1,4,3},1\}$.

Note that this is slightly different from the crossover operator discussed in [11].

After the crossover, C_{ipbest} is replaced with C_{inew} if that has a lower energy state and is taken as the new individual best position. Crossover helps the particles jump out of local optimization by sharing global information about the swarm.

Step 5: Loop: The temperature $\Theta(t)$ is calculated. If either $\Theta(t)$ is less than $\Theta(f)$ or the number of iterations completed exceeds t, the algorithm comes to a halt. The best solution found is C_{gbest}. Else it goes back to step 2.

VI) Possible extension: parameter matching and degree of association: The above algorithm can be extended to take into account the *appropriateness* of the service provider (how closely it matches the service desired by the consumer node) in cases where the types of parameters are variable. Suppose that a desired service S has parameters $\{p_1, p_2,..., p_k\}$. Also suppose that the service S is provided by Service Providers SP_1, SP_2, ..., where each of them provides the same service but with varying types of parameters. A very trivial example of varying types can be string versus integer versus floating point number. The most appropriate service provider would be the one whose parameter list matches most closely with the requested parameter list. Thus appropriateness of service provider i depends on the *degree of association* between the set $\{p_1, p_2,..., p_k\}$ and the parameter set of SP_i. Degree of association is given by:

$$D = \sum_{j=1}^{k} (p_j \Phi SP_i(p_j)) \tag{3}$$

Where, $SP_i(p_j)$ is the jth parameter in set SP_i (parameter set for the service provider providing the ith service to the service consumer) and p_j^i is the jth parameter in the parameter set for the ith service desired by the service consumer and $p_j^i \Phi SP_i(p_j)$ is the *correspondence*. The value of *correspondence* is given by:

$$p_j^i \Phi SP_i(p_j) = 1 \text{ if the type of } p_j^i \text{ exactly matches the type of } SP_i(p_j)$$
$$= 0 \text{ otherwise}$$

The degree of association can be incorporated into the definition of distance d(i) that is used in the energy function (1). Alternatively, a strategy can be used to:

i) Produce several distinct sub-optimal particles.
ii) Take the one having the maximum degree of association.

5 Simulation

Extensive simulations have been performed to judge the capability of the OSD algorithm. We have considered a sample network of 30 nodes and the existence of 10 network services. Each node provides a set of services and consumes a predefined set of services.

5.1 Implementation

We implemented the neighborhood discovery and service discovery using the nesC [5] programming language, hosted on the TinyOS [6] software platform which provides a component-based software model and an active message based communication model. The rationale behind choosing the implementation platform is to test its coding feasibility on the hardware platform (e.g., real motes like mica2, micaZ etc.) and also to utilize the interference-model provided by TOSSIM [7] to study packet-loss. nesC modules are software components that are wired together in a configuration file to form an application, much like hardware components in a schematic.

The Interference-Model: We have noticed the criticality of packet loss during transmission while simulating our scheme using the interference-model. The simulation in TOSSIM [7] considers the TOSSIM radio loss model, which is based on the empirical data (shown in Fig. 1). The loss probability captures transmitter interference using original trace that yielded the model. More detailed measurements would be required to simulate the exact transmitter characteristics; however experiments have shown the model to be very accurate.

After the nodes boot, they try to determine their neighbors. To avoid collision we have used TDMA-based approach for the nodes to transmit their neighborhood discovery messages. The implementation takes RSSI, where the signal strengths of the acknowledgement messages sent by the potential neighbors are sampled by the subject node. Our application uses a threshold value to help filter out nodes beyond a certain distance, which is directly related to the RSSI value. Results regarding relations between the RSSI values and distances have been studied in [9].

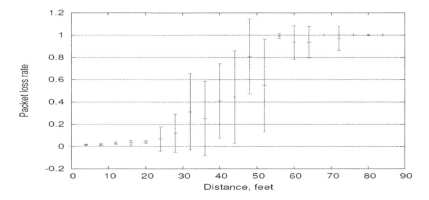

Fig. 1. TOSSIM Radio Loss Model based on empirical data

5.2 Simulation Results

The results obtained by the OSD algorithm (based on SA-PSO) were compared with results from simple PSO algorithm and a Greedy Algorithm. The PSO algorithm does not employ the notion of Simulated Annealing where as the Greedy Algorithm is more concerned only with the bundling of services from a peer.

Since all the algorithms employ an idea of random numbers the solutions produced are not at all always unique. However, the distribution of the obtained solutions varies with the algorithms. We conducted a study on this distribution, where we simulated the three algorithms for 100 times for a given network and plotted frequency of the obtained solution versus the value of energy (as in equation 1) of the obtained solution. The graph obtained is presented in figure 2.

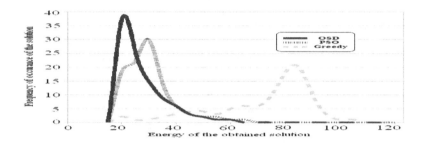

Fig. 2. Distribution of the solutions

The figure 2 shows that the graph for OSD has a greater measure of Kurtosis or *peak* than the other two. Hence the probability of the obtained optimal solution to be at a minimal energy level is greater in case of OSD, where the optimal solutions are more clustered towards the minimal energy solution. To study the merit of our approach, we performed the analysis based on the following criteria among the algorithms: a) percentage packet-loss and b) energy efficiency. The simulation was run for 50 rounds and the average number of packet losses for the three different algorithms were plotted graphically, as shown in figure 3. This simulation uses the interference-model introduced earlier. The OSD algorithm shows distinctively reliable communication compared to the others.

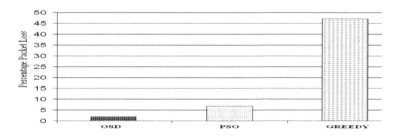

Fig. 3. Percentage packet loss for the schemes

In case of the greedy algorithm, packet loss is the maximum as communication distance is not considered. The relatively higher packet loss in PSO shows that the application of simulated annealing technique improves the OSD algorithm. The second simulation was performed for determining the energy-awareness of the three schemes.

Here, we studied the residual energy of the initiator node the number of rounds increases gradually. The energy expenditure for communication follows the first order radio model as discussed in [12]. The initiator (consumer) node is assumed to have an initial energy of 1 J. The results are shown in figure 4. The cost of communication is best in the OSD scheme. Residual energy curves show a sharper decreasing trend in the other schemes. This increases the lifetime of individual nodes resulting in increment of the network lifetime. It is clear from the above results that the OSD algorithm outperforms the other two algorithms, both in terms of higher energy conservation as well as lower packet-loss rates.

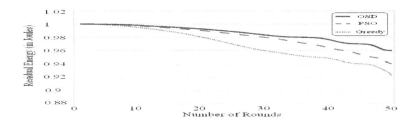

Fig. 4. Residual Mote Energy of the initiator after some rounds, for the three algorithms

6 Conclusion and Future Work

In this paper, we have presented a combined two-level strategy for nearest neighborhood and optimal service provider discoveries that would provide a single solution to this challenge. We described the OSD algorithm, a new optimization approach based on a combination of SA and PSO algorithms, which prevents getting stuck in local optimal solutions while at the same time quickly converges towards the final solution. We implemented this using the nesC programming language running on the TinyOS platform. We have shown that our results show appreciable improvements over two other conventional approaches. Developing applications using our approach offers two major advantages:

- Execution time is much shorter than when using more traditional approaches.
- The algorithm is robust, being relatively insensitive to noisy and/or missing data, as it randomly searches for the best solution over the entire solution space.

References

1. Weiser, M.: The Computer for the Twenty-First Century. Scientific Am. 265(3), 94–101 (1991)
2. Eberhart, R.C., Kennedy, J.: A new optimizer using particle swarm theory. In: The proceedings of the Sixth International Symposium on Micro machine and Human Science Nagoya, Japan, pp. 39–43 (1995)
3. Shi, Y.H., Eberhart, R.C.: A modified particle swarm optimizer. In: IEEE International Conference on Evolutionary Computation, pp. 63–73 (1998)

4. Chaojun, D., Zulian, Q.: Particle Swarm Optimization Algorithm Based on the Idea of Simulated Annealing. IJCSNS International Journal of Computer Science and Network Security 6(10) (October 2006)

5. Gay, D., Levis, P., Behren, R., Welsh, M., Brewer, E., Culler, D.: The nesC language - A holistic approach to networked embedded systems. ACM SIGPLAN Notices archive 38(5) (May 2003)

6. Levis, P., et al.: TinyOS - An Operating System for Sensor Networks. In: Ambient Intelligence. Springer, Heidelberg (2005)

7. Levis, P., Lee, N., Welsh, M., Culler, D.: TOSSIM: Accurate and Scalable Simulation of Entire TinyOS

8. Lenders, V., May, M., Plattner, B.: Service discovery in mobile ad hoc networks: A field theoretic approach. In: Pervasive and Mobile Computing. Elsevier, Amsterdam (2005)

9. Lim, J.C., Wong, K.D.: Exploring Possibilities for RSSI-Adaptive Control in Mica2-based Wireless Sensor Networks. In: ICARV 2006 (2006)

10. Kirkpatrick, S., Sorkin, G.B.: Simulated Annealing. In: The Handbook of Brain and Neural Networks. The MIT Press, Cambridge (1995)

11. Hao, Z.-F., Wang, Z.-G., Huang, H.: A Particle Swarm Optimization Algorithm with Crossover Operator. In: International Conference on Machine Learning and Cybernetics 2007, pp. 19–22 (August 2007)

12. Rabiner, W., Heinzelman, Chandrakasan, A., Balakrishnan, H.: Energy-Efficient Communication Protocol for Wireless Micro sensor Networks. In: The proceedings of the 33rd Hawaii International Conference on System Sciences (2000)

13. Whitehouse, K., Karlof, C., Culler, D.: A practical evaluation of radio signal strength for ranging-based localization. SIGMOBILE Mob. Comput. Commun. Rev. 11(1), 41–52 (2007)

ILA: Idle Listening Avoidance in Scheduled Wireless Sensor Networks

Marcin Brzozowski, Hendrik Salomon, and Peter Langendoerfer

IHP GmbH
Im Technologiepark 25
15236 Frankfurt (Oder)
Germany
{brzozowski,salomon,langendoerfer}@ihp-microelectronics.com

Abstract. There are applications that require a lifetime of several years from a sensor network and simultaneously need a guaranteed end-to-end delay. Obviously, these two parameters - lifetime and delay - contradict each other. In this work we present and evaluate a solution - Idle Listening Avoidance (ILA) - that copes with idle listening stemming from the delay between detecting that no message is transmitted and switching off the transceiver. ILA reduces idle listening from 50 to even more than 100 times, depending on the guaranteed end-to-end delays. As a result, it prolongs the lifetime by more than 50%. Moreover, the ideal solution, which requires a dedicated hardware, prolongs the lifetime by only 0.3% more than ILA, which can be applied on off-the-shelf sensor nodes.

Keywords: Sensor networks, low duty cycle, end-to-end delays, MAC protocols.

1 Introduction

Several applications, e.g. in the area of critical infrastructure protection, require guaranteed end-to-end delays. In other words, if an event occurs in the area monitored by a sensor network, the notification message must reach the sink within a predefined time. Moreover, these applications require a long lifetime of sensor nodes, even up to several years. Fulfilling both requirements is contradicting in the sense that nodes should sleep over long periods in order to maximize the lifetime but also need to shorten sleeping periods to guarantee short end-to-end delays.

To achieve a long lifetime sensor nodes use a low duty cycle (LDC) protocol, which keeps nodes sleeping most of the time. To guarantee end-to-end delays several approaches (DMAC [8] and Q-MAC [12]) maintain wake-up slots in a stacked schedule. The idea resembles the common practice of synchronizing traffic lights to turn green (wake up) just in time of the arrival of vehicles (packets) from previous intersections (hops). However, nodes wake up and listen for incoming frames even when no data is transmitted. Obviously, this causes idle listening, depletes energy and shortens the lifetime.

E. Osipov et al. (Eds.): WWIC 2010, LNCS 6074, pp. 363–374, 2010.

In this work we present a solution for idle listening avoidance (ILA). It reduces idle listening even by two orders of magnitude in LDC protocols with guaranteed end-to-end delays. In that way, ILA prolongs the lifetime by more than 50%. Moreover, we discovered that ILA achieves results very similar to the ideal solution, i.e. to the dedicated hardware. However, ILA is implemented on off-the-shelf sensor nodes and does not need any dedicated hardware.

The paper is organized as follows. Section 2 gives an overview about the scientific efforts related to end-to-end delays and low duty cycle protocols in sensor networks. We introduce the problem of idle listening and guaranteed end-to-end delays in Section 3. In section 4 we present solutions that reduce idle listening. Section 5 presents the results of our experiments. We evaluate the solutions in section 6 and conclude the paper in section 7.

2   Related Work

LDC protocols for wireless sensor networks have been extensively studied, e.g. SMAC [13], DMAC [8], B-MAC [6], Dozer [3]. However, only a few research efforts addressed the problem of limiting end-to-end delays. A general solution to low end-to-end delays resembles the idea of stacked schedule presented in DMAC [8], Q-MAC [12] and in [4]. None of these approaches addressed the problem of idle-listening reduction.

Although we did not find a reasonable solution for limiting idle listening of protocols supporting limited end-to-end delays, some work investigated the trade-off between delay and lifetime. The SMAC authors present in [13] energy savings vs. average sleep delay trade-off. The mean delay and achieved lifetime of CSMA (carrier sense multiple access) and of various TDMA (time division multiple access) approaches presents [5]. Ref. [4] introduces the trade-off relationship between the expected lifetime extension and the corresponding increase in the average detection delay achieved by different sleep scheduling algorithms. Ref. [9] explores the energy-latency trade-off for broadcast communication in sensor networks. In [1] we examined the trade-off between end-to-end delay and the lifetime of a one-hop sensor network based on IEEE 802.15.4 connected to a IEEE 802.11g network.

3   Problem Statement

3.1   End-to-End Delay

In this paper we refer to end-to-end delay as the time from an event detection on a source node to the sink notification. Apparently, it involves a multi-hop communication on the path from the source to the sink. To guarantee desired end-to-end delays nodes on the path to the sink establish a wake-up schedule presented in Figure 1, similarly to stacked schedule of DMAC [8] or Q-MAC [12]. Each node on the path arranges a receive (rx) slot to the previous node and a transmit (tx) slot to the next node. The tx slot follows the corresponding rx

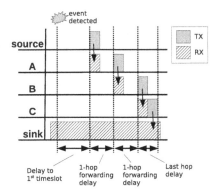

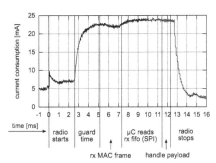

Fig. 1. End-to-end delay results from forwarding delays on intermediate nodes and the delay between event detection and the first tx slot on the source

Fig. 2. Rx slot of tmote sky sensor node (oscilloscope output: average from 2 samples); MAC frame 62 bytes, data rate 250 kbps

slot. In that way, nodes forward messages just after the reception and keep the forwarding delay very small. Therefore, the number of forwarding hops does not influence end-to-end delays considerably. Obviously, the shorter the required end-to-end delay is, the more often nodes have to wake up in order to participate in potential data transmission.

In this paper we consider an underlying MAC protocol that starts transmission exactly at the tx slot, i.e. it does not use any mechanisms like CSMA/CA (Carrier Sense Multiple Access with Collision Avoidance) or RTS/CTS (Request to Send / Clear to Send) that may postpone transmissions. Due to the scheduling approach presented here such means are not needed since the schedule is equivalent to a TDMA approach and inherently avoids contention. Additional medium access means would require longer guard times to compensate possible later transmission, causing longer idle listening.

3.2 Active and Passive Slots

To support end-to-end delays nodes must wake up at each rx slot. After waking up each node listens for a time needed to receive a frame from the previous node. If no frame arrives, the node powers down the transceiver and continues sleeping. We refer to such slots as passive slots. However, if the node receives a frame from the previous node, it forwards it to the next node towards the sink in the following tx slot. We call rx slots that trigger a transmission active.

To measure current consumption of various rx slot phases together with their duration we connected an oscilloscope to a tmote sky sensor node. Figure 2 depicts the results. In this example tmote sky receives a 62-byte long MAC frame of IEEE 802.15.4 standard. To compensate clock drift the node wakes up 2 ms earlier than the expected time of incoming frame.

Figure 3 shows the general structure of an active rx slot. After receiving a preamble[1] and the following Start Frame Delimiter (SFD) the node receives the Medium Access Control (MAC) layer payload. Then, the payload is delivered to the application, i.e. usually the transceiver drives the rx pin high and the microcontroller (µC) raises a receive interrupt (RxINT). After that, an interrupt service routine (ISR) of the operating system (OS) reads the payload from the rx buffer of the transceiver and delivers it to the application. Finally, the application calls an OS function to switch the transceiver off.

We refer to the above-mentioned approach of frame reception as the software solution.

3.3   Drawbacks of Software Solution

Passive slots. Applications running on a sensor node can only detect directly that a packet is received, when the operating system (OS) calls a rx routine, i.e. after getting the message from rx buffer. If no frame is received, the application will not know about it. The only indirect means to detect frame reception is to wait the normal time it takes from waking up till the OS calls the rx routine. The application powers down the transmitter as soon as this time interval has expired w/o any rx interrupt, see Figure 3a. However, handling RxINT and getting a frame from rx buffer may last much longer than the frame reception, see Figure 2. Moreover, if the underlying protocols use frames of various length, the application considers the max. frame length when waiting for RxINT. Obviously, the indirect detection of idle rx slots causes unnecessary long idle listening.

Active slots. In general, after receiving a frame the transceiver stays in the receive mode until µC powers it down explicitly, e.g. in CC2420 transceiver [11] µC writes a special command to the strobe register. Before software can power down the transceiver, it needs to read and process the frame payload during ISR to learn whether or not other frames will follow. After that it can signal the µC to power down the transceiver, see Figure 3a. Of course, if no frames follow the one just received, the transceiver should be powered down immediately after receiving the last byte of the incoming frame to minimize idle listening. However, a node using a software-based solution handles RxINT, reads the whole message and then powers down the transceiver. Thus, the software solution causes idle listening also in active slots.

4   Hardware Support for Idle-Listening Reduction

4.1   Idle Listening Avoidance (ILA)

Some commercial transceivers offer additional features apart from notifying a frame reception. For instance, CC2420 [11] used in tmote sky [10] sensor nodes

---

[1] Receivers use preambles to detect a new frame, the frame start/end and to synchronize bits and symbols (as the clock of sender may run with a different frequency).

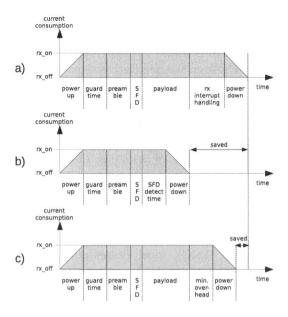

Fig. 3. a) General receive slot (software only); shortened passive (b) and active (c) slots with hardware support

captures the exact time of SFD and raises an interrupt when SFD is received[2]. Moreover, tmote sky raises an interrupt after the transceiver receives the whole MAC frame. We use these features of CC2420 and present a reasonable solution for idle listening avoidance.

Passive slots. To reduce idle listening of passive slots nodes need an indicator that determines as early as possible whether or not a frame arrives. Receiving a preamble and SFD indicates that a frame is to be received. Thus, if the node does not receive SFD in the expected time, in our example guard time + preamble, it assumes that no frame arrives in this slot, see Figure 3b. As the SFD detect time is very short on tmote sky (less than 100 µs), waiting for this time only before powering down the node shortens idle listening during passive slots considerably compared to the solution which waits until the whole frame is processed on lower layers.

Active slots. After receiving a payload, each node should power down the transceiver very quickly, if no frames follow the one just received, see Figure 3c. When tmote sky receives a frame, it raises two interrupts: the first after SFD detection and the second when it receives the whole frame. The second interrupt means only that the transceiver stored the frame in rx buffer and µC must retrieve it, which takes a few ms. However, as it takes only 90 µs to raise the

---

[2] CC2420 just sets SFD pin to high/low. In tmote sky SFD pin is connected to a µC pin that is configured to raise an interrupt on falling/rising edge.

frame reception interrupt on tmote sky, we use it to shorten active slots. Thus, after getting the interrupt, tmote sky expects SFD of the following frame. If the node does not detect SFD until $t_{next\_SFD\_time}$ time, it powers down the transceiver, as no frame follows the one just received:

$$t_{next\_SFD\_int} = t_{rx\_frame} + T_{pause} + T_{preamble} + T_{SFD} + T_{INT\_SFD} \quad (1)$$

where t_{rx_frame} is the exact frame reception time[3], T_{pause} the pause between two consecutive frames, $T_{preamble}$ preamble length of the underlying physical layer, T_{SFD} SFD length[4] and T_{INT_SFD} the time needed to raise an SFD interrupt.

4.2 ASIC Solution

The ideal solution for idle-listening reduction involves the use of an application-specific integrated circuit (ASIC), which causes minimal delays in SFD detection and switching off the transceiver. In general, such a circuit consists of a transceiver and an additional logic. To solve the mentioned idle-listening problems, such a circuit needs two additional features:

1. switch off immediately if SFD is not received within a desired time, see Figure 3b
2. power down after receiving the last frame byte; it results in a very short overhead after frame reception, see min. overhead in Figure 3c. Obviously, to power down the transceiver ASIC must discover whether the frame just received is the last one and the current frame length. In general, ASIC may read it from the MAC header. However, such a solution is tailored for a specific MAC approach, as various protocols have different headers.

In this paper we do not consider an ASIC solution in detail. We introduced it as the optimal solution - neglecting above mentioned open issues - for comparison with our solution.

5   Experiment Results

To evaluate ILA solution we carried out experiments, presented in this section, with tmote sky sensor nodes running TinyOS [7] operating system. Tmote sky consists of CC2420 transceiver (compliant to IEEE 802.15.4 standard) and MSP430 microcontroller (running at 1 MHz speed in our experiments).

In the following experiments we read a timer register to find various hardware and software delays. Since this takes some time we first evaluated the time needed to read the timer register. We stored an initial value to the timer register t_{start}. Then, we iteratively read the timer 1000x in a loop (a TinyOS function). At the

---

[3] μC captures the frame reception time with a hardware timer (no software delay).
[4] IEEE 802.15.4 using 2.4 GHz defines these values as: T_{pause} at least 6 bytes, $T_{preamble}$ 4 bytes and T_{SFD} 1 byte.

end of the experiment we read the timer register t_{end} again and estimated the average time needed to read the timer register t_{read_timer} as:

$$t_{read\_timer} = \frac{t_{end} - t_{start}}{n} \qquad (2)$$

where n equals to the number of timer read operations ($n = 1000$ in our example).

We discovered that the average time needed to read the timer register equals to approx. 26 µs, which is less than a timer tick (the timer runs with 32 768 kHz frequency, i.e. with a tick speed of 30.518 µs). Thus, we can neglect the timer read delay in experiments with significantly longer time measurements.

5.1 SFD and Frame Reception Interrupt

ILA uses SFD interrupt to detect a passive slot in a very early stage and power down the transceiver. In this experiment we measured the time T_{INT_SFD} needed from the SFD reception to the SFD interrupt handling in TinyOS, see SFD detect time in Figure 3b. The examined node received approx. 1000 messages, and collected as many T_{INT_SFD} samples. When CC2420 receives SFD of a new frame, it drives SFD pin high. Then, the µC captures the current timer value t_{SFD} and stores it in a register. In that way, the µC captures the SFD reception time very precisely, e.g. without any delay caused by software execution. Moreover, after SFD reception µC raises an SFD interrupt and TinyOS executes the appropriate handler. We captured the time t_{int} in this handler. In that way, for each received frame we collected the pair of timestamps $<t_{SFD}, t_{int}>$ and estimated the time needed to raise SFD interrupt T_{INT_SFD} as:

$$T_{INT\_SFD} = t_{int} - t_{SFD} \qquad (3)$$

In our experiment the time needed to raise an SFD interrupt was 3 ticks (approx. 91 µs) for all 1000 received messages.

As stated before, tmote sky raises an interrupt after the transceiver received the last byte. However, tmote sky uses the same pin and the same interrupt for SFD detection and for frame reception. In the first case it detects a rising edge of the pin, and a falling edge in the latter case. Thus, raising a frame reception interrupt takes as long as SFD detection, i.e. approx. 91µs .

5.2 Rx Interrupt Overhead

In this experiment we measured the time T_{RxINT} of the rx interrupt handler, i.e. the time from the frame reception on CC2420 transceiver to the function call of TinyOS that gets the payload, depicted as rx interrupt handling in Figure 3a. As the time needed to retrieve a frame from rx buffer depends on the frame size, we examined frames of various size, i.e. 42 and 127 bytes. For each payload size we collected 400 T_{RxINT} samples.

Similarly to the previous experiment, µC captured the SFD reception time t_{SFD} for each frame. Moreover, we captured the time t_{rx_TinyOS} each time

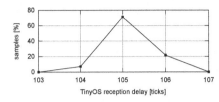 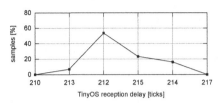

Fig. 4. Frame reception delay on tmote sky with TinyOS with different payload size (left: 42 bytes, right: 127 bytes)

TinyOS executed the function for handling of received frames. TinyOS calls this function after it handles RxINT and reads the frame payload from CC2420[5]. As we sent frames with a constant size (42 and 127 bytes), we calculated the frame length T_{frame} (approx. 44 and 133 ticks by 250 kbps data rate) and estimated T_{RxINT} as:

$$T_{RxINT} = t_{rx\_TinyOS} - t_{SFD} - T_{frame} \qquad (4)$$

Figure 4 depicts the experiment results. For the payload of 42 bytes the shortest RxINT handler took 104 ticks (3.17 ms) and the longest 106 ticks (3.23 ms). However, we noticed significantly longer times for 127-byte payload: from 271 ticks to 274 ticks (8.29 to 8.35 ms). The reason for this is the time that the µC needs to read rx buffer of the transceiver. On tmote sky the µC gets frames from the transceiver using SPI (Serial Peripheral Interface Bus) with 510 kHz SPI clock. With such a clock µC may receive 127 bytes in 2 ms, if the bytes are read one after another. However, we discovered that the µC on tmote sky waits from 50 µs to 170 µs before getting another byte, which causes such long reading of rx buffer , i.e. more than 8 ms for 127-byte frame instead of 2 ms.

6   Evaluation

In general, idle listening of rx slots stems from guard time and listening after a frame reception, see Figure 3. However, in this paper we shorten idle listening after SFD reception only, i.e. we do not consider guard times. Therefore, each time we refer to idle listening, we mean idle listening after SFD reception and not guard times.

6.1   Analysis Model

To analyze the idle-listening reduction we calculate the number of passive $N_{passive}$ and active N_{active} slots during a day, based on the slot period T_{slot} needed to guarantee the end-to-end delay d_{EtE}:

$$T_{slot} = d_{EtE} - n \cdot (T_{frame} + T_{tx\_offset}) \qquad (5)$$

---

[5] µC raises an interrupt after receiving the first payload byte and not the whole payload. Thus, TinyOS starts reading payload bytes, while the payload is still being received. In that way, the time needed for delivering frame to the software is shortened.

$$N_{active} = \frac{T_{day}}{T_{event}} \tag{6}$$

$$N_{passive} = \frac{T_{day}}{T_{slot}} - N_{active} \tag{7}$$

where n is the number of hops from the source to the sink, T_{frame} the expected receive frame length, T_{tx_offset} the time between rx and tx slots on a forwarding node and T_{event} the expected event frequency. In the next steps we calculate the idle-listening time in active and passive slots for both software and ILA solutions.

Software solution. As stated before, during passive slots a node waits for the max. frame length time T_{max_frame} and the RxINT time T_{RxINT}, before it powers down the transceiver, see Figure 3a. Thus, we estimate idle listening in passive slots $T_{passive}$ as:

$$T_{idle\_passive} = T_{max\_frame} + T_{RxINT} \tag{8}$$

During active slots RxINT handler takes T_{RxINT} time, starting from the reception of the last byte. After that, the node powers down the transceiver. However, the node should do that immediately after receiving the last byte. Thus, idle listening in active slots T_{idle_active} equals to:

$$T_{idle\_active} = T_{RxINT} \tag{9}$$

ILA. During passive slots nodes using ILA wait for the time needed to get an SFD interrupt T_{INT_SFD} before switching off the transceiver. Thus, we estimate idle listening during passive slots $T_{idle\_passive}$ as:

$$T_{idle\_passive} = T_{INT\_SFD} \tag{10}$$

As already mentioned, during active slots nodes with ILA wait the time needed for SFD interrupt of the next possible frame, see Eq. 1. If no SFD interrupt is raised, the node switches off the transceiver. Thus, we calculate idle listening during active slots T_{active} as:

$$T_{idle\_active} = T_{pause} + T_{preamble} + T_{SFD} + T_{INT\_SFD} \tag{11}$$

where T_{pause} is the pause between two consecutive frames, $T_{preamble}$ preamble length of the underlying physical layer, T_{SFD} SFD length and T_{INT_SFD} the time needed to raise an SFD interrupt.

6.2   Parameters

We examined software and hardware solutions for various end-to-end delays, as it impacts the number of receive slots and the idle listening consequently. In our simulation we considered a tree topology with a depth of five nodes, i.e. each node receives data from two neighbours and the gathering paths are 5-hops long. When a node detects an event, in our example every two minutes, it sends a message towards the sink. We examined messages with a payload size of 42 and 127 bytes (the max. frame size in IEEE 802.15.4).

As we considered tmote sky sensor node, we use current consumption values from the datasheet [10]. Moreover, we used several parameters of IEEE 802.15.4 (e.g. data rate, preamble length, min. short inter-frame spacing), as the transceiver of tmote sky is compliant to this standard.

To estimate lifetime gain of nodes using the hardware support we need to find the total energy consumption of a node. In [2] we calculated the energy consumption of nodes using our LDC protocol. Basing on this work we assume that in our scenario nodes consume approx. 2.5 mAh a day. Obviously, such an estimation does not guarantee the exact calculation of lifetime. Nonetheless, it gives an estimation about possible lifetime gain of ILA and ASIC solutions.

6.3   Results

The shorter the guaranteed end-to-end delay is, the more receive slots are needed and the longer the total idle-listening time is. For example, for an end-to-end delay of 20 seconds the software approach causes 58 seconds of idle listening a day when sending 42-byte long frames, see Figure 5. If nodes send and expect 127-byte frames, the idle-listening increases to 102 seconds.

As expected, the solutions based on hardware decrease idle listening considerably. For example, for an end-to-end delay of 20 seconds ILA shortens idle listening almost 50 times against the software solution when sending 42-byte frames, and by 85x when sending 127-byte messages, see Figure 5. Moreover, if nodes must guarantee 10 second delay, ILA decreases idle listening by two orders of magnitude when sending 127-byte frames (and by a factor of 58 for 42-byte messages)! Clearly, the shorter the guaranteed delay is, the more ILA gains against the software solution.

In Figures 6 and 7 we present the impact of shorter idle listening on energy consumption and lifetime. As mentioned, ILA shortens idle listening considerably, for example 50x for a delay of 20 seconds (42-byte frames). In that case, nodes consume 0.35 mAh less energy a day and prolong the lifetime by 118 days. This is approx. 16 per cent of the lifetime gain over the software solution. ILA achieves even better results for shorter delays. For example, it prolongs the lifetime by about 50% (more than a year) for 15 seconds delay and 127-byte frames. Moreover, ILA prolongs the lifetime for longer delays as well. For instance, for 1 minute delay ILA increases the lifetime by one month (27 days, 3%).

The ASIC solution shortens idle listening even more than ILA since it has shorter react/detection times. However, it results only in a very small lifetime gain. For longer delays, i.e. 30 seconds and more, ASIC prolongs the lifetime by only 2 days more (0.27%) than ILA, see Figure 8. Even for short delays - 10 seconds - the ASIC solution gains only slightly more than ILA. For instance, when sending 42-byte frames ASIC increases the lifetime by a bit more than a week compared to ILA. It shows clearly that the ILA achieves almost as good results

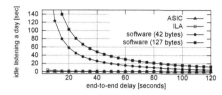

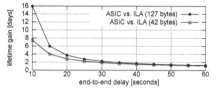

Fig. 5. Idle listening of software and hardware solutions

Fig. 6. Energy gain of ILA vs. software approach

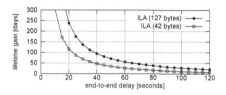

Fig. 7. Lifetime prolongation of our solution vs. software approach

Fig. 8. Lifetime gain of ASIC approach vs. our solution

as an optimal ASIC based solution. However, ILA does not require dedicated hardware and by that can be applied much simpler.

7 Conclusion

In this work we presented a solution to idle listening avoidance (ILA) in sensor networks that guarantee end-to-end delays. An off-the-shelf sensor node with ILA reduces idle listening by 50-100 times (depending on guaranteed end-to-end delay) and prolongs the lifetime by even more than 50 % for 15 seconds end-to-end delay and a message size of 127 bytes. It is evident that the potential lifetime extension to be gained with ILA depends on the guaranteed delay, i.e. the shorter the delay the higher the gain since our approach can be applied to more slots. However we discovered that support for idle listening reduction prolongs the lifetime also for longer end-to-end delays. For example, for one minute delay ILA still increases the lifetime by a month (3%).

Our evaluation revealed that an ideal solution, i.e. based on an ASIC, achieves only slightly better results than ILA e.g. prolongs the lifetime by 0.3% more. However, the ASIC solution requires a dedicated hardware, whereas ILA works on off-the-shelf sensor nodes.

Acknowledgment

The research leading to these results has received funding from the European Community's Seventh Framework Programme (FP7/2007-2013) under grant agreement n° 225186 and from the German Ministry of Education and Research under grant n° 03IP601.

References

1. Brzozowski, M., Langendoerfer, P.: On Prolonging Sensornode Gateway Lifetime by Adapting Its Duty Cycle. In: van den Berg, H., Heijenk, G., Osipov, E., Staehle, D. (eds.) WWIC 2009. LNCS, vol. 5546, pp. 24–35. Springer, Heidelberg (2009)
2. Brzozowski, M., Piotrowski, K., Langendoerfer, P.: A cross-layer approach for data replication and gathering in decentralized long-living wireless sensor networks. In: ISADS 2009: The 9th International Symposium on Autonomous Decentralized Systems (2009)
3. Burri, N., von Rickenbach, P., Wattenhofer, R.: Dozer: ultra-low power data gathering in sensor networks. In: IPSN'07: Proceedings of the 6th international conference on Information processing in sensor networks (2007)
4. Cao, Q., Abdelzaher, T., He, T., Stankovic, J.: Towards optimal sleep scheduling in sensor networks for rare-event detection. In: IPSN'05: Proceedings of the 4th international symposium on Information processing in sensor networks (2005)
5. El-Hoiydi, A.: Spatial tdma and csma with preamble sampling for low power ad hoc wireless sensor networks. In: Proceedings of the Seventh International Symposium on Computers and Communications, ISCC 2002, pp. 685–692 (2002)
6. Polastre, J., Hill, J., Culler, D.: Versatile low power media access for wireless sensor networks. In: SenSys'04: Proceedings of the 2nd international conference on Embedded networked sensor systems (2004)
7. Levis, P., Madden, S., Polastre, J., Szewczyk, R., Whitehouse, K., Woo, A., Gay, D., Hill, J., Welsh, M., Brewer, E., Culler, D.: Tinyos: An operating system for sensor networks (2005)
8. Lu, G., Krishnamachari, B., Raghavendra, C.S.: An adaptive energy-efficient and low-latency MAC for tree-based data gathering in sensor networks. Wireless Communications and Mobile Computing 7(7) (2007)
9. Miller, M.J., Sengul, C., Gupta, I.: Exploring the Energy-Latency Trade-Off for Broadcasts in Energy-Saving Sensor Networks. In: Proceedings of the 25th IEEE International Conference on Distributed Computing Systems, ICDCS 2005 (2005)
10. Moteiv Corporation. Tmote Sky Ultra low power IEEE 802.15.4 compliant wireless sensor module (2006),
    http://www.sentilla.com/pdf/eol/tmote-sky-datasheet.pdf
11. Texas Instruments. 2.4 GHz IEEE 802.15.4 / ZigBee-ready RF Transceiver (2007),
    http://focus.ti.com/docs/prod/folders/print/cc2420.html
12. Vasanthi, N.A., Annadurai, S.: Energy efficient sleep schedule for achieving minimum latency in query based sensor networks. In: SUTC '06: Proceedings of the IEEE International Conference on Sensor Networks, Ubiquitous, and Trustworthy Computing (2006)
13. Ye, W., Heidemann, J., Estrin, D.: An energy-efficient mac protocol for wireless sensor networks. In: INFOCOMM (2002)

An Efficient Authenticated-Encryption with Associated-Data Block Cipher Mode for Wireless Sensor Networks

A.A. Adekunle and S.R. Woodhead

Department of Computer and Communication Engineering,
University of Greenwich,
Chatham Maritime, Chatham, Kent ME4 4TB
{a.a.adekunle,s.r.woodhead}@gre.ac.uk

Abstract. This paper begins by presenting an analysis of the current generic schemes utilising block cipher design techniques for the provision of authenticated encryption with associated data (AEAD) security services in communication protocols. Such protocols are commonly applied in wireless sensor networks. The conclusions of this analysis are used in the design of a resourceful AEAD construct, which we term Simultaneous Combined Mode Algorithm (SCMA). Using software simulation we show that our construct can achieve improvements in processing energy requirement, processing latency and data throughput when benchmarked against the analysed schemes.

Keywords: Authenticated encryption, associated data, message authentication, modes of operation, wireless sensor networks.

1 Introduction

In Wireless Sensor Network (WSN) applications it can often be the case that when sensing nodes communicate, they require the transmitted packets to have the payload portion (wholly or partially) encrypted and authenticated (as there are dangers to unauthenticated encryption [1]) but the associated header portion unencrypted (and authenticated) so that packets can be routed expeditiously. This requirement is referred to as authenticated encryption with associated data (AEAD) and was first publicly formalised as a cryptographic primitive in its own right by Rogaway [2].

AEAD schemes can be classified as either two-pass or one-pass schemes. In a two-pass scheme, the first pass is aimed at providing privacy and the other, authenticity. One way of making a two-pass AEAD scheme is by generic composition, wherein one pass constitutes a (privacy-only) symmetric-encryption scheme, while the other pass is a message authentication code (MAC). In a one-pass scheme, a single pass is made through the data, simultaneously engendering both privacy and authenticity. Characteristically, one-pass schemes generally exhibit a lower computational cost.

E. Osipov et al. (Eds.): WWIC 2010, LNCS 6074, pp. 375–385, 2010.
© Springer-Verlag Berlin Heidelberg 2010

1.1 Motivation

A required and contemporary goal for WSN data communication security protocols is to have a non patented AEAD scheme having a computational and energy cost significantly lower than the cost for a generic composition scheme due to the majority of currently utilised WSN platforms possessing limited energy and computational resources [3]. The scheme must rely on 64-bit block ciphers as proprietary or legacy security protocols for WSN applications often utilise block ciphers with 64-bit block sizes, such as Skipjack [4] to provide all the security services required. The scheme must also be suitable, without modification, for future migration to 128-bit block ciphers.

1.2 Preliminaries

We define the goal of an AEAD protocol to be one that (wholly or partially) encrypts a message M but likewise authenticates both the message and the associated header. In particular, the header is authenticated but not encrypted. An AEAD protocol is usually built using an authenticated encryption (AE) scheme [5] that is capable of simultaneously protecting both the privacy and the authenticity/integrity of the encapsulated data.

The three generalised concepts used in AE schemes are; *Encrypt-and-MAC (E&M):* First encrypt M using key K1, to yield ciphertext C and then compute the MAC tag T; $T \leftarrow MAC_{K2}(M)$ to yield the pair (C, T). *MAC-then-Encrypt (MtE):* First MAC M using key K1 to yield MAC tag T and then encrypt the resulting pair (M,T) using key K2. *Encrypt-then-MAC (EtM):* First encrypt M using key K1 to yield ciphertext C and then compute $T \leftarrow MAC_{K2}(C)$ to yield the pair (C, T).

Decryption and verification are straightforward for each approach, for the case of MtE decrypt first, follow by authenticating. EtM and E&M need to authenticate first and then decrypt. Message authentication; we say a MAC function is considered secure if it is computationally infeasible to perform an existential forgery under an adaptive chosen text attack on it. Confidentiality; we use the indistinguishability of ciphertext from a random string under a chosen plaintext attack. This definition has been shown to be equivalent to several other definitions [6].

1.3 Our Contribution

The main contribution of this paper is the design, implementation and evaluation of a practical and secure one-pass AEAD construct utilising block cipher modes of operation. Using software simulation employing data payload lengths of 8 to 64 bytes, a range common in WSN applications; our AEAD construct indicates performance improvements in CPU instruction cycle requirements and indicated energy usage compared to the generic composition block cipher based schemes utilised in current WSN security protocols.

1.4 Outline

The remainder of this paper is organised as follows. Section 2 introduces an analysis of generalised AEAD block cipher based schemes for WSN. Section 3 explains our design philosophy and design decisions for our new construct, plus a schematic diagram representation. Section 4 details benchmark results between our new construct and a range of AEAD generic schemes currently used in security protocols for WSNs. Section 5 provides general comments and our recommendation for SCMA usage in WSN applications. Section 6 concludes and indicates our future research directions.

2   Generalised AEAD Schemes for WSN

The provision of AEAD services in WSN data communication security protocols can be achieved using block cipher modes in a range of combinations. In the interest of brevity, in this section we only analyse AEAD generic schemes that have exemplar algorithms published in open literature for security protocols in WSNs.

The generic composition scheme CBC-MAC [7] for authentication and Counter (CTR) mode encryption is used by Perring et al for their security protocol for WSNs, SPINS [8]. The construct used, utilises a 64-bit block cipher using two derived keys, one for authentication and the other for encryption.

Counter with Cipher Block Chaining Message Authentication Code [9], abbreviated to CCM is a National Institute of Standards and Technology (NIST) recommended mode based on this generic scheme. CCM is intended for use in a packet environment, i.e., when all of the data is available in storage before CCM is applied. CCM is not designed to support partial processing or stream processing and is only recommended for use with 128-bit block ciphers. The same key, K, is used for both the CTR and CBC-MAC mechanisms within CCM. Jonsson provides a proof of security for this combination [10]. In this paper we abbreviate this two-pass generic scheme as CBCTR.

TinySec [11], which is currently the de facto standard for WSN data communication security, was designed by Karlof et al utilising the generic composition scheme of a variant of CBC-MAC for authentication and CBC encryption mode for message confidentiality. This scheme uses two separate keys and a 64-bit block cipher as the underlying cryptographic primitive. The designers specifically selected CBC encryption mode for TinySec because of its robustness to information leakage when initial values (IV) repeat, in contrast to stream ciphers where a repeated IV can reveal the plaintext of both messages. In CBC mode, IV reuse reveals only the length (in blocks) of the longest shared prefix of the two messages. In this paper we abbreviate this two-pass generic scheme to CBCBC.

Li et al use a variant of the Accumulated Block Chaining (ABC) scheme [12], which they call CBC-X [13] utilising a 64-bit block cipher for their security protocol for WSNs. The CBC-X construct is a one-pass AEAD scheme that requires two keys to calculate the encryption and authentication run. The ABC generic scheme has been designed with low overhead as a goal; little extra work is required beyond that required for the electronic codebook (ECB) mode. The generic ABC scheme has infinite error propagation (i.e. an error in one ciphertext block propagates to all subsequent ciphertext blocks). A mode with this property is suited for situations where errors during transmission are either unlikely to occur or are accommodated by non-cryptographic means, such as error-detecting codes or retransmissions. These properties are contrary to the current practice of applying security services in WSNs [14], thus, we opted not to benchmark this scheme.

Doomun and Soyjaudah design and implement a one-pass hybrid CBC-MAC variant merged with CTR encryption, defined as Counter Mode Block Chaining-MAC

(CMBC-MAC) [15], to replace the CCM two-pass AEAD scheme in the IEEE 802.11i security standard [16]. CMBC-MAC can be seen as a variant of the random-ise-then-combine paradigm [17]. Initial observations of the CMBC-MAC construct point to cryptanalytic defects; mainly it is vulnerable to block wise-adaptive attacks [18] due to its linear combining method. In addition, pre-computation of the initial counter value in the CTR encryption phase, can result in lowering the effective key length of the underlying block cipher [19], which can lead to key recovery using Time Memory Trade Off (TMTO) attacks [20].

Bauer et al [21] conduct performance analyses on a number of AEAD constructs and conclude that the CCFB+H [22] construct was the most suitable for many WSN applications. CCFB+H is classified by its designer as a two-pass AEAD scheme that is claimed to be as efficient as a one-pass AEAD scheme. Despite very limited current utilisation in WSN security protocols, its simplicity of code and non patented status, plus the designer's claim of its efficiency, induces us to include it in our benchmark as a specific construct.

3   AEAD Constructs

Block cipher chaining based AEAD algorithms have their design parameters deter-mined by the known security attacks and performance requirements of the application environment in which they operate. Security is related to key length, MAC tag and packet size. Performance is determined essentially by the processing speed of the underlying block cipher employed and the AE scheme in operation. These findings all influence our AEAD construct and are discussed in the following subsections.

3.1   AEAD Model and Protocol

Throughout this paper we will consider the AEAD problem in the "symmetric-key model". AEAD schemes employ a nonce, they have to do this (or be stateful or prob-abilistic) in order to achieve semantic security. It is the responsibility of the sender not to reuse any nonce. For this purpose the sender will need to maintain state. The receiver can be stateless (replay-detection is not a part of the defined goal) and de-terministic. It is outside of the model how the associated-data H is made known to the receiver. We do not consider the associated-data to be part of the ciphertext, though the receiver will need it in order to decrypt. The same comments apply to the nonce N.

We define the AEAD protocol as consisting of two deterministic algorithms; en-cryption and decryption. The encryption algorithm is AEAD:$E_K(N, H, M)$, where N is a nonce, H is a header and M is a message to be encrypted with K, the secret key. The algorithm returns the ciphertext C and an authentication string, tag, of n bit length. The decryption algorithm AEAD:$D_K(N, H, C, tag)$ returns either INVALID or the proper message M. The adversary is allowed to manipulate both the nonce and the associated-data (subject to the constraint that no nonce is repeated), and the goal of the adversary is to successfully forge an AEAD protocol by being able to output a pair (N, H, C, tag) which is valid and (C, tag) was not the result of any prior (N, H, M) query.

3.2 Design Principle and Rational

The underlining design philosophy of our AEAD construct is a variant of the random-ise-then-combine paradigm with the randomising function being a block cipher with a non linear combination method and a keyed pseudo-random permutation transform preceding the output. It is a one-pass scheme that can be operated using a single or double key. The encrypting portion is a variant of Counter Output Feedback mode (CTR-OFB) [23] and the authentication portion is a keyed sum hash.

Bellare and Namprempre [24] systematically examined each of the three ap-proaches to AE schemes in a formal setting. Their results showed that if the MAC functions in AE schemes have a property called "strongly unforgeable", then it is possible to achieve the strongest definition of security for AE schemes only via the EtM approach. They further show that some well known encryption schemes fail to provide privacy in the AE setting when using the E&M approach and fail to provide a slightly stronger notion of privacy with the MtE approach. We therefore base our construct on the EtM scheme.

OFB mode is chosen as the encryption mode due to its desirable fault-tolerance characteristics, i.e. a ciphertext error affects only the corresponding bit(s) of the plain-text. Therefore in an error-prone environment such as wireless communication, OFB mode is particularly useful. OFB mode can produce short key stream cycles, but com-bining it with CTR mode can prevent this. We base our encryption function on a combination of CTR mode and OFB mode. Using the combined mode also has a benefit in that the underlying block cipher only needs to be operated in either the encryption or decryption direction.

The message authentication is a variant of QBC-MAC [25]. We include an extra input called a "tweak" which allows users to get several different encrypting key streams, and as a consequence different MACs, by using distinct values for this tweak input. This is closely-related to an idea of Liskov et al who introduced tweakable block ciphers [26]. A difference with our tweak is that it can be made a security parameter.

3.3 SCMA Construct

SCMA, illustrated in Figure 1, can take a message M of any length and generate tags with length up to the block size of the underlying block cipher. As a concrete exam-ple, using a 64-bit block cipher, we can distinguish a number of steps.

Message Encoding and splitting: first "encode" the message into some string M^*. All that is demanded of an encoding method is that it does not "lose" information: you can "decode" M^* to recover M, and you can recognise when a string is and is not the encoding of any message. Split the result into block width message words M_1, $M_2...M_n$.

State initialisation: fill the 64-bit state, S, with the nonce and then apply the underly-ing block cipher encryption to it using the integrity key, K1.

Chained randomising: XOR the result of the IV encryption to an incrementing counter starting at a value of 1, then ADD modulo 2^n a tweaked value (if used) to this and apply the underlying block cipher encryption to it using the encryption key, K2.

The result is XORed with the first message word M_1, with the result then ADDed modulo 2^n to an accumulator initialised by the result of encrypting the nonce. For each additional message word M_i, repeat from the XORing of the counter and ADD modulo 2^n the ciphertext of the previous block cipher encryption to the result.

Finalisation: Apply the block cipher encryption to the accumulator using the integrity key and ADD modulo 2^n the accumulator to the result. Form the tag by taking m bits of the result.

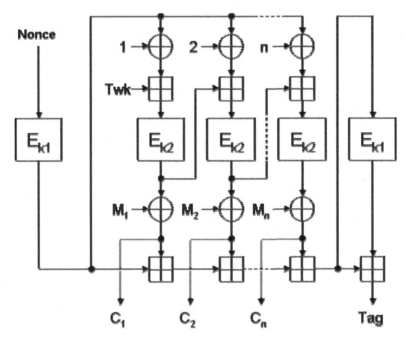

Fig. 1. SCMA schematic diagram. M1…Mn are the payload plaintext and C1…Cn the corresponding ciphertext. Twk is a tweak value chosen by the application designer.

4 Benchmarking

A software comparison between SCMA, CCFB+H, CBCTR and CBCBC modes was undertaken. CBCBC was run exactly as stated in the TinySec protocol. CBCTR authentication was implemented using the CBC-MAC variant [27] utilised in TinySec and the encryption portion used the CTR mode, where the encryption of the IV is the starting counter value. CCFB+H mode code was programmed by us form the designer's description. The de-facto packet format for WSN TinySec-AE is used as a guide.

4.1 Measurement Methodology

For simplicity and familiarity, all evaluated algorithms are implemented in the C programming language and are not optimised. The evaluation runs of the block ciphers were undertaken as a simulation of a PIC18F2320 an 8-bit RISC microcontroller simulated at a 20MHz clock frequency (200 nanosecond instruction execution). The compiler used was the MikroC v7.

4.2   Simulation Performance Metrics

The performance and evaluation of the AEAD algorithms is evaluated based on the performance metrics defined as follows:

CPU Instruction cycles per byte: A CPU instruction cycle per byte is an indication of how much total energy it takes to process the input data frame length. The instruction cycle per byte performance measurement is also used as an indication of the block cipher algorithm's energy efficiency. The performance rating increases with a lower instruction cycle count per byte.

Bits per instruction cycle: Bits per instruction cycle is an indication of process throughput depending on the packet length. The bit per instruction cycle performance measurement is also used as an indication of the AEAD modes suitability for real time applications. The performance rating increases with a higher bit count per instruction cycle.

4.3   Benchmark Performance

Figure 2 indicates from the simulation runs that SCMA requires the lowest number of CPU instruction cycles across the payload lengths and can be considered to be the quickest AEAD mode tested.

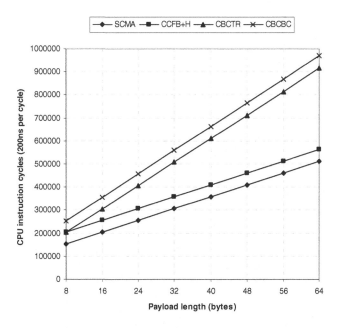

Fig. 2. CPU instruction cycles required to calculate an AEAD tag of 4 bytes for varying payload lengths on the simulated PIC18F2320 8-bit RISC microcontroller using the Skipjack block cipher

CCFB+H mode is the second quickest of the modes tested with CBCTR mode being the third. The CBCBC mode used the most instruction cycles across the various payload lengths and therefore is the slowest AEAD mode tested. Small payload lengths of 8 bytes indicate a performance improvement of SCMA in relation to CCFB+H of 6%. Figure 2 can be used to give an indication of the efficiency (and infer energy usage) of the AEAD modes tested.

Figure 3 indicates processing throughput rates of the AEAD modes tested. The mode with the highest rate is SCMA followed by CCFB+H and then CBCTR with CBCBC last. SCMA shows a 1.3 factor improvement in processing throughput in relation to CCFB+H for 8 byte payloads.

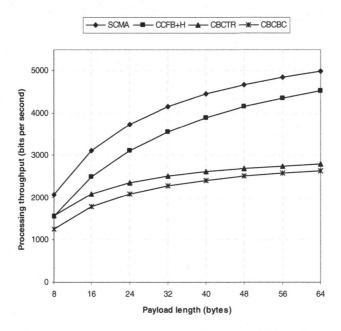

Fig. 3. Bits per CPU instruction cycle to calculate an AEAD tag of 4 bytes for varying payload lengths on the simulated PIC18F2320 8-bit RISC microcontroller using the Skipjack block cipher

5 Discussions

In this section we summarise some of the properties of SCMA and services it can be employed to provide:

Two factor message authentication codes (TF-MAC): Unlike the analysed AEAD schemes that relay on one-factor MAC (knowledge of the key), SCMA intrinsically provides TF-MAC as knowledge of a shared key and tweak value is required to generate the MAC tag. Using two factors for message authentication as opposed to one factor generally delivers a higher level of authentication assurance. A two-factor user authentication protocol for WSN is proposed by Das [28]; TF-MAC is intended for use in machine-to-machine (M2M) secured communication.

Virtual private connection (VPC): In WSN clusters the sensors all share a common group key, if two sensors share a tweaked value they would be able to establish a virtual private connection that other sensors despite having knowledge of the key can not participate unless they possess the tweaked value. This concept can be expanded to create *secured group multicast communication* as in [29].

The SCMA construct permits authenticity verification without ciphertext recovery and processing of static headers with negligible per-message cost. Authenticity verification without ciphertext recovery leads to invalid messages being rejected at half the cost of MAC generation. SCMA can be used for message integrity only by not extracting the ciphertext.

Given a repeated nonce, integrity and encryption key, two messages that have identical plaintext blocks in identical positions will produce identical ciphertext in that position for a majority of the analysed AEAD schemes. However using SCMA with different tweak values prevents this situation, as a different key stream is generated for different tweak values. SCMA provides inherent protection to IV and key reuse.

An important aspect of AEAD schemes is the authentication of the packet; when using MACs in WSN applications the critical parameter is not the amount of data processed but the number of messages authenticated by the sender using the same key. Based on our security analysis, our recommendations for using SCMA with 64-bit block ciphers are tabulated in Table 1.

Table 1. Usage parameters for SCMA utilising 64-bit block ciphers

Risk of valid forgery	Total number of processed blocks	Maximum number of key evocations
2^{-16}	2^{24}	2^{8}
2^{-24}	2^{20}	2^{12}
2^{-32}	2^{16}	2^{16}
2^{-40}	2^{12}	2^{20}
2^{-48}	2^{8}	2^{24}

Given the frequency with which networking protocols need to solve the AEAD problem and not the privacy problem, the authenticity problem or the AE-problem; we begin to view AEAD as the most appropriate solution in many WSN settings. We suggest that it is the abstract interface of an AEAD scheme that designers of secure packet-based communication protocols should, in most instances, be writing to and thinking in terms of.

6 Conclusion

In this paper we presented a resourceful AEAD construct, SCMA, which is particularly suited for use in WSN applications. We showed a graphical implementation of our AEAD construct and chart results of a simulation benchmark between it and the

AEAD generalised schemes used in current WSN security protocols. Our proposed construct proved to have advantageous performance regarding the amount of pre-processing, memory overhead, throughput plus speed for long and short messages.

Subsequent work will focus on producing a security proof for SCMA and on performance evaluation when integrated in a security framework supporting secure communication services in WSNs.

Acknowledgment

The authors would like to thank the anonymous reviewers for their useful comments that helped the overall presentation of this paper.

References

1. Joux, A., Martinet, G., Valette, F.: Blockwise-adaptive attackers. In: Yung, M. (ed.) CRYPTO 2002. LNCS, vol. 2442, pp. 17–30. Springer, Heidelberg (2002)
2. Rogaway, P.: Authenticated-encryption with associated-data. In: 9th ACM Conference on Computer and Communications Security (CCS-9). ACM Press, New York (2002)
3. Hill, J., Culler, D.: Mica: A wireless platform for deeply embedded networks. IEEE Micro 22(6), 12–24 (2002)
4. Knudsen, L.R., Wagner, D.: On the structure of Skipjack. Discrete Applied Mathematics 111, 103–116 (2001)
5. Bellare, M., Namprempre, C.: Authenticated encryption: Relations among notions and analysis of the generic composition paradigm. In: Okamoto, T. (ed.) ASIACRYPT 2000. LNCS, vol. 1976, pp. 531–545. Springer, Heidelberg (2000)
6. Bellare, M., Desai, A., Jokipii, E., Rogaway, P.: A concrete security treatment of symmetric encryption. In: Proceedings of the 38th Symposium on Foundations of Computer Science, pp. 394–403. IEEE, Los Alamitos (1997)
7. National Institute of Standards and Technology (NIST). Special Publication 800-38A: Recommendation for Block Cipher Modes of Operation – methods and techniques (2001)
8. Perrig, A., Szewczyk, R., Tygar, J.D., Wen, V., Culler, D.E.: SPINS: Security protocols for sensor networks. Wireless Networks 8(5), 521–534 (2002)
9. Whiting, D., Housley, R., Ferguson, N.: Counter with CBCMAC (CCM). RFC 3610 (2003)
10. Jonsson, J.: On the security of CTR+CBC-MAC. In: Nyberg, K., Heys, H.M. (eds.) SAC 2002. LNCS, vol. 2595, pp. 76–93. Springer, Heidelberg (2003)
11. Karlof, C., Sastry, N., Wagner, D.: TinySec: A link security architecture for wireless sensor networks. In: SenSys'04 (2004)
12. Knudsen, L.R.: Block chaining modes of operation. Technical Report, Department of Informatics, University of Bergen (2000)
13. Li, S., Li, T., Wang, X., Zhou, J., Chen, K.: Efficient link layer security scheme for wireless sensor networks. In: Proceedings of Journal on Information and Computational Science. Binary Information Press (2007)
14. Chan, H., Perrig, A.: Security and privacy in sensor networks. IEEE Computer Magazine, 103–105 (2003)

15. Razvi Doomun, M., Sunjiv Soyjaudah, K.M.: Resource saving AES-CCMP design with hybrid counter mode block chaining – MAC. IJCSNS International Journal of Computer Science and Network Security 8(10), 1–13 (2008)
16. IEEE Std 802.11i, IEEE Standard for Wireless LAN Medium Access Control (MAC) and Physical Layer Specifications (Amendment 6: Medium Access Control Security Enhancements) (2004)
17. Bellare, M., Micciancio, D.: A new paradigm for collision-free hashing: Incrementally at reduced cost. In: Fumy, W. (ed.) EUROCRYPT 1997. LNCS, vol. 1233, pp. 163–192. Springer, Heidelberg (1997)
18. Fouque, P.A., Joux, A., Poupard, G.: Blockwise adversarial model for on-line ciphers and symmetric encryption schemes. In: Handschuh, H., Hasan, M.A. (eds.) SAC 2004. LNCS, vol. 3357, pp. 212–226. Springer, Heidelberg (2004)
19. McGrew, D.A.: Counter mode security: Analysis and Recommendations. Cisco Systems (November 2002)
20. Biryukov, A., Shamir, A.: Cryptanalytic time/memory/data tradeoffs for stream ciphers. In: Okamoto, T. (ed.) ASIACRYPT 2000. LNCS, vol. 1976, pp. 1–13. Springer, Heidelberg (2000)
21. Bauer, G.R., Potisk, P., Tillich, S.: Comparing Block Cipher Modes of Operation on MICAz Sensor Nodes. In: 2009 Parallel, Distributed and Network-based Processing, pp. 371–378 (2009)
22. Lucks, S.: Two-Pass authenticated encryption faster than generic composition. In: Gilbert, H., Handschuh, H. (eds.) FSE 2005. LNCS, vol. 3557, pp. 284–298. Springer, Heidelberg (2005)
23. Sung, J., Lee, S., Lim, J.I., Lee, W., Yi, O.: Concrete security analysis of CTR-OFB and CTR-CFB modes of operation. In: Kim, K.-c. (ed.) ICISC 2001. LNCS, vol. 2288, pp. 103–113. Springer, Heidelberg (2002)
24. Bellare, M., Namprempre, C.: Authenticated encryption: Relations among notions and analysis of the generic composition paradigm. In: Okamoto, T. (ed.) ASIACRYPT 2000. LNCS, vol. 1976, pp. 531–545. Springer, Heidelberg (2000)
25. Adekunle, A.A., Woodhead, S.R.: On efficient data integrity and data origin authentication for wireless sensor networks utilising block cipher design techniques. In: Al-Begain, K. (ed.) NGMAST'09, pp. 419–424. IEEE Computer Society, Los Alamitos (September 2009)
26. Liskov, M., Rivest, R., Wagner, D.: Tweakable block ciphers. In: Yung, M. (ed.) CRYPTO 2002. LNCS, vol. 2442, pp. 31–46. Springer, Heidelberg (2002)
27. Schneier, B.: Applied Cryptography, 2nd edn. John Wiley & Sons, Chichester (1996)
28. Das, M.L.: Two-factor user authentication in wireless sensor networks. IEEE Trans. Wireless. Comm. 8(3), 1086–1090 (2009)
29. Flury, R., Wattenhofer, R.: Routing, Anycast, and Multicast for Mesh and Sensor Networks. In: IEEE International Conference on Computer Communications (INFOCOM 2007), Anchorage, Alaska, USA (May 2007)

Secure Overlays: Making Static Key Distribution Schemes Work with Mobile Base Stations in WSNs

Ioana Rodhe and Christian Rohner

Department of Information Technology, Uppsala University
Box 337, 751 05 Uppsala, Sweden
{ioana.rodhe,christian.rohner}@it.uu.se

Abstract. We introduce the concept of secure overlays over static key distribution schemes to enable the use of mobile base stations for secure data querying in wireless sensor networks. Secure overlays are key distributions initialized from fixed initialization points, allowing queries to be inserted anywhere in the network. We thereby overcome the need for re-keying when a base station moves, at the cost that a query only spreads in a limited part of the network along the key distribution.

On the example of a layered key distribution and a query dissemination protocol we argue that the use of only a few secure overlays can compensate for that artifact. Queries sent from within the area defined by the initialization points reach a significant part of the sensor nodes within the first few hops.

Keywords: Wireless sensor networks, mobile base stations, secure data querying, key distribution schemes.

1 Introduction

Sensor networks are used for sensing and collecting data from different environments. A sensor network consists of small sensor nodes and at least one base station collecting data. The limited transmission ranges of the nodes demand multi-hop communication when the deployment area is large. Queries are sent by the base station into the network and nodes answer with data. The two operations are also known as data querying.

While a base station in general can be assumed to be a powerful and tamperproof device, sensor nodes have limited resources and are prone to attacks. Secure data querying is therefore not a trivial operation. Queries have to be protected from being modified or inserted by others than the base station, in order to avoid wrong readings and to save energy. Sensor data has also to be protected from being read by others than the base station. These aspects are in particular an issue in multi-hop networks where queries and data readings are forwarded from node to node.

Secure data querying is dependent on a key distribution scheme. A common approach is to use the base station's position as an initialization point and build

E. Osipov et al. (Eds.): WWIC 2010, LNCS 6074, pp. 386–397, 2010.

a structure around it. This structure can be a tree rooted in the base station [1] or layers built considering the nodes' hop distance from it [2]. Relations and shared keys between nodes or nodes and the base station are derived from the nodes' positions in the structure. For example, in a tree, a node can share a pairwise key with its kth ancestor [1]. Also, the traffic flow follows the structure: messages are sent between layers or between a parent and its children. We refer to these distributions as static key distribution schemes.

Mobile devices, such as PDAs and mobile phones, can nowadays be used as base stations [3], [4]. A mobile base station can help to better distribute the energy consumption in the network by variating the nodes that are closest to it and thus have to forward more messages. When having a static key distribution scheme built around the base station's initial position, moving the base station requires re-keying the whole network with the new position of the base station as new itialization point.

We propose a different approach, which does not require re-keying: we consider a static key distribution as a *secure overlay* and deploy secure overlays from different *initialization points*. Note that the initialization points are chosen as locations in the deployment area and that we do not need a base station in place to use a secure overlay. Assuming knowledge of the appropriate keys, queries can be inserted from anywhere in a secure overlay, but will follow the overlay's structure and will only spread in a limited part of the network. If the key distribution, for example, follows a tree topology, the query will only spread in the subtree from where the query is inserted. By sending the query over several overlays, we can compensate for the limited spread and allow the query to spread in different directions. The base station can then freely move in the network and use the secure overlays from any point.

We will show our idea on a layered key distribution scheme, where nodes get keys assigned depending on their hop-distance to an initialization point. We estimate the limited angle of spread and show by simulation how the number of initialization points and their positions influence the number of nodes that can be reached. We show that, if the mobile base station is within the area defined by the initialization points, the queries reach a significant part of the sensor nodes within the first few hops.

2   Target Scenarios

We observed that many protocols for secure data querying consider a static base station and organize the nodes in some structure around it, e.g., a tree or layers. The cryptographic keys used for secure data querying are derived from the tree or layered structure. Considering a tree structure rooted at the base station or layers built around it, the queries will spread away from the base station and the data will be aggregated in the opposite direction towards the base station. This kind of static structures that build around base station's position are appropriate when the base station is static and in the same place for the whole life time of the sensor network. We target at introducing mobile base stations, such as mobile phones, in such scenarios and allow them to use the same key distribution schemes and security protocols.

We give a short description of a layered key distribution and a tree-based key distribution and of how they are used. These are examples of static key distribution schemes where it is hard to just introduce a mobile base station.

2.1   Layered Key Distribution

One way to organize the nodes is in layers around the base station's position: nodes i hops away from the base station comprise layer i and share a common layer key k_i. The keys are also interleaved: the nodes in layer i also know key k_{i+n}, where n is a security parameter, and the base station knows the first n keys. Figure 1 shows an example of a sensor network with five layers and $n = 2$.

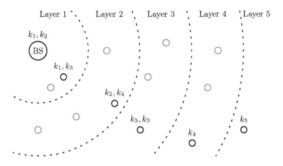

Fig. 1. Layers in a network. k_i denotes the *layer key* of layer i, which is known by all the nodes in the layer. BS is the base station and ○ are sensor nodes. The security parameter n is 2, which means that each node in, e.g., layer 2 also knows key k_4.

These keys can be used to achieve query authentication [2]: the base station constructs MACs with the first n layer keys and sends them together with the query. The nodes in the first layer will verify the query using the MAC constructed with k_1, remove this MAC from the message and add a MAC constructed with the layer key k_{1+n}. They will forward the query to the nodes in layer two. This way the query will be sent from a node in one layer to its neighbors in the next layer and MACs will be added and removed in an interleaved manner.

2.2   Tree-Based Key Distribution

Another way to organize the nodes is in a tree rooted at the base station. Keys can be distributed along the tree in the following way: each node shares a secret key with its kth ancestor. If the node does not have a kth ancestor, it will share a key with the base station. Figure 2 illustrates a small network organized as a tree where each node shares a key with its grandparent ($k = 2$).

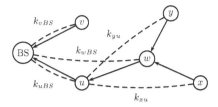

Fig. 2. A tree key distribution where each node shares a key with its grandparent (k_{ij} denotes the key shared by node i and j). The dashed lines show which nodes share a key. The arrows show connections between a node and its parent in the tree.

When homomorphic encryption is used, the data that is being aggregated is encrypted using these keys creating layers of encryption that each will be removed after k hops. At the base station, the last k keys will be removed, resulting in the aggregated data [1].

3   Secure Overlays

In this section we present our concept of secure overlays that can be applied to static key distribution schemes to make them work for sensor networks with mobile base stations.

3.1   Concept

Let us assume that the base station is, in the deployment phase, in one position and a static structure is built around it. We call the base station's initial position an *initialization point*. After the deployment phase we allow the base station to move from the initialization point, but we keep the same static key structure built around the initialization point. With knowledge of the appropriate keys, the base station can start a query, or aggregate data, from any point in the network. Because the static key structure is still built around the initialization point and the message flow still follows the static structure, queries will spread in a limited angle away from the initialization point, starting from the base station's current position, and cover only a part of the network. This is illustrated in Figure 3(a), where the initialization point is in the lower left corner of the deployment area and the nodes are divided into layers. We can see how the query spreads from one node in a layer to its neighbors in the next layer, and so on, until it reaches the most outer layer. We further refer to the nodes that get the query as *reached nodes*.

A way to spread queries in different directions from any position in the network is needed. We refer to a static key deployment with its initialization point as a *secure overlay*. We propose to have several such secure overlays deployed in the network from different initialization points. An initialization point is a location in the deployment area from where a static structure is built and it is not connected

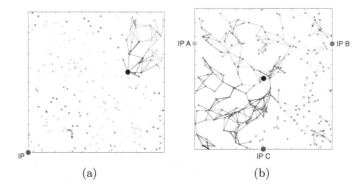

(a)   (b)

Fig. 3. Deployment area of 250 nodes (×) organized in layers around the initialization points (IP). The lines show the spreading of a query sent from a mobile base station (•). In (a) the colors represent the different layers, while in (b) the colors represent the three secure overlays. In (b) the blue × with no lines are nodes that have not been reached by the query.

to the base station's position, because the base station is mobile. For each secure overlay, the nodes are structured according to the position of its initialization point. So, when a query is inserted, it will spread in one direction away from the initialization point, for each secure overlay. Figure 3(b) shows how the query spreads in a scenario with three initialization points and the mobile base station located in the middle of the deployment area.

Which nodes are reached over a secure overlay depends on the position of the mobile base station with respect to the secure overlay's initialization point. This is why there is no guarantee that all nodes around the base station will be reached. We will further on show that a few initialization points are enough to ensure a high percentage of reached nodes within a few hops from the base station.

Taking the layered scheme as an example, from each initialization point the nodes will be organized into layers. So a node will belong to a layer in each secure overlay. The base station, when it wants to send a query, will check in which layers its current neighboring nodes are and build one query message with the appropriate keys for each secure overlay. Note that it is the same query that is sent over each secure overlay, but with different authentication information.

3.2 Initialization Cost

We discuss the cost of having s secure overlays in the network, compared with a deployment with a static base station and one secure overlay.

The nodes that share a common key in a static key distribution are usually several hops away from each other. The only known way to deploy these keys into the nodes is to have the base station collect information about the nodes' positions, construct the structure and send the keys to each node using individual pre-shared keys. When using several secure overlays, the same approach can be used. Instead of using its own position, the mobile base station will choose the initialization points, construct the structure from each of them and then distribute the keys using the individual pre-shared keys.

From our target scenarios we note that, for each secure overlay, a node needs one or two keys[1]. So when s secure overlays are deployed, each node will have s or $2s$ keys. As our simulation results show, a few initialization points are enough to achieve a high percentage of reached nodes, which results in each node having to know a small number of keys. This is feasible both in terms of saving the keys in the nodes' memory and in sending the keys from the base station to the nodes.

4   Estimating the Spreading Angle

We chose to apply and analyze the secure overlays over a layered key distribution scheme. One important advantage of using layers compared to a tree topology is that it is more resilient to node failures. A tree topology relies on a one-to-one parent-child connection for delivering messages, while a layer topology relies on a several-to-several nodes in consecutive layers connection.

When the base station sends a query into the network, the intention is to spread the query to all the nodes in the network. However, the query will only spread with a certain angle for each secure overlay. In this section we estimate that angle.

We assume a uniform node distribution with high density, allowing us to model the layers as perfect circles. We also assume ideal transmission for all nodes with range r. Let i denote the layer, with respect to the initialization point, from which the mobile base station initiates the query, and let $j_{\max}$ denote the number of hops the query spreads. Figure 4(a) illustrates a scenario with $i = 2$ and $j_{max} = 3$.

We define a spreading angle α_j as the angle spanned from the inner border of layer i, to the most outer nodes (P_{jl}, P_{jr}) that receive the query in layer $i + j$, where $0 < j < j_{max}$. Note that the points P_j are not on a line.

According to Figure 4(b), using the law of cosines, we obtain

$$\frac{\alpha}{2} = \arccos(\frac{x^2 + z^2 - r^2}{2xz}). \tag{1}$$

The spreading angle α depends on the layer i, the relationship between r and x, and the number j_{max} of considered layers. Figure 5 plots the spreading angle in relation to the distance from BS to IP for $j_{max} = 3$. We want to point out two aspects. First, larger spreading angles can be achieved in layers closer to the initialization point, and second, there is a notable difference depending on the base station's position within a layer. The closer the mobile base station is

---

[1] In a layered based distribution the nodes in the last n layers have only one key, all other nodes have two keys.

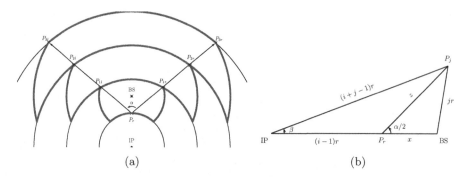

(a)   (b)

Fig. 4. (a) Spreading of the query with idealized assumptions on transmission range and node density. BS represents the mobile base station and IP the initialization point. (b) Geometrical drawing for the derivation of the spreading angle.

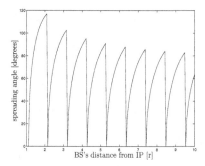

Fig. 5. Spreading angle in relation to the distance between the mobile base station and the initialization point for $j_{max} = 3$

located to the inner border of a layer, the less nodes can be reached within that layer, and therefore the spreading will be limited. In such situations, it would be favorable to send the query via the lower layer, since angles of up to 120 degrees can be achieved on the outer border of a layer.

In practice we cannot have a very high node density, so the layers will not correspond to perfect circles. In Figure 3(b) we can see the spreading of queries in a scenario where we have three initialization points A, B and C, and the mobile base station in the middle of the area. Because there are three initialization points, three queries will be sent in the network. In the figure they are shown in different colors. As we can see, the query does not reach all the nodes.

5   Simulation Results

We simulated the spreading of queries in Matlab to investigate how many nodes receive them and how the initialization points influence the spreading. We randomly distributed 250 nodes in a square area with side length 1 and adjusted their transmission range to achieve the desired node density d.

The node density d is an important parameter of the sensor network because it influences the network capacity. The optimal value for d is discussed by Hou et al. [5], who suggest $d = 6$ and $d = 8$. Xue et al. [6] shows that for a network with N nodes, the node density should be at least $5.1774 \log N$ to ensure overall connectivity, which results in $d = 12$ for our simulations.

After generating a network topology, we computed the secure overlays according to s initialization points and divided the area in 100×100 equal squares from where the mobile base station sent queries into the network. Considering all the nodes that were located within three hops from the mobile base station, we were interested in how many of them that were able to authenticate the query. Note that s query messages are sent, but they contain the same query.

5.1   Covering the Network with Several Secure Overlays

We looked at different configurations (i.e., number and position) for the initialization points to see their impact on the number of reached nodes. In the simulation results we present four scenarios, with one to four initialization points.

The results shown in Figure 6 represent the mean number of reached nodes within three hops from the mobile base station over 50 topologies for the four scenarios with $d = 12$. In this figure, the positions of the initialization points are marked with red points. In Figure 6(a), we see how the percentage of reached nodes significantly decreases as the mobile base station moves away from the single initialization point. Note that the color scale is chosen to represent high ratios dark, gradually getting lighter to be white for 50% or less nodes reached. A significant number of nodes is only reached from within the first layers from the initialization point. That result is intuitive as the query only spreads in a limited angle and away from the initialization point, so the covered area gets smaller and smaller as the mobile base station moves away from the initialization point.

By adding one more initialization point, as shown in Figure 6(b), we can see that the percentage of reached nodes does not decrease as fast when the mobile base station moves away from an initialization point. That is because of the increasing contribution from the other initialization point into the complementary direction. In Figure 6(c) with three initialization points, we can clearly recognize the shape of the triangle spanned by the three initialization points. We can again explain that by the observation that the contributions are always away from the initialization points, that is, there is only limited contribution towards the inside of the triangle if the mobile base station is outside the triangle.

The same observation can be made in the scenario with four initialization points, which form a square, presented in Figure 6(d). The percentage of reached nodes is 90% or higher within more than 70% of the square. Border artifacts can also be observed here.

The results for the triangle and square scenarios are summarized in Table 1 with the average number of reached nodes when the query is sent from the area spanned by the initialization points for $d = 7$ and $d = 12$. The proportion of reached nodes is higher for higher node density because each node has more neighbors in the upper layer and, thus, better chances to receive a query from at least one of them.

The number of reached nodes is about the same within the area spanned by both the triangle and the square for the high node density $d = 12$. In the same time, for the lower node density $d = 7$, the number of reached nodes is higher in the triangle than in the square. We explain that by the position of the initialization points in the corners of the square so that connectedness of the network from an initialization point with low node density is not always perfect. In the case of the triangle, the initialization points are not located in the corners of the network and therefore have higher probability of connectedness. In Table 2 we show the percentage of nodes that cannot be reached from an initialization point in the case of the triangle and square, for both $d = 7$ and $d = 12$. The nodes that cannot be reached from an initialization point cannot participate in the spreading of a query or data aggregation in the corresponding secure overlay. Note that the nodes that are not reached from one initialization point might be reached from other initialization points.

Table 1. Percentage of reached nodes when the query is sent from within the area spanned by the initialization points

Scenario	$d=7$	$d=12$
Triangle	85%	92%
Square	80%	91%

Table 2. Percentage of nodes that cannot be reached from an initialization point and will not be contained in a layer

Scenario	$d=7$	$d=12$
Triangle	2%	0.1%
Square	15%	1%

As we can see, only a few initialization points are enough to reach a high percentage of nodes that are a few hops away from the base station.

5.2   Choosing the Location of the Initialization Points

To further investigate how the position of the initialization points influence the number of reached nodes, we have run simulations with four initialization points randomly positioned on the side of the rectangle (one initialization point on each side). Two scenarios where used, one in which we kept the same network and just randomly moved the initialization points, and one in which we used a new network and a new set of initialization points for each run. We have made one hundred runs for each scenario. Table 3 shows the percentage of reached nodes in the whole network and within the area defined by the initialization points. As it is showed in the table, we have the same results for both scenarios, which means that the random position of the nodes does not influence the results. Also, within the area defined by the initialization points it is better coverage than in the previous square scenario (with initialization points in the corner of the area). Our conclusion from this experiments is that the position of the initialization points is not as important, but they should be positioned such that the area defined by them covers as much as possible of the deployment area.

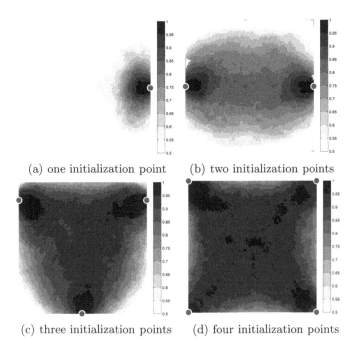

(a) one initialization point   (b) two initialization points

(c) three initialization points   (d) four initialization points

Fig. 6. Percentage of the nodes less that four hops away from the BS that are reached by the query (mean value over 50 topologies)

Table 3. Percentage of reached nodes when having four random initialization points

Scenario	Same network	Different networks
Whole network	85%	85%
Within the defined area	94%	94%

5.3   The Cost of Several Secure Overlays

As we have mentioned before, when having s secure overlays, s query messages will be sent into the network containing the same query, but different authentication information. Some nodes will receive several of these messages and will be able to use the authentication information to authenticate the query.

We have investigated by simulation the number of nodes that receive and are able to verify more than one query message and found that it is around 20% of the reached nodes. The nodes one hop away from the base station are likely to be able to verify several queries, since their position in the different secure overlays is the starting point for constructing the authentication information in the query messages. From these nodes, the query will spread in different directions, and just a few of the nodes several hops away from the base station will receive several queries. Each node should participate in spreading the query message over all possible overlays to ensure the best possible number of reached nodes. For each extra received query message that can be verified, two MAC computations are necessary: one for verifying the query and one for computing the MAC of the layer n hops away. Also the node will have to forward the query message.

6   Related Work

In this section we discuss other key distribution schemes that can be used with a mobile base station in the network.

One approach is to have all the nodes share a common secret key with the base station. This scheme can be used if the sensor networks are tamper-proof [7], otherwise, capturing one single node would reveal the secret key and allow an attacker unauthorized access to the network. As sensor networks are cheap devices, we assume that they are not tamper-proof and consider therefore that this scheme is not suitable in our scenarios.

Alternatively, each node can share an individual secret key with the base station. This approach has been used for confidential data aggregation [8]. The nodes' identities are sent together with the data, so the base station knows which nodes from the network participated in the aggregation process. This is necessary because the nodes in a sensor network are not fully reliable, so the base station needs to know which keys to use. Sending the ids of the participating nodes introduces a large overhead that can be reduced by using an interleaved approach such as the key distributions that we have described in this paper.

Another approach that would suit well is using public-key cryptography. Schemes have been proposed both for user authentication [9] and for confidential data aggregation [10]. Although Mykletun et al. [10] show that public key cryptography can be implemented more efficiently than believed before, it is still expensive. So, when dealing with frequently performed operations like query authentication or data aggregation, symmetric cryptography is still the prefered solution.

Only pairwise keys between nodes [11] cannot be used because individual nodes are not trusted in sensor networks due to the capture risk. Such keys would allow each node to either get access to the aggregated data or to modify/insert queries.

7   Conclusions

We introduced the concept of secure overlays over static key distribution schemes to enable the use of mobile base stations for secure data querying in wireless sensor networks. Enabling mobility results in a trade-off between the overhead of re-keying, and in our case, limited coverage. We apply and analyze our concept over a layered key distribution scheme and show by simulation that the use of only a few secure overlays can compensate for that artifact. Significant coverage can be achieved within the area defined by the initialization points.

Acknowledgements

This work was carried out within the Uppsala VINN Excellence Center for Wireless Sensor Networks WISENET, partly supported by VINNOVA, the Swedish Governmental Agency for Innovation Systems.

References

1. Önen, M., Molva, R.: Secure data aggregation with multiple encryption. In: Langendoen, K.G., Voigt, T. (eds.) EWSN 2007. LNCS, vol. 4373, pp. 117–132. Springer, Heidelberg (2007)
2. Rodhe, I., Rohner, C., Achtzehn, A.: n-LQA: n-layers query authentication in sensor networks. In: Proceedings of the 3rd IEEE International Workshop on Wireless and Sensor Networks Security (2007)
3. Jayaraman, P.P., Zaslavsky, A., Delsing, J.: Sensor data collection using heterogeneous mobile devices. In: IEEE International Conference on Pervasive Services (2007)
4. Ren, B., Ma, J., Chen, C.: The hybrid mobile wireless sensor networks for data gathering. In: IWCMC'06: Proceedings of the 2006 international conference on Wireless communications and mobile computing, pp. 1085–1090. ACM, New York (2006)
5. Hou, T., Li, V.: Transmission range control in multihop packet radio networks. IEEE Transactions on Communications 34(1), 38–44 (1986)
6. Xue, F., Kumar, P.R.: The number of neighbors needed for connectivity of wireless networks. Wireless Networks 10(2), 169–181 (2004)
7. Armknecht, F., Girao, J., Stoecklin, M., Westhoff, D.: Re-visited: Denial of service resilient access control for wireless sensor networks. In: Buttyán, L., Gligor, V.D., Westhoff, D. (eds.) ESAS 2006. LNCS, vol. 4357, pp. 18–31. Springer, Heidelberg (2006); Held in conjunction with ESORICS 2006
8. Castelluccia, C., Mykletun, E., Tsudik, G.: Efficient aggregation of encrypted data in wireless sensor networks. In: MOBIQUITOUS'05: Proceedings of the The Second Annual International Conference on Mobile and Ubiquitous Systems: Networking and Services (2005)
9. Benenson, Z., Gedicke, N., Raivio, O.: Realizing robust user authentication in sensor networks. In: Workshop on Real-World Wireless Sensor Networks (REALWSN), Stockholm (2005)
10. Mykletun, E., Girao, J., Westhoff, D.: Public key based cryptoschemes for data concealment in wireless sensor networks. In: IEEE International Conference on Communications, ICC 2006 (2006)
11. Eschenauer, L., Gligor, V.D.: A key-management scheme for distributed sensor networks. In: CCS'02: Proceedings of the 9th ACM conference on Computer and communications security, pp. 41–47. ACM, New York (2002)

Author Index